Seventh Edition

RACE, ETHNICITY, GENDER, & CLASS

Seventh Edition

RACE, ETHNICITY, GENDER, & CLASS

The Sociology of Group Conflict and Change

JOSEPH F. HEALEY

Christopher Newport University

EILEEN O'BRIEN

Saint Leo University

Los Angeles | London | New Delhi
Singapore | Washington DC

Los Angeles | London | New Delhi
Singapore | Washington DC

FOR INFORMATION:

SAGE Publications, Inc.
2455 Teller Road
Thousand Oaks, California 91320
E-mail: order@sagepub.com

SAGE Publications Ltd.
1 Oliver's Yard
55 City Road
London EC1Y 1SP
United Kingdom

SAGE Publications India Pvt. Ltd.
B 1/I 1 Mohan Cooperative Industrial Area
Mathura Road, New Delhi 110 044
India

SAGE Publications Asia-Pacific Pte. Ltd.
3 Church Street
#10-04 Samsung Hub
Singapore 049483

Acquisitions Editor: Jeff Lasser
Development Editor: Nathan Davidson
Editorial Assistant: Nick Pachelli
Digital Content Editor: Lauren Habib
Production Editor: Melanie Birdsall
Copy Editor: Megan Granger
Typesetter: C&M Digitals (P) Ltd.
Proofreader: Sally Jaskold
Indexer: Judy Hunt
Cover and Interior Designer: Gail Buschman
Marketing Manager: Erica DeLuca

Copyright © 2015 by SAGE Publications, Inc.

Library of Congress Cataloging-in-Publication Data

Healey, Joseph F.

Race, ethnicity, gender, and class : the sociology of group conflict and change/ Joseph F. Healey, Christopher Newport University, Eileen O'Brien, Saint Leo University, Virginia.—Seventh edition.

pages cm

Includes bibliographical references and index.

ISBN 978-1-4522-7573-4 (pbk. : acid-free paper) 1. Minorities—United States. 2. Ethnicity—United States. 3. Group identity—United States. 4. Social conflict—United States. 5. United States—Race relations. 6. United States—Ethnic relations. 7. United States—Social conditions. I. O'Brien, Eileen. II. Title.

E184.A1H415 2014b
305.800973—dc23   2014017577

This book is printed on acid-free paper.

Printed in Canada.

14 15 16 17 18 10 9 8 7 6 5 4 3 2 1

Only when lions have historians will hunters cease to be heroes.

—African Proverb

Not everything that is faced can be changed, but nothing can be changed until it is faced.

—James Baldwin

BRIEF CONTENTS

DETAILED CONTENTS

PART I: AN INTRODUCTION TO THE STUDY OF MINORITY GROUPS IN THE UNITED STATES

Newscom

2. Assimilation and Pluralism: From Immigrants to White Ethnics 30

LOC

3. Prejudice and Discrimination 68

LOC

PART II: THE EVOLUTION OF DOMINANT–MINORITY RELATIONS IN THE UNITED STATES

LOC

4. **The Development of Dominant–Minority Group Relations in Preindustrial America: The Origins of Slavery 100**

5. Industrialization and Dominant–Minority Relations: From Slavery to Segregation and the Coming of Postindustrial Society 124

PART III: UNDERSTANDING DOMINANT–MINORITY RELATIONS IN THE UNITED STATES TODAY

LOC

LOC

8. Hispanic Americans 214

iStock

9. Asian Americans 250

10. New Americans, Immigration, Assimilation, and Old Challenges 284

PART IV: OTHER GROUPS, OTHER PATTERNS

11. Gender 318

National Museum of American History,
Smithsonian Institution

National Institutes of Health

©iStockphoto.com/rrodrickbeiler

PART V: CHALLENGES FOR THE PRESENT AND THE FUTURE

14. Minority Groups and U.S. Society: Themes, Patterns, and the Future 400

©iStockphoto.com/Coast-to-Coast

PREFACE

Of all the challenges confronting the United States today, those relating to minority groups continue to be among the most urgent and the most daunting. Discrimination and rejection of "others" are part of our national heritage and—along with equality, freedom, and justice—prejudice, racism, and sexism are among our oldest values. Minority group issues penetrate every aspect of our society, and virtually every item on the national agenda—welfare and health care reform, crime and punishment, safety in the streets, the future of the family, even defense spending, foreign policy, and terrorism—has some connection with dominant–minority relations.

The issues we face will not be resolved easily or quickly. Feelings are intense, and controversy, indifference, and bitterness often swamp dispassionate analysis and calm reason. As a society, we have little hope of resolving these dilemmas unless we confront them openly and honestly; they will not disappear, and they will not resolve themselves.

This textbook contributes to the ongoing discussion by presenting information, raising questions, and probing issues. Our intent is to help students increase their knowledge, improve their understanding of the issues, and clarify their thinking regarding the inequalities related to race, ethnicity, gender, and sexual orientation. This text has been written for undergraduate students—sociology majors and nonmajors alike. It makes minimal assumptions about students' knowledge of history or sociological concepts, and the material is presented in a way that students will find accessible and coherent.

For example, a unified set of themes and concepts is used throughout the text. The analysis is consistent and continuous, even as multiple perspectives and various points of view are examined. The bulk of the conceptual framework is introduced in Parts I and II. These concepts and analytical themes are applied to a series of case studies of racial and ethnic minority groups in Part III. In Part IV, our focus shifts to gender, sexual-orientation minorities, and dominant–minority relations around the globe. Finally, in Part V, our main points and themes are summarized and reviewed, the analysis is brought to a conclusion, and some speculations are made regarding the future.

The analysis in this text is generally macro and comparative: It is focused on groups and larger social structures—institutions and stratification systems, for example—and systematically compares and contrasts the experiences and situations of America's many minorities. The text is in the tradition of conflict theory, but it is not a comprehensive statement of that tradition.

Other perspectives are introduced and applied, but no attempt is made to give equal attention to all current sociological paradigms. The text does not try to explain everything, nor does it attempt to include all possible analytical points of view. Rather, our goals are (a) to present the sociology of minority-group relations in a way that students will find understandable as well as intellectually challenging and (b) to deal with the issues and tell the stories behind the issues in a textbook that is both highly readable and a demonstration of the power and importance of thinking sociologically.

Although the text maintains a unified analytical perspective, students are exposed to a wide variety of perspectives on a number of different levels. For example, clashing points of view are presented in the Current Debates features in Chapters 1 through 12 (available at edge.sagepub.com/healey7e). The debates focus on an issue taken from the chapter but present the views of scholars and analysts from a variety of disciplines and viewpoints. Without detracting from the continuity of the main analysis, these debates reinforce the idea that no one has all the answers (or, for that matter, all the questions), and they can be used to stimulate discussion, bring additional perspectives to the classroom, and suggest topics for further research.

In addition, Chapters 1 through 12 include Narrative Portraits recounting the personal experiences and thoughts of a wide variety of people: immigrants, minority group members, journalists, sociologists, racists, and slaves, among others. These excerpts reinforce the analysis dramatically, memorably, and personally, and are integrated into the flow of the chapters. Also, the experiences of minority groups and the realities of prejudice, racism, sexism, and discrimination are documented in photos throughout the text.

This text also stresses the diversity of experiences within each minority group, especially gender differences. We also incorporate the intersectionality perspective, which explores the multiple ways race, ethnicity, social class, gender, and sexual orientation cut across one another, creating ever-shifting constellations of dominance and subordination.

Finally, we stress the ways American minority groups are inseparable from the American experience—from the early days of colonial settlements to tomorrow's headlines. The relative success of this society is due no less to the contributions of minority groups than to those of the dominant group. The nature of the minority-group experience has changed as the larger society has changed, and to understand America's minority groups is to understand some elemental truths about America. To raise the issues of difference and diversity is to ask what it means, and what it has meant, to be an American.

CHANGES IN THIS EDITION

This edition of *Race, Ethnicity, Gender, and Class* incorporates many changes.

NEW CHAPTERS

The most significant revision is the addition of three new chapters, each of which expands our analysis of diversity and difference. Chapter 11 analyzes gender, and Chapter 12 examines sexual-orientation minorities. Chapter 13 is a cross-national analysis of dominant–minority relations.

NEW IN-CHAPTER FEATURES

- *Opening vignettes* foreshadow the chapter content and arouse student interest.
- *Learning Objectives* focus student attention and help them organize the material.
- *Questions for Reflection* have been added to major sections of the text to help students analyze the material and identify crucial points.
- *Questions to Consider* have been added to each Narrative Portrait and Comparative Focus box to help students link the material to the chapter.
- An in-chapter activity called *Applying Concepts* has been added to each chapter to provide an opportunity to use key ideas.
- *Chapter summaries* have been coordinated with the learning objectives listed at the opening of the chapters.
- *Key terms* are defined in the margins of the text for convenience and ease of reference.

CHANGES IN CONTINUING FEATURES

Public Sociology Assignments (by Linda Waldron). Many sociologists have called for a more "public sociology," a sociology that is engaged in the community, the society, and the world. Although not all sociologists would endorse a call for activism and involvement, the study of American race relations will, for many people, stimulate an impulse to address social problems directly and personally. To facilitate that involvement, we have developed a number of projects for students that will lead them into their communities and the larger society and provide them with opportunities to make a positive difference in the lives of others.

The projects are presented at our website (edge.sagepub .com/healey7e), but they will be introduced at the beginning of each part of the text. Each assignment is keyed to the material covered in the chapters that follow.

These assignments should be regarded as outlines and suggestions, and participants will likely have to improvise and respond to unanticipated challenges as they arise. Nonetheless, these assignments will allow students to bridge the (sometimes large) gap between the classroom and the community and to develop and practice their own public sociology. Each assignment could be the basis for a semester-long project for individual or teams of students.

Current Debates. Chapters 1 through 12 of this text introduce Current Debates focused on a current and controversial issue facing the United States. Each debate begins with an overview, and students are directed to statements of clashing points of view. Students use the articles, materials from the chapter, and their own critical thinking skills to address a series of questions regarding the issue under debate. Instructors can choose to have students respond to the questions individually, in small-group debates, or in class discussions, and, of course, they may add their own questions.

The debate topic and a preview of the positions expressed are presented at the end of each chapter. Students can then proceed to the website for this text (edge.sagepub.com/healey7e), where they will find a more complete overview of the topic, a summary of the points of view, directions for accessing the materials, and a list of questions to consider while analyzing the issues.

OTHER CHANGES

- Research findings and data have been updated. As in the past, this edition relies on the latest information from the U.S. Census Bureau.
- There is an increased emphasis on the intersectionality perspective, particularly in Chapter 1 and new Chapters 11 and 12. In Chapter 1, for example, several new characters have been added to the "Some American Stories" section, and the biographies of other characters have been changed to illustrate a broader range of identities based on gender, class, religion, and sexual orientation.
- There is an increased emphasis on immigration, particularly in Chapter 1 and Chapters 8 through 10.
- Several new Narrative Portraits have been added to make this feature more current. Along with those in Chapters 11 and 12, new Narrative Portraits can be found in Chapters 1 and 8.
- The Current Debates feature has been updated in Chapters 3, 4, 5, 6, 7, 8, 9, and 10.
- The Comparative Focus features have been updated.
- The Internet Research Projects have been updated in Chapters 2, 4, and 6 through 10.

ANCILLARIES

$SAGE edge™

SAGE edge offers a robust online environment featuring an impressive array of tools and resources for review, study, and further exploration, keeping both students and instructors on the cutting edge of teaching and learning. SAGE edge content is open access and available on demand. Learning and teaching has never been easier!

SAGE EDGE FOR STUDENTS

SAGE edge for Students provides a personalized approach to help students accomplish their coursework goals in an easy-to-use learning environment.

- Mobile-friendly eFlashcards strengthen understanding of key terms and concepts.
- Mobile-friendly practice quizzes allow for independent assessment by students of their mastery of course material.
- An online action plan includes tips and feedback on progress through the course and materials, which allows students to individualize their learning experience.
- Learning Objectives reinforce the most important material.
- Carefully selected chapter-by-chapter video links and multimedia content enhance classroom-based explorations of key topics.
- Current Debates resource presents two or more opposing statements from scholars and analysts on controversial questions raised in the chapters (Are Indian Sports Team Mascots Offensive? Should Children Be Raised Genderless? etc.).
- Public Sociology Assignments encourage students to go beyond the classroom and engage with people, organizations, and resources in their local communities to learn more about minority groups and issues.
- Chapter Internet Research Projects guide students to use U.S. Census Bureau data to address questions related to course concepts.
- Internet Research Projects refer students to selected public websites, or direct them on guided Internet research, in order to gather data and apply concepts from the chapter.
- For Further Reading lists useful books and articles for additional study on minority groups and inter-group relations.
- EXCLUSIVE access to full-text SAGE journal articles that have been carefully selected to support and expand on the concepts presented in each chapter.

SAGE EDGE FOR INSTRUCTORS

SAGE edge for Instructors supports teaching by making it easy to integrate quality content and create a rich learning environment for students.

- Test banks provide a diverse range of pre-written options as well as the opportunity to edit any question and/or insert your own personalized questions to effectively assess students' progress and understanding.
- Sample course syllabi for semester and quarter courses provide suggested models for structuring your courses.
- Editable, chapter-specific PowerPoint® slides offer complete flexibility for creating a multimedia presentation for your course.
- Carefully selected chapter-by-chapter video links and multimedia content enhance classroom-based explorations of key topics.
- Chapter outlines follow the structure of each chapter, providing an essential reference and teaching tool.
- Exhibits from the printed book are available in an easily downloadable format for use in papers, hand-outs, and presentations.
- Photo essay ideas and suggestions with tips for instructors who assign photo essays in their classrooms.
- Current Debates resource presents two or more opposing statements from scholars and analysts on controversial questions raised in the chapters (Are Indian Sports Team Mascots Offensive? Should Children Be Raised Genderless? etc.).
- Public Sociology Assignments encourage students to go beyond the classroom and engage with people, organizations, and resources in their local communities to learn more about minority groups and issues.
- Internet Research Projects refer students to selected public websites, or direct them on guided Internet research, in order to gather data and apply concepts from the chapter.
- For Further Reading lists useful books and articles for additional study on minority groups and inter-group relations.
- A common course cartridge includes all of the instructor resources and assessment material from the student study site, making it easy for instructors to upload and use these materials in learning management systems such as Blackboard™, Angel®, Moodle™, Canvas, and Desire2Learn™.
- EXCLUSIVE access to full-text SAGE journal articles that have been carefully selected to support and expand on the concepts presented in each chapter.

ACKNOWLEDGMENTS

First and foremost, I thank Eileen O'Brien for the scholarship, expertise, and energy she has brought to this project. I would also like to thank professors Edwin H. Rhyne and Charles S. Green, the teacher-scholars who inspired me as a student, and my colleagues, past and present, in the Department of Sociology and Anthropology at Christopher Newport University: Stephanie Byrd, Cheri Chambers, Robert Durel, Marcus Griffin, Mai Lan Gustafsson, Jamie Harris, Kai Heidemann, Michael Lewis, Marion Manton, Lea Pellett, Eduardo Perez, Virginia Purtle, Andria Timmer, and Linda Waldron. They have been unflagging in their support of this project, and I thank them for their academic, logistical, and intellectual assistance. Finally, I thank Iris Price, Tracey Rausch, and Ellen Whiting for their indispensable support.

—Joseph F. Healey

I thank my department chair, Heather Parker, and dean, Mary Spoto: Their confidence in my abilities has allowed me to spread my wings in this project. Feeling supported by my superiors is something I shall never take for granted. I am also thankful for the camaraderie of my wonderful Saint Leo faculty colleagues—Patricia Campion, Mo Mathews, Janis Prince, and Chris Snead—I am truly blessed! Thanks also to Mike Armato for his enduring friendship and his assistance with suggested readings. I give special thanks to Kendall, whose fully involved coparenting made much of this project possible. To my love, D.S., where do I begin? You restored my confidence in my own abilities and reignited my passion for what I do, just by being you—and your constant inquisitiveness about this project has been its fuel and my inspiration. But above all, I am grateful to my coauthor, Joe Healey, for this wonderful opportunity, for doing more than his share, and for giving me something to look forward to by watching his example.

—Eileen O'Brien

We both thank Nathan Davidson and Jeff Lasser of SAGE Publications for their invaluable assistance in the preparation of this manuscript, and Dave Repetto, Ben Penner, and Steve Rutter, formerly of SAGE Publications, for their help in the development of this project.

This text has benefited in innumerable ways from the reactions and criticisms of a group of reviewers who proved remarkably insightful about the subject matter and about the challenges of college teaching. We thank them for the countless times when their comments led to significant improvements in the scholarship and clarity of this project. The shortcomings that remain are, of course, our responsibility, but whatever quality this text has is a direct result of the insights and expertise of these reviewers. We thank the following people:

FIRST EDITION REVIEWERS

Audwin Anderson, *University of South Alabama*
Donna Barnes, *University of Wyoming*
Norma Burgess, *Syracuse University*
Steven Cornell, *University of California, San Diego*
Gerry R. Cox, *Fort Hays State University*
Kevin Delaney, *Temple University*
Raul Fernandez, *University of California, Irvine*
Timothy Fiedler, *Carroll College*
Ramona Ford, *Southwest Texas State University*
Joni Fraser, *University of California, Davis*
Nicole Grant, *Ball State University*
Anne Hastings, *University of North Carolina, Chapel Hill*
Michael Hodge, *Georgia State University*
Ray Hutchison, *University of Wisconsin, Green Bay*
Joseph J. Leon, *California State Polytechnic University, Pomona*
Seymour Leventman, *Boston College*
Wendy Ng, *San Jose State University*
Carol Poll, *Fashion Institute of Technology*
Dennis Rome, *Indiana University*
Gerald Rosen, *California State University, Fullerton*
Ellen Rosengarten, *Sinclair Community College*
A. Seals, *Kentucky State University*
Charles Smith, *Florida A&M*
Susan Takata, *University of Wisconsin, Parkside*
Joyce Tang, *City University of New York, Queens College*
Maura I. Toro-Morn, *Illinois State University*
Diana Torrez, *University of Texas, Arlington*
Robert Williams, *Jackson State University*
Min Zhou, *University of California, Los Angeles*

SECOND EDITION REVIEWERS

JoAnn DeFiore, *University of Washington*
Linda Green, *Normandale Community College*
Jeremy Hein, *University of Wisconsin–Eau Claire*
David Matsuda, *Chabot College*
Victor M. Rodriguez, *Concordia University*
Craig Watkins, *University of Texas, Austin*
Norma Wilcox, *Wright State University*
Luis Zanartu, *Sacramento City College*
Min Zhou, *University of California, Los Angeles*

THIRD EDITION REVIEWERS

Rick Baldoz, *University of Hawaii, Manoa*
Jan Fiola, *Minnesota State University, Moorhead*
David Lopez, *California State University, Northridge*
Peggy Lovell, *University of Pittsburgh*
Gonzalo Santos, *California State University, Bakersfield*
Carol Ward, *Brigham Young University*

FOURTH EDITION REVIEWERS

Herman DeBose, *California State University, Northridge*
Abby Ferber, *University of Colorado, Colorado Springs*
Celestino Fernandez, *University of Arizona*
Samuel Leizear, *West Virginia University*
Gregory J. Rosenboom, *University of Nebraska/
    Nebraska Wesleyan University*
Peggy A. Shifflett, *Radford University*
Debbie Storrs, *University of Idaho*
Carol Ward, *Brigham Young University*
Norma Wilcox, *Wright State University*
Earl Wright, *University of Central Florida*

FIFTH EDITION REVIEWERS

Sharon Allen, *University of South Dakota*
Cathy Beighey, *Aims Community College*
Wendy H. Dishman, *Santa Monica College*
Bruce K. Friesen, *University of Tampa*

Susan E. Mannon, *Utah State University*
David McBride, *Pennsylvania State University*
Pam Brown Schachter, *Marymount College, Palos Verdes*
John Stone, *Boston University*
Merwyn L. Strate, *Purdue University*
Leigh A. Willis, *The University of Georgia*

SIXTH EDITION REVIEWERS

Tennille Allen, *Lewis University*
Steven L. Arxer, *University of Texas at Dallas*
Leslie Baker-Kimmons, *Chicago State University*
Melanie Deffendall, *Delgado Community College*
Sophia DeMasi, *Montgomery County Community College*
Creaig A. Dunton, *State University of New York, Plattsburgh*
Lisa A. Eargle, *Francis Marion University*
Kimberly H. Fortin, *Cayuga Community College*
Matasha L. Harris, *John Jay College of Criminal Justice*
C. Douglas Johnson, *Georgia Gwinnett College*
Chris Keegan, *State University of New York at Oneonta*
Janice Kelly, *Molloy College*
Patricia E. Literte, *California State University, Fullerton*
Marci B. Littlefield, *Indiana University-Purdue University*
Teri Moran, *Jackson Community College*
Gerald D. Titchener, *Des Moines Area Community College*
Deidre Ann Tyler, *Salt Lake Community College/
    The University of Utah*
Elsa Valdez, *California State University, San Bernardino*
Margaret A. M. Vaughan, *Metropolitan State University*
Elijah G. Ward, *Saint Xavier University*
Kathy Westman, *Waubonsee Community College*

SEVENTH EDITION REVIEWERS

Walter F. Carroll, *Bridgewater State University*
Wendy Dishman, *Santa Monica College*
Ramon Guerra, *University of Texas–Pan American*
Jason Hale, *Montclair State University*
Gina Logan, *Norwich University*
Yvonne Merchen Moody, *Chadron State College*
Lisa Speicher Muñoz, *Hawkeye Community College*
Deena Shehata, *Western International University*
Deidre Tyler, *Salt Lake Community College*
Judith Ann Warner, *Texas A&M International University*
Kathleen Westman, *Waubonsee Community College*

ABOUT THE AUTHORS

Joseph F. Healey is Professor Emeritus of Sociology at Christopher Newport University in Virginia. He received his PhD in sociology and anthropology from the Universityof Virginia. An innovative and experienced teacher of numerous race and ethnicity courses, he has written articles on minority groups, the sociology of sport, social movements, and violence, and he is also the author of *Statistics: A Tool for Social Research* (10th ed., 2014).

Eileen O'Brien is Associate Professor of Sociology at Saint Leo University's Virginia campus. Her BA, MA, and PhD degrees, all in sociology, are from the College of William and Mary, Ohio State University, and University of Florida, respectively. Her books include *Whites Confront Racism: Antiracists and Their Paths to Action* (2001); *White Men on Race: Power, Privilege, and the Shaping of Cultural Consciousness* (with Joe Feagin, 2003); and *The Racial Middle: Latinos and Asian Americans Living Beyond the Racial Divide* (2008).

PART i

AN INTRODUCTION TO THE STUDY OF MINORITY GROUPS IN THE UNITED STATES

The United States is a nation of groups as well as individuals. These groups vary along a number of dimensions, including size, wealth, education, race, culture, religion, and language. Some of these groups have been part of American society since colonial days, and others have formed just in the past few years.

How should all these groups relate to one another? Who should be considered American? Should we preserve the multitude of cultural heritages and languages that currently exist and stress our diversity? Should we encourage everyone to adopt Anglo-American culture and strive to become more similar and unified? Should we emphasize our similarities or celebrate our differences? Is it possible to do both?

Questions of unity and diversity are among the most pressing to face the United States today, and we begin to address these issues and many others in Chapters 1 and 2 of this text. Our goal is to develop a broader, more informed understanding of the past and present forces that have created and sustained the groups that compose U.S. society, and we will sustain this focus throughout the text.

Chapter 3 addresses prejudice and discrimination—feelings, attitudes, and actions that help maintain and reinforce the dividing lines that separate us into groups. How and why do these negative feelings, attitudes, and actions develop? How are prejudice and discrimination related to competition between groups and inequality? Can they be eliminated or at least reduced? This chapter will continue to introduce many of the sociological themes and concepts that will occupy our attention in the remainder of this text.

DIVERSITY IN THE UNITED STATES

Questions and Concepts

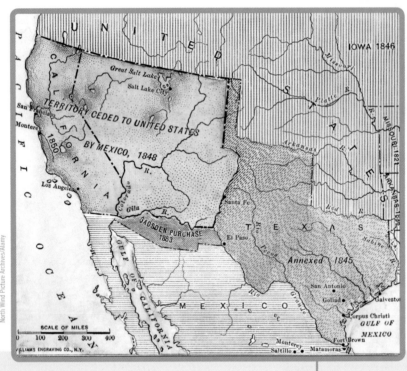

North Wind Picture Archives/Alamy

timeline

1790
The first naturalization law passes, restricting immigration to "free white persons" and excluding American Indians, indentured servants, slaves, free blacks, and Asians.

1798
Alien and Sedition Acts allow for the deportation of "dangerous aliens."

1803
Louisiana Purchase doubles the size of U.S. territory, incorporating new populations.

LOC

1819
First federal immigration legislation requires reporting of all entries.

1790   1805   1820   1835   1850   1865   1880

1848
Treaty of Guadalupe Hidalgo expands the U.S. borders to the Pacific. Mexican residents are given the option of declaring U.S. or Mexican citizenship.

1830
Indian Removal Act leads to the deportation of 100,000 Native Americans to west of the Mississippi.

1857
Dred Scott decision mandates that African Americans cannot be citizens.

Wikimedia Commons

1868
Fourteenth Amendment grants citizenship to African Americans born in the U.S.

1882
Chinese Exclusion Act prohibits entry of Chinese immigrants for 10 years.

LOC

Lucresia was falling behind, and she must have known what that meant. Her 15-year-old son tried to help, but the harsh terrain and the fast pace set by the group were too much. It was three days into the trek from Sasabe, Mexico, across the southern Arizona desert to Tucson, and it was clear that she would not fulfill her dream of reuniting with her husband, who was working in Texas. The leaders of the group decided to keep moving, taking Lucresia's daughter with them, but her son stayed with her as she died.

Lucresia's son survived and eventually returned to the family in Mexico. Lucresia's father vowed to find her remains and provide her with a decent burial. He traveled to the United States on a tourist visa and searched the desert for weeks, taking photos of likely landmarks—a distinctly shaped tree or a sandy creek bed—and sending them to his grandson in the hope that he would recognize something. He found several other bodies before he found Lucresia's. He was able to identify her by her shoes and the three rings still attached to the fleshless fingers.[1]

[1]Marosi (2005) and conversations with members of the Green Valley Samaritans, who patrol the Sonoran Desert in southern Arizona attempting to prevent deaths like Lucresia's.

LEARNING OBJECTIVES

By the end of this chapter, you will be able to do the following:

1.1 Describe the increasing racial and ethnic diversity of the United States.

1.2 Define the concept of a minority group.

1.3 Explain the sociological perspectives that will guide this text, especially as they relate to the relationships between inequality and minority-group status.

1.4 Explain the roles of race and gender in maintaining minority-group status.

1.5 Cite and explain four of the key concepts in dominant–minority relations.

1.6 Explain what is meant by a global perspective, and apply that perspective to the relationship between globalization and immigration to the United States.

1924
Johnson-Reed Act creates annual immigration quotas to limit the numbers of immigrants from Eastern Europe, the Mediterranean, and Asia.

1952
The Immigration and Nationality Act establishes limited quotas for Asian countries and other areas from which immigrants had been excluded.

1986
The Immigration Reform and Control Act provides a method for undocumented aliens to legalize their status.

1942
The Bracero Program begins, allowing Mexican citizens to work temporarily in the United States as a source of low-cost labor. The program ends in 1964.

1965
New immigration law lifts immigration restrictions based on race, creed, and nationality. No more quotas. Preference given to professionals and families of U.S. citizens.

1990
Immigration Act of 1990 increases the diversity of the immigrant flow by admitting immigrants from underrepresented countries.

1996
Illegal Immigration Reform and Immigrant Responsibility Act create more stringent immigration laws pertaining to admission and deportation.

Lucresia was just one of the millions of immigrants who have tried—sometimes unsuccessfully—to reach the United States over the past 50 years. Today, about 16% of the U.S. population was born in some other nation. Some states (California, for example) are more than 20% foreign-born, and some cities (New York, for example) are more than 30% foreign-born.

How do these immigrants affect the United States? Are they bringing new energy and revitalizing the economy? Are they draining school and welfare budgets? How do they affect African Americans, Native Americans, and other groups whose grievances remain unresolved?

Lucresia was just one person—a migrant, a woman, a wife, a mother, a Mexican. She wanted only to reunite her family, not to change American society. Most immigrants have similarly modest goals, but in their millions, could they be transforming the United States? Are they changing what it means to be an American? What kind of society are we becoming? What kind of society *can* we become? •

The United States is a nation of immigrants and groups, and since the infancy of this society we have been arguing, often passionately, about what this means, about inclusion and exclusion, and about unity and diversity. Every member of our society is an immigrant or the descendant of immigrants. Even Native Americans migrated to this continent, albeit thousands of years ago. We are all from someplace else, with roots in another part of the globe. Some came here in chains; others came on ocean liners, on jet planes, or on foot. Some arrived last week, and others have had family here for centuries. Each wave of newcomers has altered the social landscape of the United States. As many have observed, our society is continually becoming, permanently unfinished.

Today, the United States is remaking itself yet again. Large numbers of immigrants are arriving from, literally, all over the world, and their presence has raised questions about who belongs, what it means to be a U.S. citizen, and how much diversity we can tolerate.

Even as the United States debates issues of immigration, other long-standing issues of belonging, fairness, and justice remain unresolved. American Indians and African Americans have been a part of this society since its inception but largely as "others," slaves and outsiders, servants and enemies—groups outside the mainstream, not "true Americans" or full citizens. The legacies of racism and exclusion continue to affect these groups today, and, as we shall see in the chapters to come, they and other American minority groups continue to suffer from inequality, discrimination, and marginalization.

Today, the definition of "American" seems up for grabs. After all, we have twice elected a black man to the most

New Americans celebrating at a naturalization ceremony.

powerful position in our society (and, arguably, the world). To some, President Barack Obama's victories prove that the United States has finally become what it so often claimed to be: a truly open society and the last, best hope for all humanity.

Yet even a casual glance at our schools, prisons, neighborhoods, churches, corporate boardrooms—indeed, at any nook or cranny of our society—reveals pervasive inequality, differential opportunity, injustice, and unfairness. Which is the real America: the land of tolerance and opportunity or the sinkhole of narrow-mindedness and inequity?

We may be at a crossroads in this era of growing diversity, and perhaps we have an opportunity to reexamine the fundamental questions of citizenship and inclusion in this society: Can we incorporate all groups and resolve all grievances? Can we avoid fragmentation and chaotic disunity? What can hold us together? How should we approach the future? Should we celebrate our diversity or stress the need for unity?

Our understanding of these issues and our answers to these questions are partly affected by our group memberships. Each of us belongs to multiple groups and social categories, some defined by kinship, heritage, or our physical characteristics, and others linked to our social class, gender, religion, or lifestyle. Some of these group memberships are at the heart of our self-image, while others feel distant or trivial. At some level, however, all of them can influence our lives and our perceptions. They can help shape who we are and how we relate to the larger society. They can affect the ways others perceive us, the opportunities available to us, the way we think about ourselves, and our view of American society and the larger world. They affect our perception of what it means to be American.

SOME AMERICAN STORIES

To illustrate the range of these group memberships, consider some American lives. Each person introduced in the following paragraphs represents millions of others, and each exemplifies part of what it means to be an American.

• *Kim Park* is a 24-year-old immigrant from Korea. He arrived in New York City three years ago to work in his uncle's grocery store. Kim typically works a 12-hour shift, six days a week. His regular duties include stocking and cleaning, but he operates the register when necessary and is also learning how to do the bookkeeping. Instead of wages, Kim receives room and board and some spending money.

Kim is outgoing and gregarious. His English is improving, and he practices it whenever possible. He has twice enrolled in English language classes, but the demands of his job prevented him from completing the courses. Eventually, Kim wants to become a U.S. citizen, bring his siblings to America, get married and start a family, and take over the store when his uncle retires.

The store is located in a neighborhood that is changing in ethnic and racial composition. Many different minority groups have called this neighborhood home over the years. As recently as the 1950s, the area was almost exclusively Jewish. The Jewish residents have since died or moved out, and have been followed by a mixture of African Americans and Hispanic and Asian groups.

• One of Kim's regular customers is *Juan Yancy*, who is about Kim's age. The two almost always exchange greetings and, in spite of Kim's halting English, neighborhood news and gossip. Juan works in maintenance at a downtown hotel and, since the unemployment rate in the neighborhood is high, considers himself lucky to have a job.

Juan's heritage is complicated: His mother is Puerto Rican, and his father is Filipino and African American. He thinks of himself mostly as Puerto Rican but also identifies with his father's ancestry and resents the pressure from the larger society—on employment applications and other administrative forms, for example—to choose a single group membership.

• Juan lives in the apartment building where *Shirley Umphlett*, an African American, spent much of her childhood. In search of work, her family moved to New York from Alabama in the 1920s. Both her grandfather and father were construction workers, but because most labor unions and employers were white-only, they had no access to the better paying, more stable jobs and were often unemployed. Shirley's mother worked as a housekeeper and maid to help meet family expenses. Shirley did well in school, attended college on scholarship, and is now a successful executive with a multinational corporation. She is in her 40s, is married with two children, and is career oriented and ambitious. At the same time, she is committed to helping other African Americans and poor Americans in general. She and her spouse volunteer in several community action programs and maintain memberships in three national organizations that serve and represent African Americans.

• Shirley's commitment to service is partly a response to the fate of her nephew, *Dennard Umphlett*. When he was 16, Dennard was convicted of possession of crack cocaine with intent to distribute and was sentenced to a prison term of 20 years to life. Now, at age 22, he languishes in prison. Except for the support of Shirley and some other family members, Dennard feels he might lose all hope for life.

• Shirley's two children attend public school. One of their teachers is *Mary Farrell*, a fourth-generation Irish Catholic. Mary's great-grandparents came to New York as young adults in the 1880s. Her great-grandfather found work on the docks, and her great-grandmother worked as a housekeeper before marrying. They had seven children and 23 grandchildren, and Mary has more than 50 cousins living within an hour of New York City. Each generation of Mary's family tended to do a little better educationally and occupationally. Mary's father was a fireman, and her sister is a lawyer.

Mary's relations with her family were severely strained several years ago when she told them that she was a lesbian and would be moving in with Sandra, her long-time partner. Her parents, traditional Catholics, find it difficult to accept her sexual orientation, as do many of her other relatives. She brought Sandra to several family gatherings, but they both found the tension too unpleasant to bear. Mary now either attends family events alone or skips them altogether. While she has been open with her family (much to their discomfort), she mostly stays "in the closet" at work, fearing the potential repercussions from parents and administrators. Still, she and Sandra are planning to marry soon.

• In one of her fourth-grade classes, Mary took a liking to a young Native American student named *George Snyder*. George was born on a reservation in upstate New York, but his family moved to the city when he was a baby, driven away by the high unemployment rate. Mary and George kept in touch after he left elementary school, and George stopped by occasionally for a chat. Then, when George reached high school, he became rebellious and his grades began to slip. He was arrested for shoplifting and never finished school. The last time they met, Mary tried to persuade him to pursue a GED, but she got nowhere with him. She pointed out that he was still young and there were many things he could do in the future. He responded, "What's the use? I'm an Indian with a record—I've got no future."

• George's parole officer is *Hector Gonzalez*. Hector's parents came to the United States from Mexico. Every year, they crossed the border to join the stream of agricultural migrant laborers and then returned to their village in Mexico at the end of the season. With the help of a cousin, Hector's father eventually got a job as a cabdriver in New York City, where Hector was raised. Hector's mother never learned much English but worked occasionally in a garment factory in her neighborhood.

With the help of his parents, Hector worked his way through college in seven years, becoming the first member of his family to earn a bachelor's degree. Hector thinks of himself as American but is interested in his parents' home village back in Mexico, where most of his extended family still lives. Hector is bilingual and has visited the village several times. His grandmother still lives there, and he calls her once a month.

Hector is married and has a child. He and his wife are very close and often refer to each other as "best friends." Hector is bisexual and has had relationships with men in the past, a fact that his wife accepts but that he keeps hidden from his parents and grandmother.

• Hector regularly eats lunch at a restaurant around the corner from his office. Two of the three managers of the restaurant are white, most of the waitresses are black, and the kitchen workers are Latino. One of the busboys who often clears Hector's table, *Ricardo Aldana*, is in the country illegally. He left his home village in Guatemala five years ago, traveled the length of Mexico on freight trains and on foot, and crossed the border in Texas. He lives in a tiny apartment with five others and sends 40% of his wages to his family in Guatemala. He enjoys living in the United States but is not particularly interested in legalizing his status. His most fervent wish is to go home, get married, and start a family.

• The restaurant is in a building owned by a corporation headed by *William Buford III*, a white American. William invests the bulk of his fortune in real estate and owns land and buildings throughout the New York metropolitan area. The Bufords have a three-story luxury townhouse in Manhattan but rarely go into town, preferring to spend their time on their rural Connecticut estate. William attended the finest private schools and graduated from Harvard University. At age 57, he is semiretired, plays golf twice a week, vacations in Europe, and employs a staff of five to care for himself and his family. He was raised a Mormon but is not religious and has little interest in the history of his family.

These individuals belong to groups that vary along some of the most consequential dimensions within our society—ethnicity, race, immigration status, social class, sexual orientation, gender, and religion—and their lives have been shaped by these affiliations (some more than others, of course). Some of these statuses (such as William's membership in the upper class) are privileged and envied, while others (e.g., Ricardo's undocumented status) are disadvantaged and can evoke rejection and contempt from others.

Note also that each person's statuses are mixed. For example, in spite of his elite status, William has occasionally felt the sting of rejection because of his Mormon background. Dennard and George rank low on race and class but enjoy some of the advantages of being male, while Mary's chances for upward mobility in the school system are reduced by her gender and sexual orientation. Each of these individuals is privileged in some ways and limited in others—as are we all.

Finally, note that each of our group memberships can affect how we perceive others, our opportunities, the way we think about ourselves, and our view of American society and the larger world. They affect our perception of what it means to be American.

QUESTIONS FOR REFLECTION

1. Clearly, William—the wealthy, white real-estate mogul—is the highest-ranking person in this group. Can the others be placed in order below him, from high to low? Which would weigh more in such a ranking: class, gender, or race and ethnicity? How would sexual orientation affect the rankings?

2. Taking into account your own gender, racial, ethnic, and social class background, where would you rank yourself relative to these nine people? At this stage of your life, are you more "privileged" or more "disadvantaged"? Would you rank yourself higher or lower than your parents and grandparents?

THE INCREASING VARIETY OF AMERICAN MINORITY GROUPS: TRENDS AND QUESTIONS

The group memberships discussed in the previous section can shape the choices we make in the voting booth and in other areas of social life. We also need to be aware that members of different groups will evaluate these decisions in different ways. The issues will be filtered through the screens of divergent experiences, group histories, and present situations. The debates over which direction our society should take are unlikely to be meaningful or even mutually intelligible without some understanding of the variety of ways of being American.

INCREASING DIVERSITY

The choices about the future of our society are especially urgent because the diversity of U.S. society is increasing dramatically, largely due to high rates of immigration. Since the 1960s, the number of immigrants arriving in the United States each year has tripled and includes groups, literally, from all over the globe. Can our society deal successfully with this diversity of cultures, languages, and races?

Concerns about increasing diversity are compounded by other long-standing minority issues and grievances that remain unresolved. For example, charts and graphs presented in Part III of this text document continuing gaps between minority groups and national norms in income, poverty rates, and other measures of affluence and equality. In fact, in many ways, the problems of African Americans, Native Americans, Hispanic Americans, and Asian Americans today are just as formidable as they were a generation ago.

FIGURE 1.1 The U.S. Population by Race and Ethnicity, 1980–2060 (Projected)

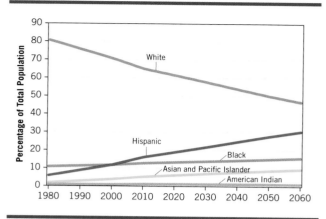

SOURCE: U.S. Census Bureau (2012b).

As one way of gauging the dimensions of diversity in our nation, consider Figure 1.1, which presents the percentage of the total U.S. population in each of five groups. We will first consider this information on its face and analyze some of its implications. Then, we will consider (and question) the terms in which this information is framed.

The chart reports the actual relative sizes of the groups for 1980 through 2010 and the projected relative sizes through 2060. Note how the increasing diversity of U.S. society is reflected in the declining numerical predominance of non-Hispanic whites. As recently as 1980, more than 8 out of 10 Americans were members of this group, but by the middle of this century, non-Hispanic whites will become a numerical minority. Several states (Texas, California, Hawaii, and New Mexico) are already "majority-minority" states and, for the first time in history, most of the babies in the United States (50.4%) are members of minority groups (U.S. Census Bureau, 2012a).

Black and American Indian populations will grow in absolute numbers but are projected to remain stable in their relative size. Hispanic American and Asian American and Pacific Islander populations, on the other hand, will grow dramatically. Asian American and Pacific Islander groups were only 2% of the population in 1980, but that will grow to 10% by midcentury. The most dramatic growth, however, will be for Hispanic Americans. This group became the largest minority group in 2002, surpassing blacks, and will grow to more than 30% of the population by 2060.

The projections into the future are just educated guesses, of course, but they forecast profound change for the United States. As this century unfolds, our society will grow more diverse racially, culturally, and linguistically. The United States will become less white, less European, and more like the world as a whole. Some see these changes as threats to traditional white, middle-class American values and lifestyles. Others see them as an opportunity for the emergence of other equally legitimate value systems and lifestyles.

WHAT'S IN A NAME?

Let's take a moment to reflect on the categories used in Figure 1.1. The group names we used are arbitrary, and none of these groups have clear or definite boundaries. We use these terms because they are convenient, familiar, and consistent with the labels found in census reports, much of the sociological research literature, and other sources of information. This does not mean that the labels are "real" or equally useful in all circumstances. In fact, these group names have some serious shortcomings, several of which we should note here.

First, the people within these groups may have very little in common with one another. Any two people in one of these categories might be as different from each other as any two people selected from different categories. They may share some general, superficial physical or cultural traits, but they will also vary by social class, religion, gender, and in thousands of other ways. People in the Asian American and Pacific Islander group, for example, represent scores of different national and linguistic backgrounds (Japanese, Samoans, Vietnamese, Pakistanis, and so forth), and the category American Indian or Alaska Native includes people from hundreds of different tribal groups.

Second, people do not necessarily use these labels when they think about their identity or who they are. In this sense, the labels are not "real" or important for all the people in these categories. For example, many whites in the United States (like William Buford) think of themselves as "just American." Many of the people we have labeled "Hispanic Americans" (like Hector Gonzalez or Juan Yancy) will identify themselves more in national terms, as Mexicans or Puerto Ricans or, even more specifically, with a particular region or village. Gay or lesbian members of any of these five groups may identify themselves more in terms of their sexual orientation than their race or ethnicity. Thus, the labels do not always reflect the ways people think about themselves, their families, or where they come from. The categories are statistical classifications created by researchers and census takers. They do not grow out of or always reflect the everyday realities of the people who happen to be in them.

Third, even though the categories in Figure 1.1 are broad, they provide no place for many groups and individuals. For example, how should we categorize Arab Americans and recent immigrants from Africa? Should Arab Americans be included with Asian Americans and Pacific Islanders? Should recent immigrants from Africa be grouped with African Americans? Of course, we don't need to have a category for every person, but we should recognize that classification schemes such as the one used in Figure 1.1 (and in many other contexts) have fuzzy boundaries and limited utility and application.

FIGURE 1.2 Interracial and Interethnic Marriages in the United States, 1980–2010

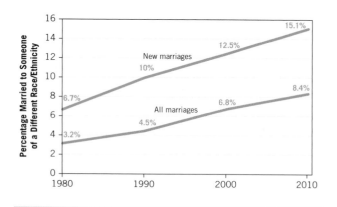

SOURCE: Wang (2012, p. 5). Reprinted with permission of Pew Research Center.

A related problem with this classification scheme will become increasingly apparent in the years to come: There is no category for the growing number of people who (like Juan Yancy) are members of more than one racial or ethnic group. The number of "mixed-group" Americans is relatively small today, slightly less than 3% of the total population. However, the number of people who chose more than one racial or ethnic category on the U.S. Census to describe themselves increased by 32% (from 2.4% to 2.9% of the total population) between 2000 and 2010 (Jones & Bullock, 2012) and is likely to continue to increase rapidly because of the growing number of marriages across group lines.

To illustrate, Figure 1.2 shows dramatic increases in the percentage of "new" marriages (couples that got married in the year prior to the survey date) and all marriages that unite members of different racial or ethnic groups (Wang, 2012, p. 5). Obviously, the greater the number of mixed marriages, the greater the number of mixed Americans. One study estimates that 21% of the population will claim membership in this category by 2050 (Smith & Edmonston, 1997, p. 119).

Finally, we should note that these categories and group names are **social constructions**, fabricated in particular historical circumstances and reflective of particular power relationships. For example, the group called American Indians today didn't exist prior to the period of European exploration and colonization of North America (and, in some ways, it doesn't exist now). Before the arrival of Europeans, there were hundreds of separate societies spread across the North American continent, each with its own language and culture. Native

Social constructions are perceptions shared by a group. These perceptions become real for the people who share them.

Americans thought of themselves primarily in terms of their tribe and had no sense of a common identity with the other peoples that inhabited North America. They became a group first in the perceptions of European conquerors, who stressed their similarities and cast them as an enemy out-group. The fact that American Indians are often defined as a single group today reflects their defeat and subordination and their status as a minority group: They became the "others" in contrast to white European colonists.

In the same way (although through different processes), African, Hispanic, and Asian Americans came to be seen as separate groups not by their own choice but as one outcome of an unequal interaction with white Americans. These groups have become "real," and much of this text is organized around a consideration of each of them (e.g., see the chapter titles in Part III). Nonetheless, we use the terms and labels as a convenience, not as a reflection of some unchangeable reality. These groups are real because they are seen as real from a particular perspective—that of the dominant group in this society: white Americans.

QUESTIONS FOR REFLECTION

1. If you were asked for your group membership, which of the groups listed in Figure 1.1 (if any) would you select? Do you feel that you belong to one and only one group? Are these groups part of your self-image, or are they just statistical categories? Do you think they affect your view of the world or shape your circle of friends? How?

2. Over the past 5 to 10 years, what signs of increasing diversity have you seen in your home community or high school? How has increasing diversity enriched everyday life in these areas? What problems or issues have arisen from rising diversity?

QUESTIONS ABOUT THE FUTURE, SOCIOLOGY, AND THE PLAN OF THIS BOOK

Even though the labels used in Figure 1.1 are arbitrary, the trends displayed have important implications for the future of the United States. What kind of society are we becoming? What should it mean to be American? In the past, opportunity and success have been far more available to white Anglo-Saxon Protestant males than to members of other groups. Most of us, even the most favored, would agree that this definition of American is far too narrow, but how inclusive should the definition be? Should we stress unity or celebrate diversity?

On Being American

Carla, now in her 20s, is finally beginning to reconcile herself to the realities of American perceptions about who she is. She is the adopted daughter of an affluent white family and grew up in the suburbs, surrounded by all the amenities of a comfortable, middle-class lifestyle. She has never met her birth parents but knows that her biological mother was Korean American, 16 years old at the time of her birth. She knows nothing about her birth father.

For much of her life, Carla felt caught between her biological heritage and her actual lifestyle. She often hesitates when asked what group she belongs to: Is she Asian American, in the terms of the U.S. Census and Figure 1.1? The only lifestyle she has ever known is white, suburban, middle class—should she check off "non-Hispanic white" when she fills out an employment application? For her, the social construction of race can be very real and, at the same time, completely false.

Here is part of what she has to say about her identity:

When I was growing up, my parents would try to teach me about my Korean heritage. We would read books about Korean history and culture, my mom learned to prepare some Korean dishes, and we even discussed taking a trip to Korea—but never did. Looking back, I really appreciate what they were trying to do, but it all felt very foreign to me, you know? Like we were discussing Bolivia or Kenya…

But then, someone would make assumptions about me based on my looks. They would think that I was good at math or nerdy or couldn't speak English. I can't tell you how many times someone has asked me, "Where are you from?" and wouldn't believe me when I said, "I'm from here," and then they would go, "No, where are you from *really*?"

I mean, I sometimes tried to "be Korean" and even attended some meetings of the Asian Student Association when I was in school, but it felt wrong—it just wasn't me. But then, something would happen…Like one time I was just walking through the mall, and some old white guy came up and said, out of the clear blue sky, "You people are ruining this country!" I mean, who did he think I was?

So, yeah, it took a long time, but now I think that I'm just me, you know? People can look at me one way and put me in all those different categories, but that's their problem. It's not who I am. It's not me!

SOURCE: Personal communication to the authors. Carla's name and exact circumstances have been fictionalized.

Questions to Consider

1. Is Carla's confusion about her identity a result of her social and physical characteristics or a result of how other people see her?
2. Would Carla's situation change if she were male? How? Would it change if her birth mother were Hispanic or black? How?

How wide can the limits be stretched before societal cohesion is threatened? How narrowly can they be defined before the desire to preserve cultural and linguistic diversity is unjustly and unnecessarily stifled?

These first few pages have raised a lot of questions. The purpose of this book is to help you develop some answers and some thoughtful, informed positions on these issues. You should be aware from the beginning that the questions addressed here are complex and the answers we seek are not obvious or easy. Indeed, there is no guarantee that we as a society will be able or willing to resolve all the problems of intergroup relations in the United States. However, we will never make progress in this area unless we confront the issues honestly and with an accurate base of knowledge and understanding. Certainly, these issues will not resolve themselves or disappear if they are ignored.

In the course of our investigation, we will rely on sociology and other social sciences for concepts, theories, and information. The first three chapters of this text introduce and define many of the ideas that will guide our investigation. Part II explores how relations between the dominant group and minority groups have evolved in American society. Part III analyzes the current situation of U.S. racial and ethnic minority groups. In Part IV, we examine group divisions based on gender and sexual orientation, and patterns of group relationships around the globe. Finally, in Part V, we bring the analysis to a close, review the challenges and issues facing our society (and the world), and see what conclusions we can develop from our investigations.

WHAT IS A MINORITY GROUP?

Before we can begin to sort out the issues, we need common definitions and a common vocabulary for discussion. We begin with the term **minority group**. Taken literally, the mathematical connotation of this term is a bit misleading because it implies that minority groups are small. In reality, a minority group can be quite large and can even be a numerical majority of the population. Women, for example, are sometimes considered to be

---

A **minority group** experiences systematic disadvantage and has a visible identifying trait. The group is self-conscious, and membership is usually determined at birth. Members tend to form intimate relations within the group.

a separate minority group, but they are a numerical majority of the U.S. population. In South Africa, as in many nations created by European colonization, whites are a numerical minority (less than 10% of the population), but they have been by far the most powerful and affluent group and, despite recent changes, retain their advantage in many ways.

Minority status has more to do with the distribution of resources and power than with simple numbers. In this text, we will be guided by a classic definition of *minority group* developed by Wagley and Harris (1958). As we shall see, not every minority group fits every criterion, but the definition still provides a useful touchstone.

According to Wagley and Harris (1958), a minority group has five characteristics:

1. The members of the group experience a pattern of disadvantage or inequality.
2. The members of the group share a visible trait or characteristic that differentiates them from other groups.
3. The minority group is a self-conscious social unit.
4. Membership in the group is usually determined at birth.
5. Members tend to form intimate relationships (close friendships, dating partnerships, and marriages) within the group.

We will examine each of these characteristics here and, a bit later, will return to examine the first two—inequality and visibility—in greater detail, because they are the most important characteristics of minority groups.

1. Inequality. The first and most important defining characteristic of a minority group is *inequality*—that is, some pattern of disability and disadvantage. The nature of the disability and the degree of disadvantage are variable and can range from exploitation, slavery, and **genocide** to slight irritants such as a lack of desks for left-handed students or a policy of racial or religious exclusion at an expensive country club. (Note, however, that you might not agree that the irritant is slight if you are a left-handed student awkwardly taking notes at a right-handed desk or if you are a golf aficionado who happens to be African American or Jewish American.)

Genocide is the deliberate attempt to exterminate an entire group.

A **dominant group** is the group that benefits from minority-group subordination.

Ethnic minority groups are distinguished by cultural traits.

Racial minority groups are distinguished by physical traits.

Whatever its scope or severity, whether it extends to wealth, jobs, housing, political power, police protection, or health care, the pattern of disadvantage is the key characteristic of a minority group. Because the group has less of what is valued by society, the term *subordinate group* is sometimes used instead of *minority group*.

The pattern of disadvantage is the result of the actions of another group, often in the distant past, that benefits from and tries to sustain the unequal arrangement. This group can be called the core group or **dominant group.** The latter term is used most frequently in this book because it reflects the patterns of inequality and the power realities of minority-group status.

2. Visibility. The second defining characteristic of a minority group is some *visible trait* or characteristic that sets members of the group apart and that the dominant group holds in low esteem. The trait can be cultural (language, religion, speech patterns, or dress styles), physical (skin color, stature, or facial features), or both. Groups that are defined primarily by their cultural characteristics are called **ethnic minority groups.** Examples of such groups are Irish Americans and Jewish Americans. Groups defined primarily by their physical characteristics are called **racial minority groups,** a term that applies to African Americans and Native Americans, for example. Note that these categories overlap. So-called ethnic groups may have (or may be thought to have) distinguishing physical characteristics (e.g., the stereotypical Irish red hair or Jewish nose), and racial groups commonly have (or are thought to have) cultural traits that differ from the dominant group (e.g., differences in dialect, religious values, or cuisine).

These distinguishing traits set boundaries and separate people into distinct groups. The traits are outward signs that identify minority-group members and help maintain the patterns of disadvantage. The dominant group has (or at one time had) sufficient power to create the distinction between groups and thus solidify a higher position for itself. These markers of group membership are crucial; without these visible signs, it would be difficult or impossible to identify who was in which group, and the system of minority-group oppression might soon collapse.

It is important to realize that the characteristics that mark the boundaries between groups usually are not significant in and of themselves. They are selected for their visibility and convenience and, objectively, may be quite trivial and unimportant. For example, scientists have concluded that skin color and other so-called racial traits have little scientific, evolutionary, medical, or biological importance. As we shall see, skin color is an important marker of group membership in our society because it was selected during a complex and lengthy historical process, not because it has any inherent significance. These markers are social constructions that become important because we attribute significance to them.

3. Awareness. A third characteristic of minority groups is that they are *self-conscious social units*, aware of their differentiation

FIGURE 1.3 Do Black Americans Have the Same Chances as White Americans to Obtain the Same Level of Employment? 1963–2011 (Responses Divided by Race)

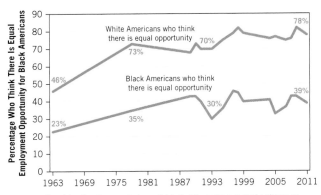

Actual Question: In general, do you think that blacks have as good a chance as white people in your community to get any kind of job for which they are qualified, or don't you think they have as good a chance?

SOURCE: Gallup (2013).

from the dominant group, their shared disabilities, and their common fate. This shared social status can provide the basis for strong intragroup bonds and a sense of solidarity, and can lead to views of the world that are markedly different from those of the dominant group and other minority groups. Minority and dominant groups can live in different cultural worlds.

For example, public opinion polls frequently show sizeable differences between dominant and minority groups in their views of the seriousness and extent of discrimination in American society. Figure 1.3 shows persistent and sizeable gaps in the percentage of nationally representative samples of whites and blacks who agree that blacks and whites have equal job opportunities. As would be expected, given their different histories, experiences, and locations in the social structure, blacks have much more negative views of racial equality, even though both groups have become somewhat more optimistic over the years. Even after the election of President Obama in 2008, the percentage of black Americans who perceived equal racial opportunity was about half that of white Americans who did.

4. Ascription. A fourth characteristic of minority groups is that membership is generally an **ascribed status**, or one acquired at birth. The traits that identify minority-group membership are typically not easy to change, and minority-group status is usually involuntary and for life.

In some cases—with "racial" minority groups, for example—this defining characteristic may seem obvious and hardly worth mentioning. Remember, however, that group labels are social constructions, based on particular historical circumstances and shared cultural perceptions. Thus, group membership can be negotiable and changeable, and a person's status at birth is not necessarily constant throughout his or her lifetime. A member of a racial minority

may be able to "pass" as a member of a different group, and a member of a religious minority may be able to change status by changing his or her faith.

It's important to keep in mind the qualification that minority status is *generally* a matter of birth. There are important exceptions to the general rule and a great deal more ambiguity regarding group membership than may appear at first glance. Also, for some groups—gays and lesbians in particular—the notion of membership by ascription can be controversial. Is homosexuality inborn or learned? We will deal with this issue later in the text.

5. Intimate Relationships. Finally, group members (dominant and minority alike) tend to form emotionally close bonds with people like themselves. That is, members tend to choose each other as close friends, dating partners, and spouses (legal and cohabitational).

For many groups, this pattern is shaped by the pervasive racial, ethnic, and class segregation of American neighborhoods, schools, and other areas of social life. In some ways, the pattern can be voluntary, but it can also be dictated by the dominant group. For example, interracial marriages were illegal in many states, and laws against **miscegenation** were declared unconstitutional by the U.S. Supreme Court less than 50 years ago, in the late 1960s (Bell, 1992).

This is a lengthy definition of minority groups, but note how inclusive it is. Although it encompasses "traditional" minority groups such as African Americans and Native Americans, it also could be applied to other groups. For instance, women arguably fit the first four criteria and can be analyzed with many of the same concepts and ideas that guide the analysis of other minority groups. Also, gay, lesbian, and transgender Americans; non-Protestants; Americans with disabilities; left-handed Americans; the aged; and Americans who are very short, very tall, or very obese could fit the definition of minority group without much difficulty, and we will consider some of these groups in Part IV of this text. Although we should not be whimsical or capricious about definitions, it is important to note that the analyses developed in this book can be applied more generally than you might realize at first and may lead to some fresh insights about a wide variety of groups and people.

QUESTIONS FOR REFLECTION

Do gay and lesbian Americans fit all five parts of this definition of minority groups? From some perspectives, gays and lesbians are seen as sinners, deviants, or mentally ill. Are all these views valid? Why or why not?

An **ascribed status** is involuntary and acquired at birth.

Miscegenation is marriage or sexual relations between members of different racial groups.

PATTERNS OF INEQUALITY

As we mentioned earlier, the most important defining characteristic of minority-group status is the pattern of inequality and discrimination. In later chapters, we document how minority group membership affects access to jobs, education, wealth, health care, and housing, and how it is associated with a lower (often much lower) proportional share of valued goods and services and more limited (often much more limited) opportunities for upward mobility.

Stratification, or the unequal distribution of valued goods and services, is a basic feature of society. Every human society, except perhaps the simplest hunter-gatherer societies, is stratified to some degree; that is, the resources of the society are distributed so that some get more and others less of whatever is valued. Societies are divided into horizontal layers (or strata), often called **social classes**, which differ from one another by the amount of resources they command. A view of the American social class system is presented in Figure 1.4. Many criteria (such as education, age, gender, and talent) may affect a person's social class position and his or her access to goods and services. Minority-group membership is one of these criteria, and it has a powerful impact on the distribution of resources in the United States and other societies.

This section begins with a brief consideration of theories about the nature and important dimensions of stratification. It then focuses on how minority-group status relates to stratification. During the discussion, we identify several concepts and themes used throughout this book.

THEORETICAL PERSPECTIVES

Sociology and the other social sciences have been concerned with stratification and human inequality since the formation of the discipline in the 19th century. An early and important contributor to our understanding of the nature and significance of social inequality was Karl Marx, the noted social philosopher and revolutionary. Half a century later, a sociologist named Max Weber, a central figure in the development of sociology, critiqued and elaborated on Marx's view of inequality. Here, we will also consider the views of Gerhard Lenski, a

---

Stratification is the system of unequal distribution of valued goods and services in society.

Social classes consist of people who have similar levels of access to valued goods and services.

The **means of production** are the materials, resources, and social relationships by which society produces and distributes goods and services.

FIGURE 1.4 Class in the United States (Gilbert–Kahn Model)

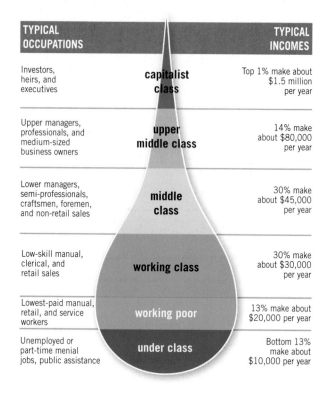

TYPICAL OCCUPATIONS		TYPICAL INCOMES
Investors, heirs, and executives	capitalist class	Top 1% make about $1.5 million per year
Upper managers, professionals, and medium-sized business owners	upper middle class	14% make about $80,000 per year
Lower managers, semi-professionals, craftsmen, foremen, and non-retail sales	middle class	30% make about $45,000 per year
Low-skill manual, clerical, and retail sales	working class	30% make about $30,000 per year
Lowest-paid manual, retail, and service workers	working poor	13% make about $20,000 per year
Unemployed or part-time menial jobs, public assistance	under class	Bottom 13% make about $10,000 per year

SOURCE: Gilbert (2011).

contemporary sociologist whose ideas about the influence of economic and technological development on social stratification have considerable relevance when comparing societies and understanding the evolution of intergroup relations. We close with a consideration of the views of another contemporary sociologist, Patricia Hill Collins, who argues that we need to view class, racial, gender, and other inequalities holistically, and take into account how each status is affected by the others.

Karl Marx. Although best known as the father of modern communism, Karl Marx was also the primary architect of a political, economic, and social philosophy that has played a major role in world affairs for more than 150 years. Marxism is a complex theory of history and social change in which inequality is a central concept and concern.

Marx argued that the most important source of inequality in society was the system of economic production. More specifically, he focused on the **means of production**, or the materials, tools, resources, and social relationships by which the society produces and distributes goods and services. In an agricultural society, the means of production include land, draft animals, and plows. In an industrial society, the means of production include factories, commercial enterprises, banks, and transportation systems, such as railroads.

Reminiscences of Carl Schurz, Vol. I, New York: McClure Publ. Co., 1907, Chap. 4, facing p. 170.

Karl Marx (1818–1883) contributed to the founding of sociology and was one of the authors of the *Communist Manifesto*.

All societies include two main social classes that struggle over the means of production. One class owns or controls the means of production, and the other is exploited and oppressed to sustain the advantage of the dominant class. In an industrial society, the two classes are the **bourgeoisie**, the capitalists who own the means of production, and the **proletariat**, or the working class. Marx believed that conflict between these classes was inevitable and that, ultimately, the working class would successfully revolt against the bourgeoisie and create a utopian society without exploitation, coercion, or inequality—in other words, a classless society.

Marxism has been extensively revised and modified over the past century and a half. Still, modern social science owes a great deal to Marx's views on inequality and his insights on class struggle and social conflict. As you shall see, Marxism remains an important body of work and a rich source of insight into group relations in industrial society.

Max Weber. One of Marx's major critics was Max Weber, a German sociologist who did most of his work around the turn of the 20th century. Weber thought that Marx's view of inequality was too narrow. Marx saw social class as a matter of economic position or relationship to the means of production, but Weber argued that inequality was more complex and included dimensions other than just the economic. Individuals

could be members of the elite in some ways but not in others. For example, an aristocratic family that has fallen on hard financial times might belong to the elite in terms of family lineage but not in terms of wealth. To use a more contemporary example, a major figure in the illegal drug trade could enjoy substantial wealth but be held in low esteem otherwise.

Weber expanded on Marx's view of inequality by identifying three separate stratification systems. First, economic inequality is based on ownership or control of property, wealth, and income. This is similar to Marx's concept of class, and in fact, Weber used the term *class* to identify this form of inequality.

A second system of stratification revolves around differences in **prestige** between groups, or the amount of honor, esteem, or respect given to us by others. Class position is one factor that affects the amount of prestige a person enjoys. Other factors might include family lineage, athletic ability, and physical appearance. In the United States and other societies, prestige is affected by the groups to which people belong, and members of minority groups typically receive less prestige than do members of the dominant group. A wealthy minority-group member might be ranked high on class or control of property, wealth, and income, but low on status or prestige.

Weber's third stratification system is **power**, or the ability to influence others, impact the decision-making process of society, and pursue and protect one's self-interest and achieve one's goals. One source of power is a person's standing in politically active organizations, such as labor unions or pressure groups, that lobby state and federal legislatures. Some politically active groups have access to great wealth and can use their riches to promote their causes. Other groups may rely more on their size and ability to mobilize large demonstrations to achieve their goals. Political groups and the people they represent vary in their abilities to affect the political process and control decision making; that is, they vary in the amount of power they can mobilize.

Typically, these three dimensions of stratification go together: Wealthy, prestigious groups will be more powerful (more likely to achieve their goals or protect their self-interest) than low-income groups or groups with little prestige. It is important to realize, however, that power is a separate dimension. Even very impoverished groups have sometimes found ways to express their concerns and pursue their goals.

The **bourgeoisie** are the elite or ruling class that owns the means of production in an industrial society.

In an industrial society, the **proletariat** are the workers.

Prestige is honor, esteem, or respect.

Power is the ability to affect the decision-making process of a social system.

Max Weber (1864–1920) was a major figure in the establishment of sociology. He took issue with many of Marx's ideas in publications such as *The Protestant Ethic* and *The Spirit of Capitalism*.

Gerhard Lenski. Gerhard Lenski is a contemporary sociologist who follows Weber and distinguishes between class (or property), prestige, and power. Lenski expands on Weber's ideas, however, by analyzing stratification in the context of societal evolution, or the **level of development** of a society (Nolan & Lenski, 2004). He argues that the nature of inequality (the degree of inequality or the specific criteria affecting a group's position) is closely related to **subsistence technology**, the means by which the society satisfies basic needs such as

The **level of development** is the stage of evolution of a society, including agrarian, industrial, and postindustrial.

A **subsistence technology** is the system by which a society satisfies basic needs.

A **postindustrial society** is dominated by service work, information-processing, and high technology.

Intersectionality stresses the cross-cutting, linked nature of inequality and the multiplicity of statuses all people occupy.

hunger and thirst. A preindustrial agricultural society relies on human and animal labor to generate the calories necessary to sustain life. Inequality in this type of society centers on control of land and labor because they are the most important means of production at that level of development.

In a modern industrial society, however, land ownership is not as crucial as control of financial, manufacturing, and commercial enterprises. At the industrial level of development, control of capital is more important than control of land, and the nature of inequality will change accordingly.

The United States and other societies have entered still another stage of development, often referred to as **postindustrial society**. In this type of society, economic growth is powered by new technology, computer-related fields, information processing, and medical and scientific research. Manufacturing jobs (e.g., producing automobiles or television sets) recede in importance and are replaced by jobs that provide services to others (e.g., teacher, financial analyst, or waitress). In the postindustrial era, economic success will be closely related to specialized knowledge, familiarity with new technologies, and education in general (Chirot, 1994, p. 88; see also Bell, 1973).

These changes in subsistence technology, from agriculture to industrialization to the "information society," alter the stratification system. As the sources of wealth, success, and power change, so do the relationships between minority and dominant groups. For example, the shift to an information-based, "hi-tech," postindustrial society means that the advantages conferred by higher levels of education will be magnified and groups that have less access to schooling will likely rank low on all dimensions of stratification.

Patricia Hill Collins. Sociologist Patricia Hill Collins (2000) calls for an approach to the study of inequality and group relations that recognizes the multiplicity of systems of inequality and privilege that operate in society. Some systems are based on social class, while others divide people by gender, race, ethnicity, sexuality, age, disability, and multiple other criteria. Almost everyone holds a mixed set of statuses, some more privileged and some less. For example, Hector, the Mexican American parole officer mentioned in the "American Stories" at the start of this chapter, is male, college educated, and a professional, all statuses that rank higher in the United States. On the other hand, his Mexican American heritage and bisexuality put him at a disadvantage in a society where whiteness and heterosexuality are more valued.

Collins stresses **intersectionality**, a view that acknowledges that everyone—like Hector—has multiple group memberships and that these crisscross and create very different realities for people with varying combinations of statuses. The realities faced by gay, blue-collar, Mexican American males are very different from those faced by heterosexual, wealthy Hispanic females, even though both would be counted as "Hispanic" in Figure 1.1. There is no singular or uniform Hispanic

Patricia Hill Collins

Patricia Hill Collins is a major contributor to the ongoing attempts by American social scientists to analyze inequality and group relations.

American (or African American or Asian American) experience, and we need to recognize how gender, class, sexual orientation, and other factors intersect with one another.

In part, Collins and other intersectionality theorists are reacting against the tendency to see inequality in terms of separate dichotomous systems, based on class (blue collar vs. white collar), race (black vs. white), gender (male vs. female), or some other criterion. The intersectionality approach analyzes how these statuses are linked to one another and form a "matrix of domination." For example, white Americans are not simply the "dominant group," undifferentiated and homogenous. Some segments of this group, such as women or poor whites, may occupy a privileged status in terms of their race but be subordinate in other ways, as defined by their gender or economic status. In the same way, minority groups are internally differentiated along lines of class and gender, and members of some segments are more privileged than others. Who is the oppressed and who is the oppressor changes across social contexts, and people can occupy both statuses simultaneously.

Everyone experiences some relative degree of advantage and disadvantage, and the separate systems of domination and subordination crosscut and overlap one another. Opportunity and individual experience are shaped by this matrix of domination. For example, as we shall see in later chapters, race and gender interact with each other and create especially disadvantaged positions for people who rank lower on both dimensions simultaneously (e.g., see Figure 6.5, which shows that black women consistently fall below black men and white men and women in terms of income).

Likewise, stereotypes and other elements of prejudice are gendered. That is, they are attached to men or women, not to the entire group. For example, some stereotypical traits might be applied to all African Americans (such as laziness; see Figure 3.3), but others are reserved for women (e.g., the "welfare queen" or "mammy") or men (e.g., the "thug" or "buffoon").

An intersectionality approach stresses the multiplicity of the systems of inequality and probes the links among them. Groups are seen as differentiated and complex, not uniform. In this text, one of our main concerns will be to explore how minority-group experience is mediated by class and gender, but you should be aware that this approach can be applied to many other dimensions of power and inequality, including disability, sexual preference, and religion.

MINORITY-GROUP STATUS AND STRATIFICATION

The theoretical perspectives we have just reviewed raise three important points about the connections between minority-group status and stratification. First, as already noted, minority-group status affects access to wealth and income, prestige, and power. A society in which minority groups systematically receive less of these valued goods is stratified, at least partly, by race and ethnicity. In the United States, minority-group status has been and continues to be one of the most important and powerful determinants of life chances, health and wealth, and success. These patterns of inequality are documented and explored in Part III, but even casual observation of U.S. society will reveal that minority groups control proportionately fewer resources and that minority-group status and stratification are intimately and complexly intertwined.

Second, although social classes and minority groups are correlated, they are separate social realities. The degree to which one is dependent on the other varies from group to group. Some groups, such as Irish or Italian Americans, enjoy considerable **social mobility** or easy access to opportunities, even though they faced considerable discrimination in the past. Furthermore, as stressed by the intersectionality approach, degrees of domination and subordination are variable and all groups are subdivided by cross-cutting lines of differentiation.

Social mobility is movement up and down the stratification system.

Social class and minority-group status are different dimensions of inequality, and they can vary independently. Some members of a minority group can be successful economically, wield great political power, or enjoy high prestige even though the vast majority of their group languishes in poverty and powerlessness. Each minority group is internally divided by systems of inequality based on class, status, or power, and in the same way, members of the same social class may be separated by ethnic or racial differences.

The third point concerning the connections between stratification and minority groups brings us back to group conflict. Dominant–minority group relationships are created by struggle over the control of valued goods and services. Minority-group structures (such as slavery) emerge so that the dominant group can control commodities such as land or labor, maintain its position in the stratification system, or eliminate a perceived threat to its well-being. Struggles over property, wealth, prestige, and power lie at the heart of every dominant–minority relationship. Marx believed that all aspects of society and culture were shaped to benefit the elite or ruling class and sustain the economic system that underlies its privileged position. The treatment of minority groups throughout American history provides a good deal of evidence to support Marx's point.

VISIBLE DISTINGUISHING TRAITS: RACE AND GENDER

In this section, we focus on the second defining characteristic of minority groups: the visible traits that denote membership. The boundaries between dominant and minority groups have been established along a wide variety of lines, including religion, language, skin color, and sexuality. Here we consider race and gender, two of the more physical and permanent—and thus more socially visible—markers of group membership.

RACE

In the past, race has been widely misunderstood, but the false ideas and exaggerated importance attached to race have not been mere errors of logic, subject to debate and refutation. At various times and in various places, they have been associated with some of the greatest tragedies in human history: massive exploitation and mistreatment, slavery, and genocide. Many myths about race survive in the present, if perhaps in diluted or muted form, and it is important to cultivate accurate understandings (although the scientific knowledge that has accumulated about race is no guarantee that race will not be used to instigate or justify further tragedies in the future).

Thanks to advances in the sciences of genetics, biology, and physical anthropology, we know more about what race is

and, more important, what race is not. We cannot address all the confusion in these few pages, but we can establish a basic framework and use the latest scientific research to dispel some of the myths.

Race and Human Evolution. Our species first appeared in East Africa about 100,000 year ago. Our ancient ancestors were hunters and gatherers who slowly wandered away from their ancestral region in search of food and other resources. Over the millennia, our ancestors traveled across the entire globe, first to what is now the Middle East and then to Asia, Europe, Australia, and North and South America.

Human "racial" differences evolved during this period of dispersion, as our ancestors adapted, physically as well as culturally, to different environments and ecological conditions. For example, consider skin color, one of the most visible "racial" characteristics. Skin color is derived from a pigment called melanin. In areas with intense sunlight, at or near the equator, melanin screens out the ultraviolet rays of the sun that cause sunburn and, more significantly, it protects against skin cancer. Thus, higher levels of melanin and darker skin colors are found in peoples who are adapted to equatorial ecologies.

In peoples adapted to areas with less intense sunlight, the amount of melanin is lower and skin color is lighter. The lower concentration of melanin may also be an adaptation to a particular ecology. It maximizes the synthesis of vitamin D, which is important for the absorption of calcium and protection against disorders such as rickets. Thus, the skin color (amount of melanin) of any group balances the need for vitamin D against the need to protect against ultraviolet rays.

Note also that our oldest ancestors were adapted to the equatorial sun of Africa. This almost certainly means that they were dark skinned (had a high concentration of melanin) and that lighter skin colors are the more recent adaptation.

The period of dispersion and differentiation, which is depicted in Figure 1.5, began to come to a close about 10,000 years ago when some of our hunting and gathering ancestors developed a new subsistence technology and settled down in permanent agricultural villages. Over the centuries, some of these settlements grew into larger societies and kingdoms and empires that conquered and absorbed neighboring societies, some of which differed culturally, linguistically, and racially from one another. The great agricultural empires of the past— Roman, Egyptian, Chinese, Aztec—united different peoples, reversed the process of dispersion and differentiation, and began a phase of consolidation and merging of human cultures and genetics. Over the next 10,000 years, human genes were intermixed and spread around the globe.

The differentiation created during the period of global dispersion was swamped by the consolidation that continues in the present. In our society, consolidation manifests in the increasing numbers of people of mixed-race descent, and similar patterns are common across the globe and throughout more

FIGURE 1.5 The Migration of Anatomically Modern Humans

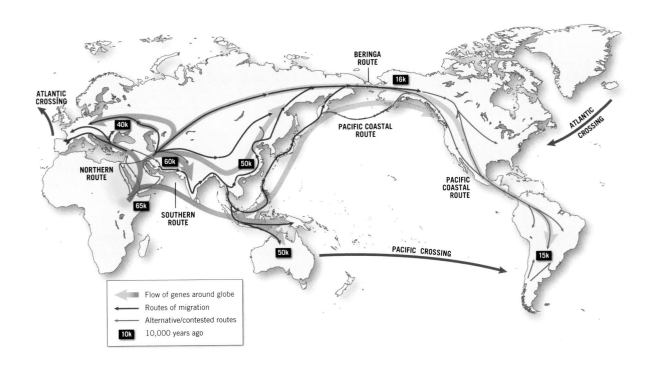

recent human history. The consolidation phase accelerated beginning about 500 years ago with the expansion of European power that resulted in the exploration and conquest of much of the rest of the world.

Race and Western Traditions. Aided by breakthroughs in navigation and ship design, the nations of western Europe began to travel to Africa, Asia, and eventually North and South America in the 1400s. Europeans had been long aware of racial variation, but the concern with race increased as they came into continuous contact with the peoples of these continents and became more aware of and curious about the physical differences they saw.

Europeans also conquered, colonized, and sometimes destroyed the peoples and cultures they encountered. From the beginning, the European awareness of the differences between the races was linked to notions of inferior and superior (conquered vs. conquering) peoples. For centuries, the European tradition has been to see race in this political and military context and to intermix biological and physical variation with judgments about the relative merits of the various races. Racist thinking was used to justify military conquest, genocide, exploitation, and slavery. The toxic form of racism that bloomed during the expansion of European power continues to haunt the world today and was the basis for the concept of race that took root in the United States.

Race and Biology. Europeans used race primarily to denigrate, reject, and exclude nonwhites, but there were also attempts to apply the principles of scientific research to the concept. These investigations focused on the construction of typologies or taxonomies, systems of classification that were intended to provide a category for every race and every person. Some of these typologies were quite elaborate and included scores of races and subraces. For example, the Caucasian race was often subdivided into Nordics (blond, fair-skinned northern Europeans), Mediterraneans (dark-haired southern Europeans), and Alpines (those falling between the first two categories).

One major limitation of these systems of classification is that the dividing lines between the so-called racial groups are arbitrary and blurred. There is no clear or definite point where, for example, "black" skin color stops and "white" skin color begins. The characteristics used to define race blend imperceptibly into one another, and one racial trait (skin color) can be blended with others (e.g., hair texture) in an infinite variety of ways. A given individual might have a skin color associated with one race, the hair texture of a second, the nasal shape of a third, and so forth.

Even the most elaborate racial typologies could not handle the reality that many individuals fit into more than one category or none at all. Although people undeniably vary in their physical appearance, these differences do not sort themselves out in a way that permits us to divide people up like species of animals. The differences between the so-called human races are not at all like the differences between elephants and butterflies. The ambiguous and continuous nature of racial characteristics makes it impossible to establish categories that have clear, non-arbitrary boundaries.

Over the past several decades, rapid advances in genetics have provided additional information and new insights into race that continue to refute many racial myths and further undermine the validity of racial typologies. Perhaps the most important single finding of modern research is that genetic variation *within* the "traditional" racial groups is greater than the variation *between* those groups (American Sociological Association, 2003). In other words, any two randomly selected members of, say, the "black" race are likely to vary genetically from each other at least as much as they do from a randomly selected member of the "white" race. No single finding could be more destructive of traditional racial categories that are, after all, supposed to group people into homogenous categories. Just as certainly, the traditional American perception of race as based primarily on skin color has no scientific validity.

The Social Construction of Race. Despite its limited scientific uselessness, race continues to animate intergroup relations in the United States and around the world. It continues to be socially important and a significant way of differentiating among people. Race, along with gender, is one of the first things people notice about one another. In the United States, we still tend to see race as a simple, unambiguous matter of skin color alone and to judge everyone as belonging to one and only one group, ignoring the realities of multiple ancestry and ambiguous classification.

How can the concept of race retain its relevance? Because of the way it developed, Western ideas about race have a social as well as biological or scientific dimension. To sociologists, race is a social construction and its meaning has been created and sustained not by science but by historical, social, economic, and political processes (see Omi & Winant, 1986; Smedley, 2007).

For example, in Chapter 4, we will analyze the role of race in the creation of American slavery and will see that the physical differences between blacks and whites became important *as a result* of the creation of that system of inequality. The elites of colonial society needed to justify their unequal treatment of Africans and seized on the obvious difference in skin color, elevated it to a matter of supreme importance, and used it to justify the enslavement of blacks. In other words, the importance of race was socially constructed in a particular historical era, and it remains important not because of objective realities but because of the widespread, shared social perception that it is important.

GENDER

You have already seen that minority groups can be internally divided by social class and other factors. An additional source of differentiation is gender. Like race, gender has both a biological and a social component and can be a highly visible and convenient way of judging and sorting people. From birth, the biological differences between the sexes form the basis for different **gender roles**, or societal expectations about proper behavior, attitudes, and personality traits. Generally, nurturance, interpersonal skills, and "emotion work" tend to be stressed for girls, while boys are expected to learn to be assertive and independent.

Gender roles and relationships vary across time and from one society to another, but gender and inequality have been closely related, and men typically claim more property, prestige, and power. Figure 1.6 provides some perspective on the variation in gender inequality across the globe. The map shows the distribution of a statistic called the Gender Inequality Index, which measures the amount of inequality between men and women across a range of variables, including education, health, and political representation. As you can see, gender equality is generally highest in the more developed, industrialized nations of North America and western Europe and lowest in the less developed, more agricultural nations of sub-Saharan Africa.

Western European and North American societies rank relatively high on gender equality, but gender discrimination continues to be a major issue, as we will see throughout this text (Chapter 11 in particular). For example, there is a consistent—and large—gender income gap in these societies, and women are decidedly underrepresented in the most lucrative and powerful occupations (e.g., see Figure 11.1). While progress has been made, gender equality will continue to be an issue in these societies for generations to come.

Part of the problem is that all societies, including western Europe and North America, have strong traditions of **patriarchy**, or male dominance. In a patriarchal society, men have more control over the economy and more access to leadership roles in business, politics, education, and other institutions. Parallel to the various forms of racism that sought to justify and continue racial inequality, women have been subjected to **sexism**, or belief systems that "explained" inequality based on gender. Women, for example, were sometimes seen in traditional cultures as "delicate flowers," too emotional and physically weak for the harsh demands of "manly" occupations outside the home. (Note that, in the American tradition, this view has a racial component and has been applied to white women only. The same men who placed white women on a pedestal did not

---

Gender roles are societal expectations regarding the behavior, attitudes, and personality traits of males and females.

Patriarchy is male dominance.

Sexism refers to belief systems that label females as inferior and rationalize their lower status.

FIGURE 1.6 Gender Inequality Worldwide

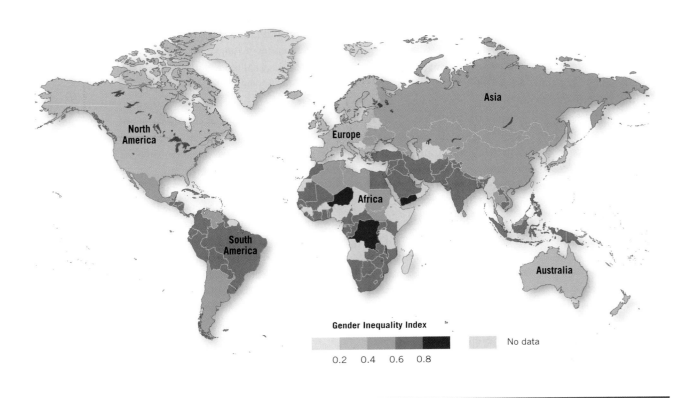

hesitate to send women of color into the fields to perform the most difficult, physically demanding, "nonfeminine" tasks.)

Even in the most progressive societies, women continue to possess many characteristics of a minority group (namely, a pattern of disadvantage based on group membership marked by a physical stigma). Thus, women could be, and in many ways should be, treated as a separate minority group. We will do this in Chapter 11, but throughout the text, we will address the divergent experiences of men and women within each minority group. We will consider how the interests and experiences of females of different groups and classes coincide with and diverge from one another and from those of the men in their groups. For example, on some issues, African American females might have interests identical to those of white females and opposed to those of African American males. On other issues, the constellations of interests might be reversed. As stressed in the intersectionality approach, the experience of minority-group membership varies by gender (along with other criteria), and the way gender is experienced is not the same for every group.

History generally has been and is written from the standpoint of the "winners"—that is, those in power. The voices of minority groups have generally been repressed, ignored, forgotten, or trivialized. Much of the history of slavery in America, for instance, has been told from the viewpoint of the slave owners. Slaves were kept illiterate by law and had few mechanisms for recording their thoughts or experiences. A more balanced and accurate picture of slavery began to emerge only in the past few decades, when scholars started to dig beneath the written records and memoirs of the slave owners and reconstruct the experiences of African Americans from nonwritten documentation such as oral traditions and the physical artifacts left by slaves.

However, our understanding of the experiences of minority groups is often based almost entirely on those of minority-group males, and the experiences of minority-group females are much less well-known and documented. If the voices of minority groups have been hushed, female minority-group members have been virtually silenced. One of the important trends in contemporary scholarship is to adjust this skewed focus and systematically incorporate gender as a factor in the minority-group experience (Baca Zinn & Thornton Dill, 1994; Espiritu, 1997).

The Social Construction of Gender. Social scientists see race as a social construction formulated in certain historical circumstances (such as the era of European colonialism) when it was needed to help justify the unequal treatment of nonwhite groups. What about gender? Is it also merely a social creation designed to rationalize the higher status of men and their easier access to power, prestige, and property? Figure 1.6 shows that all contemporary nations have some degree of gender inequality. Is this because—as many people believe—boys and men are "naturally" more aggressive and independent, and girls and women are more emotional and expressive? What is the basis of these distinctions? What connection, if any, do they have with biology and genetics?

First of all, the traits commonly seen as "typical" of men or women—aggressiveness or emotional expressiveness, for example—are not discrete categories. Every person has them to some degree, and to the extent that gender differences exist at all, they are manifested not in absolutes but in averages, tendencies, and probabilities. Aggressiveness is often thought of as a male characteristic, but many women are more aggressive than many men. Likewise, emotionality tends to be associated with women, but many males are more expressive and emotional than many females. As is the case with racial differences, research has shown that there is more variation *within* categories than between them—a finding that seriously undermines the view that gender differences are genetic or biological (Basow, as cited in Rosenblum & Travis, 2002).

Second, that gender is a social construction is illustrated by the fact that what is thought to be "appropriate" gender behavior varies from time to time and from society to society. The behavior expected of a female in Victorian England would be thoroughly out of place in 21st-century America, and the typical behavior of a contemporary male would be regarded as outrageously scandalous in Puritan America. This variability makes it difficult to argue that the differences between the genders are "hardwired" in the genetic code; if they were, the variations would be nonexistent.

Third, the essentially social nature of gender roles is further illustrated by the relationship between subsistence technology and gender inequality. As we noted previously, our species evolved in East Africa and relied on hunting and gathering to satisfy the need for food. Our distant ancestors lived in small, nomadic bands that relied on cooperation and sharing for survival. Societies at this level of development typically divide adult labor roles by gender (with men hunting and women gathering), and, although they may tend toward patriarchy, women and women's work are highly valued and gender inequality is minimal. The subordination of women is more associated with settled agricultural communities, the first of which appeared in what is now the Middle East about 10,000 years ago. Survival in preindustrial farming societies requires the combined efforts of many people, and large families are valued as a cheap labor force. Women are consigned to household and domestic duties, with a strong emphasis on producing and raising children. Since the infant mortality rate in these societies is high (perhaps 50% or more), women spend much of their lives confined and secluded, pregnant or nursing young children, far removed from the possibility of contending for leadership roles in their communities.

Industrialization and urbanization, linked processes that began in the mid-1700s in Great Britain, changed the cost/benefit ratios for childbearing. The expenses associated with having children rose in the city, and the nature of industrial work increasingly required education and literacy—qualities and abilities available to both genders. Thus, gender inequality probably reached its peak in preindustrial agrarian societies and has tended to decline as societies industrialized. It is no accident of timing that the push for gender equality and the women's liberation movement are associated with industrial societies and that gender equality is highest today in industrial and postindustrial societies (see Figure 1.6).

To be sure, biology shapes the production of personality, and researchers are still exploring the possible links between genetics and gender roles (e.g., see Hopcroft, 2009; Huber, 2007; Udry, 2000), but the key to understanding gender is social and experiential, not biological (Booth, Granger, Mazur, & Kivligham, 2006). Gender, like race, is a social construction, especially when the supposed differences between men and women are treated as categorical, "natural," and fixed, and then used to deny opportunity and equality to women.

QUESTIONS FOR REFLECTION

Are both gender and race *merely* social constructions? Aren't they *real* in some ways? In what ways do they exist apart from people's perception of them? Are they both social constructions in the same way? Are they *equally* matters of perception?

KEY CONCEPTS IN DOMINANT–MINORITY RELATIONS

Whenever sensitive issues such as dominant–minority group relations are raised, the discussion turns to (or on) matters of prejudice and discrimination. We will be very much concerned with these subjects in this book, so we need to clarify what we mean by these terms. This section introduces and defines four concepts that will help you understand dominant–minority relations in the United States.

This book addresses how individuals from different groups interact, as well as relations among groups. Thus, we need to distinguish between what is true for individuals (the psychological level of analysis) and what is true for groups or society as a whole (the sociological level of analysis). Beyond that, we must attempt to trace the connections between the two levels of analysis.

We need to make a further distinction on both the individual and group levels. At the individual level, what people think and feel about other groups and how they actually behave toward members of those groups may differ. A person might express negative feelings about other groups in private but deal fairly with members of the groups in face-to-face interactions. Groups and entire societies may display this same kind of inconsistency. A society may express support for equality in its official documents or formal codes of law and simultaneously treat minority groups in unfair and destructive ways. An example of this kind of inconsistency is the contrast between the commitment to equality stated in the Declaration of Independence ("All men are created equal") and the actual treatment of black slaves, Anglo-American women, and Native Americans at that time.

At the individual level, social scientists refer to the "thinking/feeling" part of this dichotomy as prejudice and the "doing" part as discrimination. At the group level, the term **ideological racism** describes the "thinking/feeling" dimension and **institutional discrimination** describes the "doing" dimension. Table 1.1 depicts the differences among these four concepts.

PREJUDICE

Prejudice is the tendency of an individual to think about other groups in negative ways, to attach negative emotions to those groups, and to prejudge individuals on the basis of their group memberships. Individual prejudice has two aspects: the **cognitive dimension of prejudice**, or the thinking aspect, and the **affective dimension of prejudice**, or the feeling part. A prejudiced person thinks about other groups in terms of **stereotypes** (cognitive prejudice), generalizations that are thought to apply to group members. Examples of familiar stereotypes include notions such as "women are emotional," "Jews are stingy," "blacks are lazy," "the Irish are drunks," and "Germans are authoritarian."

A prejudiced person also experiences negative emotional responses to other groups (affective prejudice). Examples of these negative emotions include contempt, disgust, arrogance, and hatred.

People vary in their levels of prejudice, and levels of prejudice can vary in the same person from one time to another and from one group to another. We can say that a person is prejudiced to the extent that he or she uses stereotypes in his or her thinking about other groups or has negative emotional reactions to other groups.

Generally, the two dimensions of prejudice are highly correlated with each other; however, they are also distinct and separate aspects of prejudice and can vary independently. One person may think entirely in stereotypes but feel no particular negative emotional response to any group. Another person may feel a very strong aversion toward a group but be unable to articulate a clear or detailed stereotype of that group.

We should note here that individual prejudice, like all aspects of society, evolves and changes. In the past, American prejudice was strongly felt, baldly expressed, and laced with clear, detailed stereotypes. Today, prejudice tends to be expressed in subtle, indirect ways. For example, it might

TABLE 1.1 Four Concepts in Dominant–Minority Relations

DIMENSION	LEVEL OF ANALYSIS	
	Individual	Group or Societal
Thinking/feeling	Prejudice	Ideological racism
Doing	Discrimination	Institutional discrimination

manifest itself in code words, as when people disparage "welfare cheats" or associate criminality with certain minority groups. We will explore these modern forms of prejudice in Chapter 3, but we need to be clear that the relative absence of blatant stereotyping or the expression of strong public emotions against minority groups in modern society does not mean that we have eliminated individual prejudice in the United States.

DISCRIMINATION

Discrimination is defined as the unequal treatment of a person or persons based on group membership. An example of discrimination is an employer who decides not to hire an individual because he or she is African American (or Puerto Rican, Jewish, Chinese, etc.). If the unequal treatment is based on the individual's group membership, the act is discriminatory.

Just as the cognitive and affective aspects of prejudice can be independent, discrimination and prejudice do not necessarily occur together. Even highly prejudiced individuals may not act on their negative thoughts or feelings. In social settings

Ideological racism refers to societal belief systems that label certain groups as inferior.

Institutional discrimination is a pattern of unequal treatment of a group that is built into the daily operation of society.

Prejudice is the tendency of individuals to think and feel negatively toward others.

The **cognitive dimension of prejudice** refers to how people think about members of other groups.

The **affective dimension of prejudice** refers to how people feel about members of other groups.

Stereotypes are generalizations that are thought to characterize groups as a whole.

Discrimination is the unequal treatment of a person based on his or her group membership.

Carolyn Kaster/Associated Press

Neo-Nazis participating in a rally. Groups such as this advocate discrimination (or worse).

regulated by strong egalitarian codes or laws (e.g., restaurants and other public facilities), people who are highly bigoted in their private thoughts and feelings may abide by the codes in their public roles.

On the other hand, social situations in which prejudice is strongly approved and supported might evoke discrimination in otherwise unprejudiced individuals. In the southern United States during the height of segregation or in South Africa during the period of state-sanctioned racial inequality called apartheid, it was usual and customary for whites to treat blacks in discriminatory ways. Regardless of a white person's actual level of prejudice, he or she faced strong social pressure to conform to the official patterns of racial superiority and participate in acts of discrimination.

QUESTIONS FOR REFLECTION

Like most Americans, you are probably familiar with the stereotypes commonly attached to various groups. Does this mean you are prejudiced against those groups? Does it mean you have negative emotions about those groups and are likely to discriminate against them?

IDEOLOGICAL RACISM

Ideological racism, a belief system that asserts that a particular group is inferior, is the group or societal equivalent of individual prejudice. These ideas and beliefs are used to legitimize or rationalize the inferior status of minority groups and are incorporated into the culture of a society and passed on from generation to generation during socialization.

Because it is a part of the cultural heritage, ideological racism exists apart from the individuals who inhabit the society at a specific time (Andersen, 1993, p. 75; See & Wilson, 1988, p. 227). An example of a racist ideology is

the elaborate system of beliefs and ideas that attempted to justify slavery in the American South. The exploitation of slaves was "explained" in terms of the innate racial inferiority of blacks and the superiority of whites.

Distinguishing between individual prejudice and societal racist ideologies naturally leads to a consideration of the relationship between these two phenomena. We will explore this relationship in later chapters, but for now we can make what is probably an obvious point: People socialized into societies with strong racist ideologies are very likely to absorb racist ideas and be highly prejudiced. It should not surprise us that a high level of personal prejudice existed among whites in the antebellum American South or in other highly racist societies, such as South Africa. At the same time, we need to remember that ideological racism and individual prejudice are different things with different causes and different locations in the society. Racism is not a prerequisite for prejudice; prejudice may exist even in the absence of an ideology of racism.

INSTITUTIONAL DISCRIMINATION

The final concept is the societal equivalent of individual discrimination. Institutional discrimination refers to a pattern of unequal treatment based on group membership that is built into the daily operations of society, whether or not it is consciously intended. The public schools, the criminal justice system, and political and economic institutions can operate in ways that put members of some groups at a disadvantage.

Institutional discrimination can be obvious and overt. For many years following the Civil War, African Americans in the American South were prevented from voting by practices such as poll taxes and literacy tests designed to ensure that they would fail. For nearly a century, well into the 1960s, elections and elected offices in the South were restricted to whites only. The purpose of this blatant pattern of institutional discrimination was widely understood by African American and white Southerners alike: It existed to disenfranchise the African American community and to keep it politically powerless.

At other times, institutional discrimination may operate more subtly and without conscious intent. If public schools use aptitude tests that are biased in favor of the dominant group, decisions about who does and does not take college preparatory courses may be made on racist grounds, even if everyone involved sincerely believes that they are merely applying objective criteria in a rational way. If a decision-making process has unequal consequences for dominant and minority groups, institutional discrimination may well be at work.

Note that although a particular discriminatory policy may be implemented and enforced by individuals, the policy is more appropriately thought of as an aspect of the operation of the

Several actual events are listed below. In the space provided, classify each as an example of cognitive prejudice, affective prejudice, individual discrimination, ideological racism, or institutional discrimination, and briefly explain your reasoning. Some incidents are ambiguous and may include elements of more than one concept.

Note: Your instructor may ask you to complete this assignment with others as a group discussion.

	INCIDENT	CONCEPT	EXPLANATION
1	Upon learning that the house next door will be purchased by an Asian American family, Mrs. Smith, a white American, says, "Well, at least they're not black."		
2	A TV commercial promoting the U.S. military recounts an incident from the 1830s when troops were dispatched to Alabama "to pacify Indians who were threatening white settlers."		
3	In a settlement with the U.S. Justice Department, a national restaurant chain admitted that black diners were purposely given poor service and made to wait longer for tables.		
4	A white voter did not vote for Obama because he feared that Obama would appoint too many unqualified blacks to his administration.		
5	A police force is sued because it has disproportionately few female officers. An investigation finds that many females had been rejected because they did not meet a requirement regarding upper-body strength.		
6	A woman who has been fired from her minimum-wage job blames "those stinking illegal aliens—they're taking all our jobs."		

TURN THE PAGE TO FIND OUR ANSWERS.

institution as a whole. Election officials in the South during segregation did not and public school administrators today do not have to be personally prejudiced themselves to implement these discriminatory policies.

However, a major thesis of this book is that both racist ideologies and institutional discrimination are created to sustain the positions of dominant and minority groups in the stratification system. The relative advantage of the dominant group is maintained from day to day by widespread institutional discrimination. Members of the dominant group who are socialized into communities with strong racist ideologies and a great deal of institutional discrimination are likely to be personally prejudiced and to routinely engage in acts of individual discrimination. The respective positions of dominant and minority groups are preserved over time through the mutually reinforcing patterns of prejudice, racism, and discrimination on both the individual and institutional levels. Institutional discrimination is but one way members of a minority group can be denied access to valued goods and services, opportunities, and rights (such as voting). That is, institutional discrimination helps sustain and reinforce the unequal positions of racial and ethnic groups in the stratification system.

A GLOBAL PERSPECTIVE

In the chapters that follow, we will focus on developing a number of concepts and theories and applying those ideas to the minority groups of the United States. However, it is important to expand our perspective beyond the experiences of just a single nation and consider the experiences and histories of other peoples and places. Thus, we will take time throughout this text to apply our ideas to other societies and non-American minority groups. Also, in Chapter 14, we will systematically examine group relationships around the globe. If the ideas and concepts developed in this text can help us make sense of these situations, we will have some assurance that they have some general applicability and that the dynamics of intergroup relations in the United States are not unique.

On another level, we must also take account of the ways group relations in the United States are shaped by economic, social, and political forces beyond our borders. As we will see, the experiences of this society cannot be understood in isolation. We are part of the global system of societies, and now, more than ever, we must take account of the complex interconnections between the domestic and the international,

	CONCEPT	EXPLANATION
1	Cognitive prejudice	Mrs. Smith seems to be thinking in terms of the traditional stereotype regarding the desirability of blacks and Asians.
2	Ideological racism	The commercial reflects the cultural assumption that Indians are outsiders who need to be pacified (or eliminated). Why were the Indians "threatening"? What were the settlers doing in Alabama? Who is the aggressor, and who is the victim?
3	Institutional discrimination	In this case, the entire company was following a discriminatory policy, not just an individual.
4	Cognitive prejudice	The voter is using stereotypes and making assumptions about what "those people" do.
5	Institutional discrimination	If the strength requirement limits the opportunities of women (or other groups), the policy is discriminatory. A possible exception might be for jobs that *truly* require upper-body strength (e.g., defensive linemen in professional football) or some other physical attribute (e.g., height for an NBA power forward).
6	Affective prejudice	She is expressing strong feelings of rejection and contempt.

particularly with respect to issues of immigration. The world is indeed growing smaller, and we must see our society as one part of a larger system. The next section illustrates one connection between the global and the local.

IMMIGRATION AND GLOBALIZATION

Immigration is a major concern in our society today, and we will address the issue on a number of occasions in the pages to come. Here, we will point out that immigration is a global phenomenon that affects virtually every nation in the world. About 214 million people—a little more than 3% of the world's population—live outside their countries of birth, and the number of migrants has increased steadily over the past several decades (United Nations Department of Economic and Social Affairs, Population Division, 2013). Figure 1.7 depicts the major population movement from 1990 to 2000 and clearly demonstrates the global nature of immigration. Note that western Europe is a major destination for immigrants, as is the United States.

What has caused this massive population movement? One very important underlying cause is globalization, or the increasing interconnectedness of people, groups, organizations, and nations. Globalization is a complex and multidimensional process, but perhaps the most powerful dimension of globalization—especially for understanding contemporary immigration—is economics and the movement of jobs and opportunity from place to place. People flow from areas of lower opportunity to those with greater opportunity, much as air flows from high- to low-pressure systems.

To illustrate, consider the southern border of the United States. For the past several decades, there has been an influx of people—like Lucresia, whose story opened this chapter—from Mexico and other Central American nations to the United States, and the presence of these newcomers has generated a great deal of emotional and political heat, especially since many migrants are undocumented.

Some Americans see these newcomers as threats to traditional American culture and the English language, and others associate them with crime, violence, and drug smuggling. Still others see them simply as people trying to survive as best they can, desperate to support themselves and their families. Few, however, see these immigrants as the human consequences of the economic globalization of the world.

What is the connection between globalization and this immigrant stream? The population pressure on the southern border is in large part a result of the North American Free Trade Agreement (NAFTA), implemented in 1994. NAFTA united the three North American nations in a single trading bloc—economically "globalizing" the region—and permitted goods and capital (but not people) to move freely among Canada, the United States, and Mexico.

Among many other consequences, NAFTA opened Mexico to the importation of food products produced at very low cost by the giant agribusinesses of Canada and the United States. This cheap food (corn in particular) destroyed the livelihoods of many rural Mexicans and forced them to leave their villages in search of work. Millions pursued the only survival strategy that seemed remotely sensible: migration north. Even the meanest job in the United States pays many times more than the average Mexican wage.

NARRATIVE PORTRAIT

A White Male Reflects on Privilege

Tim Wise is a sociologist and a prominent antiracism activist.

In this passage, Tim Wise—sociologist, lecturer, writer, and antiracism activist—reflects on his whiteness. He points out that racial privilege is largely invisible to whites because, unlike minority-group members, they don't have to deal with its restrictions. Our racist cultural traditions make whiteness "normal," the standard against which "others" are contrasted and differentiated. From the perspective of whites, only nonwhites have race and ethnicity. Does the same dynamic mean that the restrictions of traditional gender roles are visible only to females?

What does it mean to be white, especially in a nation created for the benefit of people like you? We [white people] don't often ask this question, mostly because we don't have to. Being [white]...allows one to ignore how race shapes one's life. For those of us called white, whiteness... becomes...the unspoken...norm, taken for granted, much as water can be taken for granted by a fish.

In high school, whites are sometimes asked to think about race, but rarely about whiteness. In my case, we read John Howard Griffin's classic book, *Black Like Me*, in which the author recounts his experiences in the Jim Crow South in 1959, after taking a drug that turned his skin brown and allowed him to experience apartheid for a few months from the other side of the color line.

It was a good book, especially for its time. Yet I can't help but find it a bit disturbing that it remains one of the most assigned volumes on summer reading lists dealing with race. [This popularity seems to signal] the extent to which race is considered a problem of the past...surely there are some more contemporary racial events students could discuss....[By reading the book,] whites are encouraged to think about race from the perspective of blacks,...but *Black Like Me* leaves another aspect of the discussion untouched: namely, the examination of the white experience.

[To] be white in the United States...is to have certain common experiences based solely upon race. These experiences have to do with advantage, privilege..., and belonging. We are, unlike people of color, born to belonging, and have rarely had to prove ourselves deserving of our presence here....

While some might insist that whites have a wide range of experiences, and [that] it isn't fair to make generalizations..., this is a dodge, and not a particularly artful one at that. Of course we're all different, sort of like snowflakes, which come to think of it are also white. None of us have led the exact same life. But, [regardless], all whites were placed above all persons of color when it came to the economic, social, and political hierarchies that were to form in the United States, without exception. This formal system of racial preference was codified in law from the 1600s until at least 1964, at which time the Civil Rights Act was passed....

Prior to that time we didn't even pretend to be a nation based on equality. Or rather we did pretend, but not very well; at least not to the point where the rest of the world believed it, or to the point where people of color in this country ever did. Most white folks believed it, but that's simply more proof of our privileged status. Our ancestors had the luxury of believing those things that black and brown folks could never take as givens: all that stuff about life, liberty, and the pursuit of happiness. [Today,] whites can, indeed *must*, still believe it, while people of color have little reason to join the celebration, knowing as they do that there is still a vast gulf between who we say we are as a nation and people, and who we really are.

In other words, there is enough commonality about the white experience to allow us to make some general statements about whiteness and never be too far from the mark. Returning to the snowflake analogy: although...no two white people are exactly alike, it is also true that few snowflakes have radically different experiences from those of the average snowflake. Likewise, we know a snowflake when we see one, and in that recognition we intuit, almost always correctly, something about its life experience.

SOURCE: Wise (2008, pp. 2–4). Copyright © 2011 by Tim Wise from *White Like Me: Reflections on Race from a Privileged Son*. Reprinted by permission of Counterpoint.

Questions to Consider

1. Recall Carla's issues with identity from the previous Narrative Portrait. Is Tim more certain about who he is? Why?
2. How might Tim's statement change if he were female? Working class? Gay?
3. How is racial identity "invisible" to whites? What does the author mean when he says that whiteness is "the norm" in U.S. society? How does racial privilege permit whites to ignore race?

Even as NAFTA changed the economic landscape of North America, the United States became increasingly concerned with the security of its borders (especially after the terrorist attacks of September 11, 2001) and attempted to stem the flow of people, partly by building fences and increasing the size of the Border Patrol. The easier border crossings were quickly sealed, but this did not stop the pressure from the south. Migrants moved to more difficult and dangerous crossing routes, including the deadly, forbidding Sonoran Desert in southern Arizona, resulting in an untold number of deaths on the border since the mid-1990s.

Figure 1.8 displays one count of recent deaths along the southern U.S. border. As you can see, most of the deaths—almost 1,700, including Lucresia's—have been in southern Arizona.

This number accounts only for the bodies that were discovered. Some estimates put the true number at 10 deaths for every recovered corpse.

FIGURE 1.7 Major Global Migration Flows, 1990–2000

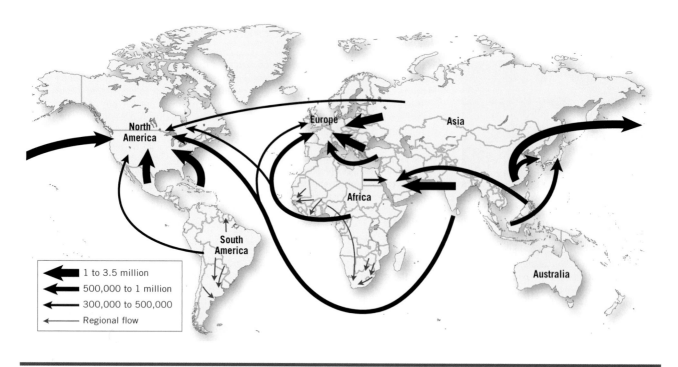

SOURCE: Adapted from *Stalker's Guide to Migration*, Peter Stalker; and World Map: Global Migration, La Documentation Française.

The relationship between NAFTA and immigration to the United States is just one aspect of a complex global relationship. Around the globe, people are moving in huge numbers from less developed nations to more developed, more affluent economies. The wealthy nations of western Europe, including Germany, Ireland, France, and the Netherlands, are also receiving large numbers of immigrants, and the citizens of these nations are concerned about their jobs and communities, housing, language, and the integrity of the national culture in much the same ways Americans are. The world is changing, and contemporary immigration must be understood in terms of changes that affect many nations and, indeed, the entire global system of societies.

FIGURE 1.8 Immigrant Deaths on the Southern Border, 2000–2010

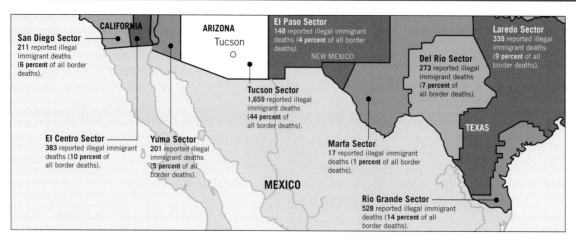

Illegal immigrant deaths, by Border Patrol sector: Covering 262 miles, the Tucson Sector has recorded nearly half of all deaths along the U.S.-Mexico border in the last decade.

SOURCE: *Arizona Daily Star.*

CONCLUSION

This chapter and this section of the book raise a lot of questions. Our intent is not so much to provide answers as to apply the sociological perspective and the concepts, theories, and body of research developed over the years to illuminate and clarify the issues. In many cases, we can identify approaches and ideas that are simply wrong and others that hold promise. Sociology can't answer all questions, but it does supply research tools and ideas that can help us think more clearly and with greater depth and nuance about the issues that face our society.

SUMMARY

This summary is organized around the Learning Objectives listed at the beginning of this chapter.

 1.1 Describe the increasing racial and ethnic diversity of the United States.

Rates of immigration are high, and, as shown in Figure 1.1, non-Hispanic white Americans are declining in relative size and will be a numerical minority of the U.S. population by midcentury. Which groups are increasing in relative size? What will America look like in the future in terms of ethnicity, race, culture, language, and cuisine?

Rates of marriage across group lines are also increasing, along with the percentage of the population that identifies with more than one racial or ethnic group. Also, groups that do not fit clearly into the categories in Figure 1.1 (e.g., Arab Americans, immigrants from Africa) are growing in size.

At the same time, many of the grievances and problems that affect the "traditional" American minority groups (African Americans, Native Americans, and Hispanic Americans) have not been resolved, as we shall see in Part III of this text. What kind of society are we becoming? What will it mean to be an American?

 1.2 Define the concept of a minority group.

A minority group has five characteristics. Members of the group

- experience a pattern of disadvantage, which can range from mild (e.g., casual snubs or insults) to severe (e.g., slavery or genocide);

- have a socially visible mark of identification, which may be physical (e.g., skin color), cultural (e.g., dress, language), or both;

- are aware of their disadvantaged status;

- are generally members from birth; and

- tend to form intimate associations within the group.

Of these traits, the first two are the most important.

 1.3 Explain the sociological perspectives that will guide this text, especially as they relate to the relationships between inequality and minority-group status.

A stratification system has three different dimensions (class, prestige, and power), and the nature of inequality in a society varies by its level of development. Minority groups and social classes are correlated in numerous and complex ways. Minority groups generally have less access to valued resources and opportunity. However, minority status and inequality are separate and may vary independently. Members of minority groups can be differentiated by gender, social class, and many other criteria; likewise, members of a particular social class can vary by gender, race, ethnicity, and along many other dimensions.

 1.4 Explain the roles of race and gender in maintaining minority-group status.

Physical differences among people—including race and gender—are widely used to identify minority-group membership and control access to privilege. These social constructions powerfully influence the way we think about one another and a person's life chances.

So-called racial characteristics, such as skin color, evolved as our ancestors migrated from East Africa and spread into new ecologies. During the period of European colonization of the globe, race became important as a marker of "us and them," conqueror and conquered. It retains importance not for biological or medical reasons but because it has become a social construction that stigmatizes nonwhites.

Similarly, gender is used as a social construction that continues to limit women's access to power, privilege, and prestige, even in the nations that are highest rated on gender equality. Sexism, like racism, continues to "explain" patterns of gender inequality in terms of the inferiority of women.

 1.5 Cite and explain four of the key concepts in dominant–minority relations.

This text analyzes dominant–minority relationships at both the individual and societal levels of analysis. Prejudice and discrimination refer to individual feelings, thoughts, and behaviors. Ideological racism and institutional discrimination are parallel concepts at the societal level.

1.6 Explain what is meant by a global perspective, and apply that perspective to the relationship between globalization and immigration to the United States.

A global perspective means that we will examine dominant–minority relations not just in the United States but in other nations as well. Also, we will be sensitive to the ways group relations in the United States are affected by economic, cultural, political, and social changes across the global system of societies. The relationship between NAFTA and immigration to the United States illustrates one of the many connections between domestic and international processes.

KEY TERMS

affective dimension of
    prejudice 21
ascribed status 11
bourgeoisie 13
cognitive dimension of
    prejudice 21
discrimination 21
dominant group 10
ethnic minority groups 10

gender roles 18
genocide 10
ideological racism 21
institutional
    discrimination 21
intersectionality 14
level of development 14
means of production 12
minority group 9

miscegenation 11
patriarchy 18
postindustrial society 14
power 13
prejudice 21
prestige 13
proletariat 13
racial minority groups 10
sexism 18

social classes 12
social constructions 8
social mobility 15
stereotypes 21
stratification 12
subsistence technology 14

REVIEW QUESTIONS

1. What is the significance of Figure 1.1? What are some of the limitations and problems with the group names used in this graph? Are the group names "social constructions"? How? In your view, does the increasing diversity of American society represent a threat or an opportunity? Should we acknowledge and celebrate our differences, or should we strive for more unity and conformity? What possible dangers and opportunities are inherent in increasing diversity? What are the advantages and disadvantages of stressing unity and conformity?

2. What groups should be considered "minorities"? The five-part definition presented in this chapter was developed with racial and ethnic minorities in mind. Does it apply to gay and lesbian Americans? How? In what ways does it apply to religious groups such as Mormons or Muslims? What about left-handed people or people who are very overweight or very tall or very short? Explain your answers.

3. What is a social construction? As social constructions, how are race and gender the same and how do they differ? What does it mean to say, "Gender becomes a social construction—like race—when it is treated as an unchanging, fixed difference and then used to deny opportunity and equality to women"?

4. Define and explain each of the terms in Table 1.1. Cite an example of each from your own experiences. How does ideological racism differ from prejudice? Which concept is more sociological? Why? How does institutional discrimination differ from discrimination? Which concept is more sociological? Why?

5. Why is it important to look beyond the United States when analyzing dominant–minority relations? What can we learn by taking a global perspective? Besides immigration, what other effects does globalization have on American dominant–minority relations?

STUDENT STUDY SITE

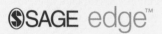

Sharpen your skills with SAGE edge at edge.sagepub.com/healey7e

SAGE edge for students provides a personalized approach to help you accomplish your coursework goals in an easy-to-use learning environment.

The following resources are available at SAGE edge:

Current Debates: Birthright Citizenship: Who Should Be an American?

The policy of birthright citizenship means that any baby born on American soil is automatically a citizen of the United States, regardless of the parents' citizenship. What are the implications of this policy? What costs does it create? Do undocumented immigrants take advantage of it? What would be the consequences of ending birthright citizenship?

On our website you will find an overview of the topic, the clashing points of view, and some questions to consider as you analyze the material.

Public Sociology Assignments

Public Sociology Assignments provide opportunities for students to address directly and personally some of the issues raised in this text.

The first two public sociology assignments on our website will lead students to confront diversity in their community. In the first assignment, you will investigate your hometown to see if you can document increases in racial and ethnic diversity consistent with Figure 1.1. In the second assignment, you will study graffiti: Does it express stereotypes and prejudice? What does it reflect about local group hierarchies?

Contributed by Linda M. Waldron

Internet Research Project

Internet research projects provide an opportunity to pursue a topic from each chapter in more depth, using the resources available on the Internet. This first project addresses the concept of race and pursues the idea that race is a social construction. Your investigation will be guided by a series of questions, and your instructor may ask you to discuss the issues in small groups.

For Further Reading

Please see our website for an annotated list of important works related to this chapter.

CHAPTER-OPENING TIMELINE PHOTO CREDITS

2

ASSIMILATION AND PLURALISM

From Immigrants to White Ethnics

Wikipedia

1826
German Jews begin entering the U.S. By 1850, the Jewish population had risen from 6,000 to 50,000. Ten years later the population is 150,000.

1881–1885
1 million Germans immigrate to the U.S.

1820   1830   1840   1850   1860   1870   1880

1845–1852
Irish potato famine leads to mass immigration to the U.S.

1848
Serfdom ends in parts of Europe, freeing many peasants to move to the U.S.

1854
The Know-Nothings, a nativist political party seeking to restrict immigration, win significant victories in Congress, a sign of popular dissatisfaction with growing immigration from Catholic Ireland.

Wikimedia Commons

NOTHING
POINT
Everybody
NOBODY.

LOC

1862
The Homestead Act provides free plots of western land to settlers, spurring an influx of immigrants from Europe seeking land of their own.

We have room for but one flag, the American flag . . . We have room for but one language and that is the English language . . . and we have room for but one loyalty and that is a loyalty to the American people.

—Theodore Roosevelt,
26th president of the United States, 1907

If we lose our language [Ojibwa] . . . , I think, something more will be lost. . . . We will lose something personal. . . . We will lose our sense of ourselves and our culture. . . . We will lose beauty—the beauty of the particular, the beauty of the past and the intricacies of a language tailored for our space in the world. That Native American cultures are imperiled is important and not just to Indians. . . . When we lose cultures, we lose American plurality—the productive and lovely discomfort that true difference brings.

—David Treuer (2012, pp. 304–305)

Welcome to America. Now, speak English.

—Bumper sticker, 2013

LEARNING OBJECTIVES

By the end of this chapter, you will be able to do the following:

2.1 Explain and analyze the concepts of assimilation and pluralism, including the "traditional" model of assimilation.

2.2 List and explain other group relationships.

2.3 Describe the timing, causes, and volume of the migration from Europe, and explain how those immigrants became "white ethnics."

2.4 Explain the patterns of assimilation and the major variations in those patterns.

2.5 Describe the status of the descendants of European immigrants today, including the "twilight of white ethnicity."

2.6 Explain how the traditional model of assimilation does or does not apply to contemporary immigrants.

1890
The demographic trends in immigration shift as immigration from southern and eastern Europe substantially increases, while the relative proportion of immigration from northern and western Europe begins to decrease.

1917
The U.S. enters World War I with anti-German sentiment rising at home.

1948
The Displaced Persons Act opens American doors to more than 200,000 Europeans who could not return to their homes after World War II.

1980–2000
Economic turmoil in the Soviet Union leads to a massive exodus of Russian and Ukrainian Jews. More than 200,000 eventually settle in the U.S.

1881–1920
2 million Eastern European Jews immigrate to the U.S.

1911
The Dillingham Commission publishes a report warning that the "new" immigration from southern and eastern Europe threatens to subvert American society.

1911–1920
2 million Italians immigrate to the U.S.

1924
The Johnson–Reed Act limits annual European immigration to 2% of the number of people from that country living in the U.S. in 1890. The act greatly reduces immigration from southern and eastern European nationalities that had only small populations in the U.S. in 1890.

1965
The Hart-Celler Act produces major changes in patterns of immigration to the U.S., eventually reducing the percentage of immigrants from Europe.

More than 300 different languages are spoken in the United States today, including more than 150 different American Indian languages. Most are spoken by relatively few people, but the sheer number of languages suggests the dimensions of contemporary American diversity.

Does this multiplicity of languages and cultures bring confusion and inefficiency? Does it enrich everyday life and spark creativity? Does it really matter if a language disappears and we lose the "lovely discomfort" of difference?

These are some of the questions Americans (and the citizens of many other nations) must ask as we confront the issues of inclusion and diversity. Should we encourage groups to retain their unique cultural heritage, including their language, or should we stress unity and conformity? How have these issues been addressed in the past? How should we approach them in the future? •

This chapter continues to look at the ways ethnic and racial groups in the United States relate to one another. Two concepts, assimilation and pluralism, are at the core of the discussion. Each includes a variety of possible group relations and pathways along which group relations might develop.

Assimilation is a process in which formerly distinct and separate groups come to share a common culture and merge together socially. As a society undergoes assimilation, differences among groups decrease. **Pluralism**, on the other hand, exists when groups maintain their individual identities. In a pluralistic society, groups remain separate, and their cultural and social differences persist over time.

In some ways, assimilation and pluralism are contrary processes, but they are not mutually exclusive. They may occur together in a variety of combinations within a particular society or group. Some groups in a society may be assimilating as others are maintaining (or even increasing) their differences. As we shall see in Part III, virtually every minority group in the United States has, at any given time, some members who are assimilating and others who are preserving or reviving traditional cultures. Some Native Americans, for example, are pluralistic. They live on or near reservations, are strongly connected to their heritage, and speak their native language. Other Native Americans are very much assimilated into the dominant society: They live in urban areas, speak English only, and know relatively little about their traditional cultures. Both

---

Assimilation is a process in which separate groups come to share a common culture and merge together socially.

In **pluralism**, groups maintain separate identities, cultures, and organizational structures.

---

assimilation and pluralism are important forces in the everyday lives of Native Americans and most other minority-group members.

American sociologists have been very concerned with these processes, especially assimilation. This concern was stimulated by the massive migration from Europe to the United States that occurred between the 1820s and the 1920s. More than 31 million people crossed the Atlantic during this time, and a great deal of energy has been devoted to documenting, describing, and understanding the experiences of these immigrants and their descendants. These efforts have resulted in the development of a rich and complex literature that we will refer to as the "traditional" perspective on how newcomers are incorporated in U.S. society.

This chapter begins with a consideration of the "traditional" perspective on both assimilation and pluralism, and a brief examination of several other possible group relationships. The traditional perspective will then be applied to European immigrants and their descendants, and we will develop a model of American assimilation based on these experiences. This model will be used in our analysis of other minority groups throughout the text and especially in Part III.

Since the 1960s, the United States has been experiencing a second mass immigration, and a particularly important issue now is whether the theories, concepts, and models based on the first mass immigration to the United States (from the 1820s to the 1920s) apply to this wave. The newest arrivals differ in many ways from those who came earlier, and ideas and theories based on the earlier experiences will not necessarily apply to the present. We will briefly note some of the issues in this chapter and explore them in more detail in the case study chapters in Part III.

Finally, at the end of this chapter, we will briefly consider the implications of these first two chapters for the exploration of intergroup relations. By the end of this chapter, you will be familiar with many of the concepts that will guide us throughout this text as we examine the variety of possible dominant–minority group situations and the directions our society (and the groups within it) can take.

ASSIMILATION

We begin with assimilation because the emphasis in U.S. group relations has historically been on this goal rather than on pluralism. This section presents some of the most important sociological theories and concepts that have been used to describe and analyze the assimilation of the 19th-century immigrants from Europe.

TYPES OF ASSIMILATION

Assimilation is a general term for a process that can follow a number of different pathways. One form of assimilation is

The melting pot has been a popular and powerful image for Americans.

the United States was designed to maintain the predominance of the English language and the British-type institutional patterns created during the early years of American society.

The stress on Anglo-conformity is clearly reflected in the quote from President Roosevelt that opens this chapter. Many Americans today agree with Roosevelt: 77% of respondents in a recent survey—the overwhelming majority—agreed that "the United States should require immigrants to be proficient in English as a condition of remaining in the U.S." Interestingly, about 60% of Hispanic Americans (vs. 80% of non-Hispanic whites and 76% of blacks) also agreed with this statement (Carroll, 2007). We should note that the apparent agreement between whites and Hispanics on the need for immigrants to learn English may flow from very different orientations and motivations. For some whites, the response may mix prejudice and contempt with support for Americanization, while the Hispanic responses may be based on direct experience with the difficulties of negotiating the monolingual institutions of American society.

Under Anglo-conformity, immigrant and minority groups are expected to adapt to Anglo-American culture as a precondition to acceptance and access to better jobs, education, and other opportunities. Assimilation has meant that minority groups have had to give up their traditions and adopt Anglo-American culture. To be sure, many groups and individuals were (and continue to be) eager to undergo Anglo-conformity, even if it meant losing much or all of their heritage. For other groups, Americanization creates conflict, anxiety, demoralization, and resentment. We assess these varied reactions in our examination of America's minority groups in Part III.

THE "TRADITIONAL" PERSPECTIVE ON ASSIMILATION: THEORIES AND CONCEPTS

American sociologists have developed a rich body of theories and concepts based on the assimilation experiences of the immigrants who came from Europe during the 1820s to the 1920s, and we shall refer to this body of work as the traditional perspective on assimilation. As you will see, the scholars working in this tradition have made invaluable contributions, and their thinking is impressively complex and comprehensive. This does not mean, of course, that they have exhausted the

expressed in the metaphor of the **melting pot**, a process in which different groups come together and contribute in roughly equal amounts to create a common culture and a new, unique society. People often think of the American experience of assimilation in these terms. This view stresses the ways diverse peoples helped construct U.S. society and made contributions to American culture. The melting-pot metaphor sees assimilation as benign and egalitarian, a process that emphasizes sharing and inclusion.

Although it is a powerful image in our society, the melting pot is not an accurate description of how assimilation actually proceeded for American minority groups (Abrahamson, 1980, pp. 152–154). Some groups—especially the racial minority groups—have been largely excluded from the "melting" process. Furthermore, the melting-pot brew has had a distinctly Anglocentric flavor: "For better or worse, the white Anglo-Saxon Protestant tradition was for two centuries—and in crucial respects still is—the dominant influence on American culture and society" (Schlesinger, 1992, p. 28).

Contrary to the melting-pot image, assimilation in the United States generally has been a coercive and largely one-sided process better described by the terms **Americanization** or **Anglo-conformity**. Rather than an equal sharing of elements and a gradual blending of diverse peoples, assimilation in

The **melting pot** is a type of assimilation in which all groups contribute in roughly equal amounts to a new culture and society.

Americanization (or **Anglo-conformity**) is a type of assimilation in which groups are pressured to conform to Anglo-American culture.

possibilities or answered (or asked) all the questions. Theorists working in the pluralist tradition and contemporary scholars studying the experiences of more recent immigrants have questioned many aspects of traditional assimilation theory and have made a number of important contributions of their own.

Robert Park. Many theories of assimilation are grounded in the work of Robert Park. He was one of a group of scholars who had a major hand in establishing sociology as a discipline in the United States in the 1920s and 1930s. Park felt that intergroup relations go through a predictable set of phases that he called a **race relations cycle**. When groups first come into contact (through immigration, conquest, etc.), relations are conflictual and competitive. Eventually, however, the process, or cycle, moves toward assimilation, or the "interpenetration and fusion" of groups (Park & Burgess, 1924, p. 735).

Park argued further that assimilation is inevitable in a democratic and industrial society. In a political system based on democracy, fairness, and impartial justice, all groups will eventually secure equal treatment under the law. In an industrial economy, people tend to be judged on rational grounds—that is, on the basis of their abilities and talents—and not by ethnicity or race. Park believed that as American society continued to modernize, urbanize, and industrialize, ethnic and racial groups would gradually lose their importance. The boundaries between groups would eventually dissolve, and a more "rational" and unified society would emerge (see also Geschwender, 1978, pp. 19–32; Hirschman, 1983).

Social scientists have examined, analyzed, and criticized Park's conclusions for years. One frequently voiced criticism

---

The **race relations cycle** is the concept that there will be a predictable cycle of group relations, from conflict to eventual assimilation.

Culture includes all aspects of the way of life of a group of people, including beliefs, values, technology, and many other components.

Social structure is the networks of relationships, groups, organizations, and institutions that organize work and connect individuals to one another.

The **primary sector** of a social structure consists of close, intimate relations.

The **secondary sector** of a social structure consists of impersonal, goal-oriented relations.

Acculturation or **cultural assimilation** is the process by which one group learns the culture of another.

Integration or **structural assimilation** is the process by which a group enters the social structure of the larger society.

---

is that he did not specify a time frame for the completion of assimilation, and therefore his idea that assimilation is "inevitable" cannot be tested. Until the exact point in time when assimilation is deemed complete, we will not know whether the theory is wrong or whether we just have not waited long enough.

An additional criticism of Park's theory is that he does not describe the nature of the assimilation process in much detail. How would assimilation proceed? How would everyday life change? Which aspects of the group would change first?

Milton Gordon. To clarify some of the issues Park left unresolved, we turn to the works of sociologist Milton Gordon, who made a major contribution to theories of assimilation in his book *Assimilation in American Life* (1964). Gordon broke down the overall process of assimilation into seven subprocesses; we will focus on the first three. Before considering these phases of assimilation, however, we need to consider some new concepts and terms.

Gordon makes a distinction between the cultural and the structural components of society. **Culture** encompasses all aspects of the way of life associated with a group of people. It includes language, religious beliefs, customs and rules of etiquette, and the values and ideas people use to organize their lives and interpret their existence. The **social structure**, or structural components of a society, includes networks of social relationships, groups, organizations, stratification systems, communities, and families. The social structure organizes the work of the society and connects individuals to one another and to the larger society.

It is common in sociology to separate the social structure into primary and secondary sectors. The **primary sector** includes interpersonal relationships that are intimate and personal, such as families and groups of friends. Groups in the primary sector are small. The **secondary sector** consists of groups and organizations that are more public, task oriented, and impersonal. Organizations in the secondary sector are often very large and include businesses, factories, schools and colleges, and bureaucracies.

Now we can examine Gordon's earliest stages of assimilation, which are summarized in Table 2.1.

1. **Acculturation** or **cultural assimilation.** Members of the minority group learn the culture of the dominant group. For groups that immigrate to the United States, acculturation to the dominant Anglo-American culture may include (as necessary) learning the English language, changing eating habits, adopting new value systems and new gender roles, and altering the spelling of the family surname.

2. **Integration** or **structural assimilation.** The minority group enters the social structure of the larger society. Integration typically begins in the secondary sector and gradually moves into the primary sector. That is, before

TABLE 2.1 Gordon's Stages of Assimilation

STAGE	PROCESS
1. Acculturation	The group learns the culture of the dominant group, including language and values.
2. Integration (structural assimilation)	
a. At the secondary level	Members of the group enter the public institutions and organizations of the dominant society.
b. At the primary level	Members of the group enter the cliques, clubs, and friendship groups of the dominant society.
3. Intermarriage (marital assimilation)	Members of the group marry with members of the dominant society on a large scale.

SOURCE: Adapted from Gordon (1964, p. 71).

people can form friendships with members of other groups (integration into the primary sector), they must first become acquaintances. The initial contact between groups often occurs in public institutions such as schools and workplaces (integration into the secondary sector). The greater their integration into the secondary sector, the more nearly equal the minority group will be to the dominant group in income, education, and occupational prestige. Once a group has entered the institutions and public sectors of the larger society, according to Gordon, integration into the primary sector and the other stages of assimilation will follow inevitably (although not necessarily quickly). Measures of integration into the primary sector include the extent to which people have acquaintances, close friends, or neighbors from other groups.

3. **Intermarriage** or **marital assimilation.** When integration into the primary sector becomes substantial, the basis for Gordon's third stage of assimilation is established. People are most likely to select spouses from among their primary relations, and thus, in Gordon's view, primary structural integration typically precedes intermarriage.

Gordon argued that acculturation was a prerequisite for integration. Given the stress on Anglo-conformity, a member of an immigrant or minority group would not be able to compete for jobs or other opportunities in the secondary sector of the social structure until he or she had learned the dominant group's culture. Gordon recognized, however, that successful acculturation does not automatically ensure that a group will begin the integration phase. The dominant group may still

exclude the minority group from its institutions and limit the opportunities available to them. Gordon argued that "acculturation without integration" (or Americanization without equality) is a common situation in the United States for many minority groups, especially the racial minority groups.

In Gordon's theory, movement from acculturation to integration is the crucial step in the assimilation process. Once that step is taken, all the other subprocesses will occur inevitably, although movement through the stages can be very slow. Gordon's idea that assimilation runs a certain course in a certain order echoes Park's conclusion regarding the inevitability of the process.

More than 50 years after Gordon published his analysis of assimilation, some of his conclusions have been called into question. For example, the individual subprocesses of assimilation that Gordon saw as linked in a certain order are often found to occur independently of one another (Yinger, 1985, p. 154). A group may integrate before acculturating or combine the subprocesses in other ways. Also, many researchers no longer think of the process of assimilation as necessarily linear or one-way (Greeley, 1974). Groups (or segments thereof) may "reverse direction" and become less assimilated over time, revive their traditional cultures, relearn their old language, or revitalize ethnic organizations or associations.

Nonetheless, Gordon's overall model continues to guide our understanding of the process of assimilation, to the point that a large part of the research agenda for contemporary studies of immigrants involves assessment of the extent to which their experiences can be described in Gordon's terms (Alba & Nee, 1997). In fact, Gordon's model will provide a major organizational framework for the case study chapters presented in Part III of this text.

Human Capital Theory. Why did some European immigrant groups acculturate and integrate more rapidly than others? Although not a theory of assimilation per se, **human capital theory** offers one possible answer to this question. This theory argues that status attainment, or the level of success achieved by an individual in society, is a direct result of educational levels, personal values and skills, and other individual characteristics and abilities. Education is seen as an investment in human capital, not unlike the investment a business might make in machinery or new technology. The greater the investment in a person's human capital, the higher the probability of success. Blau and Duncan (1967), in their pioneering

Intermarriage or **marital assimilation** is marriage between members of different groups.

Human capital theory is the view that upward mobility is a direct result of effort, personal values and skills, and investment in education.

statement of status attainment theory, found that even the relative advantage conferred by having a high-status father is largely mediated through education. In other words, high levels of affluence and occupational prestige are not so much a result of being born into a privileged status as they are the result of the superior education that affluence makes possible.

Why did some immigrant groups achieve upward mobility more rapidly than others? Human capital theory answers questions such as these in terms of the resources and cultural characteristics of the members of the groups, especially their levels of education and familiarity with English. Success is seen as a direct result of individual effort and the wise investment of personal resources. People or groups who fail have not tried hard enough, have not made the right kinds of educational investments, or have values or habits that limit their ability to compete.

More than most sociological theories, human capital theory is quite consistent with traditional American culture and values. Both tend to see success as an individual phenomenon—a reward for hard work, sustained effort, and good character. Both tend to assume that success is equally available to all and that the larger society is open and neutral in its distribution of rewards and opportunity. Both tend to see assimilation as a highly desirable, benign process that blends diverse peoples and cultures into a strong, unified whole. Thus, people or groups that resist Americanization or question its benefits are seen as threatening or illegitimate.

On one level, human capital theory is an important theory of success and upward mobility, and we will on occasion use the theory to analyze the experiences of minority and immigrant groups. On another level, the theory is so resonant with American "commonsensical" views of success and failure that we may tend to use it uncritically.

A final judgment on the validity of the theory will be more appropriately made at the end of the text, but you should be aware of the theory's major limitations from the beginning. First of all, as an explanation of minority-group experience, human capital theory is not so much "wrong" as it is incomplete. In other words, it does not take account of all the factors that affect mobility and assimilation. Second, as we shall see, the assumption that U.S. society is equally open and fair to all groups is simply wrong. We will point out other strengths and limitations of this perspective as we move through the text.

QUESTIONS FOR REFLECTION

1. What are the limitations of the melting-pot view of assimilation?

2. Why does Gordon place acculturation as the first step in the process of assimilation? Could one of the other stages occur first? Why or why not?

3. What does human capital theory leave out? In what ways is it consistent with American values?

PLURALISM

Sociological discussions of pluralism often begin with a consideration of the work of Horace Kallen. In articles published in *The Nation* magazine in 1915, Kallen argued that people should not have to surrender their culture and traditions to become full participants in American society. He rejected the Anglo-conformist, assimilationist model and contended that the existence of separate ethnic groups, even with separate cultures, religions, and languages, was consistent with democracy and other core American values. In Gordon's terms, Kallen believed that integration and equality were possible without extensive acculturation and that American society could be a federation of diverse groups, a mosaic of harmonious and interdependent cultures and peoples (Kallen, 1915a, 1915b; see also Abrahamson, 1980; Gleason, 1980).

Assimilation has been such a powerful theme in U.S. history that in the decades following the publication of Kallen's analysis, support for pluralism remained somewhat marginalized. In more recent decades, however, interest in pluralism and ethnic diversity has increased, in part because the assimilation predicted by Park (and implicit in the conventional wisdom of many Americans) has not fully materialized. Perhaps we simply have not waited long enough, but as the 21st century unfolds, distinctions among the racial minority groups in our society show few signs of disappearing, and, in fact, some members of these groups are questioning the desirability of assimilation. Also, more surprising perhaps, white ethnicity maintains a stubborn persistence, although it continues to change in form and decrease in strength.

An additional reason for the growing interest in pluralism, no doubt, is the everyday reality of the increasing diversity of U.S. society, as reflected in Figure 1.1. Controversies over issues such as "English-only" policies, bilingual education, and welfare rights for immigrants are common and often bitter. Many Americans feel that diversity or pluralism has exceeded acceptable limits and that the unity of the nation is at risk (e.g., visit www.us-english.org/, the home page of a group that advocates for English-only legislation).

Finally, interest in pluralism and ethnicity in general has been stimulated by developments around the globe. Several nation-states have disintegrated into smaller units based on language, culture, race, and ethnicity. Recent events in the Middle East, China, Eastern Europe, the former USSR, Canada, and Africa, just to mention a few, have provided dramatic and often tragic evidence of how ethnic identities and enmities can persist across decades or even centuries of submergence and suppression in larger national units.

In contemporary debates, discussions of diversity and pluralism are often couched in the language of **multiculturalism**, a general term for a variety of programs and ideas

---

Multiculturalism is a general term for pluralistic views that stress inclusion, mutual respect, and a celebration of group diversity.

that stress mutual respect for all groups and for the multiple heritages that have shaped the United States. Some aspects of multiculturalism are controversial and have evoked strong opposition. In many ways, however, these debates merely echo a recurring argument about the character of American society, a debate that will be revisited throughout this text.

TYPES OF PLURALISM

We can distinguish various types of pluralism by using some of the concepts introduced in the discussion of assimilation. **Cultural pluralism** exists when groups have not acculturated and each maintains its own identity. The groups might speak different languages, practice different religions, and have different value systems. The groups are part of the same society and might even live in adjacent areas, but in some ways, they live in different worlds. Many Native Americans are culturally pluralistic, maintaining their traditional languages and cultures and living on isolated reservations. The Amish, a religious community sometimes called the Pennsylvania Dutch, are also a culturally pluralistic group. They are committed to a way of life organized around farming, and they maintain a culture and an institutional life that is separate from the dominant culture (see Hostetler, 1980; Kephart & Zellner, 1994; Kraybill & Bowman, 2001).

Following Gordon's subprocesses, a second type of pluralism exists when a group has acculturated but not integrated. That is, the group has adopted the Anglo-American culture but does not have full and equal access to the institutions of the larger society. In this situation, called **structural pluralism**, cultural differences are minimal, but the groups occupy different locations in the social structure. The groups may speak with the same accent, eat the same food, pursue the same goals, and subscribe to the same values, but they may also maintain separate organizational systems, including different churches, clubs, schools, and neighborhoods.

Under structural pluralism, groups practice a common culture but do so in different places and with minimal interaction across group boundaries. An example of structural pluralism can be found on any Sunday morning in the Christian churches of the United States, where local parishes are often identified with specific ethnic groups or races. What happens in the various churches—the rituals, expressions of faith, statements of core values and beliefs—is similar and expresses a common, shared culture. Structurally, however, this common culture is expressed in separate buildings and by separate congregations.

A third type of pluralism reverses the order of Gordon's first two phases: integration without acculturation. This situation is exemplified by a group that has had some material success (measured by wealth or income, for example) but has not become Americanized (learned English, adopted American values and norms, etc.). Some immigrant groups have found niches in American society in which they can survive and

Mulberry Street, New York City, around 1900, a bustling marketplace for Italian immigrants.

occasionally prosper economically without acculturating very much.

Two different situations can be used to illustrate this pattern. An **enclave minority group** establishes its own neighborhood and relies on a set of interconnected businesses, each of which is usually small in scope, for its economic survival. Some of these businesses serve the group, whereas others serve the larger society. The Cuban American community in South Florida and Chinatowns in many larger American cities are examples of ethnic enclaves.

A similar pattern of adjustment, the **middleman minority group**, also relies on small shops and retail firms, but the businesses are more dispersed throughout a large area rather than concentrated in a specific locale. Some Chinese American communities fit this second pattern, as do Korean American greengroceries and Indian American–owned motels (Portes & Manning, 1986). These types of minority groups are discussed further in Part III.

The economic success of enclave and middleman minorities is partly due to the strong ties of cooperation and mutual aid within their groups. The ties are based, in turn, on cultural bonds that would weaken if acculturation took

---

Under **cultural pluralism**, groups have not acculturated or integrated and each maintains a distinct identity.

Under **structural pluralism**, a group has acculturated but not integrated.

An **enclave minority group** establishes its own neighborhood and relies on a set of interconnected businesses for economic survival.

A **middleman minority group** relies on interconnected businesses, dispersed throughout a community, for economic survival.

place. In contrast with Gordon's idea that acculturation is a prerequisite to integration, whatever success these groups enjoy is due in part to the fact that they have not Americanized. Kim Park, whom we met in the first chapter, is willing to work in his uncle's grocery store for room and board and the opportunity to learn the business. His willingness to forgo a salary and subordinate his individual needs to the needs of the group reflects the strength of his relationship to family and kin. At various times and places, Jewish, Chinese, Japanese, Korean, and Cuban Americans have been enclave or middleman minorities (see Bonacich & Modell, 1980; Kitano & Daniels, 2001).

The situation of enclave and middleman minorities—integration without acculturation—can be considered either a type of pluralism (emphasizing the absence of acculturation) or a type of assimilation (emphasizing a high level of economic equality). Keep in mind that assimilation and pluralism are not opposites but can occur in a variety of combinations. It is best to think of acculturation, integration, and the other stages of assimilation (or pluralism) as independent processes.

QUESTIONS FOR REFLECTION

1. Is the United States becoming more pluralistic? What are some of the costs and some of the benefits of increasing pluralism?

2. What are the differences between middleman and enclave minority groups? Do these groups challenge the idea that assimilation moves step-by-step in a certain order?

OTHER GROUP RELATIONSHIPS

This book concentrates on assimilation and pluralism, but there are, of course, other possible group relationships and goals. Two commonly noted goals for minority groups are separatism and revolution (Wirth, 1945). The goal of **separatism** is for the group to sever all ties (political, cultural, and geographic) with the larger society. Thus, separatism goes well beyond pluralism. Native Americans have expressed both separatist and pluralist goals, and separatism has also been pursued by some African American organizations, such as the Black Muslims.

Separatism is a minority group goal. A separatist group wishes to sever all ties with the dominant group.

Revolution is a minority-group goal. A revolutionary group wishes to change places with the dominant group and establish a new social order.

In the contemporary world, there are separatist movements among groups in French Canada, Scotland, Chechnya, Cyprus, southern Mexico, Hawaii, and scores of other places.

A minority group promoting **revolution** seeks to switch places with the dominant group and become the ruling elite or create a new social order, perhaps in alliance with members of the dominant group. Although revolutionary activity can be found among some American minority groups (e.g., the Black Panthers), this goal has been relatively rare for minority groups in the United States. Revolutionary minority groups are more commonly found in situations such as those in colonial Africa, in which one nation conquered and controlled another racially or culturally different nation.

The dominant group may also pursue goals other than assimilation and pluralism, including forced migration or expulsion, extermination or genocide, and continued subjugation of the minority group. Chinese immigrants were the victims of a policy of expulsion, beginning in the 1880s, when the Chinese Exclusion Act (1882) closed the door on further immigration and concerted efforts were made to encourage those in the country to leave (see Chapter 9). Native Americans have also been the victims of expulsion. In 1830, all tribes living east of the Mississippi River were forced to migrate to a new territory in the West (see Chapter 4). The most infamous example of genocide is the Holocaust in Nazi Germany, during which six million Jews were murdered, but there are, tragically, many other examples (see Figure 2.1). The dominant group pursues "continued subjugation" when, as with slavery in the antebellum South, it attempts to maintain a powerless and exploited position for the minority group. A dominant group may simultaneously pursue different policies with different minority groups and may, of course, change policies over time.

FROM IMMIGRANTS TO WHITE ETHNICS

In this section, we will explore the experiences of the minority groups that stimulated the development of the traditional perspective. A massive immigration from Europe began in the 1820s, and over the next century, millions of people made the journey from the Old World to the New. They came from every corner of the continent: Ireland, Greece, Germany, Italy, Poland, Portugal, Ukraine, Russia, and scores of other nations and provinces. They came as young men and women seeking jobs, as families fleeing religious persecution, as political radicals evading the police, as farmers seeking land and a fresh start, and as paupers barely able to scrape together the cost of their passage. They came as immigrants, became minority groups upon their arrival, experienced discrimination and prejudice in all its forms, went through all the varieties and stages of assimilation and pluralism, and eventually merged

FIGURE 2.1 Select Genocides Around the World, 1914 to Present

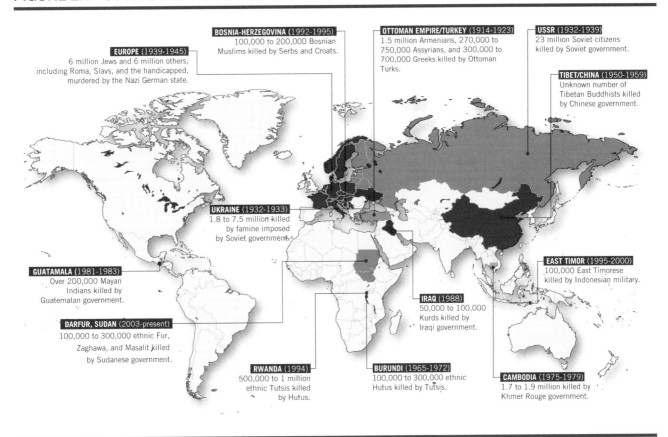

BOSNIA-HERZEGOVINA (1992-1995)
100,000 to 200,000 Bosnian Muslims killed by Serbs and Croats.

OTTOMAN EMPIRE/TURKEY (1914-1923)
1.5 million Armenians, 270,000 to 750,000 Assyrians, and 300,000 to 700,000 Greeks killed by Ottoman Turks.

USSR (1932-1939)
23 million Soviet citizens killed by Soviet government.

EUROPE (1939-1945)
6 million Jews and 6 million others, including Roma, Slavs, and the handicapped, murdered by the Nazi German state.

TIBET/CHINA (1950-1959)
Unknown number of Tibetan Buddhists killed by Chinese government.

UKRAINE (1932-1933)
1.8 to 7.5 million killed by famine imposed by Soviet government.

GUATAMALA (1981-1983)
Over 200,000 Mayan Indians killed by Guatemalan government.

EAST TIMOR (1995-2000)
100,000 East Timorese killed by Indonesian military.

DARFUR, SUDAN (2003-present)
100,000 to 300,000 ethnic Fur, Zaghawa, and Masalit killed by Sudanese government.

IRAQ (1988)
50,000 to 100,000 Kurds killed by Iraqi government.

RWANDA (1994)
500,000 to 1 million ethnic Tutsis killed by Hutus.

BURUNDI (1965-1972)
100,000 to 300,000 ethnic Hutus killed by Tutsis.

CAMBODIA (1975-1979)
1.7 to 1.9 million killed by Khmer Rouge government.

into the society that had once rejected them so viciously. Figure 2.2 shows the major European sending nations.

These immigrants were a diverse group, and their experiences in the United States varied along a number of crucial sociological dimensions. Some groups (Italians and other southern Europeans) were seen as racially inferior, while others (Irish Catholics and Jews from eastern Europe) were rejected and marginalized because of their religion. The immigration experience—from start to finish—was shaped by gender and was decidedly different for men and women.

Social class was also a major differentiating factor: Many of these immigrants brought few resources and very low human capital. They entered U.S. society at the bottom and often remained on the lowest occupational and economic rungs for generations. Other groups brought skills or financial resources that led them to a more favorable position and faster rates of upward mobility. All these factors—race, class, and gender—affected the experience in the United States and led to very different outcomes in terms of social location, mobility paths, and ultimate acceptance.

This first mass wave of immigrants shaped the United States in countless ways. When the immigration started in the 1820s, the United States was not yet 50 years old, an agricultural nation clustered along the East Coast. The nation was just coming into contact with Mexicans in the Southwest, immigration from China had not yet begun, slavery was flourishing in the South, and conflict with American Indians was intense and brutal. When the immigration ended in the 1920s, the population of the United States had increased from fewer than 10 million to more than 100 million, and the society had industrialized, become a world power, and stretched from coast to coast, with colonies in the Pacific and the Caribbean.

It was no coincidence that European immigration, American industrialization, and the rise to global prominence occurred simultaneously. These changes were intimately interlinked, the mutual causes and effects of one another. Industrialization fueled the growth of U.S. military and political power, and the industrial machinery of the nation depended heavily on the flow of labor from Europe. By World War I, for example, 25% of the nation's total labor force was foreign-born, and more than half the workforce in New York, Detroit, and Chicago consisted of immigrant men. Immigrants were the majority of the workers in many important sectors of the economy, including coal mining, steel manufacturing, the garment industry, and meatpacking (Martin & Midgley, 1999, p. 15; Steinberg, 1981, p. 36).

In the sections that follow, we explore the experiences of these groups, beginning with the forces that caused them to leave Europe and come to the United States and ending with an assessment of their present status in American society.

FIGURE 2.2 European Immigration to the United States, 1820–1920

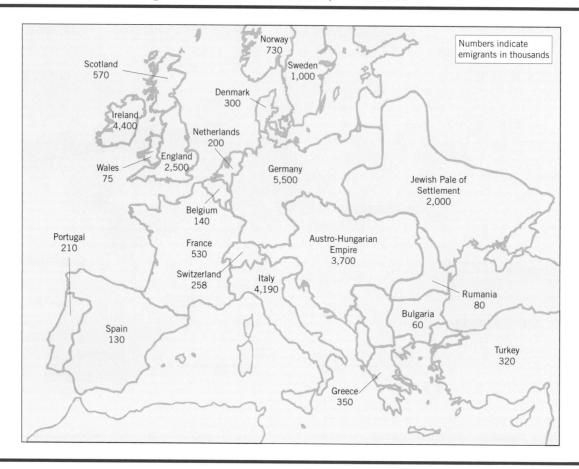

INDUSTRIALIZATION AND IMMIGRATION

What forces stimulated this mass movement of people? Like any complex phenomenon, immigration from Europe had a multitude of causes, but underlying the process was a massive and fundamental shift in subsistence technology: the **industrial revolution**. We mentioned the importance of subsistence technology in Chapter 1. Dominant–minority relations are intimately related to the system a society uses to satisfy its basic needs, and they change as that system changes. The immigrants

The **industrial revolution** is the shift in subsistence technology from labor-intensive agriculture to capital-intensive manufacturing.

Labor-intensive production is a form of work in which most of the effort is provided by people working by hand.

Capital-intensive technology replaces hand labor with machine labor. Large amounts of capital are required to develop, purchase, and maintain the machines.

were pushed out of Europe as industrial technology wrecked the traditional agricultural way of life, and they were drawn to the United States by the jobs created by the spread of the very same technology. We will consider the impact of this fundamental transformation of social structure and culture in some detail.

Industrialization began in England in the mid-1700s, spread to other parts of northern and western Europe and then, in the 1800s, to eastern and southern Europe. As it rolled across the continent, the industrial revolution replaced people and animal power with machines and new forms of energy (steam, coal, and eventually oil), causing an exponential increase in the productive capacity of society. (See pages 42–43 for a detailed timeline.)

At the dawn of the industrial revolution, most Europeans lived in small, rural villages and survived by traditional farming practices that had changed very little over the centuries. The work of production was **labor-intensive** or done by hand or with the aid of draft animals. Productivity was low, and the tasks of food production and survival required the efforts of virtually the entire family, working ceaselessly throughout the year.

Industrialization destroyed this traditional way of life as it introduced new technology, machines, and sources of energy to the tasks of production. The new technology was **capital-intensive** or dependent on machine power, and it

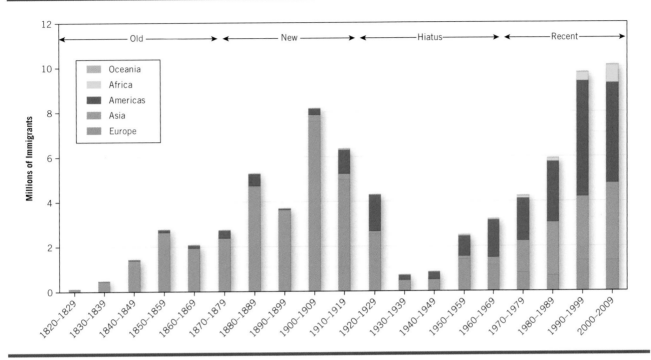

SOURCE: Data from Table 2, Persons Obtaining Legal Permanent Resident Status by Region and Selected Country of Last Residence: Fiscal Years 1820 to 2012. *Yearbook of Immigration Statistics: 2012 Legal Permanent Residents*. U.S. Department of Homeland Security.

reduced the need for human labor in rural areas as it modernized agriculture. Also, farmland was consolidated into larger and larger tracts for the sake of efficiency, further decreasing the need for human laborers. At the same time, even as survival in the rapidly changing rural economy became more difficult, the rural population began to grow.

In response, peasants began to leave their home villages and move toward urban areas. Factories were being built in or near the cities, opening up opportunities for employment. The urban population tended to increase faster than the job supply, however, and many migrants had to move on. Many of these former peasants responded to opportunities available in the New World, especially in the United States, where the abundance of farmland on the frontier kept people moving out of the cities and away from the East Coast, thereby sustaining a fairly constant demand for labor in the very areas that were easiest for Europeans to reach. As industrialization took hold on both continents, the population movement to European cities and then to North America eventually grew to become one of the largest in human history.

The timing of migration from Europe followed the timing of industrialization. The first waves of immigrants, often called the **Old Immigration**, came from northern and western Europe starting in the 1820s. A second wave, the **New Immigration**, began arriving from southern and eastern Europe in the 1880s. Figure 2.3 shows both waves and the rates of legal immigration up to 2009. Note that the "new" immigration was much more voluminous than the "old" and

that the number of immigrants declined drastically after the 1920s. We will explore the reasons for this decline later in this chapter and discuss in detail the more recent (post-1965) increase in immigration—overwhelmingly from the Americas (mostly Mexico) and Asia—in Chapters 8 through 10.

EUROPEAN ORIGINS AND CONDITIONS OF ENTRY

The immigrants from Europe varied from one another in innumerable ways. They followed a variety of pathways into the United States, and their experiences were shaped by their cultural and class characteristics, their countries of origin, and the timing of their arrival. Some groups encountered much more resistance than others, and different groups played different roles in the industrialization and urbanization of America. To discuss these diverse patterns systematically, we distinguish three subgroups of European immigrants: Protestants from northern and western Europe, the largely Catholic immigrant laborers from Ireland and from southern and eastern Europe,

The **Old Immigration** was from northern and western Europe to the United States from the 1820s to the 1880s.

The **New Immigration** was from southern and eastern Europe to the United States from the 1880s to the 1920s.

FIGURE 2.4 Timeline of the Industrial Revolution, 1712–1903

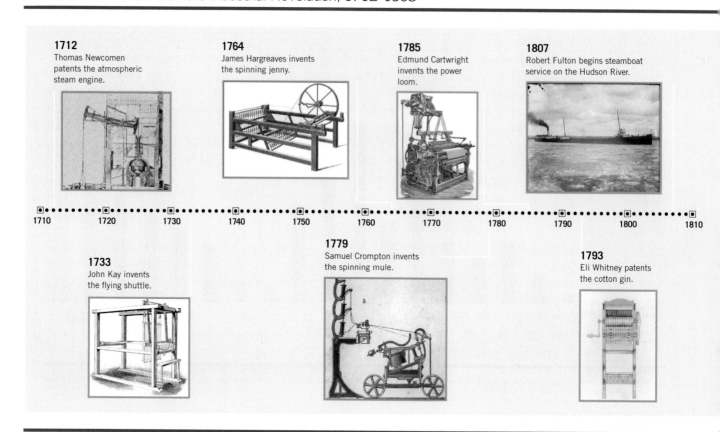

1712
Thomas Newcomen patents the atmospheric steam engine.

1764
James Hargreaves invents the spinning jenny.

1785
Edmund Cartwright invents the power loom.

1807
Robert Fulton begins steamboat service on the Hudson River.

1710 1720 1730 1740 1750 1760 1770 1780 1790 1800 1810

1733
John Kay invents the flying shuttle.

1779
Samuel Crompton invents the spinning mule.

1793
Eli Whitney patents the cotton gin.

SOURCE: Adapted from Industrial Revolution: Timeline, Facts, and Resources, Research by B. Sobey, TheFreeResource.com.

and Jewish immigrants from eastern Europe. We look at these subgroups in roughly the order of their arrival. In later sections, we will consider other sociological variables (i.e., social class, gender) that further differentiated these groups.

NORTHERN AND WESTERN PROTESTANT EUROPEANS

Northern and western European immigrants included English, Germans, Norwegians, Swedes, Welsh, French, Dutch, and Danes. These groups were similar to the dominant group in their racial and religious characteristics and also shared many cultural values with the host society, including the Protestant Ethic—which stressed hard work, success, and individualism—and support for the principles of democratic government. These similarities eased their acceptance into a society that was highly intolerant of religious and racial differences until well into the 20th century, and these immigrant groups generally experienced a lower degree of ethnocentric rejection and racist disparagement than did the Irish and immigrants from southern and eastern Europe.

Northern and western European immigrants came from nations that were just as developed as the United States; thus, they tended to be more skilled and educated than other immigrant groups, and they often brought money and other resources

with which to secure a comfortable place for themselves in their new society. Many settled in the sparsely populated Midwest and in other frontier areas, where they farmed the fertile land that had become available after the conquest and removal of American Indians and Mexican Americans (see Chapter 4). By dispersing throughout the midsection of the country, they lowered their visibility and their degree of competition with dominant-group members. Two brief case studies, first Norwegians and then Germans, outline the experiences of these groups.

Immigrants From Norway. Norway had a small population base, and immigration from this Scandinavian nation was never sizable in absolute numbers. However, "America Fever" struck here as it did elsewhere in Europe, and on a per capita basis, Norway sent more immigrants to the United States before 1890 than any other European nation except Ireland (Chan, 1990, p. 41).

The first Norwegian immigrants were moderately prosperous farmers searching for cheap land. They found abundant acreage in upper-Midwest states, such as Minnesota and Wisconsin, and then found that the local labor supply was too small to effectively cultivate the available land. Many turned to their homeland for assistance and used their relatives and friends to create networks and recruit a labor force. Thus, chains of communication and migration were established linking Norway to

1837
Samuel Morse invents the telegraph.

1876
Alexander Graham Bell invents the telephone.

1879
Thomas Edison invents the incandescent lightbulb.

1900
The zeppelin invented by Count Ferdinand von Zeppelin.

1903
The Wright Brothers make the first successful airplane flight.

1820   1830   1840   1850   1860   1870   1880   1890   1900   1910

1830
George Stephenson begins passenger rail service between Liverpool and London.

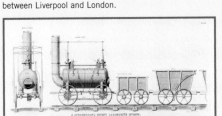

1866
Cyrus Field lays the first successful transatlantic cable.

1892
Rudolf Diesel invents the diesel-fueled internal combustion engine.

1896
Henry Ford manufactures his first motorcar.

the Northern Plains, supplying immigrants to these areas for decades (Chan, 1990, p. 41). Today, a strong Scandinavian heritage is still evident in the farms, towns, and cities of the upper Midwest.

Immigrants From Germany. The stream of immigration from Germany was much larger than that from Norway, and German Americans left their mark on the economy, the political structure, and the cultural life of their new land. In the last half of the 19th century, at least 25% of the immigrants each year were German (Conzen, 1980, p. 406), and today more Americans (about 15%) trace their ancestries to Germany than to any other country (Brittingham & de la Cruz, 2004).

The German immigrants who arrived earlier in the 1800s moved into the newly opened farmland and the rapidly growing cities of the Midwest, as had many Scandinavians. By 1850, large German communities could be found in Milwaukee, St. Louis, and other Midwestern cities (Conzen, 1980, p. 413). Some German immigrants followed the transatlantic route of the cotton trade between Europe and the southern United States and entered through the port of New Orleans, moving from there to the Midwest and Southwest. German immigrants arriving later in the century were more likely to settle in urban areas, in part because fertile land was less available. Many of the city-bound German immigrants were skilled

workers and artisans, and others found work as laborers in the rapidly expanding industrial sector. The double penetration of German immigrants into the rural economy and the higher sectors of the urban economy is reflected by the fact that by 1870, most employed German Americans were involved in skilled labor (37%) or farming (25%; Conzen, 1980, p. 413).

German immigrants took relatively high occupational positions in the U.S. labor force, and their sons and daughters were able to translate that relative affluence into economic mobility. By the dawn of the 20th century, large numbers of second-generation German Americans were finding their way into white-collar and professional careers. Within a few generations, German Americans had achieved parity with national norms in education, income, and occupational prestige.

Assimilation Patterns. By and large, assimilation for Norwegian, German, and other Protestant immigrants from northern and western Europe was consistent with the traditional model discussed earlier in this chapter. Although members of these groups felt the sting of rejection, prejudice, and discrimination, their movement from acculturation to integration and equality was relatively smooth, especially when compared with the experiences of racial minority groups. Their relative success and high degree of assimilation are suggested in Table 2.3, presented later in this chapter.

Newly arrived immigrants from Germany.

IMMIGRANT LABORERS FROM IRELAND AND SOUTHERN AND EASTERN EUROPE

The relative ease of assimilation for northern and western Europeans contrasts sharply with the experiences of non-Protestant, less educated, and less skilled immigrants. These "immigrant laborers" came in two waves. The Irish were part of the Old Immigration that began in the 1820s, but the bulk of this group—Italians, Poles, Russians, Hungarians, Greeks, Serbs, Ukrainians, Slovaks, Bulgarians, and scores of other southern and eastern European groups—made up the New Immigration that began in the 1880s.

Peasant Origins. Most of the immigrants in these nationality groups (like many recent immigrants to the United States) were peasants or unskilled laborers, with few resources other than their willingness to work. They came from rural, village-oriented cultures in which family and kin took precedence over individual needs or desires. Family life for them tended to be autocratic and male dominated, and children were expected to subordinate their personal desires and work for the good of the family as a whole. Arranged marriages were common. This cultural background was less consistent with the industrializing, capitalistic, individualistic, Protestant, Anglo-American culture of the United States and was a major reason that these immigrant laborers experienced a higher level of rejection and discrimination than did the immigrants from northern and western Europe.

The immigrant laborers were much less likely to enter the rural economy than were the northern and western European immigrants. Much of the better frontier land had already been claimed by the time most new immigrant groups began to arrive, and a large number of them had been permanently soured on farming by the oppressive and exploitative agrarian economies from which they were trying to escape.

Regional and Occupational Patterns. They settled in the cities of the industrializing Northeast and found work in plants, mills, mines, and factories. They supplied the armies of laborers needed to power the industrial revolution in the United States, although their view of this process was generally from the bottom looking up. They arrived during the decades in which the American industrial and urban infrastructure was being constructed. They built roads, canals, and railroads, as well as the buildings that housed the machinery of industrialization. For example, the first tunnels of the New York City subway system were dug, largely by hand, by laborers from Italy. Other immigrants found work in the coal fields of Pennsylvania and West Virginia and the steel mills of Pittsburgh, and they flocked by the millions to the factories of the Northeast.

Like other low-skill immigrant groups, these newcomers took jobs in which strength and stamina were more important than literacy or skilled craftsmanship. In fact, the minimum level of skills required for employment actually declined as industrialization proceeded through its early phases. To keep wages low and take advantage of what seemed like an inexhaustible supply of cheap labor, industrialists and factory owners developed technologies and machines that required few skills and little knowledge of English to operate. As mechanization proceeded, unskilled workers replaced skilled workers in the workforce. Not infrequently, women and children replaced men because they could be hired for lower wages (Steinberg, 1981, p. 35).

Many immigrants found work in coal mines.

Assimilation Patterns. Eventually, as the generations passed, the prejudice, systematic discrimination, and other barriers to upward mobility for the immigrant laborer groups weakened, and their descendants began to rise out of the working class. Although the first and second generations of these groups were largely limited to jobs at the unskilled or semiskilled level, the third and later generations rose in the American social class system. As Table 2.3 shows (later in this chapter), the descendants of the immigrant laborers achieved parity with national norms by the latter half of the 20th century.

EASTERN EUROPEAN JEWISH IMMIGRANTS AND THE ETHNIC ENCLAVE

Jewish immigrants from Russia and other parts of eastern Europe followed a third pathway into U.S. society. This group was a part of the New Immigration and began arriving in the 1880s. Unlike the immigrant laborer groups, who were generally economic refugees and included many young, single males, eastern European Jews were fleeing religious persecution and arrived as family units intending to settle permanently and become citizens. They settled in the urban areas of the Northeast and Midwest. New York City was the most common destination, and the Lower East Side became the best-known Jewish American neighborhood. By 1920, about 60% of all Jewish Americans lived in the urban areas between Boston and Philadelphia, with almost 50% living in New York City alone. Another 30% lived in the urban areas of the Midwest, particularly Chicago (Goren, 1980, p. 581).

Urban Origins. In Russia and other parts of eastern Europe, Jews had been barred from agrarian occupations and had come to rely on the urban economy for their livelihoods. When they immigrated to the United States, they brought these urban skills and job experiences with them. For example, almost two thirds of the immigrant Jewish men had been tailors and other skilled laborers in eastern Europe (Goren, 1980, p. 581). In the rapidly industrializing U.S. economy of the early 20th century, they were able to use these skills to find work.

Other Jewish immigrants joined the urban working class and took manual labor and unskilled jobs in the industrial sector (Morawska, 1990, p. 202). The garment industry in particular became the lifeblood of the Jewish community and provided jobs to about one third of all eastern European Jews residing in the major cities (Goren, 1980, p. 582). Women as well as men were involved in the garment industry. Jewish women, like the women of more recent immigrant laborer groups, found ways to combine their jobs and their domestic responsibilities. As young girls, they worked in factories and sweatshops, and after marriage, they did the same work at home, sewing precut garments together or doing other piecework such as wrapping cigars or making artificial flowers, often assisted by their children (Amott & Matthaei, 1991, p. 115).

An Enclave Economy. Unlike most European immigrant groups, Jewish Americans became heavily involved in commerce and often found ways to start their own businesses and become self-employed. Drawing on their experience in the old country, many started businesses and small independent enterprises, and developed an enclave economy. The Jewish neighborhoods were densely populated and provided a ready market for services of all kinds. Some Jewish immigrants became street peddlers or started bakeries, butcher and candy shops, or any number of other retail enterprises.

Capitalizing on their residential concentration and close proximity, Jewish immigrants created dense networks of commercial, financial, and social cooperation. The Jewish American enclave survived because of the cohesiveness of the group; the willingness of wives, children, and other relatives to work for little or no monetary compensation; and the commercial savvy of the early immigrants. Also, a large pool of cheap labor and sources of credit and other financial services were available within the community.

The Jewish American enclave grew and provided a livelihood for many of the children and grandchildren of the immigrants (Portes & Manning, 1986, pp. 51–52). As has been the case with other enclave groups that we will discuss in future chapters, including Chinese Americans and Cuban Americans, economic advancement preceded extensive acculturation, and Jewish Americans made significant strides toward economic equality before they became fluent in English or were otherwise Americanized.

Americanized Generations. One obvious way an enclave immigrant group can improve its position is to develop an educated and acculturated second generation. The Americanized, English-speaking children of the immigrants used their greater familiarity with the dominant society and their language facility to help preserve and expand the family enterprise. Furthermore, as the second generation appeared, the American public school system was expanding, and education through the college level was free or inexpensive in New York City and other cities (Steinberg, 1981, pp. 128–138). There was also a strong push for the second and third generations to enter professions, and as Jewish Americans excelled in school, resistance to and discrimination against them increased. By the 1920s, many elite colleges and universities, such as Dartmouth, had established quotas that limited the number of Jewish students they would admit (Dinnerstein, 1977, p. 228). These quotas were not abolished until after World War II.

Assimilation Patterns. The enclave economy and the Jewish neighborhoods established by the immigrants proved to be an effective base from which to integrate into American society. The descendants of the eastern European Jewish immigrants moved out of the ethnic neighborhoods years ago, and their positions in the economy—their pushcarts, stores, and jobs in the garment industry—have been taken over by more

Hester Street, New York City, was the center of the Jewish immigrant enclave a century ago.

recent immigrants. When they left the enclave economy, many second- and third-generation eastern European Jews did not enter the mainstream occupational structure at the bottom, as the immigrant laborer groups tended to do. They used the resources generated by the entrepreneurship of the early generations to gain access to prestigious and advantaged social class positions (Portes & Manning, 1986, p. 53). Studies show that Jewish Americans today, as a group, surpass national averages in income, levels of education, and occupational prestige (Sklare, 1971, pp. 60–69; see also Cohen, 1985; Massarik & Chenkin, 1973). The relatively higher status of Russian Americans shown in Table 2.3 (later in this chapter) is due in part to the fact that many Jewish Americans are of Russian descent.

CHAINS OF IMMIGRATION

All immigrant groups tend to follow "chains" established and maintained by the members of their groups. Some versions of the traditional assimilation perspective (especially human capital theory) treat immigration and status attainment as purely individual (psychological) matters. To the contrary, scholars have demonstrated that immigration to the United States was in large measure a group (sociological) phenomenon. Immigrant chains stretched across the oceans and were held together by the ties of kinship, language, religion, culture, and a sense of common peoplehood (Bodnar, 1985; Tilly, 1990). The networks supplied information, money for passage, family news, and job offers.

Here is how chain immigration worked (and continues to work today): Someone from a village in, say, Poland would make it to the United States. The successful immigrant would send word to the home village, perhaps by hiring a letter writer. Along with news and stories of his adventures, he would send his address. Within months, another immigrant from the village, perhaps a brother or other relative, would

show up at the address of the original immigrant. After his months of experience in the new society, the original immigrant could lend assistance, provide a place to sleep, help with job hunting, and orient the newcomer to the area.

Before long, others would arrive from the village in need of the same sort of introduction to the mysteries of America. The compatriots would tend to settle close to one another, in the same building or on the same block. Soon, entire neighborhoods were filled with people from a certain village, province, or region. In these ethnic enclaves, the old language was spoken and the old ways observed. Businesses were started, churches or synagogues founded, families begun, and mutual aid societies and other organizations formed. There was safety in numbers and comfort and security in a familiar, if transplanted, set of traditions and customs.

Immigrants often responded to U.S. society by attempting to re-create as much of their old world as possible. Partly to avoid the harsher forms of rejection and discrimination and

Chinatowns were the centers of social and economic life for Chinese immigrants.

NARRATIVE PORTRAIT

Entering the Promised Land

Mary Antin, author of *The Promised Land*.

Mary Antin was born a Russian Jew, grew up in a Jewish ghetto, and immigrated to the United States in 1894. Her family settled in the slums of Boston, where she was quickly identified as an outstanding student. Even though she spoke no English at her arrival, she was able to attend an elite high school and also went to Columbia University and Barnard College. In 1912, she published her memoir, The Promised Land, *which describes her childhood in Russia and her family's largely successful assimilation into American society. The book was immensely popular, perhaps because it presents her assimilation in positive terms. This passage describes her arrival in Boston and her first view of American society. Note how she consciously begins to absorb American culture, piece by piece.*

FIRST GLIMPSES OF AMERICAN SOCIETY

Mary Antin

Our initiation into American ways began with the first step on the new soil. My father found occasion to instruct or correct us even on the way...to [our new home]...in a rickety cab. He told us not to lean out of the windows, not to point, and explained the word "greenhorn."...

The first meal was an object lesson of much variety. My father produced several kinds of food, ready to eat, without any cooking, from little tin cans that had printing all over them. He attempted to introduce us to a queer, slippery kind of fruit, which he called "banana," but had to give it up for the time being....

[In] the evening..., I was delighted with the illumination of the streets. So many lamps, and they burned until morning, my father said, and so people did not need to carry lanterns....The streets were as bright as a synagogue on a holy day....

Education was free. That subject my father had written about repeatedly, as comprising his chief hope for us children, the essence of American opportunity, the treasure that no thief could touch....On our second day...a little girl from across the alley came and offered to conduct us to school. My father was out, but we five between us had a few words of English by this time. We knew the word school. We understood. This child, who had never seen us till yesterday, who could not pronounce our names,...was able to offer us the freedom of the schools of Boston!...The doors stood open for every one of us. The smallest child could show us the way....

We had to visit the stores and be dressed from head to foot in American clothing; we had to learn the mysteries of the iron stove, the washboard, and the speaking-tube; we had to learn to trade with the fruit peddler through the window, and not to be afraid of the policeman; and, above all, we had to learn English....

With our despised immigrant clothing we shed also our impossible Hebrew names. A committee of our friends ...concocted American names for us all. Those of our real names that had no pleasing American equivalents they ruthlessly discarded....My mother... was punished with the undignified nickname of Annie. Fetchke, Joseph, and Deborah issued as Frieda, Joseph, and Dora, respectively. As for poor me, I was simply cheated. The name they gave me was hardly new. My Hebrew name being Maryashe..., my friends said that it would hold good in English as *Mary*; which was very disappointing, as I longed to possess a strange-sounding American name like the others.

SOURCE: *The Promised Land* by Mary Antin (1912). Copyright, 1911 and 1912, by the Atlantic Monthly Company. Copyright, 1912, by Houghton Mifflin Company.

Questions to Consider

1. What is the single most significant act of acculturation in this passage? Why?
2. Can you identify any instances of integration?
3. What elements of chain immigration can you detect? What important roles do social networks play in Mary's adjustment to the United States?

partly to band together for solidarity and mutual support, immigrants created their own miniature social worlds within the bustling metropolises of the industrializing Northeast and West Coast. These Little Italys, Little Warsaws, Little Irelands, Greektowns, Chinatowns, and Little Tokyos were safe havens that insulated the immigrants from the larger society and allowed them to establish bonds with one another, organize a group life, pursue their own group interests, and have some control over the pace of their adjustment to American culture. For some groups and in some areas, the ethnic subcommunity was a short-lived phenomenon. For others (the Jewish enclave discussed earlier, for example), the neighborhood became the dominant structure of their lives, and the networks continued to function long after their arrival in the United States.

THE CAMPAIGN AGAINST IMMIGRATION: PREJUDICE, RACISM, AND DISCRIMINATION

Today, it may be hard to conceive of the bitterness and intensity of the prejudice that greeted the Irish, Italians, Poles, Jews, and other new immigrant groups. Even as they were becoming an indispensable segment of the American workforce, they were castigated, ridiculed, attacked, and disparaged. The Irish were the first immigrant laborers to arrive and thus the first to feel this intense prejudice and discrimination. Campaigns against immigrants were waged, Irish neighborhoods were attacked by mobs, and Roman Catholic churches and convents were burned. Some employers blatantly refused to hire the Irish, often advertising their ethnic preferences with signs that read "No Irish Need Apply." Until later arriving groups pushed them up, the Irish were mired at the bottom of the job market. Indeed, at one time they were referred to as the "niggers of Boston" (Blessing, 1980; Potter, 1973; Shannon, 1964).

Other groups felt the same sting of rejection as they arrived. Italian immigrants were particularly likely to be the victims of violent attacks, one of the most vicious of which took place in New Orleans in 1891. The city's police chief was assassinated, and rumors of Italian involvement in the murder were rampant. Hundreds of Italians were arrested, and nine were brought to trial. All were acquitted. Anti-Italian sentiment was running so high, however, that a mob lynched 11 Italians, while police and city officials did nothing (Higham, 1963).

Anti-Catholicism. Much of the prejudice against the Irish and the new immigrants was expressed as anti-Catholicism. Prior to the mid-19th century, Anglo-American society had been almost exclusively Protestant. Catholicism, with its celibate clergy, Latin masses, and cloistered nuns, seemed alien, exotic, and threatening. The growth of Catholicism, especially because it was associated with non-Anglo immigrants, raised fears that the Protestant religions would lose status. There were even rumors that the pope was planning to move the Vatican to America and organize a takeover of the U.S. government.

Although Catholics were often stereotyped as single groups, they also varied along a number of dimensions. For example, the Catholic faith as practiced in Ireland differed significantly from that practiced in Italy, Poland, and other countries. Catholic immigrant groups often established their own parishes, with priests who could speak the old language. These cultural and national differences often separated Catholic groups, despite their common faith (Herberg, 1960).

Anti-Semitism is prejudice or ideological racism directed specifically toward Jews.

Anti-Semitism. Jews from Russia and eastern Europe faced intense prejudice and racism (or **anti-Semitism**) as they began arriving in large numbers in the 1880s. Biased sentiments and negative stereotypes of Jews have been a part of Western tradition for centuries and, in fact, have been stronger and more vicious in Europe than in the United States. For nearly two millennia, European Jews have been chastised and persecuted as the "killers of Christ" and stereotyped as materialistic moneylenders and crafty businessmen.

The stereotype that links Jews and moneylending has its origins in the fact that in premodern Europe, Catholics were forbidden by the church to engage in usury (charging interest for loans). Jews were under no such restriction, and they filled the gap thus created in the economy. The ultimate episode in the long history of European anti-Semitism was, of course, the Nazi Holocaust, in which six million Jews died. European anti-Semitism did not end with the demise of the Nazi regime, however, and it remains a prominent concern throughout Europe and Russia (see Chapter 13).

Before the mass immigration of eastern European Jews began in the late 1800s, anti-Semitism in the United States was relatively mild, perhaps because the group was so small. As the immigration continued, anti-Jewish prejudice increased in intensity and viciousness, fostering the view of Jews as cunning but dishonest merchants. In the late 19th century, Jews began to be banned from social clubs and the boardrooms of businesses and other organizations. Summer resorts began posting notices: "We prefer not to entertain Hebrews" (Goren, 1980, p. 585).

By the 1920s and 1930s, anti-Semitism had become quite prominent among American prejudices and was being preached by the Ku Klux Klan and other extreme racist groups. Also, because many of the political radicals and labor leaders of the time were Jewish immigrants, anti-Semitism became fused with a fear of Communism and other anticapitalist doctrines. Some prominent Americans espoused anti-Semitic views, among them Henry Ford, the founder of Ford Motor Company; Charles Lindbergh, the aviator who was the first to fly solo across the Atlantic; and Father Charles Coughlin, a Catholic priest based in Detroit who hosted a popular radio show (Selzer, 1972).

Anti-Semitism reached a peak before World War II and tapered off in the decades following the war, but as we shall see in Chapter 3, it remains a part of U.S. society (Anti-Defamation League, 2000). Anti-Semitism also has a prominent place in the ideologies of a variety of extremist groups that have emerged in recent years, including "skinheads" and various contemporary incarnations of the Ku Klux Klan. Some of this targeting of Jews seems to increase during economic recession and may be related to the stereotypical view of Jewish Americans as extremely prosperous and materialistic.

A Successful Exclusion. The prejudice and racism directed against the immigrants also found expression in organized, widespread efforts to stop the flow of immigration. A variety of anti-immigrant organizations appeared almost as soon as the mass European immigration started in the 1820s. The strength of these campaigns waxed and waned, largely in harmony with the strength of the economy and the size of the job supply. Anti-immigrant sentiment intensified, and the strength of its organized expressions increased during hard times and depressions, and tended to soften when the economy improved.

The campaign ultimately triumphed with the passage of the National Origins Act in 1924, which established a quota system limiting the number of immigrants that would be accepted each year from each sending nation, a system that was openly racist. For example, the size of the quota for European nations was based on the proportional representation of each nationality in the United States as of 1890. This year was chosen because it predated the bulk of the New Immigration and gave the most generous quotas to northern and western European nations.

The quota system allocated nearly 70% of the available immigration slots to the nations of northern and western Europe, despite the fact that immigration from those areas had largely ended by the 1920s. Immigration from Western Hemisphere nations was not directly affected by this legislation, but immigration from Asian nations was banned altogether. At this time, almost all parts of Africa were still the colonial possessions of various European nations and received no separate quotas. In other words, the quota for immigrants from Africa was zero.

The National Origins Act drastically reduced the overall number of immigrants that would be admitted each year. The effectiveness of the numerical restrictions is clearly apparent in Figure 2.4. By the time the Great Depression took hold of the American economy in the 1930s, immigration had dropped to the lowest level in a century. The National Origins Act remained in effect until 1965.

QUESTIONS FOR REFLECTION

1. What forces motivated people to leave Europe and come to North America? How did these motives change from time to time and from place to place?

2. What motivated the forces of resistance and discrimination in the United States? How did the "exclusionists" finally triumph? What roles did class play in these processes?

PATTERNS OF ASSIMILATION

In this section, we will explore some of the common patterns in the process of assimilation followed by European immigrants and their descendants. These patterns have been well established by research conducted in the traditional perspective and are consistent with the model of assimilation developed by Gordon. They include assimilation by generation, ethnic succession, and structural mobility. We discuss each separately in this section.

THE IMPORTANCE OF GENERATIONS

People today—social scientists, politicians, and ordinary citizens—often fail to recognize the time and effort it takes for a group to become completely Americanized. For most European immigrant groups, the process took generations, and it was the grandchildren or the great-grandchildren (or even great-great-grandchildren) of the immigrants who finally completed acculturation and integration. Mass immigration from Europe ended in the 1920s, but the assimilation of some European ethnic groups was not completed until late in the 20th century.

Here is a rough summary of how assimilation proceeded for these European immigrants: The first generation, the actual immigrants, settled in ethnic neighborhoods, such as Little Italy in New York City, and made only limited movement toward acculturation and integration. They focused their energies on the network of family and social relationships encompassed within their own groups. Of course, many of them—most often the men—had to leave their neighborhoods for work and other reasons, and these excursions required some familiarity with the larger society. Some English had to be learned, and taking a job outside the neighborhood is, almost by definition, a form of integration. Nonetheless, the first generation lived and died largely within the context of the "old country," which had been re-created within the new.

The second generation, or the children of the immigrants, found themselves in a position of psychological or social marginality: They were partly ethnic and partly American but full members of neither group. They were born in America but in households and neighborhoods that were ethnic, not American. They learned the old language first and were socialized in the old ways. As they entered childhood, however, they entered the public schools, where they were socialized into the Anglo-American culture.

Very often, the world the second generation learned about at school conflicted with the one they inhabited at home. For example, the old-country family values often expected children to subordinate their self-interests to the interests of their elders and the family as a whole. Marriages were arranged by parents, or at least heavily influenced by and subject to their approval. Needless to say, these expectations conflicted sharply with American ideas about individualism and romantic love. Differences of this sort often caused painful conflict between the ethnic first generation and their Americanized children.

As the second generation progressed toward adulthood, they tended to move out of the old neighborhoods. Their geographic mobility was often motivated by social mobility.

TABLE 2.2 Some Comparisons Between Italians and WASPs

| | WASPs* | GENERATION | | |
		First	Second	Third and Fourth
1. Percentage with some college	42.4%	19%	19.4%	41.7%
2. Average years of education	12.6	9	11.1	13.4
3. Percentage white collar	34.7%	20%	22.5%	28.8%
4. Percentage blue collar	37.9%	65%	53.9%	39.0%
5. Average occupational prestige	42.5	34.3	36.8	42.5
6. Percentage of "unmixed" Italian males marrying non-Italian females	N/A	21.9%	51.4%	67.3%

SOURCE: Adapted from Alba (1985), Tables 5-3, 5-4, and 6-2. Data are originally from the NORC General Social Surveys, 1975–1980, and the Current Population Survey, 1979. Copyright © 1985 Richard D. Alba.

*White Anglo-Saxon Protestants (WASPs) were not separated by generation, and some of the differences between groups may be the result of factors such as age. That is, older WASPs may have levels of education more comparable to first-generation Italian Americans than do WASPs as a whole.

They were much more acculturated than their parents, spoke English fluently, and enjoyed a wider range of occupational choices and opportunities. Discriminatory policies in education, housing, and the job market sometimes limited them, but they were upwardly mobile, and in their pursuit of jobs and careers, they left behind the ethnic subcommunity and many of their parents' customs.

The members of the third generation, or the grandchildren of the immigrants, were typically born and raised in non-ethnic settings. English was their first (and often their only) language, and their values and perceptions were thoroughly American. Although family and kinship ties with grandparents and the old neighborhood often remained strong, ethnicity for this generation was a relatively minor part of their daily realities and self-images. Visits on weekends and holidays, and family rituals revolving around the cycles of birth, marriage, and death—these activities might have connected the third generation to the world of their ancestors, but in terms of their everyday lives, they were American, not ethnic.

The pattern of assimilation by generation progressed as follows:

- The first generation began the process and was at least slightly acculturated and integrated.
- The second generation was very acculturated and highly integrated (at least into the secondary sectors of the society).
- The third generation finished the acculturation process and enjoyed high levels of integration at both the secondary and the primary levels.

Table 2.2 illustrates these patterns in terms of the structural assimilation of Italian Americans. The educational and occupational characteristics of this group converge with those of white Anglo-Saxon Protestants (WASPs) as the generations change. For example, the percentage of Italian Americans with some college shows a gap of more than 20 points between the first and second generations and WASPs. Italians of the third and fourth generations, though, are virtually identical to WASPs on this measure of integration in the secondary sector. The other differences between Italians and WASPs shrink in a similar fashion from generation to generation.

The first five measures of educational and occupational attainment in Table 2.2 illustrate the generational pattern of integration (structural assimilation). The sixth measures marital assimilation, or intermarriage. It displays the percentage of males of "unmixed," or 100%, Italian heritage who married females outside the Italian community. Note once more the tendency for integration, now at the primary level, to increase across the generations. The huge majority of first-generation males married within their group (only 21.9% married non-Italians). By the third generation, 67.3% of the males were marrying non-Italians.

Of course, this model of step-by-step, linear assimilation by generation fits some groups better than others. For example, immigrants from northern and western Europe (except for the Irish) were generally more similar, racially and culturally, to the dominant group and tended to be more educated and skilled. They experienced relatively easier acceptance and tended to complete the assimilation process in three generations or less.

In contrast, immigrants from Ireland and from southern and eastern Europe were mostly uneducated, unskilled peasants who were more likely to join the huge army of industrial labor that manned the factories, mines, and mills. These groups were more likely to remain at the bottom of the

American class structure for generations and to have risen to middle-class prosperity only in the recent past. As mentioned earlier, eastern European Jews formed an enclave and followed a distinctly different pathway of assimilation, using the enclave as a springboard to launch the second and third generations into the larger society (although their movements were circumscribed by widespread anti-Semitic sentiments and policies).

It is important to keep this generational pattern in mind when examining immigration to the United States today. It is common for contemporary newcomers (especially Hispanics) to be criticized for their "slow" pace of assimilation, but their "progress" takes on a new aspect when viewed in the light of the generational time frame for assimilation followed by European immigrants. Especially with modern forms of transportation, immigration can be very fast. Assimilation, on the other hand, is by nature slow.

ETHNIC SUCCESSION

A second factor that shaped the assimilation experience is captured in the concept of **ethnic succession**, or the myriad ways European ethnic groups unintentionally affected one another's positions in the social class structure of the larger society. The overall pattern was that each European immigrant group tended to be pushed to higher social class levels and more favorable economic situations by the groups that arrived after them. As more experienced groups became upwardly mobile and began to move out of the neighborhoods that served as their "ports of entry," they were often replaced by a new group of immigrants who would begin the process all over again. Some neighborhoods in the cities of the Northeast served as the ethnic neighborhood—the first safe haven in the new society—for a variety of successive groups. Some neighborhoods continue to fill this role today.

This process can be understood in terms of the second stage of Gordon's model: integration at the secondary level (see Table 2.1), or entry into the public institutions and organizations of the larger society. Three pathways of integration tended to be most important for European immigrants: politics, labor unions, and the church. We will cover each in turn, illustrating with the Irish, the first immigrant laborers to arrive in large numbers, but the general patterns apply to all white ethnic groups.

Politics. The Irish tended to follow the northern and western Europeans in the job market and social class structure and were, in turn, followed by the wave of new immigrants. In many urban areas of the Northeast, they moved into the neighborhoods and took jobs left behind by German laborers. After a period of acculturation and adjustment, the Irish began to create their own connections with the mainstream society and improve their economic and social positions. They were replaced in their neighborhoods and at the bottom of the

occupational structure by Italians, Poles, and other immigrant groups arriving after them.

As the years passed and the Irish gained more experience, they began to forge more links to the larger society, and, in particular, they allied themselves with the Democratic Party and helped construct the political machines that came to dominate many city governments in the 19th and 20th centuries. Machine politicians were often corrupt and even criminal, regularly subverting the election process, bribing city and state officials, using city budgets to fill the pockets of the political bosses and their cronies, and passing out public jobs as payoffs for favors and faithful service.

Although not exactly models of good government, the political machines performed a number of valuable social services for their constituents and loyal followers. Machine politicians, such as Boss Tweed of Tammany Hall in New York City, could find jobs, provide food and clothing for the destitute, aid victims of fires and other calamities, and intervene in the criminal and civil courts.

Much of the power of the urban political machines derived from their control of the city payroll. The leaders of the machines used municipal jobs and the city budget as part of a "spoils" system (as in "to the winner go the spoils"), and as rewards for their supporters and allies. The faithful Irish party worker might be rewarded for service to the machine with a job in the police department (thus the stereotypical Irish cop) or some other agency. Private businessmen might be rewarded with lucrative contracts to supply services or perform other city business.

The political machines served as engines of economic opportunity and linked Irish Americans to a central and important institution of the dominant society. Using the resources controlled by local government as a power base, the Irish (and other immigrant groups after them) began to integrate themselves into the larger society and carve out a place in the mainstream structures of American society, as illustrated in the following Narrative Portrait.

Labor Unions. The labor movement provided a second link among the Irish, other European immigrant groups, and the larger society. Although virtually all white ethnic groups had a hand in the creation and eventual success of the movement, many of the founders and early leaders were Irish. For example, Terence Powderly, an Irish Catholic, founded one of the first U.S. labor unions, and in the early years of the 20th century, about one third of union leaders were Irish and more than 50 national unions had Irish presidents (Bodnar, 1985, p. 111; Brody, 1980, p. 615).

Ethnic succession is the process by which white ethnic groups affected one another's positions in the social class structure.

Ethnicity, Prejudice, and the Irish Political Machine

David Gray grew up a Welsh Protestant in Scranton, Pennsylvania, during the 1930s and 1940s. At that time, this coal-mining town was split along ethnic lines, and Gray (1991) recounts his socialization into the realities of in-groups and out-groups. He also describes how Scranton's Irish Catholic community responded to the Great Depression and how they used the local political machine to protect their own, generating resentment and prejudice among the Welsh.

Gray eventually earned a PhD in sociology, and became a college professor and an accomplished and respected sociologist. Among his many admiring students was one of the authors of this textbook, who grew up in Scranton's Irish Catholic community a generation after Gray.

SHADOW OF THE PAST

David Gray

I did not ask to be born Welsh Protestant in Scranton, Pennsylvania. No more than [my friend] Eddie Gilroy...asked to be born Irish Catholic. But there we both were in the heart of the anthracite coal region...during the years of the Great Depression....We were friends, good friends. [After school], he played second base and I played shortstop....We thought we were a good double-play combination and, beyond the baseball field, we respected and liked each other as well.

But, there was something wrong with Eddie Gilroy. At age ten I didn't know exactly what it was. He didn't make many errors and we often shared whatever pennies we had...at the corner candy store. Still, there was something wrong with him—vague, general, apart from real experience, but true all the same.

His fundamental defect came into sharper focus at the age of twelve. Sunday movies had just arrived in Scranton....I wanted to go with Eddie...[but] I couldn't.

"Why?"

"Because Protestants don't go to the movies on Sunday"—nor play cards, football or baseball....

"How come Eddie and Johnny can go?"

"They're Catholic."

No one quite used the word "immoral" but...the implication was clear: if Catholics did such bad things on Sunday, they surely did a lot of bad things on other days as well.

No matter, then, that Gilroy might sacrifice for even a Protestant runner to go to second,...or share his candy....His Catholicism...permeated his being,...muting his individual qualities....

...Little Welsh Protestant boys and girls learned that Catholics were somehow the enemy....

But, quite unfortunately from their vantage point, the Welsh of Scranton were not the only ones in town. While they had come to the coal regions in large numbers, others, in even larger numbers, had come also. Irish, Italian, Polish, German....With [some] exception[s]..., most were Catholic....

In this communal setting...the Great Depression arrived with particular force. [The region suffered from massive unemployment.] The coal industry...was gone....The public sector...became the primary possibility for...jobs.

And the Irish...controlled political power....[They] did their best to take care of their...own....

In Scranton's public life, the intimate relationship of religion, politics, and economics was clear....From the Mayor's office to trash collectors,...the public payroll included the names of O'Neill, Hennigan, Lydon, Kennedy, Walsh, Gerrity, and O'Hoolihan....Welsh Protestants came to know...that Lewis, Griffiths and Williams need not apply.

... Among the Welsh, the general feeling of resentment on more than one occasion was punctuated with: "Those goddam Irish Catholics."

...Jobs, homes, and lives were at stake, and religious affiliation was relevant to them all. Irish Catholic political power was a fact from which Welsh Protestant resentment followed. Prejudice there certainly was—deeply felt, poignantly articulated,...and, unfortunately, communicated to the young.

SOURCE: Gray (1991, pp. 34–38).

Questions to Consider

1. According to this passage, do the Welsh and Irish seem equally acculturated? Are they equally integrated?

2. What boundaries separate the Welsh and the Irish? How are their differences maintained? In what ways are they integrating with each other?

As the labor movement grew in strength and gradually acquired legitimacy, the leaders of the movement also gained status, power, and other resources, while the rank-and-file membership gained job security, increased wages, and better fringe benefits. The labor movement provided another channel through which resources, power, status, and jobs flowed to the white ethnic groups.

Because of the way jobs were organized in industrializing America, union work typically required communication and cooperation across ethnic lines. The American workforce at the turn of the 20th century was multiethnic and multilingual, and union leaders had to coordinate and mobilize the efforts of many different language and cultural groups to represent the interests of the workers as a social class. Thus, labor union leaders became important intermediaries between the larger society and European immigrant groups.

Women were also heavily involved in the labor movement. Immigrant women were among the most exploited segments of the labor force, and they were involved in some of the most significant events in American labor history. For example, one of the first victories of the union movement occurred in New York City in 1909. The Uprising of the 20,000 was a massive strike of mostly Jewish and Italian women (many in their teens) against the garment industry. The strike lasted four months, despite attacks by thugs hired by the bosses and abuses by the police and the courts. The strikers eventually won recognition of the union from many employers, a reversal of a wage decrease, and a reduction in the 56- to 59-hour week they were expected to work (Goren, 1980, p. 584).

One of the great tragedies in the history of labor relations in the United States also involved European immigrant women. In 1911, a fire swept through the Triangle Shirtwaist Company, a garment-industry shop located on the 10th floor of a building in New York City. The fire spread rapidly, and the few escape routes were quickly cut off. About 140 young immigrant girls died, and many chose to leap to their deaths rather than be consumed by the flames. The disaster outraged the public, and the funerals of the victims were attended by more than a quarter of a million people. The incident fueled a drive for reform and improvement of work conditions and safety regulations (Amott & Matthaei, 1991, pp. 114–116; see also Schoener, 1967).

European immigrant women also filled leadership roles in the labor movement and served as presidents and in other offices, although usually in female-dominated unions. One of the most colorful union activists was Mother Jones, an Irish immigrant who worked tirelessly to organize miners:

> *Until she was nearly one hundred years old, Mother Jones was where the danger was greatest—crossing militia lines, spending weeks in damp prisons, incurring the wrath of governors, presidents, and coal operators—she helped to organize the United Mine Workers with the only tools she felt she needed: "convictions and a voice." (Forner, 1980, p. 281)*

Women workers often faced opposition from men as well as from employers. The major unions were not only racially discriminatory but also hostile to organizing women. For example, women laundry workers in San Francisco at the start of the 20th century were required to live in dormitories and work from 6 a.m. until midnight. When they applied to the international laundry workers union for a charter, they were blocked by the male members. They eventually went on strike and won the right to an eight-hour workday in 1912 (Amott & Matthaei, 1991, p. 117).

Religion. A third avenue of mobility for the Irish and other white ethnic groups was provided by religious institutions. The Irish were the first large group of Catholic immigrants and were thus in a favorable position to eventually dominate the church's administrative structure. The Catholic priesthood became largely Irish, and as they were promoted through the hierarchy, these priests became bishops and cardinals. The Catholic faith was practiced in different ways in different nations. As other Catholic immigrant groups began to arrive, conflict within the Irish-dominated church increased. Both Italian and Polish Catholic immigrants demanded their own parishes in which they could speak their own languages and celebrate their own customs and festivals. Dissatisfaction was

Women striking for a 40-hour work week.

so intense that some Polish Catholics broke with Rome and formed a separate Polish National Catholic Church (Lopata, 1976, p. 49).

The other Catholic immigrant groups eventually began to supply priests and other religious functionaries and to occupy leadership positions within the church. Although the church continued to be disproportionately influenced by the Irish, other white ethnic groups also used the Catholic Church as part of their power base for gaining acceptance and integration into the larger society.

Other Pathways. Besides party politics, the union movement, and religion, European immigrant groups forged other not-so-legitimate pathways of upward mobility. One alternative to legitimate success was offered by crime, a pathway that has been used by every ethnic group to some extent. Crime became particularly lucrative and attractive when Prohibition, the attempt to eliminate all alcohol use in the United States, went into effect in the 1920s. The criminalization of liquor failed to lower the demand, and Prohibition created a golden economic opportunity for those willing to take the risks involved in manufacturing and supplying alcohol to the American public.

Italian Americans headed many of the criminal organizations that took advantage of Prohibition. Criminal leaders and organizations with roots in Sicily, a region with a long history of secret antiestablishment societies, were especially important (Alba, 1985, pp. 62–64). The connection among organized crime, Prohibition, and Italian Americans is well-known, but it is not so widely recognized that ethnic succession operated in organized crime as it did in the legitimate opportunity structures. The Irish and Germans had been involved in organized crime for decades before the 1920s, and the Italians competed with these established gangsters and with Jewish crime syndicates for control of bootlegging and other criminal enterprises. The pattern of ethnic succession continued after the repeal of Prohibition, and members of groups newer to urban areas, including African Americans, Jamaicans, and Hispanic Americans, have recently challenged the Italian-dominated criminal "families."

Ethnic succession can also be observed in the institution of sports. Since the beginning of the 20th century, sports have offered a pathway to success and affluence that has attracted countless millions of young men. Success in many sports requires little in the way of formal credentials, education, or English fluency, and sports have been particularly appealing to the young men in minority groups that have few resources or opportunities.

For example, at the turn of the century, the Irish dominated the sport of boxing, but boxers from the Italian American community and other new immigrant groups eventually replaced them. Each successive wave of boxers reflected the concentration of a particular ethnic group at the bottom of the class structure. The succession of minority groups continues to this day, with boxing now dominated by African American and Latino fighters (Rader, 1983, pp. 87–106). A similar progression, or "layering," of ethnic and racial groups can be observed in other sports and in the entertainment industry.

The institutions of American society, both legitimate and illegal, reflect the relative positions of minority groups at a particular moment in time. Just a few generations ago, European immigrant groups dominated both crime and sports because they were blocked from legitimate opportunities. Now, the colonized racial minority groups still excluded from the mainstream job market and mired in the urban underclass are supplying disproportionate numbers of young people to these alternative opportunity structures.

CONTINUING INDUSTRIALIZATION AND STRUCTURAL MOBILITY

We have already mentioned that dominant–minority relations tend to change along with changes in subsistence technology, and we can find an example of this relationship in the history of the European immigrant groups across the 20th century. Industrialization is a continuous process, and as it proceeded, the nature of work in America evolved and changed and created opportunities for upward mobility for the white ethnic groups. One important form of upward mobility throughout the 20th century, called **structural mobility**, resulted more from changes in the structure of the economy and the labor market than from any individual effort or desire to "get ahead."

Structural mobility refers to rising occupational and social class standing that is a result of changes in the structure of the economy and labor market, as opposed to individual efforts.

Structural mobility is the result of the continuing mechanization and automation of the workplace. As machines replaced people in the workforce, the supply of manual, blue-collar jobs that had provided employment for so many first- and second-generation European immigrant laborers dwindled. At the same time, the supply of white-collar jobs increased, but access to the better jobs depended heavily on educational credentials. For white ethnic groups, a high school education became much more available in the 1930s, and college and university programs began to expand rapidly in the late 1940s, spurred in large part by the educational benefits made available to World War II veterans. Each generation of white ethnics, especially those born after 1925, was significantly more educated than the previous generation, and many were able to translate their increased human capital into upward mobility in the mainstream job market (Morawska, 1990, pp. 212–213).

The descendants of European immigrants became upwardly mobile not only because of their individual ambitions and efforts but also because of the changing location of jobs and the progressively greater opportunities for education available to them. Of course, the pace and timing of this upward movement was highly variable from group to group and from place to place. Ethnic succession continued to operate, and the descendants of the most recent immigrants from Europe (Italians and Poles, for example) tended to be the last to benefit from the general upgrading in education and the job market.

Still, structural mobility is one of the keys to the eventual successful integration of all white ethnic groups that is displayed in Table 2.3 (later in this chapter). During these same years, the racial minority groups, particularly African Americans, were excluded from the dominant group's educational system and from the opportunity to compete for better jobs.

QUESTIONS FOR REFLECTION

1. Why is generation important for understanding assimilation?

2. What were the major institutional pathways through which European immigrants adapted to U.S. society? Can you cite evidence from your home community of similar patterns for immigrant groups today?

VARIATIONS IN ASSIMILATION

In the previous section, we discussed patterns that were common to European immigrants and their descendants. Now we address some of the sources of variation and diversity in assimilation, a complex process that is never exactly the same for any two groups. Sociologists have paid particular attention to the way degree of similarity, religion, social class, and gender shaped the overall assimilation of the descendants of the mass European immigration. They have also investigated the way immigrants' reasons for coming to this country have affected the experiences of different groups.

DEGREE OF SIMILARITY

Since the dominant group consisted largely of Protestants with ethnic origins in northern and western Europe and especially England, it is not surprising to learn that the degree of resistance, prejudice, and discrimination encountered by the different European immigrant groups varied in part by the degree to which they differed from these dominant groups. The most significant differences related to religion, language, cultural values, and, for some groups, physical characteristics (which were often seen as "racial"). Thus, Protestant immigrants from northern and western Europe experienced less resistance than the English-speaking Catholic Irish, who in turn were accepted more readily than the new immigrants, who were both non–English speaking and overwhelmingly non-Protestant.

The preferences of the dominant group correspond roughly to the arrival times of the immigrants. The most similar groups immigrated earliest, and the least similar tended to be the last to arrive. Because of this coincidence, resistance to any one group of immigrants tended to fade as new groups arrived. For example, anti-German prejudice and discrimination never became particularly vicious or widespread (except during the heat of the World Wars) because the Irish began arriving in large numbers at about the same time. Concerns about the German immigrants were swamped by the fear that the Catholic Irish could never be assimilated. Then, as the 19th century drew to a close, immigrants from southern and eastern Europe—even more different from the dominant group—began to arrive and made concerns about the Irish seem trivial.

In addition, the New Immigration was far more voluminous than the Old Immigration (see Figure 2.4). Southern and eastern Europeans arrived in record numbers in the early 20th century, and the sheer volume of the immigration raised fears that American cities and institutions would be swamped by hordes of what were seen as racially inferior, unassimilable immigrants (a fear with strong echoes in the present).

Thus, a preference hierarchy was formed in American culture that privileged northern and western Europeans over southern and eastern Europeans, and Protestants over Catholics and Jews. These rankings reflect the ease with which the groups have been assimilated and have made their way into the larger society. This hierarchy of ethnic preference is still a part of American prejudice, as we shall see in Chapter 3, although it is much more muted today than in the heyday of immigration.

RELIGION

A major differentiating factor in the experiences of the European immigrant groups, recognized by Gordon and other students of American assimilation, was religion. Protestant, Catholic, and Jewish immigrants lived in different neighborhoods, occupied different niches in the workforce, formed separate networks of affiliation and groups, and chose their marriage partners from different pools of people.

One important study that documented the importance of religion for European immigrants and their descendants (and also reinforced the importance of generations) was conducted by sociologist Ruby Jo Kennedy (1944). She studied intermarriage patterns in New Haven, Connecticut, over a 70-year period ending in the 1940s and found that the immigrant generation chose marriage partners from a pool whose boundaries were marked by ethnicity and religion. For example, Irish Catholics married other Irish Catholics, Italian Catholics married Italian Catholics, Irish Protestants married Irish Protestants, and so forth across all the ethnic and religious divisions she studied.

The pool of marriage partners for the children and grandchildren of the immigrants continued to be bounded by religion but not so much by ethnicity. Thus, later generations of Irish Catholics continued to marry other Catholics but were less likely to marry other Irish. As assimilation proceeded, ethnic group boundaries faded (or "melted"), but religious boundaries did not. Kennedy described this phenomenon as a **triple melting pot**: a pattern of structural assimilation within each of the three religious denominations (Kennedy, 1944, 1952).

Will Herberg (1960), another important student of American assimilation, also explored the connection between religion and ethnicity. Writing in the 1950s, he noted that the pressures of acculturation did not affect all aspects of ethnicity equally. European immigrants and their descendants were strongly encouraged to learn English, but they were not so pressured to change their religious beliefs. Very often, their religious faith was the strongest connection between later generations and their immigrant ancestors. The American tradition of religious tolerance allowed the descendants of the European immigrants to preserve this tie to their roots without being seen as "un-American." As a result, the Protestant, Catholic, and Jewish faiths eventually came to occupy roughly equal degrees of legitimacy in American society.

Thus, for the descendants of the European immigrants, religion became a vehicle through which their ethnicity could be expressed. For many members of this group, religion and ethnicity were fused, and ethnic traditions and identities came to have a religious expression. For example, Mary Farrell, the Irish American schoolteacher introduced in Chapter 1, still attends Mass regularly in spite of the Catholic Church's position on homosexuality and gay marriage. She feels connected

---

The **triple melting pot** is the idea that structural assimilation for white ethnic groups took place within the context of the three major American religions.

to the church, in part, because her family has always been Catholic and, by observing the rituals of the church in the present, she is honoring her connections to the past. It is not just that she is Irish Catholic American but that—for her and millions of others—being Catholic is part of being Irish in America.

SOCIAL CLASS

Social class is a central feature of social structure, and it is not surprising that it affected the European immigrant groups in a number of ways. First, social class combined with religion to shape the social world of the descendants of the European immigrants. In fact, Gordon (1964) concluded that U.S. society in the 1960s actually incorporated not three but four melting pots (one for each of the major ethnic/religious groups and one for black Americans), each of which were internally subdivided by social class. In his view, the most significant structural unit within American society was the **ethclass**, defined by the intersection of the religious, ethnic, and social class boundaries (e.g., working-class Catholic, upper-class Protestant, etc.). Thus, people were not "simply American" but tended to identify with, associate with, and choose their spouses from within their ethclasses.

Second, social class affected structural integration. The huge majority of the post-1880s European immigrants were working class, and because they "entered U.S. society at the bottom of the economic ladder, and . . . stayed close to that level for the next half century, ethnic history has been essentially working class history" (Morawska, 1990, p. 215; see also Bodnar, 1985). For generations, many groups of eastern and southern European immigrants did not acculturate to middle-class American culture but to an urban working-class, blue-collar set of lifestyles and values. Even today, ethnicity for many groups remains interconnected with social class factors, and a familiar stereotype of white ethnicity is the hard-hat construction worker.

GENDER

Anyone who wants to learn about the experience of immigration will find a huge body of literature incorporating every imaginable discipline and genre. The great bulk of this material, however, concerns the immigrant experience in general or focuses specifically on male immigrants. The experiences of female immigrants have been much less recorded and hence far less accessible. Many immigrant women came from cultures with strong patriarchal traditions, and they had much less access to leadership roles, education, and prestigious, high-paying occupations. As is the case with women of virtually all minority groups, the voices of immigrant women have been muted. The research that has been done, however, documents that immigrant women played multiple roles both during immigration and during the assimilation process. As would be expected in patriarchal societies, the roles of wife and mother were central, but immigrant women were involved in myriad other activities as well.

In general, male immigrants tended to precede women, and it was common for the males to send for the women only after they had secured lodging, jobs, and a certain level of stability. However, women immigrants' experiences were quite varied, often depending on the economic situation and cultural traditions of their home societies. In some cases, women were not only prominent among the "first wave" of immigrants but also began the process of acculturation and integration. During the 19th century, for example, a high percentage of Irish immigrants were young, single women. They came to America seeking jobs and often wound up employed in domestic work, a role that permitted them to live "respectably" in a family setting. In 1850, about 75% of all employed Irish immigrant women in New York City worked as servants, and the rest were employed in textile mills and factories. As late as 1920, 81% of employed Irish-born women in the United States worked as domestics. Factory work was the second most prevalent form of employment (Blessing, 1980; see also Steinberg, 1981).

Because the economic situation of immigrant families was typically precarious, it was common for women to be involved

Woman worker at a textile mill.

Ethclass is the group formed by the intersection of social class and ethnic or racial group.

---

in wage labor. The type and location of the work varied from group to group. Whereas Irish women were concentrated in domestic work and factories and mills, this was rare for Italian women. Italian culture had strong norms of patriarchy, and "one of the culture's strongest prohibitions was directed against contact between women and male strangers" (Alba, 1985, p. 53). Thus, acceptable work situations for Italian women were likely to involve tasks that could be done at home: doing laundry, taking in boarders, and doing piecework for the garment industry. Italian women who worked outside the home were likely to find themselves in single-sex settings among other immigrant women. Thus, women immigrants from Italy tended to be far less acculturated and integrated than those from Ireland.

Eastern European Jewish women represent still another pattern of assimilation. They were refugees from religious persecution, and most came with their husbands and children in intact family units. According to Steinberg (1981), "few were independent breadwinners, and when they did work, they usually found employment in the . . . garment industry. Often they worked in small shops with other family members" (p. 161).

Generally, immigrant women, like working-class women in general, were expected to work until they married, after which time it was expected that their husbands would support them and their children. In many cases, however, immigrant men could not earn enough to support their families, and their wives and children were required by necessity to contribute to the family budget. Immigrant wives sometimes continued to work outside the home, or they found other ways to make money. They took in boarders, did laundry or sewing, tended gardens, and were involved in myriad other activities that permitted them to contribute to the family budget and still stay home and attend to family and child-rearing responsibilities.

A 1911 report on southern and eastern European households found that about half kept lodgers and that the income from this activity amounted to about 25% of the husbands' wages. Children also contributed to the family income by taking after-school and summertime jobs (Morawska, 1990, pp. 211–212). Compared with the men, immigrant women were more closely connected to home and family, less likely to learn to read or speak English or otherwise acculturate, and significantly more influential in preserving the heritage of their groups.

When they sought employment outside the home, they found opportunities in the industrial sector and in clerical and sales work, occupations that were quickly stereotyped as "women's work." Women were seen as working only to supplement the family treasury, and this assumption was used to justify a lower wage scale. Evans (1980) reports that in the late 1800s, "whether in factories, offices, or private homes . . . women's wages were about half of those of men" (p. 135).

Finally, in addition to the myriad other roles they played, women also tended to function as the primary keepers of cultural traditions from the old country. Husbands were often more involved in the larger society and had greater familiarity with Anglo culture and the English language. Women, even when they were employed, tended to be more oriented to home, children, family, and the neighborhood, and more likely to maintain the traditional diet and dress, speak to their children in the old language, and observe the time-honored holidays and religious practices. Thus, in addition to their economic roles, the women of the immigrant groups performed crucial cultural and socialization functions and tended to be more culturally conservative and more resistant to Anglo values and practices than were the men. These gender role patterns are common in immigrant groups today, not only in the United States but also in western Europe.

SOJOURNERS

Some versions of the traditional perspective and the "taken-for-granted" views of many Americans assume that assimilation is desirable and therefore desired. However, immigrant groups from Europe were highly variable in their interest in Americanization, a factor that greatly shaped their experiences.

Some groups were very committed to Americanization. Eastern European Jews, for example, came to America because of religious persecution and planned to make America their home from the beginning. They left their homeland in fear for their lives and had no plans and no possibility of returning. They intended to stay, for they had nowhere else to go. (The nation of Israel was not founded until 1948.) These immigrants committed themselves to learning English, becoming citizens, and familiarizing themselves with their new society as quickly as possible.

Other immigrants had no intention of becoming American citizens and therefore had little interest in Americanization. These **sojourners**, or "birds of passage," were oriented to the old country and intended to return once they had accumulated enough capital to be successful in their home villages or provinces. Because immigration records are not very detailed, it is difficult to assess the exact numbers of immigrants who returned to the old country (see Wyman, 1993). We do know, for example, that a large percentage of Italian immigrants were sojourners. Although 3.8 million Italians landed in the United States between 1899 and 1924, it is estimated that around 2.1 million departed during the same interval (Nelli, 1980, p. 547).

QUESTIONS FOR REFLECTION

1. What are some of the most important variations in the ways European immigrants adjusted to U.S. society?

2. What was the "triple melting pot," and how did it function?

Sojourners are immigrants who intend to return to their country of origin.

FIGURE 2.5 Ancestry With Largest Population in Each County, 2000

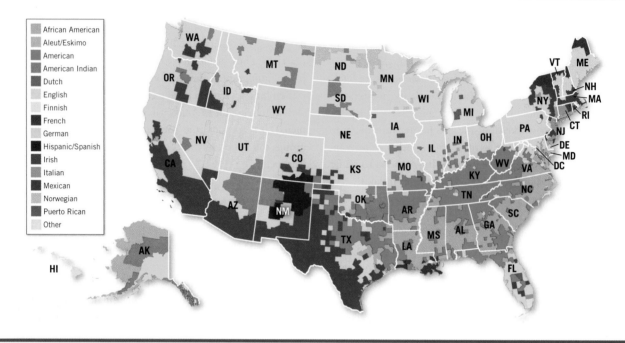

SOURCE: U.S. Census Bureau (2004a).

3. What important gender role differences existed in European immigrant groups? Would you guess that men or women would be more likely to be sojourners? Why?

THE DESCENDANTS OF THE IMMIGRANTS TODAY

GEOGRAPHICAL DISTRIBUTION

Figure 2.5 shows the geographical distribution of 15 racial and ethnic groups across the United States. The map displays the single largest group in each county. There is a lot of detail in the map, but for our purposes, we will focus on some of the groups mentioned in this chapter, including Norwegian, German, Irish, and Italian Americans (the Jewish population is too small to appear on this map).

First of all, the single largest ancestry group in the United States is German American, and this is reflected in Figure 2.5 by the predominance of yellow from Pennsylvania to California. Note also how the map reflects the original settlement areas for this group, especially in the Midwest. Likewise, Norwegian Americans (pink) are numerically dominant in some sections of the upper Midwest (e.g., northwestern Minnesota and northern North Dakota), along with Finnish Americans, another Scandinavian group. Irish Americans (blue) and Italian Americans (light green) are also concentrated in their original areas of settlement, with the Irish in Massachusetts and the Italians more concentrated around New York City.

Thus, almost a century after the end of mass immigration from Europe, many of the descendants of the immigrants have not wandered far from their ancestral locales. Of course, the map shows that the same point could be made for other groups, including blacks (concentrated in the "black belt" across the states of the old Confederacy), Mexican Americans (concentrated along the southern border from Texas to California), and Native Americans, whose concentration in the upper Midwest, eastern Oklahoma, and the Southwest reflects the locations of the reservations into which they were forced after the end of the Indian wars.

Given all that has changed in American society over the past century—industrialization, population growth, urbanization, and massive mobility—the stable location of white ethnics (and other ethnic and racial groups) seems remarkable. Why aren't people distributed more randomly across the nation's landscape?

The stability is somewhat easier to explain for some groups. African Americans, Mexican Americans, and American Indians have been limited in their geographic as well as social mobility by institutionalized discrimination, racism, and limited resources. We will examine the power of these constraints in detail in later chapters.

For white ethnics, on the other hand, the power of exclusion and rejection waned as the generations passed and the descendants of the immigrants assimilated and integrated.

Imagine you are interviewing the grandchildren (third generation) and great-grandchildren (fourth generation) of immigrants from Europe about their families' assimilation experiences. Some of the questions you might ask are listed below. Identify the stage of Gordon's model of assimilation that each question is testing.

A. What language did you speak at home when you were growing up?

B. What was your total household income last year?

C. (If married) Does your spouse share your religious faith?

D. (If married) Does your spouse share your ethnic background?

E. Did your parents have the same ethnic background? How about your grandparents?

F. Did you vote in the most recent presidential election?

G. What percentage of your friends share your ethnic background?

H. What percentage of your friends share your religious faith?

I. What is the highest level of education you have achieved?

J. Has your family name been changed or "Americanized"?

STAGE	ITEMS
Acculturation	
Integration (secondary level)	
Integration (primary level)	
Marital assimilation	

TURN THE PAGE TO FIND OUR ANSWERS.

Their current locations are perhaps more a reflection of the idea (introduced in Chapter 1) that the United States is a nation of groups as well as individuals. Our group memberships, especially family and kin, exert a powerful influence on our decisions about where to live and work and, despite the transience and mobility of modern American life, can keep people connected to their relatives, the old neighborhood, their ethnic roots, and the sites of their ancestors' struggles.

INTEGRATION AND EQUALITY

Perhaps the most important point, for our purposes, about white ethnic groups (the descendants of the European immigrants) is that they are today on the verge of being completely assimilated. Even the groups that were the most despised and rejected in earlier years are acculturated, integrated, and thoroughly intermarried.

To illustrate this point, consider Table 2.3, which shows the degree to which a variety of white ethnic groups had been integrated as far back as 1990, more than a generation ago.

The table displays data for 9 of the more than 60 white ethnic groups that people mentioned when asked to define their ancestries. The groups include the two largest white ethnic groups (German and Irish Americans) and seven more chosen to represent a range of geographic regions of origin and times of immigration (U.S. Census Bureau, 2008).

The table shows that by 1990, all nine of the groups selected were at or above national norms ("all persons") for all measures of equality. There is some variation among the groups, of course, but Table 2.3 shows that all exceeded the national averages for both high school and college education and had dramatically lower poverty rates, usually less than half the national average. All nine groups exceed the national average for median household income, some—Russians, for example, many of whom are Jewish—by a considerable margin.

In other areas, the evidence for assimilation and equality is also persuasive. For example, the distinct ethnic neighborhoods that these groups created in American cities (Little Italy, Greektown, Little Warsaw, etc.) have faded away or been taken over by other groups, and the rate of intermarriage between

STAGE	ITEMS
Acculturation	A, J
Integration (secondary level)	B, F, I
Integration (primary level)	G, H
Marital assimilation	C, D, E

members of different white ethnic groups is quite high. For example, based on data from the 1990 census, about 56% of all married whites have spouses whose ethnic backgrounds do not match their own (Alba, 1995, pp. 13–14).

THE EVOLUTION OF WHITE ETHNICITY

Absorption into the American mainstream was neither linear nor continuous for the descendants of European immigrants. Over the generations, white ethnic identity sporadically reasserted itself in many ways, two of which are especially notable. First, there was a tendency for later generations to be more interested in their ancestry and ethnicity than were earlier generations. Marcus Hansen (1952) captured this phenomenon in his **principle of third-generation interest**: "What the second generation tries to forget, the third generation tries to remember" (p. 495). Hansen observed that the children of immigrants tended to minimize or deemphasize ("forget") their ethnicity to avoid the prejudice and intolerance of the larger society and to compete on more favorable terms for jobs and other opportunities. As they became adults and started families of their own, the second generation tended to raise their children in non-ethnic settings, with English as their first and only language.

By the time the third generation reached adulthood, especially the "new" immigrant groups that arrived last, the larger society had become more tolerant of white ethnicity and diversity, and having little to risk, the third generation tried to reconnect with their grandparents and roots. These descendants wanted to remember their ethnic heritage and understand it as part of their personal identities, their sense of who they were and where they belonged in the larger society. Thus, interest in the "old ways" and the degree of identification with the ancestral

The **principle of third-generation interest** is the idea that the grandchildren of immigrants will stress their ethnicity much more than will the second generation.

group was often stronger in the more Americanized third generation than in the more ethnic second. Ironically, of course, the grandchildren of the immigrants could not recover much of the richness and detail of their heritage because their parents had spent their lives trying to forget it. Nonetheless, the desire of the third generation to reconnect with their ancestry and recover their ethnicity shows that assimilation is not a simple, one-dimensional, or linear process. This practice of ethnic recovery in later generations is illustrated in the biography of Mary Farrell, the Irish Catholic introduced in Chapter 1, who attends Mass in part because she feels that the rituals connect her with her ancestors.

In addition to this generational pattern, the strength of white ethnic identity also responded to the changing context of American society and the activities of other groups. For example, in the late 1960s and early 1970s, there was a notable increase in the visibility of and interest in white ethnic heritage, an upsurge often referred to as the ethnic revival. The revival manifested itself in a variety of ways. Some people became more interested in their families' genealogical roots, and others increased their participation in ethnic festivals, traditions, and organizations. The "white ethnic vote" became a factor in local, state, and national politics, and appearances at the churches, meeting halls, and neighborhoods associated with white ethnic groups became almost mandatory for candidates for office. Demonstrations and festivals celebrating white ethnic heritages were organized, and buttons and bumper stickers proclaiming the ancestry of everyone from Irish to Italians were widely displayed. The revival was also endorsed by politicians, editorialists, and intellectuals (e.g., see Novak, 1973), reinforcing the movement and giving it additional legitimacy.

The ethnic revival may have been partly fueled, à la Hansen's principle, by the desire to reconnect with ancestral roots, even though most groups were well beyond their third generations by the 1960s. More likely, the revival was a reaction to the increase in pluralistic sentiment in the society in general and the pluralistic, even separatist assertions of other groups. In the 1960s and 1970s, virtually every minority

TABLE 2.3 Median Household Income, Percent of Families Living in Poverty, and Educational Attainment for Selected White Ethnic Groups, 1990

	MEDIAN HOUSEHOLD INCOME	% OF FAMILIES LIVING IN POVERTY	% HIGH SCHOOL OR MORE	% BA OR MORE
ALL PERSONS	**$30,056**	**10%**	**75.2%**	**20.3%**
Russian	$45,778	3.6%	90.8%	49%
Italian	$36,060	4.9%	77.3%	21%
Polish	$34,763	4.3%	78.5%	23.1%
Ukrainian	$34,474	4%	77.5%	28.3%
Swedish	$33,881	4.5%	87.3%	27.4%
German	$32,730	5.5%	82.7%	22%
Slovak	$32,352	3.8%	78.2%	21.6%
Norwegian	$32,207	5.1%	85.9%	26%
Irish	$31,845	6.5%	79.6%	21.2%

SOURCE: U.S. Census Bureau (2008).

group generated a protest movement (Black Power, Red Power, Chicanismo, etc.) and proclaimed a recommitment to its own heritage and to the authenticity of its own culture and experience. The visibility of these movements for cultural pluralism among racial minority groups helped make it more acceptable for European Americans to express their own ethnicity and heritage.

Besides the general tenor of the times, the resurgence of white ethnicity had some political and economic dimensions that bring us back to issues of inequality and competition for resources. In the 1960s, a white-ethnic urban working class made up largely of Irish and southern and eastern European groups still remained in the neighborhoods of the industrial Northeast and Midwest, and still continued to breathe life into the old networks and traditions (see Glazer & Moynihan, 1970; Greeley, 1974). At the same time that cultural pluralism was coming to be seen as more legitimate, this ethnic working class was feeling increasingly threatened by minority groups of color. In the industrial cities, it was not unusual for white ethnic neighborhoods to adjoin black and Hispanic neighborhoods, putting these groups in direct competition for housing, jobs, and other resources.

Many members of the white ethnic working class saw racial minority groups as inferior and perceived the advances being made by these groups as unfair, unjust, and threatening. They also reacted to what they saw as special treatment and attention being accorded on the basis of race, such as school busing and affirmative action. They had problems of their own (the declining number of good, unionized jobs; inadequate schooling; and deteriorating city services) and felt that their problems were being given lower priority and less legitimacy because they were white. The revived sense of ethnicity in the

urban working-class neighborhoods was in large part a way of resisting racial reform and expressing resentment for the racial minority groups. Thus, among its many other causes and forms, the revival of white ethnicity that began in the 1960s was fueled by competition for resources and opportunities. As we will see throughout this text, such competition commonly leads to increased prejudice and a heightened sense of cohesion among group members.

THE TWILIGHT OF WHITE ETHNICITY?[1]

As the conflicts of the 1960s and 1970s faded and white ethnic groups continued to leave the old neighborhoods and rise in the class structure, the strength of white ethnic identity resumed its slow demise. Today, several more generations removed from the tumultuous 1960s, white ethnic identity has become increasingly nebulous and largely voluntary. It is often described as **symbolic ethnicity** or as an aspect of self-identity that symbolizes one's roots in the "old country" but is otherwise minor. The descendants of the European immigrants feel vaguely connected to their ancestors, but this part of their identities does not affect their lifestyles, circles of friends and neighbors, job prospects, eating habits, or other everyday routines (Gans, 1979; Lieberson &

Symbolic ethnicity is superficial, voluntary, and changeable.

---

[1] This phrase comes from Alba (1990).

Waters, 1988). For the descendants of the European immigrants today, ethnicity is an increasingly minor part of their identities that is expressed only occasionally or sporadically. For example, they might join in ethnic or religious festivals (e.g., St. Patrick's Day for Irish Americans, Columbus Day for Italian Americans), but these activities are seasonal or otherwise peripheral to their lives and self-images. The descendants of the European immigrants have choices, in stark contrast to their ancestors, members of racial minority groups, and recent immigrants: They can stress their ethnicity, ignore it completely, or maintain any degree of ethnic identity they choose. Many people have ancestors in more than one ethnic group and may change their sense of affiliation over time, sometimes emphasizing one group's traditions and sometimes another's (Waters, 1990).

In fact, white ethnic identity has become so ephemeral that it may be on the verge of disappearing altogether. For example, based on a series of in-depth interviews with white Americans from various regions of the nation, Gallagher (2001) found a sense of ethnicity so weak that it did not even rise to the level of "symbolic." His respondents were the products of ancestral lines so thoroughly intermixed and intermarried that any trace of a unique heritage from a particular group was completely lost. They had virtually no knowledge of the experiences of their immigrant ancestors or of the life and cultures of the ethnic communities they had inhabited, and for many, their ethnic ancestries were no more meaningful to them than their states of birth. Their lack of interest in and information about their ethnic heritage was so complete that it led Gallagher to propose an addendum to Hansen's principle: "What the grandson wished to remember, the great-granddaughter has never been told."

At the same time as more specific white ethnic identities are disappearing, they are also evolving into new shapes and forms. In the view of many analysts, a new identity is developing that merges the various "hyphenated" ethnic identities (German American, Polish American, etc.) into a single, generalized "European American" identity based on race and a common history of immigration and assimilation. This new identity reinforces the racial lines of separation that run through contemporary society, but it does more than simply mark group boundaries. Embedded in this emerging identity is an understanding, often deeply flawed, of how the white immigrant groups succeeded and assimilated in the past, and a view, often deeply ideological, of how the racial minority groups should behave in the present. These understandings are encapsulated in "immigrant tales": legends that stress heroic individual effort and grim determination as key ingredients leading to success in the old days. These tales feature impoverished, victimized immigrant ancestors who survived and made a place for themselves and their children by working hard, saving their money, and otherwise exemplifying the virtues of the Protestant Ethic and American individualism. They stress the idea that past generations became successful

despite the brutal hostility of the dominant group and with no government intervention, and they equate the historical difficulties faced by immigrants from Europe with those suffered by racial minority groups (slavery, segregation, attempted genocide, etc.). They strongly imply—and sometimes blatantly assert—that the latter groups could succeed in America by simply following the example set by the former (Alba, 1990; Gallagher, 2001).

These accounts mix versions of human capital theory and traditional views of assimilation with prejudice and racism. Without denying or trivializing the resolve and fortitude of European immigrants, equating their experiences and levels of disadvantage with those of African Americans, American Indians, and Mexican Americans is widely off the mark, as we shall see in the remainder of this text. These views support an attitude of disdain and lack of sympathy for the multiple dilemmas faced today by the racial minority groups and many contemporary immigrants. They permit a more subtle expression of prejudice and racism and allow whites to use these highly distorted views of their immigrant ancestors as a rhetorical device to express a host of race-based grievances without appearing racist (Gallagher, 2001).

Alba (1990) concludes as follows:

> The thrust of the [emerging] European American identity is to defend the individualistic view of the American system, because it portrays the system as open to those who are willing to work hard and pull themselves out of poverty and discrimination. Recent research suggests that it is precisely this individualism that prevents many whites from sympathizing with the need for African Americans and other minorities to receive affirmative action in order to overcome institutional barriers to their advancement. (p. 317)

What can we conclude? The generations-long journey from immigrant to white ethnic to European American seems to be drawing to a close. The separate ethnic identities are merging into a larger sense of "whiteness" that unites descendants of the immigrants with the dominant group and provides a rhetorical device for expressing disdain for other groups, especially African Americans.

QUESTIONS FOR REFLECTION

1. In what concrete ways are the descendants of the European immigrants successful?

2. What is Hansen's principle, and why is it significant? What is Gallagher's addendum to this principle, and why is it important?

3. Does white ethnic identity have a future? Why or why not?

NARRATIVE PORTRAIT

Assimilation, Then and Now

A block in Hell's Kitchen where Mario Puzo grew up.

Mario Puzo and Luis Rodriguez are both sons of immigrants, but they grew up in two very different Americas. Puzo, best known as the author of The Godfather, *grew up in the Italian American community, and his memoir of life in New York City in the 1930s illustrates some of the patterns that are at the heart of Gordon's theory of assimilation. Writing in the 1970s, Puzo remembers his boyhood and his certainty that he would escape the poverty that surrounded him. Note also his view of (and gratitude for) an America that gave people (or at least white people) the opportunity to rise above the circumstances of their birth.*

Rodriguez paints a rather different picture of U.S. society. He grew up in the Los Angeles area in the 1950s and 1960s and was a veteran of gang warfare by the time he reached high school. His memoir, Always Running: La Vida Loca *(1993), describes how his high school prepared Mexican American students for life.*

CHOOSING A DREAM: ITALIANS IN HELL'S KITCHEN

Mario Puzo

In the summertime, I was one of the great Tenth Avenue athletes, but in the wintertime I became a sissy. I read books. At a very early age I discovered libraries....My mother always looked at all this reading with a fishy Latin eye. She saw no profit in it, but since all her children were great readers, she was a good enough general to

know she could not fight so pervasive an insubordination. And there may have been some envy. If she had been able to, she would have been the greatest reader of all.

My direct ancestors for a thousand years have most probably been illiterate. Italy, the golden land,...so majestic in its language and cultural treasures..., has never cared for its poor people. My father and mother were both illiterates. Both grew up on rocky, hilly farms in the countryside adjoining Naples....My mother was told that the family could not afford the traditional family gift of linens when she married, and it was this that decided her to emigrate to America....My mother never heard of Michelangelo; the great deeds of the Caesars had not reached her ears. She never heard the great music of her native land. She could not sign her name.

And so it was hard for my mother to believe that her son could become an artist. After all, her one dream in coming to America had been to earn her daily bread, a wild dream in itself. And looking back, she was dead right. Her son an artist? To this day she shakes her head. I shake mine with her....

What has happened here has never happened in any other country in any other time. The poor, who have been poor for centuries...whose children had inherited their poverty, their illiteracy, their hopelessness, achieved some economic dignity and freedom. You didn't get it for nothing, you had to pay a price in tears, in suffering, but why not? And some even became artists.

SOURCE: Puzo, Mario (1993). "Choosing a Dream: Italians in Hell's Kitchen." In W. Brown & A. Ling (Eds.), *Visions of America*, pp. 56–57. New York: Persea. Reprinted by permission of Donadio & Olson, Inc. Copyright © 1993 Mario Puzo.

ALWAYS RUNNING: LA VIDA LOCA

Luis Rodriguez

Mark Keppel High School was a Depression-era structure with a brick and art deco facade and small, army-type bungalows in the back. Friction filled its hallways.

The Anglo and Asian upper-class students from Monterey Park and Alhambra attended the school. They were tracked into the "A" classes; they were in the school clubs; they were the varsity team members and lettermen. They were the pep squad and cheerleaders.

But the school also took in the people from the Hills and surrounding community who somehow made it past junior high. They were mostly Mexican, in the "C" track (what were called the "stupid" classes). Only a few of these students participated in school government, in sports, or in the various clubs.

The school had two principal languages. Two skin tones and two cultures. It revolved around class differences. The white and Asian kids...were from professional, two-car households with watered lawns and trimmed trees. The laboring class, the sons and daughters of service workers, janitors, and factory hands lived in and around the Hills....The school separated these two groups by levels of education: The professional-class kids were provided with college-preparatory classes; the blue-collar students were pushed into "industrial arts."...

If you came from the Hills, you were labeled from the start. I'd walk into the counselor's office and looks of disdain greeted me—one meant for a criminal, alien, to be feared. Already a thug. It was harder to defy this expectation than just accept it and fall into the trappings. It was a jacket I could try to take off, but they kept putting it back on. The first hint of trouble and the preconceptions proved true. So why not be an outlaw? Why not make it our own?

SOURCE: Rodriguez (1993, pp. 83–84).

Questions to Consider

1. What are the key sociological differences between the experiences of Puzo and Rodriguez?
2. How does the concept of segmented assimilation apply to these two different lives? What sectors of American society are Puzo and Rodriguez being prepared for? Is there any basis for Rodriguez's despair as opposed to Puzo's optimism?

Immigration and Ireland

FIGURE 2.6   Migration Into and Out of Ireland, 1987–2011

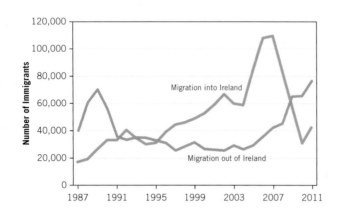

Just as the United States has been a major receiver of immigrants for the past 200 years, Ireland has been a major supplier. Mass immigration from Ireland began with the potato famines of the 1840s and continued through the end of the 20th century, motivated by continuing hard times, political unrest, and unemployment. This mass out-migration—along with the famines—cut the 1840 Irish population of 7 million in half, and the population today is still only about 4.5 million.

History rarely runs in straight lines, however. In the 1990s and into the 21st century, Ireland suddenly became a consumer of immigrants. As displayed in Figure 2.6, the number of newcomers entering Ireland soared between 1987 and 2006, and the number of people leaving decreased. Starting in about 2007, however, the trend reversed: The number of newcomers plummeted, and the historic pattern of out-migration reappeared.

What explains these patterns? Answers are not hard to find. The influx of immigrants starting in the late 1980s was largely a response to rapid economic growth. The Irish economy—the so-called "Celtic Tiger"—had entered a boom phase, spurred by investments from multinational corporations and the benefits of joining the European Economic Union. Irish nationals who had left seeking work abroad returned home in large numbers, and people from Europe and other parts of the globe also began to arrive. In addition, Ireland began to receive refugees and people seeking asylum from Africa, the Middle East, and other trouble spots.

The changes that started in 2007 have an equally obvious cause. The global economy faltered badly in that year, and the Irish economy followed suit: Banks failed, companies went bankrupt, the housing market collapsed, and jobs disappeared. The Irish returned to their historic role as a supplier of immigrants to other economies around the world.

Although the era of in-migration lasted only a few decades, it may have created some permanent changes in Irish society. For example, the number of Irish of African and Asian descent has increased by a factor of 8 since 1996 (although both groups are less than 2% of the total population). Over the centuries, many different groups (e.g., Vikings, Spanish, and Anglo-Normans) have become part of Ireland, but, for the first time in their history, the Irish are dealing with issues of racial diversity.

Questions to Consider

1. What similarities can you see between immigration to Ireland and immigration to the United States?
2. Do you suppose that immigrants to Ireland will be assimilated in the same way as immigrants to the United States? If you could travel to Ireland, what questions would you ask about the assimilation process?

CONTEMPORARY IMMIGRANTS: DOES THE TRADITIONAL PERSPECTIVE APPLY?

Does the traditional perspective—based as it is on the experiences of European immigrants and their descendants—apply to more recent immigrants? This is a key issue facing social scientists, government policymakers, and the general public today. Will contemporary immigrants duplicate the experiences of earlier groups? Will they acculturate before they integrate? Will religion, social class, and race be important forces in their lives? Will they take three generations to assimilate? More than three? Fewer? What will their patterns of intermarriage look like? Will they achieve socioeconomic parity with the dominant group? When? How?

Sociologists (as well as the general public and policymakers) are split in their answers to these questions. Some social scientists believe that the "traditional" perspective on assimilation does not apply and that the experiences of contemporary immigrant groups will differ greatly from those of European immigrants. They believe that assimilation today is fragmented or **segmented** and will have a number of different outcomes. Although some contemporary immigrant groups may integrate into the middle-class mainstream, others will find themselves permanently mired in the impoverished, alienated, and marginalized segments of racial minority groups. Still others may form close-knit enclaves based on their traditional cultures and become successful in the United States by resisting the forces of acculturation (Portes & Rumbaut, 2001, p. 45).

In stark contrast, other theorists believe that the traditional perspective on assimilation is still relevant and that contemporary immigrant groups will follow the established pathways of mobility and assimilation. Of course, the process will be variable from group to group and from place to place, but even the groups that are today the most impoverished and marginalized will, in time, move into mainstream society.

How will the debate be resolved? We cannot say at the moment, but we can point out that this debate is reminiscent of the critique of Park's theory of assimilation. In both cases, the argument is partly about time: Even the most impoverished and segmented groups may find their way into the economic mainstream eventually, at some unspecified time in the future. There are also other levels of meaning in the debate, however, related to one's perception of the nature of modern U.S. society. Is U.S. society today growing more tolerant of diversity, more open and equal? If so, this would seem to favor the traditionalist perspective. If not, this trend would clearly favor those who argue for the segmented-assimilation hypothesis. Although we will not resolve this argument in this text, we will use the debate between the traditional and segmented views on assimilation as a useful framework as we consider the experiences of these groups (see Chapters 8, 9, and 10).

QUESTIONS FOR REFLECTION

What is segmented assimilation, and why is this an important concept? How would social class and gender relate to the debate over whether contemporary assimilation is segmented?

IMPLICATIONS FOR EXAMINING DOMINANT–MINORITY RELATIONS

Chapters 1 and 2 have introduced many of the terms, concepts, and themes that form the core of the rest of this text. Although the connections between the concepts are not simple, some key points can be made to summarize these chapters and anticipate the material to come.

First, minority-group status has much more to do with power and the distribution of resources than with simple numbers or the percentage of the population in any particular category. We saw this notion expressed in Chapter 1 in the definition of *minority group* and in our exploration of inequality. The themes of inequality and differentials in status were also covered in our discussion of prejudice, racism, and discrimination. To understand minority relations, we must examine some very basic realities of human society: inequalities in wealth, prestige, and the distribution of power. To discuss changes in minority-group status, we must be prepared to discuss changes in the way society does business, makes decisions, and distributes income, jobs, health care, and opportunities.

A second area that we will focus on in the rest of the book is the question of how our society should develop. Assimilation and pluralism, with all their variations, define two broad directions. Each has been extensively examined and discussed by social scientists, by leaders and decision makers in American society, and by ordinary people from all groups and walks of life. The analysis and evaluation of these two broad directions is a thread running throughout this book.

Segmented assimilation has multiple outcomes. Some groups may eventually enter the middle class, but others may be permanently excluded, marginalized, and impoverished.

SUMMARY

This summary is organized around the Learning Objectives listed at the beginning of this chapter.

 Explain and analyze the concepts of assimilation and pluralism, including the "traditional" model of assimilation.

Assimilation and pluralism are two broad pathways of development for intergroup relations. Assimilation is a process by which groups grow more similar, and in the United States, it has generally meant Americanization or Anglo-conformity. In the traditional model, assimilation includes a number of stages: acculturation, integration at the secondary and primary levels, and intermarriage.

Under pluralism, group differences are maintained through time. In cultural (or "full") pluralism, groups differ both culturally and structurally. Under structural pluralism, groups share essentially the same culture but occupy different locations in the social structure.

2.2 List and explain other group relationships.

Group relations other than assimilation and pluralism include separatism, revolution, forced migration and expulsion, genocide, and continued subjugation.

 2.3 Describe the timing, causes, and volume of the migration from Europe, and explain how those immigrants became "white ethnics."

The period of mass European immigration stretched from the 1820s to the 1920s and included both "Old" (from northern and western Europe) and "New" (from southern and eastern Europe) phases. More than 30 million people made the journey from Europe to the United States during this time. People moved for many reasons, including the pursuit of religious and political freedom, but the underlying motive force was industrialization and urbanization. Immigrants from Europe were minority groups at first but, over a series of generations, assimilated, became upwardly mobile and integrated, and Americanized. Their experiences varied by gender, "race," and class, but, generally, most groups followed the "traditional" model of assimilation (which was based on these groups).

 2.4 Explain the patterns of assimilation and the major variations in those patterns.

Assimilation for European immigrant groups generally followed a three-generation pattern, with the grandchildren of the original immigrants completing the process. Ethnic succession occurred

when newly arrived groups of immigrants pushed older groups up in the occupational structure. The three major pathways of integration were politics, labor unions, and religion, but others included organized crime and sports. Structural mobility occurred as the American industrial economy matured and changed. Continuing mechanization and automation changed the nature of work, creating more opportunities in the middle-class, white-collar areas. The descendants of the immigrants were generally able to take advantage of expanding opportunities for education and move higher in the class structure than their parents and grandparents did. The experience of assimilation varied by the physical appearance of the group, its religion, social class, gender, and extent of sojourning.

 2.5 Describe the status of the descendants of European immigrants today, including the "twilight of white ethnicity."

These groups are, on average, at or above national norms for affluence and success. White ethnicity seems to be fading and may be in its twilight, although it remains a significant force for some people.

 2.6 Explain how the traditional model of assimilation does or does not apply to contemporary immigrants.

Research is ongoing, but, at least for some immigrant groups, assimilation today may be segmented and may have outcomes other than equality with and acceptance into the middle class. We will consider these possibilities in depth in Part III.

KEY TERMS

acculturation or cultural
  assimilation 34
Americanization (or Anglo-
  conformity) 33
anti-Semitism 48
assimilation 32
capital-intensive 40
cultural pluralism 37
culture 34
enclave minority group 37

ethclass 56
ethnic succession 51
human capital theory 35
industrial revolution 40
integration or structural
  assimilation 34
intermarriage or marital
  assimilation 35
labor-intensive 40
melting pot 33

middleman
  minority group 37
multiculturalism 36
New Immigration 41
Old Immigration 41
pluralism 32
primary sector 34
principle of third-generation
  interest 60
race relations cycle 34

revolution 38
secondary sector 34
segmented assimilation 65
separatism 38
social structure 34
sojourners 57
structural mobility 54
structural pluralism 37
symbolic ethnicity 61
triple melting pot 55

REVIEW QUESTIONS

1. Summarize Gordon's model of assimilation. Identify and explain each stage and how the stages are linked together. Explain Table 2.2 in terms of Gordon's model.

2. "Human capital theory is not so much wrong as it is incomplete." Explain this statement. What does the theory leave out? What are the strengths

of the theory? What questionable assumptions does it make?

3. What are the major dimensions along which the experience of assimilation varies? Explain how and why the experience of assimilation can vary.

4. Define pluralism, and explain the ways it differs from assimilation. Why has interest in pluralism increased? Explain the difference between and cite examples of structural and cultural pluralism. Describe enclave minority groups in terms of pluralism and in terms of Gordon's model of assimilation. How have contemporary theorists added to the concept of pluralism?

5. Define and explain segmented assimilation, and explain how it differs from Gordon's model. What evidence is there that assimilation for recent immigrants is not segmented? What is the significance of this debate for the future of U.S. society? For other minority groups (e.g., African Americans)? For the immigrants themselves?

STUDENT STUDY SITE

Sharpen your skills with SAGE edge at edge.sagepub.com/healey7e

SAGE edge for students provides a personalized approach to help you accomplish your coursework goals in an easy-to-use learning environment.

The following resources are available at SAGE edge:

Current Debates: English Only?

Should English be made the official language of the United States? Should immigrants be required to be fluent in English? Would "English-only" policies exclude and marginalize immigrants?

On our website you will find an overview of the topic, the clashing points of view, and some questions to consider as you analyze the material.

Public Sociology Assignments

Public Sociology Assignments provide opportunities for students to address directly and personally some of the issues raised in this text.

The first two public sociology assignments on our website will lead students to confront diversity in their community. In the first assignment, you will investigate your hometown to see if you can document increases in racial and ethnic diversity consistent with Figure 1.1. In the second assignment, you will study graffiti: Does it express stereotypes and prejudice? What does it reflect about local group hierarchies?

Contributed by Linda M. Waldron

Internet Research Project

For the Internet Research Project for this chapter, you will use information from the U.S. Census to assess the relative assimilation of several groups, including some white ethnic groups. Your investigation will be guided by a series of questions, and your instructor may ask you to discuss the issues in small groups.

For Further Reading

Please see our website for an annotated list of important works related to this chapter.

CHAPTER-OPENING TIMELINE PHOTO CREDITS

1845–1852: Wikimedia Commons

1854: Library of Congress Prints and Photographs Division

1862: Library of Congress Prints and Photographs Division

1881–1885: Wikipedia

1881–1920: Library of Congress Prints and Photographs Division

1911–1920: Library of Congress Prints and Photographs Division

1917: Library of Congress Prints and Photographs Division

1980–2000: Nathan Benn/Ottochrome/Corbis

3 PREJUDICE AND DISCRIMINATION

timeline

1862
The "Anti-Coolie" Act discourages Chinese immigration to California and institutes special taxes on employers who hire Chinese workers.

1880
Jim Crow Laws mandate racial segregation in all public facilities in southern states, with a separate but equal status for black Americans.

1896
The Supreme Court rules in *Plessy v. Ferguson* that "separate but equal" accommodations are constitutional.

1815   1830   1845   1860   1875   1890   1905

1830
The Indian Removal Act leads to the deportation of 100,000 Native Americans to west of the Mississippi.

1857
The Dred Scott decision mandates that African Americans cannot be citizens.

1866
The Ku Klux Klan is founded.

1836
The U.S. House of Representatives passes the first "gag rule," designed to prevent the introduction, reading, or discussion of any antislavery bill or petition.

1863
The Anti-Miscegenation Laws passed by individual states prohibit interracial marriage and interracial sex.

On August 5, 2012, Wade Michael Page walked into a Sikh[1] temple in Oak Creek, Wisconsin, and started shooting. He killed six people and wounded four others before taking his own life. As in the other mass shootings that have plagued the United States in recent years, questions abounded: Why did he do it? What kind of person could randomly slaughter strangers? How could we understand behavior so twisted and cruel?

These questions will never be fully answered, but one piece of the puzzle is clear: Page was a white supremacist, a neo-Nazi, and a member of several racist white-power rock bands. We'll never know exactly what he was thinking as he prepared his assault, but it is surely no coincidence that he targeted a setting that was populated by nonwhites, non-Christians, and recent immigrants.

_____
[1]The Sikh religion was founded in the Punjab region of India 500 years ago.

LEARNING OBJECTIVES

By the end of this chapter, you will be able to do the following:

3.1 Define and explain prejudice and discrimination.

3.2 Summarize and explain the different forms and dimensions of prejudice, and explain the theories and research related to each.

3.3 Summarize and explain the sociology of prejudice, including the role of group competition and how prejudice persists through time.

3.4 Describe and assess the seeming decline in "traditional" prejudice, and define and explain "modern" racism (is it replacing "traditional" prejudice?).

3.5 Describe the volume and nature of modern hate crimes, and explain some possible reasons for their persistence.

1943
Los Angeles erupts in the Zoot Suit Riots. American sailors cruise Mexican American neighborhoods in search of "zoot-suiters," dragging kids out of movie theaters and cafes, tearing their clothes off and viciously beating them.

1996
President Clinton signs the Federal Defense of Marriage Act (DOMA), denying same-sex couples the right to have their unions/partnerships recognized by the federal government.

2004
The Minuteman Project begins to organize anti-immigrant activists at the U.S./Mexico border. The group considers itself a citizens' border patrol, but several known white supremacists are members.

1942
Approximately 110,000 Japanese Americans are sent to internment camps.

1992
Riots erupt in Los Angeles after a jury acquits four white police officers for the videotaped beating of African American Rodney King.

1998
Matthew Shepard, a 21-year-old gay college student, is murdered, bringing hate crimes against gays into the national spotlight.

2001
Hate crimes against Arab and Asian Americans follow the terrorist attacks of September 11.

2012
Trayvon Martin, a 17-year-old African American, is fatally shot by George Zimmerman, a neighborhood watch volunteer. A national debate about racial profiling ensues.

The United States has changed a lot over the past 50 years: from a time when blatant racism was the order of the day and racial segregation was supported by the legal system, to a nation that has twice elected a black president. The progress has been impressive, but have we truly outgrown our racist past? Are hate crimes such as Page's just unfortunate reminders of those darker days, or do they signify that something in the American spirit hasn't really changed? •

Some have argued that the election of President Barack Obama proves that prejudice, skin color, and group membership have become irrelevant in our society. Others, particularly social scientists, are less willing to pronounce the death of racism: They argue that prejudice has not decreased so much as it has changed to subtler, more disguised and indirect forms. Which view is more supported by the evidence? Are prejudice and discrimination, whatever their form, still problems in America?

In this chapter, we explore these and a variety of other issues. Social scientists have developed an impressive array of theories and a huge volume of research on prejudice and discrimination, and we will review some of their most important conclusions and arguments.

We will begin by restating the difference between prejudice and discrimination, and then we will explore the two dimensions of prejudice (affective and cognitive). As we do so, we will examine some of the important individual-level theories of prejudice (see Table 3.1). We will then cover some of the central sociological perspectives on prejudice and discrimination. The emphasis will be on prejudice, but we will examine discrimination on a number of occasions in this chapter and in the chapters to come.

Toward the end of the chapter, we will return to the issues introduced above: How has American prejudice evolved and changed over the recent past? We will conclude with a look at hate crimes, one of the most vicious manifestations of bigotry and antiminority sentiment.

PREJUDICE AND DISCRIMINATION

Let's begin with definitions. Recall from Chapter 1 that prejudice is the tendency of individuals to think and feel in negative ways about members of other groups. Discrimination, on the other hand, is actual, overt, individual behavior. Although these concepts are obviously related, they do not always occur together or have a causal relationship with each other.

Table 3.1 presents four possible combinations of prejudice and discrimination in individuals. In two cases, the relationship between prejudice and discrimination is consistent. The "all-weather liberal" is not prejudiced and does not discriminate, whereas the "all-weather bigot" is prejudiced and

TABLE 3.1 Four Relationships Between Prejudice and Discrimination in Individuals

	DOES NOT DISCRIMINATE	DOES DISCRIMINATE
Unprejudiced	Unprejudiced nondiscriminator (all-weather liberal)	Unprejudiced discriminator (fair-weather liberal)
Prejudiced	Prejudiced nondiscriminator (timid bigot)	Prejudiced discriminator (all-weather bigot)

SOURCE: Adapted from Merton (1968).

does discriminate. The other two combinations, however, are inconsistent. The "fair-weather liberal" discriminates without prejudice, whereas the "timid bigot" is prejudiced but does not discriminate. These inconsistencies between attitudes and behavior are not uncommon and may be caused by a variety of social pressures, including the desire to conform to the expectations of others. They illustrate the fact that prejudice and discrimination can be independent of each other. Most of the material in this chapter is focused more on prejudice than on discrimination, but we will address the relationship between the two concepts on several occasions.

PREJUDICE

American social scientists of all disciplines have researched prejudice from a variety of theoretical perspectives and have asked many different questions. One conclusion that has emerged is that prejudice has a variety of possible causes (some more psychological and individual, others more sociological and cultural) and can present itself in a variety of forms (some blatant and vicious, others subtle and indirect). One way to begin to approach this complex subject is by examining the two main dimensions of prejudice.

THE AFFECTIVE DIMENSION

Individual prejudice is partly a set of feelings or emotions that people attach to groups, including their own. The emotions can run a wide gamut from mild to intense. At one extreme, we might find relatively mild expressions of disparagement, such as, "I don't care much for Italians" or "The Irish seem to get mean when they're drunk." At the other, we might find the dreadful rage that accompanies a lynching or other hate crime. What makes these emotions part of prejudice is their generalized association with an entire group, often in the complete absence of any actual experience with group members, and their element of prejudgment (which is, after all, the literal meaning of prejudice).

A number of psychological and social-psychological research traditions focus on the emotional or affective aspect of prejudice. Here, we will briefly examine two of these theories: the **scapegoat hypothesis** and the theory of the **authoritarian personality**.

The Scapegoat Hypothesis. This theory links prejudice to feelings of frustration and aggression. People sometimes deal with personal failure or disappointment by expressing their anger against a substitute target (or scapegoat), not against the object or person that actually caused their frustration. For example, someone who has been demoted at work might attack his or her spouse rather than the boss, or a student who received a low grade on a test might "take it out" on a pet rather than on the professor. Generally speaking, the substitute targets (spouses or pets) will be less powerful than the actual cause of the frustration and may serve as a "safe" alternative to attacking bosses or professors.

From the standpoint of members of the dominant group, minority groups can make excellent substitute targets because they, by definition, control fewer power resources. In other words, minority groups are often selected as the recipients of anger and aggression that, for whatever reason, cannot be directed at the actual cause of a person's frustration. When released against a minority group, displaced aggression is expressed as or accompanied by prejudice.

Many researchers have produced scapegoating against minority groups in laboratory settings. In a typical experiment, subjects are purposely frustrated, perhaps by being asked to complete a task that the researchers have made sure is impossible. Then, the subjects are offered the opportunity to release their anger as prejudice, sometimes by completing a survey that measures their feelings about various minority groups. Many people respond to this situation with increased feelings of rejection and disparagement against other groups (see Berkowitz, 1978; Dollard, Miller, Doob, Mowrer, & Sears, 1939; Miller & Bugleski, 1948).

Outside the laboratory, the scapegoat theory has been proposed as an explanation for a variety of political, social, and economic events. For example, the theory has been applied to the rise of the Nazi Party in Germany in the 1930s. At that time, Germany was trying to cope with its defeat in World War I, a powerful economic recession, rampant unemployment, and horrific inflation. According to this line of analysis, the success of the extremely racist, violently anti-Semitic Nazi Party was in part a result of its ability to capture these intense anxieties and fears and redirect them against Jews and other minorities (see Dollard et al., 1939).

Along the same analytical lines, Hovland and Sears (1940) argued that the rate of lynching of African Americans in the South between 1882 and 1930 was correlated with fluctuations in cotton prices. Lynchings generally increased during hard times when the price of cotton was low and (presumably)

Jewish woman and children are led to the gas chambers of Auschwitz. Jews were a favorite scapegoating target for the Nazis.

frustrations were more widespread. (For a different, more sociological view, see Beck & Clark, 2002, and Beck & Tolnay, 1990.)

Finally, scapegoating has been implicated in many hate crimes in the United States, including seemingly random attacks on Middle Easterners following the terrorist attacks of September 11, 2001. We will return to the topic of hate crimes at the end of this chapter.

The Theory of the Authoritarian Personality. This theory links prejudice to early childhood experiences and personality structure and argues that prejudice is produced by stern, highly punitive styles of parenting. On the surface, the children of authoritarian families respect and love their parents. Internally, however, they resent and fear their severe and distant parents. They can't consciously admit these negative feelings; instead, they scapegoat their fear and anger by expressing these emotions as prejudice against minority groups. Thus, prejudice provides people with authoritarian personalities a way of coping with their conflicted feelings for their parents.

The tradition of research on the authoritarian personality theory stretches back to before World War II and is supported by experiments and research projects that demonstrate a link between family structure, childhood experience, and prejudice (Adorno, Frenkel-Brunswick, Levinson, & Sanford, 1950). More recent research has examined the links between

---

The **scapegoat hypothesis** holds that people sometimes express their frustrations against substitute targets. When the substitutes are other groups, prejudice increases.

The theory of the **authoritarian personality** links prejudice to childhood experiences with stern, severe parents.

authoritarianism and gender roles (Peterson & Zurbriggen, 2010), child abuse (Rodriguez, 2010), attitudes toward international students (Charles-Toussaint & Crowson, 2010), and even leisure activities (Peterson & Pang, 2006).

Authoritarian personality theory has contributed to our understanding of individual prejudice, but it has been widely criticized for focusing solely on the internal dynamics of personality and not taking sufficient account of the social settings in which an individual is acting. Some individuals do use prejudice as a tool for handling their personality problems, but to fully understand prejudice, we need to see its connections with social structure, social class, and the context and history of group relations. The theory of the authoritarian personality is not "wrong" so much as it is incomplete. The sociological perspective, as we shall see, takes a broader approach and incorporates the social world in which the individual acts.

Do racial stereotypes shape how police work is conducted?

QUESTIONS FOR REFLECTION

1. Have you seen or experienced instances of scapegoating in your life? In your view, what substitute targets tend to be selected? Is scapegoating always expressed as prejudice?

2. Do authoritarian personalities *need* to express prejudice? Why? What would happen if they couldn't express prejudice?

3. How is the theory of the authoritarian personality incomplete? What does it omit?

THE COGNITIVE DIMENSION: STEREOTYPES

The cognitive dimension of prejudice includes stereotypes or ideas about the characteristics of other groups. Stereotypes are generalizations about groups of people that are exaggerated, overly simplistic, and resistant to disproof (Pettigrew, 1980, p. 822; see also Jones, 1997, pp. 164–202). Stereotypes stress a few traits and assume that these characteristics apply to all members of the group, regardless of individual characteristics. Highly prejudiced people will maintain their stereotypes even in the face of massive evidence that their views are wrong.

Virtually all Americans share a common set of images of the prominent ethnic, racial, and religious groups that make up U.S. society. These images include notions such as "Asians are clannish," "Jews are miserly," and "Blacks are musical." Less prejudiced people are probably familiar with these images but pay little attention to them, and they do not use them to actually judge the worth of others. More prejudiced people will

think in stereotypes, apply them to all members of a group, make sweeping judgments about the worth of others, and even commit acts of violence based solely on the group identity of another person.

For the prejudiced individual, stereotypes are an important set of cognitive categories. Once a stereotype is learned, it can shape perceptions to the point that the individual pays attention only to information that confirms that stereotype. **Selective perception**, the tendency to see only what one expects to see, can reinforce and strengthen stereotypes to the point that the highly prejudiced individual simply does not accept evidence that challenges his or her views. Thus, these overgeneralizations can become closed perceptual systems that screen out contrary information and absorb only the sensory impressions that ratify the original bias.

Types of Stereotypes and Dominant–Minority Relations. Stereotypes are, by definition, exaggerated overgeneralizations. At some level, though, even the most simplistic and derogatory stereotype can reflect some of the realities of dominant–minority group relationships. The content of a stereotype flows from the actual relationship between dominant and minority groups and is often one important way the dominant group tries to justify or rationalize that relationship.

For example, Pettigrew (1980) and others have pointed out two general stereotypes of minority groups. The first attributes extreme inferiority (e.g., laziness, irresponsibility,

---

Selective perception is the tendency to see only what one expects to see.

or lack of intelligence) to minority-group members and tends to be found in situations (such as slavery) in which a minority group is being heavily exploited and held in an impoverished and powerless status by the dominant group. This type of stereotype is a rationalization that helps justify dominant-group policies of control, discrimination, or exclusion.

The second type of stereotype is found when power and status differentials are less extreme, particularly when the minority group has succeeded in gaining some control over resources, has experienced some upward mobility, and has had some success in school and business. In this situation, credulity would be stretched too far to label the group "inferior," so their relative success is viewed in negative terms: They are seen as *too* smart, *too* materialistic, *too* crafty, *too* sly, or *too* ambitious (Pettigrew, 1980, p. 823; see also Simpson & Yinger, 1985, p. 101).

A team of psychologists has documented a similar pattern of stereotypes in the United States and other nations. They find that perceptions of groups can be arrayed in a two-dimensional space defined by perceptions of competence and feelings of warmth. Interestingly, they include groups other than minority groups in their research.

Figure 3.1 presents the results of multiple surveys of U.S. respondents. The circled clusters of scores indicate similar stereotypes. Among other findings, the researchers note two groups of ambivalent stereotypes: Some groups (the elderly, the disabled) are labeled "LC–HW" (low competence–high warmth) because they are viewed as helpless (low on competence) but also with positive affect (high on warmth). Others (Jews, Asians) are regarded as high on competence (HC) but low on warmth (LW): They are seen as capable but cunning (Cuddy et al., 2009, p. 4). The latter stereotype echoes the characterization of groups that are seen as *too* successful, a pattern these researchers label as an "envious" prejudice.

FIGURE 3.1 American Stereotypes

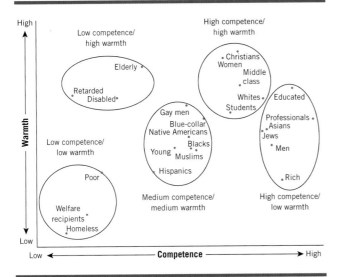

NOTE: See Cuddy et al. (2009) and Fiske, Bergsieker, Russell, and Williams (2009).

Note that African Americans and other racial minority groups fall in the same "moderately competent–moderately warm" (MC–MW) cluster as, among others, gay men and Muslims, and that "whites" are seen as more competent and warmer than the racial minorities but as less competent than the "envied" minority groups. Consistent with traditional American values, the lowest rated groups are the poor, welfare recipients, and the homeless—groups whose presumed characteristics are often seen as overlapping with those of African Americans.

While these patterns are important, you should also realize that stereotypes and prejudice can exist apart from the context of actual group relationships or the relative "success" or social standing of groups. Research shows that some individuals will readily stereotype groups about which they have little or no information. In fact, some individuals will express prejudice against groups that do not even exist! In one test, respondents were asked how closely they would associate with "Daniereans, Pireneans, and Wallonians"—all fictitious groups. A number of white respondents apparently reacted to the "foreign" sound of the names, rejected these three groups, and indicated that they would treat them about the same as other minority groups (Hartley, 1946). Clearly, the negative judgments about these groups were not made on the basis of personal experience or a need to rationalize some system such as slavery. The subjects were exhibiting a generalized tendency to reject minority groups of all sorts.

The Content of American Stereotypes. A series of studies with Princeton University undergraduates provides some interesting perspectives on the content of American stereotypes. Students were given a list of personality traits and asked to check those that applied to a number of different groups. The study was done first in 1933 and then repeated in 1951 and 1967 (Karlins, Coffman, & Walters, 1969). It is unusual to have comparable data covering such a long period of time, which makes these studies significant despite the fact that Princeton undergraduates are hardly a representative sample of American public opinion.

Several elements of these data are worth noting. First, the content of the stereotypes echoed American traditions well-known (although not necessarily endorsed) by all: The English were seen as sportsmanlike and conventional, Italians as passionate and musical, and Jews as shrewd and industrious. Second, the different kinds of stereotypes we previously discussed can be found in these results. Jews tended to be seen as successful ("intelligent") but pushy ("grasping"), whereas African Americans were seen as inferior ("lazy," "ignorant"). Third, in a recent readministration of the test (Fiske et al., 2009), the stereotypical traits ascribed to blacks included more positive traits ("loyal to family," "religious") as well as some elements of the traditional image ("musical") and some apparently negative elements ("loud").

Similar studies of stereotypical thinking have been conducted on other campuses in more recent years. Clark and Person (1982) measured white stereotypes of African Americans among undergraduates at two southeastern universities in the early 1980s. They found some continuity in the content of the stereotypes from earlier studies but also found that their subjects were more likely to characterize African Americans as having seemingly positive traits such as "loyal to family" (Clark & Person, 1982). In contrast, a study conducted by Wood and Chesser (1994) found that white students at a large Midwestern university had more negative stereotypes of African Americans. The top five most common traits selected by the sample were uniformly negative and included "loud," "aggressive," and "lazy" (Wood & Chesser, 1994). This finding was echoed in a 1995 study at the University of Wisconsin that replicated the three Princeton University tests. Three of the top five most commonly selected traits for African Americans were similar to those selected by Princeton undergraduates—"rhythmic" (vs. "musical"), "low in intelligence" (vs. "ignorant"), and "lazy"—and two were new, "athletic" and "poor" (Devine & Elliot, 1995).

These studies are informative, but, because they are based on college students, they may have little applicability to the attitudes of Americans in general. Fortunately, we can learn more about stereotypical thinking among Americans in general by reviewing research based on representative samples. One important study (Bobo & Kluegal, 1997) examined prejudice in the 1990s, and we can get a sense of how American stereotypes have changed by comparing their findings with those of a 2012 survey. In both years, respondents were asked to rate "the characteristics of people in a group" on a number of scales, including an "intelligent–unintelligent" scale and a "hard working–lazy" scale. Results for white Americans are presented in Figures 3.2 and 3.3. The first figure displays perceptions of whites and blacks as "unintelligent," and the second does the same for perceptions of "laziness." In both years, more than 95% of the respondents answered the question, indicating that the willingness to label entire groups is widespread.

FIGURE 3.2 White Americans' Perceptions of Intelligence, by Race, 1990 and 2012

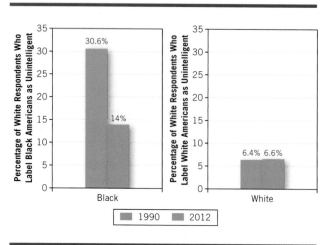

SOURCE: Adapted from Bobo and Kluegal (1997) and National Opinion Research Council (1972–2012).

FIGURE 3.3 White Americans' Perceptions of Laziness, by Race, 1990 and 2012

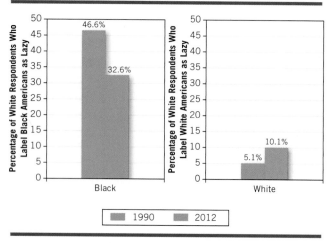

SOURCE: Adapted from Bobo and Kluegal (1997) and National Opinion Research Council (1972–2012).

Let's begin by looking at the 1990 results for "unintelligent." About 30% of whites applied this term to blacks, but only about 6% applied it to their own group, a differential of almost 25%. We can think of the size of the differential as a measure of the strength of this aspect of the traditional antiblack stereotype (Bobo & Kluegal, 1997, p. 101). In 2012, the willingness to apply this negative trait to blacks was dramatically lower (less than 15% of whites endorsed the stereotype), as was the differential between perceptions of blacks and whites (about 7%). This result might be taken as evidence of the declining strength of antiblack stereotypes among whites.

Figure 3.3 presents a less optimistic picture. Compared with the stereotype of "unintelligent," the stereotype of black laziness was more widespread in 1990 (more than 45% of whites applied this characterization to blacks) and the differential was much larger (about 42%). By 2012, the percentage of whites willing to apply this trait to blacks had declined, as had the differential (about 23%). Still, about a third of whites saw blacks as lazy, a result that indicates that this aspect of the traditional "negative" stereotype of blacks persists in American society.

Overall, these results support the idea that elements of traditional stereotypical thinking persist in the United States. The declines reflected in Figure 3.2 and 3.3 may reflect decreasing levels of prejudice or a growing unwillingness to verbalize prejudice, possibilities we will discuss later in this chapter.

COGNITIVE AND AFFECTIVE DIMENSIONS OF STEREOTYPES

Remember that individual prejudice has an affective dimension in addition to the cognitive. Robert Merton (1968), a prominent American sociologist, makes this distinction between dimensions dramatically. Merton analyzed stereotypical perceptions of Abraham Lincoln, Jews, and Japanese. In the following passage, he argues that the three "stereotypes" are identical in content but vastly different in emotional shading:

> *The very same behavior undergoes a complete change of evaluation in its transition from the in-group Abe Lincoln to the out-group Abe Cohen or Abe Kurokawa. Did Lincoln work far into the night? This testifies that he was industrious, resolute, perseverant, and eager to realize his capacities to the full. Do the out-group Jews or Japanese keep these same hours? This only bears witness to their sweatshop mentality, their ruthless undercutting of American standards, their unfair competitive practices. Is the in-group hero frugal, thrifty, and sparing? Then the out-group villain is stingy, miserly, and penny-pinching. All honor is due to the in-group Abe for his having been smart, shrewd and intelligent, and, by the same token, all contempt is owing the out-group Abes for their being sharp, cunning, crafty, and too clever by far. (p. 482)*

The stereotype of all three Abes is identical; what varies is the affect, or the emotional tone, reflected in the descriptive terms. Thus, the same stereotype evokes different emotional responses for different groups or in different individuals.

INTERSECTIONS OF RACE, GENDER, AND CLASS

The affective and cognitive dimensions of prejudice vary not only by race and ethnicity but also by gender and class, the major axes that define minority-group experience. For example, the stereotypes and feelings attached to black males differ from those attached to black females, and feelings about lower-class Mexican Americans are different from those evoked by upper-class members of the same group. We can get a sense of some of this variation by briefly reviewing three studies.

The first study asked white students at Arizona State University about their perceptions of women (Weitz & Gordon, 1993). Sharp distinctions were found between "women in general" (a label that, to the students, apparently signified white women) and African American women in particular. When asked to select traits for "American women in general," the responses were overwhelmingly positive and included "intelligent," "sensitive," and "attractive." Of the 10 most commonly selected traits, only 2 ("materialistic" and "emotional") might have had some negative connotations.

The students selected very different terms to describe African American women. The single most commonly selected trait was "loud," and only 22% of the sample saw African American women as "intelligent." Of the 10 most commonly selected traits, 5 (e.g., "talkative," "stubborn") seemed to have at least some negative affect attached to them.

The second study explores race/gender dynamics in the context of the relationships between hip-hop music and Asian American–Pacific Islanders (AAPIs) (McTaggart & O'Brien, 2013). From its origins as an expression of black, urban culture, hip-hop has grown into a diverse, global art form that transcends race, culture, language, gender, and age. A West Coast version of hip-hop began to flourish early in the movement and has long had a connection with AAPI groups, partly because it provides ways of negating dominant-group stereotypes of Asians. These stereotypes are gender specific: They depict AAPI males as soft, effeminate, and asexual, while AAPI females are seen as desirable, docile, and pliable (the ultimate fantasy of many males).

The study, based on in-depth interviews, found that for AAPI men, the hypermasculinity that is a part of hip-hop culture can be a way of compensating for and resisting the dominant-group stereotype, in much the same way as they might regard the success of NBA star Jeremy Lin as an antidote to the stereotype of AAPI males as nonathletic. For AAPI women, the youthful, urban, global aspects of hip-hop provide opportunities to break out of the narrow constraints of dominant-group images and to express themselves, even though they still have to contend with sexism and even misogyny. Thus, for its AAPI aficionados, hip-hop provides a more liberated space for self-expression and freedom from dominant-group culture.

Finally, a study by sociologist Edward Morris (2005) further illustrates how race, gender, and class can intersect in shaping feelings and thoughts of other groups. He studied an urban high school and focused on how various types of students were perceived and disciplined by school administrators and faculty. Morris found that, consistent with the notion of a "matrix of domination," mentioned in Chapter 1, stereotypes varied "not just through gender, or just through race, or just through class, but through all of these at once" (p. 44). For example, black boys were seen by school administrators and faculty as *too* masculine, extremely aggressive, and dangerous, and in need of careful watching. Black girls, in contrast, were seen as not feminine enough, too loud and aggressive, and in need of being molded into more compliant and deferential females. Other groups in the school—Latinas, Asian males, white males and females—were also the objects of clear sets of stereotypes and feelings, and tended to be subjected to forms of discipline that, ultimately, tended to reproduce the systems of inequality in the larger society.

QUESTIONS FOR REFLECTION

1. Why are Jews and Asians grouped together in the "high competence–low warmth" category of Figure 3.1? What stereotypical traits are they alleged to share? Why?

2. How have white perceptions of blacks changed? Do these changes mean that whites are less prejudiced?

3. How are stereotypes specific to race/gender combinations? Can you cite examples of these combinations from the comments of your family or friends, or from the media?

SOCIOLOGICAL CAUSES OF PREJUDICE

Prejudice is a complex phenomenon with multiple causes and manifestations. In this section, we will focus on a macrosociological approach and examine theories that stress the causes of prejudice that are related to culture, social structure, and group relationships.

THE ROLE OF GROUP COMPETITION

Every form of prejudice—even the most ancient—started at some specific point in history. If we go back far enough in time, we can find a moment that predates antiblack prejudice, anti-Semitism, negative stereotypes about Native Americans or Hispanic Americans, or antipathy against Asian Americans. What sorts of conditions create prejudice? The one common factor that seems to account for the origin of all prejudices is competition between groups—some episode in which one group successfully dominates, takes resources from, or eliminates a threat from some other group. The successful group becomes the dominant group, and the other group becomes the minority group.

Why is group competition associated with the emergence of prejudice? Typically, prejudice is more a result of the competition than a cause. Its role is to help mobilize emotional energy for the contest; justify rejection and attack; and rationalize the structures of domination, such as slavery or segregation, that result from the competition. Groups react to the competition and to the threat presented by other groups with antipathy and stereotypes about the "enemy" group. Prejudice emerges from the heat of the contest but then can solidify and persist for years (even centuries) after the end of the conflict. In chapters to come—and particularly in Chapter 4—we will often focus on the relationships between group competition and prejudice.

Robber's Cave. The relationship between prejudice and competition has been demonstrated in a variety of settings and situations, from labor strikes to international war to social psychology labs. In the chapters to come, we will examine the role of prejudice during the creation of slavery in North America, as a reaction to periods of high immigration, and as an accompaniment to myriad forms of group competition. Here, to illustrate our central point about competition and prejudice, we will examine a classic experiment from the sociological literature. The Robber's Cave experiment was conducted in the 1950s at a summer camp for 11- and 12-year-old boys.

The camp director, social psychologist Muzafer Sherif, divided the campers into two groups, the Rattlers and the Eagles (Sherif, Harvey, White, Hood, & Sherif, 1961). The groups lived in different cabins, and the staff continually pitted them against each other in a wide range of activities. Games,

sports, and even housekeeping chores were set up on a competitive basis. As the competition intensified, the groups developed and expressed negative feelings (prejudice) toward each other. Competition and prejudicial feelings grew quite intense and were manifested in episodes of name-calling and raids on the "enemy" group.

Sherif attempted to reduce the harsh feelings he had created by bringing the campers together in various pleasant situations featuring food, movies, and other treats. But the rival groups only used these opportunities to express their enmity. Sherif then came up with some activities that required the members of the rival groups to work cooperatively with each other. For example, the researchers deliberately sabotaged some plumbing to create an "emergency" that required the efforts of everyone to resolve. As a result of these cooperative activities, intergroup "prejudice" declined and, eventually, friendships were formed across groups.

In the Robber's Cave experiment, as in many actual group relationships, prejudice (negative feelings and stereotypes about other campers) arose to help mobilize feelings and justify rejection and attacks, both verbal and physical, against the out-group. When group competition was reduced, the levels of prejudice abated and eventually disappeared, again demonstrating that prejudice is caused by competition, not the other way around.

Although the Robber's Cave experiment illustrates our central point, we must be cautious in generalizing from these results. The experiment was conducted in an artificial environment with young boys (all white) who had no previous acquaintance with one another and no history of grievances or animosity. Thus, these results may be only partially generalizable to group conflicts in the real world. Nonetheless, Robber's Cave illustrates a fundamental connection between group competition and prejudice that we will observe repeatedly in the chapters to come. Competition and the desire to protect resources and status and to defend against threats from other groups are the primary motivations for the construction of traditions of prejudice and structures of inequality that benefit the dominant group.

THEORETICAL PERSPECTIVES ON GROUP COMPETITION AND PREJUDICE: POWER/CONFLICT MODELS

Many theorists have examined the dynamics of group competition and the results for prejudice and discrimination. Here we examine three of the most influential sociological perspectives on this topic.

Marxist Analysis. In Chapter 1, Marxism was discussed as a theory of social inequality. One of the tenets of Marxism is that the elites who control the means of production in a society also control the ideas and intellectual activity of the society. Ideologies and belief systems are shaped to support the dominance of the elites, and these ideologies and belief systems change when new elites come into control: "What else does the history of ideas prove, than that intellectual production changes in character in proportion as material production is changed? The ruling ideas of each age have been the ideas of its ruling class" (Marx & Engels, 1848/1967, p. 102).

Elite classes who subordinate or exploit a minority group will develop and institutionalize ideologies to justify or "explain" the arrangement. The history of the United States (and many other nations) includes numerous situations in which prejudice was used to help sustain the control of elite classes. For example, slave owners in the South used antiblack prejudice to attempt to control perceptions and justify the exploitation of the slaves. If it were commonly believed that blacks were inferior and too irresponsible to care for themselves, the constraints of slavery would seem less oppressive and unjust. People who did not benefit directly from slavery might not oppose the institution if they accepted the idea of black inferiority.

The slave owners also attempted to use Christianity to "brainwash" the slaves into accepting their powerless status. The exposure of slaves to religion was carefully controlled and emphasized those aspects of Christianity that stress the virtues of meekness and humility and promise rewards—but only in heaven. Thus, religion was used to stress obedience and to focus the attention of the slaves on the next life, not on the misery and injustice of this life.

In a more industrial example, the history of the United States for the past 150 years is replete with instances of struggle between the capitalists who control the means of production (factories, mills, mines, banks, etc.) and workers. Early in the 20th century, it was common for industrialists to try to weaken labor unions by splitting the working class along racial lines. The greater the extent to which black and white workers fought each other, the less likely there would be a unified uprising against the capitalist class. The capitalist class controlled the racially mixed working class by following a strategy of "divide and conquer" (Cox, 1948; Reich, 1986).

Split Labor Market Theory. This theory agrees with the Marxist idea that prejudice and racist ideologies serve the interest of a specific class, but it identifies a different beneficiary. In **split labor market theory**, there are three actors in the economic sector of an industrial society. First are the elites, the capitalists who own the means of production. The other two groups are segments of the working class. The labor market is divided (or split) into higher-priced labor and cheaper labor. It is in the economic self-interest of the capitalist class to use cheaper labor whenever possible. Recent immigrants and minority groups often fill the role of cheaper labor.

Higher-priced labor (usually consisting of members of the dominant group) will attempt to exclude cheaper labor from the marketplace whenever it can. Such efforts include barring minority groups from labor unions, violent attacks on minority-group communities, support for discriminatory laws, and efforts to exclude groups from the United States entirely. Prejudice is used by higher-priced labor to arouse and mobilize opposition to the cheaper labor pool represented by the minority group. The economic nature of the competition and the economic self-interests of higher-priced labor are obscured by appeals to racial or cultural unity against the "threat" represented by the minority group. The major beneficiary of prejudice is not the capitalist class but the more powerful elements of the working class (Bonacich, 1972; Bonacich & Modell, 1980).

Group Interests. A similar line of analysis was begun by American sociologist Herbert Blumer (1958), who argued that prejudice is activated when groups feel that they are threatened by other groups they see as beneath them (see also Bobo & Tuan, 2006). The dominant group—which, by definition, has the highest status in a society—is particularly likely to use prejudice as a weapon when it feels that its privileges, its sense of entitlement and high position, are in peril.

We saw in Chapter 1 that sociologist Max Weber argued that there are three separate stratification systems in society: property (the economic system that includes jobs and income), power (control of decision making and the political institution at all levels), and prestige (the allocation of honor, esteem, and respect). Perceived threat could involve any of these dimensions or any combination of the three.

An example of these dynamics can be found in the reaction of many Southern (and other) whites to the black civil rights movement of the 1950s and 1960s. We will discuss this era of race relations in some detail in Chapter 6, but, for now, we can point out that the civil rights movement challenged the Southern system of race-based privilege that was institutionalized during slavery and perpetuated during segregation, a system that granted even the lowest-status white a position superior to all blacks.

Prejudice was an important part of the attempt by whites to resist racial change. Politicians and other leaders of the white community used the most vicious stereotypes (e.g., black men as sexual threats to white women) and the most negative emotional rhetoric to motivate whites to attempt to defeat demands for racial equality and an end to segregation. Sometimes, prejudice was used to foment or justify violence—bombings, lynchings, and beatings—but even milder forms of resistance were motivated by the perceived need to maintain the superior power, prestige, and property of whites in the South, and protect their racial privilege.

Split labor market theory argues that higher-priced dominant-group labor uses prejudice and discrimination to limit the ability of lower-priced minority-group labor to compete for jobs.

A clear expression of group preferences.

Contemporary examples of how prejudice has been used to help defend group position are not difficult to locate. For example, many Americans today feel threatened by immigration (particularly by undocumented immigrants), the rising tide of diversity (see Figure 1.1), and various global threats, including the rise of China and terrorist groups such as Al Qaeda. Predictably, politicians and media figures of all persuasions have exploited—and perhaps intensified—these feelings, particularly in election campaign ads designed to (sometimes blatantly) mobilize people's fears, prejudices, and sense of threat. One widely criticized example comes from the 2010 election campaign of Senator David Vitter of Louisiana. He accused his opponent of being soft on illegal immigration and border security, and his campaign ran a TV ad in which immigrants were shown sneaking across the border and being welcomed with checks, limousine rides, and other benefits, presumably the result of the policies advocated by his opponent (see the original ad at www.youtube.com/watch?v=9uvp0Jljh6U). Vitter won the election by a wide margin.

SUMMARY AND LIMITATIONS

These theories share the conclusion that prejudice flows from struggles to control or expand a group's share of scarce resources. The primary beneficiary of prejudice is sometimes the elite class (e.g., capitalists, plantation owners, high-status groups) and sometimes another segment of the dominant group (e.g., higher-priced labor). In general, though, these

---

In the **vicious cycle**, minority-group inferiority is assumed and then forces are set in motion to create and perpetuate it.

---

perspectives agree that prejudice exists because someone or some group gains by it.

These points are persuasive and help us understand why prejudice originates in the first place, but they cannot account for prejudice in all its forms. No theory can explain everything, especially something as complex as prejudice. The origins of prejudice can be found in culture, socialization, family structure, and personality development, as well as in politics and economics. As the authoritarian personality theory reminds us, prejudice can have important psychological and social functions independent of group power relationships.

To illustrate these limitations, consider an analysis of attitudes toward immigrants. Consistent with the idea that prejudice is stimulated by group competition, Burns and Gimpel (2000) found that opposition to immigration is greater when times are hard and people feel economically threatened. However, they also found that anti-immigration prejudice cannot be explained by economics alone and that it persists even when economic conditions improve, a finding consistent with the idea that prejudice is shaped by cultural and personality factors in addition to conflict over scarce resources.

QUESTIONS FOR REFLECTION

How are the ideas presented in this section sociological? How do they differ from more psychological theories of prejudice and discrimination?

THE PERSISTENCE OF PREJUDICE

Prejudice originates in group competition of some sort but often outlives the conditions of its creation. It can persist, full-blown and intense, long after the episode that sparked it has faded from memory. How does prejudice persist through time?

THE VICIOUS CYCLE

In his classic analysis of American race relations, *An American Dilemma* (1944/1962), Swedish economist Gunnar Myrdal proposed the idea that prejudice is perpetuated through time by a self-fulfilling prophecy or a **vicious cycle**, as illustrated in Figure 3.4. The dominant group uses its power to force the minority group into an inferior status, such as slavery, as shown in the diagram in Area 1. Partly to motivate the construction of a system of racial stratification and partly to justify its existence, individual prejudice and racist belief systems are invented and accepted by the dominant group, as shown in Area 2. Individual prejudices are reinforced by the everyday observation of the inferior status of the minority group. The fact that the minority

FIGURE 3.4 Myrdal's Vicious Cycle

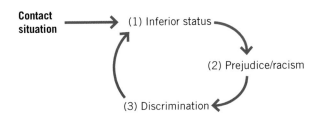

group is impoverished, enslaved, or otherwise exploited confirms and strengthens the attribution of inferiority. The belief in inferiority motivates further discrimination and unequal treatment, as shown in Area 3 of the diagram, which reinforces the inferior status, which validates the prejudice and racism, which justifies further discrimination, and so on. Over a few generations, a stable, internally reinforced system of racial inferiority becomes an integral, unremarkable, and (at least for the dominant group) accepted part of everyday life.

Culture is conservative, and once created, prejudice will be sustained over time just like any set of attitudes, values, and beliefs. Future generations will learn prejudice in the same way and for the same reasons they learn any other aspect of their culture. Thus, prejudice and racism come to us through our cultural heritage as a package of stereotypes, emotions, and ideas. We learn which groups are "good" and which are "bad" in the same way we learn table manners and religious beliefs (Pettigrew, 1958, 1971, p. 137; Simpson & Yinger, 1985, pp. 107–108). When prejudice is part of the cultural heritage, individuals learn to think and feel negatively toward other groups as a routine part of socialization. Much of the prejudice expressed by Americans—and the people of many other societies—is the normal result of typical socialization in families, communities, and societies that are, to some degree, racist. Given our long history of intense racial and ethnic exploitation, it is not surprising that Americans continue to manifest antipathy toward and stereotypical ideas about other groups.

PREJUDICE IN CHILDREN

The idea that prejudice is learned during socialization is reinforced by studies of the development of prejudice in children. Research generally shows that children become aware of group differences (e.g., black vs. white) at a very early age, perhaps as early as six months (Katz, 2003, p. 898). By age three or younger, they recognize the significance and the permanence of racial groups and can accurately classify people on the basis of skin color and other cues (Brown, 1995, pp. 121–136; Katz, 1976, p. 126). Once the racial or group categories are mentally established, children begin the

process of learning the "proper" attitudes and stereotypes to associate with the various groups, and both affective and cognitive prejudice begin to grow at an early age.

It is important to note that children can acquire prejudice even when parents and other caregivers do not teach it overtly or directly. Adults control the socialization process and valuable resources (food, shelter, praise), and children are motivated to seek their approval and conform to their expectations (at least in the early years). There are strong pressures on the child to learn and internalize the perceptions of the older generation, and even a casual comment or an overheard remark can establish or reinforce negative beliefs or feelings about members of other groups (Ashmore & DelBoca, 1976). Children need not be directly instructed about presumed minority-group characteristics; it is often said that racial attitudes are "caught and not taught."

Research also shows that children are actively engaged in their learning and that their levels of prejudice reflect their changing intellectual capabilities. Children as young as five to six months old can make some simple distinctions (e.g., by gender or race) between categories of people. The fact that this capability emerges so early in life suggests that it is not simply a response to adult teaching. "Adults use categories to simplify and make sense of their environment; apparently children do the same" (Brown, 1995, p. 126). Gross, simplistic distinctions between people may help very young children organize and understand the world around them.

The need for such primitive categorizations may decline as the child becomes more experienced in life and more sophisticated in his or her thinking. Studies from a variety of nations show that prejudice tends to be highest for younger children and declines through late childhood, up to ages 8 through 10 (Raabe & Beelman, 2011). The decline seems to be related to increased awareness of racial similarities (as well as differences) and diverse perspectives on race (see also Black-Gutman & Hickson, 1996; Bronson & Merryman, 2009; Brown, 1995, pp. 149–159; Powlishta, Serbin, Doyle, & White, 1994; Van Ausdale & Feagin, 2001). Thus, changing levels of prejudice in children may reflect an interaction between children's changing mental capacities and their environment rather than a simple or straightforward learning of racist cultural beliefs or values.

SOCIAL DISTANCE SCALES: THE CULTURAL DIMENSIONS OF PREJUDICE

Further evidence for the cultural nature of prejudice is provided by research on the concept of **social distance**, which is related to prejudice but is not quite the same thing. Social

---

Social distance refers to the degree of intimacy a person is willing to accept for members of other groups.

distance is the degree of intimacy that a person is willing to accept in his or her relations with members of other groups. On this scale, the most intimate relationship is close kinship, and the most distant is exclusion from the country. The seven degrees of social distance, as specified by Emory Bogardus (1933), the inventor of the scale, are as follows:

1. To close kinship by marriage
2. To my club as personal chums
3. To my street as neighbors
4. To employment in my occupation
5. To citizenship in my country
6. As visitors only to my country
7. Would exclude from my country

Research using social distance scales demonstrates that Americans rank other groups in similar ways across time and space. The consistency indicates a common frame of reference or set of perceptions, a continuity of vision possible only if perceptions have been standardized by socialization in a common culture.

Table 3.2 presents some results of several administrations of the scale to samples of Americans from 1926 to 2011. The groups are listed by the rank order of their scores for 1926. In that year, the sample expressed the least social distance from the English and the most distance from Asian Indians. Whereas the average social distance score for the English was 1.02, indicating virtually no sense of distance, the average score for Indians was 3.91, indicating a distance between "to employment in my occupation" and "to my street as neighbors."

As you inspect the table, note, first of all, the stability in the rankings. The actual scores (not shown) generally decrease from decade to decade, indicating less social distance and presumably a decline in prejudice over the years.

The group rankings, however, tend to be the same year after year. Considering the changes that society experienced between 1926 and 2011 (the Great Depression; World War II, the Korean War, the Vietnam War, and the Cold War with the USSR; the civil rights movement; the resumption of large-scale immigration; etc.), this overall continuity in group rankings is remarkable.

Second, note the nature of the ranking: Groups with origins in northern and western Europe are ranked highest, followed by groups from southern and eastern Europe, with racial minorities near the bottom. These preferences reflect the relative status of these groups in the U.S. hierarchy of

racial and ethnic groups, which, in turn, reflects the timing of immigration and the perceived "degree of difference" from the dominant group (see Chapter 2). The rankings also reflect the relative amount of exploitation and prejudice directed at each group over the course of U.S. history.

Although these patterns of social distance scores support the general point that prejudice is cultural, this body of research has some important limitations. The respondents were generally college students from a variety of campuses, not representative samples of the population, and the differences in actual scores from group to group are sometimes very small.

Still, the stability of the patterns cannot be ignored: The top groups are always northern European, Poles and Jews are always ranked in the middle third, and Koreans and Japanese always fall in the bottom third. African Americans and American Indians were also ranked toward the bottom until the most recent rankings.

Finally, note how the relative positions of some groups change with international and domestic relations. For example, both Japanese and Germans fell in the rankings at the end of World War II (1946). Comparing 1977 with 1946, Russians fell and Japanese rose, reflecting changing patterns of alliance and enmity in the global system of societies. The dramatic rise of African Americans in 2011 may reflect declining levels of overt prejudice in American society, and the low rankings of Muslims and Arabs in 2011 probably reflect the negative feelings generated by the terrorist attacks on September 11, 2001.

How do we explain the fact that group rankings generally are so stable from the 1920s to 2011? The stability strongly suggests that Americans view these groups through the same culturally shaped lens. A sense of social distance, a perception of some groups as "higher" or "better" than others, is part of the cultural package of intergroup prejudices we acquire from **socialization** into American society. The social distance patterns illustrate the power of culture to shape individual perceptions and preferences and attest to the fundamentally racist nature of American culture.

The power of culture to shape our perceptions is illustrated in the Narrative Portrait on page 83.

SITUATIONAL INFLUENCES

As a final point in our consideration of the persistence of prejudice, we should note the importance of the social situation in which attitudes are expressed and behavior occurs. What people think and what they do is not always the same. Even intense prejudice may not translate into discriminatory behavior, and discrimination is not always accompanied by prejudice (refer back to Table 3.1).

One of the earliest demonstrations of the difference between what people think and feel (prejudice) and what

---

Socialization is the process of physiological and social development by which a person learns his or her culture.

APPLYING CONCEPTS

Do you have a sense of social distance from different groups? Has it changed over the past 10 years? Use the seven degrees of social distance to indicate the level of intimacy you would feel comfortable sharing with members of each of the groups listed. Also, estimate the degree of social distance you would have felt for each group 10 years ago.

How did you acquire your sense of social distance? Was it from your family or community, or is it based on actual experience with members of these groups? Do you think it was "caught and not taught"? Why has it changed over the past 10 years (if it has)?

GROUP	YOUR SOCIAL DISTANCE SCORE TODAY	YOUR SOCIAL DISTANCE SCORE 10 YEARS AGO
Americans (white)		
Irish		
Russians		
Italians		
American Indians		
Jews		
Mexicans		
African Americans		
Chinese		
Muslims		

TURN TO TABLE 3.2 ON THE NEXT PAGE TO SEE THE RANKINGS OF THESE GROUPS OVER THE YEARS.

they actually do (discrimination) was provided by sociologist Robert LaPiere (1934). In the 1930s, he escorted a Chinese couple on a tour of the United States. At that time, Chinese and other Asians were the victims of widespread discrimination and exclusion, and anti-Chinese prejudice was quite high, as demonstrated by the social distance scores in Table 3.2. However, LaPiere and his companions dined in restaurants and stayed in hotels without incident for the entire trip, and experienced discrimination only once.

Six months later, LaPiere wrote to every establishment the group had patronized and inquired about reservations. He indicated that some of the party were Chinese and asked if that would be a problem. Of those establishments that replied (about half), 92% said that they would not serve Chinese and would be unable to accommodate the party.

Why the difference? Although not a definitive or particularly sophisticated method of data gathering (for example, there was no way to tell whether the correspondents were the same persons LaPiere and his associates had dealt with in person), this episode exemplifies the difference between

saying and doing and the importance of taking the situation into account. On LaPiere's original visit, anti-Asian prejudice may well have been present but was not expressed, to avoid making a scene. In a different situation, the more distant interaction of written correspondence, the restaurant and hotel staffs may have allowed their prejudice to be expressed in open discrimination because the potential for embarrassment was much less.

The situation a person is in shapes the relationship between prejudice and discrimination. In highly prejudiced communities or groups, the pressure to conform may cause relatively unprejudiced individuals to discriminate. For example, if an ethnic or racial or gender joke is told in a group of friends or relatives, all might join in the laughter. Even a completely unprejudiced person might smile or giggle to avoid embarrassing or offending the person who told the joke.

On the other hand, situations in which there are strong norms of equal and fair treatment may stifle the tendency of even the most bigoted individual to discriminate. For example, if a community vigorously enforces antidiscrimination laws,

TABLE 3.2 Social Distance Scores of Selected Groups (Ranks for Each Year)

GROUP	1926	1946	1977	2011
English (British)	1	3	2	4
Americans (white)	2	1	1	1
Canadians	3	2	3	3
Irish	5	4	7	5
Germans	7	10	11	8
Russians	13	13	29	20
Italians	14	16	5	2
Poles	15	14	18	14
American Indians	18	20	10	12
Jews	19	19	15	11
Mexicans	21	24	26	25
Japanese	22	30	25	22
Filipinos	23	23	24	16
African Americans	24	29	17	9
Turks	25	25	28	—
Chinese	26	21	23	17
Koreans	27	27	30	24
Asian Indians	28	28	27	26
Vietnamese	—	—	—	28
Muslims	—	—	—	29
Arabs	—	—	—	30
Mean (all scores)	2.14	2.12	1.93	1.68
Range	2.85	2.57	1.38	1.08

SOURCE: 1926 to 1977—Smith and Dempsey (1983, p. 588); 2011—Parrillo and Donoghue (2013).

NOTE: Values in the table are ranks for that year. To conserve space, some groups and ranks have been eliminated.

even the most prejudiced merchant might refrain from treating minority-group customers unequally. Highly prejudiced individuals may not discriminate so they can "do business" (or at least avoid penalties or sanctions) in an environment in which discrimination is not tolerated or is too costly.

SUMMARY AND LIMITATIONS

The theories and perspectives examined in this section help us understand how prejudice can persist through time. Prejudice becomes a part of the culture of a society and is passed along to succeeding generations along with other values, norms, and information.

Although cultural causes of prejudice are obviously important, considering only cultural factors may lead us to the mistaken belief that all members of the same society have similar levels of prejudice. On the contrary, no two people have the same socialization experiences or develop exactly the same prejudices (or any other attitude, for that matter). Differences in family structure, parenting style, school experiences, attitudes of peers, and a host of other factors affect the development of an individual's personality and attitude.

Furthermore, socialization is not a passive process; we are not neutral recipients of a culture that is simply forced down our throats. Our individuality, intelligence, and

NARRATIVE PORTRAIT

The Cultural Sources of Prejudice

In The Crazyladies of Pearl Street, *best-selling novelist Trevanian (2005) recounts his experiences growing up Irish Catholic in a poor neighborhood in Albany, New York, in the 1930s. Here, he recalls how his mother decided to apply for public assistance after her husband had abandoned them. Trevanian, then a boy of eight, advised her to enlist the assistance of Mr. Kane, the local grocer who had already extended them credit to buy food and other essentials. The young Trevanian saw Mr. Kane as kindly, but his mother focused on the fact that he was Jewish.*

For the author, his mother is a powerful and heroic figure. She is also, as are we all, a product of her culture. She inherited a set of attitudes and emotions about other groups and especially about Jews.

THE CRAZYLADIES OF PEARL STREET

Trevanian

Here's how things were: We were marooned on this slum street...where we didn't know anybody and...we had only a little more than five bucks to our name. But we weren't beaten. Not by a damn sight. Nobody beats [my mother]! No, sir!...Her pride had never let her seek public assistance, and it burned her up to have to do so now, but she...couldn't let pride stand in the way of us kids having food on the table. There must be agencies and people that she could turn to, just until we were on our feet again. First she'd contact them and ask them for help...make them help us, goddammit! Then she'd look for work as a waitress....But first, she had to find out the addresses of the welfare agencies.

If only she knew someone she could ask about things like this.

"What about Mr. Kane?" I suggested.

"The grocery man? Oh, I don't know. I don't think we want any more favors from his sort."

"...His sort?"

She shrugged.

"But he's nice," I said. "And smart, too."

She thought about that for a moment. She didn't like being beholden to strangers, but...Oh, all right, she'd go over to thank him for giving us credit. That was just common courtesy....

"You know, come to think of it, this Mr. Kane of yours just might help us out because if he doesn't, we won't be able to pay what we owe him. You can only count on these people if there's something in it for them."

"He'd help us anyway. He's nice."...

She often said, and honestly believed, that she was not prejudiced—well, except in the case of Italian mobsters and drunken Irish loafers and stupid Poles and snooty Yankee Protestants, but then who wasn't? Among the cultural scars left by her early years in convent school was a stereotypical view of "the people who slew Jesus." "On the other hand," she said, always wanting to be fair, "I served some very nice Jewish people in the Lake George Restaurant last season. They always chose my station. Real good tippers. But then they had to be, didn't they? To make up for things."

I accompanied her across the street, and Mr. Kane spent half the morning looking up the appropriate welfare agencies and using the pay phone at the back of

his shop to call people and make appointments for my mother....

She thanked him for his help, [and] as we crossed the street back to [the apartment] she told me that I must always be careful with these people.

"But Mr. Kane was just trying to be..."

"They have a way of worming things out of you."

"He wasn't worming any—"

"You just be careful what you tell them, and that's final. Period!"

Later that month, when we were able to begin paying something against our slate, my mother felt vindicated in her mistrust of "these people." She discovered that Mr. Kane had charged her a nickel for each call he made on her behalf. I explained that this was only fair because he had put a nickel into the slot for each call, but she waved this aside, saying she was sure he made a little something on each call. Why else would he have a phone taking up space in his shop? No, they work every angle, these people....

SOURCE: Trevanian (2005). *The Crazyladies of Pearl Street*, pp. 31–33. New York: Crown Books. Copyright © 2005 by Trevanian. Used by permission of Crown Publishers, a division of Random House, Inc.

Questions to Consider

1. What stereotypes about Jewish people does Trevanian's mother believe?
2. How does she exemplify the concept of "selective perception"? Is there anything Mr. Kane could have done to negate her assumptions about him?

---

curiosity affect the nature and content of our socialization experiences. Even close siblings may have very different experiences and, consequently, different levels of prejudice. People raised in extremely prejudicial settings may moderate their attitudes as a result of experiences later in life, just as those raised in nonprejudiced settings may develop stronger biases as time passes.

The development of prejudice is further complicated by the fact that, in the United States, we also learn egalitarian norms and values as we are socialized. Myrdal (1944/1962) was referring to this contrast when he titled his landmark

study of race relations in the United States *An American Dilemma*. We learn norms of fairness and justice along with norms that condone or even demand unequal treatment based on group membership. Typically, people develop more than one attitude about other groups, and these multiple attitudes are not set in concrete. They can change from time to time and place to place, depending on the situation and a variety of other variables. The same point could be made about other attitudes besides prejudice; people have an array of attitudes, beliefs, and values about any particular subject, and some of them are mutually contradictory.

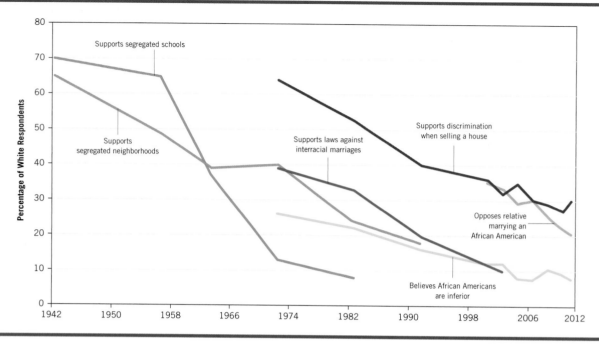

SOURCE: 1942, 1956, and 1963—Hyman and Sheatsley (1964); 1972 to 2012—National Opinion Research Council (1972–2012).

QUESTIONS FOR REFLECTION

1. What are some of the important ways prejudice is perpetuated over time? How powerful are these mechanisms? Do they mean that U.S. society will always be prejudiced?

2. How were you socialized about other groups? How did you acquire the attitudes and feelings you hold? What was the most powerful influence on your socialization: Your parents? Mass media? Your friends? Why? If you learned to be prejudiced as a child, how did you unlearn these attitudes and feelings?

RECENT TRENDS: TRADITIONAL PREJUDICE AND MODERN RACISM

One of the questions we asked at the beginning of this chapter concerned recent trends in prejudice. Is prejudice still a problem in the United States? There is a great deal of evidence documenting a decline in "traditional" prejudice: the blatant, overt feelings and ideas that have characterized American prejudice

---

Modern racism is a more subtle and indirect form of traditional prejudice.

---

virtually from the birth of the nation. Surveys and public opinion polls show that this type of prejudice is losing strength in the general population.

However, while some celebrate the decline in harsh, overt prejudice, many social scientists argue strongly that prejudice has *not* declined but, rather, has evolved into a more subtle, less obvious, but just as consequential form. This new form of prejudice has been called a number of things, including **modern racism**, symbolic racism, and color-blind racism, and there is considerable debate over its exact shape, extent, and—indeed—existence. However, even while the issues continue to be debated and researched, the evidence that prejudice, even in its more subtle and disguised forms, remains a potent force in American society continues to accumulate.

In this section, we will first investigate and document the decline in traditional prejudice and consider some of the possible causes for this decline. Second, we will consider the nature of modern racism, the newer way of expressing antipathy for other groups.

TRADITIONAL PREJUDICE: CHANGING ATTITUDES?

Some of the strongest evidence that traditional prejudice is declining comes from public opinion polls. Surveys measuring prejudice have been administered to representative samples of U.S. citizens since the early 1940s, and these polls document a consistent decrease in support for prejudicial statements, as the data in Figure 3.5 indicate.

In 1942, the huge majority—a little more than 70%—of white Americans thought that black and white children should attend different schools. Forty years later, in 1982, support for separate schools had dropped to less than 10%. In similar fashion, every survey item in Figure 3.5 shows a downward trend. By 2012, only small minorities of white Americans opposed interracial marriage or said they believed that blacks were inferior. Less than a third supported racial discrimination in housing sales, down from almost two thirds exactly four decades earlier. The overall trend is unmistakable: There has been a dramatic decline in support for prejudiced statements since World War II.

Of course, these polls also show that prejudice has not vanished. Some white Americans continue to endorse highly prejudicial sentiments and opinions. Remember also that the polls show only what people *say* they feel and think, which might be different from what they truly believe.

Assuming that the overall trend displayed in these polls is reasonably valid, what causes might be important? Here, we investigate two possible independent variables: rising levels of education and increasing contact across racial lines.

EXPLAINING THE DECLINE OF TRADITIONAL PREJUDICE 1: THE ROLE OF EDUCATION

One possible cause of declining prejudice is that Americans have become much more educated during the time period covered in Figure 3.5. Education has frequently been singled out as the most effective cure for prejudice and discrimination. Education, like travel, is said to "broaden one's perspective" and encourage a more sophisticated view of human affairs. People with higher levels of education are more likely to view other people in terms of their competence and abilities and not in terms of physical or ethnic characteristics. In some theories of assimilation (see Chapter 2), education is identified as one of the modernizing forces that will lead to a more rational, competency-based social system.

As shown in Figure 3.6, the percentage of the U.S. population with high school degrees increased almost 2.5 times

FIGURE 3.6 High School and College Graduates in the United States, Age 25 and Older, 1950–2012

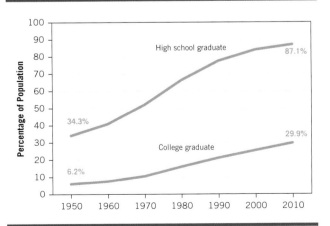

SOURCE: 1950—U.S. Census Bureau (1997); 1960 to 2010—U.S. Census Bureau (2012c, p. 151).

FIGURE 3.7 Declining Prejudicial Views of White Americans by Increased Educational Attainment, 2012

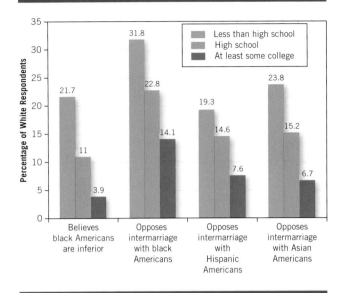

SOURCE: National Opinion Research Council (1972–2012).

between 1950 and 2010, from about 34% to 87%. In the same period, the percentage of the population with college degrees rose at an even faster rate (nearly five times), from about 6% to almost 30%. Could it be merely coincidental that prejudice declined so dramatically during the same time period?

Many studies have also found statistical correlations between an individual's level of prejudice and level of education. Figure 3.7 shows the relationships between various measures of prejudice and level of education for a representative sample of white Americans in 2012. These graphs show that support for prejudiced responses declines as education increases. White respondents with less education express greater support for the belief that blacks are inferior, and they are more opposed to marriage across group lines with blacks, Hispanics, and Asians.

The correlation between increased education and decreased prejudice supports the common wisdom that education is the enemy of (and antidote to) prejudice, but we need to consider some caveats and qualifications before we come to any conclusions. First, correlation is not the same thing as causation, and just because education and prejudice change together over time and are statistically associated does not prove that one is causing the change in the other. Perhaps people are still highly prejudiced and are simply hiding their true feelings from the public opinion pollsters, a trend that would be consistent with the arguments that traditional prejudice has morphed into modern racism.

Second, the limited set of possible responses offered to respondents (e.g., "agree" or "disagree") might not record the full range, subtlety, or complexity of people's feelings. People typically have many attitudes about a subject, especially one as emotionally charged as prejudice. As we have seen, different situations may activate different sets of attitudes, and public opinion surveys may evoke more tolerant responses. The more educated are particularly likely to be aware of the "correct" responses and more likely to express socially acceptable opinions. The bottom line is that it is hard to determine how much of the apparent reduction in prejudice has been genuine and how much is due to conformity to the prevailing and fashionable attitudes of the day (see Cribbs & Austin, 2011; Jackman, 1978, 1981; Jackman & Muha, 1984; Smith & Seelbach, 1987; Weil, 1985).

EXPLAINING THE DECLINE OF TRADITIONAL PREJUDICE 2: THE CONTACT HYPOTHESIS

Like education, contact and increased communication between groups have often been suggested as remedies for prejudice, misunderstandings, and hostile race and ethnic relations. A generic statement of this point of view might read something like this: "If only people would get together and really talk to one another, they would see that we're all the same, all human beings with hopes and dreams," and so on and so forth. Such sentiments are common, and a number of organizations at all levels of society are devoted to opening and sustaining a dialogue between groups. How effective are such efforts? Does increased contact reduce prejudice? If so, under what conditions?

First of all, contact between groups is not, in and of itself, an automatic antidote for prejudice. Contact can have a variety of outcomes and can actually increase prejudice, depending on the nature of the situation. When contact occurs in situations of group inequality, such as during American slavery or segregation, prejudice is likely to be reinforced, not reduced. On the other hand, certain forms of intergroup contact do seem to reduce prejudice.

One theory that addresses this relationship is the **equal status contact hypothesis**. This theory specifies the conditions under which intergroup contact can reduce prejudice. Intergroup contact will tend to reduce prejudice when four conditions are filled: The groups must have (a) equal status and (b) common goals, and must (c) interact intensively in noncompetitive, cooperative tasks and (d) have the active endorsement of authority figures (Pettigrew, 1998, pp. 66–67). Each of these four conditions is crucial to the reduction of prejudice.

1. *Equal status.* Only in situations in which all groups have equal resources and prestige are people likely to view one another as individuals, not as representatives of their

respective groups. When the people involved in intergroup contacts are unequal in status, they are more likely to retain or even intensify their prejudice. During slavery, for example, there was a high volume of contact across racial lines because of the nature of agricultural work. These interactions between blacks and whites were conducted in a context of massive inequality, however, and the contact did not encourage (to say the least) an honest and open sharing of views. Under the system of segregation that followed slavery, the frequency of interracial contact actually declined as blacks and whites were separated into unequal communities. By World War II, segregation was so complete that whites and blacks hardly saw each other except in situations in which blacks were clearly lower in status (Woodward, 1974, p. 118).

2. *Common goals.* The most effective contact situations for reducing prejudice are those in which members of different groups come together in a single group with a common goal. Examples of such settings include athletic teams working toward victory; study groups of students helping one another prepare for tests; and community groups organized to build a playground, combat crime, raise money for cancer research, and so forth.

3. *Intergroup cooperation and intensive interaction.* If contact is to reduce prejudice, it must occur in an atmosphere free from threat or competition between groups. When intergroup contact is motivated by competition for scarce resources, prejudice tends to increase and may even be accompanied by hatred and violence. Recall the Robber's Cave experiment and the levels of prejudice manufactured in that situation. If contact is to have a moderating effect on attitudes, it must occur in a setting where there is nothing at stake, no real (or imagined) resource that might be allocated differently as a result of the contact. If people are bound together by cooperative behavior across group lines and are motivated to achieve a common goal, they are much more likely to come to regard one another as individuals, not as caricatures or stereotypical representatives of their groups.

Furthermore, the contact has to be more than superficial. The situation must last for a significant length of time, and the participants must be fully involved. Standing next to one another at a bus stop or eating at adjoining tables in a restaurant does not meet this criterion; people of different groups must deal with one another face-to-face and on a personal level.

4. *Support of authority, law, or custom.* The greater the extent to which contact takes place with strong support from authority figures (politicians, teachers, ministers, etc.) and is backed by moral codes and values, the more likely it is to have a positive impact on intergroup attitudes.

One of the most persuasive illustrations of the contact hypothesis is the Robber's Cave experiment, discussed earlier in this chapter (Sherif et al., 1961). As you recall, rival groups

---

The **equal status contact hypothesis** argues that, under certain conditions, cooperative contacts between groups will tend to reduce prejudice.

of campers were placed in competitive situations and became prejudiced as a result. It was not until the researchers created some situations in which the rival groups had to actively cooperate to achieve common goals that prejudice began to decline. Contact, in and of itself, did not affect intergroup attitudes. Only contact that required the goal-oriented cooperation of equals in status could reduce the prejudice that the staff had created through competition.

The Robber's Cave experiment provides dramatic support for the contact hypothesis, but we must be cautious in evaluating this evidence. The experiment was conducted in a "pristine" environment in which the campers had no prior acquaintance with one another and brought no backlog of grievances and no traditions of prejudice to the situation. The study illustrates and supports the contact hypothesis but cannot prove the theory. For additional evidence, we turn to everyday life and more realistic intergroup contact situations.

In another classic study, Deutsch and Collins (1951) studied the antiblack prejudices of white residents of public housing projects. This study is significant because Deutsch and Collins were able to eliminate the problem of self-selection. In other studies, participation in the contact situation is typically voluntary. The people who volunteer for experiments in interracial contacts are usually not very prejudiced in the first place or at least are more open to change. Thus, any change in prejudice might be due to the characteristics of the people involved, not to the contact situation itself. By contrast, in the Deutsch and Collins study, some of the white participants were randomly assigned to live close to black families. The participants had no control over their living arrangement and thus were not self-selected for lower prejudice or openness to change.

A total of four public housing projects were studied. In two of the projects, black and white families were assigned to separate buildings or areas. In the remaining two, dwelling units were assigned regardless of race, and black and white families lived next to one another. As a result of proximity, the white subjects in these two housing projects had higher rates of contact with their black neighbors than did the white families assigned to "segregated" units.

The researchers interviewed the mothers of the white families and found that those living in the integrated projects were less racially prejudiced and much more likely to interact with their African American neighbors than were those living in the segregated setting. Deutsch and Collins (1951) concluded that the higher volume of interracial contact had led to lower prejudice.

More recent studies have been based on surveys administered to large, representative samples of black and white Americans and have generally supported the contact hypothesis. For example, one review of more than 500 tests conducted in a variety of nations concluded that contact has a powerful and consistent effect on prejudice, not only for racial and ethnic minorities but also for other outgroups, including gays and lesbians, and that the effects hold across nations, genders, and age groups (Pettigrew, Tropp, Wagner, & Christ, 2011, p. 271). (For more on the contact hypothesis, see Aberson, Shoemaker, & Tomolillo, 2004; Dixon, 2006; Dixon & Rosenbaum, 2004; Forbes, 1997; Katz & Taylor, 1988; Miller & Brewer, 1984; Pettigrew, 1998; Pettigrew & Tropp, 2006; Powers & Ellison, 1995; Sigelman & Welch, 1993; Smith, 1994; Wittig & Grant-Thompson, 1998; Yancey, 1999, 2007.)

Recent Trends in Intergroup Contact. Since the 1950s, concerted attempts have been made to reduce discrimination against minority groups in virtually every American social institution. In Gordon's (1964) terms, these efforts increased structural assimilation or integration (see Chapter 2) and provided opportunities for dominant- and minority-group members to associate with one another. Compared with the days of slavery and segregation, there is considerably more contact across group lines today in schools and colleges, workplaces, neighborhoods, and social gatherings.

Some of this increased contact has reduced prejudice. In other instances, contact situations that seem on paper to be likely to reduce prejudice have had no effect or have actually made matters worse. For example, schools and universities across the country have been officially integrated for decades, but these situations do not always lead to increased acceptance and the growth of friendships across group boundaries. The groups involved—whites, African Americans, Latinos, Asians, or Native Americans—sometimes minimize face-to-face interaction and contact across the social dividing lines. To illustrate, you need only visit the cafeteria of many university campuses during mealtime and observe how the seating pattern follows group lines (see Cowan, 2005; Lewis, 2012; Schofield, Hausmann, Ye, & Woods, 2010).

The contact hypothesis offers a possible explanation for this pattern of separation within integration. The student body in many schools and colleges is organized along lines that meet some, but not all, of the conditions necessary for a contact situation to lower prejudice. Even when students from the various racial and ethnic groups are roughly equal in status, they do not engage in many cooperative activities that cross group lines. Classrooms themselves are typically competitive and individualistic; students compete for grades and recognition on a one-by-one basis. Cooperation among students (either within or across groups) is not required and is not, in fact, particularly encouraged. The group separation and the lack of opportunities for cooperation often extend beyond the classroom into clubs, sports, and other activities (for an application of the contact hypothesis to high school sports teams, see Brown, Brown, Jackson, Sellers, & Manuel, 2003).

The separation might be reduced and positive contacts increased by encouraging cooperative activities among members of different groups—for example, by imitating the plumbing "emergency" fabricated during the Robber's Cave experiment. One successful attempt to increase cooperation and positive contact was made using a cooperative learning technique called the **jigsaw method** (Aronson & Gonzalez, 1988).

In this experiment, the students in a fifth-grade class were divided into groups. A certain learning task was divided into separate parts, like a jigsaw puzzle. Researchers ensured that each jigsaw group included both dominant- and minority-group children. Each student in the jigsaw group was responsible for learning one part of the lesson and then teaching his or her piece to the other students. Everyone was tested on all the pieces, not just his or her own. Each study group needed to make sure that everyone had all the information necessary to pass the test. This goal could be achieved only through the cooperation of all members of the group.

Unlike typical classroom activities, the jigsaw method satisfies all the characteristics for a positive contact experience: Students of equal status are engaged in a cooperative project in which mutual interdependence is essential for the success of all. As Aronson and Gonzalez (1988) point out, the students do not need to be idealistic, altruistic, or motivated by a commitment to equality for this method to work. Rather, the students are motivated by pure self-interest; without the help of every member of their group, they cannot pass the test (Aronson & Gonzalez, 1988, p. 307). As we would expect under true equal status contact, the results of the jigsaw method included reductions in prejudice (Aronson & Gonzalez, 1988, p. 307; see also Aronson & Patnoe, 1997). For a website devoted to this teaching method, see www.jigsaw.org.

Limitations of the Contact Hypothesis. The contact hypothesis is supported by evidence from a variety of sources and nations (Pettigrew et al., 2011). In some cases, the reduction in prejudice may be situational; that is, the changed attitudes in one situation (e.g., the workplace) may not necessarily generalize to other situations (e.g., neighborhoods). Nonetheless, equal status cooperative contact does seem to reduce prejudice and discrimination. The true challenge may be to increase the number of intergroup contacts in societies, such as the United States, that remain so segregated in so many areas of social life.

QUESTIONS FOR REFLECTION

1. What experiences have you had that are consistent with the equal status contact hypothesis? Did these situations meet all four conditions of the hypothesis? How? Did they reduce prejudice? Did the reduction seem specific to that situation, or do you think it generalized to other situations?

2. Have you had intergroup contacts that *increased* your negative feelings about other groups? What features of these situations accounted for this increase in prejudice?

The **jigsaw method** is a learning technique that requires cooperation among students.

MODERN RACISM: THE NEW FACE OF PREJUDICE?

Many scholars are investigating the idea that, rather than declining, prejudice is simply changing forms. They have been researching new forms of prejudice, variously called symbolic, color-blind, or modern racism. Whatever the label, this form of prejudice is a more subtle, complex, and indirect way of expressing negative feelings toward minority groups and opposition to change in dominant–minority relations (see Bobo, 1988, 2001; Bobo, Charles, Krysan, & Simmons, 2012; Bonilla-Silva, 2001, 2006; Kinder & Sears, 1981; Kluegel & Smith, 1982; McConahy, 1986; Sears, 1988; for a review, see Quillian, 2006).

According to sociologist Eduardo Bonilla-Silva (2006), one of the leading researchers in this area, the new form of prejudice is often expressed in seemingly neutral language or "objective" terms. For example, the modern racist might attribute the underrepresentation of people of color in high-status positions to cultural rather than biological factors ("'they' don't emphasize education enough") or explain continuing residential and school segregation by the "natural" choices people make ("'they' would rather be with their own kind"). This kind of thinking rationalizes the status quo and permits dominant-group members to live in segregated neighborhoods and send their children to segregated schools without guilt or hesitation (Bonilla-Silva, 2006, p. 28). It obscures the myriad, not-so-subtle social forces that created segregated schools, neighborhoods, and other manifestations of racial inequality in the first place and maintain them in the present (e.g., see Satter, 2009).

Modern racism has been defined in a variety of ways, but it tends to be consistent with some tenets of the traditional assimilation perspective discussed in Chapter 2, especially human capital theory and the Protestant Ethic, the traditional American value system that stresses individual responsibility and the importance of hard work. Modern racists resent and even fear minorities (especially African Americans), but they express their prejudiced attitudes and emotions indirectly. Modern racists believe the following:

- They themselves are not prejudiced.
- Serious racial, ethnic, or religious discrimination in American society no longer exists.
- Demands for preferential treatment or affirmative action for minorities are unjustified. Minority groups (especially African Americans) have already gotten more than they deserve.
- Any remaining racial or ethnic inequality is the fault of members of the minority group, who simply are not working hard enough or who suffer from other, largely self-imposed, cultural disadvantages.

The last tenet is particularly important: Cultural explanations for minority-group inequality have largely replaced the

The Contact Hypothesis and European Prejudice

Much of the research on the contact hypothesis has been conducted in the United States. How will the theory fare in other societies? Rather well, according to sociologist Lauren McLaren (2003). Professor McLaren used data from representative samples of citizens drawn from 17 European societies to study anti-immigrant sentiment.

Like the United States, European nations have experienced a sharp increase in immigration over recent decades, and there is considerable concern about the impact of these newcomers. Some Europeans wish to exclude immigrants completely, while others want to help them find their way into their new societies. What social factors might explain these varying responses?

One possibility is that people with greater equal status contacts with immigrants will be more tolerant and less likely to support expulsion. Attitudes toward legal immigrants were measured on a 5-point scale: The higher the score on this scale, the more negative the view of immigrants. Equal status contact was measured by asking respondents if they had no, some, or many friends among immigrant groups (see Figure 3.8).

McLaren (2003) found significant differences in support for expulsion by the number of immigrant friends in 16 of the 17 nations tested (the exception was Greece). Some illustrative results for 10 of the 17 nations are shown in the graph. For each nation, the average score for the respondents with "no friends" was higher than the average score for respondents with "some friends," and the latter score was generally higher than the score for people with "many friends." This pattern is very (but not perfectly) consistent with the predictions of the equal status contact hypothesis. Our confidence in the equal status contact hypothesis is increased by its strong performance in a non-U.S. arena.

Questions to Consider

1. Why would interpersonal contact reduce prejudice? What processes are involved in causing people to rethink their feelings and beliefs?

2. These results show that, in some cases, greater contact does not lead to less support for exclusion. What would explain these "negative" results? What processes might be involved?

FIGURE 3.8 Support for Excluding Immigrants From European Society Based on Levels of Friendship With Immigrants in Selected Nations, 2003

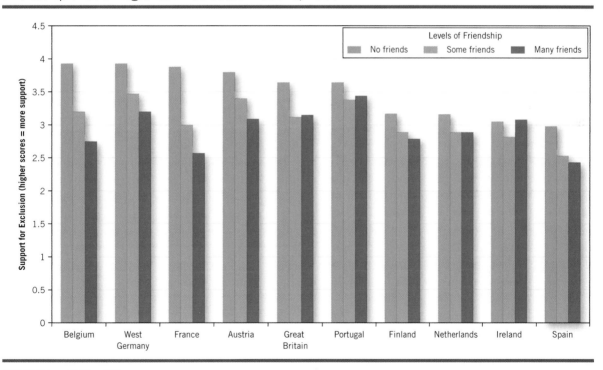

SOURCE: McLaren (2003, p. 921).

traditional biological or racial explanations. Modern racism sees group inequality as the result of the behavior or values of minority groups, not as the result of powerful historical processes and policies of the dominant group.

To illustrate the difference between traditional and modern racism, consider the results of a recent (2012) public opinion survey administered to a representative sample of Americans (National Opinion Research Council, 1972–2012). Respondents were asked to choose from among four explanations of why black people, on average, have "worse jobs, income, and housing than white people." Respondents could choose as many explanations as they wanted.

One explanation, consistent with traditional or overt anti-black prejudice, attributes racial inequality to the genetic or biological inferiority of African Americans ("The differences are mainly because blacks have less inborn ability to learn"). Less than 8% of the white respondents chose this explanation. A second explanation attributes continuing racial inequality to discrimination and a third to the lack of opportunity for education. Of white respondents, 32% chose the former and 43% chose the latter.

A fourth explanation, consistent with modern racism, attributes racial inequality to a lack of effort by African Americans ("The differences are because most blacks just don't have the motivation or willpower to pull themselves up out of poverty"). Of the white respondents, 49% chose this explanation, the most popular of the four.

Thus, the survey found support for the idea that racial inequality was the result of discrimination and lack of educational opportunities, views that are consistent with the analysis presented in this book, and relatively little support for traditional antiblack prejudice based on genetic or biological stereotypes.

However, the single most widely endorsed explanation was that the root of the problem of continuing racial inequality lies in the African American community, not the society as a whole. Modern racism asserts that African Americans could solve their problems themselves but are not willing to do so. Modern racism deflects attention away from centuries of oppression and continuing institutional discrimination in modern society. It stereotypes African Americans and other minority groups and encourages the expression of negative attitudes against them.

Researchers have consistently found that modern racism is correlated with opposition to policies and programs intended to reduce racial inequality (Bobo, 2001, p. 292; Bobo et al., 2012; Quillian, 2006). In the 2012 survey summarized earlier, for example, respondents who blamed continuing racial inequality on the lack of motivation or willpower of blacks—the "modern racists"—were the least likely to support affirmative action programs and were comparable to traditional racists (those who chose the "inborn ability" explanation) in their lack of support for government help for blacks (see Figure 3.9).

Figure 3.10 shows that the willingness to endorse traditional stereotypes is also associated with the explanation for racial inequality. Note the split in the graph: The traditional and modern racists (represented by the "ability" and "motivation" bars) are much more likely to endorse the perception that blacks are lazy and unintelligent than are respondents who believe that racial inequality is due to discrimination or lack of education. In fact, the similarly stereotypical views of traditional and modern racists support the idea that the latter form of prejudice is, at least in part, a more subtle manifestation of the former.

In the view of many researchers, modern racism has taken the place of traditional or overt prejudice. If this view is correct,

FIGURE 3.9 White Americans' Level of Support for Government Intervention Based on Explanation for Racial Inequality, 2012

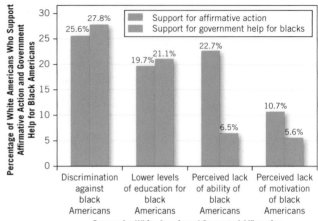

Reason for White Americans' Support of Affirmative Action and Government Help for Black Americans

the "report card" on progress in the reduction of racial hostility in the United States must be rather mixed. On one hand, we should not understate the importance of the fading of blatant, overt prejudice. On the other hand, we cannot ignore the evidence that antiblack prejudice has changed in form rather than declined in degree. Subtle and diffuse prejudice is probably preferable to the blunt and vicious variety, but it should not be mistaken for prejudice's demise. In fact, there is considerable reason to believe that "old-fashioned," blatant racism lives on and in some ways is thriving. This possibility is considered in the last section of this chapter.

LIMITATIONS

As many critics have pointed out, theories of modern racism seem to confound prejudice with political conservatism. One of the classic tenets of American conservatism, for example,

FIGURE 3.10 Belief in Stereotypical Views of Blacks by Explanation for Racial Inequality, 2012

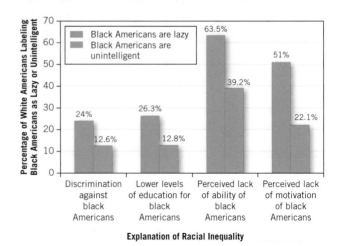

Explanation of Racial Inequality

is that government should be minimal in size and scope. So, in Figure 3.9, when people object to "government help for blacks," are they expressing prejudice against blacks or are they objecting to "big government"? The survey item is "double-barreled" and measures *both* kinds of beliefs, and it is difficult to isolate the prejudice component from political conservatism (Quillian, 2006, p. 313).

There are (at least) two possibilities here. If the item confounds prejudice with a certain political philosophy, then researchers need to do a better job of separating the two components. On the other hand, the problem may be that—at least for some people—racism has become so thoroughly intermixed with political conservatism that it can't (or shouldn't) be separated. The Current Debate introduced at the end of this chapter considers the latter possibility.

Stella and James Byrd mourn their son, the victim of a hate crime.

QUESTIONS FOR REFLECTION

What are the key differences between modern racism and traditional prejudice? Which would be the more challenging to identify and measure? Why?

HATE CRIMES

Hate crimes are attacks or other acts of intimidation motivated by the group membership of the victim or victims. Victims can be chosen randomly and are often strangers to their assailants: They are chosen as representatives of a group, not because of who they are as individuals.

These crimes are expressions of hatred or disdain, strong prejudice, and blatant racism, and they are not committed for profit or gain. In recent years, they have included assaults, arson attacks against black churches, vandalism of Jewish synagogues, cross burnings, nooses hung on the office doors of black university professors, and other acts of intimidation and harassment. Furthermore, a number of violent, openly racist extremist groups—skinheads, the Ku Klux Klan (KKK), White Aryan Resistance, the Minutemen, and Aryan Nations—have achieved widespread notoriety and maintain a prominent presence not only in some communities but also on the Internet.

Hate crimes include extreme violence and murder, such as the mass shooting at the Sikh temple we discussed in the beginning of this chapter. Other examples include two highly publicized incidents that occurred in the late 1990s. In one, James Byrd, a black man, was beaten by three white men and dragged for miles behind a pickup truck until he died. In the other, college student Mathew Shepard was beaten and tied to a fence post and left to die. His assailants selected him as a victim in part because they thought he was gay.

Do hate crimes contradict the notion that blatant prejudice is on the decline? Do they balance the shift to modern racism with an opposite shift to overt, violent racism? What causes these attacks? What are the implications?

As we will see in chapters to come, racial violence, hate crimes, and extremist racist groups are hardly new to the United States. Violence between whites and nonwhites began in the earliest days of this society (e.g., conflicts with Native Americans, the kidnapping and enslavement of Africans) and has continued, in one form or another, into the present. Contemporary racist attacks and hate crimes, in all their manifestations, have deep roots in the American past.

Also, racist and extremist groups are no strangers to American history. The KKK, for example, was founded almost 150 years ago, shortly after the Civil War, and has since played a significant role in local and state politics and in everyday life at various times and places—and not just in the South. During the turbulent 1920s, the KKK reached what was probably the height of its popularity. It had a membership in the millions and was said to openly control many U.S. senators, governors, and local politicians.

Are hate crimes increasing or decreasing? It's difficult to answer this question, though the FBI (Federal Bureau of Investigation) has been collecting and compiling information on hate crimes since the mid-1990s. Not all localities report these incidents or classify them in the same way, and, perhaps more important, not all hate crimes are reported by the victims. Thus, the actual volume of hate crimes may be many times greater than the "official" rate compiled by the FBI (for a recent analysis, see Fears, 2007).

Keeping these sharp limitations in mind, here is some of what is known. Figure 3.11 reports the breakdown of hate crimes in 2012, the most recent data available, and shows that the most common incidents were motivated by race. In the great majority of the racial cases (66.1%), blacks were the target group. Most of the religious incidents (59.7%) involved Jewish victims, and most of the antiethnic attacks (59.4%) were against Hispanics. The majority of the attacks motivated by the sexual orientation of the victim (54.6%) were directed against male homosexuals (FBI, 2013).

FIGURE 3.11 Breakdown of the 5,790 Single-Bias Hate Crime Incidents Reported in 2012

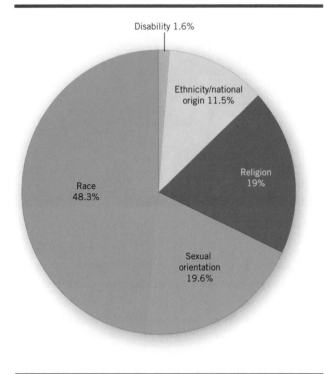

Disability 1.6%

Ethnicity/national origin 11.5%

Religion 19%

Race 48.3%

Sexual orientation 19.6%

SOURCE: FBI (2013).

The Southern Poverty Law Center tracks hate groups and hate crimes across the nation and estimates that there were about 1,007 hate groups (defined as groups that "have beliefs or practices that attack or malign an entire class of people, typically for their immutable characteristics") active in the United States in 2012 (Potok, 2013). These groups include the KKK, various skinhead and white-power groups, and black groups such as the Nation of Islam. Figure 3.12 shows that hate groups are spread across the nation and can be found in all states.

What causes hate crimes? According to some analysts, there are two main types. Many hate crimes are motivated by "thrill seeking" or the quest for excitement. These offenses are often committed by groups that search out random victims in gay bars, synagogues, or minority neighborhoods. The second common type of hate crime is "defensive": The perpetrators feel that their territory has been invaded or that members of the other group are threatening their resources or status. They strike to punish or expel the invaders, recover their rightful share of resources, or restore their prestige (Gerstenfeld, 2004, pp. 73–75).

One possible explanation for at least some hate crimes is that they are fueled by perceived threats, frustration and fear, and anger and scapegoating. Some white Americans believe that minority groups are threatening their position in the society and making unfair progress at their expense. They feel threatened by what they perceive to be an undeserved rise in the status of minority groups and fear that they may lose their jobs, incomes, neighborhoods, and schools to what they see as "inferior" groups.

Given the nature of American history, it is logical to suppose that the white Americans who feel most threatened and angriest are those toward the bottom of the stratification system: lower-class and working-class whites. It seems significant, for example, that the three murderers of James Byrd were unemployed ex-convicts with low levels of education and few prospects for economic success (at least in the conventional economy).

On a broader scale, there is evidence that males from these classes commit the bulk of hate crimes and form the primary membership of extremist racist groups (Schafer & Navarro, 2004). In the eyes of the perpetrators, attacks on minorities may represent attempts to preserve status and privilege. Some of these dynamics are illustrated in the second Narrative Portrait in this chapter.

The connection between social class and hate crimes might also reflect some broad structural changes in the economy. The United States has been shifting from an industrial, manufacturing economy to a postindustrial, information-processing economy since the mid-20th century. We will examine this transition in depth in later chapters, but here, we will note that this economic change has meant a decline in the supply of secure, well-paying, blue-collar jobs. Many manufacturing jobs have been lost to other nations with cheaper workforces; others have been lost to automation and mechanization.

The tensions resulting from the decline in desirable employment opportunities for people with lower levels of education have been exacerbated by industry downsizing, increasing inequality in the class structure, and rising costs of living. These economic forces have squeezed the middle and lower ranges of the dominant group's class system, creating considerable pressure and frustration, some of which may be expressed by scapegoating directed at immigrants and minority groups.

The idea that many hate crimes involve scapegoating is also supported by the spontaneous, unplanned, and highly emotional nature of these crimes. Consider how these themes of economic dislocation and scapegoating are illustrated in the murder of Vincent Chin, a frequently cited example of an American hate crime. Chin, who was Chinese American, was enjoying one last bachelor fling in a working-class Detroit neighborhood bar in June 1982 when he was confronted by two drunken autoworkers who blamed Japanese auto companies for their unemployment. Making no distinction between Chinese and Japanese (or American and Japanese), the autoworkers attacked and murdered Chin with a baseball bat. Apparently, any Asian would have served as a scapegoat for their resentment and anger (Levin & McDevitt, 1993, p. 58; see also U.S. Commission on Civil Rights, 1992, pp. 25–26).

FIGURE 3.12 Active Hate Groups in the United States, 2012

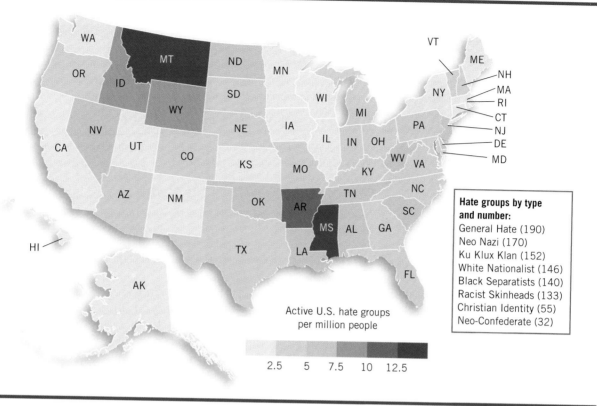

Active U.S. hate groups
per million people

Hate groups by type and number:
General Hate (190)
Neo Nazi (170)
Ku Klux Klan (152)
White Nationalist (146)
Black Separatists (140)
Racist Skinheads (133)
Christian Identity (55)
Neo-Confederate (32)

2.5   5   7.5   10   12.5

SOURCE: Reprinted with permission; originally appeared in *The Atlantic*: "The Geography of Hate" by Richard Florida, May 2011. Map by Zara Matheson, Martin Prosperity Institute. Data source: www.splcenter.org/get-information/hate-map.

Several studies also support the idea that hate crimes are motivated at least in part by scapegoating. One study found that at the state level, the rate of hate crimes increased as unemployment rose and as the percentage of the population between 15 and 19 years old increased. Also, the rate fell as average wages rose (Medoff, 1999, p. 970; see also Jacobs & Wood, 1999). Another study, based on county-level data gathered in South Carolina, found a correlation between white-on-black hate crimes and economic competition (D'Alessio, Stolzenberg, & Eitle, 2002). Finally, Arab Americans were victimized by a rash of violent attacks after September 11, 2001 (Ibish, 2003). These patterns are exactly what one would expect if the perpetrators of hate crimes tended to be young men motivated by a sense of threat and economic distress.

QUESTIONS FOR REFLECTION

1. Which theories of prejudice provide the most convincing explanations of hate crimes? Why?

2. Why are blacks victimized by hate crimes more than other groups?

3. What are some possible explanations for the regional distribution of hate groups displayed in Figure 3.12?

THE SOCIOLOGY OF PREJUDICE

We can summarize this chapter by considering the key points of the sociological approach to prejudice.

1. Prejudice has its origins in competition between groups, and it is more a result of that competition than a cause. It is created at a certain time in history to help mobilize feelings and emotional energy for competition and to rationalize the consignment of a group to minority status. It then is absorbed into the cultural heritage and is passed on to later generations as part of their taken-for-granted world, where it helps shape their perceptions and reinforce the very group inferiority that was its original cause.

2. Changes in the social environment, rising levels of education, or changing levels of intergroup contact will have relatively little impact on some types of prejudice. Prejudice that is caused by scapegoating or authoritarian personality structures, for example, is motivated by processes internal to the individual and may not respond to changes in the environment. It may be difficult to reduce these types of prejudice and impossible to eliminate them altogether. A more realistic goal might be to discourage their open expression. The greater the extent to

NARRATIVE PORTRAIT

The Dynamics of Racial Hatred

An expression of racial hatred and intimidation.

Brian Patterson was the product of a broken home and a racist father. He fell in with some racist groups and was involved in a variety of hate crimes. At the lowest point in his life, he was assisted by a black man, a complete stranger to him, and managed to turn his life around.

THE MAKING (AND UNMAKING) OF A SKINHEAD

Interview by Robert Steinback

Where were you reared and where did this story start?

I was born in...Mississippi....My dad was racist, very racist. All of his friends and everybody that I was around was racist....He was in the Klan. So was my grandfather and pretty much everybody I grew up knowing. [My father]...was violent. He liked to fight.

So violence was a part of life?

Yeah, it was routine. We were raised to be tough....Around age 9, me and my brother and my mother moved to Pensacola, Florida....I wound up going back to Tupelo at 11. I went and lived with my father until I was 15. That's where [the hate] really took root. During that time I really got indoctrinated. All of the kids in the area were indoctrinated into that way of thinking. We went to Klan rallies, and we loved it. We thought it was great....

These Klan rallies were just like campfire parties to you?

Exactly....I think they took the idea from Hitler Youth-type shit, you know. Get them while they're young....[Then], at 15,...I wound up back in Florida....So I'm basically on the streets from 15 to 18. You got the punk rock scene and the skinhead scene and that's where I wound up....We had National White Resistance and WAR, White Aryan Resistance. The Klan was real big there, too....I had fallen in with a violent group of skinheads. There were things that I did that I'm not proud of....There was a lot of fighting, a lot of beatings.

Beatings of strangers?

Mostly gang confrontations....You know, trying to keep blacks out of the neighborhoods that were predominantly white....

But then you found yourself alone. How did that happen?

I...basically wound up by myself and stuck on Pensacola Beach. They left me there....We got into it, and they left me....I'm footin' it. No money, no food....I'm just kind of drifting around...getting a little help...at the shelter. I was afraid to stay in the city....I went to the country....I got no food; I got no money; it's cold. I got no winter clothes, no blanket. So I'm sleeping in this patch of woods by this lodge....

How close to the edge were you that night?

I was thinking heavy thoughts by that time, brother. I was thinking, "I'm going to do whatever it takes from this point on to feed myself....The next motherfucker I come across is going to get it."...That was like the crossroads right there.

What happened when morning arrived?

I wake up, and I smell food. And there's a blanket on me....I look up, and there's this black guy....He's got a fire built. This dude has done throwed a blanket on me. He sees my bald head. He sees my red suspenders and my red shoelaces in my boots and my Nazi patch. This dude sees this. He still goes back to his house and gets a blanket and some food and brings it back to me....But I wake up and he's sitting there cooking me something to eat....It was his kindness [that won me over]. It was the way this man helped me despite what I was. It probably saved my life. Had he not been there, there's no telling what I would have done....

SOURCE: Southern Poverty Law Center (2010).

Questions to Consider

What ideas or theories about prejudice presented in this chapter does this passage illustrate? How does prejudice begin? How is it sustained? How can it be changed?

---

which culture, authority figures, and social situations discourage prejudice, the more likely that even people with strong personality needs for prejudice can be turned into prejudiced nondiscriminators, or "timid bigots" (see Table 3.1).

3. Culture-based or "traditional" prejudice can be just as extreme as personality-based prejudice. This type of prejudice differs not in intensity but in the degree to which it is resistant to change. A person who learns prejudice because he or she was socialized in racist environments should be more open to change than authoritarian personalities and more responsive to education and contact with members of other groups. To create more "all-weather liberals," situations that encourage or reward prejudice and discrimination must be minimized, and public opinion, the views of community and societal leaders, and the legal code must all promote tolerance. The reduction in overt prejudice over the past five or six decades, documented in Figure 3.5, is probably mainly due to a decline in traditional prejudice.

4. Intergroup conflict produces vicious, even lethal, prejudice and discrimination, but the problems here are inequality and access to resources and opportunity, not prejudice. Group

Library of Congress Prints and Photographs Division

conflicts and the prejudices they stimulate will continue as long as society is stratified along the lines of race, ethnicity, religion, and gender. Efforts to decrease hostile attitudes without also reducing inequality and exploitative relationships treat the symptoms rather than the disease.

5. Reducing prejudice will not necessarily change the situation of minority groups. The fundamental problems of minority-group status are inequality and systems of institutional discrimination and privilege that sustain the advantages of dominant groups. Prejudice is a problem, but it is not the only problem. Reducing prejudice will not, by itself, eliminate minority-group poverty or unemployment, or end institutional discrimination in schools or in the criminal justice system.

6. Individual prejudice and discrimination are not the same as racism and institutional discrimination (see Chapter 1),

and any one of these variables can change independently of the others. Thus, we should not confuse the recent reductions in overt, traditional prejudice with the resolution of American minority-group problems. Prejudice is only part of the problem and, in many ways, not the most important part.

These points are reflected in some key trends of the past several decades: Ethnic and racial inequalities persist (and may be increasing in some ways) despite the declines in overt prejudice. The verbal rejection of extreme or overt prejudice has been replaced by the subtleties of modern racism, combined with an unwillingness to examine the social, political, and economic forces that sustain minority-group inequality and institutional discrimination. Unless there are significant changes in the structure of the economy and the distribution of opportunities, we may have reached the limits of tolerance in America.

SUMMARY

This summary is organized around the Learning Objectives stated at the beginning of this chapter.

 3.1 Define and explain prejudice and discrimination.

Prejudice is the tendency to think and feel negatively about the members of other groups. Discrimination refers to negative acts motivated by a person's group membership. Prejudice and discrimination commonly occur together, but they are distinct concepts and do not necessarily cause each other.

 3.2 Summarize and explain the different forms and dimensions of prejudice, and explain the theories and research related to each.

Prejudice takes multiple forms and has a variety of causes, and no one theory accounts for all forms of prejudice. Some affective forms of prejudice are reactions to frustrations (scapegoating), and others are fundamental parts of a person's makeup (authoritarian personality). Stereotypes (the cognitive dimension) are related to the status of the minority group in the larger society. American stereotypes are plentiful and long lasting, although perhaps somewhat muted in their expression in recent decades. Some stereotypes are alleged to apply to entire groups, but others have strong gender and class dimensions.

 3.3 Summarize and explain the sociology of prejudice, including the role of group competition and how prejudice persists through time.

Prejudice can almost always be traced to a particular moment in history that featured a competition between groups over scarce resources. Prejudice can mobilize energy for the

struggle and justify the treatment of the group that loses the competition. Once created, prejudice becomes a part of the culture of the dominant group, reinforced by the discriminatory treatment of the minority group and passed on to succeeding generations as part of their "taken-for-granted" world. Also, prejudice can be highly situational.

 3.4 Describe and assess the seeming decline in "traditional" prejudice, and define and explain "modern" racism (is it replacing "traditional" prejudice?).

Traditional, overt, blatant prejudice is less commonly expressed in modern U.S. society, and its decline can be measured and documented with public opinion surveys. Some of the possible reasons for this decline include rising levels of education and intergroup contact.

Rather than declining, many analysts believe that prejudice is simply changing form. Modern racism is more subtle and indirect in its expression, and more likely to attribute continuing minority-group inequality to cultural rather than biological or genetic factors. However, so-called modern racists tend to be opposed to racial and ethnic change and fearful of and threatened by minority groups.

 3.5 Describe the volume and nature of modern hate crimes, and explain some possible reasons for their persistence.

Hate crimes and hate groups have always been a part of U.S. society and continue into the present. Hate crimes can be motivated by the search for "excitement" or by the felt need to defend a territory or status. They are commonly associated with lower-status, less-educated males who have limited prospects for success in the conventional economy.

KEY TERMS

authoritarian
personality 71

equal status contact
hypothesis 86

jigsaw method 88

modern racism 84

scapegoat
hypothesis 71

selective
perception 72

social distance 79

socialization 80

split labor
market theory 77

vicious cycle 78

REVIEW QUESTIONS

1. Distinguish between prejudice and discrimination, and explain clear examples of both. Explain the different dimensions of prejudice and differentiate between them. What are stereotypes? What forms do stereotypes take? How are stereotypes formed and maintained?

2. Explain the various causes of prejudice, including the theoretical perspectives presented in this chapter. Explain and evaluate the research evidence that has been presented. Which theories seem most credible in terms of evidence? Why? Try to think of an incident—from your own experience, the news, or popular culture—that illustrates each theory.

3. How does prejudice persist through time? What are children taught about other groups? What were you taught by your parents? How did this compare with what you learned from friends? How would your socialization experience have changed if you had been raised in another group? Have your views been changed by education or intergroup contact? How?

4. Is prejudice really decreasing, or are the negative emotions and attitudes changing into modern racism? What evidence is most persuasive in leading you to your conclusion? Why?

5. Interpret the information presented in Figure 3.9. Does this graph support the notion that modern racism is an important cause of resistance to racial change? How?

6. What forms of prejudice are involved in hate crimes? What are the roles of group competition and scapegoating? Develop an explanation for hate crimes based on these connections.

STUDENT STUDY SITE

Sharpen your skills with SAGE edge at edge.sagepub.com/healey7e

SAGE edge for students provides a personalized approach to help you accomplish your coursework goals in an easy-to-use learning environment.

The following resources are available at SAGE edge:

Current Debates: Modern Racism on Television?

How common are expressions of modern racism on television? How often are minority groups blamed for their own victimization? How do the media reflect and reinforce modern racism in the larger society?

On our website you will find an overview of the topic, the clashing points of view, and some questions to consider as you analyze the material.

Public Sociology Assignments

Public Sociology Assignments provide opportunities for students to address directly and personally some of the issues raised in this text.

The first two public sociology assignments on our website will lead students to confront diversity in their community. In the first assignment, you will investigate your hometown to see if you can document increases in racial and ethnic diversity consistent with Figure 1.1. In the second assignment, you will study graffiti: Does it express stereotypes and prejudice? What does it reflect about local group hierarchies?

Contributed by Linda M. Waldron

Internet Research Project

For the Internet Research Project for this chapter, you will investigate the idea that prejudice is a largely unconscious set of feelings that, nonetheless, greatly affect thoughts and actions. You will test your own "implicit" prejudice and review some of the information that has been amassed on the subject. Your investigation will be guided by a series of questions, and your instructor may ask you to discuss the issues in small groups.

For Further Reading

Please see our website for an annotated list of important works related to this chapter.

CHAPTER-OPENING TIMELINE PHOTO CREDITS

1857: Library of Congress Prints and Photographs Division

1866: Library of Congress Prints and Photographs Division

1880: Library of Congress Prints and Photographs Division

1896: Library of Congress Prints and Photographs Division

1942: Library of Congress Prints and Photographs Division

1943: Library of Congress Prints and Photographs Division

2004: © Saul Loeb/epa/Corbis

2012: NY Daily News/Getty Images

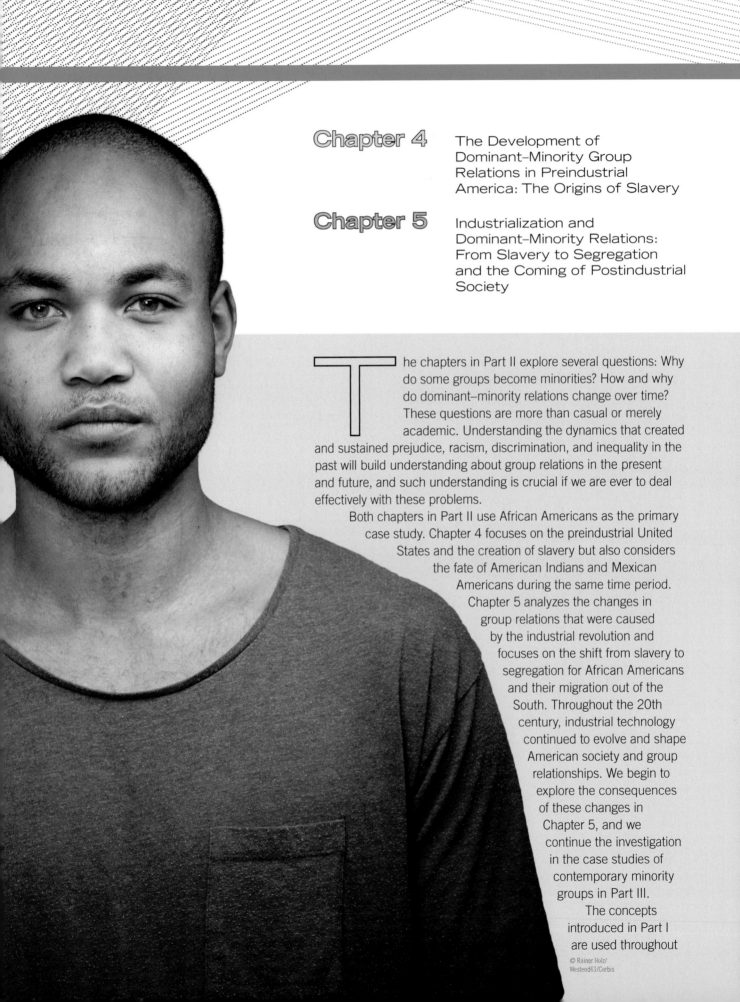

Chapter 4 The Development of Dominant–Minority Group Relations in Preindustrial America: The Origins of Slavery

Chapter 5 Industrialization and Dominant–Minority Relations: From Slavery to Segregation and the Coming of Postindustrial Society

The chapters in Part II explore several questions: Why do some groups become minorities? How and why do dominant–minority relations change over time? These questions are more than casual or merely academic. Understanding the dynamics that created and sustained prejudice, racism, discrimination, and inequality in the past will build understanding about group relations in the present and future, and such understanding is crucial if we are ever to deal effectively with these problems.

Both chapters in Part II use African Americans as the primary case study. Chapter 4 focuses on the preindustrial United States and the creation of slavery but also considers the fate of American Indians and Mexican Americans during the same time period. Chapter 5 analyzes the changes in group relations that were caused by the industrial revolution and focuses on the shift from slavery to segregation for African Americans and their migration out of the South. Throughout the 20th century, industrial technology continued to evolve and shape American society and group relationships. We begin to explore the consequences of these changes in Chapter 5, and we continue the investigation in the case studies of contemporary minority groups in Part III.

The concepts introduced in Part I are used throughout

PART ii

THE EVOLUTION OF DOMINANT–MINORITY RELATIONS IN THE UNITED STATES

Chapters 4 and 5, and some very important new concepts and theories are introduced as well. By the end of Part II, you will be familiar with virtually the entire conceptual framework that will guide us through the remainder of this text.

A Note on the Morality and the History of Minority Relations in America: Guilt, Blame, Understanding, and Communication

Very often, when people confront the kind of material presented in the next few chapters, they react on a personal level. Some might feel a sense of guilt for America's less-than-wholesome history of group relations. Others might respond with anger about the injustice and unfairness that remains in American society. Still others might respond with denial or indifference and might argue that the events discussed in Chapters 4 and 5 are so distant in time that they have no importance or meaning today.

These reactions—guilt, anger, denial, and indifference—are common, and we ask you to consider them. First, the awful things we will discuss did happen, and they were done largely by members of a particular racial and ethnic group: white Europeans and their descendants in America. No amount of denial, distancing, or disassociation can make these facts go away. African Americans, American Indians, Mexican Americans, and other groups were victims, and they paid a terrible price for the early growth and success of white American society.

Second, the successful domination and exploitation of these groups was made easier by the cooperation of members of each of the minority groups. The slave trade relied on agents and slavers who were black Africans, some American Indians aided and abetted the cause of white society, and some Mexicans helped cheat other

Mexicans. There is plenty of guilt to go around, and European Americans do not have a monopoly on greed, bigotry, or viciousness. Indeed, some white Southerners opposed slavery and fought for the abolition of the "peculiar institution." Many of the ideas and values on which the United States was founded (justice, equality, liberty) had their origins in European intellectual traditions, and minority-group protest has often involved little more than insisting that the nation live up to these ideals. Segments of the white community were appalled at the treatment of American Indians and Mexicans. Some members of the dominant group devoted (and sometimes gave) their lives to end oppression, bigotry, and racial stratification.

Our point is to urge you to avoid, insofar as is possible, a "good-guy/bad-guy" approach to this subject matter. Guilt, anger, denial, and indifference are common reactions to this material, but these emotions do little to advance understanding, and often they impede communication between members of different groups. We believe that an understanding of America's racial past is vitally important for understanding the present. Historical background provides a perspective for viewing the present and allows us to identify important concepts and principles that we can use to disentangle the intergroup complexities surrounding us.

The goal of the chapters to come is not to make you feel any particular emotion. We will try to present the often ugly facts neutrally and without extraneous editorializing. As scholars, your goal should be to absorb the material, understand the principles, and apply them to your own life and the society around you—not to indulge yourself in elaborate moral denunciations of American society, develop apologies for the past, or deny the realities of what happened. By dealing objectively with this material, we can begin to liberate our perspectives and build an understanding of the realities of American society and American minority groups.

4

THE DEVELOPMENT OF DOMINANT-MINORITY GROUP RELATIONS IN PREINDUSTRIAL AMERICA

The Origins of Slavery

LOC

timeline

1788
The U.S. Constitution is officially adopted and includes the "three-fifths" clause by which each slave is considered three-fifths of a person for the purposes of congressional representation and tax apportionment.

1641
Massachusetts becomes the first colony to legalize slavery.

1663
In Gloucester County, Virginia, the first documented slave rebellion in the colonies takes place.

1694
Rice cultivation is introduced into Carolina. Slave importation increases dramatically.

1615   1635   1655   1675   1695   1715   1735

1619
Approximately 20 Africans arrive in Virginia, the first Africans in the British North American colonies.

1636
Colonial North America's slave trade begins when the first American slave carrier, *Desire,* is built and launched in Massachusetts.

1676
In Virginia, black slaves and black and white indentured servants band together to participate in Bacon's Rebellion.

1705
The Virginia Slave Code defines all slaves as real estate, acquits masters who kill slaves during punishment, forbids slaves and free colored peoples from physically assaulting white persons, and denies slaves the right to bear arms or move abroad without written permission.

LOC

Wikipedia

The year was 1781, and the Zong, with its cargo of 471 African slaves, had been sailing for nearly three months. The ship was approaching its destination in the New World, but water was running short and disease had broken out. To deal with the dilemma, the captain ordered 54 of the sickest slaves to be chained together and thrown overboard, reasoning that they would die soon anyway. In the next two days, another 78 slaves were cast over the sides of the ship and drowned. The captain knew that the ship's insurance policy would cover losses due to drowning but not those due to "natural causes."[1]

The slave trade that brought Africans to North America was a business, subject to the calculation of profit and loss and covered by the

---

[1]This account is based on materials from a PBS documentary, *Africans in America*. See www.pbs.org/wgbh/aia/part1/1h280 .html.

LEARNING OBJECTIVES

By the end of this chapter, you will be able to do the following:

4.1 Explain the two themes stated at the beginning of the chapter.

4.2 Explain the political, economic, and social forces that led to the creation of slavery in British America.

4.3 Explain the importance of the contact situation and the relevance of the Noel and Blauner hypotheses for the development of slavery in colonial America.

4.4 Apply the concepts of paternalism, power, inequality, discrimination, prejudice and racism, and assimilation to the American system of slavery.

4.5 Explain the dynamics of gender relations under American slavery.

4.6 Apply the Noel and Blauner hypotheses and other concepts to the creation of minority-group status for American Indians and Mexican Americans.

4.7 Compare and contrast the three contact situations analyzed in this chapter. How do they differ? What are the implications of these different contact situations for relations in the present?

Cincinnati Art Museum

National Portrait Gallery

1804
The Underground Railroad is officially established in Pennsylvania.

1850
A second fugitive slave law strengthens the rights of slave owners and threatens the rights of free blacks.

1859
A group of whites and blacks, led by John Brown, conducts an unsuccessful raid on Harper's Ferry, Virginia, in an attempt to undermine slavery in the South.

1755   1775   1795   1815   1835   1855   1875   1895

1793
The first fugitive slave law is passed, allowing slave owners to cross state lines in the pursuit of fugitives and making it a penal offense to assist runaway slaves.

1800
Congress prohibits U.S. citizens from exporting slaves.

1808
Importing slaves is prohibited.

1831
Nat Turner, an enslaved Baptist preacher, leads a violent rebellion in Southampton, Virginia. At least 57 whites are killed.

1857
The Dred Scott decision mandates that African Americans cannot be citizens.

1860
The slave population is now nearly four million, making the ratio of free to enslaved Americans approximately 7:1.

1861
Harriet Jacobs's *Incidents in the Life of a Slave Girl* is the first published autobiography of an African American woman.

HORRID MASSACRE IN VIRGINIA

LOC

Wikipedia

Wikipedia

same insurance companies that backed farmers, bankers, and merchants. To the captain and owners of the *Zong*, and to others involved in the slave trade, the 132 unfortunates who were thrown over the rails were just cargo, cyphers in a ledger book.

What lay behind this cold, businesslike approach to trafficking in human beings? Was the same calculating eye for profit and efficiency behind the decision to use Africa as a source for slaves? How did the slave trade get linked to the British colonies that became the United States? How could a nation that, from its earliest days, valued liberty and freedom be founded on slavery? •

From the first settlements in the 1600s until the 19th century, most people living in what was to become the United States relied directly on farming for food, shelter, and other necessities of life. In an agricultural society, land and labor are central concerns, and the struggle to control these resources led directly to the creation of minority-group status for three groups: African Americans, American Indians, and Mexican Americans. Why did the colonists create slavery? Why were Africans enslaved but not American Indians or Europeans? Why did Native Americans lose their land and most of their population by the 1890s? How did the Mexican population in the Southwest become "Mexican Americans"? How did the experience of becoming a subordinated minority group vary by gender?

In this chapter, the concepts introduced in Part I will be used to answer these questions. Some new ideas and theories will also be introduced, and by the end of the chapter, we will have developed a theoretical model of the process that leads to the creation of a minority group. The establishment of black slavery in colonial America will be used to illustrate the process of minority-group creation. We will also consider the subordination of American Indians and Mexican Americans—two more historical events of great significance—as additional case studies. We will follow the experiences of African Americans through the days of segregation (Chapter 5) and into the contemporary era (Chapter 6). The story of the development of minority-group status for Native Americans and Mexican Americans will be picked up again in Chapters 7 and 8, respectively.

Two broad themes underlie this chapter and, indeed, the remainder of the text:

1. The nature of dominant–minority group relations at any point in time is largely a function of the characteristics of the society as a whole. The situation of a minority group will reflect the realities of everyday social life and particularly the subsistence technology (the means by which the society satisfies basic needs, such as food and shelter). As explained by Gerhard Lenski (see Chapter 1), the subsistence technology of a society acts as a

foundation, shaping and affecting every other aspect of the social structure, including minority-group relations.

2. The contact situation—the conditions under which groups first come together—is the single most significant factor in the creation of minority-group status. The nature of the contact situation has long-lasting consequences for the minority group and the extent of racial or ethnic stratification, the levels of racism and prejudice, the possibilities for assimilation and pluralism, and virtually every other aspect of the dominant–minority relationship.

THE ORIGINS OF SLAVERY IN AMERICA

By the early 1600s, the Spanish had conquered much of Central and South America, and the influx of gold, silver, and other riches from the New World had made Spain a powerful nation. Following Spain's lead, England proceeded to establish its presence in the Western Hemisphere, but its efforts at colonization were more modest than those of Spain. By the early 1600s, only two small colonies had been established: Plymouth, settled by pious Protestant families, and Jamestown, populated primarily by males seeking their fortunes.

By 1619, the British colony at Jamestown, Virginia, had survived for more than a decade. The residents of the settlement had fought with the local natives and struggled continuously to eke out a living from the land. Starvation, disease, and death were frequent visitors, and the future of the enterprise continued to be in doubt.

In August of that year, a Dutch ship arrived. The master of the ship needed provisions and offered to trade his only cargo: about 20 black Africans. Many of the details of this transaction have been lost, and we probably will never know exactly how these people came to be chained in the hold of a ship. Regardless, this brief episode was a landmark event in the

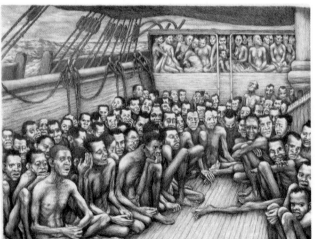

Slaves were kidnapped in Africa and transported to provide labor in the New World. The "Middle Passage" across the Atlantic could take months.

FIGURE 4.1 Slave Trade Routes, 1518–1850

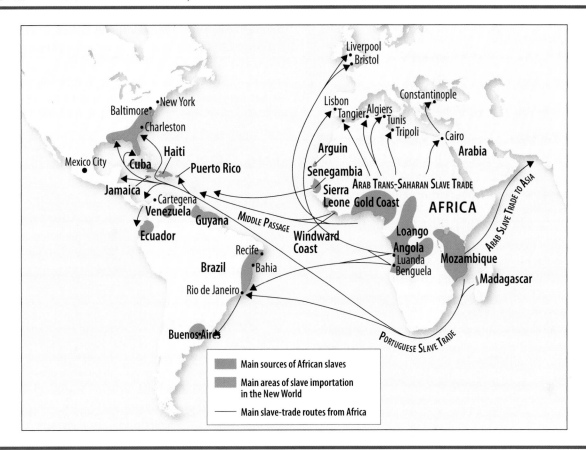

Main sources of African slaves

Main areas of slave importation
in the New World

Main slave-trade routes from Africa

SOURCE: From Williams. *Macmillan Encyclopedia of World Slavery*, 1E. © 1998 Gale, a part of Cengage Learning, Inc. Reproduced by permission. www.cengage.com/permissions.

formation of what would become the United States. In combination with the strained relations between the English settlers and American Indians, the presence of these first few Africans raised an issue that never has been fully resolved: How should different groups in this society relate to one another?

The colonists at Jamestown had no ready answer. In 1619, England and its colonies did not practice slavery, so these first Africans were probably incorporated into colonial society as **indentured servants**, contract laborers who are obligated to serve a master for a specific number of years. At the end of the indenture, or contract, the servant became a free citizen. The colonies depended heavily on indentured servants from the British Isles for labor, and this status apparently provided a convenient way of defining the newcomers from Africa, who, after all, had been treated as commodities and exchanged for food and water (see Figure 4.1 for a map of slave trade from Africa).

The position of African indentured servants in the colonies remained ambiguous for several decades. American slavery evolved gradually and in small steps; in fact, there was little demand for African labor during the years following 1619. By 1625, there were still only 23 Africans in Virginia, and that number had increased to perhaps 300 by midcentury (Franklin & Moss, 1994, p. 57). In the decades before the dawn of slavery, we know that some African indentured servants did become free citizens. Some became successful farmers and landowners

and, like their white neighbors, purchased African and white indentured servants themselves (Smedley, 2007, p. 104). By the 1650s, however, many African Americans (and their offspring) were being treated as the property of others or, in other words, as slaves (Morgan, 1975, p. 154).

It was not until the 1660s that the first laws defining slavery were enacted. In the century that followed, hundreds of additional laws were passed to clarify and formalize the status of Africans in colonial America. By the 1750s, slavery had been clearly defined in law and in custom, and the idea that a person could own another person—not just the labor or the energy or the work of a person, but the actual person—had been thoroughly institutionalized.

What caused slavery? The gradual evolution of and low demand for indentured servants from Africa suggest that slavery was not somehow inevitable or preordained. Why did the colonists deliberately create this repressive system? Why did they reach out all the way to Africa for their slaves? If they wanted to create a slave system, why didn't they enslave the American Indians nearby or the white indentured servants already present in the colonies?

Indentured servants are contract laborers who are obligated to serve a particular master for a specified length of time.

THE LABOR SUPPLY PROBLEM

American colonists of the 1600s saw slavery as a solution to several problems they faced. The business of the colonies was agriculture, and farm work at this time was labor-intensive, performed almost entirely by hand. The industrial revolution (see Chapter 2) was two centuries in the future, and there were few machines or labor-saving devices available to ease the everyday burden of work. A successful harvest depended largely on human effort.

As colonial society grew and developed, a specific form of agricultural production began to emerge. The **plantation system** was based on cultivating and exporting crops such as sugar, tobacco, and rice grown on large tracts of land using a large, cheap labor force. Profit margins tended to be small, so planters sought to stabilize their incomes by keeping the costs of production as low as possible. Profits in the labor-intensive plantation system could be maximized if a large, disciplined, and cheap workforce could be maintained by the landowners (Curtin, 1990; Morgan, 1975).

At about the same time as the plantation system began to emerge, the supply of white indentured servants from the British Isles began to dwindle. Furthermore, the white indentured servants who did come to the colonies had to be released from their indenture every few years. Land was available, and these newly freed citizens tended to strike out on their own. Thus, landowners who relied on white indentured servants had to deal with high turnover rates in their workforces and faced a continually uncertain supply of labor.

Attempts to solve the labor supply problem by using American Indians failed. The tribes closest to the colonies were sometimes exploited for manpower. By the time the plantation system had evolved, however, the local tribes had dwindled in numbers as a result of warfare and, especially, disease. Other Indian nations across the continent retained enough power to resist enslavement, and it was relatively easy for American Indians to escape back to their kinfolk.

This left black Africans as a potential source of manpower. The slave trade from Africa to the Spanish and Portuguese colonies of South America had been established in the 1500s and could be expanded to fill the needs of the British colonies as well. The colonists came to see slaves imported from Africa as

the most logical, cost-effective way to solve their vexing shortage of labor. The colonists created slavery to cultivate their lands and generate profits, status, and success. The paradox at the core of U.S. society had been established: The construction of a social system devoted to freedom and individual liberty in the New World "was made possible only by the revival of an institution of naked tyranny foresworn for centuries in the Old" (Lacy, 1972, p. 22).

THE CONTACT SITUATION

The conditions under which groups first come into contact determine the immediate fate of the minority group and shape intergroup relations for years to come. We discussed the role of group competition in creating prejudice in Chapter 3. Here, we expand some of these ideas by introducing two theories that will serve as analytical guides in understanding the contact situation.

The Noel Hypothesis. Sociologist Donald Noel (1968) identified three features of the contact situation that in combination lead to some form of inequality between groups. The Noel hypothesis states: *If two or more groups come together in a contact situation characterized by ethnocentrism, competition, and a differential in power, then some form of racial or ethnic stratification will result* (p. 163). If the contact situation has all three characteristics, some dominant–minority group structure will be created.

Noel's first characteristic, **ethnocentrism**, is the tendency to judge other groups, societies, or lifestyles by the standards of one's own culture. Ethnocentrism is probably a universal component of human society, and some degree of ethnocentrism is essential to the maintenance of social solidarity and cohesion. Without some minimal level of pride in and loyalty to one's own society and cultural traditions, there would be no particular reason to observe the norms and laws, honor the sacred symbols, or cooperate with others in doing the daily work of society.

Regardless of its importance, ethnocentrism can have negative consequences. At its worst, it can lead to the view that other cultures and peoples are not just different but inferior. At the very least, ethnocentrism creates a social boundary line that members of the groups involved will recognize and observe. When ethnocentrism exists in any degree, people will tend to sort themselves out along group lines and identify characteristics that differentiate "us" from "them."

Noel's second factor, **competition**, is a struggle over a scarce commodity. As we saw in Chapter 3, competition between groups often leads to harsh negative feelings (prejudice) and hostile actions (discrimination). In competitive contact situations, the victorious group becomes the dominant group and the losers become the minority group. The competition may center on land, labor, jobs, housing, educational opportunities, political office, or anything else that is mutually desired by both groups or that one group has and the other group wants.

The **plantation system** is a form of labor-intensive agriculture that requires large tracts of land and a large, highly controlled labor force. This was the dominant form of agricultural production in the American South before the Civil War.

Ethnocentrism is the tendency to judge other groups by the standards of one's own group, culture, or society.

Competition is a struggle between two or more parties for control of some scarce resource.

FIGURE 4.2 A Model of the Establishment of Minority-Group Status

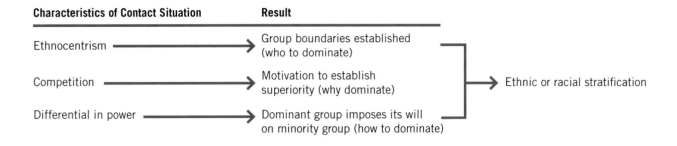

Competition provides the eventual dominant group with the motivation to establish superiority. The dominant group serves its own interests by ending the competition and exploiting, controlling, eliminating, or otherwise dominating the minority group.

The third feature of the contact situation is a **differential in power** between the groups. Power, as you recall from Chapter 1, is the ability of a group to achieve its goals even in the face of opposition from other groups. The amount of power a group commands is a function of three factors:

- First, the size of the group can make a difference, and all other things being equal, larger groups are more powerful.
- Second, in addition to raw numbers, the degree of organization, discipline, and quality of group leadership can make a difference in a group's ability to pursue its goals.
- The third component of power is resources: anything that can be used to help the group achieve its goals. Depending on the context, resources might include anything from land to information to money. The greater the number and variety of resources at the group's disposal, the greater that group's potential ability to dominate other groups.

Thus, a larger, better organized group with more resources at its disposal will generally be able to impose its will on smaller, less well-organized groups with fewer resources. The Noel hypothesis is diagrammed in Figure 4.2.

Note the respective functions of each of the three factors in shaping the contact situation and the emergence of inequality. If ethnocentrism is present, the groups will recognize their differences and maintain their boundaries. If competition is also present, the group that eventually dominates will attempt to maximize its share of scarce commodities by controlling or subordinating the group that eventually becomes the "minority" group. The differential in power allows the dominant group to succeed in establishing a superior position.

Ethnocentrism tells the dominant group *whom* to dominate, competition tells the dominant group *why* it should establish a structure of dominance, and power is *how* the dominant group imposes its will on the minority group.

The Noel hypothesis can be applied to the creation of minority groups in a variety of situations. We will also use the model to analyze changes in dominant–minority structures over time.

The Blauner Hypothesis. The contact situation also has been analyzed by sociologist Robert Blauner (1972), in his book *Racial Oppression in America*. Blauner identifies two different initial relationships—colonization and immigration—and hypothesizes that *minority groups created by colonization will experience more intense prejudice, racism, and discrimination than those created by immigration. Furthermore, the disadvantaged status of colonized groups will persist longer and be more difficult to overcome than the disadvantaged status faced by groups created by immigration.*

Colonized minority groups, such as African Americans, are forced into minority status by the superior military and political power of the dominant group. At the time of contact with the dominant group, colonized groups are subjected to massive inequalities and attacks on their cultures. They are assigned to positions, such as slave status, from which any form of assimilation is extremely difficult and perhaps even forbidden by the dominant group. Frequently, members of the minority group are identified by highly visible racial or physical characteristics that maintain and reinforce the oppressive system. Thus, minority groups created by colonization experience harsher and more persistent rejection and oppression than do groups created by immigration.

Immigrant minority groups are at least in part voluntary participants in the host society. That is, although the decision

---

A **differential in power** is any difference between groups in their ability to achieve their goals.

Colonized minority groups are created by conquest or colonization by the dominant group.

Immigrant minority groups are created by their more or less voluntary movement into the territory of the dominant group.

---

to immigrate may be motivated by extreme pressures, such as famine or political persecution, immigrant groups have at least some control over their destinations and their positions in the host society. As a result, they do not occupy positions that are as markedly inferior as those of colonized groups. They retain enough internal organization and resources to pursue their own self-interests, and they commonly experience more rapid acceptance and easier movement to equality. The boundaries between groups are not so rigidly maintained, especially when the groups are racially similar. In discussing European immigrant groups, for example, Blauner (1972) states that entering into American society

> involved a degree of choice and self-direction that was for the most part denied to people of color. Voluntary immigration made it more likely that . . . European . . . ethnic groups would identify with America and see the host culture as a positive opportunity. (p. 56)

Acculturation and, particularly, integration were significantly more possible for European immigrant groups than for the groups formed under conquest or colonization.

Blauner (1972) stresses that the initial differences between colonized and immigrant minority groups have consequences that persist long after the original contact. For example, based on measures of equality—or integration into the secondary sector, the second step in Gordon's model of assimilation (see Chapter 2)—such as average income, years of education, and unemployment rate, descendants of European immigrants are equal with national norms today (see Chapter 2 for specific data). In contrast, descendants of colonized and conquered groups (e.g., African Americans) are, on the average, below the national norms on virtually all measures of equality and integration (see Chapters 6–9 for specific data).

We should think of Blauner's two types of minority groups as opposite ends of a continuum, with intermediate positions between the extremes. One such intermediate position is held by enclave and middleman minorities (see Chapter 2). These groups often originate as immigrant groups who bring some resources and, thus, have more opportunities than do colonized minority groups. However, they are usually racially distinct from Anglos, and certain kinds of opportunities are closed to them.

For example, U.S. citizenship was expressly forbidden to immigrants from China until World War II. Federal laws restricted the entrance of Chinese immigrants, and state and local laws restricted their opportunities for education, jobs, and housing. For these and other reasons, the Asian immigrant experience cannot be equated with European immigrant patterns (Blauner, 1972, p. 55). Because they combine characteristics of both the colonized and the immigrant minority-group experience, we can predict that in terms of equality, enclave and middleman minority groups will occupy an intermediate status between the more assimilated white ethnic groups and the colonized racial minorities.

Blauner's typology has proven to be an extremely useful conceptual tool for the analysis of U.S. dominant–minority relations, and it is used extensively throughout this text. In fact, the case studies that compose Part III of this text are arranged in approximate order from groups created by colonization to those created by immigration. Of course, it is difficult to measure objectively or precisely such a thing as the extent of colonization, and the exact order of the groups is somewhat arbitrary.

THE CREATION OF SLAVERY IN THE UNITED STATES

The Noel hypothesis helps explain why colonists enslaved black Africans instead of white indentured servants or American Indians. First, all three groups were the objects of ethnocentric feelings on the part of the elite groups that dominated colonial society. Black Africans and American Indians were perceived as being different on religious as well as racial grounds. Many white indentured servants were Irish Catholics, criminals, or paupers. They not only occupied a lowly status in society but were perceived as different from the British Protestants who dominated colonial society.

Second, competition of some sort existed between the colonists and all three groups. The competition with American Indians was direct and focused on control of land. Competition with indentured servants, white and black, was more indirect; these groups were the labor force that the landowners needed to work on their plantations and to become successful in the New World.

Noel's third variable, differential in power, is the key variable that explains why Africans were enslaved instead of the other groups. During the first several decades of colonial history, the balance of power between the colonists and American Indians was relatively even and, in fact, often favored American Indians (Lurie, 1982, pp. 131–133). The colonists were outnumbered, and their muskets and cannons were only marginally more effective than bows and spears. The American Indian tribes were well-organized social units capable of sustaining resistance to and mounting reprisals against the colonists, and it took centuries for the nascent United States to finally defeat American Indians militarily.

White indentured servants, on the one hand, had the advantage of being preferred over black indentured servants (Noel, 1968, p. 168). Their greater desirability gave them bargaining power and the ability to negotiate better treatment and more lenient terms than could black indentured servants. If the planters had attempted to enslave white indentured servants, this source of labor would have dwindled even more rapidly.

Africans, on the other hand, had become indentured servants by force and coercion. In Blauner's terms, they were a colonized group that did not freely choose to enter the British colonies. Thus, they had no bargaining power. Unlike American Indians, they had no nearby relatives, no knowledge of the countryside, and no safe havens to which to escape. Table 4.1 summarizes the impact of these three factors on the three potential sources of labor in colonial America.

TABLE 4.1 The Noel Hypothesis Applied to the Origins of Slavery

POTENTIAL SOURCES OF LABOR	THREE CAUSAL FACTORS		
	Ethnocentrism	Competition	Differential in Power
White indentured servants	Yes	Yes	No
American Indians	Yes	Yes	No
Black indentured servants	Yes	Yes	Yes

QUESTIONS FOR REFLECTION

1. How do the concepts of subsistence technology and contact situation help clarify the origins of slavery in colonial America?

2. How do the three concepts in the Noel hypothesis apply to the decision to create slavery?

3. Blauner identifies two types of minority groups. How does this distinction apply to Africans in colonial America?

4. Why were African indentured servants—not white indentured servants or American Indians—selected as the labor supply for slavery?

PATERNALISTIC RELATIONS

Recall the first theme stated at the beginning of this chapter: The nature of intergroup relationships will reflect the characteristics of the larger society. The most important and profitable unit of economic production in the colonial South was the plantation, and the region was dominated by a small group of wealthy landowners. A society with a small elite class and a plantation-based economy will often develop a form of minority relations called **paternalism** (van den Berghe, 1967; Wilson, 1973).

The key features of paternalism are vast power differentials and huge inequalities between dominant and minority groups, elaborate and repressive systems of control over the minority group, caste-like barriers between groups, elaborate and highly stylized codes of behavior and communication between groups, and low rates of overt conflict.

Chattel Slavery. As slavery evolved in the colonies, the dominant group shaped the system to fit its needs. To solidify control of the labor of their slaves, the plantation elite designed and enacted an elaborate system of laws and customs that gave masters nearly total legal power over slaves. In these laws, slaves were defined as **chattel**, or personal property, rather than as persons, and they were accorded no civil or political rights. Slaves could not own property, sign contracts, bring lawsuits, or even testify in court (except against another slave). The masters were given the legal authority to determine almost every aspect of a slave's life, including work schedules,

living arrangements, and even names (Elkins, 1959; Franklin & Moss, 1994; Genovese, 1974; Jordan, 1968; Stampp, 1956).

The law permitted the master to determine the type and severity of punishment for misbehavior. Slaves were forbidden by law to read or write, and marriages between slaves were not legally recognized. Masters could separate husbands from wives and parents from children if it suited them. Slaves had little formal decision-making ability or control over their lives or the lives of their loved ones.

A Closed System. In colonial America, slavery became synonymous with race. Race, slavery, inferiority, and powerlessness became intertwined in ways that still affect the ways black and white Americans think about each other (Hacker, 1992). Slavery was a **caste system**, or closed stratification system. In a caste system, there is no mobility between social positions, and the social class you are born into is permanent. Slave status was for life and was passed on to any children a slave might have. Whites, no matter what they did, could not become slaves.

Interaction between members of the dominant and minority groups in a paternalistic system is governed by a rigid, strictly enforced code of etiquette. Slaves were expected to show deference and humility and visibly display their lower status when interacting with whites. These rigid behavioral codes made it possible for blacks and whites to work together, sometimes intimately, sometimes for their entire lives, without threatening the power and status differentials inherent in the system. Plantation and farm work required close and frequent contact between blacks and whites, and status differentials were maintained socially rather than physically.

Paternalism is form of dominant–minority relations marked by extreme inequality in power, property, and prestige. It is often associated with labor-intensive agrarian technology.

A **chattel** is a moveable item of personal property. A system of chattel slavery defines slaves as property, not people.

A **caste system** is a system of stratification in which there is virtually no movement or mobility between social positions or levels.

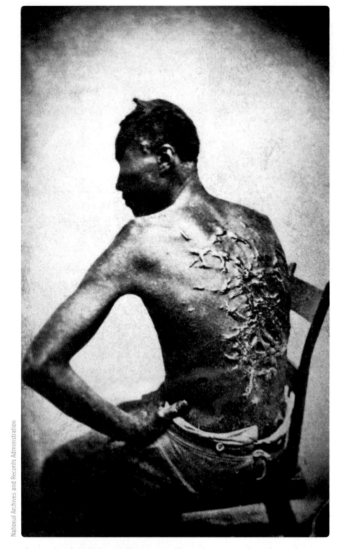

Slavery was founded on and maintained by violence. This slave shows the scars of multiple whippings.

Pseudo-Tolerance. The frequent but unequal interactions allowed the elites to maintain a pseudo-tolerance, an attitude of benevolent despotism, toward their slaves. Their prejudice and racism were often expressed as positive emotions of affection for their black slaves. The attitude of the planters toward their slaves was often paternalistic and even genteel (Wilson, 1973, pp. 52–55). For their part, black slaves often could not hate their owners as much as they hated the system that constrained them. The system defined slaves as pieces of property owned by their masters—yet they were, undeniably, human beings. Thus, slavery was founded, at its heart, on a contradiction.

> *The master learned to treat his slaves both as property and as men and women, the slaves learned to express and affirm their humanity even while they were constrained in much of their lives to accept their status as chattel. (Parish, 1989, p. 1)*

Abolitionism is the movement to abolish slavery.

Powerlessness and Resistance. The powerlessness of slaves made it difficult for them to openly reject or resist the system. Slaves had few ways they could directly challenge the institution of slavery or their position in it. Open defiance was ineffective and could result in punishment or even death. In general, masters would not be prosecuted for physically abusing their slaves.

One of the few slave revolts that occurred in the United States illustrates both the futility of overt challenge and the degree of repression built into the system. In 1831, in South-ampton County, Virginia, a slave named Nat Turner led an uprising during which 57 whites were killed. The revolt was starting to spread when the state militia met and routed the growing slave army. More than 100 slaves died in the armed encounter, and Nat Turner and 13 others were later executed.

Slave owners and white Southerners in general were greatly alarmed by the uprising and consequently tightened the system of control over slaves, making it even more repressive (Franklin & Moss, 1994, p. 147). Ironically, the result of Nat Turner's attempt to lead slaves to freedom was greater oppression and control by the dominant group.

Others were more successful in resisting the system. Runaway slaves were a constant problem for slave owners, especially in the states bordering the free states of the North. The difficulty of escape and the low likelihood of successfully reaching the North did not deter thousands from attempting the feat, some of them repeatedly. Many runaway slaves received help from the Underground Railroad, an informal network of safe houses supported by African Americans and whites involved in **abolitionism**, the movement to abolish slavery. These escapes created colorful legends and heroic figures, including Frederick Douglass, Sojourner Truth, and Harriet Tubman. The Narrative Portrait in this chapter presents the experiences of two ex-slaves who eventually escaped to the North.

Besides running away and open rebellion, slaves used the forms of resistance most readily available to them: sabotage, intentional carelessness, dragging their feet, and work slow-downs. As historian Peter Parish (1989) points out, it is difficult to separate "a natural desire to avoid hard work [from a] conscious decision to protest or resist" (p. 73), and much of this behavior may fall more into the category of noncooperation than of deliberate political rebellion. Nonetheless, these behaviors were widespread and document the rejection of the system by its victims.

An African American Culture. On an everyday basis, the slaves managed their lives and families as best they could. Most slaves were neither docile victims nor unyielding rebels. As the institution of slavery developed, a distinct African American experience accumulated, and traditions of resistance and accommodation developed side by side. Most slaves worked to create a world for themselves within the confines and restraints of the plantation system, avoiding the more vicious repression as much as possible while attending to their own needs and those of their families.

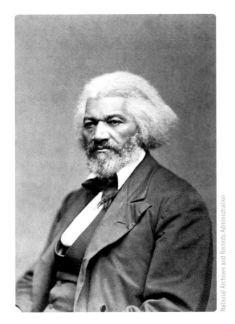

Frederick Douglass, Harriet Tubman, and Sojourner Truth were leaders of the abolitionist movement.

An African American culture was forged in response to the realities of slavery and was manifested in folklore, music, religion, family and kinship structures, and other aspects of everyday life (Blassingame, 1972; Genovese, 1974; Gutman, 1976).

QUESTIONS FOR REFLECTION

1. How did the plantation system shape slavery in colonial America?

2. Define the terms *chattel slavery* and *caste system,* and explain how they apply to the American system of slavery. Does the United States still have a racial caste system?

3. How did slaves in America resist their oppression? What risks did they run in their resistance? Were their efforts successful?

THE DIMENSIONS OF MINORITY-GROUP STATUS

The situation of African Americans under slavery can be more completely described by applying some of the concepts developed in Part I.

Power, Inequality, and Institutional Discrimination. The key concepts for understanding the creation of slavery are power, inequality, and institutional discrimination. The plantation elite used its greater power resources to consign black Africans to an inferior status. The system of racial inequality was implemented and reinforced by institutionalized discrimination and became a central aspect of everyday life in the antebellum South. The legal and political institutions of colonial society were shaped to benefit the landowners and give them almost total control over their slaves.

Prejudice and Racism. What about the attitudes and feelings of the people involved? What was the role of personal prejudice? How and why did the ideology of antiblack racism start? As we discussed in Chapter 3, individual prejudice and ideological racism are not so important as causes of the creation of minority-group status but are more the results of systems of racial inequality (Jordan, 1968, p. 80; Smedley, 2007, pp. 100–104). The colonists did not enslave black indentured servants because they were prejudiced or because they disliked blacks or thought them inferior. The decision to enslave black Africans was an attempt to resolve a labor supply problem. The primary roles of prejudice and racism in the creation of minority-group status are to rationalize and "explain" the emerging system of racial and ethnic advantage (Wilson, 1973, pp. 76–78).

Prejudice and racism helped mobilize support for the creation of minority-group status and helped stabilize the system as it emerged. Prejudice and racism can provide convenient and convincing justifications for exploitation. They can help insulate a system such as slavery from questioning and criticism and make it appear reasonable and even desirable. Thus, the intensity, strength, and popularity of antiblack southern racism actually reached its height almost 200 years after slavery began to emerge. During the early 1800s, the American abolitionist movement brought slavery under heavy attack, and in response, the ideology of antiblack racism was strengthened (Wilson, 1973, p. 79). The greater the opposition to a system of racial stratification or the greater the magnitude of the exploitation, the greater the need of the beneficiaries and their apologists to justify, rationalize, and explain.

Once created, dominant-group prejudice and racism become widespread and common ways of thinking about the minority group. In the case of colonial slavery, antiblack beliefs and feelings became part of the standard package of knowledge, understanding, and truths shared by members of the dominant group. As the decades wore on and the institution of slavery solidified, prejudice and racism were passed on from generation to generation. For succeeding generations, antiblack prejudice became just another piece of information and perspective on the world learned during socialization. Prejudice and racism began as part of an attempt to control the labor of black indentured servants, became embedded in early American culture, and were established as integral parts of the socialization process for succeeding generations (see Myrdal's "vicious cycle" in Chapter 3).

These conceptual relationships are presented in Figure 4.3. Racial inequality arises from the contact situation, as specified in the Noel hypothesis. As the dominant–minority relationship begins to take shape, prejudice and racism arise as rationalizations. Over time, a vicious cycle develops as prejudice and racism reinforce the pattern of inequality between groups, which was the cause of the prejudice and racism in the first place. Thus, as the Blauner hypothesis states, the subordination of colonized minority groups is perpetuated through time.

Assimilation. There is an enormous amount of literature on American slavery, and research on the nature and meaning of the system continues to this day. Many issues remain unsettled, however, and one of the more controversial, consequential, and interesting of these concerns is the effect of slavery on the slaves.

Apologists for the system of slavery and some historians of the South writing early in the 20th century accepted the rationalizations inherent in antiblack prejudice and argued that slavery was actually beneficial for black Africans. According to this view, British American slavery operated as a "school for civilization" (Phillips, 1918) that rescued savages from the jungles of Africa and exposed them to Christianity and Western civilization. Some argued that slavery was benevolent because it protected slaves from the evils and exploitation of the factory system of the industrial North.

These racist views were most popular a century ago, early in the development of the social sciences. Since that time, scholars have established a number of facts (e.g., Western Africa, the area from which most slaves came, had been the site of a number of powerful, advanced civilizations) that make this view untenable by anyone but the most dedicated racist thinkers.

At the opposite extreme, slavery has been compared to Nazi concentration camps and likened to a "perverted patriarchy" that brainwashed, emasculated, and dehumanized slaves, stripping them of their heritage and culture. Historian Stanley Elkins (1959) provocatively argued this interpretation in his book *Slavery: A Problem in American Institutional*

FIGURE 4.3 A Model for the Creation of Prejudice and Racism

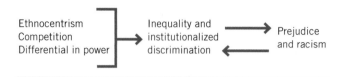

and Intellectual Life. Although his conclusions might be overdrawn, Elkins's argument and evidence are important for any exploration of the nature of American slavery. In fact, much of the scholarship on slavery since the publication of Elkins's book has been an attempt to refute or at least modify the points he made.

Still a third view of the impact of slavery maintains that through all the horror and abuse of enslavement, slaves retained a sense of self and a firm anchor in their African traditions. This point of view stresses the importance of kinship, religion, and culture in helping African Americans cope, and has been presented most poignantly in Alex Haley's (1976) semifictional family history, *Roots*, but it is also represented in the scholarly literature on slavery since Elkins (see Blassingame, 1972; Genovese, 1974).

The debate over the impact of slavery continues (see the Current Debates section at the end of this chapter), and we cannot hope to resolve the issues here. However, it is clear that African Americans, in Blauner's (1972) terms, were a "colonized" minority group who were extensively—and coercively—acculturated. Language acculturation began on the slave ships, where different tribal and language groups were mixed together to inhibit communication and lower the potential for resistance and revolt (Mannix, 1962).

The plantation elite and their agents needed to communicate with their workforce and insisted on using English. Within a generation or two, African languages died out. Some scholars argue that some African words and language patterns persist to the present day, but these survivals are trivial compared with the coerced adoption of English. To the extent that culture depends on language, Africans under slavery experienced massive acculturation.

Acculturation through slavery was clearly a process that was forced on African Americans. Because they were a colonized minority group and unwilling participants in the system, they had little choice but to adjust to the conditions established by the plantation elite as best they could. Their traditional culture was suppressed, and their choices for adjustment to the system were sharply constrained. Black slaves developed new cultural forms and social relationships, but they did so in a situation with few options or choices (Blauner, 1972, p. 66). Some African cultural elements may have survived the institution of slavery, but, given the power differentials inherent in the system, African Americans had few choices regarding their manner of adjustment.

A Slave's Life

Henry Bibb

Harriet Jacobs

Henry Bibb managed to escape slavery, and memoirs like his are an important source of information on the dynamics of the system. Here, he recounts his early life and the abuses he and his family suffered under the reign of a particularly cruel master. Bibb agonizes over leaving his daughter in bondage.

Harriet Jacobs recounts some of her experiences as a young slave. Her narrative illustrates the dynamics of power and sex in the "peculiar institution," and the very limited options she had for defending herself from the advances of her master. Like Bibb, she escaped from her bondage and penned an account of her experiences.

NARRATIVE OF THE LIFE AND ADVENTURES OF HENRY BIBB

Henry Bibb

I was born May 1815...in Shelby County, Kentucky....I was...hired out to labor for various persons and all my wages were expended for the education of [my master's daughter]. It was then I first commenced seeing and feeling that I was a wretched slave, compelled to work under the lash without wages, and often without clothes to hide my nakedness....

All that I heard about liberty and freedom...I never forgot. Among other good trades I learned the art of running away to perfection. I made a regular business of it, and never gave it up, until I had broken the bands of slavery, and landed myself safely in Canada, where I was regarded as a man, and not a thing.

[Bibb describes his childhood and adolescence, his early attempts to escape to the North, and his marriage to Malinda.] Not many months [later] Malinda made me a father. The dear little daughter was called Mary Frances....Malinda's business was to labor out in the field the greater part of her time, and there was no one to take care of poor little Frances....She was left at the house to creep under the feet of an unmerciful old mistress, Mrs. Gatewood (the owner's wife).

[We] came in from the field one day and poor little Frances...[had]...large tear drops standing in her dear little eyes....Her little face was bruised black with the whole print of Mrs. Gatewood's hand....Who can imagine the feelings of a mother and father, when looking upon their infant child whipped and tortured with impunity, and they placed in a situation where they could afford it no protection?...

On this same plantation, I was compelled to stand and see my wife shamefully scourged and abused by her master; and the manner in which this was done was so violent and inhuman that I despair in finding decent language to describe the bloody act of cruelty....

I could never look upon [my daughter] without being filled with sorrow and fearful apprehensions, of being separated by slaveholders, because she was a slave, regarded as property....But Oh! When I remember that my daughter, my only child, is still there...it is too much to bear....

SOURCE: Osofsky (1969, pp. 54–65, 80–81).

LIFE AS A SLAVE GIRL

Harriet Jacobs

During the first years of my service in Dr. Flint's family, I was accustomed to share some indulgences with the children of my mistress....But I now entered on my fifteenth year—a sad epoch in the life of a slave girl. My master began to whisper foul words in my ear....I tried to treat them with indifference or contempt....

He was a crafty man, and resorted to many means to accomplish his purposes. Sometimes he had stormy...ways that made his victims tremble; sometimes he assumed a gentleness that he thought must surely subdue....He tried his utmost to corrupt the pure principles my grandmother had instilled. He peopled my young mind with unclean images, such as only a vile monster could think of. I turned from him with disgust and hatred. But he was my master....I saw a man forty years my senior daily violating the most sacred commandments of nature. He told me I was his property; that I must be subject to his will in all things. My soul revolted against the mean tyranny. But where could I turn for protection?...There is no shadow of law to protect [me] from insult, from violence, or even from death; all these are inflicted by fiends who bear the shape of men....

SOURCE: "The Trials of Girlhood," reprinted by permission of the publishers from *Incidents in the Life of a Slave Girl: Written by Herself* by Harriet A. Jacobs, edited and with an introduction by Jean Fagan Yellin, pp. 27–30, Cambridge, Mass.: Harvard University Press, Copyright 1987, 2000 by the President and Fellows of Harvard College.

Questions to Consider

1. How do the experiences of Bibb and Jacobs illustrate the paternalism of the slave system?
2. How do the concepts of institutional discrimination and power apply to these narratives?

Gender Relations. Southern agrarian society developed into a complex social system stratified by race and gender as well as class. The plantation elite, small in number but wealthy and politically powerful, were at the top of the structure. Most whites in the South were small farmers, and relatively few of them owned slaves. In 1860, for example, only 25% of all southern whites owned slaves (Franklin & Moss, 1994, p. 123).

The principal line of differentiation in the antebellum South was, of course, race, which was largely synonymous with slave versus nonslave status. Each of the racial groups was, in turn, stratified by gender. White women were subordinate to the males of the plantation elite, and the slave community echoed the patriarchal pattern of southern society, except that the degree of gender inequality among blacks was sharply truncated by the fact that slaves had little autonomy and few resources.

At the bottom of the system were African American female slaves. Minority women are generally in double jeopardy, oppressed by their gender as well as their race. For black female slaves, the constraints were triple: "Black in a white society, slave in a free society, women in a society ruled by men, female slaves had the least formal power and were perhaps the most vulnerable group of antebellum America" (White, 1985, p. 15).

The race and gender roles of the day idealized southern white women and placed them on a pedestal. A romanticized conception of femininity was quite inconsistent with the roles women slaves were required to play. Besides domestic duties, female slaves also worked in the fields and did their share of the hardest, most physically demanding, least "feminine" farm work. Southern ideas about feminine fragility and daintiness were quickly abandoned when they interfered with work and the profit to be made from slave labor (Amott & Matthaei, 1991, p. 146).

Reflecting their vulnerability and powerlessness, women slaves were sometimes used to breed more slaves to sell. They were raped and otherwise abused by the males of the dominant group. John Blassingame (1972) expressed their vulnerability to sexual victimization:

> Many white men considered every slave cabin a house of ill-fame. Often through "gifts" but usually by force, white overseers and planters obtained the sexual favors of black women. Generally speaking, the women were literally forced to offer themselves "willingly" and receive a trinket for their compliance rather than a flogging for their refusal. (p. 83)

Note the power relationships implicit in this passage: Female slaves had little choice but to feign willing submission to their white owners.

The routines of work and everyday life differed for male and female slaves. Although they sometimes worked with the men, especially during harvest time, women more often worked in sex-segregated groups organized around domestic as well as farm chores. In addition to working in the fields, they attended the births and cared for the children of both races, cooked and cleaned, wove cloth and sewed clothes, and did the laundry. The women often worked longer hours than the men, doing housework and other chores long after the men retired (Robertson, 1996, p. 21; White, 1985, p. 122).

The group-oriented nature of their tasks gave female slaves an opportunity to develop same-sex bonds and relationships. Women cooperated in their chores, in caring for their children, in the maintenance of their quarters, and in myriad other domestic and family chores.

Their networks and interpersonal bonds could be used to resist the system. For example, slave women sometimes induced abortions rather than bring more children into bondage. They often controlled the role of midwife and were able to effectively deceive slave owners and disguise the abortions as miscarriages (White, 1985, pp. 125–126). The networks of relationships among the female slaves provided mutual aid and support for everyday problems, solace and companionship during the travails of a vulnerable and exploited existence, and some ability to buffer and resist the influence and power of the slave owners (Andersen, 1993, pp. 164–165).

Slaves in the American system were brutally repressed and exploited, but females were even more subordinated than males. Also, their oppression and exclusion sharply differentiated female slaves from white females. The white "Southern Belle"—chaste, untouchable, and unremittingly virtuous—had little in common with African American women under slavery.

QUESTIONS FOR REFLECTION

1. *The key concepts for understanding American slavery are power and inequality, not prejudice or racism.* Explain and evaluate this statement.

2. Were American slaves acculturated? Were they integrated? Under what conditions? How do these concepts relate to Blauner's distinction between immigrant and colonized minorities?

3. What, if anything, did black and white women have in common under slavery? How were their gender roles similar? How were they different?

THE CREATION OF MINORITY STATUS FOR AMERICAN INDIANS AND MEXICAN AMERICANS

Two other groups became minorities during the preindustrial period. In this section, we will review the dynamics of these processes and make some comparisons with African Americans.

Does slavery exist today? How and where? How many people are being victimized? Who are they?

In fact, the ancient institution of slavery lives on, although its dynamics are rather different, of course, from the system developed in colonial America. Slavery has been outlawed in much of the world, and modern technology has lessened the need for labor-intensive forms of work, at least in more-developed nations.

However, machines have not entirely replaced people, and the moral consensus that made slavery illegal has not spread everywhere.

Below is a brief quiz on modern slavery, and the Internet Research Project at the end of this chapter follows up on this topic. Most people would not have the information required to answer all these questions correctly—this exercise is meant to pique your interest as well as test your knowledge.

1. How many people are modern-day slaves? _____

   (To give some perspective on the numbers, it is estimated that perhaps nine million people were taken from Africa and delivered to the Western Hemisphere as slave laborers.)

2. In what form of work would most modern-day slaves be involved?
   a. Agricultural labor
   b. Sex work
   c. Other

3. Who are the primary slave owners?
   a. The state
   b. Private business

4. What region of the world has the most slaves? _____

5. What region of the world has the highest rate of slavery? _____

6. What group is the most vulnerable to slavery?
   a. Men
   b. Women
   c. Children

TURN THE PAGE TO FIND OUR ANSWERS.

As you will see, both the Noel and Blauner hypotheses provide some extremely useful insights into these experiences.

AMERICAN INDIANS

As Europeans began to penetrate the New World, they encountered hundreds of societies that had lived on this land for thousands of years. American Indian societies were highly variable in culture, language, size, and subsistence technology. Some were small, nomadic hunter-gatherer bands, whereas others were more developed societies in which people lived in settled villages and tended large gardens. Regardless of their exact nature, the inexorable advance of white society eventually devastated them all. Contact began in the East and established a pattern of conflict and defeat for American Indians that continued until the last of the tribes were finally defeated in the late 1800s. The continual expansion of white society into the West allowed many settlers to fulfill their dreams of economic self-sufficiency, but American Indians, who lost not only their lives and land but also much of their traditional way of life, paid an incalculable price.

An important and widely unrecognized point about American Indians is that there is no such thing as *the* American Indian. Rather, there were—and are—hundreds of different tribes or nations, each with its own language, culture, home territory, and unique history. There are, of course, similarities from tribe to tribe, but there are also vast differences between, for example, the forest-dwelling tribes of Virginia, who lived in longhouses and cultivated gardens, and the nomadic Plains tribes, who relied on hunting to satisfy their needs. Each tribe was and remains a unique blend of language, values, and social structure. Because of space constraints, we will not always be able to take all these differences into account. Nonetheless, it is important to be aware of the diversity and to be sensitive to the variety of peoples and histories subsumed within the general category of "American Indian."

A second important point is that many American Indian tribes no longer exist or are vastly diminished in size. When Jamestown was established in 1607, it is estimated that there were anywhere from several million to 10 million or more American Indians living in what became the United States. By 1890, when the Indian Wars finally ended, the number of American

Indians had fallen to fewer than 250,000. By the end of the nearly 300-year-long "contact situation," American Indian populations had declined by at least 75% and perhaps as much as 95% (Mann, 2011; Wax, 1971, p. 17; see also McNickle, 1973).

Very little of this population loss was due directly to warfare and battle casualties. The greatest part was caused by European diseases brought over by the colonists and by the destruction of the food supplies on which American Indian societies relied. American Indians died by the thousands from measles, influenza, smallpox, cholera, tuberculosis, and a variety of other infectious diseases (Wax, 1971, p. 17; see also Oswalt & Neely, 1996; Snipp, 1989). Traditional hunting grounds and garden plots were taken over by the expanding American society, and game such as the buffalo was slaughtered to the point of extinction. The result of the contact situation for American Indians very nearly approached genocide.

American Indians and the Noel and Blauner Hypotheses. We have already used the Noel hypothesis to analyze why American Indians were not enslaved during the colonial era. Their competition with whites centered on land, not labor, and the Indian nations were often successful in resisting domination (at least temporarily). As American society spread to the West, competition over land continued, and the growing power, superior technology, and greater resource base of the dominant group gradually pushed American Indians to near extinction.

Various attempts were made to control the persistent warfare, the most important of which occurred before independence from Great Britain. In 1763, the British Crown ruled that the various tribes were to be considered "sovereign nations with inalienable rights to their land" (see Lurie, 1982; McNickle, 1973; Wax, 1971). In other words, each tribe was to be treated as a nation-state, like France or Russia, and the colonists could not simply expropriate tribal lands. Rather, negotiations had to take place, and treaties of agreement had to be signed by all affected parties. The tribes had to be compensated for any loss of land.

This policy was often ignored but was continued by the newborn federal government after the American Revolution. The principle of sovereignty is important because it established a unique relationship between the federal government and American Indians. The fact that white society ignored the policy and regularly broke the treaties gives American Indians legal claims against the federal government that are also unique.

East of the Mississippi River, the period of open conflict was brought to a close by the Indian Removal Act of 1830, which dictated to the tribes a policy of forced migration. The law required all eastern tribes to move to new lands west of the Mississippi. Some of the affected tribes went without resistance, others fought, and still others fled to Canada rather than move to the new territory. Regardless, the Indian Removal Act "solved" the Indian problem in the East. The relative scarcity of American Indians in the eastern United States continues to the present, and the majority of American Indians live in the western two thirds of the nation.

In the West, the grim story of competition for land accompanied by rising hostility and aggression repeated itself. Wars were fought, buffalo were killed, territory was expropriated, atrocities were committed on both sides, and the fate of the tribes became more and more certain. By 1890, the greater power and resources of white society had defeated the Indian nations. All the great warrior chiefs were dead or in prison, and almost all American Indians were living on reservations controlled by agencies of the federal government. The reservations consisted of land set aside for the tribes by the government during treaty negotiations. Often, these lands were not the traditional homelands and were hundreds or even

Cheyenne warriors survey the plains.

thousands of miles away from what the tribe considered to be "home." It is not surprising that the reservations were usually on undesirable, often worthless land.

The 1890s mark a low point in American Indian history, a time of great demoralization and sadness. The tribes had to find a way to adapt to reservation life and new forms of subordination to the federal government. Although elements of the tribal way of life have survived, the tribes were impoverished and without resources, and had little ability to pursue their own interests.

American Indians, in Blauner's terms, were a colonized minority group who faced high levels of prejudice, racism, and discrimination. Like African Americans, they were controlled by paternalistic systems (the reservations) and, in a variety of ways, were coercively acculturated. Furthermore, according to Blauner, the negative consequences of colonized minority-group status persist long after the contact situation has been resolved. As we will see in Chapter 7, the experiences of this group after the 1890s provide a great deal of evidence to support Blauner's prediction.

Gender Relations. In the centuries before contact with Europeans, American Indian societies distributed resources and power in a wide variety of ways. At one extreme, some American Indian societies were highly stratified, and many practiced various forms of slavery. Others stressed equality, sharing of resources, and respect for the autonomy and dignity of each individual, including women and children (Amott & Matthaei, 1991, p. 33). American Indian societies were generally patriarchal and followed a strict gender-based division of labor, but this did not necessarily mean that women were subordinate. In many tribes, women held positions of great responsibility and controlled the wealth. For example, among the Iroquois (a large and powerful federation of tribes located in the Northeast), women controlled the land and the harvest, arranged marriages, supervised the children, and were responsible for

the appointment of tribal leaders and decisions about peace and war (Oswalt & Neely, 1996, pp. 404–405). It was not unusual for women in many tribes to play key roles in religion, politics, warfare, and the economy. Some women even became highly respected warriors and chiefs (Amott & Matthaei, 1991, p. 36).

Gender relations were affected in a variety of ways during the prolonged contact period. In some cases, the relative status and power of women rose. For example, the women of the Navajo tribe (located mainly in what is now Arizona and New Mexico) were traditionally responsible for the care of herd animals and livestock. When the Spanish introduced sheep and goats into the region, the importance of this sector of the subsistence economy increased, and the power and status of women grew along with it.

In other cases, women were affected adversely. The women of the tribes of the Great Plains, for example, suffered a dramatic loss following the contact period. The sexual division of labor in these tribes was that women were responsible for gardening, whereas men handled the hunting. When horses were introduced from Europe, the productivity of the male hunters was greatly increased. As their economic importance increased, males became more dominant and women lost status and power.

Women in the Cherokee Nation—a large tribe whose original homelands were in the Southeast—similarly lost considerable status and power under the pressure to assimilate. Traditionally, Cherokee land was cultivated, controlled, and passed down from generation to generation by the women. This matrilineal pattern was abandoned in favor of the European pattern of male ownership when the Cherokee attempted (futilely, as it turned out) to acculturate and avoid relocation under the Indian Removal Act of 1830 (Evans, 1989, pp. 12–18).

Summary. By the end of the contact period, the surviving American Indian tribes were impoverished, powerless, and clearly subordinate to white society and the federal government. Like African Americans, American Indians were sharply differentiated from the dominant group by race, and, in many cases, the tribes were internally stratified by gender. As was the case with African American slaves, the degree of gender inequality within the tribes was limited by their overall lack of autonomy and resources.

QUESTIONS FOR REFLECTION

1. What was the nature of the competition between British colonists and American Indians? How did this differ from the competition between Anglos and blacks? What were the consequences of these differences?

2. In Blauner's terms, were American Indians a colonized minority group? How?

3. How did gender relations vary from tribe to tribe? How were these relationships affected by contact with Anglo society?

MEXICAN AMERICANS

As the population of the United States increased and spread across the continent, contact with Mexicans inevitably occurred. Spanish explorers and settlers had lived in what is now the southwestern United States long before the wave of American settlers broke across this region. For example, Santa Fe, New Mexico, was founded in 1598, nearly a decade before Jamestown. As late as the 1820s, Mexicans and American Indians were almost the sole residents of the region.

By the early 1800s, four areas of Mexican settlement had developed, roughly corresponding with what would become Texas, California, New Mexico, and Arizona. These areas were sparsely settled, and most Mexicans lived in what was to become New Mexico (Cortes, 1980, p. 701). The economy of the regions was based on farming and herding. Most people lived in villages and small towns or on ranches and farms. Social and political life was organized around family and the Catholic Church, and tended to be dominated by an elite class of wealthy landowners.

Texas. Some of the first effects of U.S. expansion to the West were felt in Texas early in the 1800s. Mexico was no military match for its neighbor to the north, and the farmland of East Texas was a tempting resource for the cotton-growing interests in the American South. Anglo-Americans began to immigrate to Texas in sizable numbers in the 1820s, and by 1835, they outnumbered Mexicans 6 to 1. The attempts by the Mexican government to control these immigrants were clumsy and ineffective and eventually precipitated a successful revolution by the Anglo-Americans, with some Mexicans also joining the rebels. At this point in time, competition between Anglos and Texans of Mexican descent (called Tejanos) was muted by the abundance of land and opportunity in the area. Population density was low, fertile land was readily available for all, and the "general tone of the time was that of intercultural cooperation" (Alvarez, 1973, p. 922).

Competition between Anglo-Texans and Tejanos became increasingly intense. When the United States annexed Texas in the 1840s, full-scale war broke out, and Mexico was defeated. Under the Treaty of Guadalupe Hidalgo in 1848, Mexico ceded much of the Southwest to the United States. In the Gadsden Purchase of 1853, the United States acquired the remainder of the territory that now composes the southwestern United States. As a result of these treaties, the Mexican population of this region had become, without moving an inch from their traditional villages and farms, both a conquered people and a minority group.

Following the war, intergroup relations continued to sour, and the political and legal rights of the Tejano community were often ignored in the hunger for land. Increasingly impoverished and powerless, the Tejanos had few resources with which to resist the growth of Anglo-American domination. They were badly outnumbered and stigmatized by the recent Mexican military defeat. Land that had once been Mexican increasingly came under Anglo control, and widespread violence and lynching reinforced the growth of Anglo dominance (Moquin & Van Doren, 1971, p. 253).

California. In California, the Gold Rush of 1849 spurred a massive population movement from the East. Early relations between Anglos and Californios (native Mexicans in the state) had been relatively cordial, forming the basis for a multiethnic, bilingual state. The rapid growth of an Anglo majority after statehood in 1850 doomed these efforts, however, and the Californios, like the Tejanos, lost their land and political power.

Laws were passed encouraging Anglos to settle on land traditionally held by Californios. In such situations, the burden was placed on the Mexican American landowners to show that their deeds were valid. The Californios protested the seizure of their land but found it difficult to argue their cases in the English-speaking, Anglo-controlled court system. By the mid-1850s, a massive transfer of land to Anglo-American hands had taken place in California (Mirandé, 1985, pp. 20–21; see also Pitt, 1970).

Other laws passed in the 1850s made it increasingly difficult for Californios to retain their property and power as Anglo-Americans became the dominant group as well as the majority of the population. The area's Mexican heritage was suppressed and eliminated from public life and institutions such as schools and local government. For example, in 1855, California repealed a requirement in the state constitution that all laws be published in Spanish as well as English (Cortes, 1980, p. 706). Anglo-Americans used violence, biased laws, discrimination, and other means to exploit and repress Californios, and the new wealth generated by gold mining flowed into Anglo hands.

Arizona and New Mexico. The Anglo immigration into Arizona and New Mexico was less voluminous than that into Texas and California, and both states retained Mexican numerical majorities for a number of decades. In Arizona, most of the Mexican population were immigrants themselves, seeking work on farms, on ranches, in the mines, and on railroads. The economic and political structures of the state quickly came under the control of the Anglo population.

Only in New Mexico did Mexican Americans retain some political power and economic clout, mostly because of the relatively large size of the group and their skill in mobilizing for political activity. New Mexico did not become a state until 1912, and Mexican Americans continued to play a prominent role in governmental affairs even after statehood (Cortes, 1980, p. 706).

Thus, the contact situation for Mexican Americans was highly variable by region. Although some areas were affected more rapidly and more completely than others, the ultimate result was the creation of minority-group status for Mexican Americans (Acuña, 1999; Alvarez, 1973; Gomez, 2008; McLemore, 1973; McWilliams, 1961; Moore, 1970; Stoddard, 1973).

Wikimedia Commons

A California "49er" pans for gold.

Mexican Americans and the Noel and Blauner Hypotheses. The causal model we have applied to the origins of slavery and the domination of American Indians also provides a way of explaining the development of minority-group status for Mexican Americans. Ethnocentrism was clearly present from the very first contact between Anglo immigrants and Mexicans. Many American migrants to the Southwest brought with them the prejudices and racism they had acquired with regard to African Americans and American Indians. In fact, many of the settlers who moved into Texas came directly from the South in search of new lands for the cultivation of cotton. They readily transferred their prejudiced views to at least the poorer Mexicans, who were stereotyped as lazy and shiftless (McLemore, 1973, p. 664).

The visibility of group boundaries was heightened and reinforced by physical and religious differences. Mexicans were "racially" a mixture of Spaniards and American Indians, and the differences in skin color and other physical characteristics provided a convenient marker of group membership. In addition, the vast majority of Mexicans were Roman Catholic, whereas the vast majority of Anglo-Americans were Protestant.

Competition for land began with the first contact between the groups. However, for many years, population density was low in the Southwest, and the competition did not immediately or always erupt into violent domination and expropriation.

Nonetheless, the loss of land and power for Mexican Americans was inexorable, although variable in speed.

The size of the power differential between the groups was variable and partly explains why domination was established faster in some places than others. In both Texas and California, the subordination of the Mexican American population followed quickly after a rapid influx of Anglos and the military defeat of Mexico. Anglo-Americans used their superior numbers and military power to acquire control of the political and economic structures and expropriate the resources of the Mexican American community. In New Mexico, the groups were more evenly matched in size, and Mexican Americans were able to retain a measure of power for decades.

Unlike the case of American Indians, however, the labor as well as the land of the Mexicans was coveted. On cotton plantations, ranches, and farms, and in mining and railroad construction, Mexican Americans became a vital source of inexpensive labor. During times of high demand, this labor force was supplemented by workers who were encouraged to migrate from Mexico. When demand for workers decreased, these laborers were forced back to Mexico. Thus began a pattern of labor flow that continues to the present.

As in the case of African Americans and American Indians, the contact period clearly established a colonized status for Mexican Americans in all areas of the Southwest. Their culture and language were suppressed even as their property rights were abrogated and their status lowered. In countless ways, they, too, were subjected to coercive acculturation. For example, California banned the use of Spanish in public schools, and bullfighting and other Mexican sports and recreational activities were severely restricted (Moore, 1970, p. 19; Pitt, 1970).

In contrast to African Americans, however, Mexican Americans were in close proximity to their homeland and maintained close ties with villages and families. Constant movement across the border with Mexico kept the Spanish language and much of the Mexican heritage alive in the Southwest. Nonetheless, 19th-century Mexican Americans fit Blauner's category of a colonized minority group, and the suppression of their culture was part of the process by which the dominant culture was established.

Anglo-American economic interests benefited enormously from the conquest of the Southwest and the colonization of the Mexican people. Growers and other businessmen came to rely on the cheap labor provided by Mexican Americans and immigrant and day laborers from Mexico. The region grew in affluence and productivity, but Mexican Americans were now outsiders in their own land and did not share in the prosperity. In the land grab of the 1800s and the conquest of the indigenous Mexican population lies one of the roots of Mexican American relations with the dominant U.S. society today.

Gender Relations. Prior to the arrival of Anglo-Americans, Mexican society in the Southwest was patriarchal and maintained a clear gender-based division of labor. These characteristics tended to persist after the conquest and the creation of minority-group status.

Most Mexican Americans lived in small villages or on large ranches and farms. The women devoted their energies to the family, child rearing, and household tasks. As Mexican Americans were reduced to a landless labor force, women along with men suffered the economic devastation that accompanied military conquest by a foreign power. The kinds of jobs available to the men (mining, seasonal farm work, railroad construction) often required them to be away from home for extended periods of time, and women, by default, began to take over the economic and other tasks traditionally performed by males.

Poverty and economic insecurity placed the family structures under considerable strain. Traditional cultural understandings about male dominance and patriarchy became moot when the men were absent for long periods of time, and the decision-making power of Mexican American women increased. Also, women were often forced to work outside the household for the family to survive economically. The economics of conquest led to increased matriarchy and more working mothers (Becerra, 1988, p. 149).

For Mexican American women, the consequences of contact were variable even though the ultimate result was a loss of status within the context of the conquest and colonization of the group as a whole. Like black female slaves, Mexican American women became the most vulnerable part of the social system.

QUESTIONS FOR REFLECTION

1. What was the nature of the competition between Anglos and Mexican Americans? How did this compare and contrast with the competition between Anglos and American Indians and between Anglos and black Americans?

2. In Blauner's terms, were Mexican Americans a colonized or immigrant minority group? Why?

3. How were Mexican American gender relations affected by contact with Anglo society?

COMPARING MINORITY GROUPS

American Indians and black slaves were the victims of the explosive growth of European power in the Western Hemisphere that began with Columbus's voyage in 1492. Europeans needed labor to fuel the plantations of the mid–17th century American colonies and settled on slaves from Africa as the most logical, cost-effective means of resolving their

One of the many battles between Native Americans and U.S. soldiers.

labor supply problems. Black Africans had a commodity the colonists coveted (labor), and the colonists subsequently constructed a system to control and exploit this commodity.

To satisfy the demand for land created by the stream of European immigrants to North America, the threat represented by American Indians had to be eliminated. Once their land was expropriated, American Indians ceased to be of much concern. The only valuable resource they possessed—their land—was under the control of white society by 1890, and American Indians were thought to be unsuitable as a source of labor.

Mexico, like the United States, had been colonized by a European power—in this case, Spain. In the early 1800s, the Mexican communities in the Southwest were a series of outpost settlements, remote and difficult to defend. Through warfare and a variety of other aggressive means, Mexican citizens living in this area were conquered and became an exploited minority group.

African Americans, American Indians, and Mexican Americans, in their separate ways, became involuntary players in the growth and development of European and, later, American economic and political power. None of these groups had much choice in their respective fates; all three were overpowered and relegated to an inferior, subordinate status. Many views of assimilation (such as the "melting pot" metaphor discussed in Chapter 2) have little relevance to these situations. These minority groups had little control over their destinies, their degree of acculturation, or even their survival as groups. These three groups were coercively acculturated in the context of paternalistic relations in an agrarian economy. Meaningful integration (structural assimilation) was not a real possibility, especially for African Americans and American Indians. In Milton Gordon's (1964) terms (see Chapter 2), we might characterize these situations as "acculturation without integration" or structural pluralism. Given the grim realities described in this chapter, Gordon's terms seem a little antiseptic, and Blauner's concept of colonized minority groups seems far more descriptive.

Mexico, Canada, and the United States

Library of Congress Prints and Photographs Division

Spanish conquistadors confront the Aztec leadership in the Aztec capital city.

How do the experiences of the Spanish and the French in the Western Hemisphere compare with those of the British in what became the United States? What roles did the contact situation and subsistence technology play?[1]

The Spanish conquered much of what is now Central and South America about a century before Jamestown was founded. In 1521, they defeated the Aztec Empire, located in what is now central Mexico. The Aztec Empire was large and highly organized. The emperor ruled over scores of subject nations, and the great majority of his subjects were peasants who farmed small plots of land.

When the Spanish defeated the Aztecs, they destroyed cities and temples but not the social structure; rather, they absorbed it and used it for their own benefit. For example, the Aztec Empire had financed its central government by collecting taxes and rents from citizens. The Spanish simply grafted their own tax collection system onto this structure and diverted the flow from the Aztec elite classes (which they had, at any rate, destroyed) to themselves (Russell, 1994, pp. 29–30).

The Spanish tendency to absorb rather than destroy operated at many levels. Aztec peasants became Spanish (and then Mexican) peasants, occupying roughly the same role in the new society as they had in the old, save for paying their rents to different landlords. There was also extensive intermarriage between the groups, but, unlike the situation in the English colonies, the Spanish recognized

[1]This section is largely based on Russell (1994).

the resultant racial diversity. They recognized as many as 56 different racial groups, including mestizos (mixed European Indians) and mulattoes (mixed European Africans) (Russell, 1994, p. 35).

The society that emerged was highly race conscious, and race was highly correlated with social class: The elite classes were white, and the lower classes were nonwhite. However, the large-scale intermarriage and the official recognition of mixed-race peoples did establish the foundation for a racially mixed society. Today, the huge majority of the Mexican population is mestizo, although the elite positions continue to be monopolized by people of "purer" European ancestry.

The French began to colonize Canada at about the same time as the English established their colonies farther south. The dominant economic enterprise in the early days was not farming but trapping and the fur trade, and the French developed cooperative relations with some tribes to develop this enterprise. They, like the Spanish in Mexico, tended to absorb Native American social structures, and there was also a significant amount of intermarriage, resulting in a mixed-race group, called the Metís, who had their own identities and, indeed, their own settlements along the Canadian frontier (Russell, 1994, p. 39).

Note the profound differences in these three contact situations. The Spanish confronted a large, well-organized social system and found it expeditious to adapt Aztec practices to their own benefit. The French developed an economy that required cooperation with at least some Native American tribes, and they, too, found benefits in adaptation. The tribes encountered by the English were much smaller and much less developed than the Aztecs, and there was no particular reason for the English to adapt to or absorb their social structures. Furthermore, because the business of the English colonies was agriculture (not trapping), the competition at the heart of the contact situation was for land, and American Indians were seen as rivals for control of that most valuable resource.

Thus, the English tended to exclude American Indians, keeping them on the outside of their emerging society and building strong boundaries between their own

"civilized" world and the "savages" that surrounded them. The Spanish and French colonists adapted their societies to fit with American Indians, but the English faced no such restraints. They could create their institutions and design their social structure to suit themselves (Russell, 1994, p. 30).

As we have seen, one of the institutions created in the English colonies was slavery based on African labor. Slavery was also practiced in New Spain (Mexico) and New France (Canada), but the institution evolved in very different ways in those colonies and never assumed the importance that it did in the United States. Why? As you might suspect, the answer has a lot to do with the nature of the contact situation. Both the Spanish and French attempted large-scale agricultural enterprises that might have created a demand for imported slave labor. In the case of New Spain, however, there was a ready supply of Native American peasants available, and, although Africans became a part of the admixture that shaped modern Mexico racially and socially, demand for black slaves never matched that in the English colonies. Similarly, in Canada, slaves from Africa were sometimes used, but farmers there tended to rely on the flow of labor from France to fill their agricultural needs. The British opted for slave labor from Africa over indentured labor from Europe, and the French made the opposite decision.

Finally, we should note that many of the modern racial characteristics of these three neighboring societies were foreshadowed in their colonial origins (e.g., the greater concentration of African Americans in the United States and the more racially intermixed population of Mexico). The differences run much deeper than race alone, of course, and include differences in class structure and relative levels of industrialization and affluence. For our purposes, however, this brief comparison of the origins of dominant–minority relations underscores the importance of the contact situation in shaping group relations for centuries to come.

Questions to Consider

1. What were the key differences in the contact situations in New Spain, New France, and the British colonies? How do the concepts of competition and power apply?

2. What are some contemporary differences between Mexico, the United States, and Canada that might be traced to the contact situation?

SUMMARY

This summary is organized around the Learning Objectives listed at the beginning of this chapter.

 4.1 Explain the two themes stated at the beginning of the chapter.

These themes are explored throughout the chapter and, indeed, in much of the remainder of this text:

- Dominant–minority relations are shaped by the characteristics of society as a whole. In particular, the nature of the subsistence technology will affect group relations, culture, family structure, and virtually all aspects of social life.

- The contact situation is the single most important factor in the development of dominant–minority relations, and it will have long-term consequences.

 4.2 Explain the political, economic, and social forces that led to the creation of slavery in British America.

Slavery developed as a solution to a labor supply problem in the context of a plantation economy and labor-intensive subsistence technology. Africans became the source of slave labor in the British colonies in large part because they had less power than white indentured servants and American Indians.

4.3 Explain the importance of the contact situation and the relevance of the Noel and Blauner hypotheses for the development of slavery in colonial America.

In colonial America, the contact situation for Anglos and Africans featured ethnocentrism, competition, and a differential in power. African Americans were a colonized minority group, created by conquest and the superior power of Anglos.

 4.4 Apply the concepts of paternalism, power, inequality, discrimination, prejudice and racism, and assimilation to the American system of slavery.

Paternalistic systems of group relationships such as American slavery are characterized by extreme inequalities between groups, especially in terms of power. The minority group is controlled by a comprehensive system of discrimination and is the victim of high levels of prejudice and racism. Assimilation is not a realistic possibility in such systems, except in terms of acculturation. For example, slaves were required to learn English and adapt to British systems of work and family life.

 4.5 Explain the dynamics of gender relations under American slavery.

While white women tended to be idealized as symbols of virtue and purity, black women were often required to perform the most difficult, least "feminine" tasks. Black women had little in common with the Southern Belle and tended to be the most exploited and powerless segment of society. When not working in the fields, they performed domestic and family chores for their white owners and often worked the longest hours of any group.

 4.6 Apply the Noel and Blauner hypotheses and other concepts to the creation of minority-group status for American Indians and Mexican Americans.

The competition with American Indians centered on control of the land. American Indian tribes were conquered and pressed into a paternalistic relationship with white society. American Indians became a colonized minority group and were subjected to forced acculturation.

Mexican Americans were the third minority group created during the preindustrial era. Mexican Americans competed with white settlers over both land and labor. Like African Americans and American Indians, Mexican Americans were a colonized minority group subjected to forced acculturation.

 4.7 Compare and contrast the three contact situations analyzed in this chapter. How do they differ? What are the implications of these different contact situations for relations in the present?

The three situations vary in terms of the nature of the competition (land vs. labor), the size of the power differential, and along many other dimensions. All three groups were victims of the expansion of British power in what became the United States, and all three were colonized minority groups, subjected to paternalism and coercive acculturation.

KEY TERMS

REVIEW QUESTIONS

1. State and explain the two themes presented at the beginning of the chapter. Apply each to the contact situations between white European colonists, African Americans, American Indians, and Mexican Americans. Identify and explain the key differences and similarities among the three situations.

2. Explain what a plantation system is and why this system of production is important for understanding the origins of slavery in colonial America. Why are plantation systems usually characterized by (a) paternalism, (b) huge inequalities between groups, (c) repressive systems of control, (d) rigid codes of behavior, and (e) low rates of overt conflict?

3. Explain the Noel and Blauner hypotheses and how they apply to the contact situations covered in this chapter. Explain each of the following key terms: *ethnocentrism, competition, power, colonized minority group,* and *immigrant minority group.* How did group conflict vary when competition was over land rather than labor?

4. Explain the role of prejudice and racism in the creation of minority-group status. Do prejudice and racism help cause minority-group status, or are they caused by minority-group status? Explain.

5. Compare and contrast gender relations in regard to each of the contact situations discussed in this chapter. Why do the relationships vary?

6. What does it mean to say that under slavery, acculturation for African Americans was coerced? What are the implications for assimilation, inequality, and African American culture?

7. Compare and contrast the contact situations of Native Hawaiians and American Indians. What were the key differences in their contact situations, and how are these differences reflected in the groups' current situations?

8. Compare and contrast the contact situations in colonial America, Canada, and Mexico. What groups were involved in each situation? What was the nature of the competition, and what were the consequences?

STUDENT STUDY SITE

$SAGE edge™

Sharpen your skills with SAGE edge at edge.sagepub.com/healey7e

SAGE edge for students provides a personalized approach to help you accomplish your coursework goals in an easy-to-use learning environment.

The following resources are available at SAGE edge:

Current Debates: How Did Slavery Affect the Origins of African American Culture?

Did the institution of slavery permanently flaw African American culture? Or did African Americans create sufficient space within their subjugation to develop and sustain positive cultural norms and self-images? How was the experience of slavery different for women and men?

On our website you will find an overview of the topic, the clashing points of view, and some questions to consider as you analyze the material.

Public Sociology Assignments

Public Sociology Assignments provide opportunities for students to address directly and personally some of the issues raised in this text.

The public sociology assignments designed for Part II on our website will lead students to a study of the persistence of prejudice and discrimination in society today. The first assignment is an investigation of children's books and focuses on the depiction of race, gender, and ethnicity. Are children's books as diverse as the larger society? The second assignment analyzes patterns of cross-group interaction in local eateries, and the third looks at the depiction of historical events in contemporary cinema. How are movies based in the past affected by contemporary understandings?

Contributed by Linda M. Waldron

Internet Research Project

For the Internet Research Project for this chapter, you will investigate modern slavery. As you saw in this chapter's Applying Concepts section, slavery is a worldwide phenomenon and can be found in societies at all levels of development, including the United States. Who are the victims of modern slavery? Where are they? Who are the slave owners?

As always, this project will be guided by a series of questions, and your instructor may ask you to discuss your findings in small groups.

For Further Reading

Please see our website for an annotated list of important works related to this chapter.

CHAPTER-OPENING TIMELINE PHOTO CREDITS

1636: Library of Congress Prints and Photographs Division

1641: Library of Congress Prints and Photographs Division

1676: Wikipedia

1804: Cincinnati Art Museum/Charles T. Webber

1831: Library of Congress Prints and Photographs Division

1857: Wikipedia

1859: National Portrait Gallery/Augustus Washington

1861: Wikipedia

5

INDUSTRIALIZATION AND DOMINANT–MINORITY RELATIONS

From Slavery to Segregation and the Coming of Postindustrial Society

timeline

LOC

Wikimedia Commons

1861
The Civil War begins.

1863
The 54th Massachusetts Colored Infantry is organized. It is the first black regiment in the free states.

1868
The Fourteenth Amendment grants citizenship to African Americans born in the U.S.

1860   1864   1868   1872   1876   1880   1884

1860
Abraham Lincoln is elected president.

1861
The Union of Confederate States is formed. Jefferson Davis is elected its president.

1863
Lincoln issues the Emancipation Proclamation, freeing all slaves in areas of rebellion.

1865
The Thirteenth Amendment abolishes slavery throughout the country.

1865
The Union army defeats the Confederacy to win the Civil War.

1866
Congress passes the Civil Rights Bill to protect the rights of blacks.

1865
Lincoln is assassinated.

LOC

National Archives

LOC

LOC

THE ASSASSINATION OF PRESIDENT LINCOLN

The last Negro has left Decatur, Ind. . . . About a month ago a mob of 50 men drove out all the Negroes who were then making that city their home. Since that time the feeling against the Negro race has been intense, so much so that an Anti-Negro Society was organized.

The colored man who has just left came about three weeks ago, and since that time received many threatening letters. When he appeared on the streets he was insulted and jeered at. An attack was threatened.

The anti-negroites declare that as Decatur is now cleared of Negroes they will keep it so, and the importation of any more will undoubtedly result in serious trouble.

—*New York Times,*
July 14, 1902 (Loewen, 2005, p. 90)

LEARNING OBJECTIVES

By the end of this chapter, you will be able to do the following:

5.1 Explain the corollary to the two themes stated at the beginning of the chapter.

5.2 Describe the nature of Jim Crow segregation in the South and why this system was created.

5.3 Explain the significance of the Great Migration and the origins of black protest.

5.4 Apply the concepts of acculturation, integration, and gender to the time frame covered in this chapter.

5.5 List and explain the important trends created by the shifts to industrial and postindustrial subsistence technology, and describe how these trends affected dominant–minority relations.

5.6 Explain what is meant by the shift from paternalistic to rigid to fluid competitive group relations.

5.7 Explain and apply the concept of modern institutional discrimination to contemporary black–white relations and the issue of affirmative action.

1870
The Fifteenth Amendment is ratified, securing the right to vote for African American males.

1896
The Supreme Court rules in *Plessy v. Ferguson* that "separate but equal" accommodations are constitutional.

1914
Marcus Garvey founds the Universal Negro Improvement Association in 1914 in his native Jamaica and founds the first U.S. branch in 1916.

1880s
The Jim Crow laws mandates racial segregation in all public facilities, with a separate but equal status for black Americans.

1890–1930
An estimated 3.5 million African Americans move away from the South to escape Jim Crow and search for higher wages in the Northeast and Midwest.

1909
The NAACP is founded.

Decatur was not alone. Thousands of American towns, cities, and counties—almost all outside the South—expelled their nonwhite population between the 1890s and 1960s. These locales were sometimes called "sundown towns" because of the pervasive signs, prominently placed, that warned nonwhites to be outside city limits by the time the sun set.

Such practices make it clear that the pervasive racial residential segregation of the present day didn't "just happen," and it is not the result of some benign desire of people to be with others like themselves. It was created, deliberately and purposely—sometimes by violence, demonstrations, and attacks, and sometimes by zoning ordinances, the collusion of real-estate agents and city leaders, or other "peaceful" or hidden means. Regardless, the result was the same: massive racial segregation and the exclusion of nonwhites from opportunities for housing, jobs, and schooling. As this (and the previous) chapter demonstrates, all of today's racial inequalities have similar roots in the past. •

One theme stated at the beginning of Chapter 4 was that a society's subsistence technology shapes dominant–minority group relations. A corollary of this theme, explored in this chapter, is that *dominant–minority group relations change as the subsistence technology changes.* We saw in Chapter 4 that dominant–minority relations in the formative years of the United States were profoundly shaped by agrarian technology and the desire to control land and labor. The agrarian era ended in the 1800s, and the United States has experienced two major transformations in subsistence technology since that time, each of which has transformed dominant–minority relations and required the creation of new structures and processes to maintain racial stratification and white privilege.

The first transformation, the industrial revolution, began in the early 19th century when machine-based technologies began to develop, especially in the North. In the agrarian era, work was labor intensive, done by hand or with the aid of draft animals. During industrialization, work became capital intensive (see Chapter 2), and machines replaced people and animals.

The new industrial technology rapidly increased the productivity and efficiency of the U.S. economy and quickly began to change all other aspects of society, including the

The assembly line at a Ford Motor company plant.

nature of work, politics, communication, transportation, family life, birth and death rates, the system of education, and, of course, dominant–minority relations. The groups that had become minorities during the agrarian era (African Americans, American Indians, and Mexican Americans) faced new possibilities and new dangers, but industrialization also created new minority groups, new forms of exploitation and oppression, and, for some, new opportunities to rise in the social structure and succeed in America. In this chapter, we will explore this transformation and illustrate its effects on the status of African Americans, focusing primarily on the construction of Jim Crow segregation in the South. The impact of industrialization on other minority groups will be considered in the case studies presented in Part III.

The second transformation in subsistence technology brings us to more recent times. In the mid-20th century, the United States (and other advanced industrial societies) entered the postindustrial era, also called **deindustrialization**. This shift in subsistence technology was marked by (1) a decline in the manufacturing sector of the economy and a decrease in the supply of secure, well-paid, blue-collar, manual-labor jobs, and (2) an expansion in the service and information-based sectors of the economy and an increase in the relative proportion of white-collar and "high-tech" jobs.

Like the 19th-century industrial revolution, these changes have profound implications for every aspect of modern society, not just for dominant–minority relations. Indeed, every characteristic of American society—work, family, politics, popular culture—is being transformed as the subsistence technology continues to evolve. In the latter part of this chapter, we examine this most recent transformation in general terms and point out some of its implications for minority groups. We will examine some new concepts—especially the concept of **modern institutional discrimination**—to help us understand group relations in this new era, and we will also establish some important groundwork for the case studies in Part III, in which

Deindustrialization is the shift from a manufacturing economy to a service-oriented, information-processing economy.

Modern institutional discrimination is a more subtle and covert form of institutional discrimination.

TABLE 5.1 Three Subsistence Technologies and the United States

TECHNOLOGY	KEY TRENDS AND CHARACTERISTICS	DATES
Agrarian	Labor-intensive agriculture. Control of land and labor are central.	1607 to early 1800s
Industrial	Capital-intensive manufacturing. Machines replace animal and human labor.	Early 1800s to mid-1900s
Postindustrial	Shift away from manufacturing to a service economy. The "information society."	Mid-1900s to the present

we consider in detail the implications of postindustrial society for America's minority groups.

Table 5.1 summarizes the characteristics of the three major subsistence technologies considered in this text. As U.S. society moved through these stages, group relations and the nature of racial stratification changed.

INDUSTRIALIZATION AND THE SHIFT FROM PATERNALISTIC TO RIGID COMPETITIVE GROUP RELATIONS

The industrial revolution began in England in the mid-1700s and spread from there to the rest of Europe, then to the United States, and eventually to the rest of the world. The key innovations associated with this change in subsistence technology were the application of machine power to production and the harnessing of inanimate sources of energy, such as steam and coal, to fuel the machines. As machines replaced humans and animals, work became many times more productive, the economy grew, and the volume and variety of goods produced increased dramatically.

In an industrial economy, the close, paternalistic control of minority groups found in agrarian societies becomes irrelevant. Paternalistic relationships such as slavery are found in societies with labor-intensive technologies and are designed to organize and control a large, involuntary, geographically immobile labor force. An industrial economy, in contrast, requires a workforce that is geographically and socially mobile, skilled, and literate. Furthermore, with industrialization comes urbanization, and close, paternalistic controls are difficult to maintain in a city.

Thus, as industrialization progresses, agrarian paternalism tends to give way to a **rigid competitive group system** (see Table 5.2 later in this chapter). Under this system, minority-group members are freer to compete with dominant-group members, especially with those in the lower-class segments, for jobs and other valued commodities. As competition increases, the threatened members of the dominant group become more hostile, and attacks on the minority groups tend to increase.

Whereas paternalistic systems seek to directly dominate and control the minority group (and its labor), rigid competitive systems are more defensive in nature. The threatened segments of the dominant group seek to minimize or eliminate minority-group encroachment on jobs, housing, or other valuable goods or services (van den Berghe, 1967; Wilson, 1973).

Paternalistic systems such as slavery required members of the minority group to be active, if involuntary, participants. In contrast, in rigid competitive systems, the dominant group seeks to handicap the minority group's ability to compete effectively or, in some cases, aims to eliminate competition from the minority group altogether.

We have already considered an example of a dominant-group attempt to protect itself from a threat. As you recall, the National Origins Act was passed in the 1920s to stop the flow of cheaper labor from Europe and protect jobs and wages (see Chapter 2). In this chapter, we consider dominant-group attempts to keep African Americans powerless and impoverished—to maintain black–white racial stratification—as society shifted from an agricultural to an industrial base.

THE IMPACT OF INDUSTRIALIZATION ON THE RACIAL STRATIFICATION OF AFRICAN AMERICANS: FROM SLAVERY TO SEGREGATION

Industrial technology began to transform American society in the early 1800s, but its effects were not felt equally in all regions. The northern states industrialized first, while the plantation system and agricultural production continued to

---

A **rigid competitive group system** of group relations is one in which the dominant group seeks to exclude the minority group or limit its ability to compete for scarce resources.

Wikimedia Commons

Union soldiers at the battle of Fredricksburg.

dominate the South. This economic diversity was one of the underlying causes of the regional conflict that led to the Civil War. Because of its more productive technology, the North had more resources and defeated the Confederacy in a bloody war of attrition. Slavery was abolished, and black–white relations in the South entered a new era when the Civil War ended in April 1865.

The southern system of race relations that ultimately emerged after the Civil War was designed in part to continue the control of African American labor institutionalized under slavery. It was also intended to eliminate any political or economic threat from the African American community.

This rigid competitive system grew to be highly elaborate and inflexible, partly because of the high racial visibility and long history of inferior status and powerlessness of African Americans in the South, and partly because of the particular needs of southern agriculture. In this section, we look at black–white relations from the end of the Civil War through the ascendance of segregation in the South and the mass migration of African Americans to the cities of the industrializing North.

RECONSTRUCTION

The period of **Reconstruction**, from 1865 to the 1880s, was a brief respite in the long history of oppression and exploitation of African Americans. The Union Army and other agencies of

the federal government, such as the Freedmen's Bureau, were used to enforce racial freedom in the defeated Confederacy. Black Southerners took advantage of the Fifteenth Amendment to the Constitution, passed in 1870, which states that the right to vote cannot be denied on the grounds of "race, color, or previous condition of servitude." They registered to vote in large numbers and turned out on Election Day, and some were elected to high political office. Schools for the former slaves were opened, and African Americans purchased land and houses and established businesses.

The era of freedom was short, however, and Reconstruction began to end when the federal government demobilized its armies of occupation and turned its attention to other matters. By the 1880s, the federal government had withdrawn from the South, Reconstruction was over, and black Southerners began to fall rapidly into a new system of exploitation and inequality.

Reconstruction was too brief to change two of the most important legacies of slavery. First, the centuries of bondage left black Southerners impoverished, largely illiterate and uneducated, and with few power resources. When new threats of racial oppression appeared, African Americans found it difficult to defend their group interests. These developments are consistent with the Blauner hypothesis: Colonized minority groups face greater difficulties in improving their disadvantaged status because they confront greater inequalities and have fewer resources at their disposal.

Second, slavery left a strong tradition of racism in the white community. Antiblack prejudice and racism originated as rationalizations for slavery but had taken on lives of their own over the generations. After two centuries of slavery, the heritage of prejudice and racism was thoroughly ingrained in southern culture. White Southerners were predisposed by this cultural legacy to see racial inequality and exploitation of African Americans as normal and desirable. They were able to construct a social system based on the assumption of racial inferiority after Reconstruction ended and the federal government withdrew.

DE JURE SEGREGATION

The system of race relations that replaced slavery in the South was **de jure segregation**, sometimes referred to as the **Jim Crow system**. Under segregation, the minority group is physically and socially separated from the dominant group and consigned to an inferior position in virtually every area of social life. The phrase *de jure* ("by law") means that the system is sanctioned and reinforced by the legal code; the inferior status of African Americans was actually mandated or required by state and local laws. For example, southern cities during this era had laws requiring African Americans to ride at the back of the bus. If an African American refused to comply with this seating arrangement, he or she could be arrested.

De jure segregation came to encompass all aspects of southern social life. Neighborhoods, jobs, stores, restaurants,

---

Reconstruction followed the Civil War and lasted from 1865 until the 1880s. Many racial reforms were instituted during this time, but all were reversed during the Jim Crow era.

De jure segregation is racial segregation that is institutionalized in local and state law.

The **Jim Crow system** was the system of rigid competitive race relations in the American South that lasted from the 1880s until the 1960s.

and parks were segregated. When new social forms, such as movie theaters, sports stadiums, and interstate buses, appeared in the South, they, too, were quickly segregated.

The logic of segregation created a vicious cycle (see Figure 3.4). The more African Americans were excluded from mainstream society, the greater their objective poverty and powerlessness became. The more inferior their status and the greater their powerlessness, the easier it was to mandate more inequality. High levels of inequality reinforced racial prejudice and made it easy to use racism to justify further separation. The system kept turning on itself, finding new social niches to segregate and reinforcing the inequality that was its starting point. For example, at the height of the Jim Crow era, the system had evolved to the point that some courtrooms maintained separate Bibles for African American witnesses to swear on. Also, in Birmingham, Alabama, it was against the law for blacks and whites to play checkers and dominoes together (Woodward, 1974, p. 118).

What were the causes of this massive separation of the races? Once again, the concepts of the Noel hypothesis prove useful. Because strong antiblack prejudice was already in existence when segregation began, we do not need to account for ethnocentrism. The post-Reconstruction competition between the racial groups was reminiscent of the origins of slavery, in that black Southerners had something that white Southerners wanted: labor. In addition, a free black electorate threatened the political and economic dominance of the elite segments of the white community. Finally, after the withdrawal of federal troops and the end of Reconstruction, white Southerners had sufficient power resources to end the competition on their own terms and construct repressive systems of control for black Southerners.

THE ORIGINS OF DE JURE SEGREGATION

Although the South lost the Civil War, its basic class structure and agrarian economy remained intact. The plantation elite remained the dominant class, and they were able to use their power to build a system of racial stratification to replace slavery.

Control of Black Labor. The plantation elite retained ownership of huge tracts of land, and cotton remained the primary cash crop in the South. As was the case before the Civil War, the landowners needed a workforce to farm the land. Because of the depredations and economic disruptions of the war, the old plantation elite were short on cash and liquid capital and could not always hire workers for wages. In fact, almost as soon as the war ended, southern legislatures attempted to force African Americans back into involuntary servitude by passing a series of laws known as the "Black Codes." Only the beginning of Reconstruction and the active intervention of the federal government halted the implementation of this legislation (Geschwender, 1978, p. 158; Wilson, 1973, p. 99).

Black sharecroppers.

The plantation elite solved their manpower problem this time by developing a system of **sharecropping**, or tenant farming. The sharecroppers worked the land, which was actually owned by the planters, in return for payment in shares of the profit when the crop was taken to market. The landowner would supply a place to live and food and clothing on credit. After the harvest, tenant and landowner would split the profits (sometimes very unequally), and the tenant's debts would be deducted from his share. The accounts were kept by the landowner, who could cheat and take advantage of the tenant with great impunity. With few or no political and civil rights, black sharecroppers found it difficult to keep unscrupulous white landowners honest. The landowner could inflate the indebtedness of the sharecropper and claim that he was still owed money even after profits had been split. Under this system, sharecroppers had few opportunities to improve their situations and could be bound to the land until their "debts" were paid off (Geschwender, 1978, p. 163).

By 1910, more than half of all employed African Americans worked in agriculture, and more than half of the remainder (25% of the total) worked in domestic occupations, such as maid or janitor (Geschwender, 1978, p. 169). The manpower shortage in southern agriculture was solved, and the African American community once again found itself in a subservient status. At the same time, the white southern working class was protected from direct job competition with African Americans. As the South began to industrialize, white workers were able to exclude black workers and reserve the better-paying jobs using a combination of whites-only labor unions and strong antiblack laws and customs. White workers took advantage of the new jobs created by industrialization, while black Southerners remained a rural peasantry, excluded from participation in the modernizing job structure.

Under the **sharecropping** system of farming, the tenant (often black) worked the land and split the profits with the landowner.

In some sectors of the changing southern economy, the status of African Americans actually fell lower than it had been during slavery. For example, in 1865, 83% of the artisans in the South were African Americans; by 1900, this percentage had fallen to 5% (Geschwender, 1978, p. 170). The Jim Crow system confined African Americans to the agrarian and domestic sectors of the labor force, denied them the opportunity for a decent education, and excluded them from politics. The system was reinforced by still more laws and customs that drastically limited the options and life opportunities available to black Southerners.

Political and Civil Rights Under Jim Crow. A final force behind the creation of de jure segregation was political. As the 19th century drew to a close, a wave of agrarian radicalism known as populism spread across the country. This antielitist movement was a reaction to changes in agriculture caused by industrialization. The movement attempted to unite poor whites and blacks in the rural South against the traditional elite classes.

The economic elite were frightened by the possibility of a loss of power and split the incipient coalition between whites and blacks by fanning the flames of racial hatred. The strategy of "divide and conquer" proved to be effective (as it often had before and has since this time), and the white elite classes in states throughout the South eliminated the possibility of future threats by depriving African Americans of the right to vote (Woodward, 1974).

The disenfranchisement of the black community was accomplished by measures such as literacy tests, poll taxes, and property requirements. The literacy tests were officially justified as promoting a better-informed electorate but were shamelessly rigged to favor white voters. The requirement that voters pay a tax or prove ownership of a certain amount of property could also disenfranchise poor whites, but again, the implementation of these policies was racially biased.

The policies were extremely effective, and by the early 20th century, the political power of the southern black community was virtually nonexistent. For example, as late as 1896, in Louisiana, there were more than 100,000 registered African American voters and they were a majority in 26 parishes (counties). In 1898, the state adopted a new constitution containing stiff educational and property requirements for voting unless the voter's father or grandfather had been eligible to vote as of January 1, 1867. At that time, the Fourteenth and Fifteenth Amendments, which guaranteed suffrage for black males, had not yet been passed.

Such "grandfather clauses" made it easy for white males to register while disenfranchising blacks. By 1900, only about 5,000 African Americans were registered to vote in Louisiana, and African American voters were not a majority in any parish. A similar decline occurred in Alabama, where an electorate

The Jim Crow system of segregation encompassed water fountains and rest rooms.

of more than 180,000 African American males was reduced to 3,000 by provision of a new state constitution. This story repeated itself throughout the South, and African American political powerlessness was a reality by 1905 (Franklin & Moss, 1994, p. 261).

This system of legally mandated racial privilege was approved by the U.S. Supreme Court, which ruled in the case of *Plessy v. Ferguson* (1896) that it was constitutional for states to require separate facilities (schools, parks, etc.) for African Americans as long as the separate facilities were fully equal. The southern states paid close attention to "separate" but ignored "equal."

Reinforcing the System. Under de jure segregation, as under slavery, the subordination of the African American community was reinforced and supplemented by an elaborate system of racial etiquette. Everyday interactions between blacks and whites proceeded according to highly stylized and rigidly followed codes of conduct intended to underscore the inferior status of the African American community. Whites were addressed as "mister" or "ma'am," whereas African Americans were called by their first names or, perhaps, by an honorific title such as "aunt," "uncle," or "professor." Blacks were expected to assume a humble and deferential manner, remove their hats, cast their eyes downward, and enact the role of the subordinate in all interactions with whites. If an African American had reason to call on anyone in the white community, he or she was expected to go to the back door.

These expectations and "good manners" for black Southerners were systematically enforced. Anyone who ignored them ran the risk of reprisal, physical attacks, and even death by lynching. During the decades in which the Jim Crow system was being imposed, there were thousands of lynchings in the South. From 1884 until the end of the century, lynchings averaged almost one every other day (Franklin & Moss, 1994, p. 312). The bulk of this violent terrorism was racial

COMPARATIVE FOCUS

Jim Crow Segregation and South African Apartheid

A young black man challenges segregated busses in South Africa.

Systems of legalized, state-sponsored racial segregation like Jim Crow can be found in many nations. We will consider South African apartheid, one of the most infamous of these systems, in Chapter 13, but here we will note some of its many similarities to Jim Crow segregation.

First, and most important, both apartheid and American de jure segregation were deliberately constructed by the dominant group (whites) to control and exploit the minority group (blacks) and to keep them powerless. In both systems, segregation was comprehensive and encompassed virtually every area of life, including neighborhoods, schools, movie theaters, parks, public buildings, buses, and water fountains.

In both systems, whites benefited from a cheap, powerless labor supply in agriculture and in business. Domestically, even white families of modest means could afford servants, gardeners, and nannies.

Blacks in both systems were politically disenfranchised and closely controlled by police and other agencies of the state. Their low status was reinforced by violence and force, sometimes administered by the police, sometimes by extralegal vigilante and terrorist groups.

Elaborate rituals and customs governed interaction between the races: All were intended to overtly display and reinforce the power differential between the groups. Under both apartheid and Jim Crow segregation, blacks generally lived in abject poverty, with incomes a tiny fraction of those of the white community.

In both cases, protest movements formed in the black community and helped end the systems of racial segregation. The protests were met with extreme violence and repression from the state, and the ensuing struggles created heroes such as Martin Luther King and Nelson Mandela, among others. Also, in both cases,

state-sponsored racial oppression ended only after prolonged, intense conflict.

Of course, there were differences between the two systems, and we will explore these in Chapter 13. For now, we can note that apartheid was more repressive and more viciously defended by the white dominant group. Why? Part of the reason is simple arithmetic. Whites in South Africa were a numerical minority (no more than 10% of the total population) and felt that their privileged status was under extreme threat from the black majority. White South Africans had a "fortress mentality" and feared that they would be swamped by the black majority if they allowed even the slightest lapse in the defense of their racial privilege.

Today, South Africa continues to deal with the legacies of racial segregation, as does the United States. In both nations, racial divisions run deep, and neither has been able to completely resolve its myriad issues of fairness, justice, and equality. We will return to these concerns in Chapter 13.

Questions to Consider

1. Why did whites in South Africa and the American South respond so violently to black protest movements? What was at stake?

2. What other differences, besides the numerical one, can you identify between the two situations? For example, is it important that one system was regional and the other national? What are the implications of this difference?

and intended to reinforce the system of racial advantage or to punish real or imagined transgressors. Also, various secret organizations, such as the Ku Klux Klan, engaged in terrorist attacks against the African American community and anyone else who failed to conform to the dictates of the system.

Increases in Prejudice and Racism. As the system of racial advantage formed and solidified, levels of prejudice and racism increased (Wilson, 1973, p. 101). The new system needed justification and rationalization, just as slavery did, and antiblack sentiment, stereotypes, and ideologies of racial inferiority grew stronger. At the start of the 20th century, the United States in general—not just the South—was a very racist and intolerant society. This spirit of rejection and scorn for all out-groups

coalesced with the need for justification of the Jim Crow system and created an especially negative brand of racism in the South.

QUESTIONS FOR REFLECTION

1. How does the concept of subsistence technology clarify the shift from a paternalistic to a rigid competitive system of race relations?

2. How do the concepts of competition and differential in power in the Noel hypothesis apply to the creation of the Jim Crow system of segregation?

3. From a sociological point of view, what were the most important features of de jure segregation?

FIGURE 5.1 Distribution of the African American Population in the United States, 1790–1990

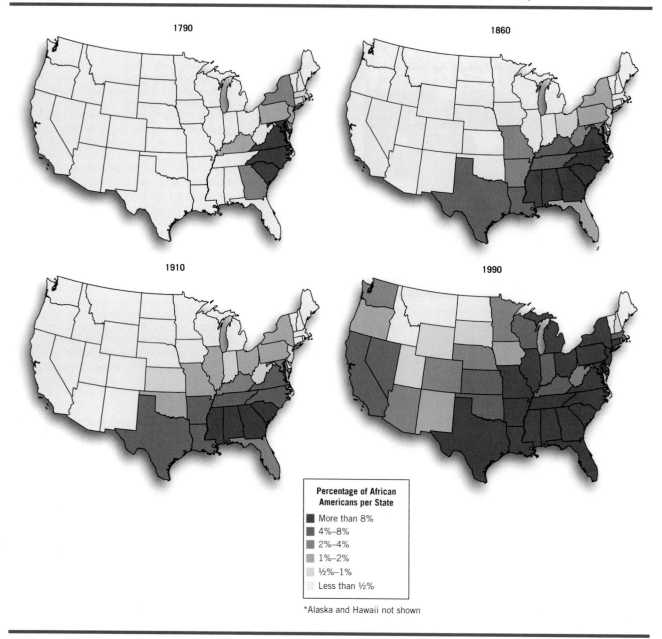

1790

1860

1910

1990

Percentage of African Americans per State

More than 8%
4%–8%
2%–4%
1%–2%
½%–1%
Less than ½%

*Alaska and Hawaii not shown

SOURCE: Bureau of the Census, U.S. Department of Commerce.

THE GREAT MIGRATION

Although African Americans lacked the power resources to withstand the resurrection of southern racism and oppression, they did have one option that had not been available under slavery: freedom of movement. African Americans were no longer legally tied to a specific master or to a certain plot of land. In the early 20th century, a massive population movement out of the South began. Slowly at first, African Americans began to move to other regions of the nation and from the countryside to the city. The movement increased when hard times hit southern agriculture and slowed down during better times. It has been said that African Americans voted against southern segregation with their feet.

As Figure 5.1 shows, the black population was highly concentrated in the South as recently as 1910, a little more than a century ago. By 1990, African Americans had become much more evenly distributed across the nation, spreading to the Northeast and the upper Midwest. Since 1990, the distribution of the black population has remained roughly the same (see Figure 6.6), although there has been some movement back to the South.

Figure 5.2 shows that, in addition to movement away from the South, the Great Migration was also a movement from the countryside to the city. A century ago, blacks were overwhelmingly rural, but today more than 90% are urban.

Thus, an urban black population living outside of the South is a 20th-century phenomenon. The significance of this population redistribution is manifold. Most important,

FIGURE 5.2 Percentage of African Americans Living in Urban Areas, 1890–2010

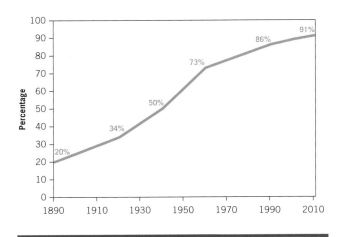

SOURCE: 1890 to 1960—Geschwender (1978); 1970, 1980, 1990—Pollard and O'Hare (1999); 2000—U.S. Census Bureau (2000c); 2010—U.S. Census Bureau (2013g).

perhaps, was the fact that by moving out of the South and into urban areas, African Americans moved from areas of great resistance to racial change to areas of lower resistance. In the northern cities, for example, it was far easier to register and vote. Black political power began to grow and eventually provided many of the crucial resources that fueled the civil rights movement of the 1950s and 1960s.

LIFE IN THE NORTH

What did African American migrants find when they got to the industrializing cities of the North? There is no doubt that life in the North was better for the vast majority of them. The growing northern African American communities relished the absence of Jim Crow laws and oppressive racial etiquette, the relative freedom to pursue jobs, and the greater opportunities to educate their children. Inevitably, however, life in the North fell far short of utopia. Many aspects of African American culture—literature, poetry, music—flourished in the heady new atmosphere of freedom, but on other fronts, northern African American communities faced massive discrimination in housing, schools, and the job market. Along with freedom and such cultural flowerings as the Harlem Renaissance came black ghettos and new forms of oppression and exploitation. In Chapter 6, we will explore these events and the workings of what has been called de facto segregation.

COMPETITION WITH WHITE ETHNIC GROUPS

It is useful to see the movement of African Americans out of the South in terms of their resultant relationships with other groups. Southern blacks began to move to the North at about the same time as the New Immigration from Europe (see Chapter 2) began to end. By the time substantial numbers

of black Southerners began arriving in the North, European immigrants and their descendants had had years, decades, and even generations to establish themselves in the job markets, political systems, labor unions, and neighborhoods of the North. Many of the European ethnic groups also had been the victims of discrimination and rejection, and, as we discussed in Chapter 2, their hold on economic security and status was tenuous for much of the 20th century. Frequently, they saw the newly arriving black migrants as a threat to their status, a perception reinforced by the fact that industrialists and factory owners often used African Americans as strikebreakers and scabs during strikes. The white ethnic groups responded by developing defensive strategies to limit the dangers presented by these migrants from the South. They tried to exclude African Americans from their labor unions and other associations and limit their impact on the political system. They also attempted, often successfully, to maintain segregated neighborhoods and schools (although the legal system outside the South did not sanction overt de jure segregation).

This competition led to hostile relations between black southern migrants and white ethnic groups, especially the lower- and working-class segments of those groups. Ironically, however, in another phase of the ethnic succession discussed in Chapter 2, the newly arriving African Americans actually helped white ethnic groups become upwardly mobile. Dominant-group whites became less contemptuous of white ethnic groups as their alarm over the presence of African Americans increased. The greater antipathy of the white community toward African Americans made the immigrants more desirable and, thus, hastened their admission to the institutions of the larger society. For many white ethnic groups, the increased tolerance of the larger society coincided happily with the coming of age of the more educated and skilled descendants of the original immigrants, further abetting the rise of these groups in the U.S. social class structure (Lieberson, 1980).

For more than a century, each new European immigrant group had helped push previous groups up the ladder of socioeconomic success and out of the old, ghettoized neighborhoods. Black Southerners got to the cities after immigration from Europe had been curtailed, and no newly arrived immigrants appeared to continue the pattern of succession for northern African Americans. Instead, American cities developed concentrations of low-income blacks who were economically vulnerable and politically weak, and whose position was further solidified by antiblack prejudice and discrimination (Wilson, 1987, p. 34).

THE ORIGINS OF BLACK PROTEST

As we pointed out in Chapter 4, African Americans have always resisted their oppression and protested their situation. Under slavery, however, the inequalities they faced were so great and their resources so meager that the protest was ineffective. With

NARRATIVE PORTRAIT

The Kitchenette

Library of Congress Prints and Photographs Division

Richard Wright, one of the most powerful writers of the twentieth century.

Richard Wright (1908–1960), one of the most powerful writers of the 20th century, lived through and wrote about many of the social changes discussed in this chapter. He grew up in the South during the height of the Jim Crow system, and his passionate hatred for segregation and bigotry is expressed in his major works, Native Son *(1940) and the autobiographical* Black Boy *(1945). In 1941, Wright helped produce* 12 Million Black Voices, *a folk history of African Americans. A combination of photos and brief essays, the work is a powerful commentary on three centuries of oppression.*

The following selection is adapted from "Death on the City Pavements," which expresses Wright's view of the African American migration out of the South, a journey he himself experienced. This bittersweet migration often traded the harsh, rural repression of the South for the overcrowded, anonymous ghettos of the North.

Housing discrimination, both overt and covert, confined African American migrants to the least desirable, most overcrowded areas of the city—in many cases, the neighborhoods that had first housed immigrants from Europe. Unscrupulous landlords subdivided buildings into the tiniest possible apartments ("kitchenettes"), and as impoverished newcomers who could afford no better, African American migrants were forced to cope with overpriced, substandard housing as best they could. Much of this passage, incidentally, could have been written about any 20th-century minority group.

DEATH ON THE CITY PAVEMENTS

Richard Wright

And the Bosses of the Buildings take these old houses and convert them into "kitchenettes," and then rent them to us at rates so high that they make fabulous fortunes.... Because we have been used to sleeping several in a room on the plantations in the South, we rent these kitchenettes and are glad to get them....

A war sets up in our emotions: One part of our feelings tells us it is good to be in the city, that we have a chance at life here, that we need but turn a corner to become a stranger, that we need no longer bow and dodge at the sight of the Lords of the Land. Another part of our feelings tells us that, in terms of worry and strain, the cost of living in the kitchenettes is too high, that the city heaps too much responsibility on us and gives too little security in return.

The kitchenette is the author of the glad tidings that new suckers are in town, ready to be cheated, plundered, and put in their places.

The kitchenette is our prison, our death sentence without a trial, the new form of mob violence that assaults...all of us, in its ceaseless attacks.

The kitchenette, with its filth and foul air, with its one toilet for thirty or more tenants, kills our black babies so fast that in many cities twice as many of them die as white babies....

The kitchenette scatters death so widely among us that our death rate exceeds our birthrate, and if it were not for the trains and autos bringing us daily into the city from the plantations, we black folk who dwell in northern cities would die out entirely over the course of a few years....

The kitchenette throws desperate and unhappy people into an unbearable closeness of association, thereby increasing latent friction, giving birth to never-ending quarrels of recrimination, accusation, and vindictiveness, producing warped personalities.

The kitchenette injects pressure and tension into our individual personalities, making many of us give up the struggle, walk off and leave wives, husbands, and even children behind to shift as best they can....

The kitchenette reaches out with fingers of golden bribes to the officials of the city, persuading them to allow old firetraps to remain standing and occupied long after they should have been torn down.

The kitchenette is the funnel through which our pulverized lives flow to ruin and death on the city pavement, at a profit.

SOURCE: Wright (1941/1988, pp. 104–111).

Questions to Consider

1. Given the grim realities described in this passage, why do you think African Americans continued to move out of the South?
2. What concepts can you apply to this passage? How does it illustrate the dynamics of this period of history?

---

the increased freedom that followed slavery, a national African American leadership developed, and spoke out against oppression and founded organizations that eventually helped lead the fight for freedom and equality. Even at its birth, the black protest movement was diverse and incorporated a variety of viewpoints and leaders.

Booker T. Washington was the most prominent African American leader prior to World War I. Washington had been born in slavery and was the founder and president of Tuskegee Institute, a college in Alabama dedicated to educating African Americans. His public advice to African Americans in the South was to be patient, to accommodate to the Jim Crow system for the time being, to raise their levels of education and job skills, and to take full advantage of whatever opportunities became available. This nonconfrontational stance earned Washington praise and support from the white community and widespread popularity in the nation. Privately, he worked behind the scenes to end discrimination and implement

Three early leaders of African American protest: Booker T. Washington, W.E.B. Du Bois, and Marcus Garvey.

full racial integration and equality (Franklin & Moss, 1994, pp. 272–274; Hawkins, 1962; Washington, 1965).

Washington's most vocal opponent was W. E. B. Du Bois, an intellectual and activist who was born in the North and educated at some of the leading universities of the day. Among his many other accomplishments, Du Bois was part of a coalition of blacks and white liberals who founded the National Association for the Advancement of Colored People (NAACP) in 1909. Du Bois rejected Washington's accommodationist stance and advocated immediate pursuit of racial equality and a direct assault on de jure segregation. Almost from the beginning of its existence, the NAACP filed lawsuits that challenged the legal foundations of Jim Crow segregation (Du Bois, 1961). As we shall see in Chapter 6, this legal strategy was eventually successful and led to the demise of the Jim Crow system.

Washington and Du Bois may have differed on matters of strategy and tactics, but they agreed that the only acceptable goal for African Americans was an integrated, racially equal United States. A third leader who emerged early in the 20th century called for a very different approach to the problems of U.S. race relations. Marcus Garvey was born in Jamaica and immigrated to the United States during World War I. He argued that the white-dominated U.S. society was hopelessly racist and would never truly support integration and racial equality. He advocated separatist goals, including a return to Africa. Garvey founded the Universal Negro Improvement Association in 1914 in his native Jamaica and founded the first U.S. branch in 1916. Garvey's organization was popular for a time in African American communities outside the South, and he helped establish some of the themes and ideas of black nationalism and pride in African heritage that would become prominent again in the pluralistic 1960s (Essien-Udom, 1962; Garvey, 1969, 1977; Vincent, 1976).

These early leaders and organizations established some of the foundations for later protest movements, but prior to the mid-20th century, they made few actual improvements in the situation of African Americans in the North or South. Jim Crow was a formidable opponent, and the African American community lacked the resources to successfully challenge the status quo until the century was well along and some basic structural features of American society had changed.

THE DIMENSIONS OF MINORITY-GROUP STATUS

ACCULTURATION AND INTEGRATION

During this era of southern segregation and migration to the North, assimilation was not a major factor in the African American experience. Rather, the black–white relations of the time are better described as a system of structural pluralism combined with great inequality. Excluded from the mainstream but freed from the limitations of slavery, African Americans constructed a separate subsociety and subculture. In all regions of the nation, African Americans developed their own institutions and organizations, including separate neighborhoods, churches, businesses, and schools. Like immigrants from Europe in the same era, they organized their communities to cater to their own needs and problems and to pursue their agenda as a group.

During segregation, a small African American middle class emerged based on leadership roles in the church, education, and business. A network of black colleges and universities was constructed to educate the children of the growing middle class, as well as other classes. Through this infrastructure, African Americans began to develop the resources and leadership that in the decades ahead would attack, head-on, the structures of racial inequality.

GENDER AND RACE

For African American men and women, the changes wrought by industrialization and the population movement to the North created new possibilities and new roles. However, as African Americans continued to be the victims of exploitation and exclusion in both the North and the South, African American women continued to be among the most vulnerable groups in society.

Following emancipation, there was a flurry of marriages and weddings among African Americans, as they were finally able to legitimatize their family relationships (Staples, 1988, p. 306). African American women continued to have primary responsibility for home and children. Historian Herbert Gutman (1976) reports that it was common for married women to drop out of the labor force and attend solely to household and family duties, because a working wife was too reminiscent of a slave role. This pattern became so widespread that it created serious labor shortages in many areas (Gutman, 1976; see also Staples, 1988, p. 307).

The former slaves were hardly affluent, however, and as sharecropping and segregation began to shape race relations in the South, women often had to return to the fields or domestic work for the family to survive. One former slave woman noted that women "do double duty, a man's share in the field and a woman's part at home" (Evans, 1989, p. 121). During the bleak decades following the end of Reconstruction, southern black families and black women in particular lived "close to the bone" (p. 121).

In the cities and in the growing African American neighborhoods in the North, African American women played a role that in some ways paralleled the role of immigrant women from Europe. The men often moved north first and sent for the women after they had attained some level of financial stability or when the pain of separation became too great (Almquist, 1979, p. 434). In other cases, African American women left the South by the thousands to work as domestic servants; they often replaced European immigrant women, who had moved up in the job structure (Amott & Matthaei, 1991, p. 168).

In the North, discrimination and racism created constant problems of unemployment for the men, and families often relied on the income supplied by the women to make ends meet. It was comparatively easy for women to find employment but only in the low-paying, less desirable areas, such as domestic work. In both the South and the North, African American women worked outside the home in larger proportions than did white women. For example, in 1900, 41% of African American women were employed, compared with only 16% of white women (Staples, 1988, p. 307).

In 1890, more than a generation after the end of slavery, 85% of all African American men and 96% of African American women were employed in just two occupational categories: agriculture and domestic or personal service. By 1930, 90% of employed African American women were still in these

African American women were often forced to work in the fields to help make ends meet.

same two categories, whereas the corresponding percentage for employed African American males had dropped to 54% (although nearly all the remaining 46% were unskilled workers; Steinberg, 1981, pp. 206–207). Since the inception of segregation, African American women have had consistently higher unemployment rates and lower incomes than African American men and white women (Almquist, 1979, p. 437). These gaps, as we shall see in Chapter 6, persist to the present day.

During the years following emancipation, some issues did split men and women, within both the African American community and the larger society. Prominent among these was suffrage, or the right to vote, which was still limited to men only. The abolitionist movement, which had been so instrumental in ending slavery, also supported universal suffrage. Efforts to enfranchise women, though, were abandoned by the Republican Party and large parts of the abolitionist movement to concentrate on efforts to secure the vote for African American males in the South. Ratification of the Fifteenth Amendment in 1870 extended the vote, in principle, to African American men, but the Nineteenth Amendment enfranchising women would not be passed for another 50 years (Almquist, 1979, pp. 433–434; Evans, 1989, pp. 121–124).

QUESTIONS FOR REFLECTION

1. Why did African Americans begin to migrate to the North in the early 20th century? Did this move improve their situation? How?

2. What African American strategies for protest were developed early in the 20th century? How were these strategies shaped by the overall situation of the group?

3. Did African Americans become more or less acculturated and integrated during the Jim Crow era? Why?

4. How was the experience of African Americans shaped by gender during this time period?

INDUSTRIALIZATION, THE SHIFT TO POSTINDUSTRIAL SOCIETY, AND DOMINANT–MINORITY GROUP RELATIONS: GENERAL TRENDS

The processes of industrialization that began in the 19th century continued to shape the larger society and dominant–minority relations throughout the 20th century. Today, the United States bears little resemblance to the society it was a century ago. The population has more than tripled in size and has urbanized even more rapidly than it has grown. New organizational forms (bureaucracies, corporations, multinational businesses) and new technologies (computers, the Internet) dominate everyday life. Levels of education have risen, and the public schools have produced one of the most literate populations and best-trained workforces in the history of the world.

Minority groups also grew in size during this period, and most became even more urbanized than the general population. Minority-group members have come to participate in an increasing array of occupations, and their average levels of education have also risen.

Despite these real improvements, however, virtually all U.S. minority groups continue to face racism, poverty, discrimination, and exclusion. As industrialization proceeded, the mechanisms for maintaining racial stratification also evolved, morphing into forms that are subtle, indirect, but, in their way, as formidable as Jim Crow segregation.

In this section, we outline the social processes that began in the industrial era and continue to shape the postindustrial stage. We note the ways these processes have changed American society and examine some of the general implications for minority groups. We then summarize these changes in terms of a transition from the rigid competitive Jim Crow era to a new stage of group relations called fluid competitive relations. The treatment here is broad and intended to establish a general framework for the examination of the impacts of industrialization and deindustrialization on group relations in the case studies that form Part III of this text.

URBANIZATION

We have already noted that urbanization made close, paternalistic controls of minority groups irrelevant. For example, the racial etiquette required by southern de jure segregation, such as African Americans deferring to whites on crowded sidewalks, tended to disappear in the chaos of an urban rush hour.

Besides weakening dominant-group controls, urbanization also created the potential for minority groups to mobilize and organize large numbers of people. As stated in Chapter 1, the sheer size of a group is a source of power. Without the freedom to organize, however, size means little, and urbanization increased both the concentration of populations and the freedom to organize.

OCCUPATIONAL SPECIALIZATION

One of the first and most important results of industrialization, even in its earliest days, was an increase in occupational specialization and the variety of jobs available in the workforce. The growing needs of an urbanizing population increased the number of jobs available in the production, transport, and sale of goods and services. Occupational specialization was also stimulated by the very nature of industrial production. Complex manufacturing processes could be performed more efficiently if they were broken down into the narrower component tasks. It was easier and more efficient to train the workforce in the simpler, specialized jobs. Assembly lines were invented, work was subdivided, the division of labor became increasingly complex, and the number of different occupations continued to grow.

The sheer complexity of the industrial job structure made it difficult to maintain rigid, caste-like divisions of labor between dominant and minority groups. Rigid competitive forms of group relations, such as Jim Crow segregation, became less viable as the job market became more diversified and changeable. Simple, clear rules about which groups could do which jobs disappeared.

As the more repressive systems of control weakened, job opportunities for minority-group members sometimes increased. However, as the relationships between group memberships and positions in the job market became more blurred, conflict between groups also increased. For example, as we have noted, African Americans moving from the South often found themselves in competition for jobs with members of white ethnic groups, labor unions, and other elements of the dominant group.

BUREAUCRACY AND RATIONALITY

As industrialization continued, privately owned corporations and businesses came to have workforces numbering in the hundreds of thousands. Gigantic factories employing thousands of workers became common. To coordinate the efforts of these huge workforces, bureaucracy became the dominant form of organization in the economy and, indeed, throughout the society.

Bureaucracies are large-scale, impersonal, formal organizations that run "by the book." They are governed by rules and regulations (i.e., "red tape") and are "rational" in that they attempt to find the most efficient ways to accomplish their tasks. Although they typically fail to attain the ideal of fully rational efficiency, bureaucracies tend to recruit, reward, and promote employees on the basis of competence and performance (Gerth & Mills, 1946).

The stress on rationality and objectivity can counteract the more blatant forms of racism and increase the array of opportunities available to members of minority groups. Although they are often nullified by other forces (see Blumer, 1965), these antiprejudicial tendencies do not exist at all or are much weaker in preindustrial economies.

The history of the concept of race illustrates the impact of rationality and scientific ways of thinking. Today, virtually the entire scientific community rejects the traditional idea that race is an important determinant of intelligence or personality traits such as dependability or competence, conclusions based on decades of research. These scientific findings undermined and contributed to the destruction of the formal systems of privilege based solely on race (e.g., segregated school systems) and traditional prejudice, which is based on the assumption that race is a crucial personal characteristic.

GROWTH OF WHITE-COLLAR JOBS AND THE SERVICE SECTOR

Industrialization changed the composition of the labor force. As work became more complex and specialized, the need to coordinate and regulate the production process increased, and as a result, bureaucracies and other organizations grew larger still. Within these organizations, white-collar occupations—those that coordinate, manage, and deal with the flow of paperwork—continued to expand throughout much of the century. As industrialization progressed, mechanization and automation reduced the number of manual or blue-collar workers, and white-collar occupations became the dominant sector of the job market in the United States.

Extractive (or primary) occupations are those that produce raw materials such as food, minerals, or lumber.

Manufacturing (or secondary) occupations are those that transform raw materials into finished products ready for the marketplace.

Service (or tertiary) occupations provide services.

The changing nature of the workforce can be illustrated by looking at the proportional representation of three different types of jobs:

1. **Extractive (or primary) occupations** are those that produce raw materials, such as food and agricultural products, minerals, and lumber. The jobs in this sector often involve unskilled manual labor, require little formal education, and are generally low paying.

2. **Manufacturing (or secondary) occupations** transform raw materials into finished products ready for sale in the marketplace. Like jobs in the extractive sector, these blue-collar jobs involve manual labor, but they tend to require higher levels of skill and are more highly rewarded. Examples of occupations in this sector include the assembly line jobs that transform steel, rubber, plastic, and other materials into finished automobiles.

3. **Service (or tertiary) occupations** do not produce "things"; rather, they provide services. As urbanization increased and self-sufficiency decreased, opportunities for work in this sector grew. Examples of tertiary occupations include police officer, clerk, waiter, teacher, nurse, doctor, and cabdriver.

The course of industrialization is traced in the changing structure of the labor market depicted in Figure 5.3. In 1840, when industrialization was just beginning in the United States, most of the workforce (70%) was in the extractive sector, with agriculture being the dominant occupation. As industrialization progressed, the manufacturing, or secondary, sector grew, reaching a peak after World War II. Today, in the postindustrial era, the large majority of U.S. jobs are in the service, or tertiary, sector.

FIGURE 5.3 The Changing U.S. Workforce: Distribution of Jobs From 1840 to 2010

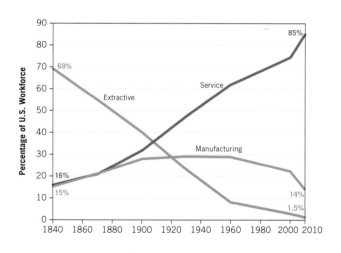

SOURCE: 1840 to 1990—adapted from Lenski, Nolan, and Lenski (1995); 2002—calculated from U.S. Census Bureau (2005, pp. 385–388); 2005—calculated from U.S. Census Bureau (2007, pp. 388–391); 2009—calculated from U.S. Census Bureau (2011a, pp. 393–395).

This shift away from blue-collar jobs and manufacturing since the 1960s is sometimes referred to as deindustrialization or the shift to a postindustrial subsistence technology. The U.S. economy has lost millions of unionized, high-paying factory jobs since the 1960s, and the downward trend continues. The industrial jobs that sustained so many generations of American workers have moved to other nations where wages are considerably lower than in the United States or have been eliminated by robots or other automated manufacturing processes (see Rifkin, 1996).

The changing structure of the job market helps clarify the nature of intergroup competition and the sources of wealth and power in society. Job growth in the United States today is largely in the service sector, and these occupations are highly variable. At one end are low-paying jobs with few, if any, benefits or chances for advancement (e.g., washing dishes in a restaurant). At the upper end are high-prestige, lucrative positions, such as Supreme Court justice, scientist, and financial analyst.

The new service-sector jobs are either highly desirable technical, professional, or administrative jobs with demanding entry requirements (e.g., physician or nurse) or low-paying, low-skilled jobs with few benefits and little security (e.g., receptionist, nurse's aide). Over the past half century, job growth in the United States has been either in areas where educationally deprived minority-group members find it difficult to compete or in areas that offer little compensation, upward mobility, or security. As we will see in Part III, the economic situation of contemporary minority groups reflects these fundamental trends.

THE GROWING IMPORTANCE OF EDUCATION

Education has been an increasingly important prerequisite for employability in the United States and in other advanced industrial societies. A high school or, increasingly, a college degree has become the minimum entry-level requirement for employment. However, opportunities for high-quality education are not distributed equally across the population. Some minority groups, especially those created by colonization, have been systematically excluded from the schools of the dominant society, and today, they are less likely to have the educational backgrounds needed to compete for better jobs.

Access to education is a key issue for all U.S. minority groups, and the average educational levels of these groups have been rising since World War II. Still, minority children continue to be much more likely to attend segregated, underfunded, deteriorated schools and to receive inferior educations (see Orfield & Lee, 2007).

A DUAL LABOR MARKET

The changing composition of the labor force and increasing importance of educational credentials has split the U.S. labor market into two segments or types of jobs. The **primary labor market** includes jobs usually located in large, bureaucratic

organizations. These positions offer higher pay, more security, better opportunities for advancement, health and retirement benefits, and other amenities. Entry requirements include college degrees, even when people with fewer years of schooling could competently perform the work.

The **secondary labor market**, sometimes called the competitive market, includes low-paying, low-skilled, insecure jobs. Many of these jobs are in the service sector. They do not represent a career and offer little opportunity for promotion or upward mobility. Very often, they do not offer health or retirement benefits, have high rates of turnover, and are part-time, seasonal, or temporary.

Many American minority groups are concentrated in the secondary job market. Their exclusion from better jobs is perpetuated not so much by direct or overt discrimination as by their lack of access to the educational and other credentials required to enter the primary sector. The differential distribution of educational opportunities, in the past as well as in the present, effectively protects workers in the primary sector from competition from minority groups.

GLOBALIZATION

Over the past century, the United States has become an economic, political, and military world power with interests around the globe. These worldwide ties have created new minority groups through population movement and have changed the status of others. Immigration to this country has been considerable for the past three decades. The American economy is one of the most productive in the world, and jobs, even those in the low-paying secondary and service sectors, are the primary goals for millions of newcomers. For other immigrants, this country continues to play its historic role as a refuge from political and religious persecution.

Many of the wars, conflicts, and other disputes in which the United States has been involved have had consequences for American minority groups. For example, both Puerto Ricans and Cuban Americans became U.S. minority groups as the result of processes set in motion during the Spanish–American War of 1898. Both World War I and World War II created new job opportunities for many minority groups, including African Americans and Mexican Americans. After the Korean War, international ties were forged between the United States and South Korea, and this led to an increase in immigration from that nation. In the 1960s and 1970s, the military involvement of the United States in Southeast Asia

---

The **primary labor market** includes jobs that are better paying, higher status, and more secure.

The **secondary labor market** includes jobs that are lower paying, lower status, and less secure.

TABLE 5.2 Characteristics of Three Systems of Group Relationships

	SYSTEMS OF GROUP RELATIONS		
	Paternalistic	**Competitive**	
		Rigid	**Fluid**
Subsistence technology	Agrarian	Industrial	Postindustrial
Stratification	*Caste.* Group determines status.	*Mixed.* Elements of caste and class. Status largely determined by group.	*Variable.* Status strongly affected by group. Inequality varies within groups.
Division of labor	*Simple.* Determined by group.	*More complex.* Jobs largely determined by group, but some sharing of jobs by different groups.	*Most complex.* Group and jobs are less related. Complex specialization and great variation within groups.
Contact between groups	*Common,* but statuses unequal.	*Less common* and mostly unequal.	*More common.* Highest rates of equal-status contact.
Overt intergroup conflict	*Rare*	*More common*	*Common*
Power differential	*Maximum.* Minority groups have little ability to pursue self-interests.	*Less.* Minority groups have some ability to pursue self-interests.	*Least.* Minority groups have more ability to pursue self-interests.

SOURCE: Based on Farley (2000, p. 109).

led to the arrival of Vietnamese, Cambodians, Hmong, and other immigrant and refugee groups from that region.

Dominant–minority relations in the United States have been increasingly played out on an international stage as the world has effectively "shrunk" in size and become more interconnected by international organizations, such as the United Nations; by ties of trade and commerce; and by modern means of transportation and communication. In a world where two thirds of the population is nonwhite and many important nations (such as China, India, and Nigeria) are composed of peoples of color, the treatment of racial minorities by the U.S. dominant group has come under increased scrutiny. It is difficult to preach principles of fairness, equality, and justice—which the United States claims as its own—when domestic realities suggest an embarrassing failure to fully implement these standards. Part of the incentive for the United States to end blatant systems of discrimination such as de jure segregation came from the desire to maintain a leading position in the world.

POSTINDUSTRIAL SOCIETY AND THE SHIFT FROM RIGID TO FLUID COMPETITIVE RELATIONSHIPS

The coming of postindustrial society brought changes so fundamental and profound that they are often described in terms of a revolution: from an industrial society, based on manufacturing, to a postindustrial society, based on information processing and computer-related or other new technologies. As the subsistence technology evolved, so did American dominant–minority relations. The rigid competitive systems (such as Jim Crow) associated with earlier phases of industrialization gave way to **fluid competitive systems** of group relations.

In fluid competitive relations, formal or legal barriers to competition—such as Jim Crow laws or apartheid—no longer exist. Both geographic and social mobility are greater, and the limitations imposed by minority-group status are less restrictive and burdensome. Rigid caste systems of stratification, in which group membership determines opportunities, adult statuses, and jobs, are replaced by more open class systems, in which the relationships between group membership and wealth, prestige, and power are weaker. Because fluid competitive systems are more open and the position of the minority group is less fixed, the fear of competition from minority groups becomes more widespread in the dominant group, and intergroup conflict increases. Table 5.2 compares the characteristics of the three systems of group relations.

Compared with previous systems, the fluid competitive system is closer to the American ideal of an open, fair system of stratification in which effort and competence are rewarded and race, ethnicity, gender, religion, and other "birthmarks" are

In **fluid competitive systems** of group relations, minority-group members are freer to compete for jobs and other scarce resources.

How have the trends discussed in this section affected you and your family? If the United States had not industrialized, where would your family live? What kind of career would your parents and grandparents have had? Would you have had the opportunity for a college education?

You can get some insight on the answers to these questions by researching your family history over the past several generations and completing the table below. You may not have all the information requested, but that might be a good reason to give your parents or grandparents a call! If you know nothing at all about your family history and have no way to get the information,

perhaps you can find someone—a roommate or friend—to interview for this exercise.

To complete the table, pick *one* ancestor from each generation, perhaps the one about which you know the most. To get you started and provide a comparison, the table is completed for one of the authors. When you get to the bottom row of the right hand side of the table, fill in the blanks in terms of your desires or plans. Would you rather live in the city, suburbs, or country? What is your ideal job or the career for which you are preparing? What degree are you pursuing?

	HEALEY			YOU		
Generations	Residence	Education	Occupation	Residence	Education	Occupation
Great-grandparent	City	Unknown	Coal miner			
Grandparent	City	Eighth grade (?)	Clerk, bar owner			
Parent	City	High school, some college	Agent for the Internal Revenue Service			
Healey	Suburbs	PhD	College professor			

TURN THE PAGE TO SEE THE PATTERNS WE PREDICT.

irrelevant. However, as we will see in chapters to come, race and ethnicity continue to affect life chances and limit opportunities for minority-group members even in fluid competitive systems. As suggested by the Noel hypothesis, people continue to identify themselves with particular groups (ethnocentrism), and competition for resources continues to play out along group lines. Consistent with the Blauner hypothesis, the minority groups that were formed by colonization remain at a disadvantage in the pursuit of opportunities, education, prestige, and other resources.

QUESTIONS FOR REFLECTION

1. Why did black–white relations shift from a rigid to a fluid competitive system? What was the role of subsistence technology in the shift?

2. What are the key changes in the shift to postindustrial subsistence technology? What are the implications of these changes for American minority groups?

MODERN INSTITUTIONAL DISCRIMINATION

In general, American minority groups continue to lag behind national averages in income, employment, and other measures

of equality, despite the greater fluidity of group relations, the end of legal barriers such as Jim Crow laws, the dramatic declines in overt prejudice (see Chapter 3), and the introduction of numerous laws designed to ensure that all people are treated without regard to race, gender, or ethnicity. After all this change, shouldn't there be more equality and less racial stratification?

As we saw in Chapter 3, many Americans attribute the persisting patterns of inequality to a lack of willpower or motivation to get ahead on the part of minority-group members. In the remaining chapters of this text, however, we argue that the major barriers facing minority groups in postindustrial, post–Jim Crow America are pervasive, subtle but still powerful forms of discrimination, which together can be called modern institutional discrimination.

As you read in Chapter 1, institutional discrimination is built into the everyday operation of the social structure of society. The routine procedures and policies of institutions and organizations are arranged so that minority-group members are automatically put at a disadvantage. In the Jim Crow era in the South, for example, African Americans were deprived of the right to vote by overt institutional discrimination and could acquire little in the way of political power.

The forms of institutional discrimination that persist in the present are more subtle and difficult to document than the blatant, overt customs and laws of the Jim Crow system.

Based on the trends discussed in this chapter, and as partially illustrated by Healey's family history, it is likely that you will see these trends in your family history:

1. Movement from rural to urban residence

2. Decrease in jobs in the primary sector (extractive jobs such as farmer or coal miner) and secondary sector (manufacturing jobs)

3. Increase in service-sector jobs

4. Increase in education

Of course, each family is unique, and it is entirely possible that your history will not agree with any of these trends. Nonetheless, given the pressures created by these macrolevel changes, the bulk of families should conform to most of these tendencies.

In fact, they are sometimes unintentional or unconscious, and are manifested more in the results for minority groups than in the intentions or prejudices of dominant-group members. Modern institutional discrimination is not necessarily linked to prejudice, and the decision makers who implement it may sincerely think of themselves as behaving rationally and in the best interests of their organizations.

THE CONTINUING POWER OF THE PAST

Many forces conspire to maintain racial stratification in the present. Some are the legacies of past discriminatory practices. Consider, for example, **past-in-present institutional discrimination**, which involves practices in the present that have discriminatory consequences because of some pattern of discrimination or exclusion in the past (Feagin & Feagin, 1986, p. 32).

One form of this discrimination is found in workforces organized around the principle of seniority. In these systems, which are quite common, workers who have been on the job longer have higher incomes, more privileges, and other benefits, such as longer vacations. The "old-timers" often have more job security and are designated in official, written policy as the last to be fired or laid off in the event of hard times. Workers and employers alike may think of the privileges of seniority as just rewards for long years of service, familiarity with the job, and so forth.

Past-in-present institutional discrimination involves patterns of inequality or unequal treatment in the present that are caused by some pattern of discrimination in the past.

Personnel policies based on seniority may seem perfectly reasonable, neutral, and fair; however, they can have discriminatory results in the present because in the past members of minority groups and women were excluded from specific occupations by racist or sexist labor unions, discriminatory employers, or both. As a result, minority-group workers and women may have fewer years of experience than do dominant-group workers and men, and may be the first to go when layoffs are necessary. The adage "last hired, first fired" describes the situation of minority-group and female employees who are more vulnerable not because of some overtly racist or sexist policy but because of the routine operation of the seemingly neutral principle of seniority.

Racial differences in homeownership provide a second example of the myriad ways the past shapes the present and maintains the moving target of racial stratification. Today, about 72% of non-Hispanic whites own their own homes, and these houses have a median value of $179,000. In contrast, only 44% of non-Hispanic blacks are homeowners, and the median value of their homes is $125,900 (U.S. Census Bureau, 2013a). Homeownership is an important source of family wealth, because home equity can be used to establish credit; finance businesses, other purchases, and investments; and fund education and other sources of human capital for the next generation. What is the origin of these huge differences in family wealth?

Part of the answer lies in events that date back 80 years. As you know, President Franklin D. Roosevelt's administration responded to the Great Depression of the 1930s, in part, by instituting the New Deal: a variety of programs that provided assistance to distressed Americans. What is not so widely known is that these programs were racially discriminatory and provided few or no benefits to African Americans (Massey, 2007, p. 60; see also Katznelson, 2005; Lieberman, 1998).

One of the New Deal programs was administered by the Federal Housing Administration (FHA): The agency offered low-interest mortgages and made homeownership possible for millions of families. However, the FHA sanctioned racially restrictive covenants that forbade whites to sell to blacks and helped institutionalize the practice of "redlining" black neighborhoods, which prevented banks from making home loans in these areas. Together, these and other discriminatory practices effectively excluded black Americans from homeownership (Massey, 2007, pp. 60–61; Massey & Denton, 1993, pp. 53–54). Thus, another racial divide was created that, over the generations, has helped countless white families develop wealth and credit but made it impossible for black families to qualify for homeownership, the "great engine of wealth creation" (Massey, 2007, p. 61).

More broadly, racial residential segregation—which is arguably the key factor in preserving racial stratification in the present—provides another illustration of modern institutional discrimination. The overt, Jim Crow–era laws and customs that created racially segregated neighborhoods and towns in the past (such as the "sundown towns" mentioned at the start of this chapter) were abolished decades ago, and racial discrimination in selling and renting houses has been illegal since the passage of the Fair Housing Act in 1968. However, blacks continue to be concentrated in all- or mostly-black neighborhoods (see, e.g., Figure 5.4), many of which are also characterized by inadequate services and high levels of poverty and crime. How is racial residential segregation maintained in an era of fair housing laws?

Some of the practices that preserve racial residential segregation have been documented by audit studies. In this technique, black and white (and sometimes Latino and Asian) customers are prepared with carefully matched background credentials (education, employment and credit histories, and finances) and sent to test the market for racial fairness. Characteristically, the black customer is steered away from white neighborhoods, required to furnish greater down payments or deposits, charged higher interest rates, or otherwise discouraged from securing a successful sale or rental. Sometimes the black customer is told that a unit is already sold or rented, or otherwise given false or misleading information (see Pager & Shepherd, 2008, for a review).

The result is that blacks are discouraged from breaking the housing color line but not directly, blatantly, or in ways that clearly violate the fair housing laws. The gatekeepers (real-estate agents, landlords, mortgage bankers) base their behavior not on race per se but on characteristics associated with race—accent, dialect, home address, and so forth—to make decisions about what levels of service and responsiveness to provide to customers. Sociologist Douglas Massey (2000, p. 4) has even demonstrated racially biased treatment based on the use of "Black English" in telephone contacts.

Audit studies have also documented racial discrimination in the job market (e.g., see Bertrand & Mullainathan, 2004). Other forms of modern institutional discrimination

FIGURE 5.4 Concentration of Whites, Blacks, and Hispanics in Chicago, 2008

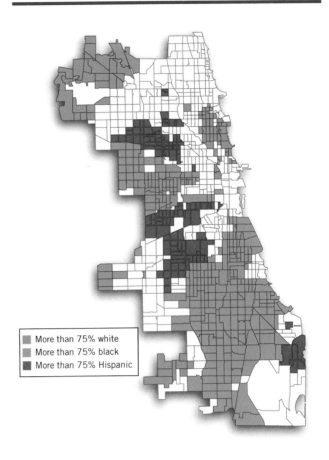

More than 75% white
More than 75% black
More than 75% Hispanic

SOURCE: Center for Governmental Studies, Northern Illinois University.

include the use of racially and culturally biased standardized tests in school systems, the pattern of drug arrests that has sent disproportionate numbers of black teenage boys and young men to jail and prison (see Chapter 6 for more on this trend), and decisions by businesspeople to move their operations away from center-city neighborhoods. Part of what makes modern institutional discrimination so challenging to document is that race, ethnicity, or gender may not be a conscious or overt part of these decision-making processes. Still, the results are that blacks and other minorities—in the past as in the present—are filtered away from opportunities and resources, and racial stratification is maintained, even in the new age of a supposedly color-blind society.

Modern institutional discrimination routinely places black Americans in less desirable statuses in education, residence and homeownership, jobs, the criminal justice system—indeed, across the entire expanse of the socioeconomic system. The result is racial stratification maintained not by monolithic Jim Crow segregation or slavery but by a subtle and indirect system that is the "new configuration of inequality" (Katz & Stern, 2008, p. 100). We will apply the concept of modern institutional discrimination throughout the case study chapters in Part III of this text.

AFFIRMATIVE ACTION

By its nature, modern institutional discrimination is more difficult to identify, measure, and eliminate, and some of the most heated disputes in recent group relations have concerned public policy and law in this area. Among the most controversial issues is **affirmative action**, a group of programs that attempt to reduce the effects of past discrimination or increase diversity in the workplace and in schools. In the 1970s and 1980s, the Supreme Court found that programs designed to favor minority employees as a strategy for overcoming past discrimination were constitutional (e.g., *Firefighters Local Union No. 1784 v. Stotts*, 1984; *Sheet Metal Workers v. EEOC*, 1986; *United Steelworkers of America, AFL-CIO-CLC v. Weber*, 1979).

Virtually all these early decisions concerned blatant policies of discrimination, which are becoming increasingly rare as we move further away from the days of Jim Crow. Even so, the decisions were based on narrow margins (votes of 5 to 4) and featured acrimonious and bitter debates. More recently, the Supreme Court narrowed the grounds on which such past grievances could be redressed (e.g., *Adarand Constructors Inc. v. Pena*, 1995).

A Case of Discrimination? The most recent case involving affirmative action programs in the work place is *Ricci v. DeStefano*, which involved firefighters in New Haven, Connecticut. In 2003, the city administered a test for promotion in the city's fire department. More than 100 people took the test, but no African American scored high enough to qualify for promotion. The city decided to throw out the test results on the grounds that its dramatically unequal racial results strongly suggested that it was biased against African Americans.

This decision is consistent with the concept of "disparate impact": If a practice has unequal results, federal policy and court precedents tend to assume that the practice is racially biased. The city feared that using these possibly "tainted" test scores might result in lawsuits by black and other minority firefighters. Instead, a lawsuit was filed by several white and Hispanic firefighters who *had* qualified for promotion, claiming that invalidating the test results amounted to reverse racial discrimination. In yet another 5-to-4 ruling, the Supreme Court ruled in favor of the white plaintiffs in 2009.

This case illustrates some of the difficult issues that accompany attempts to address modern institutional discrimination. The issue in *Ricci v. DeStefano* is not overt, Jim Crow discrimination but, rather, a test that might be discriminatory in its results, although not in its intent. New Haven was attempting to avoid racial discrimination. How far do employers need to go to ensure racial fairness? Should policies and

---

Affirmative action refers to programs that are intended to reduce the effects of past discrimination or increase diversity in workplaces and schools.

---

procedures be judged by their outcomes or their intents? What does "fairness" and "equal treatment" mean in a society in which minority groups have only recently won formal equality and still have lower access to quality schooling and jobs in the mainstream economy? Did the city of New Haven go too far in its attempt to avoid discrimination (five of the Supreme Court Justices thought so)? Can there be a truly fair, race-neutral policy for employment and promotion in the present when opportunities and resources in the past were so long allocated on the basis of race? If the problem is color coded, can the solution be color neutral?

Higher Education and Affirmative Action. Colleges and universities have been another prominent battleground for affirmative action programs. Since the 1960s, many institutions of higher education have implemented programs to increase the number of minority students on campus at both the undergraduate and graduate levels, sometimes admitting minority students who had lower grade point averages (GPAs) or test scores than those of dominant-group students who were turned away. In general, advocates of these programs have justified them in terms of redressing the discriminatory practices of the past or increasing diversity on campus and making the student body a more accurate representation of the surrounding society. To say the least, these programs have been highly controversial and the targets of frequent lawsuits, some of which have found their way to the highest courts in the land.

Recent decisions by the Supreme Court have limited the application of affirmative action by colleges and universities. In two lawsuits involving the University of Michigan in 2003 (*Grutter v. Bollinger* and *Gratz v. Bollinger*), the Supreme Court held that the university's law school *could* use race as one criterion in deciding admissions but that undergraduate admissions *could not* award an automatic advantage to minority applicants. In other words, universities could take into account an applicant's race but only in a limited way, as one factor among many.

In more recent cases involving affirmative action in higher education, the Supreme Court further narrowed the ability of universities to consider race in admissions decisions. One case, decided in June 2013, was *Fisher v. University of Texas at Austin*. The University of Texas (UT) had been using a unique admissions policy according to which the top 10% of the student body in each high school in Texas were automatically admitted. Because of the residential segregation in towns and cities across the state, the student body at many high schools is disproportionately black, white, or Hispanic, and the 10% rule guarantees substantial diversity in the UT student body. Some 80% of the students are selected by this method. The remaining 20% are selected using a variety of criteria, including race and ethnicity. It is common for selective institutions such as UT to use many criteria—not just test scores—to diversify their student body.

The case was brought by Amy Fisher, a white student who was not admitted to UT. She argued that some of the admitted minority students had lower GPAs and test scores than she did. The university argued that the educational benefit of a diverse student body justified its partial and limited use of race as one admission criterion among many.

The Supreme Court sent the case back to the federal appeals court with instructions to apply a strict standard: Race could be used as an admission criterion only if there were no workable race-neutral alternatives that would result in a diverse student body. The decision was not a death blow to affirmative action, but it appeared to continue the trend of limiting the circumstances under which affirmative action policies could be applied.

In the second recent decision (*Schuette v. BAMN*), decided in April 2014, the Supreme Court upheld an amendment to the state constitution of Michigan that banned the use of race as a factor in admissions and hiring decisions in all state agencies. This decision effectively ended affirmative action, in any form, in Michigan and in several other states with similar laws. Combined with the 2013 *Fisher* decision, it seems that the role of affirmative action in higher education has been severely curtailed.

The Future of Affirmative Action. What lies ahead for affirmative action? On one hand, there is a clear trend in court decisions to narrow the scope and applicability of these programs. Also, there is little public support for affirmative action, especially for programs that are perceived as providing specific numerical quotas for minority groups in jobs or university admissions. For example, a representative sample of Americans was asked in a 2012 survey if they supported "preferential hiring and promotion of blacks." Only 15% of white respondents expressed support, and, more surprising perhaps, less than half (43%) of black respondents supported preferential hiring (National Opinion Research Council, 1972–2012).

On the other hand, although white (and many minority-group) Americans object to fixed quotas or preferences, there is support for programs that expand the opportunities available to minority groups, including enhanced job training, education, and recruitment in minority communities (Wilson, 2009, p. 139). Programs of this sort are more consistent with traditional ideologies and value systems that stress individual initiative, personal responsibility, and equality of opportunity.

Also, many businesses and universities are committed to the broad principles of affirmative action—the need to address past injustices and the importance of providing diversity in the workplace and classroom—and they are likely to sustain their programs (to the extent allowed by court decisions and legislation) into the future. By and large, it seems that affirmative action programs, especially those that stress equality of opportunity, will continue in some form, perhaps quite limited, into the foreseeable future. The Current Debate introduced at the end of this chapter is focused on this complex and controversial topic.

QUESTIONS FOR REFLECTION

1. What is *modern* institutional discrimination, and how does it differ from *traditional* or blatant institutional discrimination? What are some of the common forms of modern institutional discrimination?

2. What is affirmative action, and what are some of the ways it has been used to combat modern institutional discrimination?

SOCIAL CHANGE AND MINORITY-GROUP ACTIVISM

This chapter has focused on the continuing industrial revolution and its impact on minority groups in general and black–white relations in particular. For the most part, changes in group relations have been presented as the results of the fundamental transformation of the U.S. economy from agrarian to industrial to postindustrial. However, the changes in the situation of African Americans and other minority groups did not "just happen" as society modernized. Although the opportunity to pursue favorable change was the result of broad structural changes in American society, the realization of these opportunities came from the efforts of the many who gave their time, their voices, their resources, and sometimes their lives in pursuit of racial justice in America. Since World War II, African Americans often have been in the vanguard of protest activity, and we focus on the contemporary situation of this group in the next chapter.

This summary is organized around the Learning Objectives listed at the beginning of this chapter.

 5.1 Explain the corollary to the two themes stated at the beginning of the chapter.

Group relations change as the subsistence technology and the level of development of the larger society change. As nations industrialize and urbanize, dominant–minority relations change from paternalistic to rigid competitive forms.

Industrialization continued throughout the 20th century and has continued to shape dominant–minority relations. As a postindustrial society began to emerge, group relations in the United States shifted from rigid to fluid competitive.

 5.2 Describe the nature of Jim Crow segregation in the South and why this system was created.

In the South, slavery was replaced by de jure segregation, a system that combined racial separation with great inequality. The Jim Crow system was intended to control the labor of African Americans and eliminate their political power. It was reinforced by coercion and intense racism and prejudice.

 5.3 Explain the significance of the Great Migration and the origins of black protest.

Black Southerners responded to segregation, in part, by moving to urban areas outside the South, particularly in the Northeast and Midwest. The African American population enjoyed greater freedom and developed some political and economic resources away from the South, but a large concentration of low-income, relatively powerless African Americans developed in the ghetto neighborhoods.

Various strategies for combatting Jim Crow segregation and improving the status of African Americans began to emerge in the early 20th century, along with protest organizations and leaders. The resources and relative freedom of blacks living outside the South became an important foundation for the various movements that dramatically changed American race relations, starting in the middle of the 20th century.

 5.4 Apply the concepts of acculturation, integration, and gender to the time frame covered in this chapter.

In response to segregation, the African American community developed a separate institutional life centered on family, church, and community. An African American middle class emerged, as well as a protest movement.

African American women remained one of the most exploited groups. Combining work with family roles, they were employed mostly in agriculture and domestic service during the era of segregation.

 5.5 List and explain the important trends created by the shifts to industrial and postindustrial subsistence technology, and describe how these trends affected dominant–minority relations.

Urbanization, bureaucratization, and other trends have changed the shape of race relations, as have the changing structure of the occupational sector and the growing importance of education. The shifts in subsistence technology created more opportunity and freedom for all minority groups but also increased the intensity of struggle and conflict.

 5.6 Explain what is meant by the shift from paternalistic to rigid to fluid competitive group relations.

The basic features of these systems of group relations are summarized in Table 5.2. Paternalistic systems are associated with an agrarian subsistence technology and the desire to control a large, powerless labor force. Under industrialization, group relationships feature more competition for jobs and status, and lower levels of contact between groups. The postindustrial subsistence technology is associated with the highest levels of openness and opportunity for minorities, along with continuing power differentials between groups.

 5.7 Explain and apply the concept of modern institutional discrimination to contemporary black–white relations and the issue of affirmative action.

Modern institutional discrimination consists of more subtle, indirect, difficult-to-document but still consequential forms of discrimination that are built into the everyday operation of society. These forms include past-in-present discrimination and other policies, such as the use of racially biased school aptitude tests and drug laws that are more punitive for minority groups. Affirmative action policies are intended, in part, to combat these forms of discrimination.

KEY TERMS

affirmative action 144

de jure segregation 128

deindustrialization 126

extractive (or primary)
  occupations 138

fluid competitive systems 140

Jim Crow system 128

manufacturing (or
  secondary) occupations
  138

modern institutional
  discrimination 126

past-in-present institutional
  discrimination 142

primary labor market 139

Reconstruction 128

rigid competitive group
  system 127

secondary labor market 139

service (or tertiary)
  occupations 138

sharecropping 129

REVIEW QUESTIONS

1. A corollary to two themes from Chapter 4 is presented at the beginning of this chapter. How exactly does the material in this chapter illustrate the usefulness of this corollary?

2. Explain paternalistic and rigid competitive relations, and link them to industrialization. How does the shift from slavery to de jure segregation illustrate the dynamics of these two systems?

3. What was the Great Migration to the North? How did it change American race relations?

4. Explain the transition from rigid to fluid competitive relations, and explain how this transition is related to the coming of postindustrial society. Explain the roles of urbanization, bureaucracy, the service sector of the job market, and education in this transition.

5. What is modern institutional discrimination? How does it differ from traditional institutional discrimination? Explain the role of affirmative action in combating each.

6. What efforts have been made on your campus to combat modern institutional discrimination? How effective have these programs been?

STUDENT STUDY SITE

Sharpen your skills with SAGE edge at edge.sagepub.com/healey7e

SAGE edge for students provides a personalized approach to help you accomplish your coursework goals in an easy-to-use learning environment.

The following resources are available at SAGE edge:

Current Debates: Affirmative Action in Higher Education (the "Mismatch" Hypothesis)

Are minority students with lesser academic credentials who are admitted to elite universities being placed in a position where they cannot hope to succeed? Are they being set up to fail? Does affirmative action create a "mismatch" between high expectations and low preparation for some of its beneficiaries?

On our website you will find an overview of the topic, the clashing points of view, and some questions to consider as you analyze the material.

Public Sociology Assignments

Public Sociology Assignments provide opportunities for students to address directly and personally some of the issues raised in this text.

The public sociology assignments designed for Part II on our website will lead students to a study of the persistence of prejudice and discrimination in society today. The first assignment is an investigation of children's books and focuses on the depiction of race, gender, and ethnicity. Are children's books as diverse as the larger society? The second assignment analyzes patterns of cross-group interaction in local eateries, and the third looks at the depiction of historical events in contemporary cinema. How are movies based in the past affected by contemporary understandings?

Contributed by Linda M. Waldron

Internet Research Project

For this Internet Research Project, you will visit a website that documents and explores the dynamics of the Jim Crow system in the American South. You will visit each of the five sections of the website and take a quiz to assess the amount of information you have absorbed. Your analysis will be guided by a series of questions, and your instructor may ask you to discuss your findings in small groups.

For Further Reading

Please see our website for an annotated list of important works related to this chapter.

CHAPTER-OPENING TIMELINE PHOTO CREDITS

1860: Library of Congress Prints and Photographs Division

1861 (Jefferson Davis): National Archives and Records Administration/ Mathew Brady

1861 (Fort Fisher): Library of Congress Prints and Photographs Division

1863 (Emancipation Proclamation): Library of Congress Prints and Photographs Division

1863 (Infantry): Wikimedia Commons

1865: Library of Congress Prints and Photographs Division

1870: Library of Congress Prints and Photographs Division

1896: Library of Congress Prints and Photographs Division

1909: Library of Congress Prints and Photographs Division

1914: Library of Congress, New York World-Telegram & Sun Collection

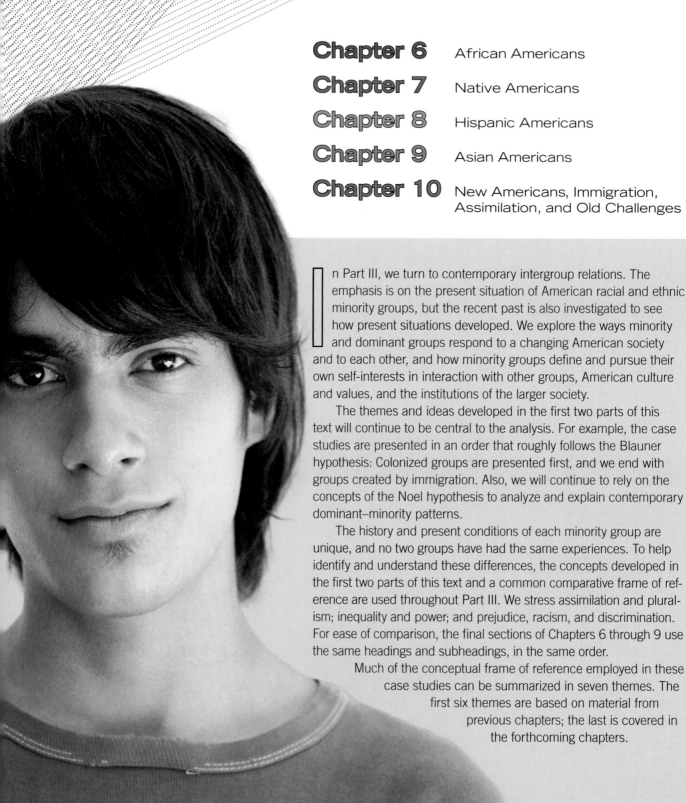

In Part III, we turn to contemporary intergroup relations. The emphasis is on the present situation of American racial and ethnic minority groups, but the recent past is also investigated to see how present situations developed. We explore the ways minority and dominant groups respond to a changing American society and to each other, and how minority groups define and pursue their own self-interests in interaction with other groups, American culture and values, and the institutions of the larger society.

The themes and ideas developed in the first two parts of this text will continue to be central to the analysis. For example, the case studies are presented in an order that roughly follows the Blauner hypothesis: Colonized groups are presented first, and we end with groups created by immigration. Also, we will continue to rely on the concepts of the Noel hypothesis to analyze and explain contemporary dominant–minority patterns.

The history and present conditions of each minority group are unique, and no two groups have had the same experiences. To help identify and understand these differences, the concepts developed in the first two parts of this text and a common comparative frame of reference are used throughout Part III. We stress assimilation and pluralism; inequality and power; and prejudice, racism, and discrimination. For ease of comparison, the final sections of Chapters 6 through 9 use the same headings and subheadings, in the same order.

Much of the conceptual frame of reference employed in these case studies can be summarized in seven themes. The first six themes are based on material from previous chapters; the last is covered in the forthcoming chapters.

PART III

UNDERSTANDING DOMINANT–MINORITY RELATIONS IN THE UNITED STATES TODAY

1. Consistent with the Noel hypothesis, the present conditions of America's minority groups reflect their contact situations, especially the nature of their competition with the dominant group (e.g., competition over land vs. competition over labor) and the size of the power differential between groups at the time of contact.
2. Consistent with the Blauner hypothesis, minority groups created by colonization experience economic and political inequalities that have lasted longer and been more severe than those experienced by minority groups created by immigration.
3. Power and economic differentials and barriers to upward mobility are especially pronounced for groups identified by racial or physical characteristics, as opposed to cultural or linguistic traits.
4. Consistent with the themes stated in Chapters 4 and 5, dominant–minority relations reflect the economic and political characteristics of the larger society and change as those characteristics change. Changes in the subsistence technology of the larger society are particularly consequential for dominant–minority relations. The shift from a manufacturing to a service economy (deindustrialization) is one of the key factors shaping dominant–minority relations in the United States today.
5. As we saw in Chapter 3, the "mood" of the dominant group over the past four decades combines a rejection of blatant racism with the belief that the modern United States is nondiscriminatory and that success is attainable for all who are willing to work hard enough. It is also common for dominant-group Americans to believe that further reforms of the larger society or special programs or treatment for minorities are unnecessary and unjustified. Efforts to address contemporary minority-group problems must deal with the pervasive "modern racism" of the dominant group.
6. The development of group relations, both in the past and for the future, can be analyzed in terms of assimilation (more unity) and pluralism (more diversity). Group relations in the past (e.g., the degree of assimilation permitted or required of the minority group) reflected mainly dominant-group needs and wishes. Although the pressure for Americanization remains considerable, there is more flexibility and variety in group relations today.
7. Since World War II, minority groups have gained significantly more control over the direction of group relationships. This trend reflects the decline of traditional prejudice in the larger society and the successful efforts of minority groups to protest, resist, and change patterns of exclusion and domination. These successes have been possible in large part because American minority groups have increased their share of political and economic resources.

6 AFRICAN AMERICANS

LOC

LOC

timeline

1954
Brown v. Board of Education of Topeka, Kansas overturns *Plessy v. Ferguson* (1896) and declares that racial segregation in schools is unconstitutional.

1960
Four black students in Greensboro, North Carolina, begin a sit-in at a segregated Woolworth's lunch counter. The event triggers many similar nonviolent protests throughout the South.

1964
President Johnson signs the Civil Rights Act, prohibiting discrimination based on race, color, religion, or national origin.

1945   1950   1955   1960   1965   1970   1975

1947
Jackie Robinson breaks Major League Baseball's color barrier when he is signed to the Brooklyn Dodgers.

1948
President Harry S. Truman issues an executive order integrating the U.S. armed forces.

1955
Rosa Parks refuses to give up her seat on a bus to a white passenger, spurring the Montgomery bus boycott.

1965
Congress passes the Voting Rights Act of 1965, making it easier for southern blacks to register to vote.

1965
In six days of rioting in Watts, a black section of Los Angeles, 35 people are killed and 883 injured.

The National Archives

LOC

1963
The March on Washington for Jobs and Freedom is attended by about 250,000 people. Martin Luther King, Jr. delivers his famous "I Have a Dream" speech.

LOC

My first victim was a woman—white, well dressed, probably in her early twenties. I came upon her late one evening on a deserted street in Hyde Park, a relatively affluent neighborhood in an otherwise mean, impoverished section of Chicago. . . . To her, the youngish black man—a broad six feet two inches with a beard and billowing hair, both hands shoved into the pockets of a bulky military jacket—seemed menacingly close. After a few more quick glimpses, she picked up her pace and was soon running in earnest. Within seconds she disappeared into a cross street.

. . . It was in the echo of that terrified woman's footfalls that I first began to know the unwieldy inheritance I'd come into—the ability to alter public space in ugly ways. It was clear that she thought herself the quarry of a mugger, a rapist, or worse. . . .

I moved to New York and . . . have remained an avid night walker. I often witness the "hunch

LEARNING OBJECTIVES

By the end of this chapter, you will be able to do the following:

6.1 Cite and explain the forces that led to the end of de jure segregation, including organizations, leaders, and legal changes.

6.2 Compare and contrast the civil rights movement with the Black Power movement.

6.3 Cite and explain the most important issues and trends that have animated black–white relations since the 1960s, including
a. the relationship between the criminal justice system and the black community,
b. class inequality within the black community,
c. modern institutional discrimination,
d. the family institution,
e. new racial identities, and
f. prejudice and discrimination.

6.4 Describe the situation of African Americans using the concepts of assimilation and pluralism, especially in terms of
a. acculturation,
b. secondary structural assimilation, and
c. primary structural assimilation.

6.5 Assess the overall situation of African Americans today based on the concepts and information presented in this chapter. Is the glass half empty or half full?

1965
Malcolm X, black Nationalist and founder of the Organization of Afro-American Unity, is assassinated.

1968
Martin Luther King, Jr. is assassinated.

1992
Riots erupt in south-central Los Angeles after a jury acquits four white police officers for the videotaped beating of African American Rodney King.

1980   1985   1990   1995   2000   2010   2015   2020

1967
The Supreme Court rules in *Loving v. Virginia* that laws prohibiting interracial marriage are unconstitutional.

1967
President Johnson appoints Thurgood Marshall to the Supreme Court. He becomes the first black Supreme Court Justice.

1978
In the case of *Bakke v. Regents of the University of California,* the U.S. Supreme Court upholds the constitutionality of affirmative action, but outlaws specific racial quotas.

1995
The Million Man March is held in Washington, D.C. to place black issues back on the nation's political agenda.

2009
Barack Obama becomes the first African American to be elected president of the United States.

posture," from women after dark. . . . They seem to set their faces on neutral and, with their purse straps strung across their chests bandolier-style, they forge ahead as though bracing themselves against being tackled. I understand, of course, that the danger they perceive is not a hallucination. Women are particularly vulnerable to street violence, and young black males are drastically overrepresented among the perpetrators of that violence. Yet these truths are no solace against the kind of alienation that comes of being ever the suspect, against being set apart, a fearsome entity with whom pedestrians avoid making eye contact.

—Brent Staples (1986)

Virtually all African American males—including President Barack Obama—have experienced this "otherness," the presumption of guilt, threat, and danger, the "unwieldy inheritance" that echoes centuries of history, crime statistics, and the gory recitations of the evening news. Shopkeepers watch young black customers with special attention; police routinely stop, question, and frisk black (and other minority-group) males; and white pedestrians cross the street when they see black males approaching.

All this might be marked down as an annoyance, something people could learn to live with, if it weren't for the high potential for escalation and tragedy, as illustrated by the 2012 case of Trayvon Martin, a black male teenager shot and killed while walking home from the store. His assailant, George Zimmerman, stopped Martin because he "looked suspicious," and their confrontation quickly turned deadly. Zimmerman, a sometimes-member of a neighborhood watch group, was acquitted of homicide charges in July 2013.

These experiences demonstrate that, on many levels, African Americans continue to be seen as outsiders, apart from and alien to the American mainstream. Certainly, there has been progress toward racial justice and inclusion, but, as this chapter will demonstrate, the struggle is far from over. •

A century ago, African Americans were primarily a southern, rural peasantry, victimized by de jure segregation, exploited by the sharecropping system of agriculture, and blocked from the better-paying industrial and manufacturing jobs in urban areas. Segregation had disenfranchised them and stripped them of the legal and civil rights they had briefly enjoyed during Reconstruction. As we saw in Chapter 5, the huge majority of African Americans had limited access to quality education, few political rights, few occupational choices, and few means of expressing their grievances to the larger society or the world.

Today, African Americans are highly urbanized, dispersed throughout the United States, and represented in every occupation. Perhaps the single most significant sign of racial progress is the election of Obama to the presidency of the United States, but African Americans are visible across the board at the highest levels of American society: from the Supreme Court to corporate boardrooms to the most prestigious universities. Some of the best-known, most successful, most respected (and wealthiest) people in the world have been African Americans: Martin Luther King Jr., Malcolm X, Michael Jordan, Bill Cosby, Toni Morrison, Michael Jackson, Maya Angelou, Muhammad Ali, Oprah Winfrey, Colin Powell, and Will Smith, to name just a few. Furthermore, some of the most important and prestigious American corporations (including Merrill Lynch, American Express, and Time Warner) have been led by African Americans.

Compared with 100 years ago, the situation of black Americans today is obviously much improved. The journey to racial equality and a truly color-blind society is, however, far from accomplished. As we shall see in this chapter, a large percentage of black Americans remain on the margins of society: excluded, segregated, and victimized by persisting inequalities in education, health care, housing, and jobs. Even the more fortunate segments of the black community remain in a tenuous situation: They have fewer resources to fall back on in hard times and weaker connections to the sources of power and privilege. The glittering success stories of the few obscure the continuing struggles of the many, and racism, prejudice, and discrimination continue to be significant problems.

To understand black–white relations in the present, we must deal with the watershed events of the recent past: the end of de jure segregation, the triumph (and limitations) of the civil rights movement of the 1950s and 1960s, the urban riots and Black Power movement of the 1960s, and the continuing racial divisions within U.S. society since the 1970s. Behind these events, we can see the powerful pressures of industrialization and modernization, the shift from rigid to fluid competitive group relations, deindustrialization and modern institutional discrimination, changing distributions of power and forms of intergroup competition, the shift from traditional prejudice to modern racism, and new ideas about assimilation and pluralism. Black–white relations changed as a direct result of protest, resistance, and the concerted actions of thousands of individuals, both black and white.

THE END OF DE JURE SEGREGATION

As a colonized minority group, African Americans entered the 20th century facing extreme inequality, relative powerlessness, and sharp limitations on their freedom. Their most visible enemy was the system of de jure segregation in the South, the rigid competitive system of group relations that controlled the lives of most African Americans.

Why and how did de jure segregation come to an end? Recall from Chapter 5 that dominant–minority relationships change as the larger society and its subsistence technology change. As the

United States industrialized and urbanized during the 20th century, a series of social, political, economic, and legal processes were set in motion that ultimately destroyed Jim Crow segregation.

The mechanization and modernization of agriculture in the South had a powerful effect on race relations. As farm work became less labor-intensive and machines replaced people, the need to maintain a large, powerless workforce declined (Geschwender, 1978, pp. 175–177). Thus, one of the primary motivations for maintaining Jim Crow segregation and the sharecropping system of farming lost force.

In addition, the modernization of southern agriculture helped spur the migration northward and to urban areas, as we discussed in Chapter 5. Outside the rural South, African Americans found it easier to register to vote and pursue other avenues for improving their situations. The weight of the growing African American vote was first felt in the 1930s and was large enough to make a difference in local, state, and even national elections by the 1940s. In 1948, for example, President Harry Truman recognized that he could not be reelected without the support of African American voters. As a result, the Democratic Party adopted a civil rights plank in the party platform—the first time since Reconstruction that a national political party had taken a stand on race relations (Wilson, 1973, p. 123).

The weight of these changes accumulated slowly, and no single date or specific event marks the end of de jure segregation. The system ended as it had begun: gradually and in a series of discrete episodes and incidents. By the mid-20th century, resistance to racial change was weakening and the power resources of African Americans were increasing. This enhanced freedom and strength fueled a variety of efforts that sped the demise of Jim Crow segregation. Although a complete historical autopsy is not necessary here, a general understanding of the reasons for the death of Jim Crow segregation is essential for an understanding of modern black–white relations.

WARTIME DEVELOPMENTS

One of the first successful applications of the growing stock of black power resources occurred in 1941, as the United States was mobilizing for war against Germany and Japan. Despite the crisis atmosphere, racial discrimination was common, even in the defense industry. A group of African Americans, led by labor leader A. Philip Randolph, head of the Brotherhood of Sleeping Car Porters, threatened to march on Washington to protest the discriminatory treatment.

To forestall the march, President Franklin D. Roosevelt signed Executive Order No. 8802, banning discrimination in defense-related industries, and created a watchdog federal agency, the Fair Employment Practices Commission, to oversee compliance with the new antidiscriminatory policy (Franklin & Moss, 1994, pp. 436–437; Geschwender, 1978, pp. 199–200). President Roosevelt's actions were significant in two ways. First, a group of African Americans not only had their grievances heard at the highest level of society but

also succeeded in getting what they wanted. Underlying the effectiveness of the planned march was the rising political and economic power of the African American community outside the South and the need to mobilize all segments of the population for a world war. Second, the federal government made an unprecedented commitment to fair employment rights for African Americans. This alliance between the federal government and African Americans was tentative, but it foreshadowed some of the dynamics of racial change in the 1950s and 1960s.

THE CIVIL RIGHTS MOVEMENT

The **civil rights movement** was a multifaceted campaign to end legalized segregation and ameliorate the massive inequalities faced by African Americans. The campaign lasted for decades and included lawsuits and courtroom battles as well as protest marches and demonstrations. We begin our examination with a look at the movement's successful challenge to the laws of racial segregation.

Brown v. Board of Education of Topeka. Undoubtedly, the single most powerful blow to de jure segregation was delivered by the U.S. Supreme Court in *Brown v. Board of Education of Topeka* in 1954. The Supreme Court reversed the *Plessy v. Ferguson* decision of 1896 (see Chapter 5) and ruled that racially separate facilities are inherently unequal and therefore unconstitutional. Segregated school systems—and all other forms of legalized racial segregation—would have to end.

The landmark Brown decision was the culmination of decades of planning and effort by the National Association for the Advancement of Colored People (NAACP) and individuals such as Thurgood Marshall, the NAACP's chief counsel (who was appointed to the Supreme Court in 1967). The strategy of the NAACP was to attack Jim Crow by finding instances in which the civil rights of an African American had been violated and then bringing suit against the relevant governmental agency.

These lawsuits were intended to extend far beyond the specific case being argued. The goal was to persuade the courts to declare segregation unconstitutional not only in the specific instance being tried but in all similar cases. The Brown (1954) decision was the ultimate triumph of this strategy. The significance of the Supreme Court's decision was not that Linda Brown—the child in whose name the case was argued—would attend a different school or even that the school system of Topeka, Kansas, would be integrated. Instead, the significance was in the rejection of the principle of de jure segregation in the South and, by implication, throughout the nation. The Brown decision changed the law and dealt a crippling blow to Jim Crow segregation.

The **civil rights movement** was the organized effort of African Americans and their allies in the 1950s and 1960s to end de jure segregation in the South.

A demonstration protesting school segregation organized by the NAACP.

The blow was not fatal, however. Southern states responded to the Brown (1954) decision by stalling and mounting campaigns of massive resistance. Jim Crow laws remained on the books for years. White Southerners actively defended the system of racial privilege and attempted to forestall change through a variety of means, including violence and intimidation. The Ku Klux Klan (KKK), largely dormant since the 1920s, reappeared, along with other racist and terrorist groups such as the White Citizens' Councils. White politicians and other leaders competed with one another to express the most adamant statements of racist resistance (Wilson, 1973, p. 128). One locality, Prince Edward County in central Virginia, chose to close its public schools rather than integrate. The schools remained closed for five years. During that time, the white children attended private, segregated academies, and the county provided no education at all for African American children (Franklin, 1967, p. 644).

Nonviolent Direct Action Protest. The principle established by Brown (1954) was assimilationist: It ordered the educational institutions of the dominant group to be opened up freely and equally to all. Southern states and communities overwhelmingly rejected the principle of equal access and shared facilities. Centuries of racist tradition and privilege were at stake, and considerable effort would be required to overcome southern defiance and resistance. The central force in this struggle was

---

Nonviolent direct action was the central tactic used by the civil rights movement to confront de jure segregation.

---

a protest movement, the beginning of which is often traced to Montgomery, Alabama, where on December 1, 1955, Rosa Parks, a seamstress and NAACP member, rode the city bus home from work, as she usually did. As the bus filled, she was ordered to surrender her seat to a white male passenger. When she refused, the police were called and Rosa Parks was jailed for violating a local segregation ordinance.

Although Mrs. Parks was hardly the first African American to be subjected to such indignities, her case stimulated a protest movement in the African American community, and a boycott of the city buses was organized. Participants in the boycott set up car pools, shared taxis, and walked (in some cases, for miles) to and from work. They stayed off the buses for more than a year, until victory was achieved and the city was ordered to desegregate its buses. The Montgomery boycott was led by the Reverend Martin Luther King Jr., the new minister of a local Baptist church.

From these beginnings sprang the protest movement that eventually defeated de jure segregation. The central strategy of the movement involved **nonviolent direct action**, a method by which the system of de jure segregation was confronted head-on, not in the courtroom or in the state legislature but in the streets. The movement's principles of nonviolence were adopted from the tenets of Christianity and from the teachings of Mohandas K. Gandhi, Henry David Thoreau, and others. Dr. King expressed the philosophy in a number of books and speeches (King, 1958, 1963, 1968). Nonviolent protest was intended to confront the forces of evil rather than the people who happened to be doing evil, and it attempted to win the friendship and support of its enemies rather than defeat or humiliate them. Above all, nonviolent protest required courage and discipline; it was not a method for cowards (King, 1958, pp. 83–84).

The movement used different tactics for different situations, including sit-ins at segregated restaurants, protest marches and demonstrations, prayer meetings, and voter registration

Rosa Parks is fingerprinted following her arrest for violoating the Montgomery, Alabama, bus segregation law.

drives. The police and terrorist groups such as the KKK often responded to these protests with brutal repression and violence, and protesters were routinely imprisoned, beaten, and attacked by police dogs. The violent resistance sometimes escalated to acts of murder, including the 1963 bombing of a black church in Birmingham, Alabama, which took the lives of four little girls, and the 1968 assassination of Dr. King. Resistance to racial change in the South was intense. It would take more than protests and marches to end de jure segregation, and the U.S. Congress finally provided the necessary tools (see D'Angelo, 2001; Halberstam, 1998; Killian, 1975; King, 1958, 1963, 1968; Lewis, 1999; Morris, 1984).

Landmark Legislation. The successes of the protest movement, combined with changing public opinion and the legal principles established by the Supreme Court, coalesced in the mid-1960s to stimulate the passage of two laws that, together, ended Jim Crow segregation. In 1964, at the urging of President Lyndon B. Johnson, the U.S. Congress passed the Civil Rights Act of 1964, banning discrimination on the grounds of race, color, religion, national origin, or gender. The law applied to publicly owned facilities such as parks and municipal swimming pools, businesses and other facilities open to the public, and any programs that received federal aid.

Congress followed this up with the Voting Rights Act in 1965, also initiated by President Johnson, which required that the same standards be used to register all citizens in federal, state, and local elections. The act banned literacy tests, whites-only primaries, and other practices that had been used to prevent African Americans from registering to vote. This law gave the franchise back to black Southerners for the first time since Reconstruction and laid the groundwork for increasing black political power.

The significance of these two laws for ending state-sponsored racial discrimination and furthering the commitment of the nation to equality and justice cannot be easily understated. The principles of the Civil Rights Act are now firmly implanted in American culture and law, and the hypocrisies of the past that granted equal rights only to whites seem like hopelessly outdated relics.

The Voting Rights Act was equally crucial in ending de jure segregation, but, unlike the Civil Rights Act, it was specifically designed as a remedy for discriminatory practices in certain states in the mid-1960s. The act had to be renewed periodically, and Congress did so, most recently in 2006 with a huge majority in the House and by a unanimous vote in the Senate.

However, in a 5-to-4 decision in 2013, the U.S. Supreme Court ruled parts of the Voting Rights Act unconstitutional on the grounds that the specific discriminatory voting practices the act was designed to remedy no longer exist. For example, Chief Justice John Roberts noted that African Americans turned out to vote at higher rates than did whites in the 2012 presidential election in most of the states originally covered by the law in 1965 (Liptak, 2013). We will consider some of the implications of this decision later in the chapter when we discuss African American political power.

The Success and Limitations of the Civil Rights Movement. Why did the civil rights movement succeed? A comprehensive list of reasons would be lengthy, but we can cite some of the most important causes of its success, especially those consistent with the general points about dominant–minority relations that have been made in previous chapters.

1. *Changing subsistence technology.* The continuing industrialization and urbanization of the society as a whole—and the South in particular—weakened the Jim Crow, rigid competitive system of minority-group control and segregation. We made this point in Chapter 5 when we discussed the impact of the changing subsistence technology and the end of paternalistic controls (see Table 5.2).

2. *An era of prosperity.* Following World War II, the United States enjoyed a period of prosperity that lasted into the 1960s. Consistent with the Noel hypothesis, this was important because it reduced the intensity of intergroup competition, at least outside the South. During prosperous times, resistance to change tends to weaken. If the economic "pie" is expanding, the "slices" claimed by minority groups can increase without threatening the size of anyone else's portions, and the prejudice generated during intergroup competition (à la Robber's Cave, Chapter 3) is held in check. Thus, these "good times" muted the sense of threat in the dominant group sparked by the demands for equality made by the civil rights movement.

3. *Increasing resources in the black community.* Some of the economic prosperity of the era found its way into African American communities and increased their pool of economic and political resources. Networks of independent, African American–controlled organizations and institutions, such as churches and colleges, were created or grew in size and power. The increasingly elaborate infrastructure of the black community included protest organizations, such as the NAACP (see Chapter 5), and provided material resources, leadership, and "people power" to lead the fight against segregation and discrimination.

4. *Assimilationist goals.* The civil rights movement embraced the traditional American values of liberty, equality, freedom, and fair treatment. It demanded civil, legal, and political rights for African Americans, rights available to whites automatically. Thus, many whites did not feel threatened by the movement because they saw it as consistent with mainstream American values, especially in contrast to the intense, often violent resistance of southern whites.

5. *Coalitions.* The perceived legitimacy of the goals of the movement also opened up the possibility of alliances with other groups (e.g., white liberals, Jews, college students). The support of others was crucial because black Southerners had few resources of their own other than their numbers and courage. By mobilizing the resources of other, more powerful groups, black Southerners

forged alliances and created sympathetic support that was brought to bear on their opposition.

6. *Mass media.* Widespread and sympathetic coverage from the mass media, particularly television, was crucial to the success of the movement. The oft-repeated scenario of African Americans being brutally attacked while demonstrating for their rights outraged many Americans and reinforced the moral consensus that eventually rejected "traditional" racial prejudice along with Jim Crow segregation (see Chapter 3).

The southern civil rights movement ended de jure segregation but found it difficult to survive the demise of its primary enemy. The confrontational tactics that had been so effective against the Jim Crow system proved less useful when attention turned to the actual distribution of jobs, wealth, political power, and other valued goods and services. Outside the South, the allocation of opportunity and resources had always been the central concern of the African American community. Let's take a look at these concerns.

QUESTIONS FOR REFLECTION

1. What forces led to the end of Jim Crow segregation? What was the role of broad social changes such as changing subsistence technology? How important were the contributions of individuals and organizations?

2. What Supreme Court decision and laws ended de jure segregation? How?

3. How do the concepts of competition and differential in power in the Noel hypothesis apply to the demise of the Jim Crow system of segregation?

4. List and explain the important reasons for the success of the civil rights movement.

DEVELOPMENTS OUTSIDE THE SOUTH

DE FACTO SEGREGATION

Chapter 5 discussed some of the difficulties encountered by African Americans as they left the rural South. Discrimination by labor unions, employers, industrialists, and white ethnic groups was common. Racial discrimination outside the South was less overt but still pervasive, especially in housing, education, and employment.

De facto segregation is racial separation and inequality that appears, on the surface, to result from voluntary choice. Often, de facto segregation is really a disguised form of de jure segregation.

The pattern of racial separation and inequality outside the South is often called **de facto segregation**: segregation resulting from what seems to be, at first glance, the voluntary choices of dominant- and minority-group members alike. As opposed to the Jim Crow system in the South or apartheid in South Africa, there are no public laws mandating racial separation, and it is often assumed that de facto segregation "just happened" as people and groups made decisions about where to live and work, or that it resulted from some benign tendency of people to be "with their own kind."

On the contrary, de facto segregation was quite intentional and is best thought of as de jure segregation in thin disguise. Racial segregation outside the South was the direct result of intentionally racist decisions made by governmental and quasi-governmental agencies, such as real-estate boards, school boards, and zoning boards (see Massey & Denton, 1993, pp. 74–114; also see Loewen, 2005). De facto segregation was created when local and state authorities actively colluded with private citizens behind the scenes, ignored racist practices within their jurisdictions, and "simply refrained from enforcing black social, economic, and political rights so that private discriminatory practices could do their work" (Massey, 2007, p. 57). For example, shortly after World War I, the real-estate board in the city of Chicago adopted a policy that required its members, on penalty of "immediate expulsion," to enforce racial residential segregation (Cohen & Taylor, 2000, p. 33). The city itself passed no Jim Crow laws, but the end result was the same: Black Americans were consigned to a separate and unequal status.

African Americans outside the South faced more poverty, higher unemployment, and lower-quality housing and schools than did whites, but there was no clear equivalent of Jim Crow to attack or blame for these patterns of inequality. Thus, the triumphs of the civil rights movement had little impact on their lives. In the 1960s, the African American community outside the South expressed its frustration over the slow pace of change in two ways: urban unrest and a movement for change that rose to prominence as the civil rights movement faded.

URBAN UNREST

In the mid-1960s, the frustration and anger of urban African American communities erupted into a series of violent uprisings. The riots began in the summer of 1965 in Watts, a neighborhood in Los Angeles, California, and over the next four years, virtually every large black urban community experienced similar outbursts. Racial violence was hardly a new phenomenon in America. Race riots had existed as early as the Civil War, and various time periods had seen racial violence of considerable magnitude.

The riots of the 1960s were different, however. Most race riots in the past had been attacks by whites against blacks, often including the invasion and destruction of African American neighborhoods (e.g., see D'Orso, 1996; Ellsworth, 1982). The urban unrest of the 1960s, in contrast, consisted largely of attacks by blacks against the symbols of their oppression and

NARRATIVE PORTRAIT

Growing Up Black and Female in the Jim Crow South

Feminist intellectual bell hooks was born in Kentucky in the 1950s, at the height of the Jim Crow system. Her family was rural and poor, but she rose from these humble beginnings to earn her doctorate in English. She has written more than 20 books and has devoted her life to a passionate critique of white supremacy, capitalism, and patriarchy. The name under which she writes is a pseudonym, and she does not capitalize it, to stress that her ideas are more important than her name or any other aspect of her identity. She teaches at City College of New York. In addition to race, what class, gender, and other differentiating factors can you identify in the passage? What is the young bell hooks learning about herself and her world?

BONE BLACK

bell hooks

We live in the country. We children do not understand that that means we are among the poor. We do not understand that the outhouses behind many of the houses are still there because running water came here long after they had it in the city.... Because we are poor, because we live in the country, we go to the country school—the little white wood-frame building where all the country kids come. They come from miles and miles away. They come so far because they are black. As they are riding the school buses they pass school after school where children who are white can attend without being bused, without getting up in the wee hours of the morning, sometimes leaving home in the dark....

School begins with chapel. There we recite the Pledge of Allegiance to the Flag. We have no feeling for the flag but we like the words; said in unison, they sound like a chant. We then listen to a morning prayer. We say the Lord's Prayer. It is the singing that makes morning chapel the happiest moment of the day. It is there I learn to sing "Red River Valley." It is a song about missing and longing. I do not understand all the words, only the feeling—warm wet sorrow, like playing games in spring rain. After chapel we go to classrooms....

Here at the country school we must always work to raise money—selling candy, raffle tickets, having shows for which tickets are sold. Sold to our parents, neighbors, friends, people without money who are shamed into buying little colored paper they cannot afford, tickets that will help keep the school going....

We learn about color with crayons. We learn to tell the difference between white and pink and a color they call Flesh. The flesh-colored crayon amuses us. Like white it never shows up on the thick Manila paper they give us to draw on, or on the brown paper sacks we draw on at home. Flesh we know has no relationship to our skin, for we are brown and brown and brown like all good things....

I must sell tickets for a Tom Thumb wedding, one of the school shows.... We get to dress up in paper wedding clothes and go through a ceremony for the entertainment of the adults. The whole thing makes me sick but no one cares. Like every other girl I want to be the bride but I am not chosen. It has always to do with money. The important roles go to the children whose parents have money to give, who will work hard selling tickets. I am lucky to be a bridesmaid, to wear a red crepe paper dress made just for me. I am not thrilled with such luck. I would rather not wear a paper dress, not be in a make-believe wedding. They tell me that I am lucky to be lighter skinned, not black black, not dark brown, lucky to have hair that is almost straight, otherwise I might not be in the wedding at all, otherwise I might not be so lucky.

This luck angers me and when I am angry things always go wrong. We are practicing in our paper dresses, walking down the aisle while the piano music plays a wedding march. We are practicing to be brides, to be girls who will grow up to be given away. My legs would rather be running, itch to go outdoors. My legs are dreaming, adventurous legs. They cannot walk down the aisle without protest. They go too fast. They go too slow. They make everything slow down. The girl walking behind me steps on the red dress; it tears. It moves from my flesh like wind moving against the running legs. I am truly lucky now to have this tear. I hope they will make me sit, but they say No we would not think of taking you out of the show. They know how much every girl wants to be in a wedding. The tear must be mended. The red dress like a woman's heart must break silently and in secret.

Questions to Consider

1. What aspects of the Jim Crow era are illustrated in this passage?
2. What gender dynamics underlie this memoir? How?

---

frustration. The most obvious targets were white-owned businesses operating in black neighborhoods and the police, who were seen as an army of occupation and whose excessive use of force was often the immediate precipitator of riots (Conot, 1967; National Advisory Commission, 1968).

THE BLACK POWER MOVEMENT

The urban riots of the 1960s were an unmistakable sign that the problems of race relations had not been resolved with the end of Jim Crow segregation. Outside the South, the problems were different and called for different solutions. Even as the civil rights movement was celebrating its victory in the South, a new protest movement rose to prominence. The **Black Power movement** was a loose coalition of organizations

---

The **Black Power movement** rose to prominence in the 1960s as a coalition of groups. Some of the central themes of the movement were Black Nationalism, autonomy for African American communities, and pride in heritage.

Buildings burning during a riot in the Watts area of Los Angeles, 1965.

and spokespersons that encompassed a variety of ideas and views, many of which differed sharply from those of the civil rights movement. Some of the central ideas included racial pride ("Black is beautiful" was a key slogan of the day), interest in African heritage, and Black Nationalism. In contrast to the assimilationist goals of the civil rights movement, Black Power groups worked to increase African American control over schools, police, welfare programs, and other public services operating in black neighborhoods.

Most adherents of the Black Power movement felt that white racism and institutional discrimination, forces buried deep in the core of American culture and society, were the primary causes of racial inequality in America. Thus, if African Americans were ever to be truly empowered, they would have to liberate themselves and do it on their own terms. Some Black Power advocates specifically rejected the goal of assimilation into white society, arguing that integration would require blacks to become part of the very system that had for centuries oppressed, denigrated, and devalued them and other peoples of color.

The Nation of Islam. The themes of Black Power voiced so loudly in the 1960s were decades, even centuries, old. Marcus Garvey had popularized many of these ideas in the 1920s, and they were espoused and further developed by the Nation of Islam, popularly known as the Black Muslims, in the 1960s.

The Black Muslims, one of the best-known organizations within the Black Power movement, were angry, impatient, and outspoken. They denounced the hypocrisy, greed, and racism of American society and advocated staunch resistance and racial separation. The Black Muslims did more than talk, however. Pursuing the goals of autonomy and self-determination, they worked hard to create a separate, independent African American economy within the United States. They opened businesses and stores in African American neighborhoods and tried to deal only with other Muslim-owned firms. Their goal

was to develop the African American community economically and supply jobs and capital for expansion using solely their own resources (Essien-Udom, 1962; Lincoln, 1961; Malcolm X, 1964; Marable, 2011; Wolfenstein, 1993).

The Nation of Islam and other Black Power groups distinguished between racial separation and racial segregation. The former is a process of empowerment whereby a group grows stronger as it becomes more autonomous and self-controlled. The latter is a system of inequality in which the African American community is powerless and controlled by the dominant group. Thus, the Black Power groups were working to find ways African Americans could develop their own resources and deal with the dominant group from a more powerful position, a strategy similar to that followed by minority groups that form ethnic enclaves (see Chapter 2).

The best-known spokesman for the Nation of Islam was Malcolm X, one of the most charismatic figures of the 1960s. Malcolm X forcefully articulated the themes of the Black Power movement. Born Malcolm Little, he converted to Islam and joined the Nation of Islam while serving a prison term. He became the chief spokesperson for the Black Muslims and a well-known but threatening figure to the white community. After a dispute with Elijah Muhammad, the leader of the Nation of Islam, Malcolm X founded his own organization, in which he continued to express and develop the ideas of Black Nationalism. In 1965, like so many other protest leaders of the era, Malcolm X was assassinated (Marable, 2011).

Malcolm X, one of the most charismatic spokesmen for the Black Power movement.

Black Power leaders such as Malcolm X advocated autonomy, independence, and a pluralistic direction for the African American protest movement. They saw the African American community as a colonized, exploited population in need of liberation from the unyielding racial oppression of white America, not integration into the system that was the source of its oppression.

PROTEST, POWER, AND PLURALISM

THE BLACK POWER MOVEMENT IN PERSPECTIVE

By the end of the 1960s, the riots had ended and the most militant and dramatic manifestations of the Black Power movement had faded. In many cases, the passion of Black Power activists had been countered by the violence of the police and other agencies, and many of the most powerful spokespersons of the movement were dead; others were in jail or in exile. The nation's commitment to racial change wavered and weakened as other concerns, such as the Vietnam War, competed for attention. Richard M. Nixon was elected president in 1968 and made it clear that his administration would not ally itself with the black protest movement. Pressure from the federal government for racial equality was reduced. The boiling turmoil of the mid-1960s faded, but the idea of Black Power had become thoroughly entrenched in the African American community.

In some part, the pluralistic themes of Black Power were a reaction to the failure of assimilation and integration in the 1950s and 1960s. Laws had been passed; court decisions had been widely publicized; and promises and pledges had been made by presidents, members of Congress, ministers, and other leaders. For many African Americans, though, little had changed. The problems of their parents and grandparents continued to constrain and limit their lives and, as far into the future as they could see, the lives of their children. The pluralistic Black Power ideology was a response to the failure to go beyond the repeal of Jim Crow laws and fully implement the promises of integration and equality.

Black Nationalism, however, was and remains more than simply a reaction to a failed dream. It was also a different way of defining what it means to be black in America. In the context of black–white relations in the 1960s, the Black Power movement served a variety of purposes. First, along with the civil rights movement, it helped carve out a new identity for African Americans. The cultural stereotypes of black Americans (see Chapter 3) stressed laziness, irresponsibility, and inferiority. This image needed to be refuted, rejected, and buried. The black protest movements supplied a view of African Americans that emphasized power, assertiveness, seriousness of purpose, intelligence, and courage.

Second, Black Power served as a new rallying cry for solidarity and unified action. Following the success of the civil rights movement, these new themes and ideas helped focus attention on "unfinished business": the black–white inequalities that remained in U.S. society.

Finally, the ideology provided an analysis of the problems of American race relations in the 1960s. The civil rights movement had, of course, analyzed race relations in terms of integration, equality of opportunity, and an end to exclusion. After the demise of Jim Crow, that analysis became less relevant. A new language was needed to describe and analyze the continuation of racial inequality. Black Power argued that the continuing problems of U.S. race relations were structural and institutional, not individual or legal. Taking the next steps toward actualizing racial equality and justice would require a fundamental and far-reaching restructuring of society. Ultimately, white Americans, as the beneficiaries of the system, would not support such restructuring. The necessary energy and commitment had to come from African Americans pursuing their own self-interests.

The nationalistic and pluralistic demands of the Black Power movement evoked defensiveness and a sense of threat in white society. By questioning the value of assimilation and celebrating a separate African heritage equal in legitimacy to white European heritage, the Black Power movement questioned the legitimacy and worth of Anglo-American values. In fact, many Black Power spokespersons condemned Anglo-American values fiercely and openly, and implicated them in the creation and maintenance of a centuries-long system of racial repression. Today, almost 50 years after the success of the civil rights movement, assertive and critical demands by the African American community continue to be perceived as threatening.

GENDER AND BLACK PROTEST

Both the civil rights movement and the Black Power movement tended to be male dominated. African American women were often viewed as supporters of men rather than as equal partners in liberation. Although African American women were heavily involved in the struggle, they were often denied leadership roles or decision-making positions in favor of men. In fact, the women in one organization, the Student Nonviolent Coordinating Committee, wrote position papers to protest their relegation to lowly clerical positions and the frequent references to them as "girls" (Andersen, 1993, p. 284). The Nation of Islam emphasized female subservience, imposing a strict code of behavior and dress for women and separating the sexes in many temple and community activities. Thus, the battle against racism and the battle against sexism were separate struggles with separate and often contradictory agendas, as the black protest movement continued to subordinate women (Amott & Matthaei, 1991, p. 177).

Library of Congress Prints and Photographs Division

Fannie Lou Hamer, a leader of the civil rights movement in Mississippi. Among other notable accomplishments, she founded the Freedom Party, which challenged the racially segregated state Democratic Party.

When the protest movements began, however, African American women were already heavily involved in community and church work, and they often used their organizational skills and energy to further the cause of black liberation. In the view of many, African American women were the backbone of the movement, even if they were often relegated to less glamorous but vital organizational work (Evans, 1979).

Fannie Lou Hamer of Mississippi, an African American who became a prominent leader in the black liberation movement, illustrates the importance of the role played by women. Born in 1917 to sharecropper parents, Hamer's life was so circumscribed that until she attended her first rally at the beginning of the civil rights movement, she was unaware that blacks could—even theoretically—register to vote. The day after the rally, she quickly volunteered to register:

I guess I'd had any sense I'd a-been a little scared, but what was the point of being scared? The only thing they could do to me was kill me and it seemed like they'd been

trying to do that a little bit at a time ever since I could remember. (Evans, 1989, p. 271)

As a result of her activism, Hamer lost her job, was evicted from her house, and was jailed and beaten on a number of occasions. She devoted herself entirely to the civil rights movement and founded the Freedom Party, which successfully challenged the racially segregated Democratic Party and the all-white political structure of the State of Mississippi (Evans, 1979; Hamer, 1967).

Much of the energy that motivated black protest was forged in the depths of segregation and exclusion, a system of oppression that affected all African Americans. Not all segments of the community had the same experience; the realities faced by the black community were, as always, differentiated by class as well as gender. A flavor of life in the Jim Crow South was presented in the Narrative Portrait earlier in this chapter.

QUESTIONS FOR REFLECTION

1. How did de facto segregation differ from de jure segregation? Were the differences merely cosmetic? Why or why not?

2. How and why did the Black Power movement differ from the civil rights movement?

3. Did the Black Power movement succeed? How?

4. What were some of the important gender dimensions of black protest?

BLACK–WHITE RELATIONS SINCE THE 1960S: ISSUES AND TRENDS

Black–white relations have changed since the 1960s, of course, but the basic outlines of black inequality and white dominance have persisted. To be sure, improvements have been made in integrating society and eliminating racial inequality. Obama's election—unimaginable just a few decades ago (and maybe a few years ago)—stands as one unmistakable symbol of racial progress, a breakthrough so stunning it has led many to conclude that America is now "postracial" and that people's fates are no longer connected to the color of their skin, an argument easily refuted by a consideration of the trends and statistics presented in this chapter.

Without denying the signs of progress, the situation of the African American community today has stagnated in many dimensions, and the problems that remain are deep-rooted and inextricably mixed with the structure and functioning of

Race in Another America

One of the key characteristics of traditional U.S. antiblack prejudice is a simple "two-race" view: Everyone belongs to one and only one race, and a person is either black or white. This perception is a legacy of the assumption of black inferiority that was at the heart of both U.S. slavery and Jim Crow segregation. The southern states formalized the racial dichotomy in law as well as custom with the "one-drop rule": Any trace of black ancestry, even "one drop" of African blood, meant that a person was legally black and subject to all the limitations of extreme racial inequality.

The U.S. perception of race contrasts sharply with the racial sensibilities in many other nations. Throughout Central and South America, for example, race is perceived as a continuum of possibilities and combinations, not as a simple split between white and black. This does not mean that these societies are egalitarian, racially open utopias. To the contrary, they incorporate a strong sense of status and position, and clear notions of who is higher and who is lower. However, other factors, especially social class, are considered more important than race as criteria for judging and ranking people. In fact, social class can affect perceptions of skin color to the extent that people of higher status can be seen as "whiter" than those of lower status, regardless of actual skin color.

One interesting comparison is between the United States and Brazil, the largest nation in South America. Like other Central and South Americans, Brazilians recognize many gradations of skin color and the different blends that are possible in people of mixed-race heritage. Commonly used terms in Brazil include *branco* (white), *moreno* (brown), *moreno claro* (light brown), *claro* (light), *pardo* (mixed race), and *negro* and *preto* (black). Some reports count scores of Brazilian racial categories, but Telles (2004, p. 82) writes that fewer than 10 are in common use. Still, this system is vastly more complex than the traditional U.S. perception of race.

Why does Brazil have a more open-ended, less rigid system than the United States? We will explore the issue in more detail in Chapter 13. Here, we can make several important points:

- The foundation for the Brazilian racial perception was laid in the distant past. The Portuguese, the colonial conquerors of Brazil, were mostly single males, and they intermarried with other racial groups, thus producing a large class of mixed-race people.
- Slavery was not so thoroughly equated with race in Brazil as it was in North America and did not carry the same presumption of racial inferiority as in North America, where slavery, blackness, and inferiority were tightly linked in the dominant ideology, an equation with powerful echoes in the present.
- After slavery ended, Brazil did not go through a period of legalized racial segregation like the Jim Crow system in the U.S. South or apartheid in South Africa. Thus, there was less need politically, socially, or economically to divide people into rigid groups in Brazil.

We should stress that Brazil is not a racial utopia, as is sometimes claimed. Prejudice is an everyday reality, and there is a high correlation between skin color and social status. Black Brazilians have much higher illiteracy, unemployment, and poverty rates, and are much less likely to have access to a university education. Whites dominate the more prestigious and lucrative occupations and the leadership positions in the economy and in politics, while blacks are concentrated at the bottom of the class system, with mixed-race people in between (Haan & Thorat, 2012; Marteleto, 2012).

It would be difficult to argue that race prejudice in Brazil is less intense than in the United States. On the other hand, given the vastly different perceptions of race in the two societies, we can conclude that Brazilian prejudice has a different content and emotional texture, and reflects a different contact situation and national history.

Questions to Consider

1. Compare and contrast the understandings of race in the United States and Brazil. Why do these differences exist?
2. What is the role of the contact situation in shaping contemporary race relations in these two societies?

modern American society. As was the case in earlier eras, racism and racial inequality today cannot be addressed apart from the trends of change in the larger society, especially changes in subsistence technology. This section examines the racial separation that continues to characterize so many areas of U.S. society and applies many of the concepts from previous chapters to present-day black–white relations.

CONTINUING SEPARATION

More than 45 years ago, a presidential commission charged with investigating black urban unrest warned that the United States was "moving towards two societies, one black, one white, separate and unequal" (National Advisory Commission, 1968). We could object to the commission's use of the phrase "moving towards," with its suggestion that U.S. society was at one time racially unified, but the warning still seems prophetic.

While race relations are clearly better today, African Americans and white Americans, in many ways, continue to live in separate worlds. The separation is especially complete when race is compounded with class and residence: The black urban poor lead lives that barely intersect with the more affluent whites of suburbia.

Each group has committed violence and hate crimes against the other, but the power differentials and the patterns of inequality that are the legacy of our racist past guarantee that African Americans will more often be seen as "invaders" pushing into areas where they do not belong and are not wanted. Sometimes, the reactions to these perceived intrusions are immediate and bloody, but other, subtler attempts to maintain the exclusion of African Americans continue to be part of everyday life, even at the highest levels of society. For example, in a lawsuit reminiscent of Jim Crow days, a national restaurant chain was accused of discriminating against African American customers by systematically providing poor service. In 2004, the company agreed to pay $8.7 million to settle the lawsuit (McDowell, 2004).

Many African Americans mirror the hostility of whites, and as the goals of full racial equality and integration continue to seem remote, frustration and anger continue to run high. While Obama's election stirred strong optimism and positive attitudes toward the future in the black community, the more typical mood is pessimistic (recall our discussion of public opinion poll results and the differences in black and white perceptions of U.S. race relations from Chapter 1).

The discontent and frustration have been manifested in violence and riots; the most widely publicized example was the racial violence that began with the 1991 arrest and beating of Rodney King by police officers in Los Angeles. The attack on King was videotaped and shown repeatedly on national and international news, and contrary to the expectations of most who saw the videotape, the police officers were acquitted of almost all charges in April 1992. On hearing word of the acquittals, African American communities in several cities erupted in violence. The worst disturbance occurred in the Watts section of Los Angeles, where 58 people lost their lives and millions of dollars of property was damaged or destroyed (Wilkens, 1992).

This aftermath of the beating of Rodney King illustrates several of the common ingredients that have sparked black collective violence and protest since the 1960s: the behavior of the police and the ubiquity of recording devices. An additional example occurred in 2009 in Oakland, California. Oscar Grant, a 23-year-old black man, was returning from New Year's Eve celebrations in San Francisco when he was caught up in an altercation at a subway station.[1] Police had Grant down on the ground when Officer Johannes Mehserle shot him in the back. Grant was not handcuffed, and Mehserle claimed that Grant was reaching for his waistband—possibly for a weapon—when he fired the fatal shot. In fact, Grant was unarmed. These events were recorded on multiple cameras and cell phones, and quickly went viral on the Internet. To many, Grant's death appeared to be an intentional, unprovoked execution.

The black community responded with both peaceful protests and violent rioting. Mehserle was eventually convicted of involuntary manslaughter and sentenced to a two-year prison term. The punishment seemed a mere slap on the wrist to many and provoked further protest, both peaceful and violent (Bulwa, 2010; Egelko, 2009).

In some ways, these events were similar to the 1960s riots. The protests and mass violence were spontaneous and expressed diffuse but bitter discontent with the racial status quo.

[1]This incident is the basis for the 2013 feature-length film *Fruitvale Station*.

They signaled the continuing racial inequality, urban poverty and despair, and the reality of separate communities, unequal and hostile.

THE CRIMINAL JUSTICE SYSTEM AND AFRICAN AMERICANS

As illustrated by the shooting of Oscar Grant, no area of race relations is more volatile and controversial than the relationship between the black community and the criminal justice system. There is considerable mistrust and resentment of the police among African Americans, and the perception that the entire criminal justice system is stacked against them is common.

A Biased Criminal Justice System? The perception of bias is not without justification: The police and other elements of the criminal justice system have a long tradition of abuse, harassment, and mistreatment of black citizens, who, in turn, commonly see the police as the enemy and the entire criminal justice system as an occupying force. For example, a 2013 nationally representative Gallup poll found that 68% of black respondents—two thirds of the sample—thought the American justice system was racially biased. Only 25% of whites agreed (Newport, 2013a). We should note that this poll was conducted shortly after George Zimmerman was acquitted of murder and manslaughter charges in the shooting death of Trayvon Martin,

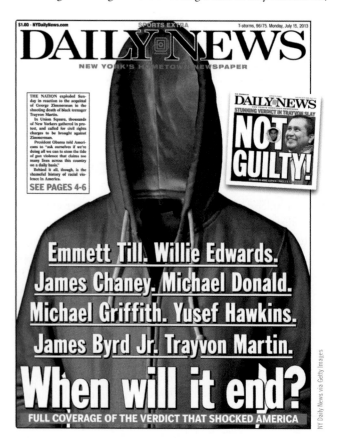

Trayvon Martin, another victim of a racially biased criminal justice system?

the case mentioned at the beginning of this chapter. We would generally expect such incidents to intensify the perception of bias. On the other hand, the percentage of black respondents who perceived bias was essentially unchanged from two previous polls, one in 2008 and the other in 1993.

The great majority of social science research has documented the continuing bias of the criminal justice system, at all levels, against African Americans (and other minorities). In a comprehensive summary of this research, Rosich (2007) concluded that, while blatant and overt discrimination has diminished over the past few decades, the biases that remain have powerful consequences for the black community, even though they often are more subtle and harder to tease out. Even slight acts of racial discrimination can have a cumulative effect throughout the stages of processing in the criminal justice system and can result in large differences in outcomes (Rosich, 2007).

The magnitude of these racial differences is documented by a report that found that, while African Americans make up 16% of all young people, they account for 28% of juvenile arrests, 34% of youths formally processed by the courts, and 58% of youths sent to adult prison (National Council on Crime and Delinquency, 2007, p. 37; see also Mauer, 2011). Civil rights advocates and other spokespersons for the black community charge that there is a dual justice system in the United States and that blacks, adults as well as juveniles, are more likely to receive harsher treatment than are whites charged with similar crimes.

The greater vulnerability of the African American community to the criminal justice system is further documented in two recent studies. The first (Pettit & Western, 2004) focused on men born between 1965 and 1969, and found that 20% of blacks, compared with 3% of whites, had been imprisoned by the time they were 30 years old. Also, the study found that education was a key variable affecting the probability of imprisonment: Nearly 60% of African American men in this cohort who had not completed high school went to prison. The second study (Pew Charitable Trust, 2008) found that black men were imprisoned at far higher rates than were white men: While less than 1% of all white men were in prison, the rate for black men was 7%. Furthermore, 11% of black men aged 20 to 34 were imprisoned.

The War on Drugs. Perhaps the most important reason for these racial differences is that, since the 1980s, black males have been much more likely than white males to get caught up in the national "get tough" policy on drugs, especially crack cocaine. Crack cocaine is a cheap form of the drug, and the street-level dealers who have felt the brunt of the national antidrug campaign disproportionately have been young African American males from less affluent areas.

Some see the "war on drugs" as a not-so-subtle form of racial discrimination. For example, until 2010, federal law required a mandatory prison term of five years for possession of five grams of crack cocaine, a drug much more likely to be dealt by poor blacks. In contrast, comparable levels of sentencing

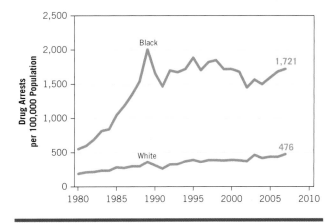

FIGURE 6.1 Drug Arrest Rates by Race, 1980–2007

SOURCE: National Center for Health Statistics (2010).

for dealing powder cocaine—the more expensive form of the drug—are not reached until the accused possesses a minimum of 500 grams (Rosich, 2007).

In 2010, the sentencing disparity was reduced by congressional action, and the mandatory five-year prison term for simple possession of crack cocaine was eliminated (Eckholm, 2010), but Figure 6.1 illustrates the much higher drug arrest rate for blacks since the early 1980s. Notice that the arrest rate for blacks spiked in the late 1980s, when the war on drugs began.

Another recent study focused on marijuana arrests and found huge racial disparities in the nation as a whole, in every state except Hawaii, and in the great majority of counties (American Civil Liberties Union, 2013). Nationally, in 2010, blacks were arrested at a rate of about 700 per 100,000 population, while the white arrest rate was slightly less than 200 per 100,000 population. Thus, blacks were roughly 3.5 times more likely to be arrested for this crime. Is this because black Americans use the drug more than do white Americans? Decidedly not. There was virtually no difference in the rate of use for blacks and whites either in the populations as a whole or among younger people.

If there is no racial difference in use of marijuana, what accounts for the huge racial disparity in arrests? Like Brent Staples, whose essay opened this chapter, blacks are more likely to be policed, watched, stopped and frisked, and profiled than are whites. Their greater vulnerability to arrest for this relatively minor offense is echoed in patterns throughout the criminal justice system and reflects the continuing "otherness" of African Americans in U.S. society.

Racial Profiling. The racial differences in vulnerability to arrest are captured by the concept of racial profiling: the police use of race as an indicator when calculating whether a person is suspicious or dangerous (Kennedy, 2001, p. 3). The tendency to focus more on blacks and disproportionately to stop, question, and follow them is a form of discrimination that generates resentment and increases the distrust (and fear) many African Americans feel toward their local police forces.

According to some, humiliating encounters with police (e.g., being stopped and questioned for "driving while black") are virtually a rite of passage for black men (Kennedy, 2001, p. 7). According to one national survey, 17% of young black men felt that they had been "treated unfairly" in dealings with the police within the previous 30 days (Newport, 2013b).

The charges of racial profiling and discrimination in the war on drugs can be controversial, but these patterns sustain the ancient perceptions of African Americans as dangerous outsiders, and in the African American community they feed the tradition of resentment and anger toward the police.

The New Jim Crow? Many of the themes and ideas in this section are presented in a provocative and important book that argues that the racial differentials in the war on drugs amount to a new racial control system that has halted the advances made during the civil rights era (Alexander, 2012). The millions of black men who have been convicted under the racially biased drug laws are not only sent to prison; they also carry the stigma of a felony conviction for their entire lives. Their prospects for legitimate employment are minis-cule, they lose the right to vote, and they are ineligible for many government programs, including student loans for college. Like the entire black population under de jure segregation, they are marginalized, excluded, second-class citizens highly controlled by the state.

INCREASING CLASS INEQUALITY

As black Americans moved out of the rural South and as the repressive force of de jure segregation receded, social class inequality within the African American population increased. Since the 1960s, the black middle class has grown, but black poverty continues to be a serious problem.

The Black Middle Class. A small African American middle class, based largely on occupations and businesses serving only the African American community, had been in existence since before the Civil War (Frazier, 1957). Has this more affluent segment benefited from increasing tolerance in the larger society, civil rights legislation, and affirmative action programs? Does Obama's election and reelection signal the continuing rise of the black middle class?

The answer to these questions appears to be no. Any progress that might have been made since the civil rights era seems to have been wiped out by the downturn in the American economy that began in 2007.

In actuality, it seems that the size and prosperity of the black middle class was always less than is sometimes assumed. Two studies illustrate this point. One (Kochhar, 2004) found that between 1996 and 2002, the percentage of blacks that

FIGURE 6.2 Wealth of the Middle Class as Defined by Level of Education and Employment

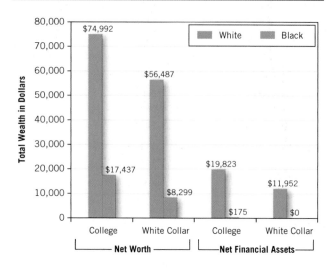

SOURCE: Oliver and Shapiro (2006, p. 96).

could be considered middle and upper class never exceeded 25% of the black population. The comparable figure for whites was almost 60%. Thus, according to this study, the black middle and upper class were less than half the size of the white middle and upper class.

The other study (Oliver & Shapiro, 2006) indicates that, prior to the 2007 economic disruption, the African American middle class was not only smaller but also much less affluent. The researchers studied racial differences in wealth, which includes not only income but all other financial assets: the value of houses, cars, savings, other property, and so forth.

Figure 6.2 compares the wealth of blacks and whites, using two different definitions of middle class and two different measures of wealth. Middle-class status is defined, first, in terms of level of education, with a college education indicating middle-class status, and, second, in terms of occupation, with a white-collar occupation indicating middle-class status.

Wealth is defined first in terms of net worth, which includes all assets (houses, cars, and so forth) minus debt. The second measure, net financial assets, is the same as net worth but excludes the value of a person's investments in home and cars. This second measure is a better indicator of the resources that are available to invest in educating the next generation or financing new businesses (Oliver & Shapiro, 2006, pp. 60–62).

By either definition, the black middle class was at a distinct disadvantage. There are huge differentials in net worth between blacks and whites, and even greater differences in net financial assets. Note, in fact, that the figure for net financial assets of blacks in white-collar occupations is exactly zero. Once their equity in houses and cars is subtracted out, they are left with no wealth at all—a statistic that strongly underscores the greater precariousness of middle-class standing for blacks.

While the bad economic times that began in 2007 have affected virtually all Americans, they appear to have had a disproportionately harsh effect on African Americans in general and the African American middle class in particular. One study found that, while both blacks and whites lost wealth after 2007, the median wealth for black families was only 10% of that for white families in 2009 (Shapiro, Meschede, & Osoro, 2013, p. 2; see also Kochhar, Fry, & Taylor, 2011).

These economic differences are due partly to discrimination in the present and partly to the racial gaps in income, wealth, and economic opportunity inherited from past generations. As we mentioned in Chapter 5, racial differences in homeownership are a key component of the racial gap in wealth (Shapiro et al., 2013, p. 4). The greater economic marginality of the African American middle class today is a form of past-in-present institutional discrimination (see Chapter 5). It reflects the greater ability of white parents (and grandparents), in large part rooted in higher rates of homeownership, to finance higher education and subsidize business ventures and home mortgages (Oliver & Shapiro, 2006).

Not only is their economic position more marginal, but middle-class African Americans commonly report that they are unable to escape the narrow straitjacket of race. No matter what their level of success, occupation, or professional accomplishments, race continues to be seen by the larger society as their primary defining characteristic (Benjamin, 2005; Cose, 1993; Hughes & Thomas, 1998). Without denying the advances of some, many analysts argue that the stigma of race continues to set sharp limits on the life chances of African Americans.

There is also a concern that greater class differentiation may decrease solidarity and cohesion within the African American community. There is greater income inequality among African Americans than ever before, with the urban poor at one extreme and some of the wealthiest, most recognized figures in the world—millionaires, celebrities, business moguls, politicians, and sports and movie stars—at the other. Will the more affluent segment of the African American community disassociate itself from the plight of the less fortunate and move away from the urban neighborhoods, taking with it its affluence, articulateness, and leadership skills? If this happens, it will reinforce the class division and further seal the fate of impoverished African Americans, who are largely concentrated in urban areas.

Urban Poverty. African Americans have become an urban minority group, and the fate of the group is inextricably bound to the fate of America's cities. The issues of black–white relations cannot be successfully addressed without dealing with urban issues, and vice versa.

As we saw in Chapter 5, automation and mechanization in the workplace have eliminated many of the manual-labor jobs that sustained city dwellers in earlier decades (Kasarda, 1989). The manufacturing, or secondary, segment of the labor force has declined in size, and the service sector has continued to expand. The more desirable jobs in the service sector have more and more demanding educational prerequisites. The service-sector jobs available to people with lower educational credentials pay low wages—often less than the minimum necessary for the basics, including food and shelter—and offer little in the way of benefits, security, and links to more rewarding occupations. This form of past-in-present institutional discrimination constitutes a powerful handicap for colonized groups such as African Americans, who have been excluded from educational opportunities for centuries.

Furthermore, many of the blue-collar jobs that have escaped automation have migrated away from the cities. Industrialists have been moving their businesses to areas where labor is cheaper, unions have less power, and taxes are lower. This movement to the suburbs, to the Sunbelt, and offshore has been devastating for the inner city. Poor transportation systems, the absence of affordable housing outside the center city, and outright housing discrimination have combined to keep urban poor people of color confined to center-city neighborhoods, distant from opportunities for jobs and economic improvement (Feagin, 2001, pp. 159–160; Kasarda, 1989; Massey & Denton, 1993).

Sociologist Rogelio Saenz (2005) analyzed the situation of blacks in the 15 largest metropolitan areas in the nation and found that they are much more likely than whites to be living in highly impoverished neighborhoods, cut off from the "economic opportunities, services, and institutions that families need to succeed" (para. 2). Saenz found that the greater vulnerability and social and geographical isolation of blacks is pervasive, however, and includes not only higher rates of poverty and unemployment but also large differences in access to cars and even phones, amenities taken for granted in the rest of society. In the areas studied by Saenz, blacks were as much as three times more likely not to have a car (and, thus, no means to get to jobs outside center-city areas) and as much as eight times more likely not to have a telephone.

Some of these industrial and economic forces affect all poor urbanites, not just minority groups or African Americans in particular. The dilemma facing many African Americans is not only due to racism or discrimination; the impersonal forces of evolving industrialization and social class structures contribute in some part as well. However, when immutable racial stigmas and centuries of prejudice (even disguised as modern racism) are added to these economic and urban developments, the forces limiting and constraining many African Americans become extremely formidable.

For the past 60 years, the African American poor have been increasingly concentrated in narrowly delimited urban areas ("the ghetto") in which the scourge of poverty has been compounded and reinforced by a host of other problems, including joblessness, high rates of school dropout, crime, drug use, teenage pregnancy, and welfare dependency. These increasingly isolated neighborhoods are fertile grounds for the development of oppositional cultures, which reject or invert the values of the larger society. The black urban counterculture may be most visible in music, fashion, speech, and other forms of popular culture, but it is also manifested in widespread lack of trust in the larger society and whites in particular. An **urban underclass**, barred from the mainstream economy and the primary labor force and consisting largely of poor African Americans and other minority groups of color, has become a prominent and perhaps permanent feature of the American landscape (Kasarda, 1989; Massey & Denton, 1993; Wilson, 1987, 1996, 2009).

Consider the parallels and contrasts between the plight of the present urban underclass and black Southerners under de jure segregation:

- In both eras, a large segment of the African American population was cut off from opportunities for success and growth.
- In the earlier era, African Americans were isolated in rural areas; now, they are isolated in urban areas, especially center cities.
- In the past, escape from segregation was limited primarily by political and legal restrictions and blatant racial prejudice; escape from poverty in the present is limited by economic and educational deficits and a more subtle and amorphous prejudice.

The result is the same: Many African Americans remain as a colonized minority group—isolated, marginalized, and burdened with a legacy of powerlessness and poverty.

MODERN INSTITUTIONAL DISCRIMINATION

The processes that maintain racial inequality in the present are indirect and sometimes difficult to document and measure. They often flow from the patterns of blatant racial discrimination in the past but are not overtly racial in the present. They operate through a series of cumulative effects that tend to filter black Americans into less desirable positions in education, housing, the criminal justice system, and the job market. Consider two areas where racial class inequalities are perpetuated: employment networks that were closed in the past and remain shut today, and the greater vulnerability of the black community to economic hardships in the larger society.

Closed Networks and Racial Exclusion. The continuing importance of race as a primary factor in the perpetuation of class inequality is dramatically illustrated in a recent research project. Royster (2003) interviewed black and white graduates

---

The **urban underclass** refers to African Americans and other minority groups of color who are marginalized and separated from the economic mainstream.

---

of a trade school in Baltimore. Her respondents had completed the same curricula and earned similar grades. In other words, they were nearly identical in terms of the credentials they brought to the world of work. Nonetheless, the black graduates were employed less often in the trades for which they had been educated, had lower wages, got fewer promotions, and experienced longer periods of unemployment. Virtually every white graduate found secure and reasonably lucrative employment. The black graduates, in stark contrast, usually were unable to stay in the trades and became, instead, low-skilled, low-paid workers in the service sector.

What accounts for these differences? Based on extensive interviews with the subjects, Royster (2003) concluded that the differences could not be explained by training or personality characteristics. Instead, she found that what really mattered was not "what you know" but "who you know." The white graduates had access to networks of referrals and recruitment that linked them to the job market in ways that simply were not available to black graduates. In their search for jobs, whites were assisted more fully by their instructors and were able to use intraracial networks of family and friends, connections so powerful that they "assured even the worst [white] troublemaker a solid place in the blue-collar fold" (p. 78).

Needless to say, these results run contrary to some deeply held American values, most notably the widespread, strong support for the idea that success in life is due to individual effort, self-discipline, and the other attributes enshrined in the Protestant Ethic. The strength of this faith is documented in a recent survey that was administered to a representative sample of adult Americans. The respondents were asked whether they thought people got ahead by hard work, luck, or a combination of the two. Fully 69% of the sample chose "hard work," and another 20% chose "hard work and luck equally" (National Opinion Research Council, 1972–2012). This overwhelming support for the importance of individual effort is echoed in human capital theory and many "traditional" sociological perspectives on assimilation (see Chapter 2).

Royster's (2003) results demonstrate that the American faith in the power of hard work alone is simply wrong. To the contrary, access to jobs is controlled by networks of personal relationships that are decidedly not open to everyone. These subtle patterns of exclusion and closed intraracial networks are more difficult to document than the blatant discrimination that was at the core of Jim Crow segregation, but they can be just as devastating in their effects and just as powerful as mechanisms for perpetuating racial gaps in income and employment.

The Differential Impact of Hard Times. Because of their greater vulnerability, African Americans are more likely to suffer the more virulent form of any illness—economic or otherwise—that strikes society: They will tend to feel the impact earlier, experience higher levels of distress, and be the last to recover. As we have seen, the recent downturn in the U.S. economy has affected almost everyone in one way or another: Americans everywhere

FIGURE 6.3 Unemployment Rate by Race in the United States, 2001–2013

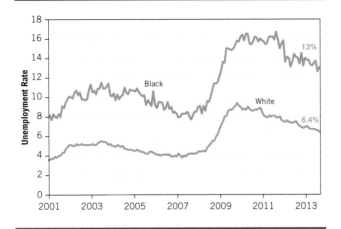

SOURCE: U.S. Bureau of Labor Statistics (2013).

have suffered from job loss, increasing poverty, home foreclosures, loss of health care coverage, and other disasters. How has the recession affected the black community?

Consider the unemployment rate, which generally runs twice as high for blacks as for whites. During the recession, the rate rose for all groups, but, as displayed in Figure 6.3, it rose earlier for blacks, rose at a steeper angle to a much higher peak, and leveled off and began to fall later than for whites. The highest rate for whites was 9.4, about 56% of the peak rate of 16.7 for blacks.

The white unemployment rate leveled off and began to fall in early 2010. The rate for blacks did not begin to decline until nearly 2 years later. These hard times affected all groups, across the board, but created a deeper economic hole for black Americans.

Another crucial area in which African Americans have been disproportionately affected by the recession is homeownership, which, as we have noted on several occasions, is a crucial source of wealth for the average American. Income enables families to get along, but financial assets such as homeownership help families get ahead, escape poverty, and become socially mobile (Oliver & Shapiro, 2008, p. A9).

Not surprisingly, black Americans have suffered more in this area, as they have in unemployment. A recent report (Oliver & Shapiro, 2008) found that black Americans and other minority groups of color, compared with whites, were more than three times as likely to be victimized by toxic, so-called "subprime" home loans and more than twice as likely to suffer foreclosure as a result. Subprime home loans were new financial instruments that enabled many previously ineligible people to qualify for home mortgages. Predatory lenders marketed the loans especially to more vulnerable populations, and the deals had hidden costs, higher interest rates, and other features that made keeping up with payments difficult. One result of the housing market's collapse was "the greatest loss of financial wealth" in the African American community (Oliver & Shapiro, 2008, p. A11).

Thus, a group that was already more vulnerable and economically marginal suffered the greatest proportional loss—an economic collapse that will take years to recover from. Societal disasters such as the recent recession are not shared equally by everyone and are especially severe for the groups that are the most vulnerable and have the most tenuous connections to prosperity and affluence. Thus, racial inequality persists decades after the end of blatant, direct, state-supported segregation.

THE FAMILY INSTITUTION AND THE CULTURE OF POVERTY

The nature of the African American family institution has been a continuing source of concern and controversy. On one hand, some analysts see the African American family as structurally weak, a cause of continuing poverty and a variety of other problems. No doubt the most famous study in this tradition was the Moynihan (1965) report, which focused on the higher rates of divorce, separation, desertion, and illegitimacy among African American families and the fact that black families were far more likely to be female headed than were white families. Moynihan concluded that the fundamental barrier facing African Americans was a family structure that he saw as crumbling, a condition that would perpetuate the cycle of poverty entrapping African Americans (p. iii). Today, many of the differences between black and white family institutions identified by Moynihan are even more pronounced. Figure 6.4, for example, compares the percentage of households headed by females (black and white) with the percentage of households headed by married couples. (Note that the trends seem to have stabilized since the mid-1990s.)

The line of analysis implicit in the Moynihan (1965) report locates the problem of urban poverty in the characteristics of

FIGURE 6.4 Composition of Family Households in the United States, 1970–2010

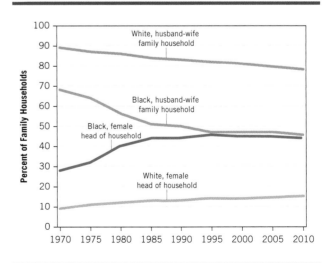

SOURCE: U.S. Census Bureau (1978, p. 43; 2007, p. 56; 2012c, p. 56).

the African American community, particularly in the African American family. These structures are "broken" in important ways and need to be "fixed." This argument is consistent with the **culture of poverty theory**, which argues that poverty is perpetuated by the particular characteristics of the poor. Specifically, poverty is said to encourage **fatalism** (the sense that one's destiny is beyond one's control) and an orientation to the present rather than the future. The desire for instant gratification is a central trait of the culture of poverty, as opposed to the ability to defer gratification, which is thought to be essential for middle-class success. Other characteristics include violence, school failure, authoritarianism, and high rates of alcoholism and family desertion by males (Lewis, 1959, 1965, 1966; for a recent reprise of the debate over the culture of poverty concept, see Small, Harding, & Lamont, 2010; Steinberg, 2011).

The culture of poverty theory leads to the conclusion that the problem of urban poverty would be resolved if female-headed family structures and other cultural characteristics correlated with poverty could be changed. Note that this approach is consistent with the traditional assimilationist perspective and human capital theory: The poor have "bad" or inappropriate values. If they could be equipped with "good" (i.e., white, middle-class) values, the problem would be resolved.

An opposed perspective, more consistent with the concepts and theories that underlie this text, sees the matriarchal structure of the African American family as the result of urban poverty—rather than a cause—and a reflection of pervasive, institutional racial discrimination and the scarcity of jobs for urban African American males. In impoverished African American urban neighborhoods, the supply of men able to support a family is reduced by high rates of unemployment, incarceration, and violence, and these conditions are, in turn, created by the concentration of urban poverty and the growth of the "underclass" (Massey & Denton, 1993; Wilson, 1996, 2009). Thus, the burden of child rearing tends to fall on females, and female-headed households are more common than in more advantaged neighborhoods.

Female-headed African American families tend to be poor, not because they are weak in some sense but because of the lower wages accorded to women in general and to African American women in particular, as documented in Figure 6.5. Note that black female workers have the lowest wages throughout the time period. Also note that the gap between black women and white men has narrowed over the years. In 1955, black women earned about a third of what white men earned. In 2012, the gap stood at about 68% (after shrinking to just

---

Culture of poverty theory argues that poverty creates certain personality traits—such as the need for instant gratification—that, in turn, perpetuate poverty.

Fatalism is the view that one's destiny is beyond one's control.

FIGURE 6.5 Median Income for Full-Time, Year-Round Workers by Race and Sex, 1956–2012

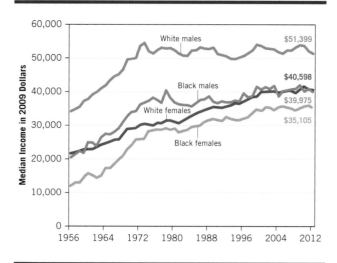

SOURCE: U.S. Census Bureau (2013d, Table P-36).

under 70% in 2005), largely because male wages (for blacks as well as whites) have been relatively flat since the 1970s, while women's wages (again for both whites and blacks) have risen. This pattern reflects the impact of deindustrialization: the shift away from manufacturing, which has eliminated many good blue-collar jobs, and the rise of employment sectors in which women tend to be more concentrated.

The poverty associated with black, female-headed households reflects the interactive effects of sexism and racism on black women, not some weakness in the black family. African American urban poverty is the result of the complex forces of past and present institutional discrimination, American racism and prejudice, the precarious position of African American women in the labor force, and continuing urbanization and industrialization. The African American family is not in need of "fixing," and the attitudes and values of the urban underclass are more the results of impoverishment than they are the causes. The solution to African American urban poverty lies in fundamental changes in the urban industrial economy and sweeping alterations in the distribution of resources and opportunities.

MIXED RACE AND NEW RACIAL IDENTITIES

As we have discussed, Americans traditionally see race as a simple dichotomy: People are either black or white, with no intermediate categories. In the past, the social convention of the "one-drop rule" meant that people of mixed racial descent were classified as black. To illustrate, consider the story of Gregory Williams (known then as Billy), a white boy growing up in the segregated South in the late 1940s and early 1950s (Williams, 1995). When Billy was 10, his father revealed that he was "half-colored." Under the one-drop rule, that made Billy black. Billy at first refused to believe: "I'm not colored, I'm white! I look white! I've always been white! I go to the 'whites only' school, 'whites only' movie theaters, and 'whites only' swimming pool" (p. 34). Gradually, he came to realize that his life—not just his life chances and his relations with others but his very identity—had been transformed by the revelation of his father's race.

In the past, mixed-race people such as Williams had few choices: Others classified him as black, and the rigid social conventions of the day forced him to accept that identity, with all its implications. Today, five decades after the formal end of Jim Crow segregation, Americans are confronting the limitations of this dichotomous racial convention. People of mixed-race descent are increasing in number and, in fact, are some of the most prominent and well-known people in society. President Obama is an obvious example of a highly visible mixed-race person, but others include professional golfer Tiger Woods (who defines himself—tongue in cheek—as Cablanasian: Caucasian, black, American Indian, and Asian), vocalist Mariah Carey, Yankees baseball star Derek Jeter, and actress Halle Berry.

How do people of multiracial descent define themselves today? How are they defined by others? Have the old understandings of race become irrelevant? Is there still pressure to place people in one and only one group? There has been a fair amount of research on this issue, and we can begin to formulate some ideas.

One important study illustrates some of the possible identities for mixed-race individuals. Rockquemore and Brunsma interviewed a sample of several hundred mixed-race college students, confining their attention to people who had one white and one black parent (Brunsma, 2005; Rockquemore & Brunsma, 2008). They found that today, unlike the situation faced by Williams, the meaning of mixed-race identity is conceptually complex and highly variable (Rockquemore & Brunsma, 2008, p. 50). They identified four main categories that their respondents used to understand their biracialism, and we present these in order from most to least common. However, the sample they assembled was not representative, and there is no reason to assume that these same percentages would characterize all biracial Americans.

1. The most common racial identity in the sample was the *border identity*. These respondents (58% of the sample) didn't consider themselves to be either black or white. They defined themselves as members of a third, separate category that is linked to both groups but is unique in itself. One respondent declared, "I'm not black, I'm biracial" (Rockquemore & Brunsma, 2008, p. 43). The authors make a further distinction:

    a. Some border identities are "validated" or recognized and acknowledged by others. These respondents see themselves as biracial, and they are also seen that way by family, friends, and the community.

    b. Other border identities are "unvalidated" by others. These individuals see themselves as biracial but are classified by others as black. For example, one respondent said, "I consider myself biracial, but I experience the world as a black person" (p. 45). This disconnect may be the result of the persistence of traditional dichotomous racial thinking and the fact that some people lack the mental category of "biracial." According to the authors, people in this category are of special interest because of the tensions created by the conflict between their self-image and the way they are defined by others.

2. The second most common identity in the sample was the *singular identity*. These individuals saw themselves not as biracial but as exclusively black (13%) or exclusively white (3%). As Williams's case illustrated, the singular black identity is most consistent with American traditional thinking about race. The authors argue that this identity *not* being the most common in their sample illustrates the complexity of racial identity for biracial people today.

3. A third identity was the *transcendent identity* (15%). The respondents in this category rejected the whole notion of race, along with the traditional categories of black and white, and insisted that they should be seen as unique individuals and not placed in a category, especially since those categories carry multiple assumptions about character, personality, intelligence, attitudes, and a host of other characteristics. Respondents with the transcendent identity were in a constant battle to avoid classification in our highly race-conscious society. One respondent's remarks are illustrative:

    I'm just John, you know? . . . I'm a good guy, just like me for that. . . . When I came here (to college), it was like I was almost forced to look at other people as being white, black, Asian, or Hispanic. And so now, I'm still trying to go, "I'm just John," but uh, you gotta be something. (p. 49)

4. The final racial identity is the least common (4%) but perhaps the most interesting. The authors describe the racial identity of these individuals as *protean*, or changing as the individual moves from group to group and through the various social contexts of everyday life. There are different "ways of being" in groups of blacks versus groups of whites, and individuals with the protean racial identity slip effortlessly from one mode to the next and are accepted by both groups as insiders. The authors point out that most people adjust their *behavior* to different situations (e.g., a fraternity party vs. a family Thanksgiving dinner), but these individuals also change their *identity* and adjust who they are to different circumstances. Respondents with the protean identity felt empowered by their ability to fit in with different groups and believed they were endowed with a high degree of "cultural savvy" (p. 47). In our increasingly diverse, multicultural, and multiracial society, the ability to belong easily to multiple groups may prove to be a unique strength.

What can we conclude? Racial identity, like so many other aspects of our society, is evolving and becoming more complex. Traditions such as the one-drop rule live on but in attenuated, weakened form. Also, racial identity, like other aspects of self-concept, can be situational or contingent on social context, not permanent or fixed. Given the world in which he lived, Williams had no choice but to accept a black racial identity. Today, in a somewhat more tolerant and pluralistic social environment, biracial people have choices and some space in which to carve out their own, unique identity. According to Rockquemore and Brunsma (2008), these identity choices are contingent on a number of factors, including personal appearance, but they are always made in the context of a highly race-conscious society with long and strong traditions of racism and prejudice.

QUESTIONS FOR REFLECTION

1. This section examined a number of issues and trends in contemporary black–white relations. In your opinion, which of these is most important? Why?

2. To what extent do blacks and whites live in different worlds? Is it fair to characterize contemporary black–white relations as "continuing separation"? Why or why not?

3. How has racial identity evolved in modern America? How is racial identity for biracial Americans different today?

PREJUDICE AND DISCRIMINATION

Modern racism, the more subtle form of prejudice that seems to dominate contemporary race relations, was discussed in Chapter 3. Although the traditional, more overt forms of prejudice have certainly not disappeared, contemporary expressions of prejudice are often amorphous and indirect. For example, the widespread belief among whites that racial discrimination has been eliminated in the United States may be a way of blaming African Americans—rather than themselves or the larger society—for the continuing reality of racial inequality.

As we saw in Chapter 5 and earlier in this chapter, a parallel process of evolution from blunt and overt forms to more subtle and covert forms has occurred in patterns of discrimination. The clarity of Jim Crow has yielded to the ambiguity of modern institutional discrimination and the continuing legacy of past discrimination in the present.

How can the pervasive problems of racial inequality be addressed in the present atmosphere of modern racism, low levels of sympathy for the urban poor, and subtle but powerful institutional discrimination? Many people advocate a "color-blind" approach to the problems of racial inequality: The legal and political systems should simply ignore skin color and treat everyone the same. This approach seems sensible to many people because, after all, the legal and overt barriers of Jim Crow discrimination are long gone and, at least at first glance, there are no obvious limits to the life chances of blacks.

In the eyes of others, however, a color-blind approach is doomed to failure. To end racial inequality and deal with the legacy of racism, society must follow race-conscious programs that explicitly address the problems of race and racism. Color-blind strategies amount to inaction. All we need to do to perpetuate (or widen) the present racial gap is nothing. This issue is taken up in the Current Debates feature introduced at the end of this chapter.

ASSIMILATION AND PLURALISM

In this section, we will use the major concepts of the Gordon model of assimilation to assess the status of African Americans. To facilitate comparisons, the same format and organization will be used in the following three chapters. Of course, we will not be able to address all aspects of these patterns or go into much depth, so these sections should be regarded as overviews and suggestions for further research.

ACCULTURATION

The Blauner hypothesis states that the culture of groups created by colonization will be attacked, denigrated, and, if possible, eliminated, and this assertion seems well validated by the experiences of African Americans. African cultures and languages were largely eradicated under slavery. As a powerless, colonized minority group, slaves had few opportunities to preserve their heritage, even though traces of African homelands have been found in black language patterns, kinship systems, music, folk tales, and family legends (see Levine, 1977; Stuckey, 1987).

Cultural domination continued under the Jim Crow system, albeit through a different structural arrangement. Under slavery, slaves and their owners worked together and interracial contact was common. Under de jure segregation, intergroup contact diminished and blacks and whites generally became more separate. After slavery ended, the African American community had somewhat more autonomy (although still few resources) to define itself and develop a distinct culture.

The centuries of cultural domination and separate development have created a unique black experience in America. African Americans share language, religion, values, beliefs, and norms with the dominant society but have developed distinct variations on the general themes.

The acculturation process may have been slowed (or even reversed) by the Black Power movement. On one hand, since the 1960s, there has been an increased interest in African culture, language, clothing, and history, and a more visible celebration

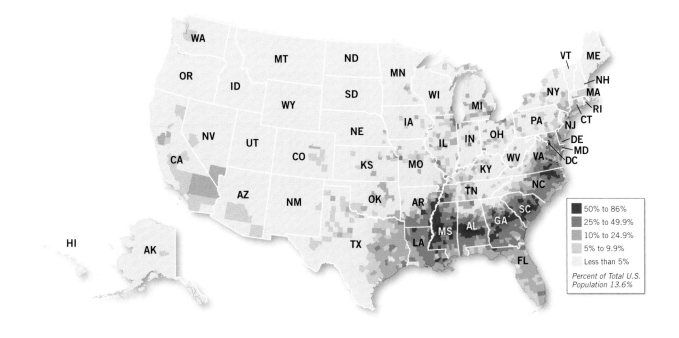

Legend:
- 50% to 86%
- 25% to 49.9%
- 10% to 24.9%
- 5% to 9.9%
- Less than 5%

Percent of Total U.S. Population 13.6%

SOURCE: Rastogi, Johnson, Hoeffel, and Drewery (2011, p. 11).

of unique African American experiences (e.g., Kwanzaa) and the innumerable contributions of African Americans to the larger society. On the other hand, many of those traditions and contributions have been in existence all along. Perhaps all that really changed was the degree of public recognition.

SECONDARY STRUCTURAL ASSIMILATION

Structural assimilation, or integration, involves two different phases. Secondary structural assimilation refers to integration in more public areas, such as the job market, schools, and political institutions. We can assess integration in this area by comparing residential patterns, income distributions, job profiles, political power, and levels of education of the different groups. Each of these areas is addressed in the next sections. We will then discuss primary structural assimilation (integration in intimate associations, such as friendship and intermarriage).

Residential Patterns. After a century of movement out of the rural South, African Americans today are highly urbanized and much more spread out across the nation. As we saw in Chapter 5 (see Figures 5.1 and 5.2), about 90% of African Americans are urban and a slight majority of African Americans continue to reside in the South. About 35% of African Americans now live in the Northeast and Midwest, overwhelmingly in urban areas. Figure 6.6 clearly shows the concentration of African Americans in the states of the old Confederacy; the urbanized

East Coast corridor from Washington, D.C., to Boston; the industrial centers of the Midwest; and, to a lesser extent, California.

Residential segregation between blacks and whites peaked toward the end of the Jim Crow era, in the 1960s and 1970s, and has decreased in recent decades (Logan & Stults, 2011). This pattern is displayed in Figure 6.7, which shows levels of residential segregation between white and black Americans for the past four census years. Scores for residential segregation between white and Hispanic Americans and white and Asian Americans are also included in the graph. We will focus on black Americans here and discuss the other groups in Chapters 8 and 9, respectively.

Figure 6.7 uses a statistic called the **dissimilarity index**, which shows the degree to which groups are *not* evenly spread across neighborhoods or census tracts. Specifically, the index is the percentage of each group that would have to move to a different tract to achieve integration. A score above 60 is considered to indicate extreme segregation.

Those seeking evidence of improving relations between blacks and whites ("the glass is half full") will note the falling scores for racial residential segregation between 1980 and 2010

The **dissimilarity index** is a measure of residential segregation. The higher the score, the greater the segregation; scores above 60 are considered to indicate extreme segregation.

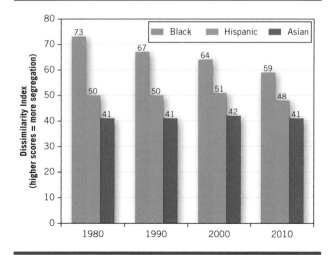

SOURCE: Logan and Stults (2011, p. 5).

and, especially, that the dissimilarity index actually dipped to slightly below 60 in the most recent year. However, those with a more negative frame of mind ("the glass is half empty") might point out that the graph shows that racial residential segregation continues to be the norm and that blacks are much more segregated from whites than are the other two groups.

As we have seen, in Chapter 5 and earlier in this chapter, the continuing patterns of residential segregation are reinforced by a variety of practices, including racial steering (guiding clients to same-race housing areas) by realtors and barely disguised discrimination. The Great Migration out of the South did little to end residential segregation, which tends to be highest in the older industrial cities of the Northeast and upper Midwest. In fact, the five most residentially segregated large metropolitan areas in 2010 were not in southern or border states but were (in rank order) in Detroit, Milwaukee, New York, Newark, and Chicago (Logan & Stults, 2011, p. 6).

Contrary to popular belief among whites, an African American preference for living in same-race neighborhoods does not play a large role in perpetuating these patterns. For example, studies generally find that African Americans prefer to live in areas split 50/50 between blacks and whites but that whites much prefer neighborhoods with low percentages of blacks or Latinos (e.g., see Krysan & Farley, 2002, p. 949; Lewis, Emerson, & Klineberg, 2011). The social class and income differences between blacks and whites are also relatively minor factors in perpetuating residential segregation, as the African American middle class is just as likely as the African American poor to be segregated (Stoll, 2004, p. 26; see also Dwyer, 2010).

School Integration. In 1954, the year of the landmark Brown desegregation decision, the great majority of African Americans lived in states operating segregated school systems. Compared with white schools, Jim Crow schools were severely underfunded and had fewer qualified teachers, shorter school years, and inadequate physical facilities. School integration was one of the most important goals of the civil rights movement in the 1950s and 1960s, and, aided by pressure from the courts and the federal government, considerable strides were made toward this goal for several decades.

In recent decades, however, the pressure from the federal government and courts has eased, and school integration is slowing and, in many areas, has even reversed. Figure 6.8 displays some of these trends for the nation as a whole for six school years, stretching from the late 1960s to the 2009–2010 school year.

The top line in the graph shows that the percentage of black students in "majority–minority" schools declined until the early 1990s and then began to rise, almost returning to the level of the late 1960s. The middle line in the graph shows a dramatic drop in the percentage of black students attending schools that were 90% to 100% minority between the 1960s and early 1990s, and then a gradual rise and leveling off. The bottom line shows a slight decrease in the percentage of black students attending schools that were virtually all minority since the early 1990s.

Figure 6.8 clearly shows that the goal of racial integration in public schools has not been achieved. What accounts for the slow progress? One very important cause is the declining number of whites in the society as a whole (see Figure 1.1) and in public schools in particular. In the 2009–2010 school year, whites were barely a majority of students (54%), down from almost 80% in the early 1970s (Orfield et al., 2012, p. 15).

FIGURE 6.8 Three Measures of School Segregation for Black Students

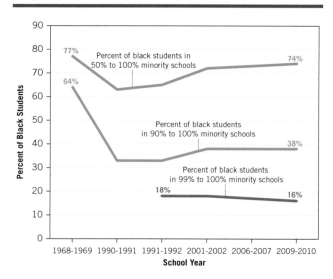

SOURCE: Orfield, Kucsera, and Siegel-Hawley (2012, p. 19).

The table below lists 10 metropolitan areas from across the nation in alphabetical order. Based on what you have learned in this chapter and Chapter 5, which ones do you think have the highest levels of racial residential segregation? Cities in the South? Cities in the Northeast or the West? Cities with a higher or lower black population?

What's your best guess? Rank order the cities from 1 (most segregated) to 10 (least segregated).

	CITY	REGION	% BLACK, 2010*	RANK
1	Atlanta, Georgia	South	32%	
2	Baltimore, Maryland	Border	29%	
3	Boston, Massachusetts	Northeast	7%	
4	Dallas–Fort Worth, Texas	Southwest	15%	
5	Kansas City, Kansas	Midwest	13%	
6	Pittsburgh, Pennsylvania	Northeast	8%	
7	Richmond, Virginia	South	38%	
8	San Diego, California	West	5%	
9	San Francisco, California	West	8%	
10	Washington, D.C.	South/border	26%	

*Percentage in entire metropolitan area, including suburbs. Data from U.S. Census Bureau (2012c, p. 31).

TURN THE PAGE TO SEE THE ACTUAL RANKS AND SCORES.

Another cause is the widespread residential segregation mentioned previously. The challenges for school integration are especially evident in those metropolitan areas that consist of a largely black-populated inner city surrounded by largely white-populated rings of suburbs.

Without a renewed commitment to integration, American schools will continue to resegregate. This is a particularly ominous trend because it directly affects the quality of education: Years of research demonstrate that the integration of schools—by social class as well as race—is related to better educational experiences and improved test scores (e.g., see Orfield et al., 2012).

In terms of the quantity of education, the gap between whites and blacks has generally decreased over the past several decades. Figure 6.9 displays the percentage of the population over 25 years old, by race and sex, with high school diplomas from 1940 to 2012, and shows a dramatic decline in the racial education gap at this level. Given the increasing demands for higher educational credentials in the job market, it is ironic that the nation has nearly achieved racial equality in high school education at a time when this credential matters less.

FIGURE 6.9 High School Graduation Rates of People 25 Years and Older in the United States, 1940–2012

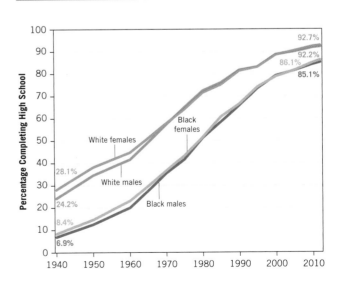

SOURCE: U.S. Census Bureau (2012c, p. 151).

Here are those 10 metro areas listed from most to least segregated. There are many American cities more segregated than Pittsburgh, and some are less segregated than San Diego. These 10 cities were selected to represent a variety of regions and race relations histories, and are not, of course, representative of the society as a whole.

	CITY	SCORE (DISSIMILARITY INDEX)
1	Pittsburgh, Pennsylvania	64.9
2	Baltimore, Maryland	62.2
3	Kansas City, Kansas	57.7
4	Boston, Massachusetts	57.6
5	Washington, D.C.	56.1
6	Atlanta, Georgia	54.1
7	San Francisco, California	50.5
8	Richmond, Virginia	49.6
9	Dallas-Fort Worth, Texas	47.5
10	San Diego, California	38.6

SOURCE: Data from Glaeser and Vigdor (2012).

At the college level, the trends parallel the narrowing gap in levels of high school education, as shown in Figure 6.10. In 1940, white males held a distinct advantage over all other race/gender groups: They were more than 4 times as likely as African American males and females to have a college degree. By 2012, the advantage of white males had shrunk, but they were still about 1.5 times more likely than black males and females to have a college degree. These racial differences grow larger with more advanced degrees, however, and differences such as these will be increasingly serious in an economy in which jobs more frequently require an education beyond high school.

Political Power. Two trends have increased the political power of African Americans since World War II. One is the movement out of the rural South, a process that concentrated African Americans in areas where it was easier for them to register to vote. As the black population outside the South grew, so did their representation at the national level. The first African American representative to the U.S. Congress (other than those elected during Reconstruction) was elected in 1928, and by 1954, there were still only three African American members in the House of Representatives (Franklin, 1967, p. 614). In 2013, there were 44 (Manning, 2013, p. 8), still fewer than the proportional share of the national population (13%).

When Obama was elected to the Senate in 2004, he was the third African American senator since Reconstruction to serve in that body. Since 2004, two African Americans have served as senators, and in the fall of 2013, Corey Booker of New Jersey was elected to the Senate.

The number of African American elected officials at all levels of government increased from virtually zero at the turn of the 20th century to more than 9,000 in 2010 (U.S. Census Bureau, 2011a, p. 258). In Virginia in 1989, Douglas Wilder became the first African American to be elected to a state governorship,

FIGURE 6.10 College Graduation Rates of People 25 Years and Older in the United States, 1940–2012

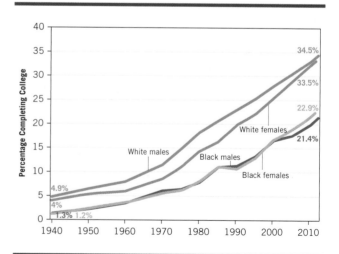

SOURCE: U.S. Census Bureau (2012c, p. 151).

and both Colin Powell and Condoleezza Rice have served as secretary of state, the highest governmental office—along with Supreme Court justice and excluding the presidency—ever held by an African American.

African American communities are virtually guaranteed some political representation because of their high degree of geographical concentration at the local level. Today, most large American cities, including Los Angeles, Chicago, Atlanta, New York, and Washington, D.C., have elected African American mayors.

The other trend that has increased black political power is the dismantling of the institutions and practices of disenfranchisement that operated during Jim Crow segregation (see Chapter 5). As we discussed earlier, the Voting Rights Act of 1965 specifically prohibited many of the practices (poll taxes, literacy tests, and whites-only primaries) traditionally used to keep African Americans politically powerless.

Since the 1960s, the number of African Americans in the nation's voting-age population has increased from slightly less than 10% to about 13%. But this increasing potential for political power has not always been fully mobilized in the past, and actual turnout has generally been lower for blacks than for whites. In the hotly contested presidential races of 2000, 2004, and 2008, however, a variety of organizations (such as the NAACP) made a concerted and largely successful effort to increase turnout for African Americans. In these years, black turnout was comparable to that of whites, and in the 2012 presidential election, the black turnout (66.2%) was slightly larger than the white turnout (64.1%) (File, 2013).

Overall, black American political power has tended to increase over the past several decades on the national, state, and local levels. One potentially ominous threat to this trend is the growth of restrictions on voting in many states in recent years. Well over half the states have considered or passed various measures that could decrease the size of the electorate in general and disproportionately lower the impact of the African American vote. For example, many states may require voters to show a government-issued photo ID—such as a driver's license—before allowing them to cast a ballot.

One of the possible consequences of the Supreme Court's decision to rule the 1965 Voting Rights Act unconstitutional is enabling states and localities to enact measures to restrict voting rights and suppress the voting power of a variety of groups. Shortly after the decision, Texas announced that a voter identification law, previously blocked, would go into effect immediately (Liptak, 2013), and North Carolina passed one of the most restrictive laws since the Jim Crow era (Brennan Center for Justice, 2013).

Proponents of restrictive voting measures argue that they prevent voter fraud, and the new laws do not, of course, mention African Americans or other minority groups, as is typical in cases of modern institutional discrimination. The result may be a dramatically lower turnout on Election Day for groups that are less likely to have driver's licenses, passports, or similar documentation, including not only African Americans but also other minority groups of color, low-income groups, senior citizens, and younger voters (see Brennan Center for Justice, 2013, for a list of efforts to restrict voting).

Jobs and Income. Integration in the job market and racial equality in income follow the trends established in many other areas of social life: The situation of African Americans has improved since the end of de jure segregation but has stopped well short of equality. Among males, whites are much more likely to be employed in the highest-rated and most lucrative occupational areas, whereas blacks are overrepresented in the service sector and in unskilled labor (U.S. Census Bureau, 2013a). One comprehensive analysis of race/gender employment trends found that, after some gains in the years following the passage of the landmark legislation of the mid-1960s, employment gains for black men and women (and white women) have been slight, and that white males continue their disproportionate hold on better jobs (Stainback & Tomaskovic-Devey, 2012, pp. 155–177).

Although huge gaps remain, we should also note that the present occupational distribution represents a rapid and significant upgrading, given that as recently as the 1930s, the majority of African American males were unskilled agricultural laborers (Steinberg, 1981, pp. 206–207). A similar improvement has occurred for African American females. In the 1930s, about 90% of employed African American women worked in agriculture or in domestic service (Steinberg, 1981, pp. 206–207). The percentage of African American women in these categories has dropped dramatically, and the majority of African American females are employed in the two highest occupational categories, although typically at the lower levels of these categories. For example, in the top-rated "managerial and professional" category, women are more likely to be concentrated in less-well-paid occupations, such as nurse or elementary school teacher (see Figure 11.1), whereas men are more likely to be physicians and lawyers.

The racial differences in education and jobs are reflected in a persistent racial income gap, as shown in Figure 6.11. The graph presents two kinds of information: the median household incomes for blacks and whites (in 2012 dollars) over the time period (read these from the left vertical axis) and the percentage of black to white household income (read this from the right vertical axis). Figure 6.11 shows that median incomes for black and white households generally moved together over the recorded time period and that both trended upward until the turn of this century. At that point, both lines flattened and then fell, a reflection of hard economic times since 2000 and especially since 2007.

Note also that incomes for black households remained well below those of white households. In the late 1960s, black household income was about 58% of white household income. The gap remained relatively steady through the 1980s, closed during the boom years of the 1990s, and, since the turn of

FIGURE 6.11 Median Household Income by Race, 1967–2012

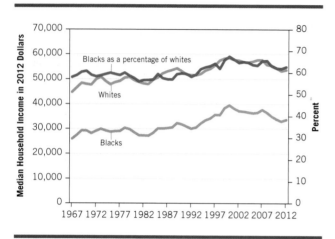

SOURCE: U.S. Census Bureau (2013c, Table H-5).

NOTE: Read income on left-hand axis and percentage on right-hand axis.

this information by comparing the distribution of income within each racial group for 2012, and highlights the differences in the percentage of each group in low-, middle-, and upper-income categories. To read this graph, note that income categories are arrayed from top to bottom and that the horizontal axis has a zero point in the middle of the graph. The percentage of white households in each income category is represented by the bars to the left of the zero point, and the same information is presented for black households by the bars to the right of the zero point.

Starting at the bottom, note that the bars representing black households are considerably wider than those for white households: This reflects the fact that black Americans are more concentrated in the lower income brackets. For example, 14.7% of black households were in the lowest two income categories (less than $10,000), 2.7 times greater than the percentage of white households (5.4%) in this range.

As we move upward, note that there is a noticeable clustering for both black and white households in the $50,000 to $124,000 categories, income ranges that would be associated with an upper-middle-class lifestyle. In this income range, however, it is the white households that are overrepresented: 39% of white households versus only 28% of black households had incomes in this range. The racial differences are even more dramatic in the two highest income ranges: About 11% of white households had incomes greater than $150,000 versus

the century, has widened again. The gap was smallest in 2000 (68%) and, in the most recent year, has grown to 63%, reflecting the differential effects of the recession on minority groups of color, as we discussed previously.

Figure 6.11 depicts the racial income gap in terms of the median, an average that shows the difference between "typical" white and black families. Figure 6.12 supplements

FIGURE 6.12 Distribution of Household Income for White and Black Americans, 2012

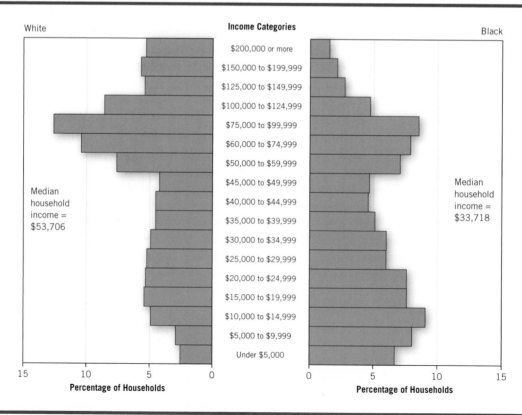

SOURCE: U.S. Census Bureau (2013f).

only 3.6% of black households. While African Americans can be found at all income levels, graphs such as this convincingly refute the notion, common among "modern racists" and many other Americans, that there are no important racial inequalities in the United States today.

Finally, poverty affects African Americans at much higher rates than it does white Americans. Figure 6.13 shows the percentage of white and black American families living below the federally established, "official" poverty level from 1967 through 2012. The poverty rate for African American families runs about 2.5 to 3 times higher than the rate for whites.

Note that there was a dramatic decrease in black poverty during the boom years of the 1990s, only to be followed by an even more sudden return to previous levels after 2000. The poverty rates for both groups have trended upward over the past decade, with a sharp spike in black poverty following the 2007 recession. Tragically, the highest rates of poverty continue to be found among children, especially African American children. Like Figure 6.12, this graph refutes the notion that serious racial inequality is a thing of the past for U.S. society.

PRIMARY STRUCTURAL ASSIMILATION

Interracial contact in the more public areas of society, such as schools or the workplace, is certainly more common today, and as Gordon's model of assimilation predicts, this has led to increases in more intimate contacts across racial lines. To illustrate, one study looked at changing intimate relationships among Americans by asking a nationally representative sample about the people with whom they discuss "important matters." Although the study did not focus on black–white relations per se, the researchers did find that the percentage of whites who included African Americans as intimate contacts increased from 9% to more than 15% between 1984 and 2004 (McPherson,

FIGURE 6.13 Families and Children Living in Poverty in the United States by Race, 1967–2012

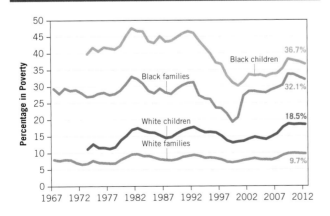

SOURCE: U.S. Census Bureau (2013e).

An integrated school, one of the few in the United States in 1955.

Smith-Lovin, & Brashears, 2006). While this increase would be heartening to those committed to a more integrated, racially unified society, these low percentages could also be seen as discouraging, as they suggest that about 85% of white Americans maintain racially exclusive interpersonal networks of friends and acquaintances.

Another interesting study (Fisher, 2008) looked at interracial friendships on a sample of 27 college campuses across the nation. First-year students were interviewed at the end of their second semester and asked about the group membership of their 10 closest friends on campus. The study found that cross-group friendships were common but that white students had the least diverse circles of friends. For whites, 76% of their friends were also white, a much higher percentage of in-group exclusiveness than Asian students (51%), Hispanic students (56%), and black students (27%).

Obviously, these percentages reflect the racial composition of the campuses (all were majority white), but it is significant that cross-group choices were positively related to more tolerant attitudes and a history of having a friend from another group in high school. Most interesting, perhaps, was that cross-group choices were positively related to greater diversity on campus. This finding supports the contact hypothesis and Gordon's assertion that integration at the secondary level leads to integration at the primary level.

Consistent with the decline in traditional, overt prejudice, Americans are much less opposed to interracial dating and marriage today. One national poll, for example, reports that 83% of a nationally representative sample approve of black–white dating (up from 48% in 1987) and 66% approve of black–white marriage (Wang, 2012, pp. 35–36). Approval of interracial dating and marriage appears to be especially high among younger people: In a 2009 poll, 88% of Americans in the 18 to 29 age range approved of interracial marriage, as opposed to 36% of those aged 65 and older (p. 38).

Behavior appears to be following attitudes, as the rates of interracial dating and marriage are increasing. A number of studies find that interracial dating is increasingly common

TABLE 6.1 Percentage Married to a Person of the Same Race, 1980 and 2008

YEAR	WHITES		BLACKS	
	Men	Women	Men	Women
1980	96%	95%	93%	97%
2008	93%	92%	77%	88%

SOURCE: Qian and Lichter (2011, p. 1072). Copyright © 2011 National Council on Family Relations. Reprinted with permission.

(see Wellner, 2007), and marriages between blacks and whites are also increasing in number, although still a tiny percentage of all marriages. According to the U.S. Census Bureau, there were 65,000 black–white married couples in 1970 (including persons of Hispanic origin), about 0.10% of all married couples. By 2010, the number of black–white married couples had increased by a factor of 8.5, to 558,000, but this is still less than 1% (0.90%) of all married couples (U.S. Census Bureau, 2012c, p. 54).

Finally, a study comparing intermarriage based on the 1980 and 2008 censuses found a slight trend toward decreasing in-marriage, particularly for black men. The results are summarized in Table 6.1. Most black males who married outside their race were married to whites (14.4%) and Hispanics (4.8%). Black women who married outside their group showed a similar pattern: 6.5% were married to whites and 2.3% to Hispanics.

QUESTIONS FOR REFLECTION

1. This section examines a variety of dimensions of acculturation and integration for African Americans. Which is most important? Why?

2. In which of these areas has there been the most progress over the past 50 years? How?

3. What evidence can you cite for the claim that "black–white relations are the best they've ever been"? What evidence can you cite against this claim?

IS THE GLASS HALF EMPTY OR HALF FULL?

The contemporary situation of African Americans is perhaps what might be expected for a group so recently "released" from exclusion and subordination. The average situation of African Americans improved vastly during the latter half of the 20th century in virtually every area of social life. As demonstrated by the data presented in this chapter, however, racial progress has stopped well short of equality.

In assessing the present situation, one might stress the improved situation of the group (the glass is half full) or the challenges that remain before full racial equality and justice are achieved (the glass is half empty). While African Americans can now be found at the highest level of the society (including the Oval Office and the Supreme Court), a large percentage of the African American population have merely traded rural peasantry for urban poverty and face an array of formidable and deep-rooted problems.

The situation of African Americans is intimately intermixed with the plight of our cities and the changing nature of the labor force. It is the consequence of nearly 400 years of prejudice, racism, and discrimination, but it also reflects broader social forces, such as urbanization and industrialization. Consistent with their origin as a colonized minority group, the relative poverty and powerlessness of African Americans has persisted long after other groups (e.g., the descendants of the European immigrants who arrived between the 1820s and the 1920s) have achieved equality and acceptance. African Americans were enslaved to meet the labor demands of an agrarian economy, became rural peasants under Jim Crow segregation, were excluded from the opportunities created by early industrialization, and remain largely excluded from the better jobs in the emerging postindustrial economy.

Progress toward racial equality has slowed since the heady days of the 1960s, and in many areas, earlier advances seem hopelessly stagnated. Public opinion polls indicate that there is little support or sympathy for the cause of African Americans (see Chapter 3). Traditional prejudice has declined only to be replaced by modern racism. In the court of public opinion, African Americans are often held responsible for their own plight. Biological racism has been replaced with indifference to racial issues or with blaming the victims.

Of course, we should not downplay the real improvements that have been made in the lives of African Americans. Compared with their forebears in the days of Jim Crow, African Americans today on the average are more prosperous and more politically powerful, and some are among the most revered of current popular heroes (the glass is half full). However, the increases in average income and education and the glittering success of the few obscure a tangle of problems for the many, problems that may well grow worse as America moves further into the postindustrial era. Poverty, unemployment, a failing educational system, residential segregation, subtle racism, and persisting discrimination continue to be inescapable realities for millions of African Americans. In many African American neighborhoods, crime, drugs, violence, poor health care, malnutrition, and a host of other factors compound these problems (the glass is half empty).

Given this gloomy situation, it should not be surprising to find in the African American community significant strength in pluralistic, nationalistic thinking, as well as some resentment and anger. Black Nationalism and Black Power remain powerful ideas, but their goals of development and autonomy for the African American community remain largely rhetorical sloganeering without the resources to bring them to actualization.

The situation of the African American community in the early 21st century might be characterized as a combination of partial assimilation, structural pluralism, and inequality—a depiction that reflects the continuing effects, in the present, of a colonized origin. The problems that remain are less visible (or perhaps just better hidden from the average white middle-class American) than those of previous eras. Responsibility is more diffused, and the moral certainties of opposition to slavery or to Jim Crow laws are long gone. Contemporary racial issues must be articulated and debated in an environment of subtle prejudice and low levels of sympathy for the grievances of African Americans. Urban poverty, modern institutional discrimination, and modern racism are less dramatic and more difficult to measure than an overseer's whip, a lynch mob, or a sign that reads "Whites Only," but they can be just as real and just as deadly in their consequences.

SUMMARY

This summary is organized around the Learning Objectives listed at the beginning of this chapter.

 6.1 Cite and explain the forces that led to the end of de jure segregation, including organizations, leaders, and legal changes.

The system of de jure segregation ended because of changing economic, social, legal, and political conditions. Continuing industrialization in the South lessened the need for a large, powerless labor force, but southern resistance to racial change was intense. Crucial events included the threat of a march on Washington during World War II (led by A. Philip Randolph), the *Brown v. Board of Education of Topeka* Supreme Court decision, the Montgomery bus boycott, and the triumphs of the civil rights movement, led by Martin Luther King Jr. and many others. The legal basis for the Jim Crow system ended with the passage of two landmark bills by the U.S. Congress: the Civil Rights Act of 1964 and the Voting Rights Act of 1965.

 6.2 Compare and contrast the civil rights movement with the Black Power movement.

The civil rights movement was primarily a southern phenomenon designed to combat legalized, state-sponsored racial segregation. Outside the South, problems were different and the strategies that had worked in the South had less relevance. Other movements, organizations, and leaders—including the Black Muslims and Malcolm X—arose to articulate these issues and channel the anger of the urban, northern black population. The civil rights movement was primarily assimilationist, but the Black Power movement had strong elements of pluralism and even separatism. Both movements relied heavily on the energy and courage of black women but tended to be male dominated.

 6.3 Cite and explain the most important issues and trends that have animated black–white relations since the 1960s, including

a. the relationship between the criminal justice system and the black community,

b. class inequality within the black community,

c. modern institutional discrimination,

d. the family institution,

e. new racial identities, and

f. prejudice and discrimination.

Black–white relations since the 1960s have been characterized by continuing inequality, separation, and hostility, along with substantial improvements in status for some African Americans.

- Relations with the criminal justice system continue to be problematic, and the black community has been victimized by the "war on drugs" on several levels.

- The African American middle class has less financial security than the white middle class, and urban poverty continues as a major problem. Class differentiation within the African American community is greater than ever before.

- The African American family has been perceived as weak, unstable, and a cause of continuing poverty. Culture of poverty theory attributes poverty to certain characteristics of the poor. An alternative view sees problems such as high rates of family desertion by men as the result of poverty, rather than the cause.

- Antiblack prejudice and discrimination are manifested in more subtle, covert forms (modern racism and institutional discrimination) in contemporary society.

6.4 Describe the situation of African Americans using the concepts of assimilation and pluralism, especially in terms of

a. acculturation,

b. secondary structural assimilation, and

c. primary structural assimilation.

- African Americans are largely acculturated, but centuries of separate development have created a unique black experience in American society.

- There have been real improvements for many African Americans, but the overall secondary structural assimilation remains low for a large percentage of the group. Evidence of continuing racial inequality in residence, schooling, politics, jobs, income, unemployment, and poverty is massive and underlines the realities of the urban underclass.

- In the area of primary structural assimilation, interracial interaction and friendships appear to be rising. Interracial marriages are increasing, although they remain a tiny percentage of all marriages.

6.5 Assess the overall situation of African Americans today based on the concepts and information presented in this chapter. Is the glass half empty of half full?

Compared with their situation at the start of the 20th century, African Americans have made significant improvements, but the distance to true racial equality remains considerable. What evidence of improvements in race relations is presented in this chapter? What evidence is provided for the argument that substantial problems remain? Which body of evidence is more persuasive? Why?

KEY TERMS

Black Power movement 159
civil rights movement 155

culture of poverty theory 170
de facto segregation 158

dissimilarity index 173
fatalism 170

nonviolent direct action 156
urban underclass 168

REVIEW QUESTIONS

1. What forces led to the end of de jure segregation? To what extent was this change a result of broad social forces (e.g., industrialization), and to what extent was it the result of the actions of African Americans acting against the system (e.g., the southern civil rights movement)? By the 1960s and 1970s, how had the movement for racial change succeeded, and what issues were left unresolved? What issues remain unresolved today?

2. Describe the differences between the southern civil rights movement and the Black Power movement. Why did these differences exist? How are the differences related to the nature of de jure versus de facto segregation? Do these movements remain relevant today? How?

3. How does gender affect contemporary black–white relations and the African American protest movement? Is it true that African American women are a "minority group within a minority group"? How?

4. According to an old folk saying, "When America catches a cold, African Americans get pneumonia." Evaluate this idea using the information, data, and analysis presented in this chapter. Is it true? Exaggerated? Untrue? What other kinds of information would be needed for a fuller assessment of the quote? How could you get this information?

5. What are the implications of increasing class differentials among African Americans? Does the greater affluence of middle-class blacks mean they are no longer a part of a minority group? Will future protests by African Americans be confined only to working-class and lower-class blacks?

6. Regarding contemporary black–white relations, is the glass half empty or half full? Considering the totality of evidence presented in this chapter, which of the following statements would you agree with? Why? (1) American race relations are the best they've ever been; racial equality has been essentially achieved (even though some problems remain). (2) American race relations have a long way to go before society achieves true racial equality.

STUDENT STUDY SITE

Sharpen your skills with SAGE edge at edge.sagepub.com/healey7e

SAGE edge for students provides a personalized approach to help you accomplish your coursework goals in an easy-to-use learning environment.

The following resources are available at SAGE edge:

Current Debates: Should the United States Be Color-Blind?

To be "color-blind" is to treat everyone the same, ignoring gender, race, and ethnicity. Would color blindness increase fairness and justice in American society? Or would it perpetuate the advantage of the dominant group?

On our website you will find an overview of the topic, the clashing points of view, and some questions to consider as you analyze the material.

Public Sociology Assignments

Public Sociology Assignments provide opportunities for students to address directly and personally some of the issues raised in this text.

There are two assignments for Part III on our website. The first looks at patterns of self-segregation in school cafeterias, and in the second, students analyze the portrayal of the American family on television in terms of race, ethnicity, sexual orientation, and other sociologically relevant characteristics.

Contributed by Linda M. Waldron

Internet Research Project

For this Internet Research Project, you will use data gathered by the U.S. Census Bureau to assess the situation of African Americans relative to the population in general and to one of the white ethnic groups you investigated in the Chapter 2 Internet Research Project. The project will be guided by a series of questions related to course concepts, and your instructor may ask you to discuss your findings in small groups.

For Further Reading

Please see our website for an annotated list of important works related to this chapter.

CHAPTER-OPENING TIMELINE PHOTO CREDITS

1947: The National Archives
1954: Library of Congress Prints and Photographs Division
1955: Library of Congress Prints and Photographs Division
1960: Library of Congress Prints and Photographs Division
1963: Library of Congress Prints and Photographs Division

1965: Library of Congress Prints and Photographs Division
1967: Library of Congress Prints and Photographs Division
1995: Wikimedia Commons
2009: Wikimedia Commons

NATIVE AMERICANS

7

Newscom

1838
Approximately 17,000 Cherokee are forcibly removed from North Carolina, Tennessee, Georgia, and Alabama to the Indian Territory, present-day Oklahoma, along the 1,200-mile "Trail of Tears." Some 4,000 to 8,000 Cherokee die during the removal process.

1876
Sitting Bull and Crazy Horse (Lakota) defeat George Custer at the Battle of the Little Bighorn.

timeline

1830	1845	1860	1875	1890	1905	1920

1830
The Indian Removal Act leads to the deportation of 100,000 Native Americans to west of the Mississippi.

1851
The Indian Appropriations Act of 1851 allocates funds to move tribes onto reservations.

LOC

1862
The Homestead Act essentially allows Americans to settle on Indian land.

1871
The Indian Appropriations Act of 1871 dissolves the status of tribes as sovereign nations.

1886
Apache leader Geronimo surrenders to U.S. troops

LOC

1887
The Dawes Act allows government to divide Indian land into individually owned parcels in an attempt to establish private ownership of Indian lands.

INDIAN LAND FOR SALE

GET A HOME
of
YOUR OWN

PERFECT TITLE
of
POSSESSION
WITHIN
THIRTY DAYS

EASY PAYMENTS

FINE LANDS IN THE WEST
IRRIGATED   GRAZING   AGRICULTURAL
IRRIGABLE   DRY FARMING

Wikimedia Commons

1890
About 300 Sioux are killed at Wounded Knee in last battle between U.S. troops and Native Americans.

LOC

Lorinda announced that the [Blessing Way ceremony for Lynette's unborn child] was about to start . . . [so we] walked into the hoghan. *A single light bulb lit the room dimly. Couches, futon mattresses, and large pillows were set against the walls for the night's sing. A coffee-maker, microwave, and crock-pot sat on a folding table against the northern wall for the midnight eating. This was the same Navajo adaptation I'd grown up seeing, the age-old ritual with modern technology.*

The hataałii *sat against the western wall. . . . He wore thick silver bracelets and a silk bandana across his brow, the knot tied off at his right temple in traditional style. A basket of* tádídíín *(sacred corn pollen) sat at his left.*

[There were] gifts: . . . a stethoscope, that the baby would have good health and might be a healer; . . . a pair of running shoes, that the child would be a strong runner; dollar bills . . . to wish the child a wealthy life; cowboy boots and work gloves so that the child would be a hard worker. . . .

The hataałii *spoke in quiet Navajo as he passed the basket of* tádídíín *to Dennis,*

LEARNING OBJECTIVES

By the end of this chapter, you will be able to do the following:

7.1 Summarize the changing population characteristics of American Indians and Alaska Natives, and some of their common cultural characteristics.

7.2 Summarize and explain the changing relationships between American Indians and the federal government, especially the changes in laws and policies and their effects, and the dynamics of Indian resistance and protest.

7.3 Cite and explain the most important issues and trends that have animated relations between American Indians and the larger society in recent decades, including

   a. struggles over natural resources,

   b. attempts to attract industry to reservations,

   c. broken treaties,

   d. gaming, and

   e. prejudice and discrimination.

7.4 Analyze the contemporary relations between American Indians and whites using the concepts of prejudice and discrimination, and assimilation and pluralism, especially in terms of

   a. acculturation,

   b. secondary structural assimilation, and

   c. primary structural assimilation.

7.5 Assess the overall situation of American Indians today based on the concepts and information presented in this chapter.

Wikipedia

1924
Federal law grants all Native Americans citizenship.

1934
The Indian Reorganization Act decreases federal control of Indian affairs and re-establishes self-governance for many tribes.

1968
The American Indian Movement, an advocacy group, is founded.

1972
The American Indian Movement sponsors the Trail of Broken Treaties, a cross-country protest presenting a 20-point list of demands from the federal government.

1978
The American Indian Movement leads the Longest Walk, a spiritual walk across the country for tribal sovereignty and to protest anti-Indian legislation.

1988
Federal legislation legalizes reservation gambling.

2005
The National Collegiate Athletic Association bans use of "hostile and abusive" American Indian mascots in postseason tournaments.

2012
Revenue from gaming on reservations reaches almost $28 billion.

LOC

LOC

who sprinkled the yellow pollen at each corner of the hoghan, *first East, South, West, then North. Then he passed the basket around the room in a clockwise order; when it came to me, I did what the others had done: I placed a pinch inside my lower lip, pressed a second pinch to my forehead, then spread the pollen in the air above in a small arch to resemble the rainbow that promises life and beauty.*

The hataałii *began the sing. Brandon and the two burly men entered the chant with accenting rhythms as articulate as wind chimes, but with the resonance of distant thunder. . . .*

Lorinda leaned forward and rocked slowly, speaking her own prayer: I heard the word hózhó *sung many times. There is no English equivalent, but mostly it means "beautiful harmony." Christians might call it grace.*

—Jim Kristofic (2011, pp. 183–184)

At the end of first grade, Jim Kristofic found himself moving from western Pennsylvania to the Navajo reservation in Arizona, where his mother had taken a job as a nurse. At first rejected and bullied by the Navajo kids, he eventually developed a deep respect for and understanding of the "Rez," the people, and the Navajo way of life. In this passage, he gives us a glimpse of a Navajo ceremony that has been practiced for centuries. Can ancient traditions such as this—and the tribes that practice them—survive? •

We discussed the contact period for American Indians in Chapter 4. As you recall, this period began in the earliest colonial days and lasted nearly 300 years, ending only with the final battles of the Indian Wars in the late 1800s. The Indian nations fought for their land and to preserve their cultures and ways of life. The tribes had enough power to win many battles, but they eventually lost all the wars. The superior resources of the burgeoning white society made the eventual defeat of American Indians inevitable, and by 1890, the last of the tribes had been conquered, their leaders had been killed or were in custody, and their people were living on government-controlled reservations.

By the start of the 20th century, American Indians were, in Blauner's (1972) terms, a conquered and colonized minority group. Like the slave plantations, the reservations were paternalistic systems that controlled American Indians with federally mandated regulations and government-appointed Indian agents.

For most of the past 100 years, as Jim Crow segregation, Supreme Court decisions, industrialization, and urbanization shaped the status of other minority groups, American Indians subsisted on the fringes of development and change—marginalized, relatively powerless, and isolated. Their links to the larger society were weaker, and, compared with African Americans,

A depiction of Custer's Last Stand, 1876. Native Americans won many battles against U.S. forces but eventually lost all of the wars.

white ethnic groups, and other minorities, they were less affected by the forces of social and political evolution. While other minority groups maintained a regular presence in the national headlines, Native Americans have been generally ignored and unnoticed, except perhaps as mascots for sports teams, including the Washington Redskins, Atlanta Braves, and Cleveland Indians.

The last decades of the 20th century witnessed some improvement in the status of American Indians in general, and some tribes, especially those with casinos and other gaming establishments, made notable progress toward parity with national standards. Also, the tribes are now more in control of their own affairs, and many have effectively used their increased autonomy and independence to address problems in education, health, joblessness, and other areas.

Despite the progress, however, large gaps remain between Native Americans and national norms in virtually every area of social and economic life. American Indians living on reservations are among the poorest groups in U.S. society.

In this chapter, we will bring the history of American Indians up to the present and explore both recent progress and persisting problems. Some of the questions we will address include, What accounts for the lowly position of this group for much of the past 100 years? How can we explain the improvements in the most recent decades? Now, early in the 21st century, what problems remain, and how does the situation of American Indians compare with that of other colonized and conquered minority groups? What are the most promising strategies for closing the remaining gaps between Native Americans and the larger society?

SIZE OF THE GROUP

How many Native Americans are there? This question has several different answers, partly because of the way census information is collected and partly because of the social and subjective nature of race and group membership. The most current answer comes from the 2010 U.S. Census.

The task of determining the size of the group is also complicated by the way the census collects information on race. As you recall, beginning with the 2000 Census, people were allowed to claim membership in more than one racial category. If we define American Indians as consisting of people who identify themselves *only* as American Indian (listed under "Alone" in Table 7.1), we will get one estimate of the size of the group. If we use a broader definition and include people who claim mixed racial ancestry (listed under "Alone or in Combination" in Table 7.1), our estimate of group size will be much larger.

TABLE 7.1 American Indians and Alaska Natives, 2010

	ALONE	ALONE OR IN COMBINATION (TWO OR MORE GROUPS)
All American Indians and Alaska Natives	2,932,248	5,220,579
American Indians	2,164,193	3,631,571
Alaska Natives	122,990	168,786
TEN LARGEST TRIBAL GROUPINGS FOR AMERICAN INDIANS		
	One Tribe Reported	**Two or More Tribes**
Cherokee	284,247	819,858
Navajo	286,731	332,129
Choctaw	103,910	195,764
Chippewa	112,757	170,742
Sioux	112,176	170,110
Apache	63,193	118,810
Blackfeet	27,279	105,304
Creek	52,948	88,332
Iroquois	42,461	81,002
Lumbee	62,957	73,691
FIVE LARGEST TRIBAL GROUPINGS FOR ALASKA NATIVES		
Yup'ik	28,927	33,889
Inupiat	24,859	33,360
Tlingit-Haida	15,256	26,080
Alaskan Athabascan	15,623	22,484
Aleut	11,920	19,282

SOURCE: Norris, Vines, and Hoeffel (2012, p. 17).

FIGURE 7.1 American Indian and Alaska Native Population, 1900–2010

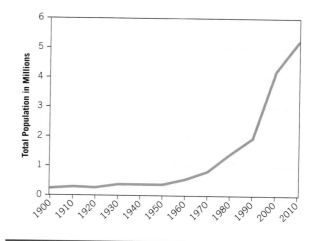

SOURCE: 1900 to 1990—Thornton (2001, p. 142); 2000 and 2010—U.S. Census Bureau (2007, p. 14; 2010) and Norris et al. (2012).

At any rate, Table 7.1 shows that more than five million people claim at least some Native American or Alaska Native ancestry, but the number is only about half that if we confine the group to people who selected one race only. By either count, the group is a tiny minority (about 1%) of the total population of the United States. Table 7.1 also presents information for American Indians and Alaska Natives separately, for the ten largest tribal groupings of American Indians and for the five largest tribal groupings of Alaska Natives.

The American Indian population has grown rapidly over the past several decades, but this fact needs to be seen in the full context of history. As we mentioned in Chapter 4, in 1492, there were anywhere from several million to more than 10 million Native Americans living in what is now the continental ("Lower 48") United States (Mann, 2011, 105–109). Losses suffered during the contact period reduced the population to fewer than 250,000 by 1900, a loss of at least 75% but probably much more.

Recent population growth has been quite rapid, especially in recent decades (see Figure 7.1). This more recent growth is largely the result of changing definitions of race in the larger society and people's much greater willingness to claim Indian ancestry, a pattern that again underscores the basically social nature of race.

AMERICAN INDIAN CULTURES

The dynamics of American Indian and Anglo-American relationships have been shaped by the vast differences in culture, values, and norms between the two groups. These differences have hampered communication in the past and continue to do so in the present. A comprehensive analysis of American Indian cultures is well beyond the scope of this text, but the past experiences and present goals of the group can be appreciated only with some understanding of their views of the world.

We must note here, as we did in Chapter 4, that there were (and are) hundreds of different tribes—each with its own language and heritage—in what is now the United States, and a complete analysis of American Indian culture would have to take this diversity into account. However, some patterns and cultural characteristics are widely shared across the tribes, and we will concentrate on these similarities.

Before exploring the content of their culture, we should note that most Native American tribes that existed in what is now the United States relied on hunting and gathering to satisfy their basic needs, although some cultivated gardens as well. This is important because, as noted by Gerhard Lenski (see Chapter 1), societies are profoundly shaped by their subsistence technology.

Hunting-and-gathering societies often survive on the thin edge of hunger and want. They endure because they stress cultural values such as sharing and cooperation, and maintain strong bonds of cohesion and solidarity. As you will see, American Indian societies are no exception to this fundamental survival strategy.

The relatively lower level of development of Native Americans is reflected in what is perhaps their most obvious difference from people in Western cultures: their ideas about the relationship between human beings and the natural world. In the traditional view of many American Indian cultures, the universe is a unity. Humans are simply a part of a larger reality, no different from or more important than other animals, plants, trees, and the earth itself. The goal of many American Indian tribes was to live in harmony with the natural world, not "improve" it or use it for their own selfish purposes—views that differ sharply from Western concepts of development, commercial farming, and bending the natural world to the service of humans. The gap between the two worldviews is evident in the reaction of one American Indian to the idea that his people should become farmers: "You ask me to plow the ground. . . . Shall I take a knife and tear my mother's bosom? You ask me to cut grass and make hay . . . but how dare I cut my mother's hair?" (Brown, 1970, p. 273).

The concept of private property, or the ownership of things, was not prominent in American Indian cultures and was, from the Anglo-American perspective, most notably absent in conceptions of land ownership. The land simply existed, and the notion of owning, selling, or buying it was foreign to American Indians. In the words of Tecumseh, a chief of the Shawnee, a man could no more sell the land than the "sea or the air he breathed" (Josephy, 1968, p. 283).

As is typical at the hunting-and-gathering level of development, American Indian cultures and societies also tended to be more oriented toward groups (e.g., the extended family, clan, or tribe) than toward individuals. The interests of the self were subordinated to those of the group, and child-rearing practices strongly encouraged group loyalty (Parke & Buriel, 2002). Cooperative, group activities were stressed over those of a competitive, individualistic nature. The bond to the group was so strong that "students [would] go hungry rather than ask their parents for lunch money, for in asking they would be putting their needs in front of the group's needs" (Locust, 1990, p. 231).

Many American Indian tribes were organized around egalitarian values that stressed the dignity and worth of every man, woman, and child. Virtually all tribes had a division of labor based on gender, but women's work was valued, and women often occupied far more important positions in tribal society than was typical for women in Anglo-American society. In many of the American Indian societies that practiced gardening, women controlled the land. In other tribes, women wielded considerable power and held the most important political and religious offices. Among the Iroquois, for example, a council of older women appointed the chief of the tribe and made decisions about when to wage war (Amott & Matthaei, 1991, pp. 34–35).

These differences in values, compounded by the power differentials that emerged, often placed American Indians at a disadvantage when dealing with the dominant group. The American Indians' conception of land ownership and their lack of experience with deeds, titles, contracts, and other Western legal concepts often made it difficult for them to defend their resources from Anglo-Americans. At other times, cultural differences led to disruptions of traditional practices, further weakening American Indian societies. For example, Christian missionaries and government representatives tried to reverse the traditional American Indian division of labor, in which women were responsible for the gardening. In the Western view, only males did farm work. Also, the military and political representatives of the dominant society usually ignored female tribal leaders and imposed Western notions of patriarchy and male leadership on the tribes (Amott & Matthaei, 1991, p. 39).

QUESTIONS FOR REFLECTION

1. Why are there different estimates for the size of the American Indian and Alaska Native population? How do these differences support the idea that race is a social construction?

2. What are the key characteristics of Native American cultures? How do these vary from Anglo culture? How did these differences shape Anglo–Indian relations?

FIGURE 7.2 American Indian Reservations in the United States

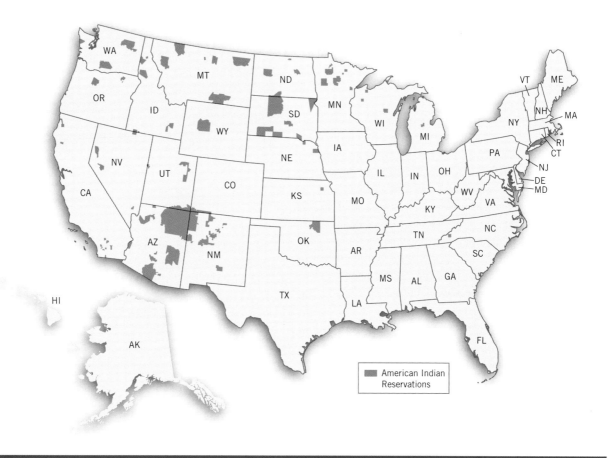

SOURCE: U.S. Parks Service.

RELATIONS WITH THE FEDERAL GOVERNMENT AFTER THE 1890S

By the end of the Indian Wars in 1890, American Indians had few resources with which to defend their self-interests. In addition to being confined to the reservations, the group was scattered throughout the western two thirds of the United States and split by cultural and linguistic differences. Politically, the power of the group was further limited by the fact that the huge majority of American Indians were not U.S. citizens and most tribes lacked a cultural basis for understanding representative democracy as practiced in the larger society.

Economically, American Indians were among the most impoverished groups in society. Reservation lands were generally of poor quality, traditional food sources such as buffalo and other game had been destroyed, and traditional hunting grounds and gardening plots had been lost to white farmers and ranchers. The tribes had few means of satisfying even their most basic needs. Many became totally dependent on the federal government for food, shelter, clothing, and other necessities.

Prospects for improvement seemed slim. Most reservations were in remote areas, far from sites of industrialization and modernization (see Figure 7.2), and American Indians had few of the skills (knowledge of English, familiarity with Western work habits and routines) that would have enabled them to compete for a place in the increasingly urban and industrial American society of the early 20th century. Off the reservations, racial prejudice and strong intolerance limited them. On the reservations, they were subjected to policies designed either to maintain their powerlessness and poverty or to force them to Americanize. Either way, the future of American Indians was in serious jeopardy, and their destructive relations with white society continued in peace as they had in war.

RESERVATION LIFE

As would be expected for a conquered and still hostile group, the reservations were intended to closely supervise American Indians and maintain their powerlessness. Relationships with the federal government were paternalistic and featured a variety of policies designed to coercively acculturate the tribes.

Paternalism and the Bureau of Indian Affairs. The reservations were run not by the tribes but by an agency of the federal government: the **Bureau of Indian Affairs** (BIA) of the U.S. Department of the Interior. The BIA and its local superintendent controlled virtually all aspects of everyday life, including the reservation budget, the criminal justice system, and the schools. The BIA (again, not the tribes) even determined tribal membership.

The traditional leadership structures and political institutions of the tribes were ignored as the BIA executed its duties with little regard for, and virtually no input from, the people it supervised. The BIA superintendent of the reservations "ordinarily became the most powerful influence on local Indian affairs, even though he was a government employee, not responsible to the Indians but to his superiors in Washington" (Spicer, 1980, p. 117). The superintendent controlled the food supply and communications with the world outside the reservation. This control was used to reward tribal members who cooperated and punish those who did not.

Coercive Acculturation: The Dawes Act and Boarding Schools. Consistent with the Blauner hypothesis, American Indians on the reservations were subjected to coercive acculturation or forced Americanization. Their culture was attacked, their languages and religions forbidden, and their institutions circumvented and undermined. The centerpiece of U.S. Indian policy was the Dawes Allotment Act of 1887, a deeply flawed attempt to impose white definitions of land ownership and transform American Indians into independent farmers by dividing their land among the families of each tribe. The intention of the act was to give each Indian family the means to survive in the manner of their white neighbors.

Although the law might seem benevolent in intent (certainly, thousands of immigrant families would have been thrilled to own land), it was flawed by a gross lack of understanding of American Indian cultures and needs, and in many ways it was a direct attack on those cultures. Most American Indian tribes did not have a strong agrarian tradition, and little or nothing was done to prepare them for their transition to peasant yeomanry. More important, American Indians had little or no concept of land as private property, and it was relatively easy for settlers, land speculators, and others to separate Indian families from the land allocated to them by this legislation. By allotting land to families and individuals, the legislation sought to destroy the broader kinship, clan, and tribal social structures and replace them with Western systems that featured individualism and the profit motive (Cornell, 1988, p. 80).

About 140 million acres were allocated to the tribes in 1887. By the 1930s, nearly 90 million of those acres—almost

American Indian pupils at Carlisle Indian Industrial school in Pennsylvania, 1900. Schools were one of the institutions through which American Indians were forcibly acculturated.

65%—had been lost. Most of the remaining land was desert or otherwise nonproductive (Wax, 1971, p. 55). From the standpoint of the Indian nations, the Dawes Allotment Act was a disaster and a further erosion of their already paltry store of resources (for more details, see Josephy, 1968; Lurie, 1982; McNickle, 1973; Wax, 1971).

Coercive acculturation also operated through a variety of other avenues. Whenever possible, the BIA sent American Indian children to boarding schools, sometimes hundreds of miles away from parents and kin, where they were required to speak English, convert to Christianity, and become educated in the ways of Western civilization. Consistent with the Blauner (1972) hypothesis, tribal languages, dress, and religion were forbidden, and to the extent that native cultures were mentioned at all, they were attacked and ridiculed. Children of different tribes were mixed together as roommates to speed the acquisition of English. When school was not in session, children were often boarded with local white families, usually as unpaid domestic helpers or farmhands, and prevented from visiting their families and revitalizing their tribal ties (Hoxie, 1984; Spicer, 1980; Wax, 1971).

American Indians were virtually powerless to change the reservation system or avoid the campaign of acculturation. Nonetheless, they resented and resisted coerced Americanization, and many languages and cultural elements survived the early reservation period, although often in altered form. For example, the traditional tribal religions remained vital throughout the period despite the fact that by the 1930s, the great majority of Indians had affiliated with one Christian faith or another. Furthermore, many new religions were founded, some combining Christian and traditional elements (Spicer, 1980, p. 118). The first Narrative Portrait in this chapter gives an intimate account of the dynamics of coercive acculturation.

The Indian Reorganization Act. By the 1930s, the failure of the reservation system and the policy of forced assimilation had become obvious to all who cared to observe. The quality of life

---

The **Bureau of Indian Affairs** is the federal agency responsible for the administration of Indian reservations.

NARRATIVE PORTRAIT

Civilize Them With a Stick

In recent decades, boarding schools for American Indian children have been much improved. Facilities have been modernized and faculties upgraded. The curriculum has been updated and often includes elements of American Indian culture and language. Still, it was not that long ago that coercive acculturation at its worst was the daily routine.

In the following passage, Mary Crow Dog, a member of the Sioux tribe who became deeply involved in the Red Power movement that began in the 1960s, recalls some of the horrors of her experiences at a reservation boarding school. As you read her words, keep in mind that she was born in 1955 and started school in the early 1960s, just a generation or two ago.

LAKOTA WOMAN

Mary Crow Dog

It is almost impossible to explain...what a typical old Indian boarding school was like; how it affected the Indian child suddenly dumped into it like a small creature from another world, helpless, defenseless, bewildered, trying desperately to survive and sometimes not surviving at all. Even now, when these schools are so much improved, when...the teachers [are] well-intentioned, even trained in child psychology—unfortunately the psychology of white children, which is different from ours—the shock to the child upon arrival is still tremendous....

In the traditional Sioux family, the child is never left alone. It is always surrounded by relatives, carried around, enveloped in warmth. It is treated with the respect due to any human being, even a small one. It is seldom forced to do anything against its will, seldom screamed at, and never beaten....And then suddenly a bus or car arrives full of strangers, who yank the child out of the arms of those who love it, taking it screaming to the boarding school. The only word I can think of for what is done to these children is kidnapping....

The mission school at St. Francis was a curse for our family for generations. My grandmother went there, then my mother, then my sisters and I. At one time or another, every one of us tried to run away. Grandma told me about the bad times she experienced at St. Francis. In those days they let students go home only for one week every year. Two days were used up for transportation, which meant spending just 5 days out of every 365 with her family....My mother had much the same experiences but never wanted to talk about them, and then there was I, in the same place....Nothing had changed since my grandmother's days. I have been told that even in the '70s they were still beating children at that school. All I got

out of school was being taught how to pray. I learned quickly that I would be beaten if I failed in my devotions or, God forbid, prayed the wrong way, especially prayed in Indian to Wakan Tanka, the Indian creator....

My classroom was right next to the principal's office and almost every day I could hear him swatting the boys. Beating was the common punishment for not doing one's homework, or for being late to school. It had such a bad effect upon me that I hated and mistrusted every white person on sight, because I met only one kind. It was not until much later that I met sincere white people I could relate to and be friends with. Racism breeds racism in reverse.

SOURCE: *Lakota Woman* (1990, pp. 28–34). Copyright © 1990 by Mary Crow Dog and Richard Erdoes. Used by permission of Grove/Atlantic, Inc.

Questions to Consider

1. How does this passage illustrate the concept of "coercive acculturation"? What other concepts seem applicable? Why?

2. What do you think about Mary Crow Dog's comment that "racism breeds racism in reverse"? Does this idea apply to other situations discussed in this text? How about to situations you have observed or experienced personally?

---

for American Indians had not improved, and there was little economic development and fewer job opportunities on the reservations. Health care was woefully inadequate, and education levels lagged far behind national standards.

The plight of American Indians eventually found a sympathetic ear in the administration of Franklin D. Roosevelt, who was elected president in 1932, and John Collier, the man he appointed to run the BIA. Collier was knowledgeable about American Indian issues and concerns, and was instrumental in securing the passage of the **Indian Reorganization Act** (IRA) in 1934.

This landmark legislation contained a number of significant provisions for American Indians and broke sharply with the federal policies of the past. In particular, the IRA rescinded the Dawes Act of 1887 and the policy of individualizing tribal lands. It also provided means by which the tribes could expand their landholdings. Many of the mechanisms of coercive Americanization in the school system and elsewhere

were dismantled. Financial aid in various forms and expertise were made available for the economic development of the reservations. In perhaps the most significant departure from earlier policy, the IRA proposed an increase in American Indian self-governance and a reduction of the paternalistic role of the BIA and other federal agencies.

Although sympathetic to American Indians, the IRA had its limits and shortcomings. Many of its intentions were never realized, and the empowerment of the tribes was not unqualified. The move to self-governance generally took place on the dominant group's terms and in conformity with the values and practices of white society. For example, the proposed increase in the decision-making power of the tribes

---

The **Indian Reorganization Act**, passed in 1934, was intended to give Indians more autonomy.

was contingent on their adoption of Anglo-American political forms, including secret ballots, majority rule, and written constitutions. These were alien concepts to those tribes that selected leaders by procedures other than popular election (e.g., leaders might be chosen by councils of elders) or that made decisions by open discussion and consensus building (i.e., decisions required the agreement of everyone with a voice in the process, not a simple majority). The incorporation of these Western forms illustrates the basically assimilationist intent of the IRA.

The IRA had variable effects on American Indian women. In tribes that were male dominated, the IRA gave women new rights to participate in elections, run for office, and hold leadership roles. In other cases, new political structures replaced traditional forms, some of which, as in the Iroquois culture, had accorded women considerable power. Although the political effects were variable, the programs funded by the IRA provided opportunities for women on many reservations to receive education and training for the first time. Many of these opportunities were oriented toward domestic tasks and other traditionally Western female roles, but some prepared American Indian women for jobs outside the family and off the reservation, such as clerical work and nursing (Evans, 1989, pp. 208–209).

In summary, the IRA of 1934 was a significant improvement over prior federal Indian policy but was bolder and more sympathetic to American Indians in intent than in execution. On one hand, not all tribes were capable of taking advantage of the opportunities provided by the legislation, and some ended up being further victimized. For example, in the Hopi tribe, located in the Southwest, the act allowed a Westernized group of American Indians to be elected to leadership roles, with the result that dominant group firms were allowed access to the mineral resources, farmland, and water rights controlled by the tribe. The resultant development generated wealth for the white firms and their Hopi allies, but most of the tribe continued to languish in poverty (Churchill, 1985, pp. 112–113). On the other hand, some tribes prospered (at least comparatively speaking) under the IRA. One impoverished, landless group of Cherokee in Oklahoma acquired land, equipment, and expert advice through the IRA, and between 1937 and 1949, they developed a prosperous, largely debt-free farming community (Debo, 1970, pp. 294–300). Many tribes remained suspicious of the IRA, and by 1948, fewer than 100 tribes had voted to accept its provisions.

The Termination Policy. The IRA's stress on the legitimacy of tribal identity seemed "un-American" to many. There was

constant pressure on the federal government to return to an individualistic policy that encouraged (or required) Americanization. Some viewed the tribal structures and communal property-holding patterns as relics of an earlier era and as impediments to modernization and development. Not so incidentally, some elements of dominant society still coveted the remaining Indian lands and resources, which could be more easily exploited if property ownership were individualized.

In 1953, the assimilationist forces won a victory when Congress passed a resolution calling for an end to the reservation system and to the special relationships between the tribes and the federal government. The proposed policy, called **termination**, was intended to get the federal government "out of the Indian business." It rejected the IRA and proposed a return to the system of private land ownership imposed on the tribes by the Dawes Act. Horrified at the notion of termination, the tribes opposed the policy strongly and vociferously. Under this policy, all special relationships—including treaty obligations—between the federal government and the tribes would end. Tribes would no longer exist as legally recognized entities, and tribal lands and other resources would be placed in private hands (Josephy, 1968, pp. 353–355).

About 100 tribes, most of them small, were terminated. In virtually all cases, the termination process was administered hastily, and fraud, misuse of funds, and other injustices were common. The Menominee of Wisconsin and the Klamath on the West Coast were the two largest tribes to be terminated. Both suffered devastating economic losses and precipitous declines in quality of life. Neither tribe had the business or tax base needed to finance the services (e.g., health care and schooling) formerly provided by the federal government, and both were forced to sell land, timber, and other scarce resources to maintain minimal standards of living. Many poor American Indian families were forced to turn to local and state agencies, which placed severe strain on welfare budgets. The experience of the Menominee was so disastrous that at the concerted request of the tribe, reservation status was restored in 1973 (Deloria, 1969, pp. 60–82; McNickle, 1973, pp. 103–110; Raymer, 1974). The Klamath reservation was restored in 1986 (Snipp, 1996, p. 394).

Relocation and Urbanization. At about the same time the termination policy came into being, various programs were established to encourage American Indians to move to urban areas. The movement to the city had already begun in the 1940s, spurred by the availability of factory jobs during World War II. In the 1950s, the movement was further encouraged with assistance programs and by the declining government support for economic development on the reservation, the most dramatic example of which was the policy of termination (Green, 1999, p. 265). Centers for American Indians were established in many cities, and various services (e.g., job training, housing assistance, English instruction) were offered to assist in the adjustment to urban life.

Termination was a federal policy intended to end the reservation system and the special relationships between Indian tribes and the federal government.

FIGURE 7.3 Urbanization of American Indians, 1900–2010

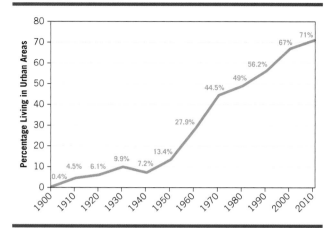

SOURCE: 1900 to 1990—Thornton (2001, p. 142); 2000 and 2010—U.S. Census Bureau (2012d, Table PCT2).

The urbanization of the American Indian population is displayed in Figure 7.3. Note the rapid increase in the movement to the city that began in the 1950s. More than 70% of all American Indians are now urbanized, and since 1950, Indians have urbanized faster than the general population. Nevertheless, American Indians are still the least urbanized minority group. The population as a whole is about 80% urbanized; in contrast, African Americans (see Figure 5.2) are about 90% urbanized.

As with African Americans, American Indians arrived in the cities after the mainstream economy had begun to deemphasize blue-collar or manufacturing jobs. Because of their relatively low average levels of educational attainment and their racial and cultural differences, American Indians in the city tended to encounter the same problems experienced by African Americans and other minority groups of color: high rates of unemployment, inadequate housing, and all the other travails of the urban underclass.

American Indian women also migrated to the city in considerable numbers. The discrimination, unemployment, and poverty of the urban environment often made it difficult for the men of the group to fulfill the role of breadwinner; thus, the burden of supporting the family tended to fall on the women. The difficulties inherent in combining child rearing and a job outside the home are compounded by isolation from the support networks provided by extended family and clan back on the reservations. Nevertheless, one study found that American Indian women in the city continue to practice their traditional cultures and maintain the tribal identity of their children (Joe & Miller, 1994, p. 186).

American Indians living in the city are, on average, better off than those living on reservations, where unemployment can reach 80% or even 90%. The improvement is relative, however. Although many individual Indians prosper in the urban environment, income figures for urban Indians as a whole are comparable to those for African Americans and well below those for whites. American Indian unemployment rates run much higher than the national average. For example, in the first half of 2010, unemployment for all American Indians was about 15%, comparable to the rate for African Americans (see Figure 6.3) and 67% higher than that for whites (Austin, 2010). Thus, a move to the city often means trading rural poverty for the urban variety, with little net improvement in life chances.

American Indians will probably remain more rural than other minority groups for years to come. Despite the poverty and lack of opportunities for schooling and jobs, the reservation offers some advantages in services and lifestyle. On the reservation, there may be opportunities for political participation and leadership roles that are not available in the cities, where American Indians are a tiny minority. Reservations also offer kinfolk, friends, religious services, and tribal celebrations (Snipp, 1989, p. 84). Lower levels of education, work experience, and financial resources combine with the prejudice, discrimination, and racism of the larger society to lower the chances of success in the city, and will probably sustain a continuing return to the reservations.

Although the economic benefits of urbanization have been slim for the group as whole, other advantages have accrued from life in the city. It was much easier to establish networks of friendship and affiliation across tribal lines in the cities, and urban Indians have been one of the sources of strength and personnel for a movement of protest that began early in the 20th century. Virtually all the organizational vehicles of American Indian protest have had urban roots.

Self-Determination. The termination policy aroused so much opposition from American Indians and was such an obvious disaster that the pressure to push tribes to termination faded in the late 1950s, although the act itself was not repealed until 1975. Since the 1960s, federal Indian policy has generally returned to the tradition set by the IRA. Termination and forced assimilation continue to be officially rejected, and within limits, the tribes have been granted more freedom to find their own way, at their own pace, of relating to the larger society.

Several federal programs and laws have benefited the tribes during the past few decades, including the antipoverty and "Great Society" campaigns launched in the 1960s. In 1970, President Richard Nixon affirmed the government's commitment to fulfilling treaty obligations and the right of the tribes to self-governance. The Indian Self-Determination and Education Assistance Act was passed in 1975. This legislation increased aid to reservation schools and American Indian students, and increased tribal control over the administration of the reservations, from police forces to schools to road maintenance.

The Self-Determination Act primarily benefited the larger tribes and those that had well-established administrative and governing structures. Smaller and less well-organized tribes have continued to rely heavily on the federal government (Snipp, 1996, p. 394). Nonetheless, in many cases, this new phase of federal policy has allowed American Indian tribes to plot their own courses free of paternalistic regulation, and just as important, it gave them the tools and resources to address their problems and improve their situations. Decision making was returned to local authorities, who were "held more accountable to local needs, conditions, and cultures than outsiders" (Taylor & Kalt, 2005, p. xi).

In the view of many, self-determination is a key reason for the recent improvements in the status of American Indians, and we will look at some of these developments after examining the American Indian protest movement.

PROTEST AND RESISTANCE

EARLY EFFORTS

As BIA-administered reservations and coercive Americanization came to dominate tribal life in the early 20th century, new forms of Indian activism appeared. The modern protest movement was tiny at first and, with few exceptions, achieved a measure of success only in recent decades. In fact, the American Indian protest movement in the past was not so much unsuccessful as simply ignored. The movement has focused on several complementary goals: protecting American Indian resources and treaty rights, striking a balance between assimilation and pluralism, and finding a relationship with the dominant group that would permit a broader array of life chances without sacrificing tribal identity and heritage.

Formally organized American Indian protest organizations have existed since the 1910s, but the modern phase of the protest movement began during World War II. Many American Indians served in the military or moved to the city to take jobs in aid of the war effort and were thereby exposed to the world beyond the reservation. Also, political activism on the reservation, which had been stimulated by the IRA, continued through the war years, and the recognition that many problems were shared across tribal lines grew.

These trends helped stimulate the founding of the National Congress of American Indians (NCAI) in 1944. This organization was pantribal (i.e., included members from many different tribes); its first convention was attended by representatives of 50 different tribes and reservations (Cornell, 1988, p. 119). The leadership consisted largely of American Indians educated and experienced in the white world. However, the NCAI's program stressed the importance of preserving the old ways and tribal institutions as well as protecting Indian welfare. An early victory for the NCAI and its allies came in 1946 when an Indian Claims Commission was created by the federal government. This body was authorized to hear claims brought by the tribes with regard to treaty violations. The commission has settled hundreds of claims, resulting in awards of millions of dollars to the tribes, and it continues its work today (Weeks, 1988, pp. 261–262).

In the 1950s and 1960s, the protest movement was further stimulated by the threat of termination and by the increasing number of American Indians living in the cities who developed friendships across tribal lines. Awareness of common problems, rising levels of education, and the examples set by the successful protests of other minority groups also increased readiness for collective action.

RED POWER

By the 1960s and 1970s, American Indian protest groups were finding ways to express their grievances and problems to the nation. The Red Power movement, like the Black Power movement (see Chapter 6), encompassed a coalition of groups, many considerably more assertive than the NCAI, and a varied collection of ideas, most of which stressed self-determination and pride in race and cultural heritage. Red Power protests included a "fish-in" in Washington State in 1965, an episode that also illustrates the nature of American Indian demands. The state of Washington had tried to limit the fishing rights of several different tribes on the grounds that the supply of fish was diminishing and needed to be protected. The tribes depended on fishing for subsistence and survival, and they argued that their right to fish had been guaranteed by treaties signed in the 1850s and it was the pollution and commercial fishing of the dominant society that had depleted the supply of fish. They organized a "fish-in" in violation of the state's policy and were met by a contingent of police officers and other law officials. Violent confrontations and mass arrests ensued. Three years later, after a lengthy and expensive court battle, the tribes were vindicated, and the U.S. Supreme Court confirmed their treaty rights to fish the rivers of Washington State (Nabakov, 1999, pp. 362–363).

Another widely publicized episode took place in 1969, when American Indians from various tribes occupied Alcatraz Island in San Francisco Bay, the site of a closed federal prison. The protesters were acting on an old law that granted American Indians the right to reclaim abandoned federal land. The occupation of Alcatraz was organized in part by the American Indian Movement (AIM), founded in 1968. More militant and radical than the previously established protest groups, AIM aggressively confronted the BIA, the police, and other forces that were seen as repressive. With the backing of AIM and other groups, Alcatraz was occupied for nearly four years and generated a great deal of publicity for the Red Power movement and the plight of American Indians.

The Indian occupation of Alcatraz Island in 1969.

In 1972, AIM helped organize a march on Washington, D.C., called the "Trail of Broken Treaties." Marchers came from many tribes and represented both urban and reservation Indians. The intent of the marchers was to dramatize the problems of the tribes. The leaders demanded the abolition of the BIA, the return of illegally taken land, and increased self-governance for the tribes, among other things. When they reached Washington, some of the marchers forcibly occupied the BIA offices. Property was damaged (by which side is disputed), and records and papers were destroyed. The marchers eventually surrendered, but none of their demands were met. The following year, AIM occupied the village of Wounded Knee in South Dakota to protest the violation of treaty rights. Wounded Knee was the site of the last armed confrontation between Indians and whites in 1890 and was selected by AIM for its deep symbolic significance. The occupation lasted more than two months and involved several armed confrontations with federal authorities. Again, the protest ended without achieving any of the demands made by the Indian leadership (Olson & Wilson, 1984, pp. 172–175). Since the early 1970s, the level of protest activity has declined, just as it has for the African American protest movement. Lawsuits and court cases have predominated over dramatic, direct confrontations.

Ironically, the struggle for Red Power encouraged assimilation as well as pluralism. The movement linked members of different tribes and forced Indians of diverse heritages to find common ground, often in the form of a "generic" American Indian culture. Inevitably, the protests were conducted in English, and the grievances were expressed in ways that were understandable to white society, thus increasing the pressure to acculturate even while arguing for the survival of the tribes. Furthermore, successful protest required that American Indians be fluent in English, trained in the law and other professions, skilled in dealing with bureaucracies, and knowledgeable about the formulation and execution of public policy. American Indians who became proficient in these areas thereby took on the characteristics of their adversaries (Hraba, 1994).

As the pantribal protest movement forged ties between members of diverse tribes, the successes of the movement and changing federal policy and public opinion encouraged a rebirth of commitment to tribalism and "Indianness." American Indians were simultaneously stimulated to assimilate (by stressing their common characteristics and creating organizational forms that united the tribes) and to retain a pluralistic relationship with the larger society (by working for self-determination and enhanced tribal power and authority). Thus, part of the significance of the Red Power movement was that it encouraged both pantribal unity and a continuation of tribal diversity (Olson & Wilson, 1984, p. 206). Today, American Indians continue to seek a way of existing in the larger society that merges assimilation with pluralism.

Table 7.2 summarizes this discussion of federal policy and Indian protest. The four major policy phases since the end of overt hostilities in 1890 are listed on the left. The thrust of the government's economic and political policies are listed in the next two columns, followed by a brief characterization of tribal response. The last column shows the changing bases for federal policy, sometimes aimed at weakening tribal structures and individualizing American Indians, and sometimes (including most recently) aimed at working with and preserving tribal structures.

QUESTIONS FOR REFLECTION

1. What are the major phases in Indian–white relations since the 1890s? What laws and federal policies shaped these changes? How did Indians respond?

2. Compare and contrast the Red Power movement with the Black Power movement discussed in Chapter 6. How were the similarities and differences shaped by the groups' situations?

TABLE 7.2 Federal Indian Policy and Indian Response

PERIOD	ECONOMIC IMPACT	POLITICAL IMPACT	INDIAN RESPONSE	GOVERNMENT APPROACH
Reservation: Late 1800s to 1930s	Land loss (Dawes Act) and welfare dependency	Government control of reservation and coerced acculturation	Some resistance; growth of religious movements	Individualistic; creation of self-sufficient farmers
Reorganization (IRA): 1930s and 1940s	Stabilized land base and supported some development of reservation	Establish federally sponsored tribal governments	Increased political participation in many tribes; some pantribal activity	Incorporated tribes as groups; creation of self-sufficient "Americanized" communities
Termination and Relocation: Late 1940s to early 1960s	Withdrawal of government support for reservations; promotion of urbanization	New assault on tribes; new forms of coercive acculturation	Increased pantribalism; widespread and intense opposition to termination	Individualistic; dissolved tribal ties and promoted incorporation into the modern, urban labor market
Self-Determination: 1960s to present	Developed reservation economies; increased integration of Indian labor force	Support for tribal governments	Greatly increased political activity	Incorporated tribes as self-sufficient communities with access to federal programs of support and welfare

SOURCE: Based on Cornell, Kalt, Krepps, and Taylor (1998, p. 5).

CONTEMPORARY AMERICAN INDIAN–WHITE RELATIONS

Conflicts between American Indians and the larger society are far from over. Although the days of deadly battle are (with occasional exceptions) long gone, the issues that remain are serious, difficult to resolve, and, in their way, just as much matters of life and death. American Indians face enormous challenges in their struggle to improve their status, but largely as a result of their greater freedom from stifling federal control since the 1970s, they also have some resources, some opportunities, and a leadership that is both talented and resourceful (Bordewich, 1996, p. 11).

NATURAL RESOURCES

Ironically, land allotted to American Indian tribes in the 19th century sometimes turned out to be rich in resources that became valuable in the 20th century. These resources include oil, natural gas, coal, and uranium, basic sources of energy in the larger society. In addition (and despite the devastation wreaked by the Dawes Act of 1887), some tribes hold title to water rights, fishing rights, woodlands that could sustain a lumbering industry, and wilderness areas that could be developed for camping, hunting, and other forms of recreation. These resources are likely to become more valuable as the earth's natural resources and undeveloped areas are further depleted in the future.

The challenge faced by American Indians is to retain control of these resources and to develop them for their own benefit. Threats to the remaining tribal lands and assets are common. Mining and energy companies continue to cast envious eyes on American Indian land, and other tribal assets are coveted by real-estate developers, fishermen (recreational as well as commercial), backpackers and campers, and cities facing water shortages (Harjo, 1996).

Some tribes have succeeded in developing their resources for their own benefit, in part because of their increased autonomy and independence since the passage of the 1975 Indian Self-Determination Act. For example, the White Mountain Apaches of Arizona own a variety of enterprises, including a major ski resort and a casino (Cornell & Kalt, 1998, pp. 3–4). On many other reservations, however, even richer stores of resources lie dormant, awaiting the right combination of tribal leadership, expertise, and development capital.

On a broader level, tribes are banding together to share expertise and negotiate more effectively with the larger society. For example, 25 tribes founded the Council of Energy Resource Tribes in 1975 to coordinate and control the development of the mineral resources on reservation lands. Since its founding, the council has successfully negotiated a number of agreements with dominant group firms, increasing the flow of income to the tribes and raising their quality of life (Cornell, 1988; Snipp, 1989). The council now encompasses more than 50 tribes and several Canadian First Nations (see their website at www.certredearth.com for more information).

Australian Aborigines and American Indians

The chief of a tribe of Australian Aborigines.

Many indigenous societies around the globe—not just American Indians—have been conquered and colonized by European societies, and similar dynamics have been at play in these episodes, even though each has its own unique history. To illustrate, we will compare the impact of European domination on Australian Aborigines and the indigenous peoples of North America.

Australia came under European domination in the late 1700s, nearly two centuries after the beginning of Anglo–American Indian relations. In spite of the time difference, however, the two contact situations shared many features. In both cases, the colonial power was Great Britain, first contact occurred in the preindustrial era, both indigenous groups were thinly spread across vast areas, and both were greatly inferior to the British in their technological development.

The Aboriginal peoples had lived in Australia for 50,000 years by the time the British arrived. They were organized into small, nomadic hunting-and-gathering bands and lacked the population base, social organization, and resources that would have permitted sustained resistance to the invasion of their land. There was plenty of violence in the contact situation, but unlike the situation in North America, there were no sustained military campaigns pitting large armies against each other.

The initial thrust of colonization was motivated by Great Britain's need for a place to send convicts; so the European population grew slowly at first and consisted mostly of prisoners. The early economic enterprises were subsistence farming and sheepherding, not large-scale operations that required forced labor.

Early relations between the English and the Aborigines centered on competition for land. The invaders pushed the Aborigines aside or killed them if they resisted. As in the Americas, European diseases took their toll, and the indigenous population declined rapidly. Because they were not desired as laborers, they were pushed away from the areas of white settlement into the fringes of development, where they and their grievances could be ignored. As in North America, they were seen as "savages": a culture that would wither away and soon disappear.

The contemporary situation of Australian Aborigines has many parallels to that of American Indians. The group is largely rural and continues to live on land that is less desirable. After the initial—and dramatic—declines, their numbers have been increasing of late, partly because of higher birthrates and partly because of changing perceptions, growing sympathy for their plight, and increased willingness of people to claim their Aboriginal heritage. The population fell to a low of fewer than 100,000 at the start of the 20th century but is now put at 517,000, or about 2.5% of the total population (Australian Bureau of Statistics, 2012).

Just as in North America, there are huge differences between the indigenous population and national norms. Life expectancy for Aborigines is as much as 12 years lower than that of the general population. They have less access to health care, and Aboriginal communities are much more afflicted with alcoholism, suicide, and malnutrition than the general population. Unemployment rates are triple that of the general population, Aboriginal housing is typically overcrowded and in poor repair, and only about 22% had completed Grade 12 in 2008 (up from 18% in 2002) (Australian Bureau of Statistics, 2012).

The issues animating Aboriginal affairs should have a familiar ring to anyone acquainted with the challenges faced by American Indians. They include concerns for the preservation of Aboriginal culture, language, and identity; self-determination and autonomy; the return of lands illegally taken by the Anglo invaders; and an end to discrimination and unequal treatment.

The Aboriginal peoples of Australia, like American Indians, face many—often overwhelming—challenges to securing a better future for themselves and their children. Their history and their present situation clearly validate both the Blauner and Noel hypotheses: They are a colonized minority group, victims of European domination, with all the consequences that status implies.

Questions to Consider

1. Compare and contrast the contact situations of American Indians and Australian Aborigines. In what ways were both colonized minorities?
2. Compare and contrast the contemporary situations of the groups. Why do these differences exist?

ATTRACTING INDUSTRY TO THE RESERVATION

Many efforts to develop the reservations have focused on creating jobs by attracting industry through such incentives as low taxes, low rents, and a low-wage pool of labor—not unlike the package of benefits offered to employers by less-developed nations in Asia, South America, and Africa. With some notable exceptions, these efforts have not been particularly successful (for a review, see Cornell, 2006; Vinje, 1996). Reservations are often so geographically isolated that transportation costs become prohibitive. The jobs that have materialized are typically low wage and have few benefits; usually, non-Indians fill the more lucrative managerial positions. Thus, the opportunities for building economic power or improving the standard of living from these jobs are sharply limited. These new jobs may transform "the welfare poor into the working poor" (Snipp, 1996, p. 398), but their potential for raising economic vitality is low.

To illustrate the problems of developing reservations by attracting industry, consider the Navajo, the second-largest American Indian tribe. The Navajo reservation spreads across Arizona, New Mexico, and Utah, and encompasses about 20 million acres, an area a little smaller than either Indiana or Maine (see Figure 7.2). The reservation seems huge on a map, but much of the land is desert not suitable for farming or other uses. As they have for the past several centuries, the Navajo today rely heavily on the cultivation of corn and sheepherding for sustenance.

Most wage-earning jobs on the reservation are with the agencies of the federal government (e.g., the BIA) or with the tribal government. Tourism is large and growing, but the jobs available in that sector are typically low wage and seasonal. There are reserves of coal, uranium, and oil on the reservation, but these resources have not generated many jobs. In some cases, the Navajo have resisted the damage to the environment that would be caused by mines and oil wells because of their traditional values and respect for the land. When exploitation of these resources has been permitted, the companies involved often use highly automated technologies that generate few jobs (Oswalt & Neely, 1996, pp. 317–351).

Figures 7.4 and 7.5 contrast Navajo income, poverty, and education with the total U.S. population. The poverty rate for the Navajo is almost three times greater than the national norm, and they are below national standards in terms of education, especially in terms of college education. Educational

FIGURE 7.5 Median Household Income and Per Capita Income for the Total Population, All American Indians and Alaska Natives (AIAN), Navajo, and Choctaw, 2012

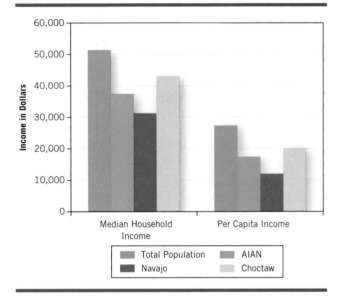

SOURCE: *We the People: American Indians and Alaska Natives in the United States: Census 2000 Special Reports* by Stella U. Ogunwole. Issued February, 2006. U.S. Census Bureau.

achievement is even lower for members of the tribe living on the reservation, where only about 64% have finished high school (vs. 73% of all Navajo; U.S. Census Bureau, 2009). Also, median household income for the Navajo is only about 60% of household income for all Americans, and their per capita income is only 43% of the national norm.

On the other hand, some tribes have managed to achieve relative prosperity by bringing jobs to their people. The Choctaw Nation of Mississippi, for example, has become one of the largest employers in the state. Tribal leaders have been able to attract companies such as McDonald's and Ford Motor Company by promising (and delivering) high-quality labor for relatively low wages. Incomes have risen, unemployment is relatively low, and the tribe has built schools, hospitals, and a television station, and administers numerous other services for its members (Mississippi Band of Choctaw Indians, 2011).

The poverty rate for the Choctaw is about half that for the Navajo (although still higher than the national norm), and their educational levels are higher than the national standard for high school education and in general much closer to the national standard for college education than are those of the Navajo or American Indians. Median household income for the Choctaw is about 80% of the national norm and more than $12,000 greater than the median income for the Navajo.

The Choctaw are not the most affluent tribe, and the Navajo are far from being the most destitute. They illustrate the mixture of partial successes and failures that typify efforts to bring prosperity to the reservations; together, these two cases suggest that attracting industry and jobs to the reservations is a possible—but difficult and uncertain—strategy for economic development.

FIGURE 7.4 Poverty Rates and Educational Attainment for the Total Population, American Indians and Alaska Natives (AIAN), Navajo, and Choctaw, 2012

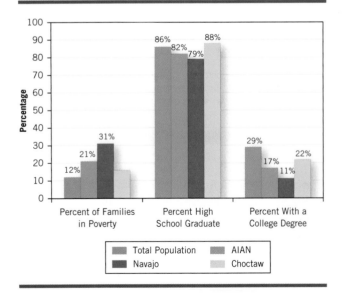

SOURCE: *We the People: American Indians and Alaska Natives in the United States: Census 2000 Special Reports* by Stella U. Ogunwole. Issued February, 2006. U.S. Census Bureau.

It is worth repeating that self-determination, the ability of tribes to control development on the reservation, seems to be one of the important keys to success. Tribes such as the Choctaw are, in a sense, developing ethnic enclaves (see Chapter 2) in which they can capitalize on local networks of interpersonal relationships. As with other groups that have followed this strategy, success in the enclave depends on solidarity and group cohesion, not Americanization and integration (see Cornell, 2006).

BROKEN TREATIES

For many tribes, the treaties signed with the federal government in the 19th century offer another potential resource. These treaties were often violated by white settlers, the military, state and local governments, the BIA, and other elements and agencies of the dominant group, and many tribes are pursuing this trail of broken treaties and seeking compensation for the wrongs of the past. For example, in 1972, the Passamaquoddy and Penobscot tribes filed a lawsuit demanding the return of 12.5 million acres of land—an area more than half the size of Maine—and $25 billion in damages. The tribes argued that this land had been illegally taken from them more than 150 years earlier. After eight years of litigation, the tribes settled for a $25 million trust fund and 300,000 acres of land. Although far less than their original demand, the award gave the tribes control over resources that could be used for economic development, job creation, upgrading educational programs, and developing other programs that would enhance human and financial capital (Worsnop, 1992, p. 391).

Virtually every tribe has similar grievances, and if pursued successfully, the long-dead treaty relationship between the Indian nations and the government could be a significant fount of economic and political resources. Of course, lawsuits require considerable (and expensive) legal expertise and years of effort to bring to fruition. Because there are no guarantees of success, this avenue has some sharp limitations and risks.

GAMING AND OTHER DEVELOPMENT POSSIBILITIES

Another resource for Native Americans is the gambling industry, the development of which was made possible by federal legislation passed in 1988. There are currently more than 400 tribes with gaming establishments (National Indian Gaming Commission, 2011), and the industry has grown many times over, from almost $5 million in revenues in 1995 to almost $28 billion in 2012 (National Indian Gaming Commission, 2012). Figure 7.6 charts the growth of revenues from gaming on American Indian reservations from 1995 to 2012.

Most operations are relatively small in scale. The 21 largest Indian casinos—about 5% of all Indian casinos—generate almost 40% of the total income from gaming, and the 71 smallest operations—about 17% of all Indian casinos—account for less than 1% of the income (National Indian Gaming Commission, 2011).

FIGURE 7.6 Gaming Revenue From American Indian Casinos, 1995–2012

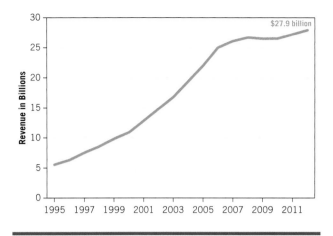

SOURCE: National Indian Gaming Commission.

The single most profitable Indian gambling operation is the Foxwoods Casino in Connecticut, operated by the Pequot tribe. The casino is one of the largest in the world and generates more revenue than the casinos of Atlantic City. The profits from the casino are used to benefit tribal members in a variety of ways, including the repurchase of tribal lands, housing assistance, medical benefits, educational scholarships, and public services such as a tribal police force (Bordewich, 1996, p. 110). Other tribes have used gambling profits to purchase restaurants and marinas and to finance the development of outlet malls, manufacturing plants, and a wide variety of other businesses and enterprises (Spilde, 2001).

The power of gaming to benefit the tribes is suggested by the information displayed in Table 7.3. The table shows that on a number of indicators, both gaming and nongaming reservations enjoyed significant improvements in their quality of life in the last decade of the 20th century but that gaming reservations improved more rapidly. For example, all reservations increased their per capita income faster than the nation as a whole (+11%), but gaming reservations improved faster (+36%) than nongaming reservations (+21%).

TABLE 7.3 Various Indicators of Improvement on Gaming vs. Nongaming Reservations, 1990–2000

INDICATOR	NONGAMING	GAMING	UNITED STATES
Per capita income	+21%	+36%	+11%
Family poverty	−7%	−12%	−1%
Unemployment	−2%	−5%	−1%
High school graduates	−1%	+2%	−1%
College graduates	+2%	+3%	+4%

SOURCE: Taylor and Kalt (2005, p. xi).

Various tribes have sought other ways to capitalize on their freedom from state regulation and taxes. Some have established small but profitable businesses selling cigarettes tax-free. Also, because they are not subject to state and federal environmental regulations, some reservations are exploring the possibility of housing nuclear waste and other refuse of industrialization—a somewhat ironic and not altogether attractive use of the remaining Indian lands.

Clearly, the combination of increased autonomy, treaty rights, natural resources, and gambling means that American Indians today have an opportunity to dramatically raise their standards of living and creatively take control of their own destinies. Some tribes have enjoyed enormous benefits, but for others, these assets remain a potential waiting to be actualized. Without denying the success stories or the improvements in recent years, the lives of many American Indians continue to be limited by poverty and powerlessness, prejudice, and discrimination. We document these patterns in the next section.

PREJUDICE AND DISCRIMINATION

Anti-Indian prejudice has been a part of American society from the beginning. Historically, negative feelings such as hatred and contempt have been widespread and strong, particularly during the heat of war, and various stereotypes of Indians have been common. One stereotype, especially strong during periods of conflict, depicts Indians as bloodthirsty, ferocious, cruel savages capable of any atrocity. The other image of American Indians is that of "the noble Red Man," who lives in complete harmony with nature and symbolizes goodwill and pristine simplicity (Bordewich, 1996, p. 34). Although the first stereotype tended to fade away as hostilities drew to a close, the latter image retains a good deal of strength in modern views of Indians found in popular culture and among environmentalist and "new age" spiritual organizations.

A variety of studies have documented continued stereotyping of Native Americans in the popular press, textbooks, the media, cartoons, and various other places (e.g., see Aleiss, 2005; Bird, 1999; Meek, 2006; Rouse & Hanson, 1991). In the tradition of "the noble Red Man," American Indians are often portrayed as bucks and squaws, complete with headdresses, bows, tepees, and other such "generic" Indian artifacts. These portrayals obliterate the diversity of American Indian culture and lifestyles.

Also, American Indians are often referred to in the past tense, as if their present situation were of no importance or, worse, as if they no longer existed. Many history books continue to begin the study of American history in Europe or with the "discovery" of America, omitting the millennia of civilization prior to the arrival of European explorers and colonizers. Contemporary portrayals of American Indians, such as in the movie *Dances With Wolves* (1990), are more sympathetic but still treat the tribes as part of a bucolic past forever lost, not as peoples with real problems in the present.

The persistence of stereotypes and the extent to which they have become enmeshed in modern culture is illustrated by continuing controversies surrounding the names of athletic teams (e.g., the Washington Redskins, the Cleveland Indians, and the Atlanta Braves) and the use of American Indian mascots, tomahawk "chops," and other practices offensive to many American Indians (see the Current Debates section at the end of this chapter for more). Protests at athletic events to increase awareness of these derogatory depictions are common, but they tend to be ridiculed or simply ignored.

There are relatively few studies of anti-Indian prejudice in the social science literature, and it is, therefore, difficult to characterize changes over the past several decades. We do not know whether there has been a shift to more symbolic or "modern" forms of anti-Indian racism, as there has been for antiblack prejudice, or whether the stereotypes of American Indians have declined in strength or changed in content.

One of the few records of national anti-Indian prejudice over time is that of social distance scale results (see Table 3.2). When the scales were first administered in 1926, American Indians were ranked in the middle third of all groups (18th out of 28), at about the same level as southern and eastern Europeans and slightly above Mexicans, another colonized group. The ranking of American Indians remained stable until 1977, when there was a noticeable rise in their position relative to other groups. In the most recent polls, the rankings of American Indians have remained stable, at about the same level as Jews and Poles but below African Americans. These shifts may reflect a decline in levels of prejudice, a change from more overt forms of racism to more subtle modern racism, or both. Remember, however, that the samples for the social distance research were college students for the most part and do not necessarily reflect trends in the general population.

Native Americans were the victims of systematic discrimination in a variety of institutions.

How much do you and Americans in general know about Native Americans? Here is a true/false quiz that tests your knowledge about the group. Some items can be answered from information presented in this chapter, but others test your knowledge "in general." How well do you think most Americans would do on this quiz? Why?

(1) Native Americans have their college expenses paid for by their tribe.

(2) Pocahontas was a real Indian princess.

(3) Native Americans scalped their enemies.

(4) The term *powwow* is a derogatory, stereotypical term used to describe negotiating sessions between Indians and whites.

(5) Native Americans practiced slavery.

(6) Native Americans use peyote in religious ceremonies.

(7) American Indians are getting rich from casinos.

(8) Anyone with an Indian ancestor is automatically a member of that tribe.

(9) American Indians were always considered U.S. citizens.

(10) Indian tribes are sovereign nations.

TURN THE PAGE TO FIND OUR ANSWERS.

Research is also unclear about the severity or extent of discrimination against American Indians. Certainly, the group's lower average levels of education limit their opportunities for upward mobility, choice of occupations, and range of income. This is a form of institutional discrimination in the sense that the opportunities to develop human capital are much less available to American Indians than to much of the rest of the population.

In terms of individual discrimination or more overt forms of exclusion, there is simply too little evidence to sustain clear conclusions (Snipp, 1992, p. 363). The situation of American Indian women is also underresearched, but Snipp reports that, like their counterparts in other minority groups and the dominant group, they "are systematically paid less than their male counterparts in similar circumstances" (p. 363).

The very limited evidence available from social distance scales suggests that overt anti-Indian prejudice has declined, perhaps in parallel with antiblack prejudice. A great deal of stereotyping remains, however, and demeaning, condescending, or negative portrayals of American Indians are common throughout the dominant culture. Institutional discrimination is a major barrier for American Indians, who have not had access to opportunities for education and employment.

QUESTIONS FOR REFLECTION

1. This section examined a number of issues in contemporary Indian–white relations. In your opinion, which of these is most important? Why?

2. Thinking about the concepts developed in this text, what is the single most important force shaping the situation of American Indians over the past century? Why?

3. Compare and contrast antiblack prejudice with anti-Indian prejudice. How and why are the two forms of prejudice different?

ASSIMILATION AND PLURALISM

In this section, we continue to assess the situation of American Indians today using the same conceptual framework used in Chapter 6. Once again, please regard this material as an overview and as starting points for further research.

Compared with other groups, information about American Indians is scant. Nonetheless, a relatively clear picture emerges. The portrait stresses a mixed picture: improvements

① False. Many tribes offer scholarships to enrolled members with strong academic qualifications, but the "urban legend" that all American Indians get a free ride to college is not true.

② True. Pocahontas was indeed a real person and may have saved the life of English colonist John Smith, as legend has it. She was the daughter of the premier chief of a large confederation of tribes, although the title of "princess" may overstate her status.

③ True, although the custom may have been introduced by Europeans.

④ False. Today, powwows are festivals celebrating American Indian culture and traditions. They are held across the nation.

⑤ True. Various forms of slavery were widespread, but none in the territory that became the United States involved exploiting a large, powerless workforce, as was true of African American slavery. Also, many runaway slaves escaped to Indian tribes.

⑥ True. For example, the Native American Church uses peyote as part of its rituals, as explained later in this chapter.

⑦ False. See the relevant sections of this chapter.

⑧ False. Tribes have specific rules about membership eligibility, and an Indian ancestor is no guarantee of acceptance.

⑨ False. American Indians were granted citizenship in 1924.

⑩ False, but tribes have considerable autonomy and the power to govern their own affairs under a variety of laws.

NOTE: These and many other ideas about American Indians are explored in A. Treuer (2012).

for some combined with continued colonization, marginalization, and impoverishment for others. Like African Americans, Native Americans can be found at every status and income level in the United States, but Indians living on reservations continue as one of the most impoverished, marginalized groups in society. American Indians as a group face ongoing discrimination and exclusion, and continue the search for a meaningful course between assimilation and pluralism.

ACCULTURATION

Despite more than a century of coercive Americanization, many tribes have been able to preserve at least a portion of their traditional cultures. For example, many tribal languages continue to be spoken on a daily basis. About 20% of American Indians and Alaska Natives speak a language other than English at home, about the same percentage as the total population. Figure 7.7 suggests the extent of language preservation. For 7 of the 10 largest tribes, less than 10% of their members speak the tribal language at home. Some tribes, however, continue to speak their native language, including about 25% of Apache and half of Navajo.

While some Native American languages have survived, it seems that even the most widely spoken of these languages is endangered. One older study (Krauss, 1996) concluded that most languages are spoken on a daily basis only by the older generation. There are very few, if any, people left who speak only a tribal language. One authority (A. Treuer, 2012, p. 80)

reports that only 20 tribal languages in the United States and Canada are spoken by children in significant numbers. If these patterns persist, Native American languages will disappear as the generations change. A number of tribes have instituted programs to try to renew and preserve their language, along with other elements of their culture, but the success of these efforts is uncertain (Schmid, 2001, p. 25; see also D. Treuer, 2012, pp. 300–305).

FIGURE 7.7 Percentage of Total Population, All American Indians and Alaska Natives (AIAN), and 10 Largest Tribes That Speak a Language Other Than English at Home, 2012

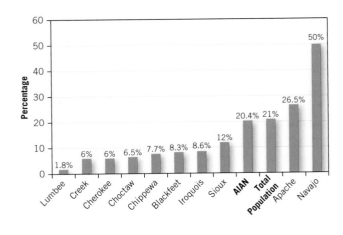

SOURCE: U.S. Bureau of the Census, 2013. American Community Survey, 2006–2012.

NARRATIVE PORTRAIT

An Indian View of White Civilization

Who's the savage? One stereotype of American Indians portrays them as "cruel, barbaric, and savage." Is it possible, however, that American Indians are more advanced than the dazzling sophisticates of urban America? In a 1972 interview, John Lame Deer, a Sioux, gives his view of the technologically advanced society that surrounds him. Through his words, we can hear the voices of the Indian cultures that have survived.

LISTENING TO THE AIR

John Lame Deer

You have made it hard for us to experience nature in the good way by being part of it. Even here [a Sioux reservation in South Dakota] we are conscious that somewhere out in those hills there are missile silos and radar stations. White men always pick the few unspoiled, beautiful, awesome spots for these abominations. You have raped and violated these lands, always saying, "gimme, gimme, gimme," and never giving anything back.... You have not only despoiled the earth, the rocks, the minerals, all of which you call "dead" but which are very much alive; you have even changed the animals,... changed them in a horrible way, so no one can recognize them. There is power in a buffalo—spiritual, magic power—but there is no power in an Angus, in a Hereford.

There is power in an antelope, but not in a goat or a sheep, which holds still while you butcher it, which will eat your newspaper if you let it. There was great power in a wolf, even in a coyote. You made him into a freak—a toy poodle, a Pekinese, a lap dog. You can't do much with a cat, which is like an Indian, unchangeable. So you fix it, alter it, declaw it, even cut its vocal cords so you can experiment on it in a laboratory without being disturbed by its cries....

You have not only altered, declawed, and malformed your winged and four-legged cousins; you have done it to yourselves. You have changed men into chairmen of boards, into office workers, into time-clock punchers. You have changed women into housewives, truly fearful creatures....You live in prisons which you have built for yourselves, calling them "homes," offices, factories. We have a new joke on the reservations: "What is cultural deprivation?" Answer: "Being an upper-middle-class white kid living in a split-level suburban home with a color TV."...

I think white people are so afraid of the world they created that they don't want to see, feel, smell, or hear it. The feeling of rain or snow on your face, being numbed by an icy wind and thawing out before a smoking fire, coming out of a hot sweat bath and plunging into a cold stream, these things make you feel alive, but you don't want them anymore. Living in boxes that shut out the heat of the summer and the chill of winter, living inside a body that no longer has a scent, hearing the noise of the hi-fi rather than listening to the sounds of nature, watching some actor on TV have a make-believe experience when you no longer experience anything for yourself, eating food without taste—that's your way. It's no good.

SOURCE: Reprinted with the permission of Simon & Schuster Adult Publisher Group from *Lame Deer, Seeker of Vision* by John (Fire) Lame Deer and Richard Erdoes. Copyright © 1972 by John (Fire) Lame Deer and Richard Erdoes. Copyright renewed © 2001 Richard Erdoes. All rights reserved.

Questions to Consider

1. Does Lame Deer's critique of mainstream American culture ring true? If you were in a debate with him, could you refute his points?

2. How does this passage support the idea that American Indian culture has survived coercive acculturation and military conquest? Is there a future for the ideas expressed by Lame Deer?

Traditional culture is retained in other forms besides language. Religions and value systems, political and economic structures, and recreational patterns have all survived the military conquest and the depredations of reservation life, but each pattern has been altered by contact with the dominant group. Cornell (1987), for example, argues that the strong orientation to the group rather than the individual is being significantly affected by the "American dream" of personal material success.

The tendency to filter the impact of the larger society through continuing, vital American Indian culture is also illustrated by the Native American Church. The Native American Church is an important American Indian religion, with more than 100 congregations across the nation.

This religion combines elements from both cultures, and church services freely mix Christian imagery and the Bible with attempts to seek personal visions by using peyote, a hallucinogenic drug. The latter practice is consistent with the spiritual and religious traditions of many tribes but clashes sharply with the laws and norms of the larger society. The difference in traditions has generated many skirmishes with the courts, and as recently as 2004, the right of the Native American Church to use peyote was upheld by the Supreme Court of Utah ("Utah Supreme Court," 2004).

American Indians have been more successful than African Americans in preserving their traditional cultures, a pattern that is partly explained by the differences in the relationship between each minority group and the dominant group. African Americans were exploited for labor, whereas the competition with American Indians involved land. African cultures could not easily survive because the social structures that transmitted the cultures and gave them meaning were largely destroyed by slavery and sacrificed to the exigencies of the plantation economy.

In contrast, Native Americans confronted the dominant group as tribal units, intact and whole. The tribes maintained integrity throughout the wars and throughout the reservation

FIGURE 7.8 Percentage of County Population Choosing American Indian or Alaska Native, Alone or in Combination, 2010

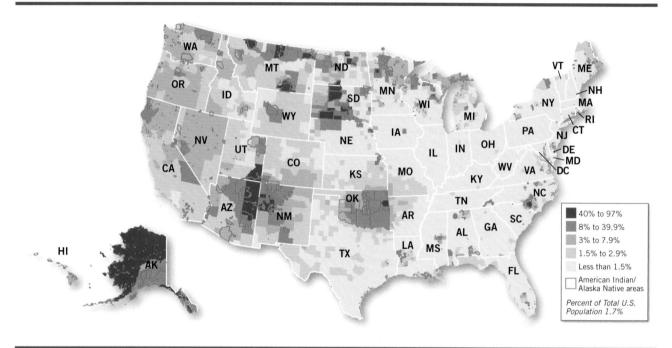

SOURCE: Norris et al., 2012; U.S. Census Bureau (2011b, Table P1).

period. Tribal culture was indeed attacked and denigrated during the reservation era, but the basic social unit that sustained the culture survived, albeit in altered form. The fact that American Indians were placed on separate reservations, isolated from one another and the "contaminating" effects of everyday contact with the larger society, also abetted the preservation of traditional languages and culture (Cornell, 1990). The second Narrative Portrait in this chapter illustrates the persistence of a distinct Indian culture and point of view.

The vitality of Indian cultures may have increased in the current atmosphere of greater tolerance and support for pluralism in the larger society, combined with increased autonomy and lessened government regulation on the reservations. However, a number of social forces are working against pluralism and the continuing survival of tribal cultures. Pantribalism may threaten the integrity of individual tribal cultures as it represents American Indian grievances and concerns to the larger society. Opportunities for jobs, education, and higher incomes draw American Indians to more developed urban areas and will continue to do so as long as the reservations are underdeveloped. Many aspects of the tribal cultures can be fully expressed and practiced only with other tribal members on the reservations. Thus, many American Indians must make a choice between "Indianness" on the reservation and "success" in the city. The younger, more educated American Indians will be most likely to confront this choice, and the future vitality of traditional American Indian cultures and languages will hinge on which option is chosen.

SECONDARY STRUCTURAL ASSIMILATION

This section assesses the degree of integration of American Indians into the various institutional structures of public life, following the general outlines of the parallel section in Chapter 6.

Residential Patterns. Since the Indian Removal Act of 1830 (see Chapter 4), American Indians have been concentrated in the western two thirds of the nation, as illustrated in Figure 7.8, although some pockets of population still can be found in the East. The states with the largest concentrations of American Indians—California, Oklahoma, and Arizona— together include about 30% of all American Indians. As Figure 7.8 illustrates, most U.S. counties have few American Indian residents. The population is concentrated in eastern Oklahoma, the upper Midwest, and the Southwest (Norris et al., 2012, p. 8).

Since American Indians are such a small, rural group, it is difficult to assess the overall level of residential segregation. An earlier study using 2000 Census data found that they were less segregated than African Americans and that the levels of residential segregation had declined since 1980 (Iceland, Weinberg, & Steinmetz, 2002, p. 23). More detailed data from the 2000 Census for the 10 metropolitan areas with the highest numbers of Native American residents shows that residential segregation was "extremely high" (dissimilarity index at or above

FIGURE 7.9 Educational Attainment for Non-Hispanic Whites, All American Indians (AIAN), and 10 Largest Tribes, 2012

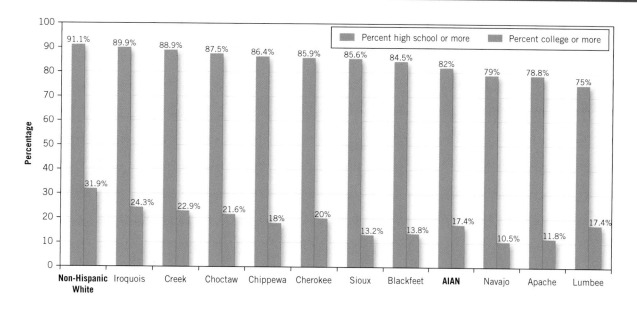

SOURCE: U.S. Census Bureau (2013a).

60) in four of the cities (New York, Phoenix, Albuquerque, and Chicago) but lower than the levels of black–white segregation. Also, a couple of the cities (Oklahoma City and Tulsa) had low scores, or a dissimilarity index at or below 30 (Social Science Data Analysis Network, n.d.).

What can we conclude? It seems that residential segregation for American Indians is less than black–white levels. However, it is difficult to come to firm conclusions because of the small size of the group and the fact that 30% live on rural reservations where the levels of isolation and racial segregation are quite high.

School Integration and Educational Attainment. As a result of the combined efforts of missionaries and federal agencies, American Indians have had a long but not necessarily productive acquaintance with Western education. Until the past few decades, schools for American Indians were primarily focused on Americanizing children, not so much on educating them.

For many tribes, the percentage of high school graduates has increased in the recent past, but American Indians as a whole are still below national levels and the levels of non-Hispanic whites, as shown in Figure 7.9. Several tribes are close to non-Hispanic whites in high school graduation rates, but none approach equality in college education. The differences in schooling are especially important because the lower levels of educational attainment limit mobility and job opportunities in the postindustrial job market.

One positive development for the education of American Indians is the rapid increase in tribally controlled colleges. There are now 37 tribal colleges: All offer two-year degrees, six

offer four-year degrees, and two offer master's degrees. These institutions are located on or near reservations, and some have been constructed with funds generated by the gaming industry. They are designed to be more sensitive to the educational and cultural needs of the group, and tribal college graduates who transfer to four-year colleges are more likely to graduate than are other American Indian students (Pego, 1998; see also His Horse Is Thunder, Anderson, and Miller, 2013).

An earlier study found that American Indian school children were less segregated than African American school children in the 2005–2006 school year but that the levels of racial isolation might be increasing (Fry, 2007). Again, it is difficult to assess trends because of the small size of the group and their concentration in rural areas.

Political Power. The ability of American Indians to exert power as a voting bloc or otherwise directly affect the political structure is limited by group size; they are a tiny percentage of the electorate. Furthermore, their political power is limited by their lower average levels of education, language differences, lack of economic resources, and fractional differences within and between tribes and reservations. The number of American Indians holding elected office is minuscule, far less than 1% (Pollard & O'Hare, 1999). In 1992, however, Ben Nighthorse Campbell of Colorado, a member of the Northern Cheyenne tribe, was elected to the U.S. Senate and served until 2005.

Jobs and Income. Some of the most severe challenges facing American Indians relate to work and income. The problems are

Housing on reservations for Native Americans is often substandard. This dilapidated trailer is home for a family of Cheyenne Indians on the Standing Rock reservation in South Dakota.

especially evident on the reservations, where jobs traditionally have been scarce and affluence rare. As mentioned previously, the overall unemployment rate for all American Indians is about double the rate for whites. For Indians living on or near reservations, however, the rate is much higher, sometimes rising to 70% to 80% on the smaller, more isolated reservations (BIA, 2005. pp. 3–39).

Nationally, American Indians are underrepresented in the higher-status, more lucrative professions and overrepresented in unskilled labor and service jobs (U.S. Census Bureau, 2013a). As is the case for African Americans, American Indians who hold white-collar jobs are more likely than whites to work in lower-income occupations, such as clerk or retail salesperson (Ogunwole, 2006, p. 10).

The data in Figure 7.10 show median household income in 2012 for non-Hispanic whites, all American Indians and Alaska Natives, and the 10 largest tribes. Median household income for American Indians and Alaska Natives is about 66% of that of non-Hispanic whites. There is a good deal of variability among the 10 largest tribes, but none approaches the incomes of non-Hispanic whites.

These income statistics reflect lower levels of education as well as the interlocking forces of past discrimination and lack of development on many reservations. The rural isolation of much of the population and their distance from the more urbanized centers of economic growth limit possibilities for improvement and raise the likelihood that many reservations will remain the rural counterparts to urban underclass ghettos.

Figure 7.11 supplements the information in Figure 7.10 by displaying the distribution of income for all American Indians and Alaska Natives compared with whites. This type of graph was introduced in Chapter 6 and follows the same format as Figure 6.12. In both graphs, the pattern of income inequality is immediately obvious. Starting at the bottom, we see that American Indians and Alaska Natives are overrepresented in the lowest income groups, as were African Americans. For example, about 12% of American Indians and Alaska Natives have incomes less than $10,000—double the percentage for whites (6%) in this range.

Moving up the figure through the lower and middle income brackets, we see that American Indian and Alaska Native households continue to be overrepresented. As was the case with Figure 6.12, there is a notable clustering of both groups in the $50,000 to $100,000 categories, but it is whites who are overrepresented at these income levels: Almost a third

FIGURE 7.10 Median Household Income for Non-Hispanic Whites, All American Indians (AIAN), and 10 Largest Tribes, 2012

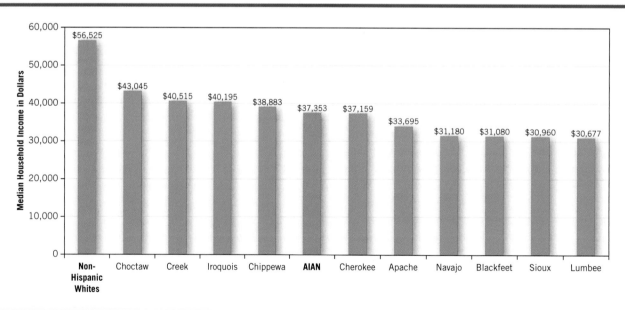

SOURCE: U.S. Census Bureau (2013a).

FIGURE 7.11 Distribution of Household Income for Non-Hispanic Whites and American Indians and Alaska Natives, 2010

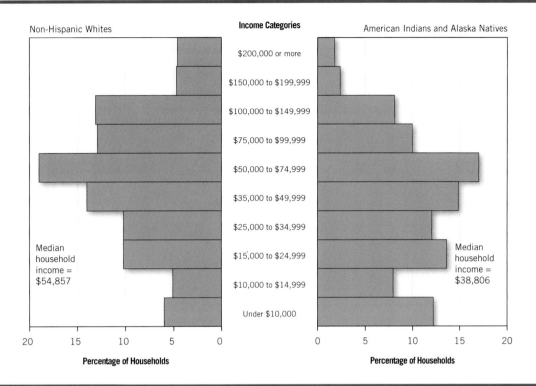

SOURCE: U.S. Census Bureau (2013h).

of white households, compared with only 27% of American Indian and Alaska Native households, are in these categories.

The income differences between the groups are especially obvious at the top of the figure. More than 22% of white households versus 12% of American Indian and Alaska Native households are in the top three income categories. Figure 7.11 also shows the median household income for both groups in 2010, and the difference of more than $16,000 further illustrates the lower socioeconomic level of American Indians.

Finally, Figure 7.12 shows the poverty levels for non-Hispanic whites, all American Indians and Alaska Natives, and the 10 largest tribes. The poverty rate for all American Indian and Alaska Native families is almost triple the rate for non-Hispanic whites, and 6 of the 10 largest tribes have an even higher percentage of families living in poverty. The poverty rates for children show a similar pattern, with very high rates for the Lumbee, Navajo, and Sioux.

Taken together, this information on income and poverty shows that despite the progress American Indians have made over the past several decades, a sizable socioeconomic gap persists.

PRIMARY STRUCTURAL ASSIMILATION

Rates of out-marriage for American Indians are quite high compared with other groups, as displayed in Table 7.4. While the overwhelming majority of whites were married to other whites

in both years, a little more than 40% of American Indians had marriage partners within the group. This pattern is partly the result of the small size of the group. As less than 1% of the total population, American Indians are numerically unlikely to find dating and marriage partners within their own group, especially in those regions of the country and urban areas where the group is small in size. For example, an earlier study found that in New England, which has the lowest relative percentage of American Indians of any region, more than 90% of Indian marriages were to partners outside the group. In the mountain states, which have a greater number of American Indians who are also highly concentrated on reservations, only about 40% of Indian marriages involved partners outside the group (Snipp, 1989, pp. 156–159).

TABLE 7.4 Percentage Married to a Person of the Same Race, 1980 and 2008

YEAR	WHITES		NATIVE AMERICANS	
	Men	Women	Men	Women
1980	96%	95%	41%	43%
2008	93%	92%	43%	42%

SOURCE: Qian and Lichter (2011, p. 1072). Copyright © 2011 National Council on Family Relations. Reprinted with permission.

FIGURE 7.12 Families and Children in Poverty for Non-Hispanic Whites, American Indians and Alaska Natives (AIAN), and 10 Largest Tribes, 2012

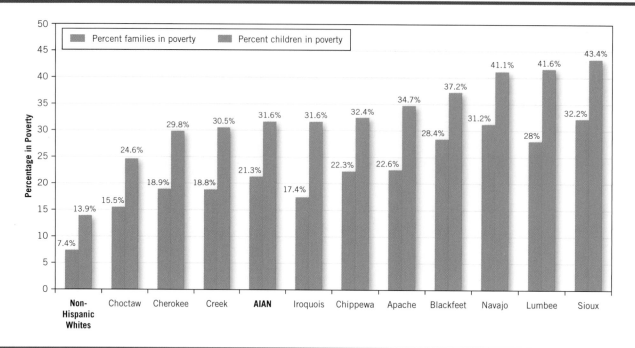

SOURCE: U.S. Census Bureau (2013a).

1. This section examined a variety of dimensions of acculturation and integration for American Indians. Which is most important? Why?

2. In which of these areas has there been the most progress over the past 50 years? How?

COMPARING MINORITY GROUPS

Comparing the experiences of American Indians with those of other groups will further our understanding of the complexities of dominant–minority relationships and permit us to test the explanatory power of the concepts and theories that are central to this text. No two minority groups have had the same experiences, and our concepts and theories should help us understand the differences and the similarities. We will make it a point to compare groups in each of the chapters in this part of the text. We begin by comparing American Indians with African Americans.

First, note the differences in the stereotypes attached to the two groups during the early years of European colonization. While Indians were seen as cruel savages, African Americans under slavery were seen as lazy, irresponsible, and in constant need of supervision. The two stereotypes are consistent with the outcomes of the contact period. The supposed irresponsibility of blacks under slavery helped justify their subordinate, highly controlled status, and the alleged savagery of American Indians helped justify their near extermination by white society.

Second, both American Indians and African Americans were colonized minority groups, but their contact situations were governed by very different dynamics (competition for labor vs. land) and a very different dominant-group agenda (the capture and control of a large, powerless workforce vs. the elimination of a military threat). These differing contact situations shaped subsequent relationships with the dominant group and the place of the groups in the larger society.

For example, consider the situations of the two groups a century ago. At that time, the most visible enemy for African Americans was de jure segregation, the elaborate system of repression in the South that controlled them politically, economically, and socially (see Chapters 5 and 6). In particular, the southern system of agriculture needed the black population— but only as a powerless, cheap workforce. The goals of African Americans centered on dismantling this oppressive system, assimilation, and equality.

American Indians, in contrast, were not viewed as a source of labor and, after their military defeat, were far too few in number and too dispersed geographically to constitute a political threat. Thus, there was little need to control them in the same way African Americans were controlled. The primary enemies of the tribes were the reservation system, various agencies of the federal government (especially the BIA), rural isolation, and the continuing attacks on their traditional cultures and lifestyles, which are typical for a colonized minority group. American Indians had a different set of problems, different resources at their disposal, and different goals in mind. They always have been more oriented toward a pluralistic relationship with the larger society and preserving what they could of their autonomy, their institutions, and their heritage. African Americans spent much of the 20th century struggling for inclusion and equality; American Indians were fighting to maintain or recover their traditional cultures and social structures. This difference in goals reflects the different histories of the two groups and the different circumstances surrounding their colonization.

PROGRESS AND CHALLENGES

What does the future hold for American Indians? Their situation has certainly changed over the past 100 years, but is it "better" or just "different," as is the case for large segments of the African American community? As the group grows in size and improves its status, the answer seems to be a little of both. To reach some conclusions, we will look at several aspects of the situation of American Indians and assess the usefulness of our theoretical models and concepts.

Since the 1960s, the decline of intolerance in society at large, the growth of pride in ancestry in many groups (e.g., Black Power), and the shift in federal government policy to encourage self-determination have all helped spark a reaffirmation of commitment to tribal cultures and traditions. As was the case with African Americans and the Black Power movement, the Red Power movement asserted a distinct and positive Indian identity, a claim for the equal validity of American Indian cultures within the broad framework of the larger society. During the same time period, the favorable settlements of treaty claims, the growth in job opportunities, and the gambling industry have enhanced the flow of resources and benefits to some reservations. In popular culture, American Indians have enjoyed a strong upsurge of popularity and sympathetic depictions. This enhanced popularity accounts for much of the growth in population size as people of mixed ancestry resurrect and reconstruct their Indian ancestors and their own ethnic identities.

Linear or simplistic views of assimilation do not fit the current situation or the past experiences of American Indians very well. Some American Indians are intermarrying with whites and integrating into the larger society; others strive to retain a tribal culture in the midst of an urbanized, industrialized society; and still others labor to use the profits from gaming and other enterprises for the benefit of the tribe as a whole. Members of the group can be found at every degree of acculturation and integration, and the group seems to be moving toward assimilation in some ways and away from it in others.

From the standpoint of the Noel and Blauner hypotheses, we can see that American Indians have struggled with conquest and colonization, experiences made more difficult by the loss of so much of their land and other resources and by the concerted, unrelenting attacks on their culture and language. The legacy of conquest and colonization was poor health and housing, an inadequate and misdirected education system, and slow (or nonexistent) economic development. For most of the 20th century, American Indians were left to survive as best they could on the margins of the larger society, too powerless to establish meaningful pluralism and too colonized to pursue equality.

Today, one key to further progress for some members of this group is economic development on reservation lands and the further strengthening of the tribes as functioning social units. Some tribes do have assets—natural resources, treaty rights, and the gambling industry—that could fuel development. However, they often do not have the expertise or the capital to finance the exploitation of these resources. They must rely, in whole or in part, on non-Indian expertise and white-owned companies and businesses. Thus, non-Indians, rather than the tribes, may be the primary beneficiaries of some forms of development (this would, of course, be quite consistent with American history). For those reservations for which gambling is not an option and for those without natural resources, investments in human capital (education) may offer the most compelling direction for future development.

Urban Indians confront the same patterns of discrimination and racism that confront other minority groups of color. Members of the group with lower levels of education and job skills face the prospects of becoming part of a permanent urban underclass. More-educated and more-skilled American Indians share with African Americans the prospect of a middle-class lifestyle that is more partial and tenuous than that of comparable segments of the dominant group.

The situation of American Indians today is vastly superior to the status of the group a century ago, and this chapter has documented the notable improvements that have occurred since 1990. Given the depressed and desperate conditions of the reservations in the early 20th century, however, it would not take much to show an improvement. American Indians are growing rapidly in numbers and are increasingly diversified by residence, education, and degree of assimilation. Some tribes have made dramatic progress over the past several decades, but enormous problems remain, both on and off the reservations. The challenge for the future, as it was in the past, is to find a course between pluralism and assimilation, and between pan-tribalism and traditional lifestyles that will balance the issues of quality of life against the importance of retaining an Indian identity.

This summary is organized around the Learning Objectives listed at the beginning of this chapter.

 7.1 Summarize the changing population characteristics of American Indians and Alaska Natives, and some of their common cultural characteristics.

Although they remain a tiny numerical minority of the population (about 1%), American Indian and Alaska Native populations are growing rapidly and, according to the 2010 Census, more than five million people now claim at least partial American Indian or Alaska Native ancestry. The increase reflects, in part, the social nature of race and the changing definitions used in the census. Traditional Indian cultures were numerous and variable. As is typical for societies at the hunting-and-gathering level of development, they commonly stressed strong group ties, cooperation with others, and egalitarian relations.

 7.2 Summarize and explain the changing relationships between American Indians and the federal government, especially the changes in laws and policies and their effects, and the dynamics of Indian resistance and protest.

After the end of armed hostilities, relations between American Indians and the larger society were paternalistic and featured coercive acculturation. At the beginning of the 20th century, American Indians faced the paternalistic reservation system, poverty and powerlessness, rural isolation and marginalization, and the Bureau of Indian Affairs. Native Americans continued to lose land and other resources. Some landmark legislation and federal policies included the Indian Reorganization Act (1934), termination, relocation, and, beginning in the 1970s, increasing self-determination. There have been organized protest movements since early in the 20th century, including a Red Power movement. American Indian protests achieved some successes and were partly assimilationist, even though they pursued some pluralistic goals and greater autonomy for the tribes.

 7.3 Cite and explain the most important issues and trends that have animated relations between American Indians and the larger society in recent decades, including

a. struggles over natural resources,

b. attempts to attract industry to reservations,

c. broken treaties,

d. gaming, and

e. prejudice and discrimination.

As a group, American Indians and Alaska Natives have experienced some improvements in quality of life, especially since the 1970s, but the progress has been uneven and enormous challenges remain.

- Some tribes and reservations have access to valuable natural resources, including oil, coal, clean water, and timber, which have sometimes been used to improve their situation.

- Some tribes (e.g., the Choctaw Nation of Mississippi) have been able to attract industry, but many reservations are too remote and inaccessible to be viable sites for development and good jobs.

- The legacy of broken treaties may provide the basis for successful lawsuits and give some tribes resources and opportunities.

- The gaming industry has benefited some tribes and has the potential to benefit others.

- Prejudice and discrimination remain potent forces limiting the opportunities for American Indians and Alaska Natives. There is some indication that anti-Indian prejudice has shifted to more "modern" forms. Institutional discrimination and access to education and employment remain major problems confronting American Indians.

 7.4 Analyze the contemporary relations between American Indians and whites using the concepts of prejudice and discrimination, and assimilation and pluralism, especially in terms of

a. acculturation,

b. secondary structural assimilation, and

c. primary structural assimilation.

- American Indians have been able to retain more of their culture than have African Americans, and the tribal languages are still spoken on some reservations. However, the forces of pantribalism and especially the attractions of education and jobs in the larger society seem to be working against the survival of traditional cultures.

- Despite recent improvements, the overall secondary structural assimilation of American Indians remains low. Inequalities persist in schooling, jobs, income, unemployment, and poverty levels.

- In terms of primary structural assimilation, intermarriages are high compared with other groups, largely as a function of the small size of the group.

 7.5 Assess the overall situation of American Indians today based on the concepts and information presented in this chapter.

The situation of American Indians today is shaped by their origin as a colonized minority group, their history of competition with the dominant group for control of land, and their recent history on the reservations. Today, the group faces an array of problems similar to those faced by all American colonized minority groups of color, as they try to find ways to raise their quality of life and continue their commitment to their tribes and to an Indian identity.

With the recent increase in self-determination and the development of resources on some reservations, the situation of some members of the group and some tribes is improved, but many others are far from equality. What evidence of improvements is presented in this chapter? What evidence of continuing inequality is presented? How does this group compare with African Americans? What important similarities and differences can you identify?

KEY TERMS

Bureau of Indian Affairs 190   Indian Reorganization Act 191   termination 192

REVIEW QUESTIONS

1. What were the most important cultural differences between American Indian tribes and the dominant society? How did these affect relations between the two groups?

2. Compare and contrast the effects of paternalism and coercive acculturation on American Indians after the end of the contact period with the effects on African Americans under slavery. What similarities and differences existed in the two situations? Which system was more oppressive and controlling? How? How did these different situations shape the futures of the groups?

3. How did federal Indian policy change over the course of the 20th century? What effects did these changes have on the tribes? Which were more beneficial? Why? What was the role of the Indian protest movement in shaping these policies?

4. What options do American Indians have for improving their position in the larger society and developing their reservations? Which strategies seem to have the most promise? Which seem less effective? Why?

5. Compare and contrast the contact situations of American Indians, African Americans, and Australian Aborigines. What are the most crucial differences in their situations? What implications did these differences have for the

development of each group's situation after the initial contact?

6. Characterize the present situation of American Indians in terms of acculturation and integration. How do they compare with African Americans? What factors in the experiences of the two groups might help explain contemporary differences?

7. What gender differences can you identify in the experiences of American Indians? How do these compare with the gender differences in the experiences of African Americans?

8. Given the information and ideas presented in this chapter, speculate about the future of American Indians. How likely are American Indian cultures and languages to survive? What are the prospects for achieving equality?

9. Given their small size and marginal status, recognition of their situations and problems continues to be a central struggle for American Indians. What are some ways the group can build a more realistic, informed, and empathetic relationship with the larger society, the federal government, and other authorities? Are there lessons in the experiences of other groups or in the various protest strategies followed in the Red Power movement?

STUDENT STUDY SITE

Sharpen your skills with SAGE edge at edge.sagepub.com/healey7e

SAGE edge for students provides a personalized approach to help you accomplish your coursework goals in an easy-to-use learning environment.

The following resources are available at SAGE edge:

Current Debates: Are Indian Sports Team Mascots Offensive?

What messages are conveyed by team names such as the Indians, Braves, and, especially, Redskins? Are these mascots offensive? Do they perpetuate stereotypes and negative views of Native Americans? Or are they harmless tributes to virtues such as bravery and honor?

On our website you will find an overview of the topic, the clashing points of view, and some questions to consider as you analyze the material.

Public Sociology Assignments

Public Sociology Assignments provide opportunities for students to address directly and personally some of the issues raised in this text.

There are two assignments for Part III on our website. The first looks at patterns of self-segregation in school cafeterias, and, in the second, students analyze the portrayal of the American family on television in terms of race, ethnicity, sexual orientation, and other sociologically relevant characteristics.

Contributed by Linda M. Waldron

Internet Research Project

For this Internet Research Project, you will use data gathered by the U.S. Census Bureau to assess the situation of all Native Americans and a tribe of your choosing. You will add this information to the data you gathered previously on African Americans and the general population. You will also search the Internet for additional information on the specific tribe you selected. The project will be guided by a series of questions related to course concepts, and your instructor may ask you to discuss your findings in small groups.

For Further Reading

Please see our website for an annotated list of important works related to this chapter.

CHAPTER-OPENING TIMELINE PHOTO CREDITS

HISPANIC AMERICANS

timeline

Everett Collection/Newscom

1942
The Bracero Program begins, allowing Mexican citizens to work temporarily in the U.S. as a source of low-cost labor. The program ends in 1964.

1953–1958
Operation Wetback results in the deportation of more than 3.8 million undocumented Mexicans.

DOL

1965
César Chávez and Dolores Huerta found the United Farm Workers association.

1910   1920   1930   1940   1950   1960   1970

1917
The Jones Act extends U.S. citizenship to Puerto Ricans.

1929
During the Great Depression, between 300,000 and 500,000 Mexicans and Mexican Americans are deported to Mexico.

1943
Los Angeles erupts in the Zoot Suit Riots. American sailors cruise Mexican American neighborhoods in search of "zoot-suiters," dragging kids out of movie theaters and cafes, tearing their clothes off and viciously beating them.

1966
The Cuban Refugee Act permits more than 400,000 people to enter the U.S.

1910
The Mexican Revolution begins; hundreds of thousands of Mexicans flee to the U.S.

LOC

LOC

Graham Avenue in [Brooklyn] was the broadest street I'd ever seen. . . . Most of these stores were . . . run by Jewish people [and there were special restaurants called delis where Jewish people ate]. . . . We didn't go into the delis because, Mami said, they didn't like Puerto Ricans in there. Instead, she took me to eat pizza.

"It's Italian," she said.

"Do Italians like Puerto Ricans?" I asked as I bit into hot cheese and tomato sauce that burned the tip of my tongue.

"They're more like us than Jewish people are," she said, which wasn't an answer.

In Puerto Rico the only foreigners I'd been aware of were Americanos. In two days in Brooklyn I had already encountered Jewish people, and now Italians. There was another group of people Mami had pointed out to me. Morenos [African Americans]. But they weren't foreigners, because they were American. They were black, but they didn't look like Puerto Rican negros. They dressed like Americanos but walked with a jaunty hop that made them look as if they were dancing down

LEARNING OBJECTIVES

By the end of this chapter, you will be able to do the following:

8.1 Summarize the population characteristics of all Hispanic Americans and the 10 largest Hispanic American groups.

8.2 Summarize and explain the history of Mexican Americans, including their cultural characteristics, their immigration patterns, changing U.S. policy and laws affecting them, their development in the United States, and their protest organizations and leaders.

8.3 Summarize and explain the history of Puerto Ricans, including their immigration patterns.

8.4 Summarize and explain the history of Cuban Americans, including their immigration patterns and the dynamics and importance of the Cuban American ethnic enclave.

8.5 Summarize how prejudice and discrimination affect Hispanic Americans.

8.6 Describe the situation of Hispanic Americans using the concepts of assimilation and pluralism, especially in terms of

a. acculturation,
b. secondary structural assimilation, and
c. primary structural assimilation

8.7 Assess the overall situation of Hispanic Americans today based on the concepts and information presented in this chapter, and assess the future of American society in terms of racial perceptions: Will the United States grow whiter or browner, or will a new racial order emerge?

1974
The Equal Educational Opportunity Act allows for bilingual education.

1994
California's Proposition 187 is approved by voters, preventing undocumented immigrants from obtaining public services. Proposition 187 is ruled unconstitutional in 1996.

2004
Hispanic Americans become the largest minority group.

2007
Massive demonstrations occur around the U.S. in support of immigrant rights.

1980
Approximately 125,000 Cubans immigrate to the U.S. during the Mariel boatlift.

2001
U.S. Senate considers the Development, Relief, and Education for Alien Minors Act, which would provide a legal path to citizenship for many undocumented immigrant minors who either attend college or serve in the military. The DREAM Act is later defeated.

2009
Sonia Sotomayor is sworn in as first Latina Justice of the U.S. Supreme Court.

2010
Arizona SB 1070 requires police to question people if there's reason to suspect they are in the U.S. illegally. Certain provisions of the law are later struck down by the Supreme Court.

1986
The Immigration Reform and Control Act creates process for undocumented immigrants to gain legal status and grants citizenship to about three million people.

the street, only their hips were not as loose as Puerto Rican men's were. According to Mami, they too lived in their own neighborhoods, frequented their own restaurants, and didn't like Puerto Ricans.

"How come?" I wondered, since in Puerto Rico, all of the people I'd ever met were either black or had a black relative somewhere in their family. I would have thought morenos *would like us, since so many of us looked like them.*

"They think we're taking their jobs."

"Are we?"

"There's enough work in the United States for everybody," Mami said.

—Esmeralda Santiago (1993, pp. 224–225)

Esmeralda Santiago (1993) moved from Puerto Rico to Brooklyn the summer before she began eighth grade. It was the 1950s, well before the surge of newcomers to the United States and New York City that began after the change in immigration policy in 1965. Still, she was overwhelmed with the variety of groups and cultures, cuisines, and languages she had to navigate. Like many Puerto Ricans who move to the mainland, she also had to deal with different ideas about the meaning of race and the importance of skin color.

Puerto Ricans have been U.S. citizens since 1917, but they live in a different cultural world. Just as Santiago was being changed by contact with U.S. culture, so have Puerto Rican and other Hispanic cultures been influenced. Now, as we shall see in this chapter, a variety of fast-growing and diverse Hispanic American groups are changing and altering Anglo lifestyles. What will American society look like a few decades from now? •

Hispanic Americans are 16.6% of the total population, which makes them the nation's largest minority group (African Americans are about 13% of the population). The group is concentrated in the West and South (particularly in California, Texas, and Florida)—where there have been large Hispanic American communities for many years—but is also growing rapidly in every region and state (Ennis, Rios-Vargas, & Albert, 2011, p. 6). Communities throughout the nation are, for the first time, hearing Spanish on their streets and finding "exotic" foods—tortillas, salsa, and refried beans—in their grocery stores. America is, once again, being reshaped and remade.

Of course, not all Hispanic American groups are newcomers. Some groups were in North America before the Declaration of Independence was signed, before slavery began,

and before Jamestown was founded. Also, Hispanic American groups are diverse and distinct from one another in many ways. These groups connect themselves to a variety of traditions; like the larger society, they are dynamic and changeable, unfinished and evolving. Hispanic Americans share a language and some cultural traits but do not generally think of themselves as a single social entity. Many identify with their national origin groups (e.g., Mexican American) rather than with broader, more encompassing labels.

In this chapter, we look at the development of Hispanic American groups over the past century, examine their contemporary relations with the larger society, and assess their current status. We focus on the three largest Hispanic groups: Mexican Americans, Puerto Ricans, and Cuban Americans. Other, smaller groups will be covered in more detail in Chapter 10.

Table 8.1 displays some information on the size and growth of Hispanic Americans and the 10 largest Latino groups as of 2012. Mexican Americans, the largest single group, are almost 11% of the total U.S. population (and almost two thirds of all Hispanic Americans), but the other groups are small in size. The relative sizes of the 10 largest Latino groups in the United States are displayed in Figure 8.1.

Latino groups are growing rapidly, partly because of their relatively high birthrates but mainly because of immigration. The number of Mexican Americans more than doubled between 1990 and 2012, and the Hispanic American population in general is growing almost twice as fast as the national average. This growth is projected to continue well into this century, and Hispanic Americans will become an increasingly important part of life in the United States. Today, 16.6 out of

FIGURE 8.1 Countries of Origin for Hispanic Population in the United States, 2012

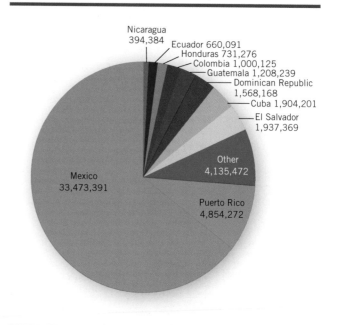

Nicaragua 394,384
Ecuador 660,091
Honduras 731,276
Colombia 1,000,125
Guatemala 1,208,239
Dominican Republic 1,568,168
Cuba 1,904,201
El Salvador 1,937,369
Other 4,135,472
Puerto Rico 4,854,272
Mexico 33,473,391

SOURCE: U.S. Census Bureau (2013a).

TABLE 8.1 Size and Growth of All Hispanic Americans and 10 Largest Groups by Origin, 1990–2012

COUNTRY OF ORIGIN	1990	2000	2012	GROWTH (NUMBER OF TIMES LARGER, 1990–2010)	PERCENTAGE OF TOTAL POPULATION, 2010
Total Hispanic American	22,355,990	35,305,818	51,866,988	2.3	16.6%
Mexico	13,496,000	20,640,711	33,473,391	2.5	10.8%
Puerto Rico*	2,728,000	3,406,178	4,854,272	1.8	1.6%
Cuba	1,044,000	1,241,685	1,904,201	1.8	< .1%
El Salvador	565,081	655,165	1,937,369	3.4	< .1%
Dominican Republic	520,521	764,945	1,568,168	3.0	< .1%
Guatemala	268,779	372,487	1,208,239	4.5	< .1%
Colombia	378,726	470,684	1,000,125	2.6	< .1%
Honduras	131,066	217,569	731,276	5.6	< .1%
Ecuador	191,198	260,559	660,091	3.5	< .1%
Nicaragua	202,658	177,684	394,384	1.9	< .1%
Percentage of U.S. Population	9.0%	12.5%	16.6%	—	—
Total U.S. Population	248,710,000	281,421,906	311,609,369	1.3	—

SOURCE: 1990—U.S. Census Bureau (1990); 2000—Ennis et al. (2011, p. 3); 2012—U.S. Census Bureau (2013a).

*Living on mainland only

every 100 Americans are Hispanic, but by 2050, this ratio is projected to almost double to more than 30 out of every 100 (see Figure 1.1). One result of these high rates of immigration is that the majority (in some cases, the great majority) of many Hispanic groups are first generation or foreign-born, as displayed in Figure 8.2.

It is appropriate to discuss Hispanic Americans at this point in the book because they include both colonized and immigrant groups, and, in that sense, combine elements of the polar extremes of Blauner's typology of minority groups. We would expect the Hispanic groups that were more colonized in the past to have much in common with African Americans and Native Americans today, and Hispanic groups whose experiences lie closer to the "immigrant" end of the continuum to have different characteristics and follow different pathways of adaptation. We test these ideas by reviewing the histories of the groups and by analyzing their current status and degree of acculturation and integration.

Two additional introductory comments can be made about Hispanic Americans:

• Hispanic Americans are partly an ethnic minority group (i.e., identified by cultural characteristics such as language) and partly a racial minority group (i.e., identified by their physical appearance). Latinos bring a variety of racial backgrounds to U.S. society. For example, Mexican Americans combine European and Native American ancestries and are

identifiable by their physical traits as well as by their culture and language. Puerto Ricans, in contrast, are a mixture of white and black ancestry, as illustrated by the excerpt from Santiago (1993) that opened this chapter. The original inhabitants of the island, the Arawak and Caribe tribes, were decimated by the Spanish conquest, and the proportion of Native American ancestry is much smaller in Puerto Rico than it is in Mexico. Africans were originally brought to the island as slaves, and there has been considerable intermarriage between whites and blacks. The Puerto Rican population today varies greatly in its racial characteristics, combining every conceivable combination of European and African ancestry. Hispanic Americans are often the victims of racial discrimination in the United States. Racial differences often (but not always) overlap with cultural distinctions and reinforce the separation of Hispanic Americans from Anglo-American society. Even members of the group who are completely acculturated may still experience discrimination based on their physical appearance.

• As is the case with all American minority groups, labels and group names are important. The term *Hispanic American* is widely applied to this group and might seem neutral and inoffensive to non-Hispanics. In fact, a recent survey shows that only about 25% of Hispanic Americans use *Hispanic* or *Latino* to describe themselves. Most (51%) identify themselves by their family's country of origin, and 21% think of themselves simply as "American" (Taylor, Lopez, Martinez, & Velasco, 2012, p. 9).

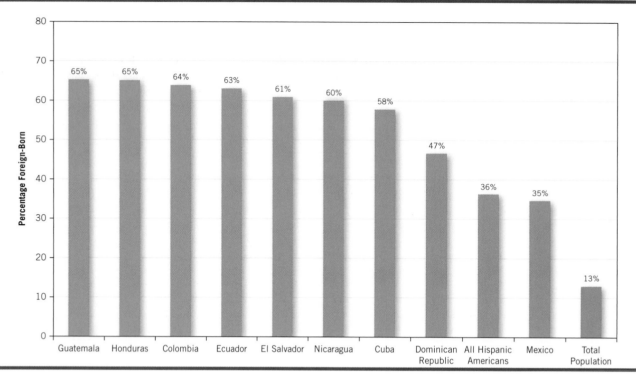

SOURCE: U.S. Census Bureau (2013a).

Further, the preferred identity varies widely by the primary language, generation, and education of the respondent. For example, almost two thirds of Spanish speakers and first-generation (foreign-born) Latinos prefer to identify themselves in terms of their countries of origin, while the "American" identity is most popular with the college-educated, the third and higher generations, and English speakers (Taylor et al., 2012, pp. 12–13). At any rate, both the *Hispanic* and *Latino* labels are similar to *American Indian*, in that they were invented and applied by the dominant group and may reinforce the mistaken perception that all Spanish-speaking peoples are the same. Also, the term *Hispanic* highlights Spanish heritage and language but does not acknowledge the roots of these groups in African and Native American civilizations. On the other hand, the *Latino* label stresses the common origins of these groups in Latin America and the fact that each culture is a unique blend of diverse traditions. Further, both labels are sometimes mistakenly applied to immigrant groups that bring French, Portuguese, or English traditions (e.g., Haitians, Brazilians, and Jamaicans, respectively). In this chapter, the terms *Latino* and *Hispanic* are used interchangeably.

MEXICAN AMERICANS

We applied the Noel and Blauner hypotheses to this group in Chapter 4. Mexicans were conquered and colonized in the 19th century and used as a cheap labor force in agriculture, ranching, mining, railroad construction, and other areas of the dominant-group economy in the Southwest. In the competition for control of land and labor, they became a minority group, and the contact situation left them with few power resources with which to pursue their self-interests.

By the dawn of the 20th century, the situation of Mexican Americans resembled that of American Indians in some ways. Both groups were small, numbering about 0.5% of the total population (Cortes, 1980, p. 702). Both differed from the dominant group in culture and language, and both were impoverished, relatively powerless, and isolated in rural areas distant from the centers of industrialization and modernization.

Mexican American beet workers.

In other ways, Mexican Americans resembled African Americans in the South: They, too, supplied much of the labor power for the agricultural economy of their region and were limited to low-paying occupations and subordinate status in the social structure. All three groups were colonized and, at least in the early decades of the 20th century, lacked the resources to end their exploitation and protect their cultural heritages from continual attack by the dominant society (Mirandé, 1985, p. 32).

There were also some important differences in the situations of Mexican Americans and the other two colonized minority groups. Perhaps the most crucial difference was the proximity of the sovereign nation of Mexico. Population movement across the border was constant, and Mexican culture and the Spanish language were continually rejuvenated, even as they were attacked and disparaged by Anglo-American society.

CULTURAL PATTERNS

Besides language differences, Mexican American and Anglo-American cultures differ in many ways. Whereas the dominant society is largely Protestant, the overwhelming majority of Mexican Americans are Catholic, and the church remains one of the most important institutions in any Mexican American community. Religious practices also vary; Mexican Americans (especially men) are relatively inactive in church attendance, preferring to express their spiritual concerns in more spontaneous, less routinized ways.

In the past, everyday life among Mexican Americans was often described in terms of the "culture of poverty" (see Chapter 6), an idea originally based on research in several different Hispanic communities (see Lewis, 1959, 1965, 1966). This perspective asserts that Mexican Americans suffer from an unhealthy value system that includes a weak work ethic, fatalism, and other negative attitudes. Today, this characterization is widely regarded as exaggerated or simply mistaken. More recent research shows that the traits associated with the culture of poverty tend to characterize people who are poor and uneducated, rather than any particular racial or ethnic group. In fact, a number of studies show that there is little difference between the value systems of Mexican Americans and other Americans with similar length of residence in the United States, social class, and educational background (e.g., see Buriel, 1993; Moore & Pinderhughes, 1993; Pew Hispanic Center, 2005, p. 20; Valentine & Mosley, 2000).

A recent survey illustrates the similarity in value systems. The survey found that Hispanic Americans were *more* supportive of "hard work" as a recipe for getting ahead—perhaps the central value in the American Creed—than was the population in general. About 75% of Hispanic Americans—versus only 58% of the general population—agreed that most people can "get ahead with hard work" (Taylor et al., 2012, pp. 18–19).

Another area of cultural difference involves **machismo**, a value system that stresses male dominance, honor, virility, and violence. The stereotypes of the dominant group exaggerate the negative aspects of machismo and often fail to recognize that it can also be expressed through being a good provider and a respected father, as well as in other nondestructive ways. In fact, the concern for male dignity is not unique to Hispanics and can be found in many cultures, including Anglo-American, in varying strengths and expressions. Thus, this difference is one of degree rather than kind (Moore & Pachon, 1985).

Compared with Anglo-Americans, Mexican Americans tend to place more value on family relations and obligations. Strong family ties can be the basis for support networks and cooperative efforts but can also conflict with the emphasis on individualism and individual success in the dominant culture. For example, strong family ties may inhibit geographical mobility and people's willingness to pursue educational and occupational opportunities distant from their home communities (Moore, 1970, p. 127).

These cultural and language differences have inhibited communication with the dominant group and have served as the basis for excluding Mexican Americans from the larger society. However, they also have provided a basis for group cohesion and unity that has sustained common action and protest activity.

IMMIGRATION

Although Mexican Americans originated as a colonized minority group, their situation since the early 1900s (and especially since the 1960s) has been largely shaped by immigration. The numbers of legal Mexican immigrants to the United

FIGURE 8.3 Legal Immigration From Mexico, 1905–2012

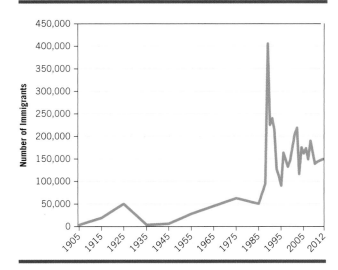

SOURCE: U.S. Department of Homeland Security (2012).

NOTES: 1. The very high number of "immigrants" in the late 1980s and early 1990s was the result of people already in the United States legalizing their status under the provisions of the Immigration Reform and Control Act.

2. Values are averages per year during each decade until 1989.

Machismo is a cultural value system that stresses male dominance and honor.

NARRATIVE PORTRAIT

The Meaning of Macho

Words as well as people can immigrate, and in both cases, the process can be transforming. In the following passage, Rose Del Castillo Guilbault (1993), a newspaper editor and columnist, reflects on the meaning of one term that has become central to the dominant group's view of Hispanic males. The image evoked by the term macho *changed from positive to negative as it found its way into American English, a process that reflects dominant–minority relations and partly defines them.*

AMERICANIZATION IS TOUGH ON "MACHO"

Rose Del Castillo Guilbault

What is *macho*? That depends on which side of the border you come from....

The Hispanic *macho* is manly, responsible, hardworking, a man in charge, a patriarch. A man who expresses strength through silence....

The American *macho* is a chauvinist, a brute, uncouth, loud, abrasive, capable of inflicting pain, and sexually promiscuous....

In Spanish, *macho* ennobles Latin males. In English it devalues them. This pattern seems consistent with the conflicts

ethnic minority males experience in this country. Typically the cultural traits other societies value don't translate as desirable characteristics in America.

I watched my own father struggle with these cultural ambiguities. He worked on a farm for 20 years. He laid down miles of irrigation pipe, carefully plowed long, neat rows in fields,...stoically worked twenty-hour days during the harvest season, accepting the long hours as part of agricultural work. When the boss complained or upbraided him for minor mistakes, he kept quiet, even when it was obvious that the boss had erred.

He handled the most menial tasks with pride. At home he was a good provider....

Americans regarded my father as decidedly un-*macho*. His character was interpreted as non-assertive....I once overheard the boss's son blame him for plowing crooked rows in a field. My father merely smiled at the lie, knowing the boy had done it....Seeing my embarrassment, my father dismissed the incident, saying, "They're the dumb ones. Imagine, me fighting with a kid."

I tried not to look at him with American eyes because sometimes the reflection hurt....

In the United States, I believe it was the feminist movement of the early '70s that changed macho's meaning. Perhaps my generation of Latin women was in part responsible. I recall Chicanas complaining about the chauvinistic nature of Latin men and the notion they wanted their women barefoot, pregnant, and in the kitchen. The generalization that Latin men embodied chauvinistic traits led to this...twist of semantics. Suddenly a word that represented something positive in one culture became a negative stereotype in another....

The impact of language in our society is undeniable. And the misuse of *macho* hints at a deeper cultural misunderstanding that extends beyond mere word definitions.

SOURCE: Guilbault (1993, pp. 163–165); *The San Francisco Chronicle,* August 20, 1989. Copyright © 1989. Reprinted with permission via Copyright Clearance Center.

Questions to Consider

1. How does this passage illustrate the cultural differences between Anglos and Mexican Americans?
2. What are the "deeper cultural misunderstandings" mentioned at the end of the passage?

States are shown in Figure 8.3. The fluctuations in the rate of immigration can be explained by conditions in Mexico; the varying demand for labor in the low-paying, unskilled sector of the U.S. economy; broad changes in North America and the world; and changing federal immigration policy. As you will see, competition, one of the key variables in Noel's hypothesis, has shaped the relationships between Mexican immigrants and the larger American society.

Push and Pull. Like the massive wave of immigrants from Europe that arrived between the 1820s and 1920s (see Chapter 2), Mexicans have been pushed from their homeland and toward the United States by a variety of sweeping changes, both domestic and global. European immigration was propelled by industrialization, urbanization, and rapid population growth. Mexican immigrants have been motivated by similarly broad forces, including continuing industrialization and globalization.

At the heart of the immigration lies a simple fact: The almost 2,000-mile-long border between Mexico and the United States is the longest continuous point of contact between a less developed and a more developed nation in the world. For the past century, the United States has developed faster than Mexico, moving from an industrial to a postindustrial society and sustaining a substantially higher standard of living. The continuing wage gap between the two nations has made even menial work in the North attractive to millions of Mexicans (and other Central and South Americans). Mexico has a large number of people who need work, and the United States offers jobs that pay more—often much more—than the wages available south of the border. Today, roughly 10% of the Mexican population lives in the United States. Just as the air flows from high to low pressure, people move from areas of lower to higher economic opportunities. The flow is not continuous, however, and has been affected by conditions in both the sending and receiving nations.

Conditions in Mexico, Fluctuating Demand for Labor, and Federal Immigration Policy. Generally, for the past 100 years, Mexico has served as a reserve pool of cheap labor for the benefit of U.S. businesses, agricultural interests, and other groups, and the volume of immigration largely reflects changing economic conditions in the United States. Immigration increases with good times in the United States and decreases when times are bad, a pattern reinforced by the policies and actions of the federal government. The most important events in the complex history of Mexican immigration to the United States are presented in Table 8.2, along with some comments regarding the nature of each event and its effects.

Prior to the early 1900s, the volume of immigration was generally low and largely unregulated. People crossed the border—in both directions—as the need arose, informally and without restriction. The volume of immigration and concern over controlling the border began to rise with the increase of political and economic turmoil in Mexico in the early decades of the 20th century, but still remained a comparative trickle.

Immigration increased in the 1920s when federal legislation curtailed the flow of cheap labor from Europe, and then decreased in the 1930s when hard times came to the United States (and the world) during the Great Depression. Many Mexicans in the United States returned home during that

Mexican American migrant workers in California, 1935.

decade, sometimes voluntarily, often by force. As competition for jobs increased, efforts to expel Mexican laborers began, just as the Noel hypothesis would predict.

TABLE 8.2 Significant Dates in Mexican Immigration

DATES	EVENT	RESULT	EFFECT ON IMMIGRATION FROM MEXICO
1910	Mexican Revolution	Political turmoil and unrest in Mexico.	Increased
Early 20th century	Mexican industrialization	Many groups (especially rural peasants) displaced.	Increased
1920s	National Origins Act of 1924	Decreased immigration from Europe.	Increased
1930s	Great Depression	Decreased demand for labor and increased competition for jobs lead to repatriation campaign.	Decreased; many return to Mexico
1940s	World War II	Increased demand for labor leads to Bracero Program.	Increased
1950s	Concern over illegal immigrants	Operation Wetback.	Decreased; many return to Mexico
1965	Repeal of National Origins Act	New immigration policy gives high priority to close family of citizens.	Increased (see Figure 8.3)
1986	Immigration Reform and Control Act	Undocumented immigrants given opportunity to legalize their status.	Many undocumented immigrants gain legal status (see Figure 8.3)
1994	North American Free Trade Agreement (NAFTA)	Borders more open; many groups in Mexico (especially rural peasants) displaced.	Increased
2007	Recession in the United States	Widespread unemployment in the United States; job supply shrinks.	Decreased

Mexican agricultural laborers admitted under the Bracero program parading in Stockton, California, with Mexican and U.S. flags, 1943.

The federal government instituted a **repatriation** campaign aimed specifically at deporting illegal Mexican immigrants. In many localities, repatriation was pursued with great zeal, and the campaign intimidated many legal immigrants and native-born Mexican Americans into moving to Mexico. The result was that the Mexican American population in the United States declined by an estimated 40% during the 1930s (Cortes, 1980, p. 711).

When the depression ended and U.S. society began to mobilize for World War II, federal policy about immigrants from Mexico changed once more as employers again turned to Mexico for workers. In 1942, the Bracero Program was initiated to permit contract laborers, usually employed in agriculture and other areas requiring unskilled labor, to work in the United States for a limited time. When their contracts expired, the workers were required to return to Mexico.

The Bracero Program continued for several decades after the war and was a crucial source of labor for the American economy. In 1960 alone, braceros supplied 26% of the nation's seasonal farm labor (Cortes, 1980, p. 703). The program generated millions of dollars of profit for growers and other employers because they were paying braceros much less than they would American workers (Amott & Matthaei, 1991, pp. 79–80).

At the same time the Bracero Program permitted immigration from Mexico, other programs and agencies worked to deport undocumented (or illegal) immigrants, large numbers of whom entered the United States with the braceros. Government efforts reached a peak in the early 1950s with **Operation Wetback**, a program under which federal authorities deported almost four million Mexicans (Grebler, Moore, & Guzman, 1970, p. 521).

During Operation Wetback, raids on Mexican American homes and places of business were common, and authorities often ignored their civil and legal rights. In an untold number of cases, U.S. citizens of Mexican descent were deported along with illegal immigrants. These violations of civil and legal rights have been a continuing grievance of Mexican Americans (and other Latinos) for decades (Mirandé, 1985, pp. 70–90).

In 1965, the overtly racist national immigration policy incorporated in the 1924 National Origins Act (see Chapter 2) was replaced by a new policy that gave a high priority to immigrants who were family and kin of U.S. citizens. The immediate family (parents, spouses, and children) of U.S. citizens could enter without numerical restriction. Some numerical restrictions were placed on the number of immigrants from each sending country, but about 80% of these restricted visas were reserved for other close relatives of citizens. The remaining 20% of the visas went to people who had skills needed in the labor force (Bouvier & Gardner, 1986, pp. 13–15, 41; Rumbaut, 1991, p. 215).

Immigrants have always tended to move along chains of kinship and other social relationships, and the new policy reinforced those tendencies. The social networks connecting Latin America with the United States expanded, and the rate of immigration from Mexico increased sharply after 1965 (see Figure 8.3) as immigrants became citizens and sent for other family members.

Most of the Mexican immigrants, legal as well as undocumented, who have arrived since 1965 continue the pattern of seeking work in the low-wage, unskilled sectors of the labor market in the cities and fields of the Southwest. For many, work is seasonal or temporary. When the work ends, they often return to Mexico, commuting across the border as they have done for decades.

In 1986, Congress attempted to deal with illegal immigrants, most of whom were thought to be Mexican, by passing the Immigration Reform and Control Act. This legislation allowed illegal immigrants who had been in the country continuously since 1982 to legalize their status. According to the U.S. Immigration and Naturalization Service (1993, p. 17), about 3 million people—75% of them Mexican—took advantage of this provision, but the program did not slow the volume of illegal immigration. In 1988, at the end of the amnesty application period, there were still almost 3 million undocumented immigrants in the United States. In 2011, the number of undocumented immigrants was estimated at 11.1 million, down from a high of 12 million in 2007 (Pew Hispanic Center, 2013, p. 2).

Recent Immigration From Mexico. Mexican immigration to the United States continues to reflect the differences in level of development and standard of living between the two societies. Mexico remains a more agricultural nation and continues to

---

Repatriation was a government-sponsored campaign during the 1930s to deport illegal immigrants back to Mexico.

Operation Wetback was a government-sponsored campaign during the 1950s to deport illegal immigrants from Mexico.

have a lower standard of living, as measured by average wages, housing quality, health care, or any number of other criteria. To illustrate, the gross national income per capita for Mexico in 2012 was $9,600, 70% higher than in 2002 but still only about a fifth of the comparable figure for the United States. About half of the Mexican population lives in poverty (World Bank, 2013). Opportunities for work are scarce, and many Mexicans are drawn to the opportunities of their affluent northern neighbor. Since the average length of schooling in their homeland is only about 8.5 years, Mexican immigrants bring much lower levels of job skills and compete for work in the lower levels of the U.S. job structure (United Nations Development Programme, 2013).

The impetus to immigrate was reinforced by the globalization of the Mexican economy. In the past, the Mexican government insulated its economy from foreign competition with a variety of tariffs and barriers. These protections have been abandoned over the past several decades, and Mexico, like many less developed nations, has opened its doors to the world economy. The result has been a flood of foreign agricultural products (cheap corn in particular), manufactured goods, and capital, which, while helpful in some parts of the economy, has disrupted social life and forced many Mexicans, especially the poor and rural dwellers, out of their traditional way of life.

Probably the most significant changes to Mexican society have come from the 1994 North American Free Trade Agreement, or NAFTA. As we discussed in Chapter 1, this policy united the three nations of North America into a single trading zone. U.S. companies began to move their manufacturing operations to Mexico, attracted by lower wages, less stringent environmental regulations, and weak labor unions. They built factories (called *maquiladoras*) along the border and brought many new jobs to the Mexican economy. However, other jobs—no longer protected from global competition—were lost, more than offsetting these gains. Mexican wages actually declined after the implementation of NAFTA, increasing the already large number of Mexicans living in poverty. One analyst estimates that more than 2.5 million families have been driven out of the rural economy because they cannot compete with U.S. and Canadian agribusinesses (Faux, 2004).

Thus, globalization in general and NAFTA in particular have reinforced the long-term relationship between the two nations. Mexico, like other nations of the less developed "South," continues to produce a supply of unskilled, less educated workers, while the United States, like other nations of the more developed and industrialized "North," provides a seemingly insatiable demand for cheap labor. Compared with what is available at home, the wages in *el Norte* are quite attractive, even when the jobs are at the margins of the mainstream economy or in the irregular, underground economy (e.g., day laborers paid off the books, illegal sweatshops in the garment industry, and sex work), and even when the journey requires Mexican immigrants to break American laws, pay large sums of money to "coyotes" to guide them across the border, and live in constant fear of raids by

A maquiladora near the U.S.–Mexican border.

La Migra. Figure 8.4 shows the dramatic increase in immigration in the 1990s that resulted from NAFTA.

The movement of people from Mexico that began in the 1960s and accelerated in the 1990s was the largest immigration from a single nation to the United States in history (Passel et al., 2012, p. 6). Some 12 million people, about 51% unauthorized, crossed the border in this period.

More recently, the historic trend has reversed. As Figure 8.4 shows, immigration from Mexico has declined dramatically since 2005. The decline is due to multiple factors, including enhanced border enforcement efforts, the growing dangers of crossing illegally (recall the story of Lucresia that opened Chapter 1), and Mexico's declining birthrate (Passel et al., 2013, p. 6). Perhaps most central to the declining numbers is

FIGURE 8.4 Legal and Unauthorized Immigration From Mexico to the United States, 1991–2010

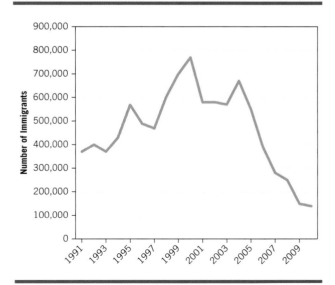

SOURCE: Passel, Cohn, and Gonzalez-Barrera (2012, p. 45).

the U.S. economic recession and the weak job market. The "pull" that attracted immigrants in the past weakened considerably, particularly after the collapse of the housing market in 2007. This relationship suggests that immigration may resume as the U.S. economy recovers.

The Continuing Debate Over Immigration Policy. Immigration has once again become a hotly debated issue in the United States. How many immigrants should be admitted? From which nations? With what skills? Should the relatives of U.S. citizens continue to receive a high priority? And perhaps the issue that generates the most passion: What should be done about unauthorized immigrants? Virtually all these questions—even those phrased in general, abstract terms—are mainly about the large volume of immigration from Mexico and the porous U.S. southern border.

The federal government continues its attempt to reduce the flow by extending the wall along the border with Mexico and beefing up the Border Patrol, with both increased personnel and more high-tech surveillance technology. Still, as we have seen, communities across the nation—not just in the southern border states—are feeling the impact of Mexican immigration and wondering how to respond. Many citizens support extreme measures to close the borders—bigger, thicker walls and even the use of deadly force—while others ponder ways to absorb the newcomers without disrupting or bankrupting local school systems, medical facilities, or housing markets.

The nation is divided on many of the issues related to immigration. Public opinion polls over the past decade show that about 40% to 50% of all Americans would like to lower the volume of immigration but that an almost equal percentage (30–40%) favor keeping the present level (Morales, 2010). Figure 8.5 shows that—perhaps surprisingly—there has been persistent support for immigration over the past decade, and

the perception that immigration is a "good thing" has increased in the most recent years.

A variety of immigration reforms have been proposed and continue to be debated. One key issue is the treatment of illegal immigrants: Should the undocumented be summarily deported, or should some provision be made for them to legalize their status, as was done in the Immigration Reform and Control Act of 1986? If the latter, should the opportunity to attain legal status be extended to all or only to immigrants who meet certain criteria (e.g., those with steady jobs and clean criminal records)? Many feel that amnesty is unjust because immigrants who entered illegally have, after all, broken the law and should be punished. Others point to the economic contributions of these immigrants and the damage to the economy that would result from summary, mass expulsions. Still others worry about the negative impact illegal immigrants might be having on job prospects for the less skilled members of the larger population, including the urban underclass that is disproportionately populated by minority-group members. We address some of these issues later in this chapter and in Chapters 9 and 10.

Immigration, Colonization, and Intergroup Competition. Three points can be made about Mexican immigration to the United States. First, the flow of population from Mexico was and is stimulated and sustained by powerful political and economic interests in the United States. Systems of recruitment and networks of communication and transportation have been established to routinize the flow of people and make it a predictable source of labor for the benefit of U.S. agriculture and other employers. The movement of people back and forth across the border was well established long before current efforts to regulate and control it. Depending on U.S. policy, this immigration is sometimes legal and encouraged and sometimes illegal and discouraged. Regardless of the label, the river of people has been steadily flowing for decades in response to opportunities for work in the North (Portes, 1990, pp. 160–163).

Second, Mexican immigrants enter a social system in which a colonized status for the group already has been established. The paternalistic traditions and racist systems that were formed in the 19th century shaped the positions that were open to Mexican immigrants in the 20th century. Mexican Americans continued to be treated as a colonized group despite the streams of new arrivals, and the history of the group in the 20th century has many parallels with those of African Americans and American Indians. Thus, Mexican Americans might be thought of as a colonized minority group that happens to have a large number of immigrants or, alternatively, as an immigrant group that incorporates a strong tradition of colonization.

Third, this brief review of the twisting history of U.S. policy on Mexican immigration should serve as a reminder that levels of prejudice, racism, and discrimination increase as competition and the sense of threat between groups increases. The very qualities that make Mexican labor attractive to employers

FIGURE 8.5 Attitudes of U.S. Adults Toward Immigration, 2001–2013

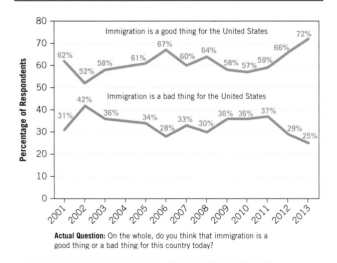

Actual Question: On the whole, do you think that immigration is a good thing or a bad thing for this country today?

SOURCE: Saad (2013).

An Immigrant's Tale

The stories of Delfino and Florentino represent the experiences of thousands of immigrants—legal as well as undocumented—who have crossed the border into the United States over the past century. Driven by the poverty of their home villages and attracted by the allure of work in el Norte, they often risk their lives to cross the border in pursuit of the dream of earning a decent wage. Many remain focused on the families they left behind. They send millions of dollars home and are the main—or even the sole—support for their kin, the hope and lifeblood for perhaps scores of relatives.

DELFINO'S DREAM

Sam Quinones

By early 2004, Delfino [who had left his Mexican village home years before and crossed the U.S. border illegally] had phony papers, a car, a shared house, a job, some English. It was then that his attention turned to other things. Back in Mexico, his family's 8-by-12-foot shack had been the most visible sign of its... low social standing. The shack had dirt floors, leaked rain, and left them unprotected from the cold. A girl's family once refused Florentino's [Delfino's brother] marriage proposal because that shack was all he could offer her.

Delfino began sending extra money home every month.... In the middle of 2004, the family moved its shack to one side—it took only a few men to lift it. On the site where the shack once stood, Delfino built the first house in his village ever paid for with dollars. It... had an indoor toilet, a kitchen, and concrete floors. The house was fronted by two smoked-glass windows so wide and tall that it looked as if the house wore sunglasses.

"I wanted it to look good when you pass," Delfino said, "and to have a nice view."

In Xocotla, nothing like it had ever been built so quickly by a youth so poor.

A few months later, Florentino [also in the United States illegally] arranged... to have a house built in the village [for himself]. All this helped change their father [Lázaro]. He had stopped drinking and discovered Alcoholics Anonymous. He was now in his 40s and tired of waking up in the pig muck.... His sons could now send him money for construction materials and know he wouldn't spend it on booze. So within a year of Delfino's arrival in the United States, Lázaro was not only sober but supervising construction of first Delfino's house, and then Florentino's....

Lázaro had never been the object of anyone's envy. He found that he liked it. He kept building those houses, telling everyone that he'd build until his sons in America told him to stop.

For a time, the Juárez brothers were the village's largest employers—spending close to 40 thousand dollars on labor and supplies. As Florentino's house went up, the family of the girl who'd refused his marriage proposal let it be known that they regretted their decision. When Delfino returned to Xocotla for a few months in late 2004, older men, who'd once laughed at his Mohawked hair, came to him to borrow money.

"Now everyone says hello," said Delfino.

SOURCE: Quinones (2007, pp. 284–286). Reprinted with permission from *Antonio's Gun and Delfino's Dream: True Tales of Mexican Migration* by Sam Quinones. Copyright © 2007 University of New Mexico Press.

Questions to Consider

1. Are the Juárez brothers living embodiments of the American Dream? Or are they criminals and fugitives who should be apprehended and deported?
2. What might happen to villages like Xocotla if immigrants like the Juárez brothers stop sending money? Should U.S. citizens be concerned with the fate of places like Xocotla? Why or why not?

---

have caused bitter resentment among those segments of the Anglo population who feel that their own jobs and financial security are threatened. Often caught in the middle, Mexican immigrants and Mexican Americans have not had the resources to avoid exploitation by employers or rejection and discrimination by others. The ebb and flow of the efforts to regulate immigration (and sometimes even deport U.S. citizens of Mexican descent) can be understood in terms of competition, differentials in power, and prejudice.

QUESTIONS FOR REFLECTION

1. How do Mexican American and Anglo cultures vary? How have these differences shaped relations between the groups?

2. Why has the volume of immigration from Mexico to the United States fluctuated?

DEVELOPMENTS IN THE UNITED STATES

As the flow of immigration from Mexico fluctuated with the need for labor, Mexican Americans struggled to improve their status. In the early decades of the 20th century, like other colonized minority groups, they faced a system of repression and control in which they were accorded few rights and had little political power.

Continuing Colonization. Early in the 20th century, Mexican Americans were largely limited to less desirable, low-wage jobs. Split labor markets, in which Mexican Americans are paid less than Anglos for the same jobs, have been common. The workforce often has been further split by gender, with Mexican American women assigned to the worst jobs and receiving the lowest wages in both urban and rural areas (Takaki, 1993, pp. 318–319).

Men's jobs often took them away from their families to work in the mines and fields. In 1930, 45% of all Mexican American men worked in agriculture, with another 28% in unskilled nonagricultural jobs (Cortes, 1980, p. 708). The women were often forced by economic necessity to enter the job market; in 1930, they were concentrated in farm work (21%), unskilled manufacturing jobs (25%), and domestic and other service work (37%) (Amott & Matthaei, 1991, pp. 76–77). They were typically paid less than both Mexican American men and Anglo women. In addition to their job responsibilities, Mexican American women had to maintain their households and raise their children, often facing these tasks without a spouse (Baca Zinn & Eitzen, 1990, p. 84).

As the United States industrialized and urbanized during the century, employment patterns became more diversified. Mexican Americans found work in manufacturing, construction, transportation, and other sectors of the economy. Some Mexican Americans, especially those of the third generation or later, moved into middle- and upper-level occupations, and some began to move out of the Southwest. Still, Mexican Americans in all regions (especially recent immigrants) tended to be concentrated at the bottom of the occupational ladder. Women increasingly worked outside the home, but their employment was largely limited to agriculture, domestic service, and the garment industry (Amott & Matthaei, 1991, pp. 76–79; Cortes, 1980, p. 708).

Like African Americans in the segregated South, Mexican Americans were excluded from the institutions of the larger society by law and by custom for much of the 20th century. There were separate (and unequal) school systems for Mexican American children, and in many communities, Mexican Americans were disenfranchised and accorded few legal or civil rights. There were "whites-only" primary elections modeled after the Jim Crow system, and residential segregation was widespread. The police and the court system generally abetted or ignored the rampant discrimination against the Mexican American community. Discrimination in the criminal justice system and civil rights violations have been continual grievances of Mexican Americans throughout the century.

Protest and Resistance. Like all minority groups, Mexican Americans have attempted to improve their collective position whenever possible. The beginnings of organized resistance and protest stretch back to the original contact period in the 19th century, when protest was usually organized on a local level. Regional and national organizations made their appearance in the 20th century (Cortes, 1980, p. 709).

Chicanismo was an ideology of the Mexican American protest movement that rose to prominence in the 1960s. It expressed militancy, impatience with injustice, and a number of pluralistic themes.

As with African Americans, Mexican Americans' early protest organizations were integrationist and reflected the assimilationist values of the larger society. For example, one of the earlier and more significant groups was the League of United Latin American Citizens (LULAC), founded in Texas in 1929. LULAC promoted Americanization and greater educational opportunities for Mexican Americans. The group also worked to expand civil and political rights and to increase equality for Mexican Americans. LULAC fought numerous court battles against discrimination and racial segregation (Moore, 1970, pp. 143–145).

The workplace has been a particularly conflictual arena for Mexican Americans. Split labor market situations increased anti–Mexican American prejudice; some labor unions tried to exclude Mexican immigrants to the United States, along with immigrants from Asia and southern and eastern Europe (Grebler et al., 1970, pp. 90–93).

At the same time, Mexican Americans played important leadership roles in the labor movement. Since early in the century, Mexican Americans have been involved in union organizing, particularly in agriculture and mining. When excluded by Anglo labor unions, they often formed their own unions to work for the improvement of working conditions. As the 20th century progressed, the number and variety of groups pursuing the Mexican American cause increased. During World War II, Mexican Americans served in the armed forces, and, as with other minority groups, this experience increased their impatience with the constraints on their freedoms and opportunities. After the war ended, a number of new Mexican American organizations were founded, including the Community Service Organization in Los Angeles and the American GI Forum in Texas. Compared with older organizations such as LULAC, the new groups were less concerned with assimilation per se, addressed a broad range of community problems, and attempted to increase Mexican American political power (Grebler et al., 1970, pp. 543–545).

Chicanismo. The 1960s were a time of intense activism and militancy for Mexican Americans. A protest movement guided by an ideology called **Chicanismo** began at about the same time as the Black Power and Red Power movements. Chicanismo encompassed a variety of organizations and ideas, united by a heightened militancy and impatience with the racism of the larger society, and strongly stated demands for justice, fairness, and equal rights. The movement questioned the value of assimilation and sought to increase awareness of the continuing exploitation of Mexican Americans; it adapted many of the tactics and strategies (marches, rallies, voter registration drives, etc.) of the civil rights movement of the 1960s.

Chicanismo is similar in some ways to the Black Power ideology (see Chapter 6). It is partly a reaction to the failure of U.S. society to implement the promises of integration and equality. It rejected traditional stereotypes of Mexican Americans, proclaimed a powerful and positive group image and heritage, and analyzed the group's past and present situation in American society in terms of victimization, continuing exploitation, and institutional discrimination. The inequalities that separated Mexican Americans from the larger society were seen as the result of deep-rooted, continuing racism and the cumulative effects of decades of exclusion. According to Chicanismo, the solution to these problems lay in group empowerment, increased militancy, and group pride, not in assimilation to a culture that had rationalized and abetted the exploitation of Mexican Americans (Acuña, 1988, pp. 307–358; Grebler et al., 1970, p. 544; Moore, 1970, pp. 149–154).

Some of the central thrusts of the 1960s protest movement are captured in the widespread adoption of **Chicanos**, which had been a derogatory term, as a group name for Mexican Americans. Other minority groups underwent similar name changes at about the same time. For example, African Americans shifted from *Negro* to *black* as a group designation. These name changes were not merely cosmetic; they marked fundamental shifts in group goals and desired relationships with the larger society. The new names came from the minority groups themselves, not from the dominant group, and they expressed the pluralistic themes of group pride, self-determination, militancy, and increased resistance to exploitation and discrimination.

Organizations and Leaders. The Chicano movement saw the rise of many new groups and leaders, one of the most important of which was Reies López Tijerina, who formed the Alianza de Mercedes (Alliance of Land Grants) in 1963. The goal of this group was to correct what Tijerina saw as the unjust and illegal seizure of land from Mexicans during the 19th century. The Alianza was militant and confrontational, and to bring attention to their cause, members of the group seized and occupied federal lands. Tijerina spent several years in jail as a result of his activities, and the movement eventually lost its strength and faded from view in the 1970s.

Another prominent Chicano leader was Rodolfo Gonzalez, who founded the Crusade for Justice in 1965. The crusade focused on abuses of Mexican American civil and legal rights, and worked against discrimination by police and the criminal courts. In a 1969 presentation at a symposium on Chicano liberation, Gonzalez expressed some of the nationalistic themes of Chicanismo and the importance of creating a power base within the group (as opposed to assimilating or integrating):

> Where [whites] have incorporated themselves to keep us from moving into their neighborhoods, we can also incorporate ourselves to keep them from controlling our neighborhoods. We ... have to understand economic revolution. ... We have to understand that liberation comes from self-determination, and to start to use the tools of nationalism to win over our barrio brothers. ... We have to understand that we can take over the institutions within our community. We have to create the community of the

César Chávez, founder of the United Farm Workers and leader of the grape boycott.

Wikimedia Commons/Joel Levine

> Mexicano here in order to have any type of power. (Moquin & Van Doren, 1971, pp. 381–382)

A third important leader was José Angel Gutiérrez, organizer of the party La Raza Unida (The People United). La Raza Unida offered alternative candidates and ideas to those of Democrats and Republicans. Its most notable success was in Crystal City, Texas, where, in 1973, it succeeded in electing its entire slate of candidates to local office (Acuña, 1988, pp. 332–451).

Without a doubt, the best-known Chicano leader of the 1960s and 1970s was the late César Chávez, who organized the United Farm Workers, the first union to successfully represent migrant workers. Chávez was as much a labor leader as a leader of the Mexican American community, and he also organized African Americans, Filipinos, and Anglo-Americans. Migrant farmworkers have few economic or political resources, and the migratory nature of their work isolates them in rural areas and

Chicanos is a group name for Mexican Americans that is associated with the ideology of Chicanismo.

CHAPTER 8 • HISPANIC AMERICANS 227

makes them difficult to contact. In the 1960s (and still today), many were undocumented immigrants who spoke little or no English and returned to the cities or to their countries of origin at the end of the season. As a group, farmworkers were nearly invisible in the social landscape of the United States in the 1960s, and organizing this group was a demanding task. Chávez's success in this endeavor is one of the more remarkable studies in group protest.

Like Dr. Martin Luther King Jr., Chávez was a disciple of Gandhi and a student of nonviolent direct protest (see Chapter 6). His best-known tactic was the boycott; in 1965, he organized a grape-pickers' strike and a national boycott of grapes. The boycott lasted five years and ended when the growers recognized the United Farm Workers as the legitimate representative of farmworkers. Chávez and his organization achieved a major victory, and the agreement provided for significant improvements in the situation of the workers (for a biography of Chávez, see Levy, 1975).

Gender and the Chicano Protest Movement. Mexican American women were heavily involved in the Chicano protest movement. Jessie Lopez and Dolores Huerta were central figures in the movement to organize farmworkers and worked closely with César Chávez. However, as was the case for African American women, Chicano women encountered sexism and gender discrimination within the movement even as they worked for the benefit of the group as a whole. Their dilemmas are described by activist Sylvia Gonzales:

> Along with her male counterpart, she attended meetings, organized boycotts, did everything asked of her. . . . But, if she [tried to assume leadership roles], she was met with the same questioning of her femininity which the culture dictates when a woman is not self-sacrificing and seeks to fulfill her own needs. . . . The Chicano movement seemed to demand self-actualization for only the male members of the group. (Amott & Matthaei, 1991, p. 83)

Despite these difficulties, Chicano women contributed to the movement in a variety of areas. They helped organize poor communities and worked for welfare reform. Continuing issues include domestic violence, child care, the criminal victimization of women, and the racial and gender oppression that limits women of all minority groups (Amott & Matthaei, 1991, pp. 82–86; see also Mirandé & Enríquez, 1979, pp. 202–243).

MEXICAN AMERICANS AND OTHER MINORITY GROUPS

Like the Black Power and Red Power movements, Chicanismo began to fade from public view in the 1970s and 1980s. The movement could claim some successes, but perhaps the clearest victory was in raising the awareness of the larger society about

Mexican workers cultivating lettuce, 2013. Agricultural labor remains a primary draw for migrant laborers.

the grievances and problems of Mexican Americans. Today, many Chicanos continue to face poverty and powerlessness, and exploitation as a cheap agricultural labor force. The less educated, urbanized segments of the group share the prospect of becoming a permanent urban underclass with other minority groups of color.

Over the course of the 20th century, the ability of Chicanos to pursue their self-interests has been limited by both internal and external forces. Like African Americans, the group has been systematically excluded from the institutions of the larger society. Continuing immigration from Mexico has increased the size of the group, but these immigrants bring few resources with them that could be directly or immediately translated into economic or political power in the United States.

Unlike immigrants from Europe, who settled in the urban centers of the industrializing East Coast, Mexican Americans tended to work and live in rural areas distant from and marginal to urban centers of industrialization and opportunities for education, skill development, and upward mobility. They were a vitally important source of labor in agriculture and other segments of the economy but only to the extent that they were exploitable and powerless. As Chicanos moved to the cities, they tended to continue their historic role as a colonized, exploited labor force concentrated at the lower end of the stratification system. Thus, the handicaps created by discrimination in the past were reinforced by continuing discrimination and exploitation in the present, perpetuating the cycles of poverty and powerlessness.

At the same time, however, the flow of immigration and the constant movement of people back and forth across the border kept Mexican culture and the Spanish language alive. Unlike African Americans under slavery, Chicanos were not cut off from their homeland and native culture. Mexican American culture was attacked and disparaged, but, unlike African culture, it was not destroyed.

Clearly, the traditional model of assimilation—which was based largely on the experiences of European immigrant groups—does not effectively describe the experiences of Mexican Americans. They have experienced less social mobility than European immigrant groups but have maintained their traditional culture and language more completely. Like African Americans, the group is split along lines of social class. Although many Mexican Americans (particularly of the third generation and later) have acculturated and integrated, a large segment of the group continues to fill the same economic role as their ancestors did: an unskilled labor force for the development of the Southwest, augmented with new immigrants at the convenience of U.S. employers. In 2010, more than 16% of employed Mexican Americans—more than double the percentage for non-Hispanic whites—were in the construction and farm sectors of the labor force (U.S. Census Bureau, 2013a). For the less educated and for recent immigrants, cultural and racial differences combine to increase their social visibility, mark them for exploitation, and rationalize their continuing exclusion from the larger society.

QUESTIONS FOR REFLECTION

1. Are Mexican Americans a colonized or immigrant minority group? Both? Neither? Why?

2. Compare Chicanismo with Black and Red Power. How and why do these protest movements differ? Describe the key ideas, leaders, and organizations of Mexican American protest.

PUERTO RICANS

Puerto Rico became a territory of the United States in 1898, after the defeat of Spain in the Spanish–American War. The island was small and impoverished, and it was difficult for Puerto Ricans to avoid domination by the United States. Thus, the initial contact between Puerto Ricans and U.S. society was made in an atmosphere of war and conquest. By the time Puerto Ricans began to migrate to the mainland in large numbers, their relationship to U.S. society was largely that of a colonized minority group, and they generally retained that status on the mainland.

MIGRATION (PUSH AND PULL) AND EMPLOYMENT

At the time of initial contact, the population of Puerto Rico was overwhelmingly rural and supported itself with subsistence farming and by exporting coffee and sugar. As the century wore on, U.S. firms began to invest in and develop the island economy, especially the sugarcane industry. These agricultural endeavors took more and more of the land. Opportunities for economic survival in the rural areas declined, and many peasants were forced to move into the cities (Portes, 1990, p. 163).

Movement to the mainland began gradually and increased slowly until the 1940s. In 1900, about 2,000 Puerto Ricans were living on the mainland. By the eve of World War II, this number had grown to only 70,000, a tiny fraction of the total population. Then, during the 1940s, the number of Puerto Ricans on the mainland increased more than fourfold, to 300,000, and during the 1950s, it nearly tripled, to 887,000 (U.S. Commission on Civil Rights, 1976, p. 19).

This massive and sudden population growth was the result of a combination of circumstances. First, Puerto Ricans became citizens of the United States in 1917; so their movements were not impeded by international boundaries or immigration restrictions. Second, unemployment was a major problem on the island. The sugarcane industry continued to displace the rural population, urban unemployment was high, and the population continued to grow. By the 1940s, a considerable number of Puerto Ricans were available to seek work off the island and, like Chicanos, could serve as a cheap labor supply for U.S. employers.

Third, Puerto Ricans were pulled to the mainland by the same labor shortages that attracted Mexican immigrants during and after World War II. Whereas the latter responded to job opportunities in the West and Southwest, Puerto Ricans moved to the Northeast. The job profiles of these two groups were similar: Both were concentrated in the low-wage, unskilled sector of the job market. However, the Puerto Rican migration began many decades after the Mexican migration, at a time when the United States was much more industrialized and urbanized. As a result, Puerto Ricans were more concentrated in urban labor markets than were Mexican immigrants (Portes, 1990, p. 164).

Movement between the island and the mainland was facilitated by the commencement of affordable air travel between San Juan and New York City in the late 1940s. New York had been the major center of settlement for Puerto Ricans on the mainland even before annexation. A small Puerto Rican community had been established in the city, and as with many groups, organizations and networks were established to ease the transition and help newcomers with housing, jobs, and other issues. Although they eventually dispersed to other regions and cities, Puerto Ricans on the mainland remain centered in New York City. About 53% now reside in the Northeast, with 23% in New York alone (Brown & Patten, 2013d, p. 2).

Economics and jobs were at the heart of the move to the mainland. The rate of Puerto Rican migration has followed the cycle of boom and bust, just as the rate for Mexican immigrants has. The 1950s, the peak decade for Puerto Rican migration, was a period of rapid U.S. economic growth. Migration was encouraged, and job recruiters traveled to the island to attract workers. By the 1960s, however, the supply of jobs on the island had expanded appreciably, and the average number of migrants declined from the peak of 41,000 per year in the 1950s to about 20,000 per year. In the 1970s, the U.S. economy faltered, unemployment grew, and the flow of Puerto Rican migration actually reversed itself, with the number of returnees exceeding the number of migrants in various years (U.S. Commission on Civil Rights, 1976, p. 25). However, movement to the mainland has continued, and in 2011 almost five million Puerto Ricans, about 57% of all Puerto Ricans, were living on the mainland (Brown & Patten, 2013d, p. 1).

As the U.S. economy expanded and migration accelerated after World War II, Puerto Ricans moved into a broad range of jobs and locations in society, and the group grew more economically diversified and more regionally dispersed. Still, the bulk of the group remains concentrated in lower-status jobs in the larger cities of the Northeast. Puerto Rican men have often found work as unskilled laborers or in service occupations, particularly in areas where English language facility is not necessary (e.g., janitorial work). The women often have been employed as domestics, hotel maids, or seamstresses for the garment industry in New York City (Portes, 1990, p. 164).

TRANSITIONS

Although Puerto Ricans are not "immigrants," the move to the mainland does involve a change in culture and language (Fitzpatrick, 1980, p. 858). Despite nearly a century of political affiliation, Puerto Rican and Anglo cultures differ along many dimensions. Puerto Ricans are overwhelmingly Catholic, but the religious practices and rituals on the mainland are quite different from those on the island. Mainland Catholic parishes often reflect the traditions and practices of other cultures and groups. On the island, "Religious observance reflects the spontaneous and expressive practices of the Spanish and the Italian and not the restrained and well-organized worship of the Irish and Germans" (p. 865). Also, there has been a shortage of Puerto Rican priests and Spanish-speaking clergy on the mainland; thus, members of the group often feel estranged from and poorly served by the church (Fitzpatrick, 1987, pp. 117–138). Although the overwhelming majority of Latinos are Catholic, only about 6% of Catholic priests are Latinos (Olivo & Eldeib, 2013).

A particularly unsettling cultural difference between the island and the mainland involves skin color and perceptions of race. Puerto Rico has a long history of racial intermarriage. Slavery was less monolithic and total, and the island had no periods of systematic, race-based segregation like the Jim Crow system. Thus, although skin color prejudice still exists in Puerto Rico, it has never been as categorical as on the mainland. On the island, race is perceived as a continuum of possibilities and combinations, not as a simple dichotomous split between white and black.

Furthermore, in Puerto Rico, other factors such as social class are considered to be more important than race as criteria for judging and classifying others. In fact, as we discussed in the Chapter 6 Comparative Focus, social class can affect perceptions of skin color, and people of higher status might be seen as lighter skinned. Coming from this background, Puerto Ricans find the rigid racial thinking of U.S. culture disconcerting and even threatening.

The confusion and discomfort that can result was documented and illustrated by a study of Puerto Rican college students in New York City. Dramatic differences were found between the personal racial identification of the students and their perceptions of how Anglos viewed them. When asked for their racial identification, most of the students classified themselves as "tan," with one third labeling themselves "white" and only 7% considering themselves "black." When asked how they thought they were racially classified by Anglos, however, none of the students used the "tan" classification: 58% felt that they were seen as "white," and 41% felt that they were seen as "black" (Rodriguez, 1989, pp. 60–61; see also Rodriguez & Cordero-Guzman, 1992; Vargas-Ramos, 2005).

Another study documented dramatic differences in the terms used by women on the mainland and those in Puerto Rico to express racial identity. The latter identified their racial identities primarily in terms of skin color: black, white, or *trigueña* (a "mixed-race" category with multiple skin tones), while mainland women identified themselves in nonracial terms, such as Hispanic, Latina, Hispanic American, or American. In the view of the researchers, these labels serve to deflect the stigma associated with black racial status in the United States (Landale & Oropesa, 2002; see also Vargas-Ramos, 2012).

In the racially dichotomized U.S. culture, many Puerto Ricans feel that they have no clear place. They are genuinely puzzled when they first encounter prejudice and discrimination based on skin color, and are uncertain about their own identities and self-image. The racial perceptions of the dominant culture can be threatening to Puerto Ricans to the extent that they are victimized by the same web of discrimination and disadvantage that affects African Americans. There are still clear disadvantages to being classified as black in U.S. society. Institutionalized racial barriers can be extremely formidable, and in the case of Puerto Ricans, they may combine with cultural and linguistic differences to sharply limit opportunities and mobility.

PUERTO RICANS AND OTHER MINORITY GROUPS

Puerto Ricans arrived in the cities of the Northeast long after the great wave of European immigrants and several decades after African Americans began migrating from the South. They have often competed with other minority groups for housing, jobs, and other resources. In some neighborhoods and occupational areas, a pattern of ethnic succession can be seen in which Puerto Ricans have replaced other groups that have moved out (and sometimes up).

Because of their more recent arrival, Puerto Ricans on the mainland were not subjected to the more repressive paternalistic or rigid competitive systems of race relations such as slavery or Jim Crow. Instead, the subordinate status of the group is manifested in their occupational, residential, and educational profiles, and by the institutionalized barriers to upward mobility that they face. Puerto Ricans share many problems with other urban minority groups of color: poverty, failing educational systems, and crime. Like African Americans, Puerto Ricans find their fate to be dependent on the future of the American city, and a large segment of the group is in danger of becoming part of a permanent urban underclass.

Like Mexican Americans, Puerto Ricans on the mainland combine elements of both an immigrant and a colonized minority experience. The movement to the mainland is voluntary in some ways, but in others, it is strongly motivated by the transformations in the island economy that resulted from modernization and U.S. domination. Like Chicanos, Puerto Ricans tend to enter the labor force at the bottom of the occupational structure and face similar problems of inequality and marginalization. Also, Puerto Rican culture retains a strong vitality and is continually reinvigorated by the considerable movement back and forth between the island and the mainland.

QUESTIONS FOR REFLECTION

1. Would you say that Puerto Ricans are more an immigrant or colonized minority group? Why?

2. What are some of the key differences between Puerto Rican and Anglo cultures? How have these differences shaped relations between the groups?

CUBAN AMERICANS

The contact period for Cuban Americans, as for Puerto Ricans, dates back to the Spanish–American War. At that time, Cuba was a Spanish colony but became an independent nation as a result of the war. Despite Cuba's nominal independence, the United States remained heavily involved in Cuban politics and economics for decades, and U.S. troops actually occupied the island on two different occasions.

The development of a Cuban American minority group bears little resemblance to the experience of either Chicanos or Puerto Ricans. As recently as the 1950s, there had not been much immigration from Cuba to the United States, even during times of labor shortages, and Cuban Americans were a very small group, numbering no more than 50,000 (Perez, 1980, p. 256).

IMMIGRATION (PUSH AND PULL)

The conditions for a mass immigration were created in the late 1950s, when a revolution brought Fidel Castro to power in Cuba. Castro's government was decidedly anti-American and began to restructure Cuban society along socialist lines. The middle and upper classes lost political and economic power, and the revolution made it impossible for Cuban capitalists to continue "business as usual." Thus, the first Cuban immigrants to the United States tended to come from the more elite classes and included affluent and powerful people who controlled many resources. They were perceived as refugees from Communist persecution (the immigration occurred at the height of the Cold War) and were warmly received by the government and the American public.

The United States was a logical destination for those displaced by the revolution. Cuba is only 90 miles from southern Florida, the climates are similar, and the U.S. government, which was as anti-Castro as Castro was anti-American, welcomed the new arrivals as political refugees fleeing from Communist tyranny.

Prior social, cultural, and business ties also pulled the immigrants in the direction of the United States. Since gaining its independence in 1898, Cuba has been heavily influenced by its neighbor to the north, and U.S. companies helped develop the Cuban economy. At the time of Castro's revolution, the Cuban political leadership and the more affluent classes were profoundly Americanized in their attitudes and lifestyles (Portes, 1990, p. 165). Furthermore, many Cuban exiles viewed southern Florida as an ideal spot from which to launch a counterrevolution to oust Castro.

Immigration was considerable for several years. More than 215,000 Cubans arrived between the end of the revolution and 1962, when an escalation of hostile relations resulted in the cutoff of all direct contact between Cuba and the United States. In 1965, an air link was reestablished, and an

Fidel Castro, leader of the Cuban Revolution.

NARRATIVE PORTRAIT

Gender Images of Latinas

One part of the minority-group experience is learning to deal with the stereotypes, images, and expectations of the larger society. Of course, everyone (even white males) has to respond to the assumptions of others, but given the realities of power and status, minority-group members have fewer choices and a narrower range in which to maneuver: The images imposed by society are harder to escape and more difficult to deny.

In her analysis, Judith Ortiz Cofer (1995), a writer, poet, professor of English, and Puerto Rican, describes some of the images and stereotypes of Latinas with which she has had to struggle and some of the dynamics that have created and sustained those images. She writes from her own experiences, but the points she makes illustrate many of the sociological theories and concepts that guide this text.

THE ISLAND TRAVELS WITH YOU

Judith Ortiz Cofer

On a bus trip...a young man...spotted me and as if struck by inspiration went down on his knees in the aisle. With both hands over his heart he broke into a...rendition of "María" from *West Side Story*. My...fellow passengers gave [him a] round of gentle applause....I managed my version of an English smile: no show of teeth, no extreme contortions of the facial muscles....But María had followed me to London, reminding me of a prime fact of my life: you can leave the Island, master the English language, and travel as far as you can, but if you are a Latina,...the Island travels with you....

As a Puerto Rican girl growing up in the United States and wanting like most children to "belong," I resented the stereotype that my Hispanic appearance called forth from many people I met.

Our family lived in...New Jersey during the sixties....We spoke in Spanish, we ate Puerto Rican food bought at the bodega, and we practiced strict Catholicism....

As a girl, I was kept under strict surveillance, since virtue and modesty were... the same as family honor. As a teenager, I was instructed on how to behave as a proper señorita. But it was a conflicting message girls got, since the Puerto Rican mothers also encouraged their daughters to look and act like women and to dress in clothes our Anglo friends found too "mature" for our age....At Puerto Rican festivals, neither the music nor the colors we wore could be too loud. I still experience a vague sense of letdown when I'm invited to a "party" and it turns out to be a marathon conversation in hushed tones rather than a fiesta with salsa, laughter, and dancing— the kind of celebration I remember from my childhood....

Mixed cultural signals have perpetuated certain stereotypes—for example, that of the Hispanic woman as the "Hot Tamale" or sexual firebrand....

It is custom, however,...that leads us to choose scarlet over pale pink. As young girls, we were influenced in our decisions about clothes and colors by the women— older sisters and mothers who had grown up on a tropical island where the natural environment was a riot of primary colors, where showing your skin was one way to keep cool as well as to look sexy. Most important of all, on the island, women perhaps felt freer to dress and move more provocatively, since...they were protected by the traditions, mores, and laws of a Spanish/Catholic system of morality and machismo whose main rule was: *You may look at my sister, but if you touch her I will kill you.* The extended family and church structure could provide a young woman with a circle of safety in her small pueblo on the island; if a man "wronged" a girl,

everyone would close in to save her family honor....

Because of my education and proficiency with the English language, I have acquired many mechanisms for dealing with the anger I experience. This [is] not...true for the many Latin women working at menial jobs who must put up with stereotypes about our ethnic group such as: "They make good domestics."...María, the housemaid or counter girl, is now indelibly etched into the national psyche. The big and the little screens have presented us with the picture of the funny Hispanic maid, mispronouncing words and cooking up a spicy storm in a shiny California kitchen....

There are thousands of Latinas without the privilege of an education or the entrée into society that I have. For them, life is a struggle against the misconceptions perpetuated by the myth of the Latina as whore, domestic, or criminal. My personal goal in my public life is to try to replace the old pervasive stereotypes and myths about Latinas....Every time I give a reading [of my poetry], I hope the stories I tell, the dreams and fears I examine in my work, can achieve some universal truth which will get my audience past the particulars of my skin color, my accent, or my clothes.

SOURCE: *From the Latin Deli: Prose & Poetry* by Judith Ortiz Cofer. Copyright 1993 by Judith Ortiz Cofer. Reprinted by permission of the University of Georgia Press.

Questions to Consider

1. What differences between Puerto Rican and Anglo culture are examined in this passage? How might these differences affect or distort communications between cultures?
2. How does this passage illustrate the idea, introduced in Chapter 3, that stereotypes can be "gendered"?

---

additional 340,000 Cubans made the journey. When the air connection was terminated in 1973, immigration slowed to a trickle once more.

In 1980, the Cuban government permitted another period of open immigration. Using boats of every shape, size, and

degree of seaworthiness, about 124,000 Cubans crossed to Florida. These immigrants are often referred to as the ***marielitos***, after the port of Mariel from which many of them departed. This wave of immigrants generated a great deal of controversy in the United States because the Cuban government used the opportunity to rid itself of a variety of convicted criminals and outcasts. The reception for this group was decidedly less favorable than for the original wave of Cuban immigrants. Even the established Cuban American community distanced itself from

---

Marielitos were refugees from Cuba who arrived in the United States in 1980.

the *marielitos*, who were largely products of the new Cuba, having been born after the revolution, and with whom they lacked kinship or friendship ties (Portes & Shafer, 2006, pp. 16–17).

REGIONAL CONCENTRATIONS

The overwhelming majority of Cuban immigrants settled in southern Florida, especially in Miami and the surrounding Dade County. Today, Cuban Americans remain one of the most spatially concentrated minority groups in the United States, with 70% of all Cuban Americans residing in Florida alone (Bowen & Patten, 2013d, p. 2). This dense concentration has led to a number of disputes and conflicts between the Hispanic, Anglo-, and African American communities in the area. Issues have centered on language, jobs, and discrimination by the police and other governmental agencies. The conflicts often have been intense, and on more than one occasion, they have erupted into violence and civil disorder.

SOCIOECONOMIC CHARACTERISTICS

Compared with other streams of immigrants from Latin America, Cubans are, on the average, unusually affluent and well educated. Among the immigrants in the early 1960s were large numbers of professionals, landowners, and business-people. In later years, as Cuban society was transformed by the Castro regime, the stream included fewer elites—largely because there were fewer left in Cuba—and more political dissidents and working-class people. Today (as displayed in the figures presented later in this chapter), Cuban Americans rank higher than other Latino groups on a number of dimensions, a reflection of the educational and economic resources they brought with them from Cuba and the favorable reception they enjoyed in the United States (Portes, 1990, p. 169).

These assets gave Cubans an advantage over Chicanos and Puerto Ricans, but the differences between the three Latino groups run deeper and are more complex than a simple accounting of initial resources would suggest. Cubans adapted to U.S. society in a way that is fundamentally different from the experiences of the other two Latino groups.

THE ETHNIC ENCLAVE

Most of the minority groups we have discussed to this point have been concentrated in the unskilled, low-wage segments of the economy in which jobs are not secure and not linked to opportunities for upward mobility. Many Cuban Americans have bypassed this sector of the economy and much of the discrimination and limitation associated with it. Like several other groups, such as Jewish Americans, Cuban Americans are an enclave minority (see Chapter 2). An ethnic enclave is a social, economic, and cultural subsociety controlled by the group itself. Located in a specific geographical area or neighborhood inhabited solely or largely by members of the group, the enclave encompasses sufficient economic enterprises and social institutions to permit the group to function as a self-contained entity, largely independent of the surrounding community.

The first wave of Cuban immigrants brought with them considerable human capital and business expertise. Although much of their energy was focused on ousting Castro and returning to Cuba, they generated enough economic activity to sustain restaurants, shops, and other small businesses that catered to the exile community.

As the years passed and the hope of a return to Cuba dimmed, the enclave economy grew. Between 1967 and 1976, the number of Cuban-owned firms in Dade County increased ninefold, from 919 to about 8,000. Six years later, the number had reached 12,000. Most of these enterprises were small, but some factories employed hundreds of workers (Portes & Rumbaut, 1996, pp. 20–21). By 2001, there were more than 125,000 Cuban-owned firms in the United States, and the rate of Cuban-owned firms per 100,00 population was 4 times greater than the rate for Mexican Americans and 14 times greater than the rate for African Americans (Portes & Shafer, 2006, p. 14).

In addition to businesses serving their own community, Cuban-owned firms are involved in construction, manufacturing, finance, insurance, real estate, and an array of other activities. Over the decades, Cuban-owned firms have become increasingly integrated into local economies and increasingly competitive with firms in the larger society. The growth of economic enterprises has been paralleled by a growth in the number of other types of groups and organizations, and in the number and quality of services available (schools, law firms, medical care, funeral parlors, etc.). The enclave has become a largely autonomous community capable of providing for its members from cradle to grave (Logan, Alba, & McNulty, 1994; Peterson, 1995; Portes & Bach, 1985, p. 59).

That the enclave economy is controlled by the group itself is crucial; it separates the ethnic enclave from "the ghetto," or neighborhoods that are impoverished and segregated. In ghettos, members of other groups typically control the local economy; the profits, rents, and other resources flow out of the neighborhood. In the enclave, profits are reinvested and kept in the neighborhood. Group members can avoid the discrimination and limitations imposed by the larger society, and can apply their skills, education, and talents in an atmosphere free from language barriers and prejudice. Those who might wish to venture into business for themselves can use the networks of cooperation and mutual aid for advice, credit, and other forms of assistance. Thus, the ethnic enclave provides a platform from which Cuban Americans can pursue economic success independent of their degree of acculturation or English language ability.

The effectiveness of the ethnic enclave as a pathway for adaptation is illustrated by a study of Cuban and Mexican immigrants, all of whom entered the United States in 1973.

At the time of entry, the groups were comparable in levels of skills, education, and English language ability. The groups were interviewed on several different occasions, and although they remained comparable on many variables, there were dramatic differences between the groups that reflected their different positions in the labor market. The majority of the Mexican immigrants were employed in the low-wage job sector. Less than 20% were self-employed or employed by another person of Mexican descent. Conversely, 57% of the Cuban immigrants were self-employed or employed by another Cuban (i.e., they were involved in the enclave economy). Among the subjects in the study, self-employed Cubans reported the highest monthly incomes ($1,495), and Cubans otherwise employed in the enclave earned the second-highest monthly incomes ($1,111). The lowest monthly incomes ($880) were earned by Mexican immigrants employed in small, non-enclave firms—many of whom worked as unskilled laborers in seasonal, temporary, or otherwise insecure jobs (Portes, 1990, p. 173; see also Portes & Bach, 1985).

A more recent study confirms the advantages that accrue from forming an enclave. Using 2000 Census data, Portes and Shafer (2006) compared the incomes of several groups in the Miami–Fort Lauderdale metropolitan area, including the original Cuban immigrants (who founded the enclave), their children (the second generation), Cuban immigrants who arrived after 1980 (the *marielitos* and others), and several other groups. Some of the results of the study for males are presented in Figure 8.6.

The founders and primary beneficiaries of the Cuban enclave are the self-employed, pre-1980 Cuban immigrants (far-left bar). The income for this group is higher than for all other Cuban groups included in the graph, and only slightly less than for non-Hispanic whites (not shown). The sons of the founding generation (U.S.-born Cuban Americans) also enjoy a substantial benefit, both directly (through working in

the enclave firms started by their fathers) and indirectly (by translating the resources of their families into human capital, including education, for themselves). The incomes of post-1980 Cuban immigrants are the lowest on the graph and, in fact, are comparable to incomes for non-Hispanic blacks (not shown).

The ability of most Hispanic (and other) immigrants to rise in the class system and compete for place and position is constrained by discrimination and their own lack of economic and political power. Cuban immigrants in the enclave do not need to expose themselves to American prejudices or to rely on the job market of the larger society. They constructed networks of mutual assistance and support, and linked themselves to opportunities more consistent with their ambitions and qualifications.

The link between the enclave and economic equality (an aspect of secondary structural integration) challenges the predictions of some traditional assimilation theories and the understandings of many Americans. The pattern has long been recognized by some leaders of other groups, however, and is voiced in many of the themes of Black Power, Red Power, and Chicanismo that emphasize self-help, self-determination, nationalism, and separation.

However, ethnic enclaves cannot be a panacea for all immigrant or other minority groups. They develop only under certain limited conditions—namely, when business and financial expertise and reliable sources of capital are combined with a disciplined labor force willing to work for low wages in exchange for on-the-job training, future assistance and loans, or other delayed benefits. Enclave enterprises usually start on a small scale and cater only to other ethnics. Thus, the early economic returns are small, and prosperity follows only after years of hard work, if at all. Most important, eventual success and expansion beyond the boundaries of the enclave depend on the persistence of strong ties of loyalty, kinship, and solidarity. The pressure to assimilate might easily weaken these networks and the strength of group cohesion (Portes & Manning, 1986, pp. 61–66).

FIGURE 8.6 Family Incomes for Self-Employed and Wage/Salaried Male Workers From Three Cuban American Groups, 2000

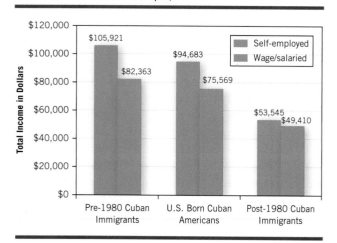

SOURCE: Portes and Shafer (2006, p. 42).

CUBAN AMERICANS AND OTHER MINORITY GROUPS

The adaptation of Cuban Americans contrasts sharply with the experiences of colonized minority groups and with the common understanding of how immigrants are "supposed" to acculturate and integrate. Cuban Americans are neither the first nor the only group to develop an ethnic enclave, and their success has generated prejudice and resentment from the dominant group and from other minority groups. Whereas Puerto Ricans and Chicanos have been the victims of stereotypes labeling them "inferior," higher-status Cuban Americans have been stereotyped as "too successful," "too clannish," and "too ambitious." The former stereotype commonly emerges to rationalize exploitative relationships; the latter expresses

In a classic article, anthropologist Jane Hill (1995) analyzed "mock Spanish"—phrases such as "no problemo," "hasty banana," and "buenos nachos." Mock Spanish is distinct from the blending of Spanish and English ("Spanglish") common in the borderlands of the Southwest among people who speak both languages, in that it is used by mono-English speakers and intended to be a form of humorous, light-hearted banter.

Hill (1995) argues that this seemingly innocent butchering of Spanish is a form of racism that relies on negative stereotypes of Hispanics (particularly Mexicans) for its humor. For example, calling something "el cheapo" will conjure in the minds of many Anglos images of lazy, lower-class Mexicans. Furthermore, an analysis of mock Spanish reveals a linguistic double standard: Spanish speakers are disparaged or ridiculed for using incorrect English, but English speakers abuse and misuse Spanish with impunity.

Mock Spanish is common in everyday language and in media. Some examples are listed below. Can you identify the source and the speaker?*

1. "Hasta la vista, baby."

2. "You got a lot of 'splainin' to do."

3. "Nurse Espinosa and her nursitas want more dinero."

4. "I need a lift in el trucko to el towno."

5. "I'm promoting myself to 'El Tigre Numero Uno.'"

*Many of these examples are based on materials presented on the website Teaching Resources: Teaching Linguistic Anthropology, at teach.linguisticanthropology.org/tag/mock-spanish.

TURN THE PAGE TO FIND THE ANSWERS.

disparagement and rejection of groups that are more successful in the struggle to acquire resources (see Chapter 3). Nonetheless, the stereotype of Cubans is an exaggeration and a misperception that obscures the fact that poverty and unemployment are major problems for many members of this group, especially for the post-1980 immigrants (see the figures at the end of this chapter).

QUESTIONS FOR REFLECTION

1. Would you say that Cuban Americans are more an immigrant or colonized minority group? Why?

2. Are Cuban Americans an enclave minority? What are the most important advantages enjoyed by enclave minority groups? Are there any disadvantages?

PREJUDICE AND DISCRIMINATION

The American tradition of prejudice against Latinos was born in the 19th-century conflicts that created minority-group status for Mexican Americans. The themes of the original anti-Mexican stereotypes and attitudes were consistent with the nature of the contact situation: As Mexicans were conquered and subordinated, they were characterized as inferior, lazy, irresponsible, low in intelligence, and dangerously criminal (McWilliams, 1961, pp. 212–214). The prejudice and racism, supplemented with the echoes of the racist ideas and beliefs brought to the Southwest by many Anglos, helped justify and rationalize the colonized, exploited status of the Chicanos.

These prejudices were incorporated into the dominant culture and transferred to Puerto Ricans when they began to arrive on the mainland. However, this stereotype does not fit the situation of Cuban Americans very well. Instead, their affluence has been exaggerated and perceived as undeserved or achieved by unfair or "un-American" means, a characterization similar to the traditional stereotype of Jews but just as prejudiced as the perception of Latino inferiority.

There is some evidence that the level of Latino prejudice has been affected by the decline of explicit American racism (discussed in Chapter 3). For example, social distance scale results show a decrease in the scores of Mexicans, although their group ranking tends to remain stable.

On the other hand, anti-Latino prejudice and racism tend to increase during times of high immigration. In particular, there is considerable, though largely anecdotal, evidence that the surge in immigration that began in the 1990s sparked high levels of anti-Latino prejudice in the "borderlands," or the areas along the U.S.–Mexican border. Extreme, racist rhetoric was common, and the activities of various hate groups were prominently featured in the media. Many observers see racism in Arizona's widely publicized State Bill 1070 (which, if ever implemented, would allow police to check anyone for proof of citizenship) and its state-mandated ban on ethnic studies programs in public schools. At any rate, the level of immigrant bashing and anti-Latino sentiments along the border demonstrates that American prejudice, although sometimes disguised as a subtle modern racism, is alive and well.

In Chapter 5, we mentioned that audit studies have documented the persistence of discrimination against blacks in the housing and job markets: Many of the same studies also demonstrate anti-Hispanic biases (see Quillian, 2006, for a review). Discrimination of all kinds, institutional as well as individual, against Latino groups has been common, but it has not been as rigid or as total as the systems that controlled African American labor under slavery and segregation. However, discrimination against Latinos persists across the United States. Because of their longer tenure in the United States and their original status as a rural labor force, Mexican Americans probably have

been more victimized by the institutionalized forms of discrimination than have other Latino groups.

ASSIMILATION AND PLURALISM

As in previous chapters, we will use the central concepts of this text to review the status of Latinos in the United States. Where relevant, comparisons are made between the major Latino groups and the minority groups discussed in previous chapters.

ACCULTURATION

Latinos are highly variable in their extent of acculturation but are often seen as "slow" to change, learn English, and adopt Anglo customs. Contrary to this perception, research shows that Hispanics are following many of the same patterns of assimilation as European groups did. Their rates of acculturation increase with length of residence and are higher for the native-born (Espinosa & Massey, 1997; Goldstein & Suro, 2000; Valentine & Mosley, 2000).

The dominant trend for Hispanic groups, as for immigrants from Europe in the past (see Chapter 2) is that language acculturation increases over the generations as the length of residence in the United States increases and as education increases. One study (Hakimzadeh & Cohn, 2007), which combines six different surveys conducted since 2000 and is based on more than 14,000 respondents, illustrates these points. Results are displayed in Figures 8.7 and 8.8.

A different study showed that the values of Hispanics come to approximate the values of society as a whole as the

One of the many organized demonstrations protesting Arizona Senate Bill 1070.

Immigration to Europe Versus Immigration to the United States

The volume of immigration in the world today is at record levels. About 232 million people, an increase of more than 50% since 1990, live outside their countries of birth, and there is hardly a nation or region that has not been affected (United Nations Department of Economic and Social Affairs, Population Division, 2013). The United States currently hosts the largest number of migrants (about 20% of the total), but it is only one of many destinations, and the issues of immigration and assimilation being debated so fervently here are echoed in many other nations.

In particular, the nations of western Europe, with their highly developed economies and high standards of living, are prime destinations for immigrants. Like the United States, these nations offer myriad opportunities for economic survival, even though the price may be to live on the margins or take jobs scorned by the native-born. Another powerful factor is that western European nations have very low birthrates, and in some cases (e.g., in Germany and Spain), their populations are actually projected to decline in coming decades (Population Reference Bureau, 2013). The labor force shortages thus created will continue to attract immigrants to western Europe for decades to come.

The immigrant stream to western Europe is varied and includes people from all walks of life, from highly educated professionals to peasant laborers. The most prominent flows include movements from Turkey to Germany, from Africa to Spain and Italy, and from many former British colonies (Jamaica, India, Nigeria, etc.) to the United Kingdom. This immigration is primarily an economic phenomenon motivated by the search for jobs and survival, but the stream also includes refugees and asylum seekers fleeing civil wars, genocides, and political unrest.

In terms of numbers, the volume of immigration to western Europe is smaller than the flow to the United States, but its proportional impact is comparable. About 13% of the U.S. population is foreign-born, and many western European nations (including Germany, the United Kingdom, and France) have a similar profile (United Nations Department of Economic and Social Affairs, Population Division, 2013). Thus, it is not surprising that in both cases, immigration has generated major concerns and debates about handling newcomers and managing a pluralistic society, including national language policy, the limits of religious freedom, and the criteria for citizenship.

To focus on one example, Germany has the largest immigrant community of any western European nation and has been dealing with a large foreign-born population for decades. Beginning in the 1960s, Germany began to allow large numbers of immigrants to enter as temporary workers or guest workers (*Gastarbeiter*) to help staff its expanding economy. Most of these immigrants came from Turkey, and they were seen by Germans as temporary workers only, people who would return to their homeland when they were no longer needed. Thus, the host society saw no particular need to encourage immigrants to acculturate and integrate.

However, many guest workers settled permanently, and many of their descendants today speak only German and have no knowledge of or experience with their "homeland." Although largely acculturated, they are not fully integrated, and, in fact—in contrast to the United States—they were denied the opportunity to become citizens until recently.

A German law passed a century ago reserved citizenship for people who had at least one German parent, regardless of place of birth. Thus, Turks living in Germany were not eligible for citizenship regardless of how long they or their families had been residents. This law was changed in 2000 to permit greater flexibility in qualifying for citizenship, but still more recently, Germany has passed new laws that make it harder for foreigners to enter the country. Immigrants see these new laws as a form of rejection, and there have been bitter (and sometimes violent) demonstrations in response.

Clashes of this sort have been common across western Europe in recent years, especially with the growing Muslim communities. Many Europeans see Islamic immigrants as unassimilable, too foreign or exotic ever to fit into the mainstream of their society. These conflicts have been punctuated by violence and riots in France, Germany, the Netherlands, and other places.

Across Europe, just as in the United States and Canada, nations are wrestling with issues of inclusion and diversity: What should it mean to be German or French or British or Dutch? How much diversity can be tolerated before national cohesion is threatened? What is the best balance between assimilation and pluralism? Struggles over the essential meaning of national identity are increasingly common throughout the developed world.

Questions to Consider

1. What similarities and differences between the United States and western Europe can you cite in terms of immigration?
2. Do you think the United States is more or less successful in dealing with immigrants than are the nations of western Europe? Why?

generations pass. Figure 8.9 shows some results of a 2002 survey of Latinos and compares cultural values by English language proficiency, which increases with length of residence and by generation. For example, most Latinos who speak predominantly Spanish (72%) are first generation, while most who speak predominantly English (78%) are third generation. The second generation is most likely to be bilingual.

Figure 8.9 shows the results for four different survey items that measure values and opinions. The values of predominantly Spanish speakers are distinctly different from those of non-Latinos, especially on the item that measures support for the statement that "children should live with their parents until they are married." Virtually all the predominantly Spanish speakers supported the statement, but English-speaking Latinos approximate the more individualistic values of Anglos. For each of the other three items, a similar acculturation to American values occurs.

Even while acculturation continues, however, Hispanic culture and the Spanish language are revitalized by immigration. By its nature, assimilation is a slow process that can require

FIGURE 8.7 Percentage of Hispanic Americans Who Speak English "Very Well" by Generation

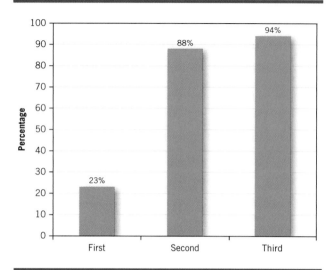

SOURCE: Hakimzadeh and Cohn (2007).

decades or generations to complete. In contrast, immigration can be fast, often accomplished in less than a day. Thus, even as Hispanic Americans acculturate and integrate, Hispanic culture and language are sustained and strengthened. What is perceived to be slow acculturation for these groups is mostly the result of fast and continuous immigration.

Furthermore, colonized minority groups such as Chicanos and Puerto Ricans were not encouraged to assimilate in the past. Valued primarily for the cheap labor they supplied, they were seen as otherwise inferior or undesirable and unfit for integration. For much of the 20th century, Latinos were excluded from the institutions and experiences (e.g., school) that could have led to greater equality and higher rates of acculturation. Prejudice, racism, and discrimination combined to keep most Latino groups away from the centers of modernization and change, and away from opportunities to improve their situation.

Finally, for Cubans, Dominicans, Salvadorans, and other groups, cultural differences reflect that they are largely recent immigrants. Their first generations are alive and well, and as is typical for immigrant groups, they keep their language and traditions alive.

SECONDARY STRUCTURAL ASSIMILATION

In this section, we survey the situation of Latinos in the public areas and institutions of American society, following the same format as the previous two chapters. We begin with where people live.

Residence. Figure 8.10 shows the regional concentrations of Latinos in 2010. The legacies of the varied patterns of entry and settlement for the largest groups are evident. The higher concentrations in the Southwest reflect the presence

of Mexican Americans, those in Florida are the result of the Cuban immigration, and those in the Northeast display the settlement patterns of Puerto Ricans.

Figure 8.11 highlights the areas of the nation where Latinos are growing fastest. A quick glance at the map will reveal that many of the high-growth areas are distant from the traditional points of entry for these groups. In particular, the Hispanic American population is growing rapidly in parts of New England, the South, the upper Midwest, the Northwest, and even Alaska. Among many other forces, this population movement is a response to the availability of jobs in factories, mills, chicken-processing plants and slaughterhouses, farms, construction, and other low-skilled areas of the economy.

Within each of these regions, Latino groups are highly urbanized, as shown in Figure 8.12. With the exception of Mexican Americans, more than 90% of each of the 10 largest Hispanic American groups live in urban areas, and this percentage approaches 100% for some groups. Mexican Americans are more rural than the other groups, but in sharp contrast to their historical role as an agrarian workforce, the percentage of the group living in rural areas is tiny today.

The extent of residential segregation for Hispanic Americans was displayed in Figure 6.7, using the dissimilarity index for each of the last four census years. Residential segregation is much lower for Hispanics than for blacks: None of the scores for Hispanics in Figure 6.7 approach the "extreme" segregation denoted by a dissimilarity index of 60 or more.

Note that, contrary to the decreasing levels of black–white segregation, Hispanic–white residential segregation has held steady, with minor increases or decreases. Among other factors, this is a reflection of high rates of immigration and "chain"

FIGURE 8.8 Percentage of Hispanic Americans Who Speak English "Very Well" by Years of Residence and Level of Education

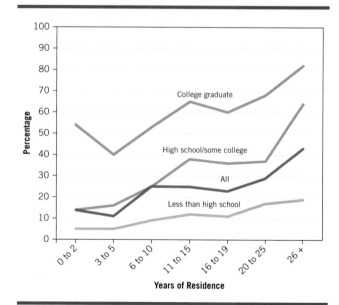

SOURCE: Hakimzadeh and Cohn (2007).

patterns of settlement, which concentrate newcomers in ethnic neighborhoods. In other words, levels of residential segregation for Hispanics remain relatively steady because weakening barriers to integration in the larger society are counteracted by the continuing arrival of newcomers, who tend to settle in predominantly Hispanic neighborhoods.

FIGURE 8.9 Percentage of Hispanic Americans and Non-Latinos Agreeing on Select Issues by Primary Language

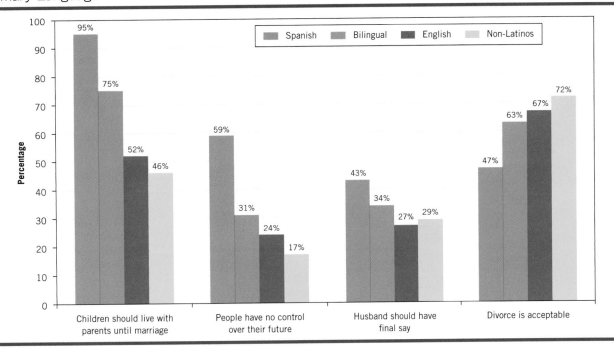

SOURCE: Pew Hispanic Center (2004).

NOTE: Full text of survey items:

"It is better for children to live in their parents' home until they are married."

"It doesn't do any good to plan for the future because you have no control over it."

"In general, the husband should have the final say in all family matters."

"Divorce is acceptable."

FIGURE 8.10 Geographic Distribution of Hispanic Americans by County, 2010 (Percentage Share of County Population)

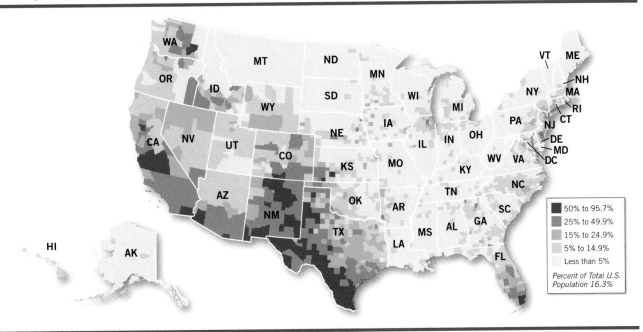

SOURCE: Ennis et al. (2011, p. 10); U.S. Census Bureau (2011b).

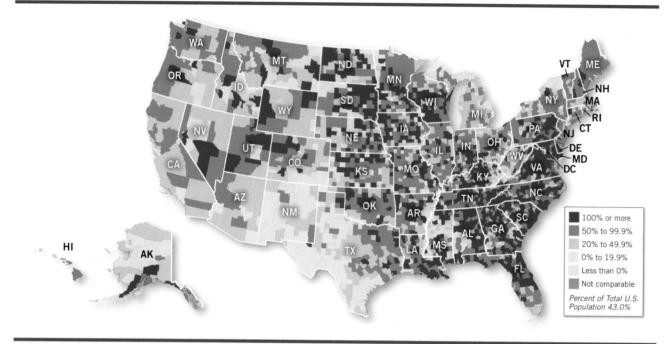

Education. Figure 8.13 displays the extent of school segregation for Hispanic Americans using the same format as Figure 6.8. Five different school years are used, along with three different measures. The top line shows that the overwhelming—and increasing—majority of Hispanic students attended "majority–minority" schools over this time period. By this measure, Hispanic students are actually more segregated than black students. The middle line shows an increasing percentage of Hispanic students attending schools that are 90% to 100% minority, and the bottom line shows a slight decrease in the percentage attending schools that are virtually all minority. The first two trends reflect recent high rates of immigration and the tendency for newcomers to reside in the same neighborhoods as their coethnics.

Levels of education for Hispanic Americans have risen in recent years but still are far below national standards, as displayed in Figure 8.14. Hispanic Americans in general and all subgroups, except Colombian Americans, fall well below non-Hispanic whites for high school education. In particular, less than 60% of Mexican Americans and only about half of Honduran, Salvadoran, and Guatemalan Americans have high school degrees. At the college level, Colombian and Cuban Americans approximate national norms, but the other groups and Hispanic Americans as a whole are far below non-Hispanic whites.

The lower levels of education for Mexican Americans and Puerto Ricans are the cumulative results of decades of systematic discrimination and exclusion. These levels have been further reduced by the high percentage of recent immigrants from Mexico, the Dominican Republic, El Salvador, and other nations that have modest educational backgrounds.

Given the role that educational credentials have come to play in the job market, these figures are consistent with the idea that assimilation may be segmented for some Hispanic groups (see Chapters 2 and 10), who may contribute in large numbers, along with African Americans and Native Americans, to the growth of an urban underclass.

FIGURE 8.12   Percentage of 10 Largest Hispanic American Groups and Non-Hispanic Whites Living in Urbanized Areas, 2000

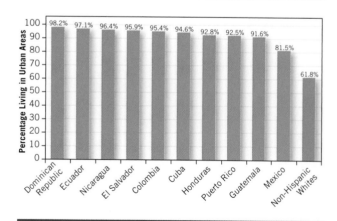

Political Power. The political resources available to Hispanic Americans have increased over the years, but the group is still proportionally underrepresented. Nationally, Hispanic Americans rose from about 6% of those eligible to vote in 1996 to almost 11% in 2012. However, this increase in potential political power was limited by lower rates of registration and lower voter turnout: Less than half (48%) of Hispanic Americans eligible to vote actually cast a ballot in the 2012 presidential election (File, 2013, pp. 3–5). Clearly, the impact of the Latino vote on national politics will increase as the group grows in size, but participation is likely to remain lower than for other groups for some time because of the large percentage of recent, non-English-speaking immigrants and noncitizens in the group.

At the national level, there are now 37 Hispanic Americans in the U.S. Congress, about 7% of the total membership and more than double the number in 1990. There are 33 Hispanic members of the House of Representatives (26 of them Democrats) and 4 senators (3 of them Republicans) (Manning, 2013). On the local and state level, the number of public officials identified as Hispanic increased by more than 65% between 1985 and 2008, from 3,147 to 5,240 (U.S. Census Bureau, 2011a, p. 259).

Although Hispanic Americans are still underrepresented, these figures suggest that they will become increasingly important in American political life as their numbers continue to grow and rates of naturalization rise. Even with a smaller turnout, Hispanic voters were an important part of the coalition that reelected President Barack Obama, and competition

FIGURE 8.13 Three Measures of School Segregation for Hispanic Students

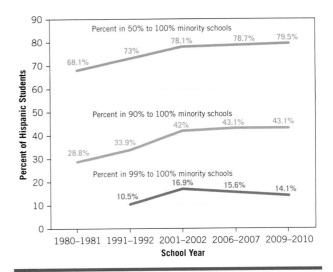

SOURCE: Orfield, Kucsera, and Siegel-Hawley (2012, p. 19).

between the Republican and Democratic Party for this growing segment of the electorate will continue.

Jobs and Income. The economic situation of Hispanic Americans is quite mixed. Many Latinos, especially those who have been in the United States for several generations, are doing "just fine. They have, in ever increasing numbers, accessed opportunities in education and employment and have carved out a niche of American prosperity for

FIGURE 8.14 Educational Attainment for All Hispanic Americans, Non-Hispanic Whites, and 10 Largest Hispanic American Groups, 2012

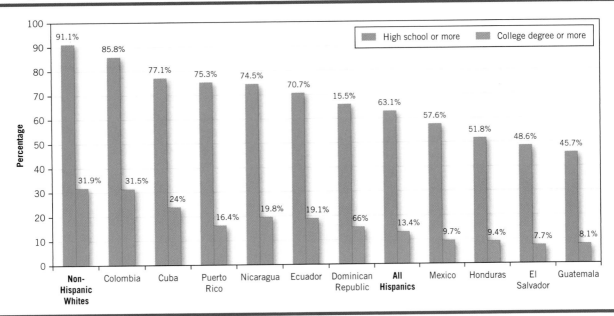

SOURCE: U.S. Census Bureau (2013a).

themselves and their children" (Camarillo & Bonilla, 2001, pp. 130–131). For others, however, the picture is not so bright. They face the possibility of becoming members of an impoverished, powerless, and economically marginalized urban underclass, like African Americans and other minority groups of color.

Occupationally, Hispanic Americans who are recent immigrants with modest levels of education and job skills are concentrated in the less desirable, lower-paid service and unskilled segments of the job market. Those with higher levels of human capital and education compare more favorably with the dominant group.

Unemployment, low income, and poverty continue to be issues for all Hispanic groups. The official unemployment rates for Hispanic Americans run about 50% higher than the rate for non-Hispanic whites (U.S. Bureau of Labor Statistics, 2013).

Figure 8.15 compares median household incomes for non-Hispanic whites and all Hispanic Americans across five decades. The size of the income gap fluctuates but generally remains in the low to mid-70%. In the most recent years, however, it has fallen to just below 70%.

As a group, Hispanic Americans historically have been intermediate between blacks and whites in the stratification system, and this is reflected by the fact that the Hispanic–white income gap is smaller than the black–white income gap (which was 63% in 2012; see Figure 6.11). This smaller gap also reflects the more favorable economic circumstances of Hispanics (especially those more "racially" similar to the dominant group) who have been in the United States for generations and are thoroughly integrated into the mainstream economy.

Figure 8.16 shows that there is a good deal of income variability from group to group, but Hispanic Americans in general and all subgroups have, on the average, dramatically lower median household incomes than do non-Hispanic whites, especially the groups with large numbers of recent immigrants who bring low levels of human capital.

Figure 8.17 supplements the information on median income by displaying the overall distribution of income for Hispanic Americans and non-Hispanic whites for 2012. The figure shows a greater concentration (wider bars) of Hispanics in the lower-income categories and a lower concentration (narrower bars) in the income groups at the top of the figure. There is a noticeable concentration of both groups in the $50,000 to $125,000 categories, but whites outnumber Hispanics by about 40% to 32% in these income ranges. In the three highest income categories, whites outnumber Hispanic Americans more than 2 to 1 (16% to 7%).

Recent detailed income information is not available for the separate subgroups, but we can assume that—although all groups have members in all income categories—Mexican Americans, Dominican Americans, and Puerto Ricans would be disproportionately represented in the lowest income categories,

and Cuban Americans—especially, as we have seen, those that benefit from the enclave economy—in the higher groups.

Figure 8.18 finishes the socioeconomic profile by displaying the varying levels of poverty for Hispanic Americans, a pattern that is consistent with previous information on income and education. The poverty rate for all Hispanic families is almost three times the rate for non-Hispanic white families but lower than that of African Americans (see Figure 6.13). However, there is considerable diversity across the subgroups, with Colombians and Cubans closest to non-Hispanic whites, and Dominicans and Hondurans the most impoverished. For all groups, children have higher poverty rates than do families.

These socioeconomic profiles reflect the economic diversity of Latinos. Some are "doing just fine," but others are concentrated in the low-wage sector of the economy. As a group, Cuban Americans rank higher than Mexican Americans and Puerto Ricans—the two other largest groups—on virtually all measures of wealth and prosperity. As we saw previously, this relative prosperity is even more pronounced for the earlier immigrants from Cuba and their children.

We should also note that the income gap and the picture of economic distress would be much greater if we focused on recent immigrants and, especially, undocumented immigrants, who are concentrated in the informal, irregular economy. These groups are sometimes paid "off the books" and less than minimum wage. As we have discussed, they tend to be focused on their families and villages back home, and live as frugally as possible—5 or even 10 to a room, for example—to maximize the money they can send home. Since they tend to live "below the radar," they are less likely to be included in the data-gathering efforts that supply the information for the figures in this chapter. If they were included, the results for average wages

FIGURE 8.15 Median Household Incomes for Non-Hispanic White and All Hispanic Households, 1972–2012

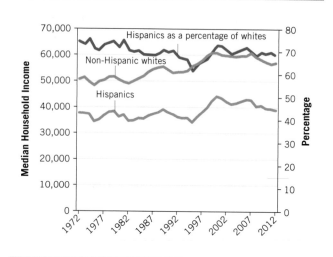

SOURCE: U.S. Census Bureau (2013a).

FIGURE 8.16 Median Household Income for Non-Hispanic Whites, All Hispanic Americans, and 10 Largest Hispanic Groups, 2012

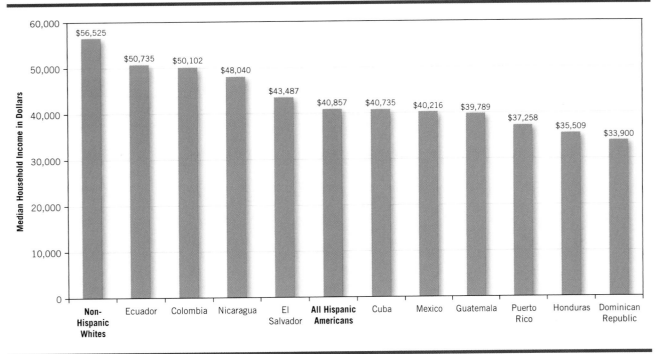

SOURCE: U.S. Census Bureau (2013a).

would be lower and rates of poverty higher for virtually all Latino groups in the United States.

Gender and Inequality. There is a split labor market differentiated by gender within the dual market differentiated by race and ethnicity. Hispanic women—like minority-group women in general—are among the lowest paid, most exploitable, and least protected segments of the U.S. labor force. The impact of poverty is especially severe for Latino women because they often find themselves with the sole responsibility of caring for their children. In 2012, about 21% of all Hispanic American households were female headed (vs. about 13% in the total population), but this percentage ranged from a low of 15% for Cuban Americans to a high of about 36% for Dominicans

FIGURE 8.17 Distribution of Household Income for White and Hispanic Americans, 2012

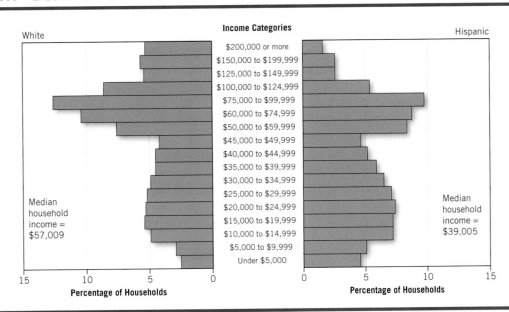

SOURCE: U.S. Census Bureau (2013f).

FIGURE 8.18 Poverty Rates for Non-Hispanic Whites, All Hispanic Americans, and 10 Largest Hispanic American Groups, 2012

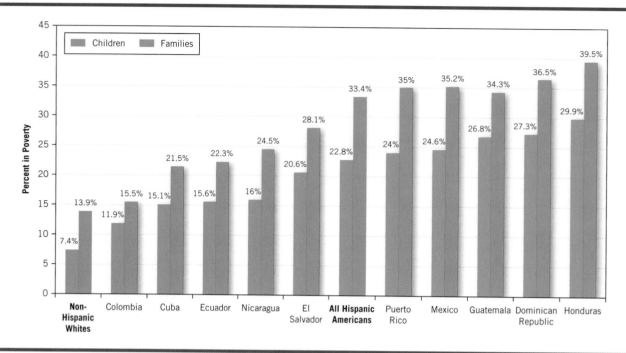

SOURCE: U.S. Census Bureau (2013a).

(U.S. Census Bureau, 2013a). This pattern is the result of many factors, among them the status of Latino men in the labor force. The jobs available to Latino men often do not pay enough to support a family, and many jobs are seasonal, temporary, or otherwise insecure.

Female-headed Latino families face a triple economic handicap: They have only one wage earner, whose potential income is limited by discrimination against both women and Latinos. The result of these multiple disadvantages is an especially high rate of poverty. Whereas 24% of non-Hispanic white, female-headed households fall below the poverty line, the percentage is about 41% for Hispanic households headed by females (U.S. Census Bureau, 2013a).

Summary. The socioeconomic situation of Latinos is complex and diversified. Many members of the group have successfully entered the mainstream economy, but others face poverty and exclusion. Highly concentrated in deteriorated urban areas (barrios), segments of these groups, like other minority groups of color, face the possibility of permanent poverty and economic marginality.

PRIMARY STRUCTURAL ASSIMILATION

Overall, the extent of intimate contact between Hispanic Americans and the dominant group probably has been higher than for either African Americans or American Indians (e.g., see Quillian & Campbell, 2003; Rosenfeld, 2002). This pattern may reflect the fact that Latinos are partly ethnic minority groups and partly racial minority groups. Some studies report that contact is greater for the more affluent social classes, in the cities, and for the younger generations (who are presumably more Americanized; Fitzpatrick, 1976; Grebler et al., 1970, p. 397; Rodriguez, 1989, pp. 70–72). On the other hand, the rate of contact probably has been decreased by the rapid increase in immigration and the tendency of the first generation to socialize more with coethnics.

Rates of intermarriage are higher for Latinos than for African Americans, but neither are a very high percentage of all marriages. Black and white interracial couples make up less than 1% of all marriages, and the comparable figure for Latinos is 4% of all marriages (U.S. Census Bureau, 2012c, p. 54).

Table 8.3 shows that rates of in-marriage for Hispanics are lower than those for whites. This is partly a function of simple arithmetic: The larger group (white Americans) is more likely to find partners within the group. However, note that the rate of Latino in-marriage is also lower than that of blacks (see Table 6.1), a group of about the same size. This pattern may reflect the tenacity of racial (vs. ethnic) barriers to integration in this institutional area.

Also note that rates of in-marriage for Latinos are affected by nativity. In both years, the foreign-born were more likely to marry within the group than were the U.S.-born. This pattern, like so many others, reflects the high rates of immigration and the tendency of recent immigrants to socialize within the ethnic subcommunity. For both years, Hispanics who married outside their group were most likely to marry whites.

TABLE 8.3 Percentage of Whites and Latinos Married to a Person of the Same Group, 1980 and 2008

| YEAR | WHITES | | LATINOS | | | |
| | Men | Women | Men | | Women | |
			Foreign-Born	U.S.-Born	Foreign-Born	U.S.-Born
1980	96%	95%	80%	67%	84%	70%
2008	93%	92%	83%	58%	83%	59%

SOURCE: Qian and Lichter (2011, p. 1072). Copyright © 2011 National Council on Family Relations. Reprinted with permission.

QUESTIONS FOR REFLECTION

1. This section examined a variety of dimensions of acculturation and integration for Hispanic Americans. Which is most important? Why?

2. Which Hispanic groups have been more successful in U.S. society and why? Do you agree with the definitions of "success" used in this section? What other definitions might be useful, and how might these change your ideas about which group is most successful?

ASSIMILATION AND HISPANIC AMERICANS

As test cases for what we have called the traditional view of American assimilation, Latinos fare poorly. Almost two centuries after the original contact period, Mexican Americans tend to be concentrated in the low-wage sector of the labor market, a source of cheap labor for the dominant group's economy. Puerto Ricans, who are more recent arrivals, occupy a similar profile and position.

The fundamental reality faced by both groups, in their histories and in their present situations, is their colonized status in U.S. society. Even while many Mexican Americans and Puerto Ricans have risen in the social class and occupational structure of the larger society, many share the problems of other urban minority groups of color.

The traditional views of the nature of assimilation likewise fail to describe the experiences of Cuban Americans. They are more prosperous, on the average, than either Mexican Americans or Puerto Ricans, but they became successful by remaining separate and developing an ethnic enclave in South Florida.

There is no single Hispanic American experience or pattern of adjustment to the larger society. We have focused mainly on three of the many Latino groups in the United States, and the diversity of their experiences suggests the variety and complexity of what it means to be a minority group in U.S. society. Their experiences also illustrate some of the fundamental forces that shape the experiences of minority groups: the split labor market and the U.S. appetite for cheap labor, the

impact of industrialization, the dangers of a permanent urban underclass, the relationships between competition and levels of prejudice and rejection, and the persistence of race as a primary dividing line between people and groups.

HISPANIC AMERICANS AND THE EVOLUTION OF THE AMERICAN RACIAL ORDER

The United States has, virtually since its birth, been organized into two communities: black and white, separate and unequal. This structural relationship has been reinforced and solidified by the traditional perception that there are *only* two races. What will happen to this tradition as groups that are neither black nor white—Latinos, Asian Americans, and others—continue to grow in numbers and significance in the everyday life of U.S. society?

One possibility, which we will call the whitening thesis, hypothesizes that Latinos (and Asian Americans) eventually will be accepted as white, while African Americans remain relegated to the perpetual black. An opposing position, called the browning thesis, predicts that all "peoples of color" will band together and threaten the dominance of whites. We consider each of these views below, as well as a third possible future for the racial order of the United States.

WHITENING

In this model, Latinos and Asian Americans will become part of the white American racial group while blacks will remain disproportionately unequal, powerless, and marginalized. The racial identities of Latinos and Asians will become "thinner," declining in salience for them as they increasingly access the privileges of whiteness, much like the Irish and Italians before them. As they assimilate, the "white" racial identity will grow more prominent and their sense of ethnicity will become largely symbolic.

This prediction is consistent with Gordon's assimilation model and the notion that immigrants move through a series of stages and become more incorporated into the dominant society in a relatively linear fashion. Once a group has completed acculturation, integration, and intermarriage, they will begin to racially identify with the dominant group.

George Yancey (2003) has tested the whitening thesis on a nationally representative data set, and his analysis places Latinos and Asian Americans in the middle stages of assimilation, because their residential patterns, marital patterns, and several key political beliefs align more closely with white Americans than they do with black Americans. If Gordon's model holds true, these groups will come to identify as white over the next several generations.

Another research project (Murguia & Foreman, 2003) focused on Mexican Americans and found that they tend to prefer spouses, neighbors, coworkers, and friends who are either Puerto Rican or white, not black. The researchers also found that Mexican Americans tend to endorse modern racism (see Chapter 3): the belief that racism is not much of a barrier to success and that people of color are largely responsible for their own hardships. This consistency with the ideology of the dominant group also positions Mexican Americans on the path to whiteness.

Finally, note that an important part of the whitening process is to distance oneself from the perpetually stigmatized black group. To the extent that a whitening process occurs for Latino and Asian Americans, these groups will tend to use both traditional and modern antiblack racism to emphasize their differences and align themselves more with the attitudinal and cultural perspectives of the dominant group. We discussed this type of dynamic in our coverage of the racial identity of Puerto Ricans who come to the mainland.

BROWNING

The browning thesis argues that whites will gradually lose their dominant status as Latino and Asian American groups grow in numbers. The balance of power will tip toward the nonwhite groups, who will use their greater numbers to challenge whites for position in the society.

Some theorists see the loss of white dominance as very negative, a threat to the integrity of Anglo-American culture. This version of the browning thesis has been presented by political scientist Samuel Huntington (2004), among many others (see the Current Debate at the end of this chapter). Some proponents of this perspective argue that Latinos are "unassimilable" due to their alleged unwillingness to learn English and absorb other aspects of U.S. culture, a view based largely on nativism, ethnocentrism, and prejudice, and refuted by much of the evidence presented in this chapter (e.g., see Figures 8.8 through 8.10). Nevertheless, this version of the browning thesis has gained momentum in popular culture and on some talk radio and cable TV shows. It also manifests itself in the political arena in debates over immigration policy and in the movement to make English the "official" language of the nation (see Chapter 2).

A different version of the browning thesis has taken hold among some sociologists. For example, Feagin and O'Brien

(2004) put a positive spin on the idea of the declining white numerical majority. They believe that as nonwhite groups grow in size, whites will be forced to share power in a more democratic, egalitarian, and inclusive fashion. This shift will be more likely to the extent that minority groups can forge alliances with one another. These combinations may be foreshadowed by studies of generational differences in the racial attitudes of immigrants, some of which show that native-born or second-generation Latinos and Asian Americans are more likely to express solidarity with African Americans than are the foreign-born and recently arrived members of their group (Murguia & Foreman, 2003). In contrast to the whitening thesis, this view of the browning thesis expects Latinos and Asian Americans to embrace a more color-conscious worldview and find ways to leverage their growing numbers, in alliance with African Americans, to improve their status in American society.

This version of the browning thesis also adopts a more global perspective. It recognizes that the world is occupied by many more "people of color" than by whites of European descent and that the growing numbers of nonwhites in the United States can be an important resource in the global marketplace. For example, people around the world commonly speak several languages on a daily basis, but Americans are almost entirely monolingual; this places them at a disadvantage in a global marketplace that values linguistic diversity. The United States might improve its position if it encourages the "fluent bilingualism" of its Latino and Asian American citizens, rather than insisting on "English only" (see Chapter 2).

SOMETHING ELSE?

Still another group of scholars challenges both the browning and the whitening theses and foresees a three-way racial dynamic. These scholars focus on the tremendous diversity within the Latino and Asian American communities in the United States in terms of relative wealth, skin color and other "racial" characteristics, religion, and national origins. This diversity leads them to conclude that only some Latino and Asian Americans will "whiten."

For example, Eduardo Bonilla-Silva (2003) sketches out a future racial trichotomy: whites, honorary whites, and the collective black. In this schema, well-off and light-skinned Latinos and Asians would not "become white" but, rather, would occupy an intermediary "honorary whites" status. This status would afford them much of the privilege and esteem not widely accorded to people of color, but it would still be a conditional status, which potentially could be revoked in times of economic crisis or at any other time when those in power found it necessary. Bonilla-Silva predicts that groups such as Chinese Americans and lighter-skinned Latinos would fit into the honorary white category, while darker-skinned Latinos and Asians would fit into the collective black category, along with, of course, American blacks.

Murguia and Foreman (2003) provide some findings from their study of Mexican Americans that can be used to illustrate this process. They point out that skin color and educational level make a difference in whether or not Latinos ally with blacks. Mexican Americans with darker skin and higher educational levels and those born in the United States are less likely to buy into the antiblack stereotypes of the larger culture and more likely to recognize the significance of racism in their own lives. Attitudes such as these may form the basis of future alliances among some (but not all) Latinos, Asian Americans, and African Americans.

HOW WILL THE RACIAL ORDER EVOLVE?

Will the United States grow browner or whiter? In the face of high levels of immigration and the growing importance of groups that are in the "racial middle"—those that are neither black nor white—it seems certain that the traditional, dichotomous black–white racial order cannot persist. What will replace it? Whichever thesis proves correct, it seems certain that new understandings of race and new relationships among racial groups will emerge in the coming decades.

SUMMARY

This summary is organized around the Learning Objectives listed at the beginning of this chapter.

 Summarize the population characteristics of all Hispanic Americans and the 10 largest Hispanic American groups.

The label "Hispanic American" includes a variety of different groups who trace their origins to Central and South America and the Caribbean. Taken as a whole, they are the largest U.S. minority group and are growing rapidly, largely as a result of high rates of immigration. Most Hispanic groups have a high percentage of first-generation members. Mexican Americans are the largest Hispanic group, followed by Puerto Ricans and Cuban Americans, but there are many other groups.

 Summarize and explain the history of Mexican Americans, including their cultural characteristics, their immigration patterns, changing U.S. policy and laws affecting them, their development in the United States, and their protest organizations and leaders.

Mexican Americans became a minority group in the 19th century as a result of military conquest. Culturally, Mexican Americans vary from the Anglo mainstream in terms of religion, the importance attached to family, and in many other areas. Since first contact with the dominant group, Mexican American culture has been sustained by immigration, which has fluctuated in volume as the result of conditions in Mexico, the demand for labor in the United States, and federal policy. In recent decades, immigration has been affected by the 1965 change in U.S. immigration policy, the implementation of NAFTA, and the downturn in the U.S. economy.

Domestically, Mexican Americans mix elements of both colonized and immigrant minority groups. A protest movement has been in existence since the 19th century, and the Chicanismo movement became prominent in the 1960s. Notable leaders include César Chávez.

 Summarize and explain the history of Puerto Ricans, including their immigration patterns.

Puerto Ricans became an American minority group as a result of the defeat of Spain in the Spanish–American War of 1898. Movement to the mainland began in significant numbers after World War II and centered on the urban Northeast, where members of the group had to adjust to Anglo culture, including differing ideas and perceptions regarding race. Puerto Ricans combine elements of both colonized and immigrant minority-group experiences, and tend to be concentrated in the lower levels of the occupational structure.

 Summarize and explain the history of Cuban Americans, including their immigration patterns and the dynamics and importance of the Cuban American ethnic enclave.

Cubans began immigrating to the United States in large numbers after the Cuban Revolution of 1959. They are residentially concentrated in Florida and especially in Miami-Dade County. The early immigrant stream included many middle- and upper-class people. They brought capital and business expertise and started business enterprises, at first to serve the group but gradually to serve the larger community. The enclave provided an arena in which the first generation and their children could avoid the prejudice of the larger society and capitalize on their business experience. Cuban Americans, in large part because of the enclave economy, tend to rank higher in levels of education and income.

 Summarize how prejudice and discrimination affect Hispanic Americans.

The overall levels of anti-Hispanic prejudice and discrimination seem to have declined, along with the general decline in explicit, overt racism in American society. However, recent high levels of immigration seem to have increased anti-Hispanic prejudice and discrimination, especially in the borderlands and other areas with large numbers of immigrants.

8.6 Describe the situation of Hispanic Americans using the concepts of assimilation and pluralism, especially in terms of

    a. acculturation,

    b. secondary structural assimilation, and

    c. primary structural assimilation.

- Hispanic American cultures and the Spanish language are very much intact. Mexican American and Puerto Rican cultures are sustained by the close proximity of the homeland and frequent migration back and forth. The immigration of other groups, including Cuban Americans, is recent, and culture and language remain intact, at least for the first generation. Language acculturation tends to increase as the generations pass and with length of residence and level of education.

- The secondary structural assimilation of Hispanic Americans is variable from group to group. Recent immigrants with low levels of education rank low in social class, but many Latinos whose families have been in the United States for generations are thoroughly integrated.

- Primary structural assimilation is also highly variable, although generally higher than for African Americans. Recent immigrants with lower levels of education rank lower on this dimension.

8.7 Assess the overall situation of Hispanic Americans today based on the concepts and information presented in this chapter, and assess the future of American society in terms of racial perceptions: Will the United States grow whiter or browner, or will a new racial order emerge?

Hispanic American groups are following a variety of pathways in their relationships with the larger society. Some seem to be following the "traditional" three-generation assimilation model, although the movement toward mainstream society tends to be balanced by the arrival of newcomers; Cuban Americans are an enclave minority; and others may be moving toward permanent marginalization and membership in the urban underclass.

The traditional dichotomous racial order seems destined to change, but what will replace it? Will Latinos and Asian Americans become white? Will whites lose their dominant position as the society grows "browner"? Or will a different racial order emerge, with whites, honorary whites, and perpetual blacks?

KEY TERMS

Chicanismo 226

Chicanos 227

machismo 219

marielitos 232

Operation Wetback 222

repatriation 222

REVIEW QUESTIONS

1. At the beginning of this chapter, it was stated that Hispanic Americans "combine elements of the polar extremes [immigrant and colonized] of Blauner's typology of minority groups" and that they are "partly an ethnic minority group and partly a racial minority group." Explain these statements in terms of the rest of the material presented in the chapter.

2. What important cultural differences between Mexican Americans and the dominant society have shaped the relationships between the two groups?

3. How does the history of Mexican immigration demonstrate the usefulness of Noel's concepts of differentials in power and competition?

4. Compare and contrast the protest movements of Mexican Americans, American Indians, and African Americans. What similarities and differences existed in Chicanismo, Red Power, and Black Power? How do the differences reflect the unique experiences of each group?

5. In what ways are the experiences of Puerto Ricans and Cuban Americans unique compared with those of other minority groups? How do these differences reflect other differences, such as variations in the contact situation?

6. The Cuban American enclave has resulted in a variety of benefits for the group. Why don't other minority groups follow this strategy?

7. What images of Latinas are common in U.S. society? How do these images reflect the experiences of these groups?

8. Describe the situation of the major Hispanic American groups in terms of acculturation and integration. Which groups are closest to equality? What factors or experiences might account for the differences between groups? In what ways might this statement be true: "Hispanic Americans are remaining pluralistic even while they assimilate"?

Sharpen your skills with SAGE edge at edge.sagepub.com/healey7e

SAGE edge for students provides a personalized approach to help you accomplish your coursework goals in an easy-to-use learning environment.

The following resources are available at SAGE edge:

Current Debates: Are Hispanic Americans Assimilating, or Are They Changing American Culture?

Will Hispanic immigrants—especially those from Mexico—ultimately adapt to American culture? Or will they transform the fundamental values of U.S. society? Is American society being "Hispanicized"?

On our website you will find an overview of the topic, the clashing points of view, and some questions to consider as you analyze the material.

Public Sociology Assignments

Public Sociology Assignments provide opportunities for students to address directly and personally some of the issues raised in this text.

There are two assignments for Part III on our website. The first looks at patterns of self-segregation in school cafeterias, and, in the second, students analyze the portrayal of the American family on television in terms of race, ethnicity, sexual orientation, and other sociologically relevant characteristics.

Contributed by Linda M. Waldron

Internet Research Project

For this Internet Research Project, you will use data gathered by the U.S. Census Bureau to assess the situation of all Hispanic Americans and a Latino group of your choosing. You will add this information to the data you gathered previously on African Americans, Native Americans, and the general population. The project will be guided by a series of questions related to course concepts, and your instructor may ask you to discuss your findings in small groups.

For Further Reading

Please see our website for an annotated list of important works related to this chapter.

CHAPTER-OPENING TIMELINE PHOTO CREDITS

1910: Library of Congress Prints and Photographs Division

1942: Everett Collection/Newscom

1943: Library of Congress Prints and Photographs Division

1965: Department of Labor

2001: Reuters/Jeff Topping

2007: ©iStockphoto.com/rrodrickbeiler

2009: Collection of the Supreme Court of the United States/Steve Petteway

2010: ©iStockphoto.com/jcamilobernal

9

ASIAN AMERICANS

Wikimedia

timeline

1847
Yung Wing becomes first Chinese to graduate from U.S. college (Yale).

1862
The "Anti-Coolie" Act discourages Chinese immigration to California and institutes special taxes on employers who hire Chinese workers.

1924
The Johnson-Reed A effectively prohibits immigration of all Asians.

| 1760 | 1850 | 1865 | 1880 | 1895 | 1910 | 1925 |

1763
The first recorded settlement of Asians in the U.S. are Filipinos in Louisiana.

LOC

1848
The California Gold Rush leads to first large-scale Chinese immigration.

Wikimedia Commons

1882
The Chinese Exclusion Act suspends immigration of Chinese laborers for 10 years.

LOC

1914–1918
Many Asian Americans serve in World War I and are awarded naturalization for their service.

1907–1908
Under the Gentleman's Agreement, Japan denies passports to laborers seeking to enter the U.S.

I had flown from San Francisco . . . and was riding a taxi to my hotel to attend a conference on multiculturalism. My driver and I chatted about the weather and the tourists. . . . The rearview mirror reflected a white man in his forties. "How long have you been in this country?" he asked. "All my life," I replied, wincing. "I was born in the United States." With a strong Southern drawl, he remarked: "I was wondering because your English is excellent!" . . . I explained: "My grandfather came here from Japan in the 1880s. My family has been here for over a hundred years." He glanced at me in the mirror. Somehow, I did not look "American" to him; my eyes and complexion looked foreign.

—Ronald Takaki (1993, p. 2),
professor of Asian American studies

LOC

LEARNING OBJECTIVES

By the end of this chapter, you will be able to do the following:

9.1 Summarize the population characteristics of all Asian Americans and the 10 largest Asian American groups.

9.2 Summarize and explain the history of Chinese and Japanese Americans, including their cultural characteristics, their immigration patterns, their development in the United States, and the nature and importance of the enclave for each.

9.3 Explain the patterns of the recent immigration from Asia.

9.4 Summarize how prejudice and discrimination affect Asian Americans.

9.5 Describe the situation of Asian Americans using the concepts of assimilation and pluralism, especially in terms of

a. acculturation,

b. secondary structural assimilation, and

c. primary structural assimilation

9.6 Assess the overall situation of Asian Americans today based on the concepts and information presented in this chapter, and assess the idea that Asian Americans are a "model minority." Are Asian Americans "whitening," "blackening," or becoming "honorary whites"?

1942
Approximately 110,000 Japanese Americans are sent to internment camps during World War II.

2001
Hate crimes against Arab and Asian Americans follow the September 11 terrorist attacks.

1940   1955   1970   1985   2000   2015

1943
Congress repeals Chinese Exclusion Act and grants naturalization rights.

1988
The Civil Liberties Act of 1988 pays surviving Japanese-American internees $20,000 each.

2012
Asians surpass Hispanics as the largest group of new immigrants in the U.S.

Ronald Reagan Presidential Library

Wikimedia Commons

These few seconds of conversation speak deeply to U.S. perceptions of Asian Americans (and other minority groups). The taxi driver certainly meant no insult, but his casual question revealed his view, widely shared, that the United States is a white, European society. At the time of the conversation, Professor Takaki was a distinguished professor at a prestigious West Coast university, a highly respected teacher and internationally renowned expert in his area of study. Very possibly, his family had been in the United States longer than the taxi driver's family; yet the driver automatically assumed he was an outsider. •

Asian Americans, like other peoples of color, continually find themselves set apart, excluded, and stigmatized—whether during the 19th-century anti-Chinese campaign in California, after the 1922 Supreme Court decision (*Takao Ozawa v. United States*) that declared Asians ineligible for U.S. citizenship, or by the racist reactions to the crowning of Nina Davulari, an American of Indian descent, as Miss America in September 2013 (Oldenburg, 2013). The stereotypes are sometimes "positive"—as in the view that Asian Americans are "model minorities"—but the "othering" is real, painful, and consequential.

In this chapter, we begin with an overview of Asian American groups and then briefly examine the traditions and customs they bring with them to America. For much of the chapter, we will focus on the two oldest groups, Chinese Americans and Japanese Americans.

Throughout, we will be especially concerned with the perception that Asian Americans in general and Chinese and Japanese Americans in particular are "model minorities": successful, affluent, highly educated people who do not suffer from the problems usually associated with minority-group status. How accurate is this view? Have Asian Americans forged a pathway to upward mobility that could be followed by other groups? Do the concepts and theories that have guided this text (particularly the Blauner and Noel hypotheses) apply? Does the success of these groups mean that the United States is truly an open, fair, and just society? We explore these questions throughout the chapter.

Asian American groups vary in their languages, in their cultural and physical characteristics, and in their experiences in the United States. Some of these groups are truly newcomers to America, but others have roots in this country stretching back more than 150 years. As was the case with American Indians and Hispanic Americans, "Asian American" is a convenient label imposed by the larger society (and by government agencies such as the U.S. Census Bureau) that deemphasizes the differences

TABLE 9.1 Size and Growth of All Asian Americans* and 10 Largest Asian American Groups, by Origin, 1990–2012

GROUP	1990	2000	2012	GROWTH (NUMBER OF TIMES LARGER), 1990–2010	PERCENTAGE OF TOTAL POPULATION, 2010
Total Asian American	6,908,638	11,070,913	17,817,803	2.6	5.6%
China	1,645,472	2,879,636	4,224,293	2.6	1.3%
Philippines	1,406,770	2,364,815	3,480,437	2.5	1.1%
India	815,447	1,899,599	3,208,387	3.9	1.0%
Vietnam	614,547	1,223,736	1,842,851	3.0	< 1%
Korea	798,849	1,228,427	1,748,287	2.2	< 1%
Japan	847,562	1,148,932	1,320,157	1.6	< 1%
Pakistan	N/A	204,309	401,707	—	< 1%
Cambodia	147,411	206,052	310,964	2.1	< 1%
Hmong**	90,082	186,310	263,072	2.9	< 1%
Laos	149,014	198,203	249,108	1.7	< 1%
Percentage of U.S. Population	2.8%	3.9%	5.6%		
Total U.S. Population	248,710,000	281,422,000	311,609,369	1.2	

SOURCE: 1990—U.S. Census Bureau (1990); 2000—U.S. Census Bureau (2000c); 2012—U.S. Census Bureau (2013a).

*Asian Americans, alone and in combination with other groups.

**The Hmong are from various Southeast Asian nations, including Laos and Vietnam.

between the groups. Table 9.1 lists some information about size and growth rates for the 10 largest Asian American groups and all Asian Americans.

Several features of Table 9.1 are worth noting. First, Asian Americans are a small fraction of the total U.S. population. Even when aggregated, they account for only 5.6%. In contrast, African Americans are 13% and Hispanic Americans 16%.

Second, most Asian American groups have grown dramatically in recent decades, largely because of high rates of immigration since the 1965 changes in U.S. immigration policy. All the groups listed in Table 9.1 grew faster than the total population between 1990 and 2012. Japanese Americans grew at the slowest rate (largely because immigration from Japan has been low in recent decades), but the number of Asian Indians almost quadrupled, and nearly all the other groups doubled or tripled their populations.

This rapid growth is projected to continue for decades to come, and the impact of the Asian American population on everyday life and American culture will increase accordingly. As we saw in Figure 1.1, projections show that, by midcentury, 1 out of every 10 Americans will be of Asian descent. The relative sizes of the largest Asian American groups are presented in Figure 9.1.

Like Hispanic Americans, most Asian American groups have a high percentage of foreign-born members, as displayed in Figure 9.2. The majority of 8 of the 10 groups listed in the graph are first generation, and even Japanese Americans, the lowest-ranked group, are almost double the national norm for foreign-born members. The vast majority of Asian Americans (88%) are either immigrants or the second-generation children of immigrants (Pew Research Center, 2013c, p. 23).

We pointed out in Chapter 8 that most Hispanic Americans identify themselves in terms of their family's country of origin, and the same is true of Asian Americans. According to a recent survey, about 62% describe themselves in terms of their country of origin, about 20% describe themselves as "Asian American," and 14% describe themselves as just "American." There are large differences in self-description by nativity: Almost 70% of the foreign-born (vs. 43% of the native-born) describe themselves in terms of their country of origin (Pew Research Center, 2013c, pp. 88–89).

ORIGINS AND CULTURES

Asian Americans bring a wealth of traditions to the United States. They speak many different languages and practice religions as diverse as Buddhism, Confucianism, Islam, Hinduism, and Christianity. Asian cultures predate the founding of the United States by centuries or even millennia. Although no two of these cultures are the same, some general similarities can be identified. These cultural traits have shaped the behavior of

FIGURE 9.1 Asian Groups in the United States by Countries of Origin, 2012

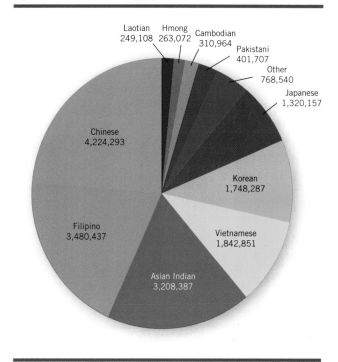

Laotian 249,108
Hmong 263,072
Cambodian 310,964
Pakistani 401,707
Other 768,540
Japanese 1,320,157
Korean 1,748,287
Vietnamese 1,842,851
Asian Indian 3,208,387
Filipino 3,480,437
Chinese 4,224,293

SOURCE: U.S. Census Bureau (2013a).

Asian Americans, as well as the perceptions of members of the dominant group, and compose part of the foundation on which Asian American experiences have been built.

Asian cultures tend to stress group membership over individual self-interest. For example, Confucianism, which was the dominant ethical and moral system in traditional China and had a powerful influence on many other Asian cultures, counsels people to see themselves as elements in larger social systems and status hierarchies. Confucianism emphasizes loyalty to the group, conformity to societal expectations, and respect for one's superiors.

In traditional China, as in other Asian societies, the business of everyday life was organized around kinship relations, and most interpersonal relations were with family members and other relatives (Lyman, 1974, p. 9). The family or the clan often owned the land on which all depended for survival, and kinship ties determined inheritance patterns. The clan also performed a number of crucial social functions, including arranging marriages, settling disputes between individuals, and organizing festivals and holidays.

Asian cultures stress sensitivity to the opinions and judgments of others, and the importance of avoiding public embarrassment and not giving offense. Especially when discussing Japanese culture, these cultural tendencies are often contrasted with Western practices in terms of "guilt versus shame" and the nature of personal morality (Benedict, 1946). In Western cultures, individuals are encouraged to develop and abide by a conscience, or an inner moral voice, and behavior is guided by

FIGURE 9.2 Foreign-Born Population for Asian Americans (Select Countries of Origin), 2012

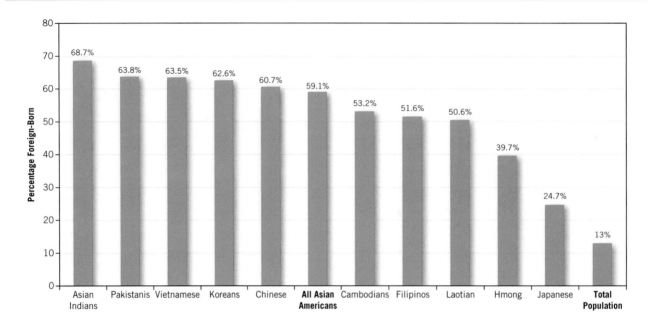

SOURCE: U.S. Census Bureau (2013a).

one's personal sense of guilt. In contrast, Asian cultures stress the importance of maintaining the respect and good opinion of others, and avoiding shame and public humiliation. Group harmony, or *wa* in Japanese, is a central concern, and displays of individualism are discouraged. These characteristics are reflected in the Japanese proverb, "The nail that sticks up must be hammered down" (Whiting, 1990, p. 70). Asian cultures emphasize proper behavior, conformity to convention and the judgments of others, and avoiding embarrassment and personal confrontations ("saving face").

A possible manifestation of this tendency to seek harmony and avoid confrontation was documented by Chou and Feagin (2008) in interviews with Asian Americans from a variety of groups. They found that their subjects commonly used "compliant conformity" to cope with white racism, discrimination, and rejection (p. 222). Their respondents often expressed the belief that their conformity and hard work would bring recognition and acceptance from the larger society. The parents of the respondents, even those who had experienced substantial discrimination, commonly pressured their children to conform to white expectations and Anglo values in the hope that their success (e.g., in school) would protect them from negative treatment and stereotyping. Chou and Feagin suggest that this strategy has had limited success (at best) and that, ultimately, it sustains white prejudicial values and the conventional racial hierarchy in U.S. society by complying with rather than challenging racism (p. 222).

Traditional Asian cultures were male dominated, and women were consigned to subordinate roles. A Chinese woman was expected to serve first her father, then her husband,

and, if widowed, her eldest son. Confucianism also decreed that women should observe the Four Virtues: chastity and obedience, shyness, a pleasing demeanor, and skill in the performance of domestic duties (Amott & Matthaei, 1991, p. 200). Women of high status in traditional China symbolized their subordination by binding their feet. This painful, crippling practice began early in life and required women to wrap their feet tightly to keep them artificially small. The bones in the arch were broken so that the toes could be bent under the foot, further decreasing the size of the foot. Bound feet were considered beautiful, but they also immobilized women and were intended to prevent them from "wandering away" from domestic and household duties (Jackson, 2000; Takaki, 1993, pp. 209–210).

The experiences of Asian Americans in the United States modified these patriarchal values and traditional traits. For the groups with longer histories in U.S. society, such as Chinese Americans and Japanese Americans, the effects of these values on individual personality may be slight, but for more recently arrived groups, the effects may be more powerful.

The cultural and religious differences among the Asian American groups also reflect the recent histories of each of the sending nations. For example, Vietnam was a Chinese colony for 1,000 years, but for much of the past century, it was a French colony. Although Vietnamese culture has been heavily influenced by China, many Vietnamese are Catholic, a result of the efforts of the French to convert them. The Philippines and India were also colonized by Western nations—the former by Spain and then the United States, and the latter by Great Britain. As a result, many Filipinos are Catholic, and many Indian immigrants are familiar with English and Anglo culture.

Do Asian Americans and Anglo-Americans behave differently because of their cultural differences? Do these different reactions lead to misunderstandings and problems for Asian Americans?

Below is a series of statements you might hear on a college campus. Although any of them might be spoken by a student of any background, which are more likely to be said by an Asian American student? Which are more reflective of Anglo culture?

STATEMENT	ASIAN	ANGLO
"I really love the social life on this campus—I really enjoy chatting with all different kinds of people, making small talk, and trading gossip."		
"It's really important to show respect to our professors and the college administrators."		
"I was so proud to be recognized in front of everyone—the entire class—for my research project."		
"I don't like to talk in class when I am directly called on."		
"I don't think that people should bottle their emotions—let it all hang out!"		

TURN THE PAGE TO FIND OUR ANSWERS.

These examples are, of course, the merest suggestion of the diversity of these groups. In fact, Asian Americans, who share little more than a slight physical resemblance and some broad cultural similarities, are much more diverse than Hispanic Americans, who are overwhelmingly Catholic and share a common language and historical connection with Spain (Min, 1995, p. 25).

QUESTIONS FOR REFLECTION

1. What are some of the key differences between Asian and Anglo cultures? How have these differences shaped relations between the groups?

2. Which group is the most diverse: African Americans, Native Americans, Hispanic Americans, or Asian Americans? How? Given the levels of diversity, does it make sense to discuss these groups as a single entity? Why or why not?

CONTACT SITUATIONS AND THE DEVELOPMENT OF THE CHINESE AMERICAN AND JAPANESE AMERICAN COMMUNITIES

The earliest Asian groups to arrive in substantial numbers were from China and Japan. Their contact situations not only shaped their own histories but also affected the present situation of all Asian Americans in many ways. As we will see, the contact situations for both Chinese Americans and Japanese Americans featured massive rejection and discrimination. Both groups adapted to the racism of the larger society by forming enclaves, a strategy that eventually produced some major benefits for their descendants.

CHINESE AMERICANS

Early Immigration and the Anti-Chinese Campaign. Immigrants from China to the United States began to arrive in the early 1800s and were generally motivated by the same kinds of social and economic forces that have inspired immigration everywhere for the past two centuries. Chinese immigrants were "pushed" to leave their homeland by the disruption of traditional social relations, caused by the colonization of much of China by more industrialized European nations and by rapid population growth (Chan, 1990; Lyman, 1974; Tsai, 1986). At the same time, these immigrants were "pulled" to the West Coast of the United States by the Gold Rush of 1849 and by other opportunities created by the development of the West.

The Noel hypothesis (see Chapter 4) provides a useful way to analyze the contact situation that developed between Chinese and Anglo-Americans in the mid-19th century. As you may recall, Noel argues that racial or ethnic stratification will result when a contact situation is characterized by three conditions: ethnocentrism, competition, and a differential in power. Once all three conditions were met on the West Coast, a vigorous campaign against the Chinese began, and the group was pushed into a subordinate, disadvantaged position.

STATEMENT	ASIAN	ANGLO
"I really love the social life on this campus—I really enjoy chatting with all different kinds of people, making small talk, and trading gossip."		X
Asian American values place less emphasis on spontaneity, sociability, and flexibility, and more on self-control and discipline.		
"It's really important to show respect to our professors and college administrators."	X	
Asian Americans are more likely to stress obedience to authority, while Anglos are more likely to stress questioning authority.		
"I was so proud to be recognized in front of everyone—the entire class—for my research project."		X
Asian American values prize humility, cooperation with others, and shared responsibility, not individual achievement.		
"I don't like to talk in class when I am directly called on."	X	
In Anglo culture, individual visibility is acceptable, even encouraged. Asian American culture places more value on the collective.		
"I don't think that people should bottle their emotions—let it all hang out!"		X
Anglo culture places more stress on "telling it like it is" and openly expressing all emotions.		

Could these differences in values be a problem for Asian American students? How about in situations where students are graded for their contributions to class discussion or expected to speak out and express their ideas? More broadly, might there be issues in situations where students face racism, must make contact across ethnic or racial lines, or desire to date someone from another group? How?

NOTE: This exercise is largely based on Japanese American Citizens League (2009).

Ethnocentrism based on racial, cultural, and language differences was present from the beginning, but at first, competition for jobs between Chinese immigrants and native-born workers was muted by a robust, rapidly growing economy and an abundance of jobs. At first, politicians, newspaper editorial writers, and business leaders praised the Chinese for their industriousness and tirelessness (Tsai, 1986, p. 17).

Before long, however, the economic boom slowed and the supply of jobs began to dry up. The Gold Rush petered out, and the transcontinental railroad, which thousands of Chinese workers had helped build, was completed in 1869. The migration of Anglo-Americans from the East continued, and competition for jobs and other resources increased. An anti-Chinese campaign of harassment, discrimination, and violent attacks began. In 1871, in Los Angeles, a mob of "several hundred whites shot, hanged, and stabbed 19 Chinese to death" (Tsai, 1986, p. 67). Other attacks against the Chinese occurred in Denver; Seattle; Tacoma; and Rock Springs, Wyoming (Lyman, 1974, p. 77).

As the West Coast economy changed, the Chinese came to be seen as a threat, and elements of the dominant group tried to limit competition. The Chinese were a small group—there were only about 100,000 in the entire country in 1870—and by law, they were not permitted to become citizens. Hence, they controlled few power resources with which to withstand these attacks. During the 1870s, Chinese workers were forced out of most sectors of the mainstream economy, and in 1882, the anti-Chinese campaign experienced its ultimate triumph when the U.S. Congress passed the **Chinese Exclusion Act**, banning virtually all immigration from China. The act was one of the first restrictive immigration laws and was aimed solely at the Chinese. It established a rigid competitive relationship between the groups (see Chapter 5) and eliminated the threat

The **Chinese Exclusion Act**, passed by the U.S. Congress in 1882, banned virtually all immigration from China.

presented by Chinese labor by excluding the Chinese from American society.

Consistent with the predictions of split labor market theory (see Chapter 3), the primary antagonists of Chinese immigrants were native-born workers and organized labor. White owners of small businesses, feeling threatened by Chinese-owned businesses, also supported passage of the Chinese Exclusion Act (Boswell, 1986). Other social classes, such as the capitalists who owned larger factories, might actually have benefited from the continued supply of cheaper labor created by immigration from China. Conflicts such as the anti-Chinese campaign can be especially intense because they confound racial and ethnic antagonisms with disputes between different social classes.

The ban on immigration from China remained in effect until World War II, when China was awarded a yearly quota of 105 immigrants in recognition of its wartime alliance with the United States. Large-scale immigration from China did not resume until federal policy was revised in the 1960s.

Population Trends and the "Delayed" Second Generation. Following the Chinese Exclusion Act, the number of Chinese in the United States actually declined (see Figure 9.3) as some immigrants passed away or returned to China and were not replaced by newcomers. The huge majority of Chinese immigrants in the 19th century had been young adult male sojourners who intended to work hard, save money, and return to their homes in China (Chan, 1990, p. 66). After 1882, it was difficult for anyone from China, male or female, to enter the United States, and the Chinese community in the United States remained overwhelmingly male for many decades. At the end of the 19th century, for example, males outnumbered females by more than 25 to 1, and the sex ratio did not approach parity for decades (Wong, 1995, p. 64; see also Ling, 2000). The scarcity of Chinese women in the United States delayed the second generation (the first generation born in the United States), and it wasn't until the 1920s, 80 years after immigration began, that as many as one third of all Chinese in the United States were native-born (Wong, 1995, p. 64).

The delayed second generation may have reinforced the exclusion of the Chinese American community, which began as a reaction to the overt discrimination of the dominant group (Chan, 1990, p. 66). The children of immigrants are usually much more acculturated, and their language facility and greater familiarity with the larger society often permit them to represent the group and speak for it more effectively. In the case of Chinese Americans (and other Asian groups), members of the second generation were citizens of the United States by birth, a status from which the immigrants were barred, and they had legal and political rights not available to their parents. Thus, the decades-long absence of a more Americanized, English-speaking generation increased the isolation of Chinese Americans.

FIGURE 9.3 Population Growth for Chinese and Japanese Americans, 1850–2012

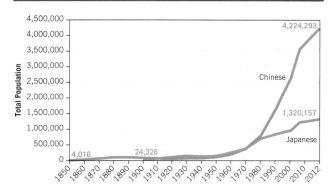

SOURCE: Hoeffel, Rastogi, Kim, and Shahid (2012, p. 4); Kitano (1980, p. 562); Lee (1998, p. 15).

The Ethnic Enclave. The Chinese became increasingly urbanized as the anti-Chinese campaign and rising racism took their toll. Forced out of towns and smaller cities, they settled in larger urban areas, especially San Francisco, which offered the safety of urban anonymity and neighborhoods where the old ways could be practiced and contact with the hostile larger society minimized. Chinatowns had existed since the start of the immigration, and they now took on added significance as safe havens from the storm of anti-Chinese venom. The Chinese withdrew to these neighborhoods and became an "invisible minority" (Tsai, 1986, p. 67).

These early Chinatowns were ethnic enclaves like those founded by Jews on the East Coast and the more recently founded Cuban community in Miami, and a similar process formed them. The earliest urban Chinese included merchants and skilled artisans who, like the early wave of Cuban immigrants, were experienced in commerce (Chan, 1990, p. 44). They established businesses and retail stores that were typically small in scope and modest in profits. As the number of urban Chinese increased, the market for these enterprises became larger and more spatially concentrated. New services were required, the size of the cheap labor pool available to Chinese merchants and entrepreneurs increased, and the Chinatowns became the economic, cultural, and social centers of the community.

Within the Chinatowns, elaborate social structures developed that mirrored traditional China in many ways. The enforced segregation of the Chinese in America helped preserve much of the traditional food, dress, language, values, and religions of their homeland from the pressures of Americanization. The social structure was based on a variety of types of organizations, including family and clan groups and *huiguan*, or associations based on

Huiguan were associations based on the region of China from which immigrants originated. They performed various social and welfare functions.

Children of an affluent family in the streets of Chinatown, San Francisco.

the region or district in China from which the immigrants had come. These organizations performed various, often overlapping, social and welfare services, including settling disputes, aiding new arrivals from their regions, and facilitating the development of mutual aid networks (Lai, 1980, p. 221; Lyman, 1974, pp. 32–37, 116–118).

Life was not always peaceful in Chinatown, and there were numerous disputes over control of resources and the organizational infrastructure. In particular, secret societies called **tongs** contested the control and leadership of the merchant-led *huiguan* and the clan associations. These sometimes bloody conflicts were sensationalized in the American press as "Tong Wars," and they contributed to the popular stereotypes of Asians as exotic, mysterious, and dangerous (Lai, 1980, p. 222; Lyman, 1974, pp. 37–50).

Despite these internal conflicts, American Chinatowns evolved into highly organized, largely self-contained communities, complete with their own leadership and decision-making structures. The internal "city government" of Chinatown was the Chinese Consolidated Benevolent Association (CCBA).

Tongs were secret societies in Chinatown that sometimes fought with each other and with other organizations for control of resources.

Dominated by the larger *huiguan* and clans, the CCBA coordinated and supplemented the activities of the various organizations and represented the interests of the community to the larger society.

The local CCBAs, along with other organizations, also attempted to combat the anti-Chinese campaign, speaking out against racial discrimination and filing numerous lawsuits to contest racist legislation (Lai, 1980, p. 223). The effectiveness of the protest efforts was handicapped by the lack of resources in the Chinese community and the fact that Chinese immigrants could not become citizens. Attempts were made to mobilize international pressure to protest the treatment of the Chinese in the United States. At the time, however, China was itself colonized and dominated by other nations (including the United States). The country was further weakened by internal turmoil and could mount no effective assistance for its citizens in the United States (Chan, 1990, p. 62).

Survival and Development. The Chinese American community survived despite the widespread poverty, discrimination, and pressures created by the unbalanced sex ratio. Members of the group began to seek opportunities in other regions, and Chinatowns appeared and grew in New York, Boston, Chicago, Philadelphia, and many other cities.

The patterns of exclusion and discrimination that began during the 19th-century anti-Chinese campaign were common throughout the nation and continued well into the 20th century. Chinese Americans responded by finding economic opportunity in areas where dominant-group competition for jobs was weak, continuing their tendency to be an "invisible" minority group. Very often, they started small businesses that either served other members of their own group (e.g., restaurants) or relied on the patronage of the general public (e.g., laundries). The jobs provided by these small businesses were the economic lifeblood of the community but were limited in the amount of income and wealth they could generate. Until recent decades, for example, most restaurants served primarily other Chinese, especially single males. Since their primary clientele were poor, the profit potential of these businesses was sharply limited. Laundries served the more affluent dominant group, but the returns from this enterprise declined as washers and dryers became increasingly present in homes throughout the nation. The population of Chinatown was generally too small to sustain more than these two primary commercial enterprises (Zhou, 1992, pp. 92–94).

As the decades passed, the enclave economy and the complex subsociety of Chinatown evolved. However, discrimination, combined with defensive self-segregation, ensured the continuation of poverty, limited job opportunities, and substandard housing. Relatively hidden from general view, Chinatown became the world in which the second generation grew to adulthood. Some of this experience is captured in the next Narrative Portrait.

The Second Generation. Whereas the immigrant generation largely retained its native language and customs, the second generation was much more influenced by the larger culture. The institutional and organizational structures of Chinatown were created to serve the older, mostly male immigrant generation, but younger Chinese Americans tended to look beyond the enclave to fill their needs. They came in contact with the larger society through schools, churches, and voluntary organizations such as the YMCA and YWCA.

They abandoned many traditional customs and were less loyal to and interested in the clan and regional associations that the immigrant generation had constructed. They founded organizations of their own that were more compatible with their Americanized lifestyles (Lai, 1980, p. 225).

As with other minority groups, World War II was an important watershed for Chinese Americans. During the war, job opportunities outside the enclave increased, and after the war, many of the 8,000 Chinese Americans who served in the armed forces were able to take advantage of the GI Bill to further their education (Lai, 1980, p. 226). In the 1940s and 1950s, many second-generation Chinese Americans moved out of the enclave, away from the traditional neighborhoods, and pursued careers in the larger society. This group was mobile and Americanized, and with educational credentials comparable to the general population, they were prepared to seek success outside Chinatown.

In another departure from tradition, the women of the second generation also pursued education, and as early as 1960, median years of schooling for Chinese American women were slightly higher than for Chinese American men (Kitano & Daniels, 1995, p. 48). Chinese American women also became more diverse in their occupational profile as the century progressed. In 1900, three quarters of all employed Chinese American women worked in manufacturing (usually in garment industry sweatshops or in canning factories) or in domestic work. By 1960, less than 2% were in domestic work, 32% were in clerical occupations, and 18% held professional jobs, often as teachers (Amott & Matthaei, 1991, pp. 209–211).

The men and women of the second generation achieved considerable educational and occupational success, and helped establish the idea that Chinese Americans are a "model minority." A closer examination reveals, however, that the old traditions of anti-Chinese discrimination and prejudice continued to limit the life chances of even the best-educated members of this generation. Second-generation Chinese Americans earned less, on the average, and had less-favorable occupational profiles than did comparably educated white Americans, a gap between qualifications and rewards that reflects persistent discrimination. Kitano

and Daniels (1995, p. 50) conclude, for example, that although well-educated Chinese Americans could find good jobs in the mainstream economy, the highest, most lucrative positions—and those that required direct supervision by whites—were still closed to them (see also Hirschman & Wong, 1984).

Furthermore, many Chinese Americans, including many of those who stayed in the Chinatowns to operate the enclave economy and the immigrants who began arriving after 1965, do not fit the image of success at all. A large percentage of these Chinese Americans face many of the same problems as do members of colonized, excluded, exploited minority groups of color. For survival, they rely on low-wage jobs in the garment industry, the service sector, and the small businesses of the enclave economy, and are beset by poverty and powerlessness, much like the urban underclass segments of other groups.

Thus, Chinese Americans can be found at both ends of the spectrum of success and affluence, and the group is often said to be "bipolar" in its occupational structure (see Barringer, Takeuchi, & Levin, 1995; Min, 2006; Takaki, 1993, pp. 415–416; Wong, 1995, pp. 77–78; Zhou & Logan, 1989). Although a high percentage of Chinese Americans are found in more desirable occupations—sustaining the idea of Asian success—others, less visible, are concentrated at the lowest levels of society. Later in this chapter, we will again consider the socioeconomic status of Chinese Americans and the accuracy of the image of success and affluence.

JAPANESE AMERICANS

Immigration from Japan began to increase shortly after the Chinese Exclusion Act of 1882 took effect, in part to fill the gap in the labor supply created by the restrictive legislation (Kitano, 1980). The 1880 Census counted only a few hundred Japanese in the United States, but the group increased rapidly over the next few decades. By 1910, the Japanese in the United States outnumbered the Chinese, and they remained the larger of the two groups until large-scale immigration resumed in the 1960s (see Figure 9.3).

The Anti-Japanese Campaign. The contact situation for Japanese immigrants resembled that of the Chinese. They immigrated to the same West Coast regions as the Chinese, entered the labor force in a similar position, and were a small group with few power resources. Predictably, the feelings and emotions generated by the anti-Chinese campaign transferred to them. By the early 1900s, an anti-Japanese campaign to limit competition was in full swing. Efforts were being made to establish a rigid competitive system of group relations and to exclude Japanese immigrants in the same way the Chinese had been barred (Kitano, 1980, p. 563; Kitano & Daniels, 1995, pp. 59–60; Petersen, 1971, pp. 30–55).

Growing Up in Chinatown

Murals in Chinatown.

Ben Fong-Torres grew up in the China-town enclave of Oakland, California, in the 1940s and 1950s. His seemingly Hispanic family name originated when his father, unable to enter the United States legally because of immigration restrictions, moved first to the Philippines, where he worked for several years. There he purchased Filipino identity papers on the black market before moving to the United States.

In his memoir, The Rice Room, *Fong-Torres recounts some of his experiences as a young boy and remembers the challenges of negotiating the social and cultural spaces between his Chinese heritage and the larger society. Also note his descriptions of the institutions, organizations, networks, and customs that helped Chinatown function as a subsociety. How did his family begin to absorb the surrounding culture? How did they resist Americanization? Can you detect any gender dimensions in his account?*

Fong-Torres grew up to become an editor for Rolling Stone *magazine and a well-known journalist, DJ, television personality, and author.*

NEGOTIATING CHINESE AND AMERICAN CULTURES

Ben Fong-Torres

Our parents had a mission in life: to instill Chinese culture in us. While Japanese Americans, stung by their experiences in internment camps during World War II, were more determined than ever to assimilate into the American mainstream, first-generation Chinese had no such goals. . . .

Their children, they would grudgingly allow, were Americans as well as Chinese. Ideally, they would succeed—the boys as doctors, dentists, or lawyers; the girls as wives of doctors, dentists, or lawyers. Still, they'd be Chinese at the core.

And so, as each of us turned 8, [we] found our school days lengthened by several hours in Chinese school at the nearby Chinese Community Center . . . [where] teachers taught language, calligraphy, culture, and history and, not incidentally, manners. . . . We sat attentively through lectures about Sun Yat-sen, and we learned calligraphy by copying characters into books with pages of squares in vertical rows. We learned to hold a Chinese brush pen straight up, to dip it into black ink soaked in cotton balls in little bottles. We traced large characters onto tissue paper. . . .

American holidays came as a shock to my parents. Two months after her arrival in Oakland, my mother was home one evening when her doorbell rang. She pulled back the curtain on the front door window and found herself confronted by two children—one dressed as a ghost, the other a witch. Even though they were clearly children, they frightened Mom, and she hurried to the telephone to call [her friend] Grace Fung.

"What is this?" she asked. "Children in make-believe clothes at my front door!"

Grace told my mother about Halloween. For good measure, she also explained Thanksgiving and Christmas. . . .

But while we had tricks and treats and Thanksgiving and Christmas, we also had Chinese New Year every February. . . . I knew that, no matter how far from home, the children were expected to gather for dinner on those days in a show of family unity. Every year, our parents would put out their round, lacquered, wood platter . . . with eight compartments for a variety of sweets—candied melon (for health), sugared coconut strips (togetherness), kumquat (prosperity), lichee nuts (strong family ties), melon seeds (dyed red to symbolize happiness), lotus seeds (many children), and longan (many good sons).

All over the house, there'd be bowls and platters piled high with oranges and tangerines, which meant good luck and wealth, and wherever Chinese visited during the 2 weeks of New Year celebration, they would bring gifts of fruit and go through an exercise of manners that befuddled us.

The hosts would chide the visitors for bringing oranges. "Oh, not necessary," they would say, knowing full well that the gift was almost mandatory in Chinese tradition.

The guests would insist; the hosts would relent. Then, at the end of the visit, the hosts would pile the guests up with oranges and tangerines.

"Oh, no, no," the departing guests would protest, fully prepared to accept the exchange of fruit, which they would bring to their next hosts.

At dinner, every course . . . was laden with symbolism and purpose. We had to have chicken, simply steamed and presented whole, indicating completeness. The same reasoning applied to fish, roast suckling pig with thick, crunchy skin and an even thicker layer of fat, and, as a yin-yang balance, a vegetarian dish called "Buddha's monk stew," composed of Chinese vermicelli (noodles, uncut, symbolize long life), fermented bean curd, tiger lily flowers, and gingko nuts.

Before dinner, we'd set off firecrackers outside the house—to ward off evil spirits—and create an echo of what for most Chinese was the highlight of New Year's: the parade through Chinatown. . . . On Webster and surrounding streets, teams of young lion dancers . . . made the rounds of business establishments and family associations, which hired the lions to chase off bad influences with their supernatural powers. While neighbors and passersby gathered to watch, they performed amidst gongs, drums, and exploding firecrackers, and, at show's end, climbed high . . . to snatch a string of *hoong bow*—red envelopes containing dollar bills—payment to the lions for warding off the demons.

I was fascinated by the lion's head, with the blinding primary colors, the bulging, bejeweled, fur-brewed eyes and the pom-poms springing out of its forehead. . . . Back at [the family restaurant], I'd take a cardboard box that had held eggs and, with paper, water colors, crayons, string, and fabrics . . . fashion my own lion's head, complete with a flapping lower lip. Barry and Shirley were happy to pound on garbage can lids . . . while I pranced around the backyard. Our parents were delighted that we would embrace Chinese New Year with such enthusiasm.

SOURCE: Fong-Torres (1995, pp. 44–49). Copyright © 2011 by Ben Fong-Torres. Published by the University of California Press. Reprinted with permission.

Questions to Consider

1. Was the separation between Chinatown and the surrounding society complete? How did the Anglo society penetrate the lives of the Fong-Torres family?

2. What Asian American values were most important in the Chinatown described in this passage? How did these differ from Anglo-American values?

3. Do you think the young Ben was being well prepared for life in the larger society? Why or why not?

Japanese immigration was partly curtailed in 1907 when a "gentlemen's agreement" was signed between Japan and the United States limiting the number of laborers Japan would allow to immigrate (Kitano & Daniels, 1995, p. 59). This policy remained in effect until the United States changed its immigration policy in the 1920s and barred immigration from Japan completely. The end of Japanese immigration is largely responsible for the slow growth of the Japanese American population displayed in Figure 9.3.

Most Japanese immigrants, like the Chinese, were young male laborers who planned to return eventually to their homeland or bring their wives after they were established in their new country (Duleep, 1988, p. 24). The agreement of 1907 curtailed the immigration of men, but because of a loophole, females were able to continue immigrating until the 1920s. Japanese Americans were thus able to maintain a relatively balanced sex ratio, marry, and begin families, and a second generation of Japanese Americans began to appear without much delay. Native-born Japanese numbered about half the group by 1930 and were a majority of 63% on the eve of World War II (Kitano & Daniels, 1995, p. 59).

The anti-Japanese movement also attempted to dislodge the group from agriculture. Many Japanese immigrants were skilled agriculturists, and farming proved to be their most promising avenue for advancement (Kitano, 1980, p. 563). In 1910, between 30% and 40% of all Japanese in California were engaged in agriculture; from 1900 to 1909, the number of independent Japanese farmers increased from fewer than 50 to about 6,000 (Jibou, 1988, p. 358).

Most of these immigrant farmers owned small plots of land, and they made up only a minuscule percentage of West Coast farmers (Jibou, 1988, pp. 357–358). Nonetheless, their presence and relative success did not go unnoticed and eventually stimulated discriminatory legislation, most notably the **Alien Land Act**, passed by the California legislature in 1913 (Kitano, 1980, p. 563). This bill made aliens who were ineligible for citizenship (effectively meaning only immigrants from Asia) also ineligible to own land. The act did not achieve its goal of dislodging the Japanese from the rural economy. They were able to dodge the discriminatory legislation through various devices, mostly by putting land titles in the names of their American-born children, who were citizens by law (Jibou, 1988, p. 359).

The Alien Land Act was one part of a sustained campaign against the Japanese in the United States. In the early decades of this century, the Japanese were politically disenfranchised and segregated from dominant-group institutions in schools and residential areas. They were discriminated against in movie houses, swimming pools, and other public facilities (Kitano & Daniels, 1988, p. 56). The Japanese were excluded from the mainstream economy and confined to a limited range of poorly paid occupations (see Yamato, 1994). Thus, there were strong elements of systematic discrimination, exclusion, and colonization in their overall relationship with the larger society.

The Ethnic Enclave. Spurned and disparaged by the larger society, the Japanese, like the Chinese, constructed a separate subsociety. The immigrant generation, called **Issei** (from the Japanese word *ichi*, meaning "one"), established an enclave in agriculture and related enterprises, a rural counterpart of the urban enclaves constructed by other groups we have examined.

By World War II, the Issei had come to dominate a narrow but important segment of agriculture on the West Coast, especially in California. Although the Issei were never more than 2% of the total population of California, Japanese American–owned farms produced as much as 30% to 40% of various fruits and vegetables grown in the state. As late as 1940, more than 40% of the Japanese American population was involved directly in farming, and many more were dependent on the economic activity stimulated by agriculture, including the marketing of their produce (Jibou, 1988, pp. 359–360). Other Issei lived in urban areas, where they were concentrated in a narrow range of businesses and services, such as domestic work and gardening, some of which catered to other Issei and some of which served the dominant group (p. 362).

Japanese Americans in both the rural and urban sectors maximized their economic clout by doing business with other Japanese-owned firms as often as possible. Gardeners and farmers purchased supplies at Japanese-owned firms; farmers used other members of the group to haul their produce to market; and businesspeople relied on one another and mutual credit associations, rather than dominant-group banks, for financial services. These networks helped the enclave economy grow and also permitted the Japanese to avoid the hostility and racism of the larger society. However, these very same patterns helped sustain the stereotypes that depicted the Japanese as clannish and unassimilable. In the years before World War II, the Japanese American community was largely dependent for survival on their networks of cooperation and mutual assistance, not on Americanization and integration.

The Second Generation (Nisei). In the 1920s and 1930s, anti-Asian feelings continued to run high, and Japanese Americans continued to be excluded and discriminated against despite (or perhaps because of) their relative success. Unable to find acceptance in Anglo society, the second generation, called **Nisei**, established clubs, athletic leagues, churches, and a multitude of other social and recreational organizations within their own communities (Kitano & Daniels, 1995, p. 63). These organizations reflected the high levels of Americanization of

---

The **Alien Land Act**, passed by the California legislature in 1913, declared that aliens ineligible for citizenship (meaning Asian immigrants) could not own land.

The **Issei** were first-generation immigrants from Japan.

The **Nisei** were second-generation Japanese Americans.

the Nisei and expressed values and interests quite compatible with those of the dominant culture. For example, the most influential Nisei organization was the Japanese American Citizens League, whose creed expressed an ardent patriotism that was to be sorely tested: "I am proud that I am an American citizen. . . . I believe in [American] institutions, ideas, and traditions; I glory in her heritage; I boast of her history, I trust in her future" (p. 64).

Although the Nisei enjoyed high levels of success in school, the intense discrimination and racism of the 1930s prevented most of them from translating their educational achievements into better jobs and higher salaries. Many occupations in the mainstream economy were closed to even the best-educated Japanese Americans, and anti-Asian prejudice and discrimination did not diminish during the hard times and high unemployment of the Great Depression in the 1930s. Many Nisei were forced to remain within the enclave, and in many cases, jobs in the produce stands and retail shops of their parents were all they could find. Their demoralization and anger over their exclusion were eventually swamped by the larger events of World War II.

The Relocation Camps. On December 7, 1941, Japan attacked Pearl Harbor, killing almost 2,500 Americans. President Franklin D. Roosevelt asked Congress for a declaration of war the next day. The preparations for war stirred up a wide range of fears and anxieties among the American public, including concerns about the loyalty of Japanese Americans. Decades of exclusion and anti-Japanese prejudice had conditioned the dominant society to see Japanese Americans as sinister, clannish, cruel, unalterably foreign, and racially inferior. Fueled by the ferocity of the war itself and fears about a Japanese invasion of the mainland, the tradition of anti-Japanese racism laid the groundwork for a massive violation of civil rights.

Two months after the attack on Pearl Harbor, President Roosevelt signed Executive Order 9066, which led to the relocation of Japanese Americans living on the West Coast. By the late summer of 1942, more than 110,000 Japanese Americans, young and old, male and female—virtually the entire West Coast population—had been transported to **relocation camps**, where they were imprisoned behind barbed-wire fences patrolled by armed guards. Many of these people were American citizens, yet no attempt was made to distinguish between citizen and alien. No trials were held, and no one was given the opportunity to refute the implicit charge of disloyalty.

The government gave families little notice to prepare for evacuation and secure their homes, businesses, and belongings. They were allowed to bring only what they could carry, and many possessions were simply abandoned. Businesspeople sold their establishments and farmers sold their land at panic-sale

A Japanese American family prepares to be transported to a relocation camp.

prices. Others locked up their stores and houses and walked away, hoping that the evacuation would be short-lived and their possessions undisturbed.

The internment lasted for nearly the entire war. At first, Japanese Americans were not permitted to serve in the armed forces, but, eventually, more than 25,000 escaped the camps by volunteering for military service. Nearly all of them served in segregated units or in intelligence work with combat units in the Pacific Ocean. Two all-Japanese combat units served in Europe and became the most decorated units in American military history (Kitano, 1980, p. 567). Other Japanese Americans were able to get out of the camps by different means. Some, for example, agreed to move to militarily nonsensitive areas far away from the West Coast (and far from their former homes). Still, when the camps closed at the end of the war, about half the original internees remained (Kitano & Daniels, 1988, p. 64).

The strain of living in the camps affected Japanese Americans in a variety of ways. Lack of activities and privacy, overcrowding, boredom, and monotony were all common complaints. The next Narrative Portrait summarizes the experiences of one Japanese American.

The camps disrupted the traditional forms of family life, as people had to adapt to barracks living and mess-hall dining. Conflicts flared between those who counseled caution and temperate reactions to the incarceration, and those who wanted to protest in more vigorous ways. Many of those who advised moderation were Nisei intent on proving their loyalty and cooperating with the camp administration.

Despite the injustice and dislocations of the incarceration, the camps did reduce the extent to which women were relegated to a subordinate role. Like Chinese women, Japanese women were expected to devote themselves to the care of the males of their family. In Japan, for example, education for females was not intended to challenge their intellect so much as to make them better wives and mothers. In the camps, however, pay for the few jobs available was the same for both men and women,

---

Japanese Americans were held at **relocation camps** during World War II.

NARRATIVE PORTRAIT

The Relocation

A Japanese American relocation camp.

Joseph Kurihara was born in Hawaii in 1895. He moved to California at age 20 and served with the U.S. Army in World War I, completed a college education, and was a businessman working within the Japanese American enclave until World War II. He worked actively to promote acculturation and better relations with the larger society during the interwar years.

He was sent to the relocation camp at Manzanar, California, in the spring of 1942 and continued to play an active role in the dislocated Japanese American community. Although he had never visited Japan and had no interest in or connection with the country of his parents' birth, his experiences in the camp were so bitter that he renounced his American citizenship and expatriated to Japan following the war.

WE WERE JUST JAPS

Joseph Kurihara

[The evacuation] . . . was really cruel and harsh. To pack and evacuate in 48 hours was an impossibility. Seeing mothers completely bewildered with children crying from want and peddlers taking advantage and offering prices next to robbery made me feel like murdering those responsible without the slightest compunction in my heart.

The parents may be aliens but the children are all American citizens. Did the government of the United States intend to ignore their rights regardless of their citizenship? Those beautiful furnitures [*sic*] which the parents bought to please their sons and daughters, costing hundreds of dollars were robbed of them at the single command, "Evacuate!" . . . Having had absolute confidence in Democracy, I could not believe my very eyes what I had seen that day. America, the standard bearer of Democracy had committed the most heinous crime in its history. . . .

The desert [where the camp was located] was bad enough. The . . . barracks made it worse. The constant cyclonic storms loaded with sand and dust made it worst. After living in well-furnished homes with every modern convenience and suddenly forced to live the life of a dog is something which one cannot so readily forget. Down in our hearts we cried and cursed this government every time when we were showered with sand.

We slept in the dust; we breathed the dust; and we ate the dust. Such abominable existence one could not forget, no matter how much we tried to be patient, understand the situation, and take it bravely. Why did not the government permit us to remain where we were? Was it because the government was unable to give us the protection? I have my doubt. . . . It was not the question of protection. It was because we were Japs! Yes, Japs!

After corralling us like a bunch of sheep in a hellish country, did the government treat us like citizens? No! We were treated like aliens regardless of our rights. Did the government think we were so without pride to work for $16.00 a month when people outside were paid $40.00 to $50.00 a week in the defense plants? . . .

My American friends . . . no doubt must have wondered why I renounced my citizenship. This decision . . . dates back to the day when General DeWitt ordered evacuation. It was confirmed when he flatly refused to listen even to the voices of the . . . veterans and it was doubly confirmed when I entered Manzanar. We who already had proven our loyalty by serving in the last World War should have been spared. The veterans asked for special consideration but their requests were denied. They too had to evacuate like the rest of the Japanese people, as if they were aliens. . . .

I expected that at least the Nisei would be allowed to remain. But to General DeWitt, we were all alike. "A Jap's a Jap. Once a Jap, always a Jap." . . . I swore to become a Jap 100% and never to do another day's work to help this country fight this war. My decision to renounce my citizenship there and then was absolute.

[Just before he left for Japan (in 1946), Kurihara wrote:]

It is my sincere desire to get over there as soon as possible to help rebuild Japan politically and economically. The American Democracy with which I was infused in my childhood is still unshaken. My life is dedicated to Japan with Democracy my goal.

SOURCE: Swaine and Nishimoto (1946).

Questions to Consider

1. Why didn't Kurihara's efforts to succeed and acculturate protect him—and others like him—from the relocation?
2. Do you think Kurihara's bitterness was justified? Was his decision to move to Japan reasonable?

and the mess halls and small living quarters freed women from some of the burden of housework. Many took advantage of the free time to take classes to learn more English and other skills. The younger women were able to meet young men on their own, weakening the tradition of family-controlled, arranged marriages (Amott & Matthaei, 1991, pp. 225–229).

Some Japanese Americans protested the incarceration from the start and brought lawsuits to end the relocation program. Finally, in 1944, the Supreme Court ruled that detention was unconstitutional. As the camps closed, some Japanese American individuals and organizations began to seek compensation and redress for the economic losses the

A woman works in the Manzanar relocation camp.

group had suffered. In 1948, Congress passed legislation to authorize compensation to Japanese Americans. About 26,500 people filed claims under this act. These claims were eventually settled for a total of about $38 million—less than one tenth of the actual economic losses. Demand for meaningful redress and compensation continued, and in 1988, Congress passed a bill granting reparations of about $20,000 in cash to each of the 60,000 remaining survivors of the camps. The law also acknowledged that the relocation program had been a grave injustice to Japanese Americans (Biskupic, 1989, p. 2879).

The World War II relocation devastated the Japanese American community and left it with few material resources. The emotional and psychological damage inflicted by this experience is incalculable. The fact that today, only seven decades later, Japanese Americans are equal or superior to national averages on measures of educational achievement, occupational prestige, and income is one of the more dramatic transformations in minority-group history.

Japanese Americans After World War II. In 1945, Japanese Americans faced a world very different from the one they had left in 1942. To escape the camps, nearly half the group had scattered throughout the country and lived everywhere but on the West Coast. As Japanese Americans attempted to move back to their former homes, they found their fields untended, their stores vandalized, their possessions lost or stolen, and their lives shattered. In some cases, there was simply no Japanese neighborhood to return to; the Little Tokyo area of San Francisco, for example, was now occupied by African Americans who had moved to the West Coast to take jobs in the defense industry (Amott & Matthaei, 1991, p. 231).

The **Sansei** and **Yonsei** are, respectively, third- and fourth-generation Japanese Americans.

Japanese Americans themselves had changed as well. In the camps, the Issei had lost power to the Nisei. The English-speaking second generation had dealt with the camp administrators and held the leadership positions. Many Nisei had left the camps to serve in the armed forces or to find work in other areas of the country. For virtually every American minority group, the war brought new experiences and a broader sense of themselves, the nation, and the world. A similar transformation occurred for the Nisei. When the war ended, they were unwilling to rebuild the Japanese community as it had been before.

Like second-generation Chinese Americans, the Nisei had a strong record of success in school, and they also took advantage of the GI Bill to further their education. When anti-Asian prejudice began to decline in the 1950s and the job market began to open, the Nisei were educationally prepared to take advantage of the resultant opportunities (Kitano, 1980, p. 567).

The Issei-dominated enclave economy did not reappear after the war. One indicator of the shift away from an enclave economy was the fact that the percentage of Japanese American women in California who worked as unpaid family laborers (i.e., worked in family-run businesses for no salary) declined from 21% in 1940 to 7% in 1950 (Amott & Matthaei, 1991, p. 231). Also, between 1940 and 1990, the percentage of the group employed in agriculture declined from about 50% to 3%, and the percentage employed in personal services fell from 25% to 5% (Nishi, 1995, p. 116).

By 1960, Japanese Americans had an occupational profile very similar to that of whites except that they were actually overrepresented among professionals. Many were employed in the primary economy, not in the ethnic enclave, but there was a tendency to choose "safe" careers (e.g., in engineering, optometry, pharmacy, accounting) that did not require extensive contact with the public or supervision by whites (Kitano & Daniels, 1988, p. 70).

Within these limitations, the Nisei, their children (**Sansei**), and their grandchildren (**Yonsei**) have enjoyed relatively high status, and their upward mobility and prosperity have contributed to the perception that Asian Americans are a model minority group. An additional factor contributing to the high status of Japanese Americans (and to the disappearance of Little Tokyos) is that, unlike Chinese Americans, immigrants from Japan have been few in number and the community has not had to devote many resources to newcomers. Furthermore, recent immigrants from Japan tend to be highly educated professionals whose socioeconomic characteristics add to the perception of success and affluence.

The Sansei and Yonsei are highly integrated into the occupational structure of the larger society. Compared with their parents, their connections with their ethnic past are more tenuous, and in their values, beliefs, and personal goals, they resemble dominant-group members of similar age and social class (Kitano & Daniels, 1995, pp. 79–81; see also Spickard, 1996).

Japan's "Invisible" Minority

By the definition stated in Chapter 1, two of the most important characteristics of minority groups are that they (1) are the objects of a pattern of disadvantage and (2) are easily identifiable, either culturally or physically. These two traits work in tandem: Members of the dominant group must be able to determine a person's group membership quickly and easily so the discrimination that is the hallmark of minority-group status can be practiced.

Visibility is such an obvious precondition for discrimination that it almost seems unnecessary to state it. However, every generalization seems to have an exception, and the members of at least one minority group, the Burakumin of Japan, have been victimized by discrimination and prejudice for hundreds of years but are virtually indistinguishable from the general population. How could such an "invisible" minority come into being? How could the disadvantaged status be maintained through time?

The Burakumin were created centuries ago, when Japan was organized into a caste system (see Chapter 4) based on occupation. The ancestors of today's Burakumin did work that brought them into contact with death (e.g., as gravediggers) or required them to handle meat products (e.g., as butchers). These occupations were regarded as very low in status, "unclean," or polluted.

The Burakumin were required to live in separate villages and to wear identifying leather patches (thus raising their social visibility). They were forbidden to marry outside their caste, and any member of the general population who touched a member of the Burakumin had to be ritually purified or cleansed of pollution (Lamont-Brown, 1993, p. 137).

The caste system was officially abolished in the 19th century, at about the time Japan began to industrialize, and most observers today agree that the overall situation of the Burakumin has improved (Ball, 2009). But the Burakumin maintain their minority status, and prejudice against them continues (Neary, 2003, p. 288).

The Burakumin are a small group, about 2% or 3% of Japan's population. About 1 million still live in traditional villages, and another 2 million or so live in non-Burakumin areas, mostly in larger cities. They continue to be seen as "filthy," "not very bright," and "untrustworthy"—stereotypical traits often associated with minority groups mired in subordinate and unequal positions (see Chapter 3). Also, as is the case for many American minority groups, the Burakumin have a number of protest organizations—including the Buraku Liberation League (www.bll.gr.jp/eng.html)—that are dedicated to improving conditions.

The situation of the Burakumin might seem puzzling. If the group is indistinguishable from the general population, why don't the Burakumin simply blend in and disappear? What keeps them attached to their group?

Some Burakumin are proud of their heritage and refuse to surrender to the dominant culture. They have no intention of trading their identity for acceptance or opportunity. For others, even those attempting to pass, the tie to the group and a subtle form of social visibility are maintained by the ancient system of residential segregation. The identity of the traditional Burakumin areas of residence are well-known, and this information—not race or culture—is what establishes the boundaries of the group and forms the ultimate barrier to Burakumin assimilation.

There are reports that Japanese firms use lists of local Burakumin addresses to screen out potential employees. Also, the telltale information may be revealed when applying to rent an apartment (some landlords refuse to rent rooms to Burakumin because of their alleged "filthiness") or purchase a home (banks may be reluctant to provide loans to members of a group that is widely regarded as "untrustworthy").

Another line of resistance can arise with marriage. It is common for Japanese parents to research the family history of a child's fiancé, a process which is sure to unearth any secret Burakumin connections. Thus, members of the Burakumin who pass undetected at work and in their neighborhood are likely to be "outed" if they attempt to marry outside the group.

This link to the traditional Burakumin residential areas means that this group is not really invisible: There is a way to determine group membership, a mark or sign of who belongs and who doesn't. Consistent with our definition, this "birth-mark" is the basis for a socially constructed boundary that differentiates "us" from "them," and for the discrimination and prejudice associated with minority-group status.

Questions to Consider

1. Are the Burakumin unique? What other minority groups are similarly "invisible"?
2. Are the Burakumin advocacy groups justified in attempting to preserve the group's heritage? Should they be working for greater assimilation?
3. What do you suppose the future holds for the Burakumin? Will they disappear and assimilate into the larger society? Why?

COMPARING MINORITY GROUPS

What factors account for the differences in the development of Chinese and Japanese Americans and other racial minority groups? First, unlike the situation of African Americans in the 1600s and Mexican Americans in the 1800s, the dominant group had no desire to control the labor of these groups. The contact situation featured economic competition (e.g., for jobs) during an era of rigid competition between groups (see Table 5.2), and Chinese and Japanese Americans were seen as a threat to security that needed to be eliminated, not as a labor pool that needed to be controlled.

Second, unlike American Indians, Chinese and Japanese Americans in the early 20th century presented no military danger to the larger society; so there was little concern with their activities once the economic threat had been eliminated. Third, Chinese and Japanese Americans had the ingredients and experiences necessary to form enclaves. The groups were allowed to "disappear," but unlike other racial minority groups, the urban location of their enclaves left them with opportunities for starting small businesses and providing an education for the second and later generations. As many scholars argue, the particular mode of incorporation developed by Chinese Americans and Japanese Americans is the key to understanding the present status of these groups.

QUESTIONS FOR REFLECTION

1. What forces shaped the immigration of Chinese and Japanese Americans? Compare and contrast these patterns with those of Hispanic immigration and the 1820s to 1920s immigration from Europe. What are the key differences and similarities?

2. Compare and contrast the development of the Chinese American community with the development of the Japanese American community. What are the most important differences and similarities? What accounts for these patterns? Did both groups form enclaves? Why and how?

3. Are Japanese and Chinese Americans colonized or immigrant groups? Why?

CONTEMPORARY IMMIGRATION FROM ASIA

Figure 9.4 displays the volume of immigration from Asia since 1900. The green line represents the number of immigrants (read these values from the left vertical axis) and shows the decline in rates after the restrictive legislation of the 1920s—almost to zero—and the steep increases following the change in U.S. immigration policy in the mid-1960s. Immigration from Asia has steadily increased in volume since the 1960s and continued to increase even as the flow of immigrants from Hispanic nations has declined. Starting in 2009, Asia became the largest supplier of immigrants to the United States.

The blue line shows the percentage of all immigrants in each time period that came from Asia. This line (read from the right vertical axis) shows that Asian immigration was rare—less than 5% of all immigrants—until the mid-1960s. The percentage increased until the 1980s and then declined in the 1990s as the volume of immigration from Mexico and Central and South America exploded. The percentage is now more than 35%, a reflection of the continued flow from Asia and the declining flow of Hispanic groups.

Figure 9.5 shows that Asian immigration since the 1950s has been heaviest from China, India, and the Philippines but that Korea and Vietnam have also made sizable contributions.

FIGURE 9.4 Immigration From Asia, 1900–2012

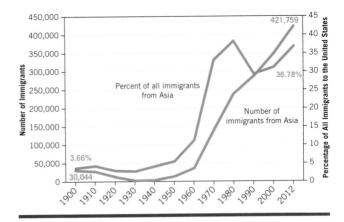

SOURCE: U.S. Department of Homeland Security (2012).

As noted previously, immigration from Japan has been relatively low since the initial influx a century ago (see Figure 9.3).

As is the case with Hispanic immigrants, the sending nations (other than Japan) are less developed than the United States, and the primary motivation for most of these immigrants is economic. However, unlike Hispanic immigration, the Asian immigrant stream also includes a large contingent of highly educated professionals seeking opportunities to pursue their careers and expand their skills.

These more elite immigrants contribute to the image of "Asian success," but many Asian immigrants are less skilled and less educated, and often undocumented. Thus, this stream of immigrants, like Chinese Americans, is "bipolar" and includes a healthy representation of people from both the top and the bottom of the occupational and educational hierarchies.

Of course, other factors besides economics attract these immigrants. The United States has maintained military bases throughout the region (including in South Korea, Japan, and the Philippines) since the end of World War II, and many Asian immigrants are the spouses of American military personnel.

Also, U.S. involvement in the war in Southeast Asia in the 1960s and 1970s created interpersonal ties and governmental programs that drew refugees from Vietnam, Cambodia, and Laos, many of whom lived in camps and relocation centers for years before arriving in the United States. Because of the conditions of their escape from their homelands, they typically brought little in the way of human or material capital.

Among the refugee groups are the Hmong, hill people from Laos and other Southeast Asian nations who fought alongside the American forces in the Vietnam War. Their group is relatively small in number (see Table 9.1) and faces some unique challenges in adjustment to U.S. society. Their culture is very traditional and, in many ways, far removed from the modernized, Western world in which they find themselves. Prior to the Vietnam War, the Hmong were at the hunter-gatherer level of subsistence technology and brought

FIGURE 9.5 Relative Sizes of Immigrant Groups From Asia, 1950–2012

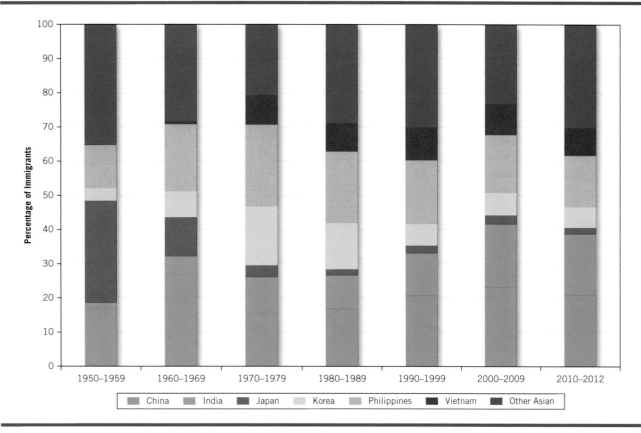

SOURCE: U.S. Department of Homeland Security (2012).

very little social and cultural capital with them. The scope of the challenges they face in making the transition to the United States is illustrated by anthropologist Anne Fadiman (1998) in her account of the fate of an epileptic Hmong girl. According to traditional Hmong cultural understandings, illness is caused by spirits and needs to be treated in the time-honored way, by shamans and traditional healers. The girl's parents found it difficult to accept and follow the instructions of the Western doctors that attempted to treat the girl's epileptic condition. The resultant tragedy underscores the distance between the Hmong and the Western world, and illustrates the challenges of acculturation for this group (Fadiman, 1998). Contrary to the image of Asian American success, the Hmong generally display a socioeconomic profile more consistent with America's colonized minority groups.

Another striking contrast is between immigrants from India, many of whom are highly educated and skilled, and Vietnamese Americans, who have a socioeconomic profile that more resembles those of non-Asian racial minorities in the United States. Part of the difference between these two groups relates to their contact situations and can be illuminated by applying the Blauner hypothesis. Immigrants from India are at the "immigrant" end of Blauner's continuum.

They tend to bring strong educational credentials and to be well equipped to compete for favorable positions in the occupational hierarchy.

The Vietnamese, in contrast, began their American experience as a refugee group fleeing the turmoil of war. Although they do not fit Blauner's "conquered or colonized" category, most Vietnamese Americans had to adapt to American society with few resources and few contacts with an established immigrant community. The consequences of these vastly different contact situations are suggested by the data presented in the figures at the end of this chapter. We will address some of these groups in more detail in Chapter 10.

QUESTIONS FOR REFLECTION

1. Identify the major groups of recent immigrants from Asia. How do they differ from Chinese and Japanese Americans?

2. How did the motivation for immigration vary for the different Asian groups? How have these differences affected their relationship with U.S. society?

3. Are these groups colonized or immigrant groups? Why?

PREJUDICE AND DISCRIMINATION

American prejudice against Asians first became prominent during the anti-Chinese movement of the 19th century. The Chinese were believed to be racially inferior, docile, and subservient, but also cruel and crafty, despotic, and threatening (Lai, 1980, p. 220; Lyman, 1974, pp. 55–58). The Chinese Exclusion Act of 1882 was justified by the idea that the Chinese were unassimilable and could never be part of U.S. society. The Chinese were seen as a threat to the working class, to American democracy, and to other American institutions. Many of these stereotypes and fears transferred to the Japanese later in the 19th century and then to other groups as they, in turn, arrived in the United States.

The social distance scores presented in Table 3.2 provide the only long-term record of anti-Asian prejudice in society as a whole. In 1926, the five Asian groups included in the study were grouped in the bottom third of the scale, along with other racial and colonized minority groups. Twenty years later, in 1946, the Japanese had fallen to the bottom of the rankings and the Chinese had risen seven positions, changes that reflect America's World War II conflict with Japan and alliance with China.

This suggests that anti-Chinese prejudice may have softened during the war as distinctions were made between "good" and "bad" Asians. For example, an item published in a 1941 issue of *Time* magazine, "How to Tell Your Friends From the Japs," provided some tips for identifying "good" Asians: "The Chinese expression is likely to be more placid, kindly, open; the Japanese more positive, dogmatic, arrogant. . . . Japanese are nervous in conversation, laugh loudly at the wrong time" (p. 33).

In more recent decades, the average social distance scores of Asian groups have fallen even though the ranking of the groups has remained relatively stable. The falling scores probably reflect the society-wide increase in tolerance and the shift from blatant prejudice to modern racism that we discussed in Chapter 3. However, the relative position of Asians in the American hierarchy of group preferences has remained remarkably consistent since the 1920s. This stability may reflect the cultural or traditional nature of much of the anti-Asian prejudice in America.

There are numerous reports of violent attacks and other forms of harassment against Asian Americans, especially recent immigrants. High school and middle school students of Asian descent report that they are stereotyped as "high-achieving students who rarely fight back," making them excellent candidates for bullying and scapegoating by other groups (Associated Press, 2005). The level of harassment at one high school in New York rose to such severe levels that the U.S. Department of Justice intervened, at the request of school officials (Associated Press, 2005). Incidents such as these suggest

During and after World War II, anti-Japanese prejudice was often openly expressed.

that the tradition of anti-Asian prejudice is close to the surface and could be reactivated under the right combination of competition and threat.

On the other hand, a recent survey suggests that discrimination and prejudice are not perceived as major problems by most Asian Americans. According to the survey, which was administered to a representative sample, only 13% of the Asian Americans interviewed said that discrimination was a "major problem," with results ranging from 24% for Korean Americans to only 8% for Japanese Americans (Pew Research Center, 2013c, p. 110). Also, only about 20% said they had personally experienced discrimination because of their Asian origin, and only 10% said they had been called offensive names (p. 114). These levels are far below those of African Americans and Hispanic Americans when asked similar questions. For example, 43% of a representative sample of African Americans said there was "a lot" of discrimination against their group, and 61% of Hispanic Americans said discrimination was a "major problem" for them (p. 115).

What might account for these differences? One possibility is that Asian Americans are downplaying the extent of their negative experiences, in conformity with the cultural tendency to avoid confrontation and stress harmony.

Another possibility is that these reports are accurate and Asian Americans truly experience less discrimination than do other racial minorities. As we discussed in Chapter 8, some analysts argue that Asian Americans (along with lighter-skinned, more affluent Latinos) will become "honorary whites," positioned between whites and blacks (and darker-skinned, less affluent Latinos) in the American racial order. If society is actually evolving in this direction, we would expect Asian Americans to feel somewhat less victimized than blacks and some Hispanic Americans.

A final possibility, closely related to the second, is that Asian Americans benefit from "positive" stereotypes and are seen in a more favorable light than other racial minorities.

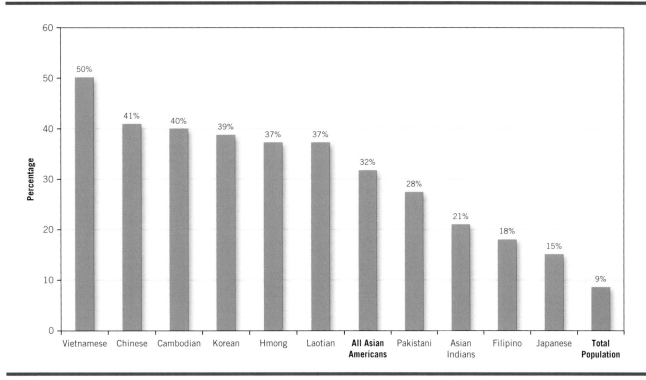

The perception of Asian Americans as a "model minority"—polite, successful, and deferential—could explain their lower levels of discrimination.

As we shall see, the "model-minority" image is a stereotype, exaggerated and overstated. For some Asian American groups, the image is simply false. The label has been applied to these groups by the media, politicians, and others. It is not an identity the Asian American groups themselves have developed or advocated—in fact, many virulently oppose it because it obscures many of the problems that exist in Asian American communities. As you might suspect, people who apply this label to Asian Americans have a variety of hidden moral and political agendas, and we will explore these dynamics later in this chapter.

ASSIMILATION AND PLURALISM

In this section, we continue to assess the situation of Asian Americans today using the same conceptual framework used in the previous three chapters.

ACCULTURATION

The extent of acculturation of Asian Americans is highly variable from group to group. Japanese Americans represent one extreme. They have been a part of American society for more than a century, and the current generations are highly acculturated.

Immigration from Japan has been low and has not revitalized the traditional culture or language. As a result, Japanese Americans are the most acculturated of the Asian American groups, as illustrated in Figure 9.6, and have the lowest percentage of members who speak English less than "very well."

Filipino and Indian Americans also have low percentages of members who are not competent English speakers, but for different reasons. The Philippines has had a strong American presence since the Spanish–American War of 1898, while India is a former British colony in which English remains an important language in higher education and among the educated elite.

Chinese Americans, in contrast, are highly variable in the extent of their acculturation. Many are members of families who have been American for generations and are highly acculturated. Others, including many recent undocumented immigrants, are newcomers who have little knowledge of English or Anglo culture. On this dimension, as in occupations, Chinese Americans are "bipolar." This great variability within the group makes it difficult to characterize their overall degree of acculturation.

Also note that the groups who are refugees from the 1960s and 1970s wars in Southeast Asia (Vietnamese, Cambodians, Hmong, and Laotians) are less acculturated. They, along with the Chinese and Koreans, have many foreign-born members (see Figure 9.2) and are still largely in their first generation.

Gender and Physical Acculturation: The Anglo Ideal. Anglo-conformity can happen on levels other than the cultural. A number of studies document the feelings of inadequacy and

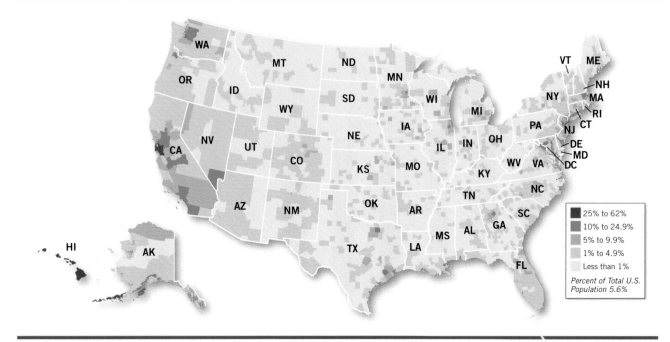

SOURCE: Hoeffel et al. (2012, p. 10).

negative self-images that often result when minority-group members—especially women—compare themselves with the Anglo standards of attractiveness and beauty that dominate U.S. culture.

Some of the studies in this tradition are classics of the social science literature, including the "doll studies" conducted by social psychologists Kenneth and Mamie Clark in the 1930s and 1940s. The Clarks showed pairs of white and black dolls to a sample of young African American children and asked them a series of questions, including, "Which doll is pretty?" "Which doll is nice?" "Which doll would you like to play with?" and "Which doll is ugly?"

They documented a preference for the white doll, which they interpreted as evidence that the children had internalized white standards of beauty and developed negative self-images as a consequence. Contemporary "replications" of the Clark doll study include a YouTube video titled "A Girl Like Me," by then-17-year-old Kiri Davis (see www.youtube.com/watch?v=YWy I77Yh1Gg), and a documentary by Chris Rock titled *Good Hair*.

Asian American women, like all women in this still paternalistic society, are pressured by the cultural message that physical beauty should be among their chief concerns. As racial minorities, they are also subjected to the additional message that they are inadequate by Anglo standards and that some of their most characteristic physical traits (e.g., their small, "slanted" eyes and flat noses) are devalued—indeed, ridiculed—in the larger society (Kaw, 1997).

These messages generate pressures for minority women to conform not only culturally but also physically. For example, African Americans have spent millions of

dollars on hair straightening and skin bleaching. For Asian American women, the attempt to comply with Anglo standards of beauty may include cosmetic surgery to sculpt their noses or "open" their eyes.

Eugenia Kaw (1997) studied these issues by conducting in-depth interviews with medical practitioners and with a small sample of Asian American women, most of whom had undergone surgery on their eyelids or noses. The women tended to see their surgeries as simply their personal choice, not unlike putting on makeup. However, Kaw found that they consistently described their presurgical features in negative terms. They uniformly said "that 'small, slanty' eyes and a 'flat' nose suggest" a person who is dull and passive "and a mind that is narrow and 'closed.'" For example, one subject said that she considered eyelid surgery while in high school to "'avoid the stereotype of the Oriental bookworm' who is 'dull and doesn't know how to have fun.'" Kaw concludes that the decision of Asian American women to change the shape of their eyes and noses was greatly influenced by racist stereotypes and patriarchal norms: an attempt—common among all racial minority groups—to acculturate on a physical as well as cultural level.

SECONDARY STRUCTURAL ASSIMILATION

We will cover this complex area in the same order followed in previous chapters.

Residence. Figure 9.7 shows the regional concentrations of all Asian Americans in 2010. The tendency to reside on either

FIGURE 9.8 Percentage Change in Asian American Population, 2000–2010

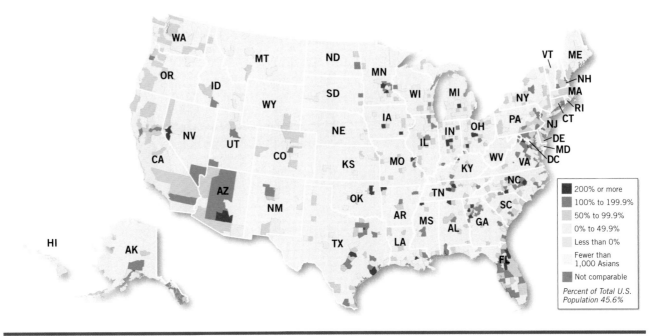

SOURCE: Hoeffel et al. (2012, p. 11).

coast and around Los Angeles, San Francisco, and New York stands out clearly. Note also the sizable concentrations in a variety of metropolitan areas, including Chicago, Atlanta, Miami, Denver, and Houston.

The various Asian American groups are concentrated in different regions, with the huge majority of Filipino and Japanese Americans residing in the West, along with about half of Chinese and Vietnamese Americans. Asian Indians have the highest percentage living in the Northeast (30%), and Vietnamese Americans have the highest percentage in the South (32%), mostly concentrated in the fishing industry on the Texas and Louisiana coasts. The Hmong, alone among Asian American groups, are concentrated in the upper Midwest, especially in Wisconsin and Minnesota (Hoeffel et al., 2012, pp. 18–20).

Figure 9.8 shows that Asian Americans, like Hispanic Americans, are moving away from their "traditional" places of residence into new regions. Between 2000 and 2010, the Asian American population increased especially rapidly along the East and West Coast, in Arizona, and in some areas of the upper Midwest.

Asian Americans in general are highly urbanized, a reflection of the entry conditions of recent immigrants as well as the appeal of ethnic neighborhoods, such as Chinatowns, with long histories and continuing vitality. As displayed in Figure 9.9, all but 2 of the 10 largest Asian American groups were more than 90% urbanized in 2000, and several approach the 100% mark.

As we saw in Figure 6.7 in Chapter 6, Asian Americans are much less residentially segregated than either African Americans or Hispanic Americans. The levels of residential

segregation for Asian Americans have been well below "high" (dissimilarity scores greater than 60) but tend to be slightly higher in cities with more concentrated Asian populations. The level of residential segregation is holding steady, a reflection of high rates of immigration and the tendency of newcomers to settle close to other members of their group. Also, these lower scores may reflect the more favored position for Asian Americans—as opposed to blacks and darker-skinned Hispanic Americans—which we noted earlier when discussing their lower levels of reported discrimination.

Asian Americans are also moving away from their traditional neighborhoods and enclaves and into the suburbs of metropolitan areas, most notably in the areas surrounding Los Angeles, San Francisco, New York, and other cities where the groups are highly concentrated. For example, Asian Americans have been moving in large numbers to the San Gabriel Valley, just east of Downtown Los Angeles. Once a bastion of white, middle-class suburbanites, these areas have taken on a distinctly Asian flavor in recent years. Monterey Park, once virtually all white, is now majority Chinese American and is often referred to as "America's first suburban Chinatown" or the "Chinese Beverly Hills" (Fong, 2002, p. 49; see also Chowkwanyun & Segall, 2012).

Education. Asian American children experience less school segregation than Hispanic and Black American children (Fry, 2007), although the extent of segregation for this population may have increased in recent years because of high rates of immigration and residential concentration, particularly in larger cities.

FIGURE 9.9 Urbanization of 10 Largest Asian American Groups, All Asian Americans, and Total Population, 2000

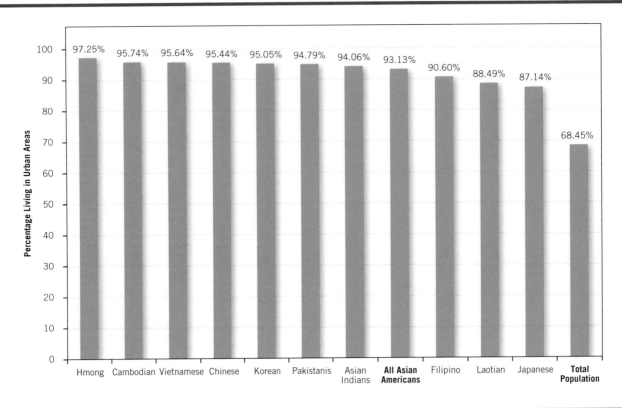

SOURCE: U.S. Census Bureau (2000a).

FIGURE 9.10 Educational Attainment for All Asian Americans, 10 Largest Asian American Groups, and Non-Hispanic Whites, 2012

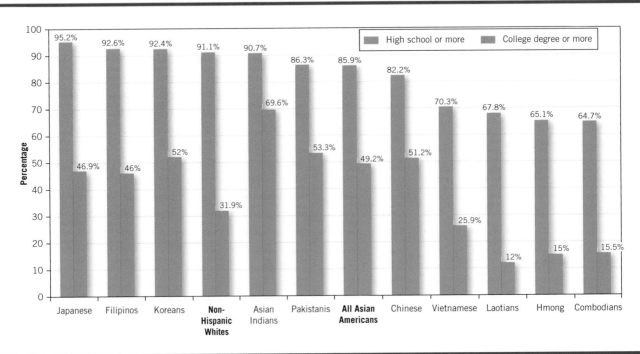

SOURCE: U.S. Census Bureau (2013a).

FIGURE 9.11 Percentage Hispanic Americans, African Americans, American Indians, Non-Hispanic Whites, All Asian Americans, and 10 Largest Asian American Groups With Less Than a High School Education, 2012

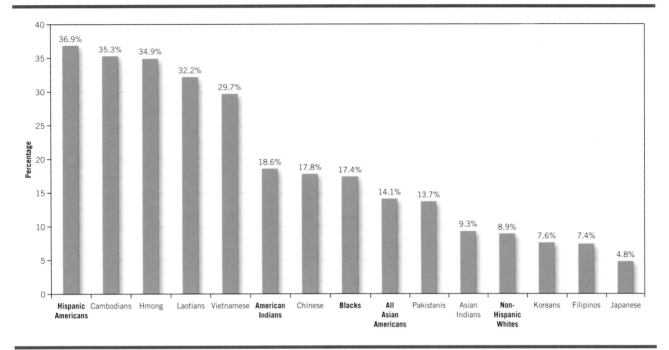

SOURCE: U.S. Census Bureau (2013a).

The extent of schooling for Asian Americans is very different from that for other U.S. racial minority groups, at least at first glance. Asian Americans as a whole compare favorably with society-wide standards for educational achievement, and they are above those standards on many measures.

Figure 9.10 shows that 3 of the 10 Asian American groups are higher than non-Hispanic whites in high school education and that 6 of the 10 are higher in college education, a pattern that has been reinforced by the high education levels of many recent Asian immigrants.

A quick glance at Figure 9.10 might sustain the image of Asian American success, but note that several groups are relatively low in educational attainment. Asian Americans display a full range of achievement: While it is true that some groups (or at least some elements of some groups) are quite successful, others have profiles that are closer to those of colonized racial minority groups.

This more balanced view of Asian Americans is further explored in Figures 9.11 and 9.12. The former shows the percentage of each group with *less than* a high school education and includes Hispanic Americans, African Americans, American Indians, and non-Hispanic whites for comparison. As we saw in Chapter 8, recent Hispanic immigrants tend to bring modest educational credentials, and the same point can be made for several of the Asian American groups, all of which have a high percentage of foreign-born members and include many refugees from the wars in Southeast Asia. On this measure of educational attainment, the Southeast Asian groups actually fare worse than African Americans and American Indians, both colonized racial minorities. Information such as this presents a serious challenge to glib characterizations of Asian Americans as successful "model minorities."

Figure 9.12 further challenges the "model-minority" image by comparing the educational attainment of Chinese Americans and non-Hispanic whites. More than 50% of Chinese Americans hold college and graduate degrees, far outnumbering whites (31%) at this level. Note, however, that Chinese Americans are also disproportionately concentrated at the lowest level of educational achievement. About 18% of the group has less than a high school diploma, as opposed to a little less than 10% of non-Hispanic whites. Many of these less educated Chinese Americans are recent immigrants (many undocumented), and they supply the unskilled labor force—in retail shops, restaurants, and garment industry "sweatshops"—that staffs the lowest levels of the Chinatown economy.

Assessments of Asian American success must also differentiate between the native-born and foreign-born members of the groups. The native-born are generally better educated, and the foreign-born are split between highly educated professionals and those who bring lower levels of human capital. For example, according to a recent survey, almost all (98%) native-born Chinese Americans were high school graduates and 73% had college degrees. In contrast, only 77% of foreign-born Chinese Americans had finished high school and only 41% had earned a college degree (computed from Pew Research Center, 2013c).

FIGURE 9.12 Educational Attainment for Non-Hispanic Whites and Chinese Americans, 2012

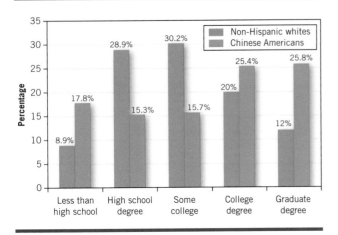

SOURCE: U.S. Census Bureau (2013a).

As illustrated by these examples, the image of success for Asian Americans needs to be balanced with the recognition that there is a full range of achievement in the group and average levels of educational attainment are "inflated" for some groups by recent immigrants who are highly educated, skilled professionals.

Political Power. The ability of Asian Americans to pursue their group interests has been sharply limited by a number of factors, including their relatively small size, institutionalized discrimination, and the same kinds of racist practices that have limited the power resources of other minority groups of color. However, and contrary to the perception that Asian Americans are a "quiet" minority, the group has a long history of political action, including a civil rights movement in the 1960s and 1970s (Fong, 2002, pp. 273–281).

The political power of Asian Americans today is also limited by their high percentage of foreign-born members and, for some groups, lack of facility in English. Rates of political participation for the group (e.g., voting in presidential elections) are considerably lower than national norms. For example, as was the case with Hispanic Americans, less than half (47%) of Asian Americans voted in the 2012 presidential election (vs. about two thirds of non-Hispanic whites and blacks). This level of participation was about the same as in the 2008 presidential election, although slightly higher than in earlier presidential elections (File, 2013, pp. 3–5). Like Hispanic Americans, the impact of this group on national politics will likely increase as more members Americanize, learn English, and become citizens.

There are signs of the group's growing power, especially in areas where they are most residentially concentrated. Of course, Asian Americans have been prominent in Hawaiian politics for decades, but they are increasingly involved in West Coast political life as well. At present, there are 12 Asian and Pacific Islanders in the U.S. House of Representatives (about 2% of the membership) and one in the Senate, Senator Mazie Hirono of Hawaii, the first Asian American female to serve in the Senate (Manning, 2013, p. 8).

Jobs and Income. The economic situation of Asian Americans is mixed and complex, as it is for Hispanic Americans. On some measures, Asian Americans as a whole exceed national norms, a reflection of the high levels of academic achievement combined with the impressive educational credentials of many new arrivals. However, overall comparisons can be misleading, and we must also recognize the economic diversity of Asian Americans.

Starting with occupational profiles, the image of success is again sustained. Both males and females are overrepresented in the highest occupational categories, a reflection of the high levels of educational attainment for the group. Asian American males are underrepresented among manual laborers, but, otherwise, the occupational profiles of the groups are in rough proportion to society as a whole (U.S. Census Bureau, 2013a).

Figure 9.13 shows median household incomes for Asian Americans and whites for the past 25 years and reveals that Asian Americans have *higher* median household incomes, a picture of general affluence in dramatic contrast to the other racial minority groups we have examined in this text. The gap fluctuates, but Asian Americans' median household income is generally 115% of whites.'

This image of success, glittering at first glance, becomes more complicated and nuanced when we look at the separate subgroups within the Asian American community. Figure 9.14 displays median household incomes for all non-Hispanic whites, all Asian Americans, and the 10 largest subgroups, and we can see immediately that economic success is not universally shared: Half of Asian American groups are below the average income for non-Hispanic whites.

A still more telling picture emerges when we consider income per capita (or per person) as opposed to median incomes

FIGURE 9.13 Median Household Income for Non-Hispanic Whites and All Asian Americans, 1987–2012

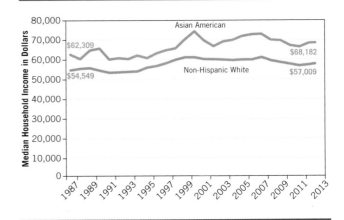

SOURCE: U.S. Census Bureau (2013c).

FIGURE 9.14 Median Household Incomes for All Asian Americans, 10 Largest Asian American Groups, and Non-Hispanic Whites, 2012

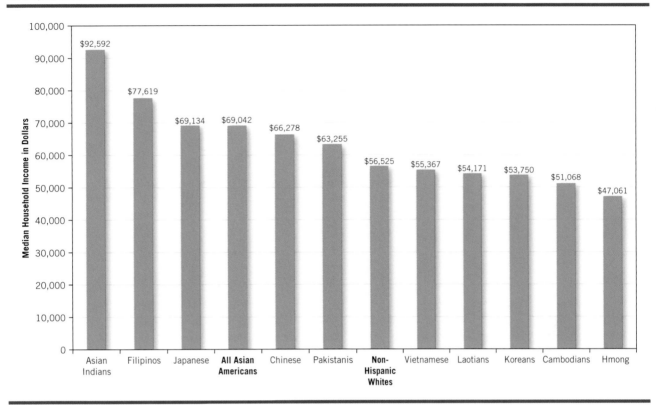

SOURCE: U.S. Census Bureau (2013a).

for entire households. This is an important comparison because the apparent prosperity of so many Asian American families is linked to their ownership of small businesses in the enclave. These enterprises typically employ the entire family for many hours each day, with children adding their labor after school and on weekends and other relatives (many new immigrants, a percentage of whom are undocumented) contributing as well. The household unit may post a high income as a result of these collective efforts, but, when spread across many family members, the glow of "success" is muted.

Figure 9.15 shows that, on per capita income, only two Asian American groups exceed non-Hispanic whites. The other eight groups (including Chinese and Korean Americans, the groups most dependent on small-business ownership) enjoy much lower levels of relative prosperity. In particular, the Southeast Asian groups with high percentages of refugees from the Vietnam War (especially the Hmong) are below national norms on this measure.

Figure 9.16 provides additional evidence that the image of a "model minority"—uniformly prosperous and success-ful—is greatly exaggerated. Asian Americans, unlike other racial minority groups, are overrepresented in the three high-est income categories: 24% of all Asian Americans are in these categories compared with only 16% of non-Hispanic whites. However, note that Asian Americans are also overrepresented

in the lowest income category, a reflection of the "bipolar" dis-tribution of Chinese Americans and some other groups.

Figures 9.17 and 9.18 finish the economic portrait of Asian Americans and reinforce the picture of complexity and diversity. While the poverty levels of all Asian Americans, con-sidered as a single group, are comparable to non-Hispanic whites, several of the groups have much higher rates of pov-erty, especially for children. As we have seen in other figures, Japanese Americans, Filipino Americans, and Asian Indians are "successful" on this indicator, but other groups have poverty levels comparable to colonized racial minority groups.

Figure 9.18 examines the situation of several Asian American groups in terms of their nativity. Once again, we see the great diversity from group to group, with for-eign-born Vietnamese Americans (largely refugees) and Korean Americans exhibiting the highest percentage of mem-bers earning less than $30,000. For all six groups, in fact, the native-born have much lower percentages of members with low incomes, and in some cases (e.g., for Chinese Americans) the difference is quite dramatic.

These socioeconomic profiles reflect the diversity of Asian American groups. Some are, indeed, prosperous and successful and exceed national norms, sometimes by a consid-erable margin. Other groups resemble other American racial minority groups. Japanese and Chinese Americans have the

FIGURE 9.15 Per Capita Income for All Asian Americans, 10 Largest Asian American Groups, and Non-Hispanic Whites, 2012

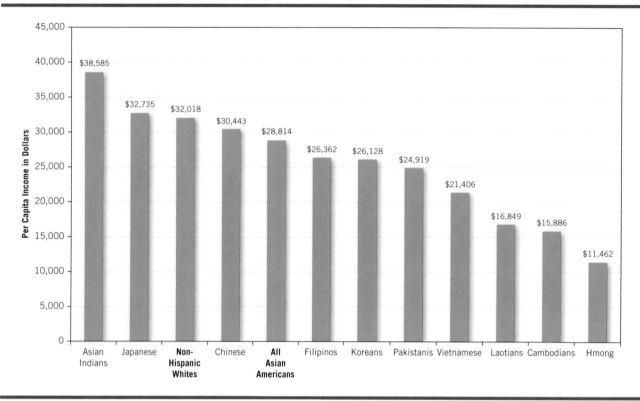

SOURCE: U.S. Census Bureau (2013a).

longest histories in the United States and generally rank at the top in measures of wealth and prosperity. Other groups—particularly those that include large numbers of refugees from Southeast Asia—have not fared as well and present pictures of poverty and economic distress. Some "bipolar" groups, such as

Chinese Americans, fit in both categories. We should also note that the picture of economic distress for these groups would be much greater if we focused on undocumented immigrants, who are numerous in the community and concentrated in the informal, irregular economy.

FIGURE 9.16 Distribution of Household Income for Non-Hispanic Whites and Asian Americans, 2012

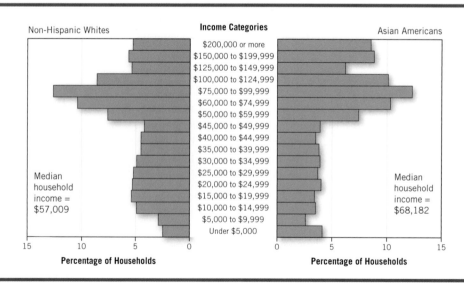

SOURCE: U.S. Census Bureau (2013f).

FIGURE 9.17 Percentage of Families and Children in Poverty for All Asian Americans, 10 Largest Asian American Groups, and Non-Hispanic Whites, 2012

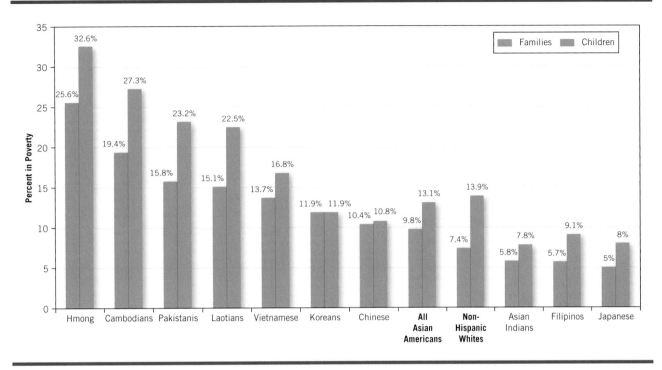

SOURCE: U.S. Census Bureau (2013a).

PRIMARY STRUCTURAL ASSIMILATION

Levels of integration at the primary level for Asian Americans are, once again, highly variable from group to group. Japanese Americans tend to be the most integrated on this dimension. One study found that, of the six Asian American groups studied, Japanese Americans were the most likely to have friends outside their group and to marry across group lines (Pew Research Center, 2013c, pp. 98, 32). The same study found that, as would be expected, integration at the primary level was lower for the foreign-born and those with less English language ability.

Generally, rates of primary integration tend to be higher than for other groups but are declining as the number of Asian Americans grows and the percentage of foreign-born increases (Passel, Wang, & Taylor, 2010, p. 17). This pattern reflects the tendency of newcomers to marry within their group.

Table 9.2 compares in-marriage trends in 1980 and 2008 following the same format used in previous chapters. Asian Americans have much lower rates of in-marriage than do African Americans and Hispanic Americans, although they have somewhat higher rates than Native Americans. Again, this is partly a function of the relative sizes of these groups but also reflects the more favored position of Asian Americans in the dominant group's perceptions.

Also note that the percentage of foreign-born Asian Americans marrying within the group increased for both men and women. This is consistent with high rates of immigration in recent years and the idea that the first generation tends to socialize more with coethnics.

FIGURE 9.18 Percentage of Selected Native-Born and Foreign-Born Asian American Groups and Non-Hispanic Whites With Incomes Less Than $30,000, 2012

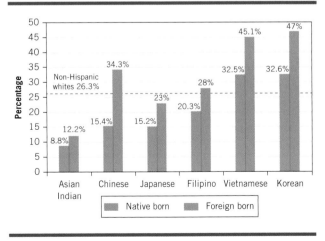

SOURCE: Computed from Pew Research Center (2013c).

TABLE 9.2 Percentage of Whites and Asian Americans Married to a Person of the Same Group, 1980 and 2008

| YEAR | WHITES | | ASIAN AMERICANS | | | |
| | Men | Women | Men | | Women | |
			Foreign-Born	U.S.-Born	Foreign-Born	U.S.-Born
1980	96%	95%	58%	57%	45%	51%
2008	93%	92%	77%	53%	55%	52%

SOURCE: Qian and Lichter (2011, p. 1072). Copyright © 2011 National Council on Family Relations. Reprinted with permission.

QUESTIONS FOR REFLECTION

1. In this section, we examined a variety of dimensions of acculturation and integration for Asian Americans. Which is most important? Why?

2. What evidence is presented to support the idea that Asian Americans are a "model minority"? What evidence is presented against this characterization? Which argument is more convincing? Why?

COMPARING MINORITY GROUPS: EXPLAINING ASIAN AMERICAN SUCCESS

To conclude this chapter, let's return to a question raised in the opening pages: How can we explain the apparent success of some Asian American groups? Relative affluence and high status are not characteristic of the other racial minority groups we have examined, and at least at first glance, there seems to be little in our theories and concepts to help us understand the situation of Asian Americans. Of course, as we have noted on several occasions, we need to recognize that the "success" label is simplistic and even incorrect for some groups, especially for Southeast Asian groups with a high percentage of refugees, who have profiles that resemble those of colonized racial minority groups.

To better focus this discussion, we will concentrate on the groups with the longest histories in the United States: Chinese and Japanese Americans. The Current Debates section for this chapter presents several different views on the nature and causes of "success" for these groups. In this section, we compare Chinese and Japanese Americans with European immigrant groups and colonized minority groups. What crucial factors differentiate the experiences of these groups? Can we understand these differences in terms of the framework provided by the Blauner and Noel hypotheses and the other concepts developed in this text?

The debate over the causes of Asian American success often breaks down into two different viewpoints. One view offers a cultural explanation, which accepts the evidence of Asian American success at face value and attributes it to the "good values" of traditional Asian cultures that we briefly explored at the beginning of this chapter. These values—including respect for elders and authority figures, hard work and thriftiness, and conformity and politeness—are highly compatible with U.S. middle-class Protestant value systems and presumably helped Asian Americans gain acceptance and opportunities. The cultural explanation is consistent with traditional assimilation theory and human capital theory, and an example of it can be found in the selection by Professor Harry Kitano in this chapter's Current Debates section.

The second point of view stresses the ways Chinese and Japanese Americans entered American society and their reactions to the racism and exclusion they faced. This approach could be called a "structural explanation," and it emphasizes contact situations, modes of incorporation, enclave economies, group cohesion, position in the labor market, and institutionalized discrimination, rather than cultural values.

Also, the structural approach questions the notion that Asian Americans are "successful" and stresses the realities of Asian American poverty and the continuing patterns of racism and exclusion. The structural approach is more compatible with the theories and concepts used throughout this text, and it identifies several of the important pieces needed to solve the puzzle of Asian "success" and put it in perspective. This is not to suggest that the cultural approach is wrong or irrelevant, however. The issues we raise are complex and will probably require many approaches and perspectives before they are fully resolved.

ASIAN AMERICANS AND WHITE ETHNICS

Chinese and Japanese immigrants arrived in America at about the same time as immigrants from southern and eastern Europe (see Chapter 2). Both groups consisted mainly of sojourning young men who were largely unskilled, from rural backgrounds, and not highly educated. Immigrants from Europe, like those from Asia, encountered massive discrimination and rejection and were also victims of restrictive legislation. Yet the barriers to upward mobility for European immigrants (or at least for their descendants) fell away more rapidly than did the barriers for immigrants from Asia. Why?

Some important differences between the two immigrant experiences are clear, the most obvious being the greater racial visibility of Asian Americans. Whereas the cultural and linguistic markers that identified eastern and southern Europeans faded with each passing generation, the racial characteristics of the Asian groups continued to separate them from the larger society.

Thus, Asian Americans are not "pure immigrant" groups (see Blauner, 1972, p. 55). For most of the 20th century, Chinese and Japanese Americans remained in a less favorable position than did European immigrants and their descendants, excluded by their physical appearance from the mainstream economy until the decades following World War II.

Another important difference relates to position in the labor market. Immigrants from southern and eastern Europe entered the industrializing East Coast economy, where they took industrial and manufacturing jobs. Although such jobs were poorly paid and insecure, this location in the labor force gave European immigrants and their descendants the potential for upward mobility in the mainstream economy. At the very least, these urban industrial and manufacturing jobs put the children and grandchildren of European immigrants in positions from which skilled, well-paid, unionized jobs were reachable, as were managerial and professional careers.

In contrast, Chinese and Japanese immigrants on the West Coast were forced into ethnic enclaves and came to rely on jobs in the small-business and service sector, and, in the case of the Japanese, in the rural economy. By their nature, these jobs did not link Chinese and Japanese immigrants or their descendants to the industrial sector or to better-paid, more secure, unionized jobs. Furthermore, their exclusion from the mainstream economy was reinforced by overt, racially based discrimination from both employers and labor unions (see Fong & Markham, 1991).

ASIAN AMERICANS AND COLONIZED RACIAL MINORITY GROUPS

Comparisons between Asian Americans and African Americans, American Indians, and Hispanic Americans have generated a level of controversy and a degree of heat and passion that may be surprising at first. An examination of the issues and their implications, however, reveals that the debate involves some thinly disguised political and moral agendas, and evokes sharply clashing views on the nature of U.S. society. What might appear on the surface to be merely an academic comparison of different minority groups turns out to be an argument about the quality of American justice and fairness and the very essence of the U.S. value system.

What is not in dispute in this debate is that some Asian groups (e.g., Japanese Americans) rank far above other racial minority groups on all the commonly used measures of secondary structural integration and equality. What is disputed is how to interpret these comparisons and assess their meanings. Of course, gross comparisons between entire groups can be misleading. If we confine our attention to averages (mean levels of education or median income), the picture of Asian American success is sustained. However, if we also observe the full range of differences within each group (e.g., the "bipolar" nature of occupations among Chinese Americans), we see that the images of success have been exaggerated and need to be placed in a proper context (see the selection by Min in this chapter's Current Debates section).

Even with these qualifications, however, discussion often slides onto more ideological ground, and political and moral issues begin to cloud the debate. Asian American success is often taken as proof that American society is truly the land of opportunity and that people who work hard and obey the rules will get ahead.

When we discussed modern racism in Chapter 3, we pointed out that a belief in the openness and fairness of the United States can be a way of blaming the victim and placing the responsibility for change on the minority groups rather than on the structure of society or on past-in-present or institutionalized discrimination. Asian success has become a "proof" of the validity of this ideology. The none-too-subtle implication is that other groups (African Americans, Hispanic Americans, and American Indians) could achieve the same success as Asian Americans but, for various reasons, choose not to. Thus, the relative success of Chinese and Japanese Americans has become a device for scolding other minority groups.

A more structural approach to investigating Asian success begins with a comparison of the history of the various racial minority groups and their modes of incorporation into the larger society. When Chinese and Japanese Americans were building their enclave economies in the early part of the 20th century, African and Mexican Americans were concentrated in unskilled agricultural occupations. American Indians were isolated from the larger society on their reservations, and Puerto Ricans had not yet begun to arrive on the mainland. The social class differences between these groups today flow from their respective situations in the past.

Many of the occupational and financial advances made by Chinese and Japanese Americans have been due to the high levels of education achieved by their second generations. Although education is traditionally valued in Asian cultures, the decision to invest limited resources in schooling is also quite consistent with the economic niche occupied by these immigrants. Education is one obvious, relatively low-cost strategy to upgrade the productivity and profit of a small-business economy and improve the economic status of the group as a whole. An educated, English-speaking second generation could bring expertise and business acumen to the family enterprises and lead them to higher levels of performance. Education might also be the means by which the second generation could enter professional careers. This strategy may have been especially attractive to an immigrant generation that was itself relatively uneducated and barred from citizenship (Hirschman & Wong, 1986, p. 23; see also Bonacich & Modell, 1980, p. 152; Sanchirico, 1991).

The efforts to educate the next generation were largely successful. Chinese and Japanese Americans achieved educational parity with the larger society as early as the 1920s. One study found that for men and women born after 1915, the median years of schooling completed were actually higher for Chinese and Japanese Americans than for whites (Hirschman & Wong, 1986, p. 11).

Before World War II, both Asian groups were barred from the mainstream economy and from better jobs. When anti-Asian prejudice and discrimination declined in the 1950s, however, the Chinese and Japanese American second generations had the educational background necessary to take advantage of the increased opportunities.

Thus, there was a crucial divergence in the development of Chinese and Japanese Americans and the colonized minority groups. At the time when native-born Chinese and Japanese Americans reached educational parity with whites, the vast majority of African Americans, American Indians, and Mexican Americans were still victimized by Jim Crow laws and legalized segregation, and excluded from opportunities for anything but rudimentary education. The Supreme Court decision in *Brown v. Board of Education of Topeka* (1954) was decades in the future, and American Indian schoolchildren were still being subjected to intense Americanization in the guise of a curriculum.

Today, these other racial minority groups have not completely escaped from the disadvantages imposed by centuries of institutionalized discrimination. African Americans have approached educational parity with white Americans only in recent years (see Chapter 6), and American Indians and Mexican Americans remain far below national averages (see Chapters 7 and 8, respectively).

The structural explanation argues that the recent upward mobility of Chinese and Japanese Americans is the result of the methods by which they incorporated themselves into American society, not so much their values and traditions. The logic of their enclave economy led the immigrant generation to invest in the education of their children, who would then be better prepared to develop their businesses and seek opportunities in the larger society.

As a final point, note that the structural explanation is not consistent with traditional views of the assimilation process. The immigrant generation of Chinese and Japanese Americans responded to the massive discrimination they faced by withdrawing, developing ethnic enclaves, and becoming "invisible" to the larger society. Like Jewish and Cuban Americans, Chinese and Japanese Americans used their traditional cultures and patterns of social life to create and build their own subcommunities, from which they launched the next generation. Contrary to traditional ideas about how assimilation is "supposed" to happen, we see again that integration can precede acculturation and that the smoothest route to integration may be the creation of a separate subsociety independent of the surrounding community.

SUMMARY

This summary is organized around the Learning Objectives listed at the beginning of this chapter.

 9.1 Summarize the population characteristics of all Asian Americans and the 10 largest Asian American groups.

Asian Americans are very diverse and include groups from all over Asia and the Pacific Islands. As a whole, Asian Americans are 5.6% of the population, but that percentage is expected to increase to 10% by midcentury. Like Hispanic Americans, Asian Americans have a high percentage of first-generation members and are growing more rapidly than the population as a whole. Asian Americans have accounted for the largest stream of immigrants to the United States since 2009, when they outpaced Hispanic Americans. The largest groups are Chinese, Filipino, and Indian Americans, and the groups with the longest history in the United States are Chinese and Japanese Americans.

 9.2 Summarize and explain the history of Chinese and Japanese Americans, including their cultural characteristics, their immigration patterns, their development in the United States, and the nature and importance of the enclave for each.

Asian cultures tend to be less individualistic and more focused on maintaining harmonious interpersonal relations than is Anglo culture. Also, they tend to be more group and family oriented.

Chinese Americans began immigrating in significant numbers in the 1840s. Tolerated at first, they became the victims of a massive campaign of discrimination and exclusion. They responded by constructing enclaves. Chinatowns became highly organized communities, largely run by the local Chinese Consolidated Benevolent Association and other groups. The second generation faced many barriers to employment in the dominant society, although opportunities increased after World War II.

Japanese immigration began in the 1890s and stimulated a campaign that attempted to oust the group from agriculture and curtail immigration from Japan. The Issei formed an enclave, but during World War II, Japanese Americans were forced into relocation camps, an experience that devastated the group economically and psychologically. The group has since made a strong recovery and is, today, probably the most assimilated Asian American group.

 9.3 Explain the patterns of the recent immigration from Asia.

Recent immigration from Asia has been voluminous and diverse. Some immigrants are highly educated professionals, while others more closely resemble the "peasant laborers" who have come from Mexico in recent decades and from Italy, Ireland, Poland, and scores of other nations in the past. This second group of immigrants forms the unskilled workforce for the enclave economy and in other areas.

 9.4 Summarize how prejudice and discrimination affect Asian Americans.

Overall levels of anti-Asian prejudice and discrimination have probably declined in recent years but remain widespread. A recent survey suggests that prejudice and discrimination are perceived as being less of a problem for Asian Americans than for other racial minority groups. Among other possibilities, this might reflect "positive" stereotypes of Asian Americans and/or the movement of the group toward "honorary" whiteness.

 9.5 Describe the situation of Asian Americans using the concepts of assimilation and pluralism, especially in terms of

    a. acculturation,

    b. secondary structural assimilation, and

    c. primary structural assimilation.

- Levels of acculturation are highly variable. Some groups, such as Japanese Americans, are highly

acculturated, while others, especially those with many first-generation members, have barely begun the process. Continuing high levels of immigration help sustain the various Asian American cultures.

- Secondary structural assimilation is also highly variable. Members of these groups whose families have been in the United States longer tend to be highly integrated. Recent immigrants from China, however, are "bipolar": Many are highly educated and skilled, but a sizable number are "immigrant laborers" who bring modest educational credentials and are likely to be living in poverty.

- Levels of primary assimilation are also highly variable. Asian Americans who have had family in the United States for a long time tend to rank high on primary assimilation, while recent immigrants who reside in the enclave tend to rank low. Rates of intermarriage with other groups are higher than for African and Hispanic Americans, but this is dependent on nativity, among other variables.

 9.6 Assess the overall situation of Asian Americans today based on the concepts and information presented in this chapter, and assess the idea that Asian Americans are a "model minority." Are Asian Americans "whitening," "blackening," or becoming "honorary whites"?

First, the notion that Asian Americans are a "model minority" is exaggerated, but comparisons with European immigrants and colonized minority groups suggest some of the reasons for the relative "success" of these groups.

Second, Asian American groups occupy various relations with the larger society, encompassing multiple forms of assimilation and pluralism. Some groups, or segments of groups, may be "whitening," others may be perpetuating an enclave, while still others are being marginalized and, perhaps, moving toward a position in the urban underclass. At any rate, traditional, linear notions of assimilation do not describe the situations of these groups, at least at present.

KEY TERMS

Alien Land Act 261	*huiguan* 257	relocation	tongs 258
Chinese Exclusion	Issei 261	camps 262	Yonsei 264
Act 256	Nisei 261	Sansei 264	

REVIEW QUESTIONS

1. Describe the cultural characteristics of Asian American groups. How did these characteristics shape relationships with the larger society? Did they contribute to the perception of Asian Americans as "successful"? How?

2. Compare and contrast the contact situations for Chinese Americans, Japanese Americans, and Cuban Americans. What common characteristics led to the construction of ethnic enclaves for all three groups? How and why did these enclaves vary from one another?

3. In what sense was the second generation of Chinese Americans "delayed"? How did this affect the group's relationship with the larger society?

4. Compare and contrast the campaigns that arose in opposition to the immigration of Chinese and Japanese people. Do the concepts of the Noel hypothesis help explain the differences? Do you see any similarities with the changing federal policy toward Mexican immigrants across the 20th century? Explain.

5. Compare and contrast the Japanese relocation camps with Indian reservations in terms of paternalism and coerced acculturation. What impact did this experience have on the Japanese Americans economically? How were Japanese Americans compensated for their losses? Does the compensation paid to Japanese Americans provide a precedent for similar payments (reparations) to African Americans for their losses under slavery? Why or why not?

6. How do the Burakumin in Japan illustrate "visibility" as a defining characteristic of minority-group status? How is the minority status of this group maintained?

7. What gender differences characterize Asian American groups? What are some of the important ways the experiences of women and men vary?

8. Describe the situation of the Chinese and Japanese Americans in terms of prejudice and discrimination, acculturation, and integration. Are these groups truly "success stories"? How? What factors or experiences might account for this "success"? Are all Asian American groups equally successful? Describe the important variations from group to group. Compare the integration and level of equality of these groups with other American racial minorities. How would you explain the differences? Are the concepts of the Noel and Blauner hypotheses helpful? Why or why not?

STUDENT STUDY SITE

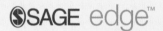

Sharpen your skills with SAGE edge at edge.sagepub.com/healey7e

SAGE edge for students provides a personalized approach to help you accomplish your coursework goals in an easy-to-use learning environment.

The following resources are available at SAGE edge:

Current Debates: Asian American "Success": What Are the Dimensions, Causes, and Implications for Other Minority Groups?

Considered as a whole, Asian Americans tend to exceed national norms in education, income, and other measures of success. How accurate is this picture? What truths are obscured by the myth of Asian success? What are the implications for other minority groups?

On our website you will find an overview of the topic, the clashing points of view, and some questions to consider as you analyze the material.

Public Sociology Assignments

Public Sociology Assignments provide opportunities for students to address directly and personally some of the issues raised in this text. There are two assignments for Part III on our website. The first looks at patterns of self-segregation in school cafeterias, and, in the second, students analyze the portrayal of the American family on television in terms of race, ethnicity, sexual orientation, and other sociologically relevant characteristics.

Contributed by Linda M. Waldron

Internet Research Project

For this Internet Research Project, you will use data gathered by the U.S. Census Bureau to assess the situation of all Asian Americans and an Asian American group of your choosing. You will add this information to the data you gathered previously on African Americans, Native Americans, Hispanic Americans, and the general population. The project will be guided by a series of questions related to course concepts, and your instructor may ask you to discuss your findings in small groups.

For Further Reading

Please see our website for an annotated list of important works related to this chapter.

CHAPTER-OPENING TIMELINE PHOTO CREDITS

1763: Library of Congress Prints and Photographs Division

1847: Wikimedia/Fred Hsu

1848: Wikimedia Commons

1882: Library of Congress Prints and Photographs Division

1924: Library of Congress Prints and Photographs Division

1942: Library of Congress Prints and Photographs Division

1988: Ronald Reagan Presidential Library

2012: Wikimedia Commons/Eric R. Bechtold

10

NEW AMERICANS, IMMIGRATION, ASSIMILATION, AND OLD CHALLENGES

LOC

timeline

1875
In search of opportunity, a small number of Arab Muslims emigrate from the Ottoman Empire and settle in New York.

1907
Executive Order 589 prevents Japanese and Koreans from entering U.S. mainland.

1946
Luce-Celler Act permits Filipinos and Indians to immigrate and grants them naturalization rights.

1874   1886   1898   1910   1922   1934

1893
The first substantial migration of Muslims to the U.S. begins.

1924
The Supreme Court rules that Asian Indians cannot be naturalized.

1952
Muslims in the U.S. military sue the government to be allowed to identify themselves as Muslims. Until then, Islam was not recognized as a legitimate religion.

1952
The Immigration and Nationality Act drastically reduces number of Caribbean farm workers allowed to enter the U.S.

LOC

Sade and four of his twenty-something friends are at a hookah cafe almost underneath the Verrazano-Narrows Bridge in Brooklyn. It's late, but the summer heat is strong and hangs in the air. They sit on the sidewalk in a circle, water pipes bubbling between their white plastic chairs.

Sade is upset. He recently found out that his close friend of almost four years was an undercover police detective sent to spy on him, his friends, and his community. Even the guy's name . . . was fake, which particularly irked the twenty-four-year-old Palestinian American. . . .

"I was very hurt," he says. "Was it friendship, or was he doing his job?" He takes a puff from his water pipe. "I felt betrayed." The smoke comes out thick and smells like apples. . . . He shakes his head. . . .

Informants and spies are regular conversation topics [among Arab Americans] in the age of terror,

1965
The Hart-Celler Act, a new immigration law, launches a new wave of immigration from the Caribbean. Pakistanis, Bangladeshis, and Arabs from the professional classes also immigrate, helping to establish Islam in America.

1977–1981
60,000 Haitians land in South Florida by boat, fleeing the brutal political repression of the Duvalier dictatorship. Thousands are returned to Haiti.

2001
Hate crimes against Arab and Asian Americans follow the September 11 terrorist attacks.

1956
Dalip Singh Saund of California becomes the first Indian American in Congress.

1975
The Vietnam War ends, leading to large migration of Southeast Asians.

1979–1992
During El Salvador's civil war, between 500,000 and one million immigrate to the U.S.

1980
Ethiopians become the largest group of Africans to immigrate to the U.S. under the provisions of the Refugee Act of 1980.

1986
40,000 Haitians seeking political asylum are given permanent resident status.

2008
The number of undocumented immigrants begins to decline in response to economic hard times in the U.S., falling to less than 11 million in 2012.

2012
The Obama administration creates a program by which the children of undocumented immigrants ("DREAMers") can apply to stay in the U.S. without fear of deportation.

a time when friendships are tested, trust disappears, and tragedy becomes comedy. If questioning friendship isn't enough, Sade has also had other problems to deal with. Sacked from his Wall Street job, he is convinced that the termination stemmed from his Jerusalem birthplace. Anti-Arab and anti-Muslim invectives were routinely slung at him there, and he's happier now in a technology firm owned and staffed by other hyphenated Americans. But the last several years have taken their toll. I ask him about life after September 11 for Arab Americans. "We're the new blacks," he says. "You know that, right?"

—Moustafa Bayoumi (2008, pp. 1–2)

Sade's comparison between Arab Americans and blacks may be overstated, but there is no question that America finds itself in a new era of group relations today. The "traditional" minority groups—black Americans, Mexican Americans, and others—have been joined by new groups from places that most Americans could not find on a map: Armenia, Zimbabwe, Bhutan, Guyana, and Indonesia to name but a few.

What do these newcomers bring? What do they contribute, and what do they cost? How are they changing the United States? What will the country look like in 50 years? We asked at the beginning of this text: "What does it mean to be an American?" How will that question be answered in the future? •

The world is on the move as never before, and migration connects even the remotest villages of every continent in a global network of population ebb and flow. As we have seen, people are moving everywhere, but the United States remains the single most popular destination. Migrants will pay huge amounts of money—thousands of dollars, veritable fortunes in economies where people survive on dollars a day—and undergo considerable hardship for the chance to find work in the United States.

What motivates this population movement? How does it differ from migrations of the past? What impact will the newcomers have on U.S. society? Will they absorb American culture? What parts? Will they integrate into American society? Which segments?

We have been asking questions like these throughout the text. In this chapter, we focus specifically on current immigrants and the myriad issues stimulated by their presence. We mentioned some groups of new Americans in Chapters 8 and 9. In this chapter, we begin by addressing recent immigration in general terms and then consider some additional groups of new Americans, including Hispanic, Caribbean, and Asian groups; Arabs and Middle Easterners; and immigrants from sub-Saharan Africa. A consideration of these groups will broaden your understanding of the wide cultural variations, motivations, and human capital of the current immigrant stream to the United States.

We will next address the most important and controversial immigration issues facing U.S. society and conclude with a brief return to the "traditional" minority groups: African Americans, Native Americans, and other peoples of color who continue to face issues of equality and full integration and must now pursue their long-standing grievances in an atmosphere where public attention and political energy are focused on other groups and newer issues.

CURRENT IMMIGRATION

As you know, the United States has experienced three different waves of mass immigration. In Chapter 2, we discussed the first two waves (see Figure 2.2). As you recall, the first wave lasted from the 1820s to the 1880s and consisted of mostly northern and western European immigrants, while the second, from the 1880s to the 1920s, brought primarily southern and eastern European immigrants. During these two periods, more than 37 million people immigrated to the United States, an average rate of about 370,000 per year. These waves of newcomers transformed American society on every level: its neighborhoods and parishes and cities, its popular culture, its accents and dialects, its religion, and its cuisine.

The third wave of mass immigration promises to be equally transformative. This wave began after the 1965 change in U.S. immigration policy and includes people from every corner of the globe. Since the mid-1960s, well over 30 million newcomers have arrived (not counting undocumented immigrants)—a rate of more than 600,000 per year, much higher than the earlier period (although the rate is lower as a percentage of the total population). Also, Figure 10.1 shows that the number of

FIGURE 10.1 Number of Legal Immigrants to the United States, 1960–2012

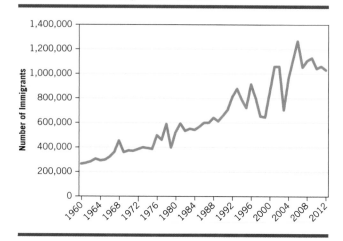

SOURCE: U.S. Department of Homeland Security (2012).

FIGURE 10.2 Number of Legal Immigrants for Top 25 Sending Nations, 2012

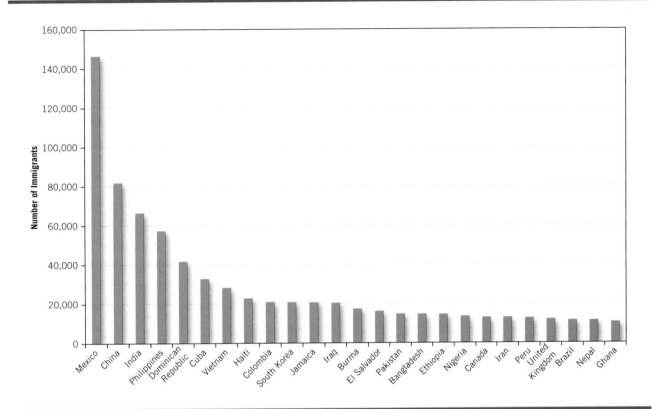

SOURCE: U.S. Department of Homeland Security (2012).

legal immigrants per year generally increased over this period, at least until the U.S. economy turned sour in recent years.

The official record for most immigrants in a year was set in 1907, when almost 1.3 million people arrived on U.S. shores. That number was almost equaled in 2006, but if undocumented immigrants had been included in the count, the 1907 record would have been eclipsed several times since the 1960s.

The more recent wave of immigration is much more diverse than the first two. In 2012 alone, immigrants arrived from more than 200 separate nations—from Afghanistan and Albania to Zambia and Zimbabwe. Only about 8% of the newcomers were from Europe, about a third were from North America (mostly Mexico), and 40% were from the nations of Asia. The numbers for the top 25 sending nations for 2012 are displayed in Figure 10.2. Note that the number of Mexican immigrants is almost double the number from China, the next-highest sending nation. Also note the variety of nations and regions of origin. Immigration to the United States is truly a global phenomenon!

How will this new wave of immigration transform the United States? How will these new immigrants be transformed by the United States? What do they contribute? What do they cost? Will they adopt the ways of the dominant society? What are the implications if assimilation fails?

We begin by reviewing several case studies of new Americans, focusing on information and statistics comparable to those used in Chapters 6 through 9. Each of the groups covered in this chapter has had some members in the United States for decades, some for more than a century. However, in all cases, the groups were quite small until the latter third of the 20th century. Although they are growing rapidly now, all remain relatively small, and none are larger than 1% of the population. Nonetheless, some will have a greater impact on American culture and society in the future, and some groups—Muslims and Arab and Middle Eastern Americans—have already become a focus of concern and controversy because of the events of September 11 and the ensuing war on terrorism.

QUESTIONS FOR REFLECTION

1. What are some of the key differences between the first two waves of mass immigration from the 1820s to the 1920s and the current, post-1965 wave?

2. Why is the current wave of immigration so diverse? What are the implications of this diversity for the future of American society?

NEW HISPANIC GROUPS: IMMIGRANTS FROM THE DOMINICAN REPUBLIC, EL SALVADOR, AND COLOMBIA

Immigration from Latin America, the Caribbean, and South America has been considerable, even excluding Mexico. As with other sending nations, the volume of immigration from these regions increased after 1965 and has averaged about 200,000 per year. Generally, Latino immigrants—not counting those from Mexico—have been about 25% of all immigrants since the 1960s (U.S. Department of Homeland Security, 2012).

The sending nations for these immigrants are economically less developed, and most have long-standing relations with the United States. In Chapter 8, we discussed the roles that Mexico and Puerto Rico have historically played as sources of cheap labor and the ties that led Cubans to immigrate to the United States. Each of the other sending nations has been similarly linked to the United States, the dominant economic and political power in the region.

Although the majority of these immigrants bring educational and occupational qualifications that are modest by U.S. standards, they tend to be more educated, more urbanized, and more skilled than the average citizens of the nations from which they come. Contrary to widely held beliefs, these immigrants do not represent the poorest of the poor, the "wretched refuse" of their homelands. They tend to be rather ambitious, as evidenced by their willingness to attempt to succeed in a society that has not been notably hospitable to Latinos or people of color in the past. Most of these immigrants are not only fleeing poverty or joblessness but also are attempting to pursue their ambitions and seek opportunities for advancement that are simply not available in their countries of origin (Feliciano, 2006; Portes & Rumbaut, 1996, pp. 10–11).

This characterization applies to legal and unauthorized immigrants alike. In fact, the latter may illustrate the point more dramatically because the cost of illegally entering the United States can be considerable, much higher than the cost of a legal entry. The venture may require years of saving or the combined resources of a large kinship group. Forged papers and other costs of being smuggled into the country can easily amount to many thousands of dollars, a considerable sum in nations where the usual wage is a tiny fraction of the U.S. average. Also, the passage can be extremely dangerous and can require a level of courage (or desperation) not often associated with the undocumented and illegal.

Rather than attempting to cover all South and Central American groups, we will select three of the largest to serve as "case studies" and consider immigrants from the Dominican Republic, El Salvador, and Colombia. Together, these three groups have made up 7% to 8% of all immigrants in recent years and about 30% of the immigrants from Central and South America and the Caribbean. These groups had few members in the United States before the 1960s, and all have had high rates of immigration over the past four decades. However, the motivation of the immigrants and the immigration experience has varied from group to group, as we shall see later.

THREE CASE STUDIES

Some basic information about these three groups is presented in Table 10.1. Some of this information was also presented in Chapter 8 but is repeated here to provide a common frame of reference for all the groups covered in this chapter.

Each of these groups has a high percentage of foreign-born members, and, predictably with so many members in the first generation, proficiency in English is an important issue. Although Colombian Americans approach national norms in education, the other two groups have relatively low levels of human capital (education) and are well below national norms in terms of affluence, income, and poverty.

TABLE 10.1 Selected Characteristics of Three Hispanic American Groups and Non-Hispanic Whites, 2012

GROUP	SIZE	PERCENTAGE WITH LESS THAN HIGH SCHOOL DIPLOMA	PERCENTAGE WITH COLLEGE DEGREE OR MORE	PERCENTAGE FOREIGN-BORN	PERCENTAGE WHO SPEAK ENGLISH LESS THAN "VERY WELL"	MEDIAN HOUSEHOLD INCOME	PERCENTAGE OF FAMILIES IN POVERTY
Non-Hispanic whites	—	8.9	31.9	3.9	1.7	$56,525	7.4
Dominicans	1,568,168	34.0	15.5	46.6	44.0	$33,900	27.3
Salvadorans	1,937,369	51.4	7.7	60.9	52.3	$43,487	20.6
Colombians	1,000,125	14.2	31.5	63.9	39.0	$50,102	11.9

SOURCE: U.S. Census Bureau (2013a).

Although these groups share some common characteristics, there are also important differences. They differ in their "racial" characteristics, with Dominicans being more African in appearance, Colombians more European, and Salvadorans more Indian. The groups tend to settle in different places. Colombians are clustered in the South (49%), particularly in Florida, and in the Northeast (33%), mostly in New York and New Jersey (Brown & Patten, 2013a, p. 2). Dominicans are very much concentrated in the Northeast (78%), with almost half living in New York alone (Brown & Patten, 2013b, p. 2). In contrast, Salvadorans tend to reside in the West (40%), mostly in California, and the South, mostly in Texas (Brown & Patten, 2013c, p. 2).

Finally, the groups differ in the conditions of their entry or contact situations—a difference that, as we have seen, is consequential. Salvadorans are more likely to be political refugees who fled a brutal civil war and political repression, while Dominicans and Colombians are more likely to be motivated by economics and the employment possibilities offered in the United States. We will consider each of these groups briefly and further explore some of their differences.

Dominicans. The Dominican Republic shares the Caribbean island of Hispaniola with Haiti. The island economy is still largely agricultural, although the tourist industry has grown in recent years. Unemployment and poverty are major problems, and Dominicans average about five years of education (NationMaster, 2014). Dominican immigrants, like those from Mexico, are motivated largely by economics, and they compete for jobs with Puerto Ricans, other immigrant groups, and native-born workers with lower levels of education and job skills.

Although Dominicans are limited in their job options by the language barrier, they are somewhat advantaged by their willingness to work for lower wages, and they are especially concentrated in the service sector, as day laborers (men) or domestics (women). Dominicans maintain strong ties with home and are a major source of income and support for the families left behind.

In terms of acculturation and integration, Dominicans are roughly similar to Mexican Americans and Puerto Ricans, although some studies suggest that they are possibly the most impoverished immigrant group (see Table 10.1, as well as Figures 8.16 and 8.18). A high percentage of Dominicans are undocumented, and many spend a great deal of money and take considerable risks to get to the United States. If these less visible members of the community were included in the official, government-generated statistics used in the figures presented later in this chapter, the portrait of poverty and low levels of education and job skills likely would be even more dramatic.

Salvadorans. El Salvador, like the Dominican Republic, is a relatively poor nation, with a high percentage of the population relying on subsistence agriculture for survival. It is estimated that about 36% of the population lives below the poverty level

(Central Intelligence Agency, 2013), and there are major problems with unemployment and underemployment. About 80% of the population is literate, and the average number of years of school completed is a little more than five (NationMaster, 2014).

El Salvador, like many sending nations, has a difficult time providing sufficient employment opportunities for its population, and much of the pressure to migrate is economic. However, El Salvador also suffered through a brutal civil war in the 1980s, and many of the Salvadorans in the United States today are actually political refugees. The United States, under the administration of President Ronald Reagan, refused to grant political refugee status to Salvadorans, and many were returned to El Salvador. This federal policy resulted in high numbers of undocumented immigrants and also stimulated a sanctuary movement, led by American clergy, to help Salvadoran immigrants, both undocumented and legal, stay in the United States. As is the case with Dominicans, if the undocumented immigrants from El Salvador were included in official government statistics, the picture of poverty would become even more extreme.

Colombians. Colombia is somewhat more developed than most other Central and South American nations but has suffered from more than 40 years of internal turmoil, civil war, and government corruption. The nation is a major center for the production and distribution of drugs to the world in general and the United States in particular, and the drug industry and profits are complexly intertwined with domestic strife.

Colombian Americans are closer to U.S. norms of education and income than are other Latino groups (see Table 10.1, as well as Figures 8.14, 8.16, and 8.18), and recent immigrants are a mixture of less-skilled laborers and well-educated professionals seeking to further their careers. Colombians are residentially concentrated in urban areas, especially in Florida and the Northeast, and often settle in areas close to other Latino neighborhoods. Of course, the huge majority of Colombian Americans are law-abiding and not connected with the drug trade, but still they must deal with the pervasive stereotype that portrays Colombians as gangsters and drug smugglers (not unlike the Mafia stereotype encountered by Italian Americans).

NON-HISPANIC IMMIGRANTS FROM THE CARIBBEAN

Immigrants from the Western Hemisphere bring a variety of traditions to the United States other than Hispanic ones. Two of the largest non-Latino groups come from Haiti and Jamaica in the Caribbean. Both nations are much less developed than the United States, and this is reflected in the educational and occupational characteristics of their immigrants. A statistical profile of both groups is presented in Table 10.2, along with that of non-Hispanic whites for purposes of comparison.

TABLE 10.2 Selected Characteristics of Two Non-Hispanic Caribbean Groups and Non-Hispanic Whites, 2012

GROUP	SIZE	PERCENTAGE WITH LESS THAN HIGH SCHOOL DIPLOMA	PERCENTAGE WITH COLLEGE DEGREE OR MORE	PERCENTAGE FOREIGN-BORN	PERCENTAGE WHO SPEAK ENGLISH LESS THAN "VERY WELL"	MEDIAN HOUSEHOLD INCOME	PERCENTAGE OF FAMILIES IN POVERTY
Non-Hispanic whites	—	8.9	31.9	3.9	1.7	$56,525	7.4
Haitians	898,484	22.8	19.0	59.2	37.2	$42,275	19.5
Jamaicans	1,016,037	15.5	25.0	59.3	1.2	$49,310	12.5

SOURCE: U.S. Census Bureau (2013a).

TWO CASE STUDIES

Haitians. Haiti is the poorest country in the Western Hemisphere, and most of the population relies on small-scale subsistence agriculture for survival. An estimated 80% of the population lives below the poverty line, and less than one third of adults hold formal jobs (Central Intelligence Agency, 2013). Less than half the population is literate, and Haitians average less than three years of formal education (NationMaster, 2014). The already difficult conditions in Haiti were intensified by a massive earthquake in January 2010, and it will take years for the tiny nation to recover fully.

Haitian migration was virtually nonexistent until the 1970s and 1980s, when thousands began to flee the brutal repression of the Duvalier dictatorship, which—counting both father ("Papa Doc") and son ("Baby Doc")—lasted until the mid-1980s. In stark contrast to the treatment of Cuban immigrants (see Chapter 8), however, the U.S. government defined Haitians as economic refugees ineligible for asylum, and an intense campaign was begun to keep Haitians out of the United States. Thousands were returned to Haiti, some to face political persecution, prison, and even death. Others have been incarcerated

Hatian refugees attempting to sail to the Florida. Note the overcrowded, unsafe conditions.

in the United States, and in the view of some, "during the 1970s and 1980s, no other immigrant group suffered more U.S. government prejudice and discrimination than Haitians" (Stepick, Stepick, Eugene, Teed, & Labissiere, 2001, p. 236).

What accounts for this cold, negative reception? Some reasons are not hard to identify. Haitian immigrants brought low levels of human capital and education. This created concerns about their ability to support themselves in the United States and also meant that they had relatively few resources with which to defend their self-interests. In addition, although French is the language of the educated elite, most Haitians speak a version of Creole that is spoken only by Haitians, and a high percentage of Haitian immigrants spoke English poorly or not at all. Perhaps the most important reason for the rejection, however, is that Haitians are black and must cope with the centuries-old traditions of rejection, racism, and prejudice that are such an integral part of American culture (Stepick et al., 2001).

Haitian Americans today are still mostly first-generation, recent immigrants. Overall, they are comparable to Hispanic Americans in terms of such measures of equality as income and poverty (see Table 10.2, as well as Figures 8.16 and 8.18 for information on the status of Hispanic Americans). Still, research shows that some Haitians continue to face the exclusion and discrimination long associated with nonwhite ancestry.

One important study of Haitians in South Florida found that a combination of factors—their hostile reception, poverty and lack of education, and racial background—combined to lead the Haitian second generation (the children of the immigrants) to a relatively low level of academic achievement and a tendency to identify with the African American community. "Haitians are becoming American but in a specifically black ethnic fashion" (Stepick et al., 2001, p. 261). The ultimate path of Haitian assimilation will unfold in the future, but these tendencies suggest that some members of the second generation are unlikely to move into the middle class and that their assimilation may be segmented.

Jamaicans. The Jamaican economy is more developed than Haiti's, and this is reflected in the higher levels of education of Jamaican immigrants (see Table 10.2). However, as is true throughout the less developed world, the Jamaican economy has faltered in recent decades, and the island nation has been unable to provide full-employment opportunities to its population. Jamaica is a former British colony, and its immigrants have journeyed to the United Kingdom in addition to the United States. In both cases, the immigrant stream tends to be more skilled and educated, and represents something of a "brain drain," a pattern we have seen with other groups, including Asian Indians (Feliciano, 2006). Needless to say, the loss of the more educated Jamaicans to migration can exacerbate problems of development and growth on the island.

Jamaicans typically settle on the East Coast, particularly in the New York City area. Because they come from a former British colony, they have the advantage of speaking English as their native tongue. On the other hand, they are black, and like Haitians, they must face the barriers of discrimination and racism faced by all nonwhite groups in the United States. On the average, they are significantly higher than Haitians (and native-born African Americans) in socioeconomic standing, but poverty and institutionalized discrimination limit upward mobility for a segment of the group. Some, like other groups of color in the United States, face the possibility of segmented assimilation and permanent exclusion from the economic mainstream. On the other hand, at least one study shows that many second-generation Jamaicans are moving into the mainstream economy and taking jobs comparable to others with their level of education, at least in New York City, where many of them live (Kasinitz, Mollenkopf, Waters, & Holdaway, 2008).

CONTEMPORARY IMMIGRATION FROM ASIA

Immigration from Asia has been considerable since the 1960s, averaging close to 300,000 people per year and running about 35% to 40% of all immigrants (U.S. Department of Homeland Security, 2012). As was the case with Hispanic immigrants, the sending nations are considerably less developed than the United States, and the primary motivation for most of these immigrants is economic. As we pointed out in Chapter 9, however, the Asian immigrant stream is "bipolar" and includes many highly educated professionals along with the less skilled and less educated. Also, many Asian immigrants are refugees from the war in Southeast Asia in the 1960s and 1970s, and others are spouses of U.S. military personnel who have been stationed throughout the region.

As before, rather than attempting to cover all Asian immigrant groups, we will concentrate on four case studies and consider immigrants from India, Vietnam, Korea, and the Philippines. Together, these four groups make up about half of all immigrants from Asia (U.S. Department of Homeland Security, 2012).

FOUR CASE STUDIES

The four groups considered here are small, and they all include a high percentage of foreign-born members. They are quite variable in their backgrounds, occupational profiles, levels of education, and incomes. In contrast to Hispanic immigrants, however, they tend to have higher percentages of members who are fluent in English, members with higher levels of education, and relatively more members prepared to compete for good jobs in the American economy. A statistical profile of the groups is presented in Table 10.3, along with that of non-Hispanic whites for purposes of comparison.

The four groups vary in their settlement patterns. Most are concentrated along the West Coast, but Asian Indians are roughly equally distributed on both the East and West Coast, and Vietnamese have a sizable presence in Texas, in part related to the fishing industry along the Gulf Coast.

Asian Indians. India is the second most populous nation in the world, and its huge population of more than 1.2 billion people incorporates a wide variety of different languages (India has

TABLE 10.3 Selected Characteristics of Four Asian American Groups and Non-Hispanic Whites, 2012

GROUP	SIZE	PERCENTAGE WITH LESS THAN HIGH SCHOOL DIPLOMA	PERCENTAGE WITH COLLEGE DEGREE OR MORE	PERCENTAGE FOREIGN-BORN	PERCENTAGE WHO SPEAK ENGLISH LESS THAN "VERY WELL"	MEDIAN HOUSEHOLD INCOME	PERCENTAGE OF FAMILIES IN POVERTY
Non-Hispanic whites	—	8.9	31.9	3.9	1.7	$56,525	7.4
Asian Indians	3,208,387	9.3	69.6	68.7	21.1	$92,592	5.8
Koreans	1,748,287	7.6	52.0	62.6	38.8	$53,750	11.9
Filipinos	3,480,437	7.4	46.0	51.6	18.1	$77,619	5.7
Vietnamese	1,842,851	29.7	25.9	63.5	50.2	$53,367	13.7

SOURCE: U.S. Census Bureau (2013a).

22 official languages, including English), religions, and ethnic groups. Overall, the level of education is fairly low: The population averages about five years of formal schooling (NationMaster, 2014) and is about 63% literate (Central Intelligence Agency, 2013). However, according to recent reports, about 20% of the college-age Indian population is enrolled in some form of higher education ("College Enrollment in India Expands Rapidly," 2012). This means there are millions of educated Indians looking for careers commensurate with their credentials. Because of the relative lack of development in the Indian economy, many college-educated Indians must search for career opportunities abroad, and not just in the United States.

It is also important to note that as a legacy of India's long colonization by the British, English is the language of the educated. Thus, Indian immigrants tend to be not only well educated but also English speaking, as shown in Table 10.3.

Immigration from India to the United States was low until the mid-1960s, and the group was quite small at that time. The group almost quadrupled in size between 1990 and 2012 (see Table 9.1), and Indians are now the third-largest Asian American group (behind Chinese and Filipinos).

Immigrants from India tend to be a select, highly educated, and skilled group, as shown in Table 10.3 and Figures 9.10 and 9.14. According to the 2000 Census, Indians are overrepresented in some of the most prestigious occupations, including computer engineering, medicine, and college teaching (U.S. Census Bureau, 2000c). Immigrants from India are part of a worldwide movement of educated peoples from less-developed countries to more-developed countries. One need not ponder the differences in career opportunities, technology, and compensation for long to get some insight into the reasons for this movement. Other immigrants from India are more oriented to commerce and small business, and there is a sizable Indian ethnic enclave in many cities (Kitano & Daniels, 1995, pp. 96–111; Sheth, 1995).

Koreans. Immigration from South Korea to the United States began early in the 20th century, when laborers were recruited to help fill the void in the job market left by the 1882 Chinese Exclusion Act. This group was extremely small until the 1950s, when the rate of immigration rose because of refugees and "war brides" after the Korean War. Immigration did not become substantial, however, until the 1960s, and the number of immigrants from Korea peaked in the late 1980s (Min, 2006, p. 232). The size of the group increased fivefold in the 1970s and more than doubled between 1990 and 2012 (see Table 9.1), although it is still much less than 1% of the total population.

Like the immigrant stream from India, South Korean immigrants include many middle-class, more educated, professional people, many of whom were "pushed" from their homeland by a repressive military government. Korea transitioned to a more Western-style democracy in the late 1980s, and immigration declined as a direct result (see Figure 9.5).

Although differences in culture, language, and race make Koreans visible targets of discrimination, the high percentage of Christians among them (about 70%) may help them appear more "acceptable" to the dominant group. Certainly, Christian church parishes play a number of important roles for the Korean American community, offering assistance to newcomers and the less fortunate, serving as a focal point for networks of mutual assistance, and generally assisting in the completion of the myriad chores to which immigrant communities must attend (e.g., government paperwork, registering to vote, etc.; Kitano & Daniels, 2001, p. 123).

Korean American immigrants have formed an enclave, and the group is heavily involved in small businesses and retail stores—particularly fruit and vegetable retail stores, or greengroceries. According to one study, Koreans had the second-highest percentage of self-employment among immigrant groups (Greeks were the highest), with about 23% of the group in this occupational category (Min, 2006, pp. 238–239). However, Korean Americans are typically more visible than many other entrepreneurial groups because of their size and concentration in the largest metropolitan areas.

As is the case for other groups that have pursued this course, the enclave allows Korean Americans to avoid the discrimination and racism of the larger society and to survive in an economic niche in which lack of English fluency is not a particular problem. However, the enclave has its perils and its costs. For one thing, the success of Korean enterprises depends heavily on the mutual assistance and financial support of other Koreans and the willingness of family members to work long hours for little or no pay (recall the story of Kim Park from Chapter 1). These resources would be weakened or destroyed by acculturation, integration, and the resultant decline in ethnic solidarity. Only by maintaining a distance from the dominant culture and its pervasive appeal can the infrastructure survive.

Furthermore, the economic niches in which mom-and-pop greengroceries and other small businesses can survive are often in deteriorated neighborhoods populated largely by other minority groups. There has been a good deal of hostility and resentment expressed against Korean shop owners by African Americans, Puerto Ricans, and other urbanized minority groups. For example, anti-Korean sentiments were widely apparent in the 1992 Los Angeles riots that followed the acquittal of the policemen charged in the beating of Rodney King. Korean-owned businesses were some of the first to be looted and burned, and when asked why, one participant in the looting said simply, "Because we hate 'em. Everybody hates them" (Cho, 1993, p. 199). Thus, part of the price of survival for many Korean merchants is to place themselves in positions in which antagonism and conflict with other minority groups is common (Kitano & Daniels, 1995, pp. 112–129; Light & Bonacich, 1988; Min, 2006; see also Hurh, 1998).

Filipino Americans. Ties between the United States and the Philippines were established in 1898 when Spain ceded the territory after its defeat in the Spanish–American War. The Philippines achieved independence following World War II, but the United States has maintained a strong military presence there for much of the past 60 years. The nation has been heavily influenced by American culture, and English remains one of two official languages. Thus, Filipino immigrants are often familiar with English, at least as a second language (see Table 10.3).

Today, Filipinos are the second-largest Asian American group, but their numbers became sizable only in the past few decades. There were fewer than 1,000 Filipinos in the United States in 1910, and by 1960, the group still numbered fewer than 200,000. Most of the recent growth has come from increased post-1965 immigration. The group more than doubled in size over the past several decades (see Table 9.1).

Many of the earliest immigrants were agricultural workers recruited for the sugar plantations of Hawaii and the fields of the West Coast. Because the Philippines was a U.S. territory, Filipinos could enter without regard to immigration quotas until 1935, when the nation became a self-governing commonwealth.

The most recent wave of immigrants is diversified, and like Chinese Americans, Filipino Americans are "bipolar" in their educational and occupational profiles. Many recent immigrants have entered under the family preference provisions of the U.S. immigration policy. These immigrants are often poor and compete for jobs in the low-wage secondary labor market (Kitano & Daniels, 1995, p. 94).

More than half of all Filipino immigrants since 1965, however, have been professionals, many of them in the health and medical fields. Many female immigrants from the Philippines were nurses actively recruited by U.S. hospitals to fill gaps in the labor force. In fact, nurses have become something of an export commodity in the Philippines. Thousands of trained nurses leave the Philippines every year to work all over the world. About a third of the world's nurses are Filipino, and the United States currently employs more than 50,000 registered nurses from the Philippines (Kaye, 2010, pp. 30–34). Thus, the Filipino American community includes some members in the higher-wage primary labor market and others who are competing for work in the low-wage secondary sector (Agbayani-Siewert & Revilla, 1995; Espiritu, 1996; Kitano & Daniels, 1995, pp. 83–94; Min, 2006; Posadas, 1999).

Vietnamese. A flow of refugees from Vietnam began in the 1960s as a direct result of the war in Southeast Asia. The war began in Vietnam but expanded when the United States attacked communist forces in Cambodia and Laos. Social life was disrupted, and people were displaced throughout the region. In 1975, when Saigon (the South Vietnamese capital) fell and the U.S. military withdrew, many Vietnamese and other Southeast Asians who had collaborated with the United States and its allies fled in fear for their lives. This group included high-ranking officials and members of the region's educational and occupational elite.

Later groups of refugees tended to be less well educated and more impoverished. Many Vietnamese waited in refugee camps for months or years before being admitted to the United States, and they often arrived with few resources or social networks to ease their transition to the new society (Kitano & Daniels, 1995, pp. 151–152). The Vietnamese are the largest of the Asian refugee groups, and contrary to Asian American success stories and notions of model minorities, they have incomes and educational levels that are somewhat comparable to those of colonized minority groups (see Table 10.3 and Figures 9.10, 9.11, 9.14, 9.15, and 9.17). The story of one Vietnamese refugee family is recounted in the following Narrative Portrait.

MIDDLE EASTERN AND ARAB AMERICANS

Immigration from the Middle East and the Arab world began in the 19th century but has never been particularly large. The earliest immigrants tended to be merchants and traders, and the Middle Eastern community in the United States has been constructed around an ethnic, small-business enclave. The number of Arab and Middle Eastern Americans has grown rapidly over the past several decades but still remains a tiny percentage of the total population. Table 10.4 displays some statistical information on the group, broken down by the ancestry subgroup with which individuals identify. The "Arab American" category is a general one and includes Lebanese, Egyptian, and Syrian Americans, along with many smaller groups.

Table 10.4 shows that these groups tend to rank relatively high in income and education. All groups rank higher than non-Hispanic whites in terms of college graduates, and some (Egyptians and Iranians) are far more educated. Although poverty is a problem (especially for the general "Arab American" category), most of these groups compare quite favorably in terms of median household income.

Many recent Middle Eastern immigrants are, like Asian immigrants, highly educated people who take jobs in the highest levels of the American job structure. Also, consistent with the heritage of being an enclave minority, the groups are overrepresented in sales and underrepresented in occupations involving manual labor. One study, using 1990 Census data and a survey mailed to a national sample of Arab American women in 2000, found that immigrant Arab American women have a very low rate of employment, the lowest of any immigrant group. The author's analysis of this data strongly suggests that this pattern is due to traditional gender roles and family norms regarding the proper role of women (Read, 2004).

Arab and Middle Eastern Americans are diverse and vary along a number of dimensions. For example, not all Middle Easterners are Arabic; Iranians, for example, are Persian. They bring different national traditions and cultures and also vary in

Refugees

Vietnamese refugees are picked up by a U.S. Navy ship after spending eight days at sea.

C. N. Le was a young boy when his family left Vietnam. They were in the first wave of refugees who left their homeland as the U.S.-supported South Vietnamese government collapsed. Although they had to leave all their possessions and their life savings behind, Le's family brought a number of resources, including the ability to speak English, and—unlike many refugee families—they made a successful transition to America. Notice the role played by ethnic networks and extended family in the adjustment process. Le became a sociologist and currently maintains the Asian-Nation website (www .asian-nation.org).

FROM SAIGON TO SUBURBIA

C. N. Le

Our "ticket" out of Viet Nam...was my mother's employment with the U.S. government....Her superiors...arranged for us to be evacuated. We...were [picked up by] a cargo ship....

As the ship approached, everyone tried to use whatever vessels they could find, steal, or rent to make their way to the ship. People were swimming in the sea and jumping from boat to boat in their efforts to board....In this frantic confusion, my mother's mother and her brother and his family failed to get on board and were left behind. She would not see them again for almost 20 years....

Conditions were very crowded [on the ship]....Because [we] had to leave all [our] possessions behind, my family literally had nothing besides the clothes on [our] backs....

When I asked [them] how they felt [about being] relocated in the United States,...my mother said that she was quite distraught, depressed, and in a state of shock worrying over what would become of her brother and mother....As she put it, her sadness overshadowed any feelings of coming to the United States.

My father was also very sad at having to leave his home, his business, and our life savings back in Viet Nam, and at the thought that he probably would never see Viet Nam again....He also mentioned that he was worried about the prospects for a good life in the United States. As he put it, "I was thinking about whether my skills could feed a family of five and could my children get along in school speaking a different language and having a different culture."...His pragmatism and vision fortunately compensated for my mother's feelings of distress....

We were flown to one of the four relocation centers that the U.S. government had set up to process the approximately 125,000 refugees who left Viet Nam. We...began our life in the United States on May 15, 1975....

[My] family moved to Camp Pendleton in California to take custody of my 2-year-old cousin, who had become separated from her family....Our sponsor agency...eventually found us an apartment [near]...Los Angeles, on September 25, 1975. We were part of a group of 16 other families that were settled in the same apartment complex, the first group of refugees being settled into that area. The sponsor agency arranged for our first month's rent, along with a supply of groceries.

Since my mother knew enough English, she began working as a teacher's aide in an English class that all refugees [had] to attend....She went on to take...classes [and obtained] her GED. After my father's mother arrived to look after my sisters and me, she was able to...take nursing courses....She became an RN in 1983. She now works as an auditor for the Los Angeles County hospital system.

My father also immediately went to find employment, riding the bus to the unemployment office and all around the greater metropolitan area....After a month, he found a position as a mechanical drafter. Eventually, [he found work] as a mechanical and structural engineer.

My parents were able to borrow enough money from relatives so that, combined with their savings (which they regularly added to for just this occasion), we were eventually able to move to a...quiet, middle-class [neighborhood]....

Everyone in our family is now a citizen of the United States, my parents having applied for citizenship in 1982, seven years after we came to the United States. When I asked each parent why they wanted to become citizens, my mother [said that] she wanted to be a citizen of a free country...with its better opportunities and benefits, which gave our family the chance to achieve the "American dream."

Since our arrival in the United States, we have sponsored two groups of Vietnamese immigrants. In 1981, we sponsored my father's niece and her husband [and] a year later...we sponsored my mother's cousin and her husband. To this day, both my parents are very active in the Vietnamese community...assisting recent immigrants and refugees.

SOURCE: Le (2005, pp. 348–351). Reprinted by permission of Pearson Education, Inc., Upper-Saddle River, NJ.

Questions to Consider

1. Compare and contrast Le's experience with that of an immigrant who entered an enclave (e.g., Ben Fong-Torres's father, described in the first Narrative Portrait in Chapter 9). What differences and similarities can you identify? What are the implications for adjustment to the larger society?
2. Immigrants tend to move along chains of communication and interpersonal networks. How does this idea apply to Le's narrative?
3. Le's family had nothing but the clothes on their backs as they left Vietnam. What resources did they have that helped them adjust to the United States?

TABLE 10.4 Selected Characteristics of Arab Americans, Middle Eastern Americans, and Non-Hispanic Whites, 2012

GROUP	SIZE	PERCENTAGE WITH LESS THAN HIGH SCHOOL DIPLOMA	PERCENTAGE WITH COLLEGE DEGREE OR MORE	PERCENTAGE FOREIGN-BORN	PERCENTAGE WHO SPEAK ENGLISH LESS THAN "VERY WELL"	MEDIAN HOUSEHOLD INCOME	PERCENTAGE OF FAMILIES IN POVERTY
Non-Hispanic whites	—	8.9	31.9	3.9	1.7	$56,525	7.4
Arab Americans	1,740,266	11.4	46.1	43.0	21.1	$52,447	18.3
Lebanese	496,599	7.4	47.5	21.9	8.1	$66,779	9.7
Egyptians	215,511	4.1	66.4	60.6	24.4	$60,606	16.0
Syrians	159,558	10.1	41.3	24.6	12.4	$59,579	10.3
Iranians	470,227	7.7	59.4	64.9	29.4	$63,059	10.8
Turks	197,550	9.4	53.9	55.5	24.1	$59,023	9.2

SOURCE: U.S. Census Bureau (2013a).

religion. Most are Muslim, but many are Christian. Also, about two thirds of all Muslims in the United States are immigrants, and about 23% are African American (Pew Research Center, 2011, pp. 13, 16; see also Muslim West Facts Project, 2009).

Residentially, Arab and Middle Eastern Americans are highly urbanized, and almost 50% live in just five states (California, New Jersey, New York, Florida, and Michigan).

This settlement pattern is not too different from that of other recent immigrant groups, except for the heavy concentration in Michigan, especially in the Detroit area. These settlement patterns reflect chains of migration, some set up decades ago. Figure 10.3 shows the regional distribution of the group in 2000 and clearly displays the clusters in Michigan, Florida, and Southern California.

FIGURE 10.3 Regional Distribution of Arab Americans, 2000

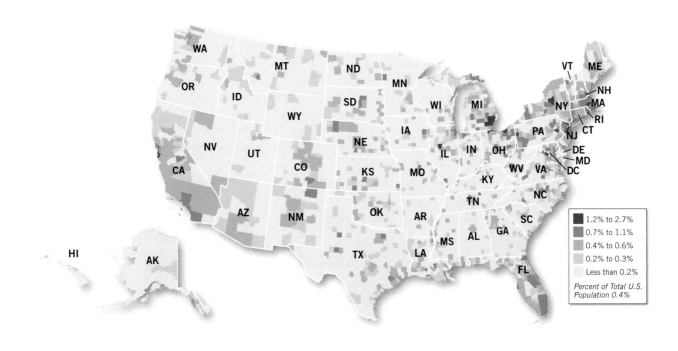

SOURCE: de la Cruz and Brittingham (2003, p. 6).

DETROIT'S ARAB AMERICAN COMMUNITY

Dr. Steven Gold

The greater Detroit area has long been a center of Arab American life. It continues to display vitality, with growing numbers of businesses, continued arrivals from the Middle East, and the creation of communal institutions such as the Arab American National Museum and the Islamic Center of America, the nation's largest Muslim house of worship. The population, which traces its local presence back 100 years, is large and continues to grow. However, due to recent arrivals, difficulties in enumeration, and the effects of intermarriage, estimates of the population are subject to debate. While the 2000 U.S. Census counted some 130,000 people of Arab origin in the tricounty Detroit area, the Zogby Worldwide polling firm pegs the community at more than 400,000.

Major nationality groups making up the Arab American population include Lebanese, Iraqi, Palestinian, and Yemeni. In addition, these groups reflect considerable religious diversity associated with several traditions, including Chaldean, Melkite, Maronite, and Roman Catholics; Protestants and Orthodox Christians; as well as Sunni and Shi'a Muslims. Local enclaves based on nationality and religion can be found throughout Metro Detroit's three counties, revealing significant diversity in housing, class membership, and way of life.

Detroit's Arab Americans have created a broad array of organizations that address the population's social service, cultural, religious, health, educational, political, and economic needs. Among the most well-known is ACCESS (Arab Community Center for Economic and Social Services). Established in the early 1970s, ACCESS is the largest Arab American human services nonprofit in the United States. With eight locations and more than 100 programs, it caters to a diverse population. Ismael Ahamed, the organization's founder, has gone on to serve as the director of the Michigan Department of Human Services—the state government's second-largest agency—and is currently associate provost of the University of Michigan at Dearborn. While inclusive and large-scale organizations such as ACCESS maintain a communitywide focus, others reflect particular concerns associated with the population's varied subgroups.

Arab Detroit is noted for its extensive self-employment. The population is estimated to own some 5,000 enterprises—with Chaldeans (Iraqi Catholics) and Lebanese having especially high rates of entrepreneurship. The growth of Arab American businesses is most evident in Dearborn, where thousands of Arabic signs advertise a whole range of goods and services to local customers. At the same time, Arab-owned shops, restaurants, car dealerships, gas stations, and professionals serve consumer needs throughout the region in neighborhoods ranging from the inner city to affluent suburbs.

Business success is enabled by a wide range of resources, including familial and communal ties and personal experience with self-employment. In addition, the population's generally high levels of education and intact families are known to facilitate proprietorship. Indeed, Middle Eastern–origin groups have long revealed a propensity toward self-employment in the United States. In 1911, the Dillingham Commission of the U.S. Congress found that more than 75% of male Syrian immigrants (who would now be classified as Lebanese) in New York were self-employed. Recent evidence suggests that the trend endures. According to the 1990 U.S. Census, 6 of the 10 nationality groups with the highest rates of self-employment in the United States were from the Middle East.

Finally, a variety of ethnic organizations, including the Arab American Chamber of Commerce, Chaldean Federation of America, Arab American Women's Business Council, Chaldean American Chamber of Commerce, Chaldean American Bar Association, Chaldean American Association for Health Professionals, and Lebanese American Chamber of Commerce, provide services and contacts for Arab American entrepreneurs in Southeast Michigan.

Despite the community's size, wealth, and influence, a number of activists and observers contend that the population suffers from significant hostility and discrimination. This includes both racial profiling and surveillance conducted by U.S. government agencies since September 11, 2001, as well as discrimination and violence from members of the American public. The net impact of these trends causes Arab Americans to feel unsafe in their own homes, deprecated for their national and religious origins, pressured to apologize for acts

Images of the Arab American community in Detroit, Michigan.

they had nothing to do with, and compelled to cooperate with intrusive surveillance activities.

Based on decisions made by federal agencies, South Asians and Middle Easterners in the United States are treated as a special population. In the years following the September 11 attacks, more than 1,200 persons—who were neither named nor charged with crimes—were detained, with about half being deported. At the same time, numerous ethnic and religious organizations representing the same nationalities have been accused of assisting terrorists—generally with little or no evidence—an action that permits the freezing of their assets and the criminalization of their members.

In addition to dealing with criminal justice and migration officials, Arab Americans also confront various forms of hostility, including insults, vandalism, and violence, as they go about their daily lives. This is evidenced by the cancellation of the Dearborn Arab International Festival in 2013, an event that for the previous 18 years brought together hundreds of thousands of people from throughout the United States and the world to enjoy Middle Eastern food and culture and family-friendly entertainment.

The festival was targeted by fundamentalist Christian groups as a setting where they could confront Arabs and Muslims. These missionaries—who included Florida Pastor Terry Jones, best known for the public burning of a Quran (the Muslim holy book)—brought with them a pig's head and signs insulting Islam's prophet. When the fundamentalist protestors won a 2010 lawsuit protecting their First Amendment rights, the city of Dearborn withdrew its support of the festival. Instead, officials encouraged the festival's organizers to hold it in a park where public order could be more easily maintained.

Representatives of the Arab American community rejected this option because they favored the event's previous location, adjacent to numerous Arab businesses that have been vital to improving the city's (and region's) economic and cultural vitality. With too little time to make alternative arrangements, the popular and highly successful event had to be cancelled.

In sum, Detroit's Arab community continues to grow and prosper, bringing vitality and development to a location more commonly associated with economic decline and population loss. Yet, even as its members seek to celebrate their successful participation in American life, the circumstances of their religion, heritage, and regional origins often result in their being denied access to opportunities that groups with different origins might take for granted.[1]

A protest against the construction of an Islamic Mosque in Temecula, California.

9/11 AND ARAB AMERICANS

There always has been at least a faint strain of prejudice directed at Middle Easterners in American culture (e.g., see the low position of Turks in the 1926 social distance scales presented in Chapter 3; most Americans probably are not aware that Turks and Arabs are different groups). These vague feelings have intensified in recent decades as relations with various Middle Eastern nations and groups have worsened. For example, in 1979, the U.S. Embassy in Tehran, Iran, was attacked and occupied, and more than 50 Americans were held hostage for more than a year. The attack stimulated a massive reaction in the United States, in which anti-Arab and anti-Muslim feelings figured prominently. Continuing anti-American activities across the Middle East in the 1980s and 1990s stimulated a backlash of resentment and growing intolerance in the United States.

These earlier events pale in comparison, of course, to the events of September 11, 2001. Americans responded to the attacks by Arab terrorists on the World Trade Center and the Pentagon with an array of emotions that included bewilderment, shock, anger, patriotism, deep sorrow for the victims and their families, and—perhaps predictably in the intensity of the moment—increased prejudicial rejection of Middle Easterners, Arabs, Muslims, and any group that seemed even vaguely associated with the perpetrators of the attacks.

In the nine weeks following September 11, more than 700 violent attacks were reported to the Arab American Anti-Discrimination Committee, followed by another 165 violent incidents in

[1]Suggestions for further reading:

Bakalian, Anny, and Mehdi, Bozorgmehr. 2009. *Backlash 9/11*. Berkeley: University of California Press.

Gold, Steven J., and Mehdi, Bozorgmehr. 2007. Middle East and North Africa. In Mary Waters and Reed Ueda (with Helen B. Marrow) (Eds.), *The New Americans: A Guide to Immigration Since 1965* (pp. 518–533). Cambridge, MA: Harvard University Press.

Schopmeyer, Kim. 2011. Arab Detroit After 9/11: A Changing Demographic Portrait. In Nabeel Abraham, Sally Howell, and Andrew Shryock (Eds.), *Arab Detroit 9/11: Life in the Terror Decade* (pp. 29–63). Detroit, MI: Wayne State University Press.

Shryock, Andrew, Abraham, Nabeel, and Howell, Sally. 2011. The Terror Decade in Arab Detroit: An Introduction. In Nabeel Abraham, Sally Howell, and Andrew Shryock (Eds.), *Arab Detroit 9/11: Life in the Terror Decade* (pp. 1–25). Detroit, MI: Wayne State University Press.

the first nine months of 2002 (Arab American Anti-Discrimination Committee, 2002). In this same time period, there were more than 80 incidents in which Arab Americans were removed from aircraft after boarding because of their ethnicity, more than 800 cases of employment discrimination, and "numerous instances of denial of service, discriminatory service, and housing discrimination" (Ibish, 2003, p. 7).

Anti-Arab passions may have cooled somewhat since the multiple traumas of 9/11, but the Arab American community still faces a number of issues and problems, including profiling at airport security checks and greater restrictions on entering the country. Also, the USA Patriot Act, passed in 2001 to enhance the tools available to law enforcement to combat terrorism, allows for long-term detention of suspects, a wider scope for searches and surveillance, and other policies that many (not just Arab Americans) are concerned will encourage violations of due process and suspension of basic civil liberties.

Thus, although the Arab and Middle Eastern American communities are small in size, they have assumed a prominent place in the attention of the nation. The huge majority of these groups denounce and reject terrorism and violence, but, like Colombians and Italians, they are victimized by a strong stereotype that is often applied uncritically and without qualification. A recent survey of Muslim Americans, a category that includes the huge majority of Arab and Middle Eastern Americans, finds them to be "middle class and mostly mainstream." They have a positive view of U.S. society and espouse distinctly American values. At the same time, they are very concerned about becoming scapegoats in the war on terror, and a majority (53%) say that it became more difficult to be a Muslim in the United States after 9/11 (Pew Research Center, 2007).

Relations between Arab Americans and the larger society are certainly among the most tense and problematic of any minority group, and given the U.S. invasions of Iraq and Afghanistan and the threat of further terrorist attacks, they will not ease anytime soon. Some of the consequences of these relationships are discussed in the next Narrative Portrait.

IMMIGRANTS FROM AFRICA

Our final group of new Americans consists of immigrants from Africa. Immigration from Africa has been quite low over the past 50 years. However, there was the usual increase after the 1960s, and Africans were about 5% of all immigrants after 1960 and have been almost 10% since 2000.

Table 10.5 shows the total number of sub-Saharan Africans in the United States in 2012, along with the two largest national groups. The number of native Africans in the United States has more than doubled since 1990, and this rapid growth suggests that these groups may have a greater impact on U.S. society in the future.

The category "sub-Saharan Africans" is extremely broad and encompasses destitute black refugees from African civil wars and relatively affluent white South Africans. In the remainder of this section, we will focus on Nigerians and Ethiopians rather than on this very broad category.

Clearly, although they may be growing, Nigerians and Ethiopians are tiny minorities: Neither group is as much as 0.1% of the total population. They are recent immigrants and have a high representation of first-generation members. They both compare favorably to national norms in education, an indication that this is another example of a "brain drain" from the countries of origin. Nigerian and Ethiopian immigrants tend to be highly skilled and educated, and they bring valuable abilities and advanced educational credentials to the United States. Like some other groups, many of the immigrants from Nigeria and Ethiopia are motivated by a search for work, and they compete for positions in the higher reaches of the job structure.

TABLE 10.5   Selected Characteristics of Sub-Saharan African Groups and Non-Hispanic Whites, 2012

GROUP	SIZE	PERCENTAGE WITH LESS THAN HIGH SCHOOL DIPLOMA	PERCENTAGE WITH COLLEGE DEGREE OR MORE	PERCENTAGE FOREIGN-BORN	PERCENTAGE WHO SPEAK ENGLISH LESS THAN "VERY WELL"	MEDIAN HOUSEHOLD INCOME	PERCENTAGE OF FAMILIES IN POVERTY
Non-Hispanic whites	—	8.9	31.9	3.9	1.7	$56,525	7.4
All sub-Saharan Africans	2,908,097	13.3	31.2	41.4	13.5	$41,213	20.9
Ethiopians	209,816	15.8	25.9	72.3	34.4	$41,547	18.0
Nigerians	265,782	3.4	61.8	60.4	9.6	$58,534	10.8

SOURCE: U.S. Census Bureau (2013a).

9/11 and Middle Eastern Americans

Amir Marvasti and Karyn McKinney are sociologists who, between 2002 and 2004, conducted in-depth interviews with 20 Middle Eastern Americans. The interviews covered a variety of topics, but most centered on the reactions of the respondents to the attacks of 9/11, the ensuing public reaction, and their own rethinking of what it means to be an American. What follows are the personal reactions of the respondents, knit together by the narrative written by Marvasti and McKinney.

MIDDLE EASTERN AMERICANS AND THE AMERICAN DREAM

Amir Marvasti and Karyn McKinney

Difficulty with cultural assimilation is a common experience for most ethnic groups, but being designated public enemy number one is not. In the hours following the tragic attacks of September 11, 2001, being or just looking Middle Eastern became an instant offense. For members of this group, this was a turning point in terms of both the way they were viewed by others and the way they defined themselves. While the feeling of shock is similar to what everyone must have felt that day, in the case of Middle Eastern Americans, there was also a feeling of impending doom, the knowledge that their lives would never be exactly the same....

As the day went by, a chasm began to form between Middle Eastern Americans and their fellow citizens. The perception that Middle Easterners were the aggressors and Americans the victims began to take hold, and out of this perception grew anger:

> Wherever you went you always—that day even among my friends there was talk about anger and they looked really angry....There was talk about "We should bomb Palestine." And "Who cares about these people now." In a way, I understood their anger because of what had just happened. I guess it was kind of lonely that day.

In the days following the attacks, Middle Eastern Americans had to accept the fact that they were seen by many as legitimate targets of anger. The news media were full of messages about hate being an acceptable emotion under the circumstances. In that atmosphere, it was indeed very "lonely" to be Middle Eastern American....

Perhaps the most significant realization for many Middle Eastern Americans was the awareness that their right to be part of the American Dream could be taken away for actions that they were not in any way responsible for. With this realization came the sense of not belonging and the real possibility of being physically separated from the rest of society and placed in an internment camp. One young Middle Eastern American remembered,

> I really thought I was going to be sent to like a camp....It didn't—for those couple of days—it didn't feel like we were going to be back to normal again....I thought my life was never going to be the same. I no longer had a home here.

As this respondent puts it, realizing that one no longer has a home here was tantamount to realizing that the American Dream applied to some more than others....

September 11 was an important turning point in the psyche of Middle Eastern Americans to the extent that it caused them to reevaluate their place in American society and its promises of freedom and equality. Consider, for example, how this Pakistani American woman...rethinks her status as an American in light of how she and her family have been treated since September 11:

> My brother was assaulted three days after September 11th. It was part of the backlash....I feel I'm even considered an outsider a lot of the times. I sound just as American as anyone else, and I was born and raised here....[After September 11] I think a lot of people thought that if you're not going to consider me American, why am I going to consider myself an American....

According to this respondent,...it became particularly apparent that the ideals of equality in the American Dream did not apply to her and her family. Her ethnicity transcends her identity as an American and places her in the position of a second-class citizen....

One of the most profound effects of September 11 on the lives of Middle Eastern Americans was the realization that their daily routines...would be subjected to scrutiny and potentially make them vulnerable to acts of violence. An Iranian American man describes how September 11 affected his life:

> I actually canceled a trip....And that's when I realized there's a difference in this war [the war on terrorism]. There is a new order....We can't go somewhere and play our own music. We like our own music, we like our own dance, we like our own food and tradition so we couldn't do that therefore I canceled that trip. That's when it occurred to me there's a difference.

Collectively, these post-9/11 experiences have caused some Middle Eastern Americans to question the meaning of the American Dream and the extent to which its lofty promises apply to them. They have recognized that full assimilation into American culture will not provide protection against acts of ignorance and that their future in this country is uncertain.

Questions to Consider

1. What theories of prejudice and discrimination (see Chapter 3) can you apply to the experiences described in this narrative?
2. In the passage that opened this chapter, Sade says that Arabs are "the new blacks." Does this narrative—and other material in this chapter—tend to support or refute that comparison? How?

Nigeria is a former British colony, so the relatively high level of English fluency among its immigrants is not surprising. Table 10.5 shows that, on the average, members of the group have been able to translate their relatively high levels of human capital and English fluency into a favorable position in the U.S. economy. They compare quite favorably with national norms in their income levels and poverty rates.

Compared with Nigerians, Ethiopians rank lower in their English fluency and are more mixed in their backgrounds. They include refugees from domestic unrest along with the educated elite. These facts are reflected in Table 10.5. Although Ethiopians compare favorably with national norms in education, they have much higher rates of poverty and much lower levels of income. These contrasts suggest that Ethiopians are less able to translate their educational credentials into higher-ranked occupations.

MODES OF INCORPORATION

As the case studies included in this chapter (and those in Chapters 8 and 9) demonstrate, recent immigrant groups occupy a wide array of different positions in U.S. society. One way to address this diversity is to look at the contact situation, especially the characteristics the groups bring with them (e.g., their race and religion, the human capital with which they arrive) and the reaction of the larger society. There are three main modes of incorporation for immigrants in the United States: entrance through the primary labor market, the secondary labor market (see Chapter 5), or the ethnic enclave. We will consider each pathway separately and relate them to the groups discussed in this chapter.

IMMIGRANTS AND THE PRIMARY LABOR MARKET

The primary labor market includes the more desirable jobs with greater security, higher pay, and more benefits, and the immigrants entering this sector tend to be highly educated, skilled professionals and businesspeople. Members of this group are generally fluent in English, and many were educated at U.S. universities. They are highly integrated into the global urban-industrial economy, and in many cases they are employees of multinational corporations transferred here by their companies. These immigrants are affluent, urbane, and dramatically different from the peasant laborers so common in the past (e.g., from Ireland and Italy) and in the present (e.g., from the Dominican Republic and Mexico). The groups with high percentages of members entering the primary labor market include Indian, Egyptian, Iranian, and Nigerian immigrants.

Because they tend to be affluent, immigrants with professional backgrounds usually attract less notice and fewer racist reactions than do their more unskilled counterparts. Although they come closer to Blauner's pure immigrant group than most other minority groups we have considered, racism can still complicate their assimilation. In addition, Arab American Islamic groups must confront discrimination and prejudice based on their religious affiliation.

IMMIGRANTS AND THE SECONDARY LABOR MARKET

This mode of incorporation is more typical for immigrants with lower levels of education and fewer job skills. Jobs in this sector are less desirable and command lower pay, little security, and few benefits, and are often seasonal or in the underground or informal economy. This labor market includes jobs in construction or the garment industry in which workers are paid "off the books" and working conditions are unregulated by government authorities or labor unions; domestic work; and some forms of criminal or deviant activity, such as drug sales and sex work. The employers who control these jobs often prefer to hire undocumented immigrants because they are easier to control and less likely to complain to the authorities about abuse and mistreatment. The groups with high percentages of members in the secondary labor market include Dominicans, Haitians, and the less skilled and less educated kinfolk of the higher-status immigrants.

IMMIGRANTS AND ETHNIC ENCLAVES

As we have seen, some immigrant groups—especially those that can bring financial capital and business experience—have established ethnic enclaves. Some members of these groups enter U.S. society as entrepreneurs and become owners of small retail shops and other businesses; their less skilled and less educated coethnics serve as a source of cheap labor to staff the ethnic enterprises. The enclave provides contacts, financial and other services, and social support for the new immigrants of all social classes. Korean Americans and Arab Americans, like Cuban Americans and Jewish Americans in the past, have been particularly likely to follow this path.

SUMMARY

This classification suggests some of the variety in relationships between the new Americans and the larger society. The contemporary stream of immigrants entering the United States is extremely diverse and includes people from the most sophisticated and urbane to the most desperate and despairing. This variety can be seen in a list of occupations in which recent immigrants are overrepresented. For men, the list includes biologists and other natural scientists, taxi drivers, farm laborers, and waiters. For women, the list includes chemists, statisticians, produce packers, laundry workers, and domestics (Kritz & Girak, 2004).

Listed below are five nations, the number of immigrants each sent to the United States in 2012, and the level of literacy for each. How familiar are you with these new Americans? Can you identify the geographical region from which each group comes and the most common religious affiliation in its homeland? Also, what's your best guess as to whether immigrants from each group are above or below national averages for education, income, and poverty levels?

NATION OF ORIGIN	NUMBER OF IMMIGRANTS, 2012	PERCENTAGE LITERATE, HOME NATION	REGION OF THE WORLD	MOST COMMON RELIGION	PERCENTAGE WITH COLLEGE DEGREE OR MORE	MEDIAN HOUSEHOLD INCOME	PERCENTAGE FAMILIES IN POVERTY
Nepal	10,198	57			__ Above __ Below	__ Above __ Below	__ Above __ Below
Ghana	10,592	72			__ Above __ Below	__ Above __ Below	__ Above __ Below
Guyana	5,683	92			__ Above __ Below	__ Above __ Below	__ Above __ Below
Peru	12,609	90			__ Above __ Below	__ Above __ Below	__ Above __ Below
Ukraine	7,642	100			__ Above __ Below	__ Above __ Below	__ Above __ Below

TURN THE PAGE TO FIND THE ANSWERS.

QUESTIONS FOR REFLECTION

1. List and describe the characteristics of the largest groups of immigrants from Central America, the Caribbean, Asia, the Middle East, and Africa.

2. Which of these groups is most likely to assimilate into the primary labor market? Why? Which group is most likely to be incorporated into the secondary labor market? Why? Which is most likely to be an enclave minority? Why?

IMMIGRATION: ISSUES AND CONTROVERSIES

THE ATTITUDES OF AMERICANS

One factor that affects the fate of immigrant groups is the attitude of the larger society, particularly of the groups that have the most influence with governmental policymakers. Overall, American public opinion is split on the issue of immigration: Today, the majority of Americans regard immigration as a positive force, and this percentage has increased in the past few years (see Figure 8.5).

Many Americans, however, are vehemently opposed to immigration and immigrants—and it is the latter whose voices seem to be more prominent in everyday discourse. The history of this nation is replete with anti-immigrant and nativist groups and activities, including those that opposed the immigration from Europe (Chapter 2), Mexico (Chapter 8), and China and Japan (Chapter 9). The present is no exception: As immigration increased over the past several decades, so did the number and visibility of anti-immigrant groups, particularly in the states along the Mexican border.

The contemporary anti-immigrant movements have generated a number of state laws. The most controversial and widely publicized of these laws was State Bill 1070, passed by the Arizona legislature in the spring of 2010. Among other provisions, the bill required law enforcement officers to check the immigration status of anyone they stopped, detained, or arrested if they had a "reasonable" suspicion that the person might be in the country illegally. Supporters of the legislation argued that it would help control illegal immigration, but opponents raised fears of racial profiling and legalized anti-Hispanic discrimination. There was also considerable concern that the legislation would deter Hispanic Americans from reporting crimes or otherwise cooperating with the police.

NATION OF ORIGIN	NUMBER OF IMMIGRANTS, 2012	PERCENTAGE LITERATE, HOME NATION	REGION OF THE WORLD	MOST COMMON RELIGION	PERCENTAGE WITH COLLEGE DEGREE OR MORE	MEDIAN HOUSEHOLD INCOME	PERCENTAGE FAMILIES IN POVERTY
Nepal	10,198	57	South Asia	Hindu (81%)	X Above __ Below	__ Above X Below	X Above __ Below
Ghana	10,592	72	Western Africa	Christian (71%)	X Above __ Below	__ Above X Below*	X Above __ Below
Guyana	5,683	92	Northern South America	Christian (56%), Hindu (28%)	__ Above X Below	X Above __ Below	Equal
Peru	12,609	90	Western South America	Catholic (81%)	__ Above X Below**	__ Above X Below	X Above __ Below
Ukraine	7,642	100	Eastern Europe	Eastern Orthodox (77%)	X Above __ Below	X Above __ Below	__ Above X Below

SOURCE: Number of immigrants—U.S. Department of Homeland Security (2012); percentage literate and dominant religion—Central Intelligence Agency (2013); education, income, and poverty—U.S. Census Bureau (2013a).

*The Ghanaian median household income is only $40 less than the national average.

**The difference is less than 1%.

Most of the provisions of Arizona S.B. 1070 were invalidated by the Supreme Court in June 2012, by which time several other states had passed similar bills. Alabama's House Bill 56 was passed in 2011 and has been considered particularly punitive. Among other provisions, it required schools to verify the immigration status of students in grades K–12, banned undocumented immigrants from soliciting work, and made it a crime to give the undocumented rides or rent apartments to them. Most of the provisions of the law were effectively repealed in the fall of 2013 (Vock, 2013).

Consistent with the idea that Americans are ambivalent about immigration, other states passed legislation favorable to immigrants during the same period. Some states (e.g., Colorado and Oregon) extended in-state tuition to undocumented immigrants who graduated from their high school system, and others (e.g., Georgia and Illinois) began to allow them to get driver's licenses (Wogan, 2013).

What factors might account for people's anti-immigration views? Research has identified a number of important causes, many of them consistent with the ideas we have examined throughout this text. Prejudice and racism are linked to competition between groups for scarce resources (jobs, political power, control of neighborhoods, and so forth) and a sense of threat. Guided by the results of the Robber's Cave experiment (Chapter 3) and the Noel hypothesis (Chapter 4),

we would expect that negative feelings toward immigrants would be strongest among the most economically vulnerable Americans and those who feel most threatened by the increase in immigration over the past several decades (e.g., see Wallace & Figueroa, 2012).

On the other hand, some research projects (Hainmueller & Hiscox, 2010; Reyna, Dobria, & Wetherell, 2013) do not support the idea that prejudice and group competition are closely related. These projects found little correlation between a person's anti-immigrant feelings and personal economic situation. Rather, they found that both high- and low-status respondents were less concerned with their own pocketbooks and more focused on the potential costs of low-skill immigrants—for schooling, health care, and other services—and their impact on the U.S. economy in general.

Of course, "competition" can be much broader than fights over jobs and votes. Many opponents to immigration in the United States (and Europe) seem to be motivated by a collective sense of threat, the idea that the newcomers will compromise the way of life and cultural integrity of the host nation. These defensive forms of prejudice can stimulate powerful emotions, as we have seen repeatedly throughout this text.

Finally, we have seen that prejudice and negative feelings toward other groups can be motivated by a variety of factors, not just competition. Anti-immigrant attitudes are highly correlated with other forms of prejudice and are caused by the same processes we examined in Chapter 3—for example, exposure to racist cultural norms and values during childhood, and low levels of education (Pettigrew, Wagner, & Christ, 2007).

Is everyone who has reservations and questions about immigration a racist? Emphatically no. While anti-immigrant feelings, prejudice, and a sense of threat seem to be linked, this does not mean that all who oppose immigration are bigots or that all proposals to decrease the flow of immigrants are racist. These are serious and complex issues, and it is not helpful simply to label people as bigots or dismiss their concerns as prejudiced.

On the other hand, we need to clearly recognize that anti-immigrant feelings—particularly the most extreme—are linked to some of the worst, most negative strains of traditional American culture: the same racist and prejudicial views that helped justify slavery and the near genocide of Native Americans. In popular culture, on some talk radio and cable TV "news" shows, in letters to the editor, and so forth, these views are regularly used to demonize immigrants, blame them for an array of social problems, and stoke irrational fears and rumors, such as the idea that Latino immigrants are aiming to return parts of the Southwest to Mexico. At any rate, when American traditions of prejudice and racism are linked to feelings of group threat and individual insecurity, the possibilities for extreme reactions, hate crimes, and poorly designed policy and laws become formidable.

THE IMMIGRANTS

One survey of immigration issues (National Public Radio, 2004) included a nationally representative sample of immigrant respondents. Not surprisingly, the researchers found that their attitudes and views differed sharply from those of native-born respondents on a number of dimensions. For example, immigrant respondents were more likely to see immigration as a positive force for the larger society and more likely to say that immigrants work hard and pay their fair share of taxes. The survey also showed that immigrants are grateful for the economic opportunities available in the United States, with 84% agreeing that there are more opportunities to get ahead here than in their countries of origin.

A more recent survey (Taylor, Cohn, Livingston, Funk, & Morin, 2013) documents the willingness of immigrants to take advantage of opportunities through a commitment to hard work. Large majorities of both Hispanic (78%) and Asian (68%) immigrants supported the idea that hard work results in success, an endorsement of the Protestant Ethic that exceeds that of the general public (58%) (p. 85). On the other hand, the survey also showed that immigrants are ambivalent about U.S. culture and values. For example, only 32% of Hispanic immigrants and 14% of Asian immigrants believed that the family is stronger in the United States than in their homelands, and less than half (44% of Hispanic and 36% of Asian immigrants) said that moral values are better in the United States (p. 77).

Another helpful report (Motel & Patten, 2013) used census data to compile a statistical portrait of the 40 million Americans—about 13% of the total population—who are foreign-born or first-generation immigrants. As you would expect, Mexicans are the single largest segment of this group (29%), with Asian immigrants being the second largest (25%). Almost 40% of the foreign-born immigrated before 1990 (this category includes the surviving members of the last great wave of European immigrants), but an almost equal percentage (36%) are true newcomers, having arrived since 2000.

Most (58%) of the foreign-born are married (vs. 47% of the native-born), and they have a higher fertility rate than the general population. As we have seen, facility with English is an important issue for immigrants: Only about one third of immigrants speak English "very well." As we have also seen, there is a great deal of diversity among the foreign-born in terms of education. Overall, 16% of the foreign-born (vs. 18% of the native-born) are college educated, but this percentage varies from about 4% for immigrant Mexican Americans to almost 30% for immigrants from Asia. Occupation, income, and poverty are also highly variable from group to group.

What can we conclude? Synthesizing the information in this and previous chapters, we can say that the immigrant stream is highly diversified and that the United States is growing more diverse as a result. The "typical immigrant" is from Mexico, China, or another Asian or Central American nation, and is motivated primarily by economics and the absence of viable opportunities at home. Those that come from less-developed nations bring little human capital, education, or job skills, but others bring glowing educational and professional credentials.

As is typical of the first generation, they are often more oriented to their homes than to the United States. Many, especially the "low-skilled" immigrants, don't have the time, energy, or opportunity to absorb much of Anglo culture or the English language, while others—the more skilled and educated—move easily between their native cultures and American lifestyles. Like past waves of immigrants, even the least skilled and educated are determined to find a better way of life for themselves and their children, even if the cost of doing so is living on the margins of the larger society.

QUESTIONS FOR REFLECTION

1. Are Americans particularly welcoming of newcomers? What are some of the ways states have attempted to deal with immigrants, particularly the undocumented? Have these attempts been successful?

2. What are some of the causes of anti-immigrant sentiment? Is it fair to label Americans as prejudiced against immigrants? Why or why not?

3. What characteristics do immigrants bring? What is their motivation for immigrating?

COSTS AND BENEFITS

Many Americans believe that immigration is a huge drain on the economic resources of the nation. Common concerns include the ideas that immigrants take jobs from native-born workers; strain societal institutions, including schools, housing markets, and medical facilities; and do not pay taxes. These issues are complex and hotly debated at all levels of U.S. society—so much so that passion and intensity of feeling on all sides often compromise the objective analysis of data.

The debate is further complicated because conclusions about these economic issues can vary depending on the type of immigrants being discussed and the level of analysis being used. For example, conclusions about costs and benefits can be very different depending on whether we focus on less-skilled or undocumented immigrants on one hand or the highly educated professional immigrants entering the primary job market on the other. Immigrants in their 20s and 30s are more likely to make a net contribution (especially if they have no children) than those who are over 65 and out of the workforce. Also, national studies might lead to different conclusions than studies of local communities, since the former spreads the costs of immigrants over the entire population while the latter can concentrate those costs in a specific locality.

Contrary to widespread beliefs, many studies, especially those done at the national level, find that immigrants are not a particular burden. For one thing, most immigrants are ineligible for most publically funded services (such as Medicaid and food stamps), and undocumented immigrants are ineligible for virtually all such services. The exceptions are the American-born children of immigrants, who are eligible for many programs targeted at children, and schools—U.S. schools must educate all children regardless of legal status (West, 2011, pp. 433–434).

Various studies (e.g., Smith & Edmonston, 1997) find that immigrants are a positive addition to the economy. They add to the labor supply in areas as disparate as the garment industry, agriculture, domestic work, and higher education. Other researchers find that low-skilled immigrants tend to find jobs in areas of the economy in which few U.S. citizens work or in the enclave economies of their own groups, taking jobs that would not have existed without the economic activity of their coethnics (Heer, 1996, pp. 190–194; Smith & Edmonston, 1997), and thus do not have a negative effect on the employment of native-born workers (Kochhar, 2006; Meissner, 2010). One important recent study of the economic impact of immigrants concluded that there is a relatively small effect on the wages and employment of native workers, although there may be negative consequences for earlier immigrants and for less-skilled African American workers (Bean & Stevens, 2003).

Another concern is the strain immigrants place on taxes and services such as schools and welfare programs. Again, these issues are complex and far from settled, but many research projects show that immigrants generally "pay their own way." Taxes are automatically deducted from their paychecks (unless, of course, they are being paid "under the table"), and their use of public services is actually lower than their proportional contributions. This is particularly true for undocumented immigrants, whose use of services is sharply limited by their vulnerable legal status (Marcelli & Heer, 1998; Simon, 1989). Bean and Stevens (2003, pp. 66–93) found that immigrants are not overrepresented on the welfare rolls; rather, the key determinant of welfare use is refugee status. Groups such as Haitians, Salvadorans, and Vietnamese—who arrive without resources and, by definition, are in need of assistance on all levels—are the most likely to be on the welfare rolls.

In general, immigrants—undocumented as well as legal—pay local, state, and federal taxes, and make proportional contributions to Social Security and Medicare. The undocumented are the most likely to be paid "off the books" and receive their wages tax free, but estimates are that the majority (at least 50%) and probably the huge majority (up to 75%) of them pay federal and state taxes through payroll deduction (White House, 2005). Also, all immigrants pay sales taxes and the other taxes (e.g., on gas, cigarettes, and alcohol) that are levied on consumers. (See this chapter's Current Debates section for a reprise of many of these issues.)

Also, evidence suggests that immigrants play a crucial role in keeping the Social Security system solvent. This source of retirement income is being severely strained by the "baby boomers"—the large number of Americans born between 1945 and 1960 who are now retiring. This group is living longer than previous generations, and since the U.S. birthrate has stayed low over the past four decades, there are relatively fewer native-born workers to support them and replace the funds they withdraw as Social Security and Medicare benefits. Immigrants may supply the much-needed workers to take up the slack in the system and keep it solvent. In particular, most undocumented immigrants pay into the system but (probably) will never draw any money out because of their illegal status. They thus provide a tidy surplus—perhaps as much as $7 billion a year or more—to help subsidize the retirements of the baby boomers and keep the system functioning (Porter, 2005; see also Dewan, 2013).

Final conclusions about the impact and costs of immigration must await ongoing research, and there is no question that many local communities are experiencing real distress as they try to deal with the influx of newcomers in their housing markets, schools, and health care facilities. Concerns about the economic impact of immigrants are not unfounded, but they may be confounded with and exaggerated by prejudice and racism directed at newcomers and strangers. The current opposition to immigration may be a reaction to "who" as much as to "how many" or "how expensive."

Finally, we can repeat the finding of many studies (e.g., Bean & Stevens, 2003) that immigration is generally a positive force in the economy and that, as has been true for decades, immigrants—legal and illegal—continue to find work and niches in American society in which they can survive. The highly skilled immigrants fill gaps in the primary labor market—in schools and universities, corporations, hospitals, and hundreds of other sectors of the economy. Less-skilled immigrants provide cheap labor for the low-wage secondary job market, and, frequently, the primary beneficiaries of this long-established system are not the immigrants (although they are often grateful for the opportunities) but employers, who benefit from a cheaper, more easily exploited workforce, and American consumers, who benefit from lower prices in the marketplace and reap the benefits virtually every time they go shopping, have a meal in a restaurant, pay for home repairs or maintenance, or place a loved one in a nursing home.

Wes Bramhall, age 83, demonstrates his support for tighter security along the U.S.–Mexican border.

UNDOCUMENTED IMMIGRANTS

Americans are particularly concerned with undocumented immigrants but, again, are split in their attitudes. A recent poll (Saad, 2010) asked about people's concerns regarding undocumented immigrants and found that 61% of respondents were concerned with the burden on schools, hospitals, and government services; 55% were concerned that "illegal immigrants might be encouraging others to move here illegally"; and 53% were concerned that undocumented immigrants are lowering wages for native-born workers. At the same time, 64% of respondents proclaimed themselves to be "very" or "somewhat" sympathetic toward undocumented immigrants. Only 17% said they were "very unsympathetic."

The high level of concern is certainly understandable, because the volume of illegal immigration has been huge over the past few decades. As displayed in Figure 10.4, the estimated number of undocumented immigrants increased

from 8.4 million in 2000 to a high of 12 million in 2007, an increase of more than 40%. The number has declined during the recession and is now about 10.7 million. About 55% of all unauthorized immigrants are from Mexico (Passel, Cohn, & Gonzalez-Barrera, 2013).

Some undocumented immigrants enter the country on tourist, temporary worker, or student visas and simply remain in the nation when their visas expire. In 2012 alone, the Department of Homeland Security processed more than 165 million tourists, businesspeople, temporary workers, and foreign students entering the United States (Monger, 2012). These numbers suggest how difficult it is to keep tabs on this avenue of illegal immigration. Others cross the border illegally in the hopes of evading the Border Patrol and finding their way into some niche in the American economy. The fact that people keep coming, even in hard economic times, suggests that most succeed.

One of the reasons the supply of unauthorized immigrants is so high is because of the continuing demand for cheap labor in the U.S. economy. As we have noted on several occasions, the Global South—and Mexico in particular—has functioned as a reserve labor force for the U.S. economy for decades. Even in 2010, after several years of economic recession, undocumented immigrants provided a sizable percentage of the workforce in many states and were as much as 10% of the workers in several of them (see Figure 10.5).

The demand for cheap (undocumented) labor varies by the sector of the economy, and one of the biggest users has been the agricultural sector. Arturo Rodriguez (2011), president of the United Farm Workers of America (the union founded by César Chávez and mentioned in Chapter 8), estimates that as much as 70% of the two million agricultural workers in the United States—the people who pick the crops and prepare them to be shipped to market—are undocumented immigrants. U.S. agriculture and the food supply would collapse without the contributions of undocumented workers.

FIGURE 10.4 Undocumented Immigration to the United States: Total Number Versus Mexican Immigrants, 1990–2012

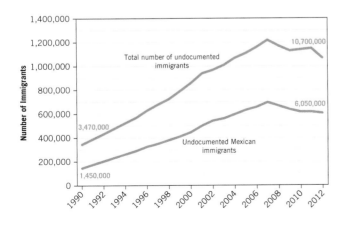

SOURCE: Passel et al. (2013).

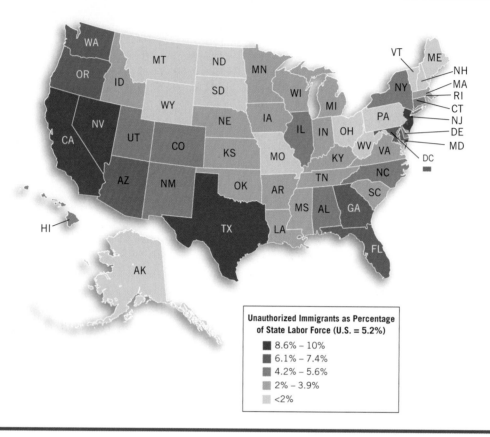

Unauthorized Immigrants as Percentage of State Labor Force (U.S. = 5.2%)

- 8.6% – 10%
- 6.1% – 7.4%
- 4.2% – 5.6%
- 2% – 3.9%
- <2%

SOURCE: Passel and Cohn (2011).

A variety of efforts continue to be made to curtail and control the flow of illegal immigrants. Various states have attempted to lower the appeal of the United States by limiting benefits and opportunities. Other than the aforementioned State Bill 1070 in Arizona, one of the best known of these attempts occurred in 1994, when California voters passed Proposition 187, which would have denied educational, health, and other services to illegal immigrants. The policy was declared unconstitutional, however, and was never implemented.

Other efforts to decrease the flow of illegal immigration have included proposals to limit welfare benefits for immigrants, denial of in-state college tuition to the children of illegal immigrants, increases in the size of the Border Patrol, and the construction of taller and wider walls along the border with Mexico. Over the past decade, a variety of proposals to reform the national immigration policy have been hotly debated at the highest levels of government, but none have been passed.

Although Americans will continue to be concerned about this problem, many people wonder if much can be done (within the framework of a democratic, humane society) to curtail the flow of people. The social networks that deliver immigrants—legal as well as illegal—are too well established, and the demand for cheap labor in the United States is simply insatiable. In fact, denying services, as envisioned in Proposition 187, may make illegal immigrants *more* attractive as a source of labor by reducing their ability to resist exploitation. For example, if the children of illegal immigrants were not permitted to attend school, they would become more likely to join the army of cheap labor on which some employers depend. Who would benefit from barring access to public schools or denying in-state college tuition for the children of illegal immigrants?

DREAMers

In 2001, the U.S. Senate considered the Development, Relief, and Education for Alien Minors (DREAM) Act. This act, like so many attempts to address immigration issues, stalled and was never passed, but it did give a name (DREAMers) to a population that has increased in size since that time and remains a continuing concern: the children of undocumented immigrants who were brought to the United States as young children.

DREAMers are in the United States illegally but not because of any choice of their own. They are not citizens of the United States (unlike the children born to undocumented immigrants in the United States), and, in many ways, they are not citizens of their "native" land either. Many have never visited their "homeland" and are unfamiliar with its customs or even its language.

Students in Phoenix, Arizona, demonstrate in support of the DREAM Act.

They are caught in the middle—residents of the United States but not citizens, strangers to the homelands of their parents. They live in fear of deportation, and their illegal status can prevent them from competing for jobs in the primary labor market, getting a driver's license, attending college, or receiving unemployment benefits or food stamps. Where do the roughly two million DREAMers (most of them Mexican) belong?

Attempts to revive the 2001 bill have failed, as have various alternative measures. Because of the political gridlock at the highest levels of government, many members of the group feared that their situation would never be reasonably addressed, let alone resolved.

Then, in June 2012, the Obama administration enacted a program under which the children of undocumented immigrants can apply to stay in the United States without threat of deportation. Those that meet the conditions of the program (e.g., they must be high school graduates with no significant criminal violations) can get driver's licenses, work permits, and attend college. More than 500,000 people have applied to and been approved for the program.

The program grants a two-year, renewable reprieve from deportation for the DREAMers (but not for their parents and other relatives). It does not offer permanent legal status or a pathway to citizenship. More permanent and comprehensive immigration programs continue to be proposed in the U.S. Congress.

QUESTIONS FOR REFLECTION

1. Do immigrants cost more than they contribute? What are some of the factors that have to be taken into account in dealing with this issue?

2. Has the number of undocumented immigrants grown in recent years? What factors affect the size of this population? Will it continue to grow in the future?

3. Who are the DREAMers? What should be done to resolve their situation?

IS CONTEMPORARY ASSIMILATION SEGMENTED?

In Chapter 2, we reviewed the patterns of acculturation and integration that typified the adjustment of Europeans who immigrated to the United States before the 1930s. Although their process of adjustment was anything but smooth or simple, these groups eventually acculturated and achieved levels of education and affluence comparable to national norms.

Will contemporary immigrants experience similar success? Will their sons and daughters and grandsons and granddaughters rise in the occupational structure to a position of parity with the dominant group? Will the cultures and languages of these groups gradually fade and disappear?

Final answers to these questions must await future developments. In the meantime, there is considerable debate on these issues. Some analysts argue that the success story of the white ethnic groups will not be repeated and that assimilation for contemporary immigrants will be segmented: Some will enjoy success and rise to middle-class prosperity, but others will find themselves mired in the urban underclass, beset by crime, drugs, school failure, and marginal, low-paid menial jobs (Haller, Portes, & Lynch, 2011, p. 737).

Other analysts find that the traditional perspective on assimilation—particularly the model of assimilation developed by Milton Gordon—continues to be a useful framework for describing the experience of contemporary immigrants and that these groups will eventually reproduce the successes of earlier immigrants. We will review some of the most important and influential arguments from each side of this debate and, finally, attempt to come to some conclusions about the future of American assimilation.

THE CASE FOR SEGMENTED ASSIMILATION

This thesis has attracted many advocates, including some of the most important researchers in this area of the social sciences. Here, we will focus on two of the most important works. The first presents an overview, and the second is based on an important, continuing research project on the second generation, the children of contemporary immigrants.

Assimilation Now Versus Assimilation Then. Sociologist Douglas Massey (1995) argued that there are three crucial differences between past (before the 1930s) and contemporary (after the mid-1960s) assimilation experiences. Each calls the traditional perspective into question.

First, the flow of immigrants from Europe to the United States slowed to a mere trickle after the 1920s because of restrictive legislation, the worldwide depression of the 1930s, and World War II (see Figure 2.2). Immigration in the 1930s, for example, was less than 10% of the flow in the early 1920s. Thus, as the children and grandchildren of the European immigrants Americanized and grew to adulthood in the 1930s and 1940s, few new immigrants fresh from the old country replaced them in the ethnic neighborhoods. European cultural traditions and languages weakened rapidly with the passing of the first generation and the Americanization of their descendants.

It is unlikely, argues Massey, that a similar hiatus will interrupt contemporary immigration. As we saw in Figure 10.5, for example, the number of undocumented immigrants remained high even after the economic recession that began in 2007. Immigration has become continuous, argues Massey, and as some immigrants (or their descendants) Americanize and rise to affluence and success, new arrivals will replace them and revitalize the ethnic cultures and languages.

Second, the speed and ease of modern transportation and communication will maintain cultural and linguistic diversity. A century ago, immigrants from Europe could maintain contact with the old country only by mail, and many had no realistic expectation of ever returning. Modern immigrants, in contrast, can return to their homes in a day or less and can use telephones, television, e-mail, and the Internet to stay in intimate contact with the families and friends they left behind. Thus, the cultures of modern immigrants can be kept vital and whole in ways not available (or even imagined) 100 years ago.

Third, and perhaps most important, contemporary immigrants face an economy and a labor market that are vastly different from those faced by European immigrants of the 19th and early 20th centuries. The latter group generally rose in the class system as the economy shifted from manufacturing to service (see Figure 5.3). Today, rates of upward mobility have decreased, and just when the importance of education has increased, schools available to the children of immigrants have fallen into neglect (Massey, 1995, pp. 645–646).

For the immigrants from Europe a century ago, assimilation meant a gradual rise to middle-class status and suburban comfort, a process often accomplished in three generations. Massey fears that assimilation today is segmented and that a large percentage of the descendants of contemporary immigrants—especially many of the "peasant immigrants," such as some Hispanic groups, Haitians, and other peoples of color—face permanent membership in a growing underclass population and continuing marginalization and powerlessness.

The Second Generation. An analysis of the second generation of recent immigrant groups (Haller et al., 2011) also found support for the segmented assimilation model. The researchers interviewed the children of immigrants in the Miami and San Diego areas at three different times—when they were average age 14 in the early 1990s, again 3 years later, and a final time 10 years later, when the respondents were an average age 24. The sample was large (more than 5,000 respondents at the beginning) and representative of the second generation in the two metropolitan areas where the study was conducted. This is an important study because its longitudinal design permits the researchers to track these children of immigrants in precise detail.

The researchers, consistent with Massey (1995) and with many of the points made previously in this text, argue that contemporary immigrants face a number of barriers to successful adaptation, including racial prejudice (since the huge majority are nonwhite), a labor market sharply split between a primary sector that requires high levels of education and a secondary sector that is low paid and insecure, and a widespread criminal subculture based on gangs and drug sales that can provide an attractive alternative to the conventional pursuit of success through education.

Whether immigrants and their descendants are able to overcome these obstacles depends decisively on three factors, which are listed at the far left of Figure 10.6. The figure also depicts several different projected pathways of mobility across the generations.

Immigrants who arrive with high levels of human capital enter the primary labor market, and their descendants generally enter the economic and social mainstream by the third generation (see the top row of the figure). The descendants of immigrants with lower levels of human capital can succeed if they benefit from strong families and strong coethnic communities that reinforce parental discipline. This pathway, depicted in the middle row of the figure, also results in full acculturation and integration in the economic mainstream by the third generation.

The bottom row of the figure outlines a very different pathway for a large percentage of some contemporary immigrant groups. The mode of incorporation for these immigrants does not place them in a strong coethnic community, and they may also experience weaker family structures, sometimes because of their undocumented status or because the family is split between the United States and their home country. The result is lower educational achievement and economic marginalization and, potentially, assimilation into gangs, the drug subculture, and other deviant lifestyles.

The researchers present a variety of evidence in support of segmented assimilation theory. For example, the second generations of different groups have very different experiences in school, very different income levels, and very different interactions with the criminal justice system. Some of these differences are presented in Figure 10.7, which shows large variations in the percentage of second-generation individuals who do *not* pursue education beyond high school, and in Figure 10.8, which shows patterns of incarceration by group.

As the researchers point out, these and the other patterns they examine are not random; rather, they reflect large differences in the human capital of the immigrant generation and variations in modes of incorporation (especially in terms of legal status and racial prejudice). They show that large percentages of the second (and third and later) generations of

FIGURE 10.6 Paths of Immigrant Mobility Across Generations

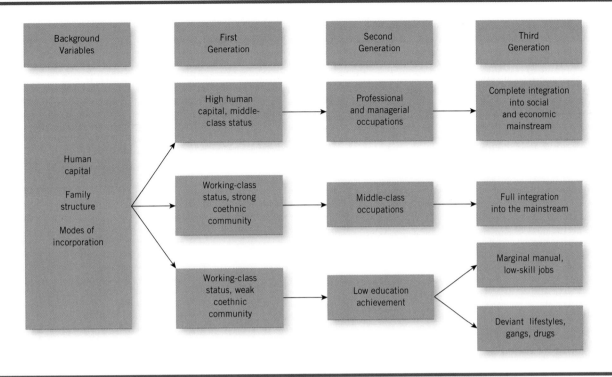

SOURCE: Based on Haller et al. (2011, p. 738).

FIGURE 10.7 Percentage of Second-Generation Americans With a High School Diploma or Less

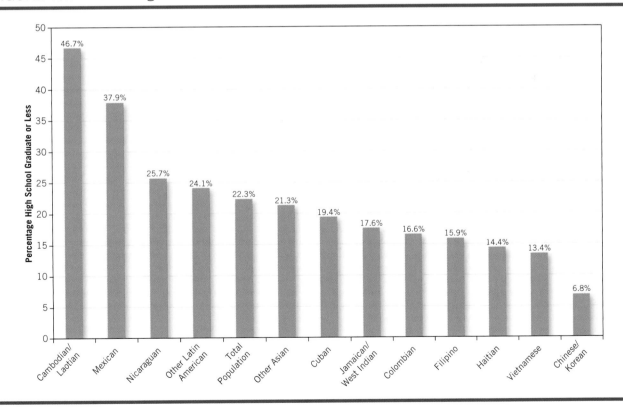

SOURCE: Based on Haller et al. (2011, p. 742).

NOTES:

Chinese and Korean Americans were combined, as were Cambodian and Laotian Americans, because of similar patterns and to create groups large enough for statistical analysis.

"Other Latin American" consists mostly of Salvadoran and Guatemalan Americans.

"Other Asian" is a diverse group that includes many nationalities.

FIGURE 10.8 Incarceration Rates for Second-Generation American Males

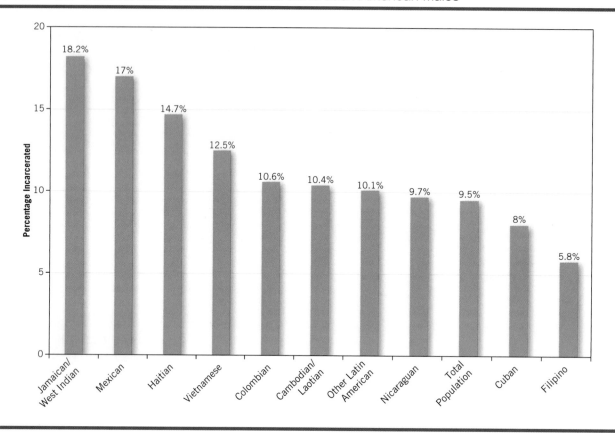

SOURCE: Based on Haller et al. (2011, p. 742).

NOTES: Cambodian and Laotian Americans were combined because of similar patterns and to create a group large enough for statistical analysis.

"Other Latin American" consists mostly of Salvadoran and Guatemalan Americans.

some groups are destined for assimilation into low-status, marginalized, or deviant sectors of American society, in direct contradiction to the patterns predicted by some versions of traditional assimilation theory.

Another important recent study reinforces some of these points. Sociologists Telles and Ortiz (2008) studied a sample of Mexican Americans who were interviewed in 1965 and again in 2000. They found evidence of strong movements toward acculturation and integration on some dimensions (e.g., language) but not on others. Even fourth-generation members of their sample continued to live in "the barrio" and marry within the group, and did not reach economic parity with Anglos. The authors single out institutional discrimination (e.g., underfunding of schools that serve Mexican American neighborhoods) as a primary cause of the continuing separation, a point consistent with Massey's (1995) conclusion regarding the decreasing rates of upward mobility in American society.

THE CASE FOR TRADITIONAL ASSIMILATION THEORY

Other recent studies come to a very different conclusion regarding the second generation: They are generally rising relative to

their parents. This contradicts the segmented assimilation thesis and resurrects the somewhat tattered body of traditional assimilation theories. These studies (e.g., Alba & Nee, 2003; Bean & Stevens, 2003; Kasinitz et al., 2008; White & Glick, 2009) argue that contemporary assimilation will ultimately follow the same course as that of European immigrant groups 100 years ago and as described in Gordon's theory (see Chapter 2).

For example, two studies (Alba & Nee, 2003; Bean & Stevens, 2003) find that most contemporary immigrant groups are acculturating and integrating at the "normal" three-generation pace. Those groups that appear to be lagging behind this pace (notably Mexicans) may take as many as four to five generations, but their descendants will eventually find their way onto the primary job market and the cultural mainstream.

Studies of acculturation show that values Americanize and that English language proficiency grows with time of residence and generation (Bean & Stevens, 2003, p. 168). We discussed some of these patterns in Chapter 8 (see Figures 8.7 through 8.9).

In terms of structural integration, contemporary immigrant groups may be narrowing the income gap over time, although many groups (e.g., Dominicans, Mexicans, Haitians, and Vietnamese) are handicapped by very low levels of human capital at the start (Bean & Stevens, 2003, p. 142). Figures 10.9

FIGURE 10.9 Wage Differentials of Mexican American Male Workers Relative to White Male Workers by Generation

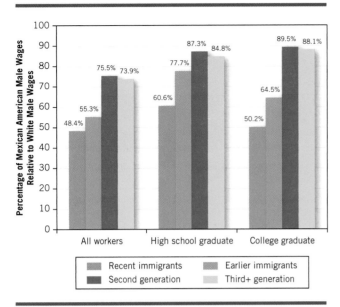

SOURCE: Bean and Stevens (2003, p. 139).

and 10.10 illustrate this process with respect to wage differentials between Mexican and white non-Hispanic males and females of various generations and levels of education. In these figures, complete income equality with non-Hispanic whites would be indicated if the bar touched the 100% line at the top of the graph.

Looking first at all male workers (the leftmost bars in Figure 10.9), recent Mexican immigrants earned a little less than half of what white males earned. The difference in income is less for earlier immigrants and less still for Mexican males of

FIGURE 10.10 Wage Differentials of Mexican American Female Workers Relative to White Female Workers by Generation

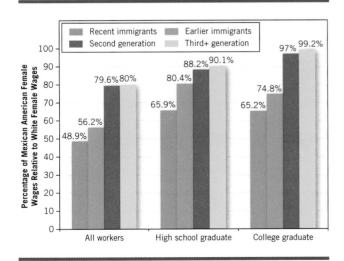

SOURCE: Bean and Stevens (2003, p. 139).

the second and third generations. Separating out males with high school degrees (the middle bars) and college degrees (the rightmost bars), the wage differential is generally lower for the more educated members of each generation. In other words, income equality tends to increase over the generations and as education increases.

On the other hand, note that third-generation males do not rise relative to their parents' generation. This contradicts the view that assimilation will proceed in a linear, stepwise fashion across the generations, and is reminiscent of the findings of Telles and Ortiz (2008) cited earlier. For females (Figure 10.10), the wage differential also shrinks as the generations pass and as level of education increases. Note that for third-generation, college-educated females, the wage differential shrinks virtually to zero, indicating integration on this variable (at least compared with dominant-group females).

Another study (Taylor et al., 2013) used census data to compare immigrants and their children, and generally found that the latter rose in the society relative to the former. The second generation had higher incomes and levels of education, and lower levels of poverty. For example, for Hispanics, median household income rose from $34,600 for the immigrant generation to $48,400 for the second generation. Levels of education showed a similar upgrade: Almost half the immigrant generation had less than a high school education compared with only 17% of the second generation. The study found similar but less dramatic improvements for Asians, largely because of the high levels of human capital brought by the immigrant generation (e.g., 50% had college degrees).

These patterns generally support the traditional perspective on assimilation. Income and education tend to improve by generation, even though the pattern is not linear or complete. The second and third generations seem, on the average, to be moving toward the economic mainstream, even though they do not close the gap completely. Bean and Stevens (2003) conclude that the patterns in Figures 10.9 and 10.10 are substantially consistent with the "three-generation model." The assimilation trajectory of Mexican Americans and other recent immigrant groups is not toward the urban poor, the underclass, or the disenfranchised, disconnected, and marginalized. Assimilation is not segmented but is substantially repeating the experiences of the European groups on which Gordon (1964) based his theory.

SUMMARY

How can we reconcile the directly contradictory conclusions supported by the segmented and traditional perspectives on assimilation? In large part, this debate concerns the nature of the evidence and judgments about how much weight to give various facts and trends. On one hand, Massey's (1995) points about the importance of the postindustrial economy, declining opportunities for less-educated workers, and the neglect that seems typical of inner-city schools are well taken, as is the evidence supplied by other studies that generally support the segmented assimilation thesis.

On the other hand, it seems that even the least-educated immigrant groups have been able to find economic niches in which they and their families can survive and eke out an existence long enough for their children and grandchildren to rise in the social structure, a pattern that has been at the core of the American immigrant experience for almost two centuries.

Of course, this debate will continue, and new evidence and interpretations will appear. Ultimately, however, these disputes may continue until immigration stops (which is very unlikely to happen, as Massey points out) and the fate of the last immigrant groups' descendants is measured.

QUESTIONS FOR REFLECTION

1. Summarize the arguments and evidence for the segmented assimilation model and traditional assimilation theory.

2. Which of these perspectives is more convincing? Why? What questions would have to be answered before one of them could be discarded?

RECENT IMMIGRATION IN HISTORICAL AND GLOBAL CONTEXT

The current wave of immigration to the United States is part of a centuries-old process that spans the globe. Underlying this immense and complex population movement is the powerful force of continuing industrialization, economic development, and globalization. The United States and other advanced industrial nations are the centers of growth in the global economy, and immigrants flow to the areas of greater opportunity. In the 19th century, population moved largely from Europe to the Western Hemisphere. Over the past 50 years, the movement has been from the Global South to the Global North. This pattern reflects the simple geography of industrialization and opportunity, and the fact that the more developed nations are in the Northern Hemisphere.

The United States has been the world's dominant economic, political, and cultural power for much of the century, and the preferred destination of most immigrants. Newcomers from around the globe continue the collective, social nature of past population movements (see Chapter 2). The direction of their travels reflects contemporary global inequalities: Labor continues to flow from the less developed nations to the more developed nations. The direction of this flow is not accidental or coincidental; it is determined by the differential rates of industrialization and modernization

across the globe. Immigration contributes to the wealth and affluence of the more developed societies and particularly to the dominant groups and elite classes of those societies.

The immigrant flow is also a response to the particular dynamics of globalization, especially since the 1980s (Sen & Mamdouh, 2008). The current era of globalization has been guided by the doctrine of neoliberalism, or free trade, which urges nations to eliminate barriers to the free movement of goods and capital. The North American Free Trade Agreement (NAFTA), which we have mentioned on several occasions in this book, is an example of a neoliberal policy. These policies open less-developed nations such as Mexico to consumer goods manufactured and controlled by large, transnational corporations. These corporations are often able to undersell indigenous goods, driving small-scale local farmers and manufacturers out of business.

In addition, the international agencies that regulate the global economy pressure states to reduce the size of their governmental sector. This often means that the national budget for health and education is slashed and that services once controlled and subsidized by the government (e.g., water, electricity) are sold to private businesses. The combined result of these global forces is an increasingly vulnerable population in less-developed nations, unable to provide for themselves, educate their children, or afford the simplest of daily necessities.

Americans tend to see immigrants as individuals acting of their own free will and, often, illegally ("They chose to come to the United States and break the law"), but the picture changes when we see immigration as the result of these powerful, global economic and political forces. While domestic economies and social systems crumble, the victims of neoliberal globalization are left with few choices: They cross borders not only to the United States but to other advanced industrial nations, illegally if they have to, because "it is the best choice to achieve a dignified life—if not for themselves, then for their children" (Sen & Mamdouh, 2008, p. 7).

When viewed through the lens of globalization, it is clear that this population movement will continue because immigrants simply have no choice. It is unlikely that they can be stopped by further militarization of the border or by building bigger and taller walls. They come to the United States in their numbers, as immigrants did in the past, because the alternatives are unacceptable or nonexistent.

This perspective suggests that the tendency of many citizens of the more-developed world to reject, demonize, and criminalize immigrants is self-defeating. Punitive, militaristic policies will not stem the flow of people from the Global South to the Global North. Globalization, in its neoliberal form, is incomplete: It allows for the free movement of goods and capital but not of people. It benefits transnational corporations and the mega-businesses that produce consumer goods but victimizes the vulnerable citizens of the less-developed nations. As long as these forms of globalization hold, the population pressure from South to North will continue.

NEW IMMIGRANTS AND OLD ISSUES

In this chapter, we focused on some of the issues raised by high levels of immigration since the 1960s. As we discuss, debate, and consider these issues, we need to remember a fundamental fact about modern American society: The issues of the "traditional" minority groups—African Americans and American Indians, for example—have not been resolved. As we saw in earlier chapters, these groups have been a part of American society from the beginning, but they remain, in many ways, far from achieving complete equality and integration.

Many of the current issues facing these groups relate to class as well as race. The urban underclass is disproportionately made up of peoples of color and remains marginal to the mainstream society in access to education and job opportunities, decent housing, and good health care. While it is probably true that American society is more open and tolerant than ever before, we must not mistake a decline in blatant racism or a reduction in overt discrimination for its demise. In fact, as we have seen, abundant evidence shows that racism and discrimination have not declined but have merely changed form, and that the patterns of exclusion and deprivation sustained in the past continue in the present.

Similarly, gender issues and sexism remain on the national agenda. Blatant sexism and overt discrimination against women are probably at a historic low, but, again, we cannot mistake change for disappearance. Most important, minority women remain the victims of a double jeopardy and are among the most vulnerable and exploited segments of society. Many female members of the new immigrant groups find themselves in similarly vulnerable positions.

These problems of exclusion and continuing prejudice and sexism are exacerbated by a number of trends in the larger society. For example, the continuing shift in subsistence technology away from manufacturing to the service sector privileges groups that, in the past as well as today, have had access to education. The urban underclass consists disproportionately of groups that have been excluded from education in the past and have unequal access in the present.

The new immigrant groups have abundant problems of their own, of course, and need to find ways to pursue their self-interests in their new society. Some segments of these groups—the well-educated professionals seeking to advance their careers in the world's most advanced economy—will be much more likely to find ways to avoid the harshest forms of American rejection and exclusion. Similarly, the members of the "traditional" minority groups that have gained access to education and middle-class status will enjoy more opportunities than previous generations could have imagined (although, as we have seen, their middle-class position will be more precarious than that of their dominant-group counterparts).

Will we become a society in which ethnic and racial groups are permanently segmented by class, with the more favored members enjoying a higher, if partial, level of acceptance while other members of their groups languish in permanent exclusion and segmentation? What does it mean to be an American? What should it mean?

SUMMARY

This summary is organized around the Learning Objectives listed at the beginning of this chapter.

 Summarize the volume and diversity of recent immigration to the United States.

The third wave of mass immigration to the United States began in the mid-1960s. This wave surpasses the first two in both number of immigrants per year (especially if undocumented immigrants are included in the count) and diversity. While the earlier waves were mostly European, contemporary immigrants are much more global and come from every continent and nearly every society.

 Summarize the general characteristics of recent immigrants, especially new Hispanic and Asian groups, groups from the Caribbean, Middle Eastern and Arab groups, and immigrants from Africa.

Recent immigrant groups include Salvadorans, Dominicans, Haitians, Vietnamese, Filipinos, Syrians, Lebanese, Nigerians, and literally scores of other groups. Most new Hispanic and Caribbean groups tend to resemble the "peasant laborers" of old and have characteristics similar to those of Mexicans. Other groups tend to be "bipolar," including less-skilled laborers and refugee groups as well as highly educated professionals. All together, these groups bring an impressively diverse array of languages, cultural norms, background experiences, and desires. They also face multiple issues, including institutionalized discrimination, racism, and a changing U.S. economy. Arab Americans remain a special target for discrimination and rejection.

 Characterize the new immigrant groups in terms of whether they are entering through the primary or secondary labor markets or through ethnic enclaves.

The primary labor market consists of more-desirable jobs with higher pay and greater security. Immigrants entering this sector are highly educated professionals and businesspeople, and include, among others, many immigrants from India, Iran, and Nigeria. Jobs in the secondary sector are less desirable and command lower pay, little security, and few benefits. These jobs are filled by immigrants with lower levels of education and job skills, including Dominicans and Haitians. Some groups, including Korean and Arab Americans, have established ethnic enclaves consisting mostly of small retail shops and other businesses. The pathway of each group is strongly influenced by the amount of human capital its members bring, their racial background, the attitude of the larger society, and many other factors.

 10.4 Explain the attitudes of the American public as well as the values and statistical characteristics of the immigrants.

Americans are split in their opinions on immigration. The majority sees immigration as positive, but there is a large and vociferous opposition. The contemporary anti-immigrant movement has sponsored various bills at the state level. Group competition and a sense of threat may be important motivators for those opposed to immigration. The immigrants are eager to exploit the economic opportunities offered in the United States but often have reservations about American values. The immigrant stream is highly diversified in terms of education, occupation, and motivation.

 10.5 Summarize the various positions regarding the costs and benefits of immigration, undocumented immigrants, and DREAMers.

Prominent immigration issues include relative costs and benefits, the fate of undocumented immigrants, and the situation of DREAMers. Immigration is thought to be a generally positive force in the economy, but research continues to explore this controversial and complex issue. The size of the undocumented population seems to have fallen in recent years, but there is still a great deal of debate over public policy on this matter. DREAMers are illegal immigrants who were brought to the United States as children. An executive order in 2012 allows DREAMers who meet certain criteria to stay in the United States for a renewable two-year term, without fear of deportation.

 10.6 Explain the points of view and evidence regarding whether contemporary immigration will be segmented.

Segmented assimilation theory, in direct contrast to traditional assimilation theory, predicts that not all immigrants will rise to the middle class but that some will become part of a permanent, marginalized underclass. At present, there is evidence supporting both theories.

 10.7 Place current immigration in the context of globalization, and cite some of the implications of immigration for "traditional" American minority groups.

Current immigration to the United States is part of a global population movement that reflects global inequalities and is stimulated, in part, by neoliberal globalization. Goods and capital but not people are free to move internationally. Also, national governments in the Third World are being pressured to open their borders and reduce the protections they offer their people. Immigration is partly a response to globalization.

REVIEW QUESTIONS

1. What differences exist among these new Americans in terms of their motivations for coming to the United States? What are the implications of these various "push" factors for their reception and adjustment to the United States?

2. Compare and contrast the Hispanic and Asian immigrant groups discussed in this chapter. What important differences and similarities can you identify in terms of modes of incorporation and human capital? What are the implications of these differences for the experiences of these groups?

3. Compare Arab and Middle Eastern immigrant groups with those from the Caribbean. Which group is more diverse? What differences exist in their patterns of adjustment and assimilation? Why do these patterns exist?

4. Compare and contrast African immigrants with the other groups. How do they differ? What are the implications of these differences for their adjustment to the larger society?

5. What, in your opinion, are the most important issues facing the United States in terms of immigration and assimilation? How are these issues playing out in your community? What are the implications of these issues for the future of the United States?

6. Will assimilation for contemporary immigrants be segmented? After examining the evidence and arguments presented by both sides, and using information from this and previous chapters, which side of the debate seems more credible? Why? What are the implications of this debate? What will the United States look like in the future if assimilation is segmented? How will the future change if assimilation follows the "traditional" pathway? Which of these scenarios is more desirable for immigrant groups? For society as a whole? For various segments of U.S. society (e.g., employers, labor unions, African Americans, consumers, the college educated, the urban underclass, etc.)?

Sharpen your skills with SAGE edge at edge.sagepub.com/healey7e

SAGE edge for students provides a personalized approach to help you accomplish your coursework goals in an easy-to-use learning environment.

The following resources are available at SAGE edge:

Current Debates: Is Immigration Harmful or Helpful to the United States?

What do immigrants cost American taxpayers? What do they contribute to the economy? Do the costs exceed the contributions?

On our website you will find an overview of the topic, the clashing points of view, and some questions to consider as you analyze the material.

Public Sociology Assignments

Public Sociology Assignments provide opportunities for students to address directly and personally some of the issues raised in this text.

There are two assignments for Part III on our website. The first looks at patterns of self-segregation in school cafeterias, and, in the second, students analyze the portrayal of the American family on television in terms of race, ethnicity, sexual orientation, and other sociologically relevant characteristics.

Contributed by Linda M. Waldron

Internet Research Project

For this Internet Research Project, you will choose any two of the new American groups covered in this chapter and use data gathered by the U.S. Census Bureau to assess their situation. You will add this information to the data you gathered previously on African Americans, Native Americans, Hispanic Americans, Asian Americans, and the general population. The project will be guided by a series of questions related to course concepts, and your instructor may ask you to discuss your findings in small groups.

For Further Reading

Please see our website for an annotated list of important works related to this chapter.

CHAPTER-OPENING TIMELINE PHOTO CREDITS

OTHER GROUPS, OTHER PATTERNS

In this part, we go beyond minority groups defined by race and ethnicity, and beyond the United States. Chapter 11 considers gender as a dimension of minority-group status, and Chapter 12 analyzes minority groups defined by sexual orientation: lesbian, gay, and bisexual (LGB) Americans. Chapter 13 examines dominant–minority group situations across the globe, in nations from a variety of regions. In all cases, we continue to apply the analytical framework (with some modifications) developed in the first three parts of this text.

We need to say a word here about labels and our extensive use of the LGB acronym in Chapter 12. It is common to see sexual-orientation minorities identified as LGBTQ or even LGBTQQ. The first acronym includes transgender (T) people (those whose gender does not match their biological sex) and queer (Q) people (a broad category that includes anyone who's gender expression does not conform to societal expectations). The second Q is broader still and refers to anyone who questions societal gender conventions or is uncertain or in transition in his or her own gender expression.

We use LGB rather than either of the longer acronyms for a couple of reasons. Transgender people are covered in Chapter 11, since they are defined in terms of a mismatch between gender and biological sex. Our focus in Chapter 12 is on lesbian and gay Americans and, to a lesser extent, bisexual Americans because data and other information are more available for these groups. All these categories (including queer and questioning) are important, however, because they underline the reality that sexual identity and sexual orientation are evolving, open-ended, and, ultimately, social constructions.

11

GENDER

National Portrait Gallery/Smithsonian Institution

LOC

timeline

1843
Isabella Baumfree takes the name Sojourner Truth and goes on to become a famed abolitionist and women's rights activist.

1881
Clara Barton founds the American Red Cross.

1840 1852 1864 1876 1888 1900 1912

1839
Mississippi becomes first state to grant married women right to hold property in their own names, independent of their husbands.

1848
The first women's rights convention is held in Seneca Falls, N.Y.

1869
The first women's suffrage law is passed in Wyoming.

1872
Susan B. Anthony is arrested for trying to vote.

1890
Wyoming becomes the first state to grant women the right to vote in all elections.

Wikimedia Commons

Maria's parents always told her she could grow up to be anything she wanted to be. She and her brother, Malcolm, were both bright students, but Malcolm sometimes struggled with behavior issues, so Maria had better grades. Maria knew that girls and boys were equally smart, strong, and capable, but her life was not the same as her brother's. While she babysat neighborhood kids for $3 to $5 an hour, Malcolm was mowing the neighbors' lawns for $25 to $50 each. Malcolm's curfew was later than hers, and her parents set stricter limits on her social life.

Maria and Malcolm were both interested in math and computer science, and although Maria got into the "better" college, they both enrolled in the same major. But Maria's computer classes were male dominated, and she struggled to form a social network among her peers. She had always loved working with children, so she picked up a second major in education. When the two siblings graduated from college, within a year of each other, Malcolm took a job as a computer programmer,

1920
The Nineteenth Amendment gives women the right to vote.

1963
The Equal Pay Act is passed by Congress to close gender pay gap.

1972
Title IX bans sex discrimination in schools.

1973
In *Roe v. Wade,* the Supreme Court protects a woman's right to terminate pregnancy.

2009
President Obama signs into law the Lilly Ledbetter Fair Pay Act, intended to reduce the pay gap between men and women.

1924   1936   1948   1960   1972   1984   1996   2008

1932
Amelia Earhart becomes the first woman to fly solo across the Atlantic.

1938
The Fair Labor Standards Act establishes minimum wage without regard to gender.

1963
Betty Friedan's *The Feminine Mystique* is published.

1964
Title VII of Civil Rights Act of 1964 prohibits employment discrimination on basis of race, color, religion, national origin, or sex.

1982
For the first time, more women than men receive bachelor's degrees.

1998
The Supreme Court rules that employers are liable for workplace sexual harassment.

1981
Sandra Day O'Connor becomes the first woman Supreme Court justice.

starting at $65,000 a year, and Maria took a job teaching high school math and computers for $35,000 a year.

Maria and Malcolm both want to marry and have children eventually. They both also happen to be mixed race (Latino, African American, and white). Both attended predominantly white colleges, but while Malcolm enjoyed an active dating life, Maria did not conform to the "white" standard of beauty confronting her in media images and the surrounding culture, and thus had a harder time finding suitable mates.

Maria feels more pressure to conform to a certain "look" than Malcolm ever did. Both wonder whether their future relationships will bear any resemblance at all to their parents' marriage. Their family was able to get by primarily on their father's income, while their mother worked part-time and was heavily involved in their schooling and extracurricular activities. Right now, not even Malcolm would be able to buy a house on his own without some additional income or assets, much less Maria . . .

Siblings can be drastically different, even when raised by the same parents, due to variations in personality and temperament. However, what other social factors are at play here, influencing the two siblings' divergent paths? How much of their different lifestyles can we attribute to their biochemical makeup and how much to socialization, culture, or the structure of society? What, if anything, can be done to change these inequalities? Does anything need to be changed? •

This chapter examines how gender shapes stratification and inequality in our social lives. While certain biological factors distinguish the sexes of the human species from each other, most of the gender dynamics we observe in everyday life are the outcomes of human social arrangements. As with other types of stratification we analyze in this text, when society has designated certain groups (in this case, women) as minorities, this impacts how all of us relate to one another across virtually every social institution.

The term **sex** refers to those biological variations that differentiate "male" from "female." Sex includes genitalia, hormones, and chromosomes, and it is often determined before, or right at the time of, birth. Once our sex is named

---

Sex refers to biological characteristics.

Gender refers to social characteristics.

Androgynous refers to someone with a combination of "male" and "female" characteristics.

---

and noted, it bears a close relationship to our **gender**. Gender connotes physical appearance, behaviors, and ways of interacting in the world that are typically socially constructed as masculine, feminine, or some combination of both. People who combine both "male" and "female" gender traits are sometimes called **androgynous.** (See the Applying Concepts section in this chapter for an opportunity to find out more about your gender role.)

The social expectations are that a person with a male sex exhibits whatever his society labels as masculine self-presentation and behaviors, while those with a female sex display a feminine gender. Such gender/sex correspondence is enforced through cultural and structural sanctions that are sometimes not noticeable, especially to those who are convinced that their gender is "natural." However, the many cases of people whose gender does not line up with their sex—from tomboys and "sissy" boys to "metrosexual" stay-at-home dads and powerful women in pantsuits—serve to illustrate the distinction between sex and gender.

Gender is a social construction that varies across time, culture, and society. The admonition to "be a man!"—or to do whatever is regarded as masculine—has quite a different meaning to a Japanese American elder in the 20th century than to a young African American man in the 21st century. And the ideal "feminine" image was quite different for a white upper-class woman in the 19th century than it is for a Latina woman today. You might be surprised to see in early American family portraits that young boys were often photographed wearing what look like white gowns, and you may be shocked when a European tourist asks if your baby (wearing a pink dress and bows in her hair) is a boy or a girl. The various ways we have learned, often subconsciously, to announce and mark our sex correspond with our own particular society's constructions of gender. We have often conformed so well to these norms that we use the terms *sex* and *gender* interchangeably in everyday language.

Yet the fusion between sex and gender that proscribes everyday life does not have to be an inescapable straightjacket. A young female in Afghanistan may find it inconceivable to envision a life where she receives a formal education, chooses a well-paid profession, and selects her own life partner. A young man in urban America may find it impossible to cry when he is sad, to choose to become a professional ballet dancer, or to stay at home with his children while his partner fulfills the role of breadwinner. But because gender is a social construction, it is also possible to create social change—both within the cultural expectations for gendered behaviors and in the social structures that assign differential rewards and life chances based on gender. Some changes can be attained through hard-won political and legal struggles, while others will have to be addressed more creatively through the processes by which we socialize our citizens and in the cultural norms we uphold throughout various institutions—the family, religion, schools, and media, just to name a few.

This chapter begins with an examination of the history and background of gender relations. We will analyze how society's economic development and transitions have had a significant impact on how gender relations are structured in each period. Next, we will examine the various protest and resistance movements that have sought to lessen gender stratification. These efforts toward social change and gender equality are often referred to in the modern context as **feminism**. However, we will also consider the diversity of what is meant by the term *feminism* and the sometimes problematic relationship between the label itself and the various individuals and groups that have sought gender equality.

As with the various racial and ethnic minorities we have already studied here, there exists continued discrimination against women in terms of their economic and political power as a worldwide minority group. In this chapter, we will examine but a few examples from the United States and worldwide of how gender discrimination continues to impact women's lives, thereby exemplifying the relationship between sexism and modern society. We will also touch on how sexism cannot be fully understood without taking into account intersectionality—as gender relations operate quite differently depending on one's race, class, and sexual orientation. Not all men benefit from sexism equally, nor do all women feel its sting in quite the same ways.

Finally, at the end of this chapter, we will apply the concepts of assimilation and pluralism that we have carried throughout this text, with an eye toward evaluating how the experiences of women as a minority group have been both similar to and different from other groups we have studied. In certain sectors of society, such as education in many Western nations, the notion of a gender gap is almost passé; in others, it persists, with life-and-death consequences. By the end of this chapter, you will be familiar with historical as well as contemporary gender relations and will be able to understand how stratification operates in this particular area of social life.

HISTORY AND BACKGROUND OF GENDER RELATIONS

Although gender relations in any society often seem taken for granted, as if things have always operated that way, a quick review of history allows us to examine how gender stratification can be organized quite differently depending on the society's primary mode of subsistence. Typically, as global economic shifts happen, gender relations shift accordingly.

HUNTING AND GATHERING

Only recently in human history have societies moved away from hunting and gathering in favor of growing their own food. A few small hunting-and-gathering societies remain today, but this is an all-but-disappeared mode of social organization. When humans rely on hunting and gathering for primary resources, they cannot easily settle anywhere permanently, for when the food source depletes, they must move.

The nomadic nature of hunting-and-gathering societies means that their population growth stays low; so reproductive activities are a relatively small part of the total life course. This is significant to gender relations since so much of the inequality that develops in more modern economies revolves around the two sexes' divergent relationships to childbirth and child rearing. Forming huge families, with time and space dedicated to them, is a luxury hunter-gatherers cannot afford.

Out of necessity and practicality, the organization of hunting-and-gathering societies often allowed men and women to engage in parallel activities. Food had to be produced daily, and both males and females found themselves providing for their kin. Both had to work to produce food, and both had to cooperate to survive. Although men engaged primarily in hunting and fishing, animal products accounted for only a small percentage of the unit's total needs. Also, due to the lack of any surplus in this type of society, there were few resources to acquire and horde, and this made it extremely difficult for men to gain any power over women—or vice versa (Lenski, 1984).

These characteristics of hunting-and-gathering societies are important to sociologists of gender stratification because they challenge the ideological basis of the argument that a male breadwinner/female caregiver is the traditional, natural, or primal gender arrangement. Indeed, this historical (and for some, current) mode of subsistence illustrates that it is possible for men and women to have relatively equal power in society and to work cooperatively toward survival.

AGRARIAN

As societies moved from hunting and gathering to agriculture based, tasks became more gender specific. Although the equipment necessary to farm required greater physical strength and this is one reason for the emergence of a gendered division of labor (women inside the home, men outside), the most fundamental shift undergirding gender inequality was the emergence of private property. Now that societies could produce their own food and sustenance, rather than having to depend on the whims of the hunt, there was an opportunity to accumulate surplus. Animals became domesticated, and men needed to keep track of their property. The structure of a patriarchal family emerged so a man could be certain which children "belonged" to him, because with private property, resources get passed down from one generation to the next (Engels, 1884/2010).

Feminism refers to all the movements that have sought to reduce gender stratification.

At the agrarian level of development, work was labor intensive.

With the origin of private property came the emergence of capitalism. People no longer just exchanged goods; now goods were also a way to make money. It was during the agrarian era that early capitalism first emerged, and along with it the doctrine of "separate spheres." This ideology asserted that man's place is primarily in the field and the marketplace, while women's activities should be concentrated within the domestic sphere. Women certainly made ample contributions to production (e.g., milking cows, culling wheat), but their activities were less likely to engage the marketplace directly. Families also began to have more children, who were more likely than ever to survive to adulthood, which meant a greater proportion of women's time had to be spent in child-rearing activities, further confining them to the domestic sphere (Gray, 2000).

Despite the sexual inequality in the different roles men and women played in agrarian societies, agricultural work required all participants to contribute, and the outputs of labor were immediately tangible in their impact. Men and women, girls and boys alike were up early doing chores, and the various tasks that needed doing continued into nightfall. It was not until industrialization that a distinct labor force—with categories of employed and unemployed—emerged, fusing unpaid labor with the domestic sphere and paid labor with the public sphere, and thus further entrenching sexism in the separate spheres ideology (Padavic & Reskin, 2002).

We should also note that many societies today are organized around an agricultural mode of production, with all the gender inequality that implies. The higher scores on gender inequality for many African, South American, and other nations displayed in Figure 1.6 reflect their agrarian subsistence technology.

INDUSTRIAL

By the middle of the 19th century, with the advent of the sewing machine, telegraph, transcontinental railroad, and automobile, the industrial revolution was in full swing and with it urbanization. As employment became urbanized, women's and children's participation in the labor force declined. Work was no longer just out in the field or the local marketplace; it was now in a central city that required some travel time to reach, and it typically excluded young children. Thus, in an industrialized, urbanized society, the workplace becomes decidedly gendered as a "masculine" space (Padavic & Reskin, 2002).

With industrialization came a labor force with a tiered wage structure. In the United States and other Western societies, the highest-paying jobs were reserved for white men. Unions developed to curb labor exploitation and fight for humane working conditions, but, as we have seen in previous chapters, unions also functioned to restrict those on the lower end of the stratification ladder from entering the skilled labor pool. Those persons excluded from unions for much of the early history of labor in the United States include women, immigrants, and nonwhites.

Along with the profile of the ideal worker as white and male came the practice of paying a "family wage." Employers such as Henry Ford of Ford Motor Company realized that to retain good employees, they could pay their (typically) male workers a wage sufficient to support their entire families, ideally eliminating the need for wives and children to work. This would lessen the likelihood of employees migrating in search of work. While rational from the perspective of capitalist, male business owners, the family wage assumed a two-parent family headed by a white male. Female workers who were helping support their families or even just trying to support themselves worked at a substantially lower wage than their male counterparts, due in large part to the family wage and the assumptions behind it.

Only those in the middle class and higher could afford to approximate this ideal family structure of the male breadwinner and female homemaker. Immigrant and nonwhite women, whether single or married, continued to labor at low-wage work, as their income was sorely needed to supplement the poorly compensated labor of the men in their families.

This ideal family structure was upheld universally but was an unrealistic standard for many. It constructed an ideology that drew stark contrasts between masculinity and femininity. The ideal husband was a "good provider" whose domain was mainly outside the home and who showed little emotion while inside the home, leaving the child rearing primarily to the woman. Juxtaposed with this was the "cult of true womanhood": Women who did not do manual labor were the guardians of all things domestic, and it was their job to make sure their husbands came home to a sanctuary of domestic orderliness after their hard day's work.

Such ideals were much more than mere stereotypes; they were encoded into law, and sanctions existed for those who deviated from them. For example, up until the 1970s, prior to no-fault divorce laws, one had to have "grounds" for a divorce.

A man was able to divorce his wife on the grounds that she was not an adequate homemaker. Acceptable grounds for women also conformed to the ideal: A wife could divorce her husband if he was not an adequate breadwinner or wage earner (Schwartz & Scott, 1997).

Despite these gender-role proscriptions, as the industrial era continued to roll forward, significant events contributed to the slow but steady increase in the involvement of women in all institutional areas of society. For example, in 1920, after a suffrage movement that had been building for decades, women were granted the right to vote in the United States, following the lead of several European and other countries.

Women's involvement in the paid labor force also rose over the decades. As was the case with many other minority groups we have discussed, the job opportunities available to women increased during World War II. Their contributions were encouraged and celebrated with wartime propaganda such as the now-famous image of Rosie the Riveter.

Civil rights and feminist movements of the 1960s also encouraged more women toward financial independence. As late as the 1970s, however, a married woman could not get a driver's license, credit card, or even library card unless it was in her husband's name, and it was not until the 1970s, with the advent of deindustrialization, that women's participation in the labor force dramatically increased.

Images such as this encouraged and celebrated the contributions of women to the war effort during World War II.

POSTINDUSTRIAL

Deindustrialization and globalization transformed gender relations along with relations between racial and ethnic groups. Everywhere, even in the most patriarchal, male-dominated societies, women have been moving away from their traditional wife and mother roles, taking on new responsibilities, and facing new challenges. In the United States, the transition to a postindustrial society has changed gender relations and the status of women on a number of levels.

Women and men are now equal in terms of education levels (U.S. Census Bureau, 2012c, p. 151), and the shift to fluid competitive group relations has weakened the barriers to gender equality, along with those to racial equality, although formidable obstacles remain. The changing role of women is also shaped by other characteristics of a modern society: smaller families, higher divorce rates, and rising numbers of single mothers who must work to support their children as well as themselves.

One of the most fundamental changes in U.S. gender relations has been the increasing participation of women in the paid labor force, a change related to both demographic trends (e.g., lower birthrates) and changing aspirations. Women are now employed at almost the same levels as men. In 2010, for example, 63% of single women (vs. about 67% of single men) and about 61% of married women (vs. about 76% of married men) had jobs outside the home (U.S. Census Bureau, 2012c, p. 384). Furthermore, between 1970 and 2009, the workforce participation of married women with children increased from a little less than 40% to almost 70% (p. 385).

One reflection of changing aspirations is that U.S. women are entering a wider variety of careers. In the past, women were largely concentrated in a relatively narrow range of female-dominated jobs such as nurse and elementary school teacher. Figure 11.1 focuses on four pairs of careers and illustrates both the traditional pattern and recent changes. Each pair includes a female-dominated occupation and a comparable but higher-status, more lucrative, traditionally male-dominated occupation. While the "women's" careers remain largely female, the percentage of females in the higher-status occupations has increased dramatically (even though, except for university professor, the more lucrative careers remain disproportionately male).

The changing status of women in postindustrial society is also reflected in other measures of secondary structural integration. We will analyze these trends later in this chapter, following much the same format as used in the chapters in Part III.

QUESTIONS FOR REFLECTION

1. Is the glass half empty or half full for today's women? Consider how the comparison group we choose—women of the past versus men of the present—might influence our answer to that question.

2. Consider how race, class, sexual orientation, and religion might have affected the gender advances and restrictions described in this section. For example, are men of every class, race, and background excelling over comparable women? Are all women able to take advantage of educational and occupational opportunities, regardless of religion, sexual orientation, and other categories?

MOVEMENTS FOR GENDER EQUALITY

Although it was not until after 1970 that women's labor force participation increased in the United States and the gender gap in earnings began to decline, it was not for women's lack of trying in earlier periods. Several movements for gender equality have been making strides for more than a century, marked by periods of significant social change and legal achievements alternating with "doldrum" periods, when women were still organizing but more quietly and under more repression (Rupp & Taylor, 1987).

The term *feminism* has come to represent various social movements for gender equality, and historians have identified three major "waves" of feminism. The first wave consists of what is often referred to as the suffragists, who worked in both the

United States and several other Western industrialized nations during the late 19th and early 20th centuries. Their main goal was to secure the vote for women and the right of women to run for political office (see Figure 11.2 on page 327 for a timeline of when women won the right to vote in various nations).

The second wave occurred during the period when the word *feminist* actually emerged, in the late 1960s to early 1970s. This wave culminated in various achievements, including the Equal Pay Act, the acceptance of women into virtually all previously all-male colleges and universities, and Title IX, which dealt with gender equality in school and university sports.

The third wave is generally dated from the 1980s to the present. Third-wave feminists are the first to take advantage of the many legal and other institutional advances for which the second wave fought. The third-wave period is also characterized by a heightened diversity of gender experiences— encompassing multiracial feminism, postmodern feminism, and transgender activism, among others. Below we consider each wave in turn.

SUFFRAGISTS (FIRST WAVE)

In the mid-1800s, women who were engaged in the abolitionist movement to end slavery began to consider the question of human equality under the law more broadly. In 1848, the

FIGURE 11.1 Percentage of Females in Selected Occupations, 1983–2010

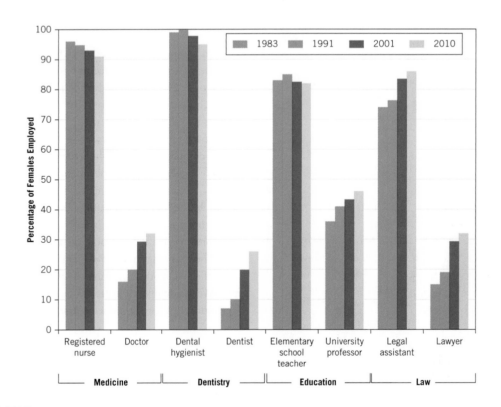

SOURCE: 1983 and 1991—calculated from U.S. Census Bureau (1993, pp. 392–393); 2001—calculated from U.S. Census Bureau (2002, pp. 587–588); 2010—calculated from U.S. Census Bureau (2012c, pp. 393–394).

APPLYING CONCEPTS

What's your gender type? Do you conform to the societal expectations attached to your biological sex, or do you challenge those expectations? Are you a gender conformist or a gender pioneer, making your own way regardless of convention and custom? You can find out, and perhaps acquire some useful self-knowledge, by completing the "gender traits" test below. This test is a way of judging just how "male" or "female" you are in your behavior and feelings.

Using the following scale, rank the traits below as to how well they describe you.

1 = Never or almost never true

2 = Usually not true

3 = Sometimes but infrequently true

4 = Occasionally true

5 = Often true

6 = Usually true

7 = Always or almost always true

_____ Adaptable	_____ Affectionate	_____ Aggressive
_____ Conceited	_____ Compassionate	_____ Assertive
_____ Conscientious	_____ Eager to soothe hurt feelings	_____ Defends own beliefs
_____ Conventional	_____ Gentle	_____ Dominant
_____ Jealous	_____ Loves children	_____ Forceful
_____ Moody	_____ Sensitive to the needs of others	_____ Has leadership abilities
_____ Reliable	_____ Sympathetic	_____ Independent
_____ Secretive	_____ Tender	_____ Strong personality
_____ Tactful	_____ Understanding	_____ Willing to take a stand
_____ Truthful	_____ Warm	_____ Willing to take risks

TURN THE PAGE TO CALCULATE YOUR SCORE.

SOURCE: Reproduced by special permission of the Publisher, MIND GARDEN, Inc., www.mindgarden.com from the Bem Sex Role Inventory - Short Form by Sandra Bem. Copyright 1978, 1981 by Consulting Psychologists Press, Inc. Further reproduction is prohibited without the Publisher's written consent.

Seneca Falls Convention was held, and Elizabeth Cady Stanton, Lucretia Mott, Frederick Douglass, and many others drafted the Declaration of Sentiments, which included demands for women's right to vote (Kraditor, 1981). The document also included a number of statements that reflected compromises between the delegates and were the results of heated debates and negotiations. Not all abolitionists believed in gender equality, and not all suffragists endorsed racial equality (Davis, 1983).

The abolitionist movement met its primary goal during the Civil War. Although it is often said that the 1865 Emancipation Proclamation granted black men the right to vote in the United States—55 years before women attained the same legal right in 1920—the reality was that the Jim Crow terrorism that followed the war in the South (see Chapter 5) made it virtually impossible for black men to exercise that right, nor were black women able to do so in many states even after 1920. It would take the concerted efforts of the second wave of feminists to secure voting rights for all women, not just in theory but in practice.

However, the first wave was concerned with much more than just voting rights. Women's economic independence was also a central concern. In the United States, women could not own property, and it was perfectly legal to pay women much less than men for the same work.

Moreover, particularly for women in the white upper classes—who had the most time, resources, and education to be the voice of the early movement—their reproductive capacity and homemaking seemed to be their only source of societal worth. Sociologist Charlotte Perkins Gilman wrote eloquently during the late 1800s and early 1900s about the excessive "sex distinction" between men and women. While acknowledging that women were the only ones capable of giving birth to

First, calculate your score:

Total the second and third columns.

The first column is what might be called a dummy column, meant to keep you from skewing the test while you're taking it.

Total from the second column is Score A.

Total from the third column is Score B.

Subtract Score B from Score A for the Difference Score.

Second, use the following table to determine your gender trait score:

For instance,

if your A score is 90 and your B score is 70, it would be 90 − 70 = +20 (positive 20);

if your A score is 70 and your B score is 90, it would be 70 − 90 = −20 (negative 20).

Masculine	−20 and under
Nearly masculine	−19 to −10
Androgynous	−9 to +9
Nearly feminine	+9 to +19
Feminine	+20 and over

If you scored in the "masculine" range, you tend to be assertive and independent: The higher the numerical value of your score (disregarding the negative sign), the more "masculine" you tend to be. Likewise, scores of +10 or more mean that you are in the "feminine" range and tend to be affectionate and empathetic.

Note that people who are very masculine or very feminine have some important strengths and some notable weaknesses. For example, a highly masculine person would be able to stand up for himself or herself when necessary but might not be of much use when a grief-stricken friend needs comforting. A very feminine person would have the opposite strengths and weaknesses.

This brings us to the middle range of scores: Androgynous people combine the traits traditionally associated with masculine and feminine gender roles in Western societies. They can be assertive when necessary and tender when appropriate. Thus, it may be that androgynous people are better equipped for modern life than those who are very masculine or very feminine, because they can deal with a broader array of situations.

Do you agree that androgynous people can be happier and more successful in everyday life? Doesn't this idea contradict the conventional wisdom that "boys should be boys, and girls should be girls"? If these ideas about androgyny are valid, what are the implications for gender-role socialization?

children, Gilman critiqued a society that relegated so many of the other domestic tasks to women, when either men or women could easily perform them. She further argued that keeping half the human race from engaging in productive mental and public labor was limiting the progress of humans as a species. She also pointed out that, due to lack of economic independence, women were reduced to using "sex attraction" to pursue a gold ring (marriage), since at that time the only way women could access property and various other rights was through their husbands (Appelrouth & Edles, 2012).

Without the ability to control their own reproductive capacities, women's economic independence would continue to prove elusive. Recognizing this connection, Margaret Sanger opened the first birth-control clinic in the United States in 1916, shortly before the Nineteenth Amendment to the U.S. Constitution

granted women the right to vote. Not unlike the racial tensions inherent in the struggle for suffrage, women's involvement in the fight for access to birth control was tainted by its association with the eugenics movement. Finding herself a target of hostility and death threats for her work and desperate for allies, Sanger accepted support from white supremacists who saw birth control as an ideal way to curb the reproduction of those they deemed "lesser races," including Jews, blacks, eastern Europeans, many other immigrants, Native Americans, and anyone else not fitting their limited ideas of "racial purity" (Davis, 1983). Although it is debated whether her allies' ideology corresponded with her own personal views, the public affiliation between the two movements separated white women and women of color, a division that continued to be of considerable consequence during the second and even third wave of the movement.

FIGURE 11.2 When Women Won the Right to Vote in Selected Countries, 20th Century

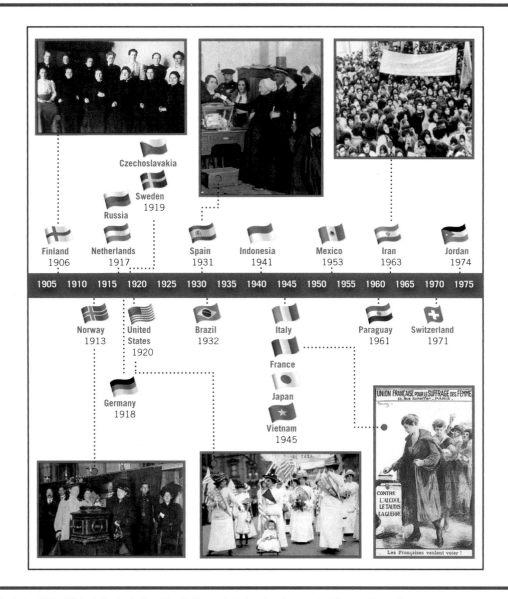

SOURCE: Ministry for Foreign Affairs of Finland; Gipuzkoako Foru Aldundiko Kultura eta Euskara Departamentua; Oslo Museum; Library of Congress.

WOMEN'S LIBERATION MOVEMENT (SECOND WAVE)

Although it was the vision of their foremothers in the 1800s that women be able to own property independent of their husbands, women continued to be subjected to men in various areas of social life, both domestic and public, well into the mid-1950s. Gender equality was not a popular political issue, particularly during the "doldrum" period of 1945 to 1960 (Rupp & Taylor, 1987). During this time, the "cult of domesticity" reigned supreme. "Ideal" womanhood meant a stay-at-home mother complete with all the trappings of a suburban household, such as a refrigerator, washing machine, and even dishwasher! While industrial society seemed to be advancing rapidly, a woman was still clearly the property of her husband. The concept of "marital rape" was still an oxymoron—a woman owned by her husband did not need to give consent. And an unmarried woman past a certain age was still socially stigmatized and shunned.

A number of factors converged to spur the rise of the second wave against these oppressive conditions. Young women were heavily involved in the student liberation movements and civil rights movement in the South during the 1960s, not unlike the abolitionist movements of the previous era. Yet many women fought sexism within these social movements (see Chapter 6) as they struggled to be taken as seriously as the men with whom they worked (Evans, 1980).

While some young, unmarried women were growing restless with their subordinate status in the civil rights movement, some married women were becoming restless with their suburban domesticity. The publication of Betty Friedan's *Feminine Mystique* in 1963 gave voice to many women's dissatisfaction

Some leaders of the women's movement—including Billie Jean King, Bella Abzug, and Betty Friedan—participate in the passing of a torch that was carried by runners from New York to Houston for the 1977 Women's Convention.

with being reduced to homemaking without a choice and is often cited as one of the catalysts for the second wave.

This women's liberation movement that began in the 1960s had many goals. For years, the loftiest aim (never achieved) was an Equal Rights Amendment to the U.S. Constitution. This amendment would have made unequal treatment for men and women unconstitutional, with far-reaching implications for jobs, income, education, and virtually every other area of social life. The amendment passed both the houses of Congress but failed to generate the required approval of 38 of the 50 states.

However, many other advances were achieved by the movement and its activists. Between 1963 and 1968, several measures strengthened women's economic independence, including the Equal Pay Act (1963), the 1967 executive order that applied what is known as "affirmative action" to employment for women, and a 1968 Supreme Court ruling that finally made illegal the practice of separate "Help Wanted: Men" and "Help Wanted: Women" job ads. Besides these employment measures, several legal reforms having to do with gender equality in education were achieved in the 1970s, such as the Women's Educational Equity Act and Title IX, which attempted to equalize funding for women's and girls' athletics.

Like the first wave, the second wave continued to push for greater reproductive rights and domestic equality. In 1965, the U.S. Supreme Court in *Griswold v. Connecticut* finally outlawed the state bans on use of birth control by married couples, and in the 1970s, no-fault divorce laws began, doing away with the gender-specific grounds for divorce described earlier in this chapter. By the mid-1970s, several U.S. states began adopting laws against marital rape and opening domestic violence and rape crisis centers.

Cultural feminism is the movement to change the values and norms of patriarchal societies.

Such legal reforms, though, were only part of what the second-wave feminists aimed to accomplish. **Cultural feminism** also sought to change the values and norms associated with patriarchal societies, where "masculine" traits are considered superior and "feminine" traits are devalued. Within patriarchy, women are negatively sanctioned for being tough and independent, even though those are precisely the traits associated with success in the dominant society.

Likewise, men in a patriarchal society are negatively sanctioned for displaying qualities considered feminine—such as being emotional, crying, or appearing too docile. Feminists who advocated cultural as well as legal changes could often be found protesting in social spaces where women were treated as devalued sex objects. For example, feminist journalist Gloria Steinem became famous for her undercover work as a Playboy bunny after she wrote scathing exposés on the sexist treatment of women in that environment, and Robin Morgan led the first of many protests of the Miss America beauty pageant.

Some of the diversity of the second wave is captured by sociologist Judith Lorber's (2001) distinction among three different types of feminism: gender reform, gender resistance, and gender rebellion. The first two types were prominent during the second wave, and the third emerged during the third wave.

The first type includes feminists whose work aimed primarily at making sure institutions treated women and men equally. These reformers would include liberal, Marxist, and postcolonial feminists.

On the other hand, the gender-resistance feminists—who become more prominent in the second wave—focused not just on legal change but also on cultural change. While gender-reform feminists generally see the existing social structure and institutions as suitable provided that women can participate as equals alongside men, gender-resistance feminists take issue with many of the premises on which American society is based. Indeed, these feminists might argue that if a patriarchal structure were replaced with some of the socially defined "feminine" values—for instance, cooperation and consensus building as opposed to cutthroat competitiveness—the world would be a better place.

Thus, while gender-reform feminists were fighting to get women equal footing in politics and the economy, gender-resistance feminists were demanding female-centered spaces, such as rape crisis centers and battered women's shelters, where the unique needs of women could be considered. They also created cultural spaces such as *Ms. Magazine* and eventually women's studies programs at colleges and universities to focus on the unique contributions women have made to society—overlooked and overshadowed by a patriarchal curriculum (Lorber, 2001).

The achievements of the second-wave feminists cannot be overstated, nor can the weight of the societal resistance they had to overcome. Their efforts coincided with a historical moment that was ripe for civil rights and a time when the economy was relatively stable. Yet even with these factors on their side, those in power often subscribed to a chauvinism that was difficult to sidestep. Feminists, and their male allies in the movement, often took stances that were unpopular with the mainstream—simply to earn basic rights that many of today's young women now take for granted. The stigma of the "feminist" label that existed in this middle era continues into the modern period—the third wave—where many new names and terms are emerging to represent those who continue to struggle for gender equality.

POSTMODERN AND POSTINDUSTRIAL MOVEMENTS FOR GENDER EQUALITY (THIRD WAVE)

While the second wave made great strides toward equality, some felt that the movement did not speak for everyone. For example, the National Organization for Women pushed for abortion rights, but many women of color believed that their major reproductive rights struggle was to control their own fertility, not be involuntarily sterilized, and avoid a situation where they had to raise other women's children as domestic workers. Women of color were more interested in having and caring for their own children, a right they had often been effectively denied by the power of Jim Crow state institutions or the economic exigencies of their lives.

These were altogether different problems from the typical white suburban housewife's plight as described in Friedan's *Feminine Mystique* (e.g., being discouraged from paid labor while staying home to raise children and not having access to the legal right to birth control). Women of color, even when married, did not have the luxury of dropping out of the paid labor force to raise their children because of the large discrepancy between white men's salaries and the incomes of men of color (see Figure 6.5). It seemed that the issues of white middle-class women were defining the feminist movement's agenda, while the pressing social and economic gender-related concerns were left unaddressed by the movement at large (Davis, 1983).

In response, a "womanist" movement was born. In the mid- to late 1980s, scholars/activists such as Angela Davis (1983), Barbara Smith (1983/2000), bell hooks (1984/2000), and Gloria Anzaldúa (1987/1999), among others, published a flurry of works that became the foundation for what Lorber (2001) calls multiracial feminism. These women argued that one cannot simply speak of "men" and "women" without taking into account the myriad differences within those categories—age, class, race, sexual orientation, religion, and so on. By the 1990s, this approach became known as intersectionality, which we introduced in the opening chapter of this text and have used throughout.

Though intersectionality became a relevant scholarly lens, it emerged only after the powerful social movement for change that preceded it. Black women had been arguing since

During the third wave of the movement for gender equality, the movement sought a broader focus, including demands by women of color to have and care for their own children.

the early 1970s that neither the black liberation movement nor the women's movement fully addressed their struggles. By 1983, Alice Walker had coined the term *womanist* to refer to "a black feminist or feminist of color" but also to someone who is "committed to survival and wholeness of entire people, male *and* female" (p. xii; emphasis in original). Walker's quote characterizes the mood of the third-wave generation: "Womanist is to feminist as purple is to lavender" (p. xii). The third wave saw second-wave feminists as narrowly focused on empowering suburban white women and sought to be more inclusive and broader in its agenda.

If the first wave was about women being equal to men in the existing structure and the second wave emphasized dismantling that patriarchal structure in a more feminine-friendly way, the third wave questions the very idea of "men" and "women" altogether. Acknowledging the vastly different experiences of white men and men of color, for example, multicultural feminists ask the questions, "Which men?" and "Which women?"

However, other types of feminists in Lorber's (2001) "gender rebellion" category (the third wave) remind us that the social constructions of "man" and "woman" serve to greatly reduce the substantial diversity of humanity that exists between what is called "male" and what is called "female." For example, social-constructionist feminists stress that we "do" gender as performance, as opposed to the idea of gender flowing directly out of biological sex. Postmodern feminists likewise challenge the gender binary, suggesting that gender is fluid and people can occupy different gender spaces depending on context.

Transgender activists in particular have been a force shaping these more recent feminist issues. Of course, there have been "gender benders" throughout human history, but as we shall see in the next chapter, the gay liberation movement gained traction and broadened to include transgender persons within its range of advocacy. The existence of transgender persons encourages us to think more critically about dividing up societal resources and cultural socialization along the lines of male/female and masculine/feminine when such a range of diversity exists between those two poles.

For example, Anne Fausto-Sterling (1993) wrote an article titled "The Five Sexes" in which she presented the scientific evidence for a range of chromosomal, hormonal, and genital variations that have existed in human live births, besides just the standard male/female dichotomy around which most societies have organized themselves. Estimates are that between 1% and 5% of the population is **intersexed** (has biological characteristics from more than one sex category), and in a dichotomous-gender society, life becomes quite challenging for these individuals.

Thus, for reasons that are biological, social, or both, more persons than many of us realize do not fit comfortably into either gender "box." Third-wave feminists in particular are more likely to take issue not just with male/female inequality or patriarchy but with this entire dichotomous gender structure. They may advocate for changes such as unisex restroom options in public places and more than two "sex" options on government forms such as birth certificates and driver's licenses.

Some college campuses—such as the University of Iowa, University of Pennsylvania, and University of Missouri–Kansas City—have been at the forefront of these social changes, allowing for multiple gender categories on applications and even providing dormitory spaces for transgender persons. They use the term *cisgender* to refer to individuals for whom biological sex and gender identity "match," and *non-cisgender* to refer to both transgender and transsexual individuals for whom the relationship between biological sex and gender identity is not as clear-cut (Schulman, 2013).

The contribution of transgender and multiracial feminists to the third-wave movement is that they question the simple assertion that "men" have it better than "women" in contemporary societies. They also alert us to the fact that, in a postmodern world, efforts to achieve gender equality must be context and society specific. Just as we cannot see an individual man and assume he is a privileged oppressor—his class, race, or sexual orientation might not place him in the dominant/majority group—we also cannot assume that someone who appears to be a "man" was born that way sexually or has had a relatively easy time being accepted by society due to his gender.

In the same way, we cannot assume that someone who appears to be a "woman" has led a linear life of being biologically female or faces the same gender-related struggles as any other woman. If the slogan of the second wave was "sisterhood is powerful," the third wave insists that feminism be "multigendered" as well as "multiracial, multicultural, and multi-issue"

Intersexed people have the biological characteristics of more than one sex.

(www.thirdwavefoundation.org). The shift in terminology for university academic departments (founded as a result of second-wave activism) once called "women's studies" and now called "gender studies" is also indicative of the historical transition from second- to third-wave feminist ideals. A dichotomous notion of women versus the patriarchy is no longer viable within the diverse landscape of the third wave.

The diversity of gender expression along with that of racial, class, and sexual-orientation issues that encompass third-wave feminism sometimes lead to multiple, complex positions. For example, while second-wave feminism was characterized by a relatively homogenous voice speaking out against pornography and sex work as exploitation of women, the third wave includes some "sex-positive" feminists who may view sex work as empowering when undertaken freely and without coercion.

At the same time, third-wave feminists would wholeheartedly reject sex slavery and human trafficking, where the notion of choice is virtually nonexistent. Third-wave feminists include "girlie" young women espousing girl power alongside masculine women and/or women of color who reject makeup and high heels as oppressive (Baumgardner & Richards, 2000). One important goal of these modern feminists is that all human beings be able to freely choose their own forms of productive work, their own relationships, their own life, liberty, and pursuit of happiness, without regard to their gender, race, class, or other form of difference. This "postmodern" version of feminism acknowledges that issues of gender inequality are complex and diverse and that a one-size-fits-all feminist agenda is no longer viable in a postindustrial, globalized world.

QUESTIONS FOR REFLECTION

1. Before reading this section, what pictures would come into your head when you heard the word *feminist*? Where do you think these images come from? Are they stereotypes? How would you revise your previously held picture after reading this brief history?

2. What examples of second- or third-wave feminism from your campus or home community can you cite? To find examples, you might look at university documents that deal with sex discrimination or at the titles, course descriptions, or syllabi of courses.

RECENT TRENDS AND ISSUES

Despite the many achievements of the first, second, and third waves of feminism, many areas of gender inequality in social life remain, both in the United States and globally. It would be impossible for us to tackle all such issues thoroughly in a single chapter, but here we explore three: employer sex discrimination

NARRATIVE PORTRAIT

Growing Up Transgender

At her birth in 1949, Leslie Feinberg was identified as female. Early on, however, she realized that there was, in our terms, a mismatch between her sex and her gender. She grew up in the 1950s, well before the rigid molds of racial and gender conformity would be challenged by the movements for black, gay, and women's liberation. She struggled to find a clear sense of herself and longed for acceptance. Feinberg survived her conflicted childhood and became a novelist, journalist, and transgender activist.

I MUST BE A MARTIAN

Leslie Feinberg

When I was born in 1949, the doctor confidently declared, "It's a girl." That might have been the last time anyone was so sure. I grew up a very masculine girl. It's a simple statement to write, but it was a terrifying reality to live.

I was raised in the 1950s—an era marked by rigidly enforced social conformity and fear of difference....

I tried to mesh two parallel worlds as a child—the one I saw with my own eyes and the one I was taught. For example, I witnessed powerful adult women in our working-class [housing] projects handling every challenge of life, while coping with too many kids and not enough money. Although I hated seeing them so beaten down by poverty, I loved their laughter and their strength. But, on television I saw women depicted as foolish

and not very bright. Every cultural message taught me that women were only capable of being wives, mothers, housekeepers—seen, not heard. So, was it true that women were the "weak" sex?...

And I learned very early on that boys were expected to wear "men's" clothes, and girls were not. When a man put on women's garb, it was considered a crude joke. By the time my family got a television, I cringed as my folks guffawed when "Uncle Miltie" Berle donned a dress. It hit too close to home. I longed to wear the boys' clothing I saw in the Sears catalog.

My own gender expression felt quite natural. I liked my hair short and I felt most relaxed in sneakers, jeans and a t-shirt. However, when I was most at home with how I looked, adults did a double-take or stopped short when they saw me. The question, "Is that a boy or a girl?" hounded me throughout my childhood. The answer didn't matter much. The very fact that strangers had to *ask* the question already marked me as a gender outlaw.

My choice of clothing was not the only alarm bell that rang my difference. If my more feminine younger sister had worn "boy's" clothes, she might have seemed stylish and cute. Dressing all little girls and all little boys in "sex-appropriate" clothing actually called attention to our gender differences. Those of us who didn't fit stuck out like sore thumbs.

Being different in the 1950s was no small matter. McCarthy's anti-communist

witch hunts were in full frenzy. Like most children, I caught snippets of adult conversations....The lesson seeped down: keep your mouth shut; don't rock the boat....

...I learned that my survival was my own responsibility. From kindergarten to high school, I walked through a hail of catcalls and taunts in school corridors. I pushed past clusters of teenagers on street corners who refused to let me pass. I endured the stares and glares of adults. It was so hard to be a masculine girl in the 1950s that I thought I would certainly be killed before I could grow to adulthood. Every gender image—from my Dick and Jane textbooks in school to the sitcoms on television—convinced me that I must be a Martian.

SOURCE: Feinberg (1996, pp. 3–6).

Questions to Consider

1. Compare Leslie's Narrative Portrait with those of Carla and Tim in Chapter 1. Is Leslie's uncertainty comparable to Carla's? How? How does she differ from Tim?

2. Do you suppose that Leslie would have comparable difficulties if she were growing up today? Why or why not? How about if she were black or Hispanic instead of white? Would that compound or lessen her discomfort?

---

on the part of a multinational, multibillion-dollar–grossing corporation (Wal-Mart); sexual harassment and sexual assault in the U.S. military; and issues of reproductive rights.

INSTITUTIONAL SEX DISCRIMINATION

As discussed in Chapter 1, discrimination can exist on an individual as well as institutional level. In the Applying Concepts exercise for that chapter, we mentioned a national restaurant chain that was found guilty of institutional discrimination toward many of its black customers, as a result of which the plaintiffs won a class action suit against the company (Labaton, 1994).

When an instance of discrimination is local and isolated, the victimized individual can be awarded damages for the specific violation of law. Occasionally, however, class action suits

arise in which victims charge that the pattern of discrimination is more widespread, across many sites of the organization. Often in such cases, supervisors, managers, and other powerful persons in the organization have turned a blind eye to the patterns of discrimination. Sometimes it may even be a matter of off-the-record policy among the leadership of the organization that certain types of discrimination will be practiced covertly.

For example, in another successful race-related class action suit, a major oil and gas company had used racial slurs and prejudiced statements during private board meetings. When recordings of these statements became public, they served to substantiate employees' claims of unfair treatment by their corporate employer (Mulligan & Kraul, 1996). Female employees of Wal-Mart have been fighting a similar, ongoing battle over charges of companywide practices of institutional discrimination. They have experienced a variety of victories and setbacks along the way.

In 2001, a middle-aged African American woman named Betty Dukes became the first female Wal-Mart worker to legally charge her employer with gender discrimination. In the course of investigating her allegations, her attorneys found that she was not alone in her experience, and eventually she joined several other women in a class action suit against the corporation.

Dukes represents a telling example of how race, class, and gender intersect, because although the official basis of her legal case is gender discrimination, Dukes reports that she feels compelled to speak on behalf of low-wage workers everywhere and singles out particular discriminatory incidents that occurred during her tenure at Wal-Mart that may have been racially motivated as well (Elias, 2010; Jamieson, 2012).

A number of women of various racial backgrounds followed Dukes's lead in speaking out about their treatment as employees of the company. As the cases built, legal counsel retained statisticians that revealed a troubling pattern for women at the company—both for hourly wage employees and particularly for salaried women. Even though women tended to have lower turnover rates, staying with the company longer, and even had higher average performance evaluations than men, male employees were still promoted and tracked into management training faster than female employees (Drogin, 2003). Thus, what began as a simple case of individual discrimination, upon inspection, revealed a larger, more systematic pattern of institutional discrimination.

The U.S. judicial system has struggled with how to deal fairly with such massive cases of discrimination. At the national level, the fact that more than a million women could have been considered part of the "class" in the class action suit seemed to overwhelm the Supreme Court, which threw the case out on that basis. However, at state and local levels, class action suits continue to be filed. In 2010, the Equal Employment Opportunity Commission was successful in securing back wages for a group of female Wal-Mart employees in London, Kentucky, and in 2011, charges were filed in San Francisco in a suit that could cover more than 40,000 California women (Hines, 2012; Jamieson, 2012).

This corporation, though larger than most, is not alone in its participation in a "race to the bottom" in the postindustrial, globalized economy, seeking to cut its labor costs in any way possible (Pincus, 2011). As we shall see in a subsequent section on jobs and income, the glass ceiling that blocks women from receiving promotions and salary increases within corporations existed well before Wal-Mart entered the corporate landscape. Indeed, by singling out an employer whose influence and scope is so widespread, proponents of gender equality hope to send an amplified message about battles they have long fought.

Because employment discrimination law is handled only in civil court, the penalty is monetary damages, which would not do much to alter this particular corporation's dominance in the global economic landscape. Thus, the successfully litigated cases are largely symbolic and serve as a warning to others who may be harder hit by the penalties of continuing such discriminatory practices.

Protestors rally to denounce the decision by Air Force General Franklin to overturn the conviction of Lt. Col. Wilkerson for sexual assault.

SEXUAL HARASSMENT AND ASSAULT IN THE MILITARY

Just as institutional sex discrimination and the glass ceiling are not limited to a single corporation, the evidence is clear that sexual harassment and assault exist in many other institutions besides the U.S. military. However, this particular institution provides an interesting case study for students of social inequalities because the military is unique in its relatively high levels of racial integration and has often been held up as a model of equal opportunity for all—especially for those who cannot afford higher education (Moskos & Butler, 1997).

The military is often regarded as one of the few true meritocratic institutions, where anyone can make it if he or she tries. It is known for its uniformity of standards and its privileging of internal rank order over any other social/demographic distinctions. Despite the long struggle to get women fully incorporated into military academies and on the front lines in combat zones, some research shows that white women in the military actually report greater job satisfaction and self-assessed quality of life than their civilian counterparts (Lundquist, 2008). Yet even with these great strides in inclusiveness, the military culture remains patriarchal and in some respects creates an atmosphere that makes the reporting and sanctioning of sexual assault and harassment cases extremely difficult (Steinhauer, 2013).

The primary aims of both sexual assault and sexual harassment are power, control, and dominance, but sometimes these crimes are misunderstood as being motivated by sexual attraction. Victims are controlled not only by perpetrators but by a culture that often blames the victim and works to silence those affected, making it extremely challenging to bring offenders to justice. Indeed, a Defense Department study found that less than 10% of all those who experienced sexual assault in the military even reported it (Briggs, 2013).

In a time of repeated deployments due to ongoing conflicts in Iraq and Afghanistan, government officials grew increasingly outspoken about this troubling pattern of sexual abuse among service members, fearing it could pose threats to their ability to complete their missions effectively. With the military handling complaints and punishments for sexual abuse "in house," it is perhaps not surprising that more than half of those surveyed who did report abuse felt that they had experienced some type of retaliation for coming forward (O'Toole, 2013).

Certain expressions of power become institutionalized, or at least tacitly accepted, within the ranks of such authoritarian organizational cultures. Not unlike the situation of police officers of color who participate in racial profiling of blacks and other minorities, some male offenders in the military have also chosen to sexually victimize other men, regardless of their sexual orientation. Moreover, because women make up only about 15% of the total U.S. military force, it follows that, in terms of raw numbers of claims, males have actually reported more unwanted sexual contact (from other men) than women have. Such offenders also tend to identify as heterosexual (Dao, 2013; Lundquist, 2008).

Guilt and shame often work to silence victims of both genders, and cultural sexual scripts about what behaviors are socially acceptable for each gender contribute to the problem. A congressional bill, introduced in both the U.S. House and Senate in 2013, is intended to reform the military structure of reporting and sanctioning such crimes so that, regardless of gender, offenders will be more likely to be brought to justice (Briggs, 2013). The problem of sexual harassment and assault that plagues the larger society nevertheless stands out as a major blemish for an institution such as the military, where racial and gender gaps in promotions, pay equity, and job satisfaction are smaller than in the civilian sector. Due to the global reach of the nation's military, even those analysts who do not particularly identify as feminists agree that, from a national security standpoint, this acute problem cannot remain publicly unaddressed.

REPRODUCTIVE RIGHTS AND FREEDOMS

Establishing control over one's own reproductive capacities is hardly a new gender inequality issue. As we noted previously, feminists of the first, second, and third waves all tackled various legal and cultural barriers to achieving reproductive freedom. In societies where women are unable to give legal consent to sexual activity and/or control the timing of childbirth, men are able to exert great dominance over the female sex. Reproductive freedom continues to be a political issue of paramount importance both nationally and globally.

Political junkies in the United States might equate the term "reproductive rights" to abortion and the now four-decades-old *Roe v. Wade* (1973) Supreme Court ruling that preserved a woman's right to privacy in first trimester abortions. The 2012 presidential campaign and subsequent Obama term featured plenty of political mudslinging along these lines—including one political commentator referring to a law student who wanted birth control pills covered by health insurance as a "slut" and a "prostitute" (Geiger, 2012), and a Congressman erroneously claiming that "legitimate rape" would somehow automatically protect a woman from unwanted pregnancy (Whiteman, 2012).

However, across the globe, reproductive rights are defined much more broadly than just as access to abortions and contraceptives. Reproductive freedom includes a woman's right to access maternal health care—as in the landmark case of a poor Afro-Brazilian woman whose death during childbirth could have been prevented, a case that has been taken up pro bono by the Center for Reproductive Rights as a symbol of the struggles of women everywhere to receive adequate care in pregnancy and childbirth (Cook, 2013). Reproductive freedom also includes the right to resist child marriage, which tends to be most common in the least-developed nations, where poverty is widespread and the education rate for women and girls is dismally low (Prois, 2013).

Indeed, most advocates for women's equality globally argue that the key factor in reducing gender inequality, particularly in developing countries, is ensuring that women have more control over their reproductive functions. For example, during a speaking engagement in Saudi Arabia—a country that ranks close to last in gender equality among nations—Bill Gates was asked about what could be done to advance the nation technologically. The founder of Microsoft and perhaps the world's richest person bluntly replied that Saudi Arabia would be handicapped in its development efforts as long as half the population was not allowed to participate in the creative process of the economy. As long as Saudi women were restricted to the roles of wives and mothers, the nation would never reach its full potential for growth (Quigley, 2013).

The same point can be made for Western democracies such as the United States: Being married off at an early age and/or quickly foisted into childbirth and parenting without a chance to educate and better oneself further deepens gender inequality and limits development and growth. Greater access to contraceptive education and services is of paramount importance in many societies around the world. Although the most critical areas of public policy vary from nation to nation, the unifying concern of reproductive rights, broadly defined, will continue to be a pressing issue of gender inequality as long as the economic, political, and educational inequalities we discuss in the following sections persist.

QUESTIONS FOR REFLECTION

1. How might current civil rights legislation be reformed to better address the ongoing problem of institutional discrimination, since the current model expects plaintiffs to file individual lawsuits suing for damages against the company responsible for the discrimination?

2. What do you suspect would affect greater reductions in sexual assaults in the military—changes to the culture of military life or organizational changes to the punitive structure for such offenses? Why?

3. Develop a systematic list of reproductive rights and freedoms, for both women and men. Which seem to be of greater concern among your peers and local community, and which tend to get less media/popular attention? Why?

SEXISM AND DISCRIMINATION

Some people argue that there is no longer a need for feminism or gender-related social change. Despite the evidence we review in this chapter—showing that women are a minority in areas such as the economy, political power, and even some aspects of education—there are those who claim that as many stereotypes exist about men as about women, and that men have no particular overall advantages in society. Yet social science evidence supports the concept of sexism—that is, a system of oppression that confers overall advantages to men over women in social life.

To convey the systemic nature of sexist oppression, feminist writer Marilyn Frye (1983) uses the metaphor of a bird cage. She points out that if we focus only on one wire in the cage, we may wonder why the bird simply does not fly around that wire. Yet if we step back and take a wider view, we realize that each single wire on its own adds up to a network that cannot be easily subverted.

The advantaged group in an oppressive system may face some isolated wires but nothing it cannot get around. Frye notes that some confuse examples such as "men aren't allowed to cry" as oppression, but it is more appropriate to think about the drawbacks faced by men as unfortunate limitations. If they "fly" the other way, not crying at all, they will be socially approved—allowing them to get around that one single wire. In contrast, a minority group faces a **double bind**: No matter what choice is made, there are negative consequences. For women in a patriarchal society, crying earns them the stigma of being too emotional or irrational, yet *not* crying opens them to accusations of being frigid, uptight, or even a "bitch" (Frye, 1983).

Additionally, as we noted in several earlier chapters (Chapters 1 and 4, for example), oppressive systems are held

---

A **double bind** is a situation in which negative consequences ensue regardless of the choice that is made.

Pink-collar occupations are those that have been predominantly female.

The **glass escalator** (as opposed to the glass ceiling) is an occupational setting in which the dominant group (e.g., men) enjoys a distinct advantage.

---

in place by an ideology. The ideology that undergirds sexism tells us that those traits, characteristics, behaviors, and activities associated with men are more highly valued. Thus, taking the "men can't cry" example a bit further, some point out that U.S. society today is harder on boys because there is no longer much stigma associated with girls who want to "cross" the gender divide and become more athletic or play with cars. Boys who want to play dress-up or dolls, on the other hand, are harassed, bullied, and taunted. What this example really demonstrates, however, is the relative value society continues to place on male and female activities. Since "masculine" activities are more valued, women can enact them with little or no stigma, but men enacting the less valued "feminine" activities receive far stronger sanctions and much more stigma.

In Chapter 3, we discussed how stereotypes exist for many different racial groups, and on a micro level, many of us hold prejudices about different groups, whether majority or minority. Likewise, there indeed exist negative stereotypes about both sexes and prejudices about what they can and cannot do; for example, men are assumed not to know how to cook or clean properly, and women are assumed to be useless when it comes to machinery. Yet, taken together, the assumptions add up to a collective advantage for men, both culturally and structurally, by elevating whatever is deemed "masculine" and attaching greater material rewards to that category.

One of the most striking examples of this pattern can be found in the research of Christine Williams (1992, 2013), who examined the experience of men in traditionally feminine (**pink-collar**) occupations such as nurse, librarian, social worker, and elementary school teacher. We know that sometimes society attaches negative stigmas to males who choose these professions. The popular films *Meet the Parents* and *Meet the Fockers* famously depict this, as Robert DeNiro's character relentlessly ridicules Ben Stiller's character about his feminine career choice of nurse.

Likewise, some of Williams's interviewees reported facing negative prejudices, including being called "sissy" and enduring antigay slurs. Yet these men ironically experienced a **glass escalator** in their respective professions. That is, they were often fast-tracked to the upper-level (higher-paying) spots in their profession, well ahead of their female counterparts with more experience. Male elementary school teachers were quickly moved to principal or the school board office; male librarians were quickly moved away from the desk and shelves and toward the prestigious position of library director. Despite the negative stigma attached to the pursuit of "female" occupations, the power and privilege of being a member of the dominant group asserted themselves.

Analyzing sexism and discrimination in modern times is complex. Much like modern racism, official legal barriers to employment discrimination against women have been removed, but inequalities persist. Token women have achieved greater successes than ever before—heads of state, Fortune 500 CEOs—but an overall pattern of female disadvantage in these fields is undeniable. Not unlike color-blind racism (see Chapter 3), this seeming paradox leads some to use **modern sexism** to explain continued gender inequality. Modern sexism, like modern racism, assumes that gender discrimination is a thing of the past and that any continuing inequalities are the fault of the minority group.

The modern sexist has negative feelings but expresses them indirectly and symbolically. The old-fashioned sexist believes that gender inequality is natural and even desirable; the modern sexist denies the existence of sexual discrimination and inequality, and trivializes or dismisses the concerns of women. Modern sexism is harder to detect and measure, in part because it is often expressed in the language of equality and fairness. For example, the modern sexist might express opposition to affirmative action programs for women by arguing that such programs are unfair to men, rather than invoking notions of female inferiority or incompetence (Beaton, Tougas, & Joly, 1996).

Some research findings suggest that modern sexism is one important factor in the continued maintenance of gender inequality. These studies indicate that modern sexists are less likely to perceive instances of sexist discrimination and more likely to dismiss complaints of sexism as trivial (e.g., see Barreto & Ellemers, 2005; Cameron, 2001; Swim, Mallett, & Stangor, 2004). Also, modern sexists are less likely to identify instances of sexist discrimination and more likely to use sexist language.

Another study (Swim & Cohen, 1997) examined reactions to several situations involving charges of sexual harassment (e.g., an offer to trade career assistance for sexual favors and a work situation in which male employees displayed sexually explicit photos or made sexual comments to female employees). The subjects in the study, all male, were asked to judge the seriousness of these various scenarios. Subjects who scored higher on modern sexism were less likely to classify the incidents as sexual harassment, had less sympathy for victims, were more likely to see the female victims as overreacting, and were less likely to recommend harsh punishments for perpetrators.

Of course, men are not the only ones who subscribe to modern sexism. Just as people of color can internalize racism, women also can resort to this lens to interpret the relative lack of success of their own group. One example of a modern sexist belief is the assumption that women simply choose restricted career paths, either because they are not as ambitious or they have other priorities, such as marriage and family. The chief operating officer of Facebook, Sheryl Sandberg (2013), notably perpetuated this argument with her book *Lean In.* Although she argues that women are capable of being just as successful as men in business, she mainly implicates individual women's choices rather than the structure of society for continued gender inequality. For example, she suggests women need to be smarter in selecting a spouse who will be an equal partner in domestic tasks and need to fight harder for themselves in corporate negotiations. Factors such as institutional discrimination, particularly in the low-wage sector of the economy, and

sexual harassment receive notably less attention in Sandberg's "manifesto" (hooks, 2013). Modern sexism can distract our attention from the more systematic transformations needed to bring about greater gender equality in society.

QUESTIONS FOR REFLECTION

1. In the context of sexism and gender oppression, what are double binds and how do they limit women more than men? Why is it less stigmatizing for women to cross the gender divide than for men?

2. What is the "glass escalator," and how does it benefit men?

3. What is modern sexism, and how does it help maintain the structures of male privilege? Can women be modern sexists? How?

ASSIMILATION AND PLURALISM

In this section, we use the major concepts of Gordon's model of assimilation to assess the status of women, as we have done in previous chapters with other minority groups.

ACCULTURATION

In previous chapters, we discussed acculturation in terms of Americanization or Anglo conformity (the process of the minority group learning the dominant-group culture), or the degree of similarity between the languages, values systems, and norms of the minority and dominant groups. Obviously, this approach does not fit the cultural differences between men and women. Instead, we will focus on how culture influences males and females through socialization.

In a society where gender was no longer the basis for social stratification, insults such as "You throw like a girl" or descriptors such as "Mr. Mom" would have no meaning. Yet, despite the removal of multiple legal barriers to gender equality in many modern societies, gender roles—society's expectations for how women and men should behave—continue to exist. These expectations are reinforced through **gender socialization**—the process by which a society's expectations

---

Modern sexism, like modern racism, is an indirect, more subtle way of expressing prejudice against women.

Gender socialization refers to the processes by which boys and girls are taught expectations for appropriate gendered behaviors.

NARRATIVE PORTRAIT

The Invisible Privileges of Maleness

As we have noted on several occasions, white privilege tends to be invisible to its beneficiaries, largely because Western and U.S. cultural traditions make whiteness "normal."

This point was notably made by Peggy McIntosh (1989) in her classic article "White Privilege: Unpacking the Invisible Knapsack," in which she listed 50 ways whites are privileged in everyday life.

A parallel point can be made about male privilege. In this passage, Barry Deutsch adapts McIntosh's list and describes some of the everyday privileges of being male. To fit this space, we have edited his original list to only 15 items.

A CHECKLIST OF MALE PRIVILEGE

Barry Deutsch

In 1990, Wellesley College professor Peggy McIntosh wrote an essay [in which she] observes that whites in the U.S. are "taught to see racism only in individual acts of meanness, not in invisible systems conferring dominance...." To illustrate these...systems, McIntosh wrote a list of...invisible privileges whites benefit from.

As McIntosh points out, men also tend to be unaware of their own privileges. ...In the spirit of McIntosh's essay, I...compile[d] a list...focusing on the invisible privileges benefiting men.

Since I first compiled...the list... critics (usually, but not always, male) have pointed out men have disadvantages too—being drafted into the army, being expected to suppress emotions, and so on. These are indeed bad things—but I never claimed that life for men is all ice cream sundaes....

Pointing out that men are privileged *in no way denies that sometimes bad things happen to men.*

Several critics have also argued that the list somehow victimizes women. I disagree; pointing out problems is not the same as perpetuating them. It is not a "victimizing" position to acknowledge that injustice exists; on the contrary, without that acknowledgment it isn't possible to fight injustice.

An...acquaintance of mine once wrote, "The first big privilege which whites, males, people in upper economic classes, the able bodied, the straight...can work to alleviate is the privilege to be oblivious to privilege." This checklist is, I hope, a step towards helping men to give up the "first big privilege."

THE MALE PRIVILEGE CHECKLIST

1. I can be confident that my co-workers won't think I got my job because of my sex—even though that might be true.
2. I am far less likely to face sexual harassment at work than my female co-workers are.
3. On average, I am taught to fear walking alone after dark in...public spaces much less than my female counterparts are.
4. If I have children but do not provide primary care for them, my masculinity will not be called into question.
5. When I ask to see "the person in charge," odds are I will face a person of my own sex. The higher-up in the organization the person is, the surer I can be.
6. As a child, chances are I was encouraged to be more active and outgoing than my sisters.
7. If I'm careless with my driving it won't be attributed to my sex.
8. Even if I sleep with a lot of women, there is no chance that I will be

seriously labeled a "slut," nor is there any male counterpart to "slut-bashing."

9. If I'm not conventionally attractive, the disadvantages are relatively small and easy to ignore.
10. I can be loud with no fear of being called a shrew. I can be aggressive with no fear of being called a bitch.
11. My ability to make important decisions and my capability in general will never be questioned depending on what time of the month it is.
12. The decision to hire me will not be based on assumptions about whether or not I might choose to have a family sometime soon.
13. Most major religions argue that I should be the head of my household, while my wife and children should be subservient to me.
14. If I have children with my girlfriend or wife, I can expect her to do most of the basic childcare such as changing diapers and feeding.
15. I have the privilege of being unaware of my male privilege.

SOURCE: Deutsch (n.d.).

Questions to Consider

1. Can you add to Deutsch's list? What unconscious or "invisible" male privileges have you observed?
2. Some might criticize lists such as this as frivolous or trivial. Do you agree? Why or why not?
3. How would you respond to Deutsch's point (quoting McIntosh) about racism (and sexism) as "individual acts" versus "invisible systems"? Which of these levels of analysis is emphasized in this chapter and this text? How?

---

for masculine behavior for males and feminine behavior for females are inscribed on individuals. Various socialization agents work together to program these expectations into members of society, in ways that often go unnoticed and typically are taken for granted. These agents include parents, teachers, peers, and media, among many others. We will discuss these influences in terms of the life cycle.

Infancy and Childhood. Even before birth, parents and others attach myriad assumptions about the physical and psychological

makeup of their baby once they find out its sex, based on the cultural assumptions attached to that gender in their society. (See the Current Debates section for this chapter to consider a case in which parents tried to deflect these cultural assumptions.) Experimental studies in which adults are informed or misinformed of a baby's sex and then asked to describe the baby often produce highly stereotypical descriptions of the baby and its behavior (e.g., Delk, Madden, Livingston, & Ryan, 1986). For example, when told that a female baby is male, people are likely to say that the child is tough, strong, and adventurous. Given

COMPARATIVE FOCUS

Women's Status in Global Perspective

On October 9, 2012, in the Swat region of Pakistan, an armed assailant attacked 15-year-old Malala Yousafzai while she was riding a bus to school. Her attacker sought her out and even asked for her by name. He shot at her three times, one bullet passing through her left eye and out her shoulder.

The reason for the attack? Malala wanted an education and was an outspoken advocate for schooling for girls. The gunman was sent by the Taliban to punish Malala because she flaunted, publicly and repeatedly, the organization's ideas regarding the proper place of women.

Malala survived the attack and was transported to the United Kingdom, where she underwent a lengthy and painful recovery. Far from being intimidated, she resumed her advocacy for education and was frequently featured by the mass media in western Europe, the United States, and around the globe. In recognition of her courage, eloquence, and passion, she was nominated for the Nobel Peace Prize in 2013, becoming the youngest person to be so recognized.

Why was Malala willing to risk her life? How oppressed are women in Pakistan? How does the status of Pakistani women compare to that of women in other nations?

In Pakistan and around the globe, women are moving out of their traditional and often highly controlled and repressed status. According to United Nations (2013) statistics, rates of early marriage and childbirth are falling, and education levels and participation in the paid labor force are rising. Today, almost 50% of all women worldwide are in the paid labor force (vs. 72% of all men), although they still tend to be concentrated in lower-status, less-lucrative, and more-insecure jobs everywhere (pp. 8, 20–22).

The women of Pakistan are not as repressed as women in many other nations, including Saudi Arabia, where women are not allowed to drive a car or vote. Some simple statistics will illustrate the range of possibilities. The table below provides information on women's status in four nations representing various levels of development, locations, and religious backgrounds.

As we have noted, the status of women is partly a function of subsistence technology. Mali is the most agricultural of these four nations (with 80% of its workforce in farming), and the women there have more children, earlier in life, and are far more likely to die in childbirth. They are also much less educated than the women of other nations and the men of their own nation.

Pakistan is less agricultural than Mali, and the status of women is relatively higher, although they are indeed much less likely than men to be educated. Note, also, that the statistics suggest that Pakistani women are still largely focused on producing and maintaining large families.

Women's status generally rises as industrialization and urbanization proceed, as indicated by the profiles of Chile and Sweden. Sweden is more industrialized than Chile, and Swedish women have fewer children, later in life, and are just as educated as men in their nation.

Why does the status of women generally improve as societies move away from agricultural subsistence technology? One reason, no doubt, is the changing economies of childbearing: Large families are useful in the labor-intensive economies of agrarian nations, but children become increasingly expensive in modern urban-industrial economies. Also, consistent with Malala's point, more-educated women tend to make different choices about career and family and about their own life goals.

Questions to Consider

1. From the statistics presented in Table 11.1, what can you infer about the lives of women in Mali? Would they live in the city or countryside? Would they attend school at all? What power would they have regarding decisions about family size? What kinds of activities would they pursue during the day? What dreams would they have for their daughters? For their sons? How would their lives compare with those of women in Sweden?

2. How important is Malala's cause? Why would education have such a powerful effect on women? Earlier in the chapter, we noted Bill Gates's comment regarding the importance of education for women. Why would he (and many others) say that the way to develop or advance a society is to educate women?

TABLE 11.1 Status of Women in Select Nations, 2013

	NATION			
VARIABLES	**Mali**	**Pakistan**	**Chile**	**Sweden**
Percentage of labor force in agriculture	80	45.1	13.2	1.1
Mother's mean age at first birth	18.6	22.7	23.7	28.6
Maternal mortality rate (deaths of mothers per 100,000 live births)	540	260	25	4
Total fertility rate (average number of children per woman, lifetime)	6.25	2.96	1.85	1.67
Percentage literate				
Males	43	68	99	99
Females	25	40	99	99

SOURCE: Central Intelligence Agency (2013).

the tendency of children to want to live up to their parents' expectations, we can easily see how these gender-role expectations become self-fulfilling prophecies in the lives of many.

If parents were the only socialization agent in the primary process, some dedicated parents with feminist ideals might be able to subvert this gender stereotyping altogether. However, the media, the economy (especially toy marketing), teachers/schools, and peer groups all contribute to reinforcing the internalization of these societally sanctioned gender roles. Despite the rising number of female athletes in the wake of Title IX, an athletic girl might still be considered a "tomboy" and a nonathletic throw is still known as "throwing like a girl." And even the most open-minded of parents are likely to be concerned when their male child shows too much interest in items culturally marked as "feminine"—such as nail polish, makeup, dolls, and dresses. Both positive and negative sanctions work together to quickly steer us away from activities and interests that do not fit our gender-role proscriptions and toward those that do.

Before we know it, such gender roles—clearly originating externally from our society's proscriptions—become so ingrained in us that it is difficult to tell where our own interests and proclivities end and where society's begin. Mattel was once forced to recall a Barbie doll that said "math class is tough," because it perpetuated the stereotype that women are not good at math. Yet, despite evidence of equal math abilities between the sexes, society's stereotypes persist; not only do teachers assume boys are better at math, but young men and women tend to underestimate or overestimate their abilities according to the stereotypes (Correll, 2004; Quaid, 2008). There is concern that young adults are influenced in their choice of careers by these gender stereotypes, and some tangible results of this can be seen in Figure 11.1 earlier in this chapter.

Adolescence and Adulthood. What begins in infancy and childhood continues into adolescence and adulthood. As dating begins, **sexual scripts**—gender-based blueprints for sexual behavior—and their sexual double standard become evident. A young man with multiple partners is more likely to be deemed within the realm of masculine acceptability—a stud, a Romeo—while a young woman with the same number of partners is often labeled much more negatively—a slut or whore (Tanenbaum, 1999). This societal tolerance for male sexual conquest has been termed **rape culture** and is deemed responsible for the high level of sexual victimization of American women. For example, it is estimated that one in four college women have survived sexual assault (Warshaw, 1994).

Sexual scripts are gender-based verbal expectations.

Rape culture is a patriarchal culture in which male violence and rape are tolerated.

Students assemble to raise awareness of sexual violence and rape on college campuses.

A female learns quickly that society will judge her on her appearance and that this will matter more for her life than for her male counterparts. Indeed, studies of personal ads and dating sites have shown that while women tend to seek financial security in a partner, men tend to seek physical attractiveness as the primary characteristic desirable in a woman (Davis, 1990).

Likewise, studies of gender differences in the corporate world reveal that physical attractiveness and appropriate height/weight ratio matter far less to a man's career success than to a woman's (Quast, 2012). As a result, gender socialization nudges women to pay close attention to their appearance. This is the cultural sexism that the second-wave feminists fought so hard to undo. They argued that if women were able to spend less time on primping and more on cultivating their minds and talents, the world would be a better place (Wolf, 2002).

The near-impossible standard of beauty elevated in many Western cultures has been blamed for alarmingly high incidences of eating disorders—with sometimes deadly consequences—among modern young women (Thompson, 1996). Third-wave feminists have critiqued unrealistic female body images in advertising by creating alternative ad campaigns, such as The Body Shop's campaign centered on a voluptuous doll named Ruby ("There are 3 billion women who don't look like supermodels and only 8 who do") and Dove's Real Beauty campaign featuring average-sized women wearing plain white cotton undergarments and little to no makeup (Bahadur, 2014; Callimachi, 2005).

Despite these alternative voices, young women and girls continue to evaluate themselves against mass media images of beauty. Interestingly, in one study, both white teens and teenagers of color found such images to be unrealistic, but the white teens incorporated those negative evaluative schemas into their own self-concepts, chastising themselves for not being able to achieve the depicted ideal. By contrast, nonwhite young women had a clearer sense that they were never going to achieve the depicted ideal and thus substituted more attainable standards of beauty for themselves (Milkie, 1999).

Studies of men and gender roles also exhibit great variability with respect to race and class. While toughness and aggressiveness are associated with masculinity in general, the boundaries within which one is permitted and expected to express these traits are often defined by one's social status. There exists a **hegemonic masculinity**—the expression of masculinity that is most privileged in society—and this is usually associated with middle- to upper-class white, heterosexual men. When men of color or men of lower socioeconomic status exhibit an "over-the-top" bravado or machismo, it may be considered cartoonish or buffoonish and not "refined" enough for the hegemonic ideal.

Michael Messner's (1990) study of how young men constructed their masculinities through organized sports, for example, demonstrated how middle- to upper-class white boys knew at some level that sports was but one avenue of expression for them and that educational and economic success was another. In contrast, the youth of lower socioeconomic status were not socialized to believe that there were multiple avenues of success for them; so they often pursued sports with a one-dimensional intensity, and with all the "feel-no-pain" ethic that comes with that arena. Men's studies, an outgrowth of third-wave feminism, has joined multiracial feminism in pointing out how much of the cultural sexism that undergirds gender inequality is also influenced by race, class, and sexual orientation.

Young men and women grow up to form families of their own, and gender socialization continues. Again, even with the best of intentions, men and women who desire an egalitarian ideal struggle with societal pressures and cultural expectations for what their family role should be (Gerson, 2009). Despite the rising number of dual-earner couples and even stay-at-home fathers, the task of child rearing is still assumed to be the mother's primary role, lending meaning to the label "Mr. Mom"—a man performing what is assumed to be the feminine parenting role in society. Mass-media images still reinforce the notion of a feminine domestic sphere. Progressive men brought attention to this cultural sexism by critiquing (and boycotting) a 2012 Huggies diapers ad that depicted men as clueless when it came to taking care of babies—not unlike an image of several confused-looking men on cell phones in the baby food aisle that PBS Parents posted to its Facebook page the same year (Belkin, 2012).

These gender-role expectations are of particular concern to feminist advocates of gender equality, because even when legal barriers are removed, these very strong gender expectations in Western and U.S. culture continue to exert pressure and negative sanctions on those who dare to subvert them. Public policy such as laws against gender-based wage discrimination and policies for gender-neutral family leave are obviously important. However, as long as gender-role differences remain so prominent in the culture's fabric, these policies alone will not be able to do the work of achieving gender equity.

SECONDARY STRUCTURAL ASSIMILATION

This section will cover the various dimensions of secondary structural assimilation in the same order as the chapters in Part III did, although some topics (residential and school segregation, for example) are not relevant here.

Education. Today, the males and females of every group we have considered in this text are equal in terms of levels of education. We saw in Figures 6.9 and 6.10 that there is virtually no gender gap in high school or college education for either blacks or whites (although a notable gap remains between the races). The same holds true for the other groups we discussed in Part III: Although the groups vary with respect to each other (e.g., Hispanic Americans are lower and Asian Americans are higher), there are no gender gaps within the groups (U.S. Census Bureau, 2012c, p. 151).

On the other hand, sexism persists in education in sometimes subtle ways. The tradition of patriarchy in Western society tends to place more weight on the education of males, even in these relatively enlightened times. In elementary school classrooms, for example, boys tend to be called on more than girls, praised more, and given more attention from the teacher (Sadker & Zittleman, 2009). Also, at all levels of education, girls tend to be steered toward traditionally female fields of study (e.g., nursing, education, social work) and away from such areas as engineering, physics, and math. The result is continuing sex segregation of college majors and adult occupations, as we discussed in connection with Figure 11.1.

Political Power. As we have mentioned, U.S. women acquired the right to vote in 1920 with the ratification of the Nineteenth Amendment and have been increasing their involvement in politics ever since. In fact, in recent decades, women have tended to vote at higher rates than men, at least in presidential elections (Center for American Women and Politics, 2011). For example, about 53% of eligible women voted in the 2012 presidential election, compared with only 47% of men (Roper Center, 2012).

The voting power of women may be equal to that of men, but they are less represented in elected office. For example, in 2010, women held only 71 (less than 4%) of the almost 1,900 elected state and local public offices across the nation. Representation in state legislatures ranged from lows of 10% (South Carolina) and 11% (Oklahoma) to highs of 37% (New Hampshire and Vermont) and 38% (Colorado), but no state has reached a 50/50 gender balance (U.S. Census Bureau, 2012c, p. 262). At the national level, only 19% of the members of the U.S. Congress are women (Manning, 2013, p. 7).

Hegemonic masculinity is the privileged, dominant expression of masculinity in a society.

Overall, the political power of women is increasing, but continued imbalances in representation remain, especially at the highest levels of power. The first female Supreme Court justice (Sandra Day O'Connor) was nominated in 1981, and today three of the nine justices are female. In 2008, Sarah Palin became only the second woman candidate of a major political party for the vice presidency of the United States (Geraldine Ferraro was the first, in 1984). Some remaining barriers to the election of women to the highest offices may fall in the next few election cycles.

Jobs and Income. As is the case with many other minority groups, the economic status of women has improved over the past few decades but has stopped well short of equality. For example, as displayed in Figure 11.3, there is a persistent, although decreasing, gender gap in income. The graph can be read in the same way as Figure 6.11: It shows median incomes (in 2012 dollars to control for inflation) for both males and females (read from the left vertical axis) and the percentage of female to male incomes (read from the right vertical axis). Note that only full-time, year-round workers are included in the graph.

On the average, women workers today earn about 79% of what male workers earn, up from about 65% in 1955. The relative increase in women's income is due to a variety of factors, including the movement of women into more lucrative careers, as reflected in Figure 11.1. Another cause of women's rising income is that some of the occupations in which women are highly concentrated have benefited from deindustrialization and the shift to a service economy. For example, job opportunities in the FIRE (finance, insurance, and real estate) sector of the job market have expanded rapidly since the 1960s, and since a high percentage of the workers in this sector are female, this has tended to elevate average salaries for women in general (Farley, 1996, pp. 95–101).

A third reason for the narrowing gender income gap has more to do with men's wages than women's. Before deindustrialization began to transform U.S. society, men monopolized the more desirable, higher-paid, unionized jobs in the manufacturing sector. For much of the 20th century, these blue-collar jobs paid well enough to subsidize a comfortable lifestyle, a house in the suburbs, and vacations, with enough left over to save for a rainy day or the kids' college education. However, with deindustrialization, many of these desirable jobs were lost to automation and cheaper labor forces outside the United States, and were replaced, if at all, by low-paying jobs in the service sector. The result, reflected in Figure 11.3, is that while women's wages increased steadily between the 1950s and about 2000, men's wages have remained virtually level since the early 1970s.

These large-scale, macrolevel forces have tended to raise the status of women and narrow the income gap, but they have not equalized gender relations. Far from it! For example, although women and men are now equal in terms of education, women tend to get lower returns on their investment in human capital. Figure 11.4 compares men and women who were full-time workers in 2012 and shows a wage gap at every level of education. Wages rise as education rises for both sexes, but the wage gap persists.

A recent study showed that the gender wage gap for each level of education appears to be reproduced for jobs that require different skill levels. The researchers divided jobs into three skill levels, based on criteria used by the U.S. Department of Labor. Jobs were also classified as male dominated if they were more than 75% male, female dominated if they were more than 75% female, and "mixed" if they fell between these two categories.

Table 11.2 shows a sizable gender gap in pay for each skill level, with the largest gap for high-skilled jobs. The researchers note that this gender gap between occupations compounds the gap within occupations, creating a kind of double income jeopardy for women: Women earn less than comparably qualified men in the same occupation and are paid less because they are in jobs dominated by women (Hegeswisch, Liepmann, Hayes, & Hartmann, 2010, p. 13).

Continuing gender income inequality is also documented in Figure 11.5, which compares the income distribution for male and female workers in 2012. This figure is similar to income pyramids in earlier chapters (e.g., see Figure 6.12) and shows that, as with most minority groups, women tend to be overrepresented in the lower income categories and notably underrepresented in the higher income brackets. For example, 12.4% of women workers earn less than $20,000 per year (vs. only 8.3% of male workers), and less than 8% of women workers are in the highest income group (vs. more than 17% of men).

A gender gap in economic status seems to be universal, but the size of the gap varies from group to group and from time to time. To illustrate, Table 11.3 shows the gender income gap for various groups, along with the gap between each group and non-Hispanic white men. Hispanic and black Americans have the smallest gender income gaps, perhaps because the men and women of both groups are overrepresented in the low-wage, low-skill sectors of the economy (see Chapters 6 and 8).

FIGURE 11.3 Median Income for Full-Time, Year-Round Workers by Sex, 1955–2012

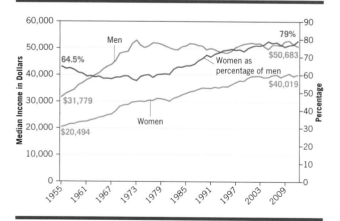

SOURCE: U.S. Census Bureau (2013d).

FIGURE 11.4 Mean Annual Income for Full-Time, Year-Round Workers Age 25–64 by Sex and Educational Attainment, 2012

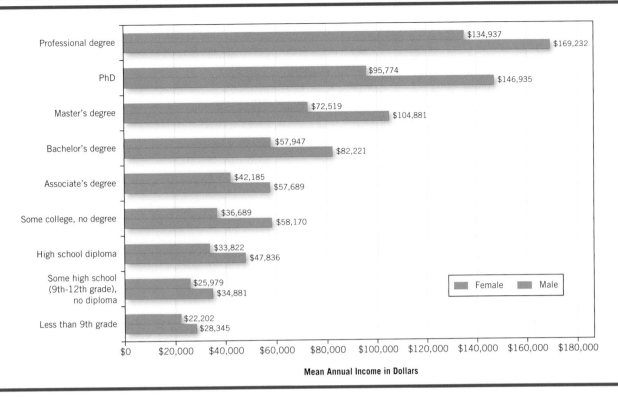

Mean Annual Income in Dollars

SOURCE: U.S. Census Bureau (2013b).

Asian American males and females have the highest average incomes of their respective genders for these four groups, a reflection of the higher levels of education of both the native-born and immigrants (but remember the "bipolar" nature of many Asian American groups, as discussed in Chapter 9). But even in this most "successful" group, a gender gap in income persists, roughly equal in size to the gap for non-Hispanic whites.

The continuing gender income gap is partly a function of the persistent concentration of women in less-well-paid occupations, illustrated in Figure 11.1, which, in turn, is partly the result of outright occupational discrimination and the pervasive pressure to funnel young women into "appropriate" jobs, as mentioned earlier. This pattern is also a result of the choices women

make to balance the demands of their jobs and family obligations. Whereas men are expected to make a total commitment to their jobs and careers, women have been expected to find ways to continue fulfilling their domestic roles even while working full-time, and many "female" jobs offer some flexibility in this area. For example, some women become elementary school teachers because the job offers long summer breaks, which can help women meet their child-care and other family responsibilities. We see this demonstrated in the divergent paths of the similarly educated siblings Maria and Malcolm in the opening vignette of this chapter. This pattern of gender occupational segregation testifies to the persistence of minority status for women and the choices they make to reconcile the demands of career and family.

TABLE 11.2 Median Weekly Earnings in Occupations by Skill Level and Gender Composition, 2009

SKILL LEVEL	MALE DOMINATED	MIXED	FEMALE DOMINATED	EARNINGS IN FEMALE-DOMINATED OCCUPATIONS AS A PERCENTAGE OF EARNINGS IN MALE-DOMINATED OCCUPATIONS
Low	$553	$435	$408	73.8
Medium	$752	$735	$600	79.8
High	$1,424	$1,160	$953	66.9

SOURCE: Hegeswisch et al. (2010, p. 10). Based on IWPR analysis of data from U.S. Department of Labor, Bureau of Labor Statistics. 2009. "Household Data Annual Averages. Table 39."

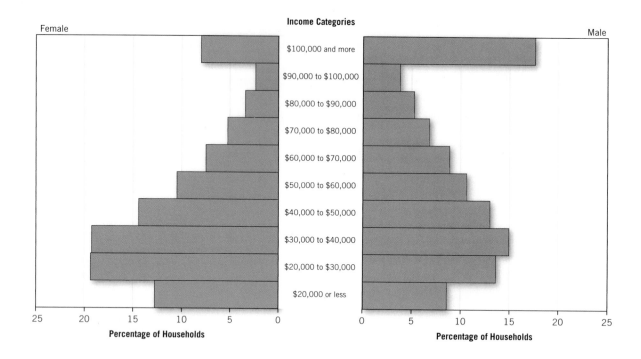

Income Categories

Female

Male

$100,000 and more

$90,000 to $100,000

$80,000 to $90,000

$70,000 to $80,000

$60,000 to $70,000

$50,000 to $60,000

$40,000 to $50,000

$30,000 to $40,000

$20,000 to $30,000

$20,000 or less

Percentage of Households

Percentage of Households

SOURCE: U.S. Census Bureau (2013g).

Women, along with minority groups in general, are also limited by the **glass ceiling**, or the discriminatory practices that limit opportunities to rise to higher levels in their careers, qualify for promotions, and earn higher salaries. These practices are, today, usually subtle, unspoken, and unwritten but effective in maintaining gender inequality, including income inequality. Decisions about promotions or raises will not overtly mention gender, but the glass ceiling is maintained, for example, by giving women less access to key mentors or sponsors and fewer opportunities for training

TABLE 11.3 Median Incomes for Full-Time, Year-Round Workers by Gender and Racial or Ethnic Group, 2012

GROUP	MEDIAN INCOME	PERCENTAGE OF WHITE MALES	PERCENTAGE OF FEMALES TO MALES IN THEIR GROUP
Non-Hispanic white males	$56,247	—	75.0
Non-Hispanic white females	$42,171	75.0*	
Black males	$39,975	71.1	87.8
Black females	$35,105	62.4	
Asian males	$59,531	105.8	77.7
Asian females	$46,241	82.2	
Hispanic males	$32,516	57.8	90.8
Hispanic females	$29,508	52.5	

SOURCE: U.S. Census Bureau (2013g).

NOTE: Blacks and Asians are "alone and in combination" with other groups.

*This gap is not strictly comparable with the one reported in Figure 11.3. The two data sources are slightly different, as are the groups involved (all women and men in Figure 11.3 vs. non-Hispanic white men and women in Table 11.3).

and other experiences needed to qualify for higher-level jobs (Federal Glass Ceiling Commission, 1995, p. 8; Ridgeway, 2011, pp. 109–117).

One recent cross-national study demonstrated the reality of gender discrimination in business. The researchers followed a group of men and women who held MBAs from prestigious universities and found that the women in the sample started in lower positions, earned less over the course of their careers, and were far less likely to rise to the top in their companies (Carter & Silva, 2010).

Another recent study of the Fortune 500 largest corporations found that women were woefully underrepresented among top business leaders and absent from the executive suites and boardrooms. Women made up almost half of the total workforce in these companies but were only about 15% of executive officers and board members, and less than 8% of top earners (Soares, Combopiano, Regis, Shur, & Wong, 2010).

PRIMARY STRUCTURAL ASSIMILATION

Gordon's model of assimilation cites marital assimilation as the final stage of the assimilation process, and we have applied this idea to a variety of American minority groups in previous chapters. For women and men, we must revise this routine, since the two groups already intermarry (even though the institution of marriage often has been the locus and even the very embodiment of female oppression).

Instead, we will consider other areas of primary socialization and relationships in which women still fall short of full assimilation in society. Just because men and women marry each other does not mean that women are viewed and treated as equals in all areas of life.

Interestingly, some aspects of the contact hypothesis (see Chapter 3), which predicts that cross-group contact between status equals over a prolonged period of time can reduce intergroup prejudice, can be applied to gender relations as well. For example, some research suggests that boys who grow up with female siblings are less likely to perpetuate violence against women than are those who grow up primarily with other boys as peers (Lefkowitz, 1998).

Also, research shows that some college fraternities are more misanthropic and "rape-prone" than others. One key factor in determining negative attitudes and behaviors toward women is the extent to which cross-gender socialization is encouraged on campus: The more sexual segregation is encouraged, the more likely abuse is to occur (Boswell & Spade, 1996). This evidence has led some universities to consider encouraging more coed fraternities—even doing away with single-sex fraternities altogether—as a way to cut down on campus sexual assaults (Theen & Staley 2012).

Patterns forged in adolescence and early adulthood continue into adults' occupational lives as well. Consider workplace sexual harassment. As predicted by the contact hypothesis, the more men socialize with women as peers and equals, the less likely they will be to objectify them and treat them as pawns to be manipulated sexually in the workplace. Cohen (2013) points out that careers that are highly sex-segregated—such as auto mechanic or airline pilot—are more prone to cases of sexual harassment. Interestingly, one study found that claims of sexual harassment by white women had actually begun to go down slightly by the early 2000s, yet the numbers of such claims were going up for women of color (Joyce, 2004). Because the informal networks of white men include even fewer women of color than they do white women, this evidence would seem to support the hypothesis that the absence of cross-gender socialization in informal platonic settings creates an atmosphere where abuses—particularly of the less familiar (to white men) women of color—are more likely to occur.

As we have explored throughout this text, discrimination can occur in overt acts—such as abuse and harassment—but also in more subtle ways, through the conference of privilege and advantage, whereby members of the more dominant groups continue doing what has always been more comfortable for them and thus marginalizing those left outside the network of privilege. As a case in point, consider the typical golf course in the United States. It is known to be an arena where business and political contacts are solidified, and even where deals are made. Yet, for the majority of the nation's history, most golf courses excluded both women and nonwhites, thus barring members of these groups from opportunities for deal making and socializing.

In one study of corporate employees, about half of businesswomen surveyed named lack of access to informal networks as the most important obstacle to their success, and the top informal network cited was golf (Andrews, 2012). Elliott and Smith (2004) refer to this as **homosocial reproduction** and point out that white men have greater access to these informal networks of power than does any other race/gender group. This social network advantage pays dividends in terms of promotion advances. For example, Gail McGuire's study of one of the United States' largest financial institutions found that even where level of experience and tenure with the company were the same, men were able to parlay their informal network connections into promotions with the firm in a way that women could not (Reaney, 2010).

The **glass ceiling** refers to practices that limit opportunities for women or for other minority groups.

Homosocial reproduction is the tendency of male elites to select candidates for advancement who are most like themselves.

Access and position in these networks not only affect one's pace of advancement within the workplace but also determine whether one learns about job opportunities at all. Particularly at the highest levels, research shows that white males have greater access to job availability information than does any other group, due to their routine conversations with informal-network peers (McDonald, Lin, & Ao, 2009). These inequalities in contacts are highly problematic because they cannot be legislated away through public policy and will require more innovative solutions to remedy. Yet the evidence is clear: The more cross-gender socialization occurs in platonic/intimate spaces, in addition to romantic/marriage relationships, the more attainable gender equality will be.

QUESTIONS FOR REFLECTION

1. According to the evidence, in which areas of social life or in which social institutions would you say women have come closest to full assimilation? Alternatively, which areas seem to need the most work or attention?

2. In the vignette that opened this chapter, we discussed Maria and Malcolm. If you were their parents, what actions, if any, might you have taken to bring greater equality to the siblings' experiences? (Keep in mind that some actions might be on the micro level in terms of your individual parenting choices, but others would require you to get involved in politics and public policy.)

CONCLUSIONS AND IMPLICATIONS FOR DOMINANT–MINORITY RELATIONS

In Chapter 6, after considering the situation of African Americans, we asked if the glass was half empty or half full, and the same question can be asked of women. Considerable progress toward equality has been made over the past few decades, but enormous challenges remain at every level of society and in every institutional sector.

It is clear that generalizations about "all women" or "all men" need to be carefully qualified. For example, the size of the gender income gap varies by racial and ethnic group, as we have seen, as do levels of education and occupational segregation. Systems of gender inequality and oppression are not the same for all women, and the quality and nature of gender privilege is not the same for all men. Nor do the terms *women* and *men* alone capture all people's gendered experiences, as the writers of the third wave of the feminist movement have pointed out. At any rate, women of all groups and social classes—and all those who are not included in the dominant gender—face considerable resistance to further progress, especially in the context of economic recession, globalization of employment, and deindustrialization. We should be careful not to let our celebration of progress in some areas blind us to the barriers that remain throughout the social structure and across the life course.

SUMMARY

This summary is organized around the Learning Objectives listed at the beginning of this chapter.

 11.1 Explain and analyze the concepts of sex and gender, and the social context of the latter.

Sex refers to biological differences between males and females, yet much of what we observe in everyday life as differences between these two groups is a result of gender distinctions rather than solely biological sex. Gender socialization is so all encompassing, we may begin to perceive this social conditioning as natural and immutable. Gender-role socialization also varies greatly by race, class, religion, and nationality.

 11.2 List and explain key historical and economic events that have shaped gender relations.

Shifts from hunting-and-gathering societies to agrarian economies to industrial-based economies to the postindustrial globalized service economies have all affected transitions in gender relations worldwide. Societies create ideologies for culturally acceptable divisions of labor that rationalize various inequalities and divides. For example, industrial society emphasized a "separate spheres" doctrine that in some ways was even more damaging to gender equality than were the ideologies of eras that came before it. And when the economy becomes more globally interdependent, new forms of gender exploitation emerge that capitalize on readily available cheap labor. At the same time, historical events such as women in other industrialized nations obtaining the right to vote and the 1960s civil rights movement for African Americans have pushed the United States to take legal and political strides toward greater gender equality.

 11.3 Describe feminism as a social movement, its varieties, its achievements, and its challenges.

Feminism is generally defined as the social movement for gender equality, though it exists in many different forms. Lorber's distinctions between gender reform, gender resistance, and gender rebellion movements are useful, and correspond roughly to the historic periods of the first, second, and third waves of feminism. The first wave accomplished voting rights and some economic and reproductive reforms, while the second wave extended more economic and reproductive gains, along with a host of cultural shifts in terms of how women were regarded by the patriarchal society. The ongoing third wave conceptualizes gender as less dichotomous and more fluid, and is more cognizant of gender diversity. Some are reluctant to identify with feminism for fear of appearing too radical, or because they do not think the movement addresses their group's unique gender concerns. Others hold the misconception that gender equality has already been achieved and feminism is no longer needed. However, a plethora of feminist organizations exist today, both domestically and internationally, concentrating on a host of varied gender-related issues.

11.4 Identify and explain the key evidence and causes of gender inequality today.

While women in postindustrialized nations experience many signs of equality that, relative to the past and industrializing nations, are unparalleled historically, they nonetheless continue to face barriers to full equality. Such inequalities are evidenced in statistics such as the wage gap and the percentages of women in the highest political and corporate offices. Yet women worldwide, regardless of type of society, continue to face threat of sexual violence and to lack full reproductive control. Various forms of cultural sexism, exacerbated by gender socialization as well as institutional sex discrimination, all contribute to these continued inequalities.

11.5 Describe how race, class, sexual orientation, and religion impact gender inequality.

Although males are generally considered privileged in patriarchal societies, many gay men, men of color, poor/

working-class men, and men who are religious minorities may not feel very privileged. Structurally, examining the gender wage gap, white males tend to enjoy a comfortable wage advantage over all other groups, whether male or female. Culturally, male gender-role socialization that encourages dangerous risk-taking behavior tends to be more pronounced for boys and men in communities of color and lower socioeconomic status. Heterosexual marriage privileges accord elite white women (often married to elite white men) a degree of social status that women of other backgrounds (e.g., lesbians, women of color) cannot as readily access. And certain religions' norms and values are particularly damaging to gender equality. Sweeping generalizations about all women or all men are seldom accurate—the data show us that such statements usually need to be contextualized by race, class, sexual orientation, and religion, among other characteristics.

11.6 Explain how the concepts of assimilation and pluralism apply to women's experiences as a minority group in society.

Gender socialization creates very different cultural expectations for males and females at each stage of the life cycle, although these experiences are mediated by social class, race, and ethnicity. These expectations remain powerful forces in social life, in spite of the efforts of public policy to encourage gender neutrality. In the United States (and many other advanced industrial nations), women and men are equal in terms of years of education, but persistent and important gender gaps remain in the quality of education, occupational profiles, income, political power, and virtually every institutional area. The extent of gender inequality varies by social class, race, and ethnicity. In terms of primary structural assimilation, patterns of inequality persist in terms of access to the informal social networks that often control upward mobility.

KEY TERMS

androgynous 320
cultural feminism 328
double bind 334
feminism 321
gender 320

gender socialization 335
glass ceiling 343
glass escalator 334
hegemonic
  masculinity 339

homosocial
  reproduction 343
intersexed 330
modern sexism 335
pink collar 334

rape culture 338
sex 320
sexual scripts 338

REVIEW QUESTIONS

1. Define and explain the difference between sex and gender. What does it mean to say that gender is a "social construction"?

2. How do changes in subsistence technology affect gender relations? At what level of development are gender relations most unequal? Why?

3. Define and explain androgyny. What advantages does androgyny bring in modern Western urban-industrial society? Would these same advantages apply to non-Western societies or those at lower levels of development? Why or why not?

4. What movements for gender equality have been active over the past several centuries? What were the goals of these movements? What are the three waves of feminism? Did each succeed? How?

5. Summarize and explain each of the three recent gender trends and issues cited in this chapter. What public policies might be developed to better address these issues?

6. With regard to gender relations today, is the glass half empty or half full? What evidence of persistent gender inequality is presented in this chapter? How serious are these problems? What are some useful approaches to addressing these problems?

STUDENT STUDY SITE

Sharpen your skills with SAGE edge at edge.sagepub.com/healey7e

SAGE edge for students provides a personalized approach to help you accomplish your coursework goals in an easy-to-use learning environment.

The following resources are available at SAGE edge:

Current Debates: Should Children Be Raised Genderless?

Should all children be raised in the same way, without regard to their biological sex? Should children be free to choose their own gender expressions? Is it possible to socialize boys and girls outside of societal gender expectations?

On our website you will find an overview of the topic, the clashing points of view, and some questions to consider as you analyze the material.

Public Sociology Assignments

Public Sociology Assignments provide opportunities for students to address directly and personally some of the issues raised in this text.

There are four assignments for Part IV on our website. In the first assignment, students will use the information available from the Pew Research Center to examine religion as a source of diversity in American life. In the second assignment, groups of students will analyze the lyrics of popular songs. Do the lyrics reflect stereotypes of racial or ethnic groups? What messages are being conveyed about gender or sexual orientation?

The third assignment focuses on a film and website that probe the reality of bullying in America's schools. The fourth assignment is an analysis of the thousands of languages around the world that are in danger of becoming extinct.

Contributed by Linda M. Waldron

Internet Research Project

For this Internet Research Project, you will use information gathered by the U.S. Census Bureau to learn more about gender differences and gender inequality for all Americans and two groups of your own choosing. The groups you choose can be any racial or ethnic group or subgroup covered in this text, including white ethnics, black Americans, Native Americans, Hispanic or Asian Americans, or one of the "New American" groups covered in Chapter 10. The project will be guided by a series of questions related to course concepts, and your instructor may ask you to discuss your findings in small groups.

For Further Reading

Please see our website for an annotated list of important works related to this chapter.

12

LESBIAN, GAY, AND BISEXUAL AMERICANS

Getty

Wikimedia Commons

timeline

1955
The Daughters of Bilitis, a lesbian organization, is founded.

1957
The Kinsey Report estimates that 10% of the male population is predominantly homosexual.

1969
Patrons of the Stonewall Inn in Greenwich Village riot when police officers attempt to raid the popular gay bar.

1979
An estimated 75,000 people participate in the National March on Washington for Lesbian and Gay Rights.

1940   1946   1952   1958   1964   1970   1976

1943
The U.S. military bars gays and lesbians from serving in the Armed Forces.

1953
Executive order bans homosexuals from working for the federal government or any of its private contractors.

1960
The first U.S. public gathering of lesbians occurs at San Francisco's Daughters of Bilitis national convention.

1973
The board of the American Psychiatric Association votes to remove homosexuality from its list of mental illnesses.

1978
Harvey Milk, an openly gay San Francisco city council member and promoter of gay rights, is murdered.

1948
The Kinsey Report finds that 4% of men identify as exclusively homosexual while 37% have had sexual relationships with other men.

Evelyn and Hope Johnson have been together for 20 years and have two children—Mariah and Paul. The Johnson parents tried to be as involved as possible in their children's schooling but occasionally were met with palpable hostility by certain teachers and administrators—including one teacher who said that it was against her religion to welcome both of Mariah's parents to the classroom party at the end of the year. Usually, reactions were more "subtle" but equally frustrating. Some teachers would make eye contact with one parent but ignore the other during conferences, and forms and class projects almost always included references to "mom" and "dad." The result was that the children were often uncomfortable sharing the details of their loving family with their classmates and teachers.

This lack of acceptance came to a head last year when Evelyn was in a car accident and spent

LEARNING OBJECTIVES

By the end of this chapter, you will be able to do the following:

 12.1 Identify and analyze the difference between sexual orientation, sexual identity, and sexual behavior or practices.

 12.2 List and explain the key events that have impacted how lesbian, gay, and bisexual persons are viewed by society and have experienced society.

 12.3 Describe key moments in the struggle for gay liberation.

 12.4 Identify and explain the patterns of sexual orientation inequality in society today.

 12.5 Describe how race, class, gender, and religion impact sexual-orientation inequality.

National Institutes of Health

1987
The Names Project unveils the AIDS Memorial Quilt on the Capitol Mall in Washington, D.C.

Wikipedia

1998
Matthew Shepard, a 21-year-old gay college student, is murdered, bringing hate crimes against gays into the national spotlight.

Reuters

2008
California voters approve Proposition 8, making same-sex marriage in California illegal. In 2010, Prop 8 is found unconstitutional.

2014
18 states plus Washington, D.C. allow gay marriage.

1982   1988   1994   2000   2006   2012   2018   2024

1987
The National March on Washington for Lesbian and Gay Rights draws over 500,000 people, making it the largest civil rights demonstration in U.S. history.

Associated Press

1993
The Department of Defense enacts the "Don't Ask, Don't Tell" policy for military applicants.

2004
Massachusetts becomes the first state to legalize same-sex marriage.

1996
President Clinton signs the Federal Defense of Marriage Act (DOMA), denying same-sex couples the right to have their unions/partnerships recognized by the federal government.

2009
The Matthew Shepard Act is passed, expanding the 1969 U.S. Federal Hate Crime Law to include crimes motivated by a victim's sexual orientation.

2010
The "Don't Ask, Don't Tell" policy is repealed, allowing gays and lesbians to serve openly in the U.S. military.

2013
The Boy Scouts lift ban on gay youth.

2013
The U.S. Supreme Court strikes down DOMA.

The White House

several weeks in the hospital in critical condition. Because the hospital records showed that it was Hope who gave birth to Mariah and Paul, hospital staff would not allow the children to visit their critically ill mother, despite the fact that Evelyn is a legal guardian and shares their last name. (Because of the laws of their state, Evelyn is unable to formally adopt the children she has coparented and provided for since birth.) Scarier still, it took several days of legal battles and heartache before even Hope was allowed to be at Evelyn's bedside, because the hospital did not consider her "family."

Evelyn and Hope got married in New York, but they live in North Carolina, which does not recognize their marriage. Their medical bills are astronomical since they have to carry the cost of two different family health insurance policies. In addition, they now face the legal bills from the rushed medical power of attorney and various other documents Hope cobbled together to fight the hospital, lest she be separated from her spouse in what might have been her final days.

The Johnsons tried to shield their children as much as possible from these struggles, but as the children got older, they came to understand how their family was viewed by many in their town. Both children are passionate about fighting sexual-orientation discrimination, are now majoring in public policy and law, and are heavily involved in various projects and organizations dedicated to making society more accepting and tolerant.

There are many types of family in the United States today, and the "traditional" nuclear family—husband and wife with children—is only one of multiple possibilities. What challenges do the Johnsons face that other types of families do not? What dynamics of prejudice and discrimination described in the above vignette resemble those faced by the racial/ethnic minorities we have studied thus far? Which are different? In this chapter, we will explore these and many other related questions. •

This chapter examines how society is stratified by sexual orientation, in its culture, its social structure, and its institutions. We will review the various, often unconscious privileges heterosexual individuals enjoy and the societal stigma placed on lesbians, gays, and bisexuals (LGBs). While some major cultural shifts have occurred in the United States and some other Western nations in recent years, particularly in the younger generations,

inequalities and differences in treatment based on sexual orientation continue across virtually all areas of social life.

We begin with a consideration of sexual orientation and then examine the history of sexual orientation as an organizing principle for stratification. We will analyze how changes in subsistence technology and level of development have affected the patterns of inequality for LGB individuals, and the various protest and resistance movements that have sought to lessen stratification based on sexual orientation.

We will also consider some of the issues that are central to relations between LGB persons and the larger society, and, following our usual approach, we will end the chapter by applying some of the concepts we have used throughout the text to compare LGBs to other minority groups we have studied. Throughout the chapter, we will use intersectionality to examine the relationships between sexual orientation and inequality. Antigay prejudice and the marginalization of LGB persons operate quite differently depending on race, class, and gender. Not all heterosexuals benefit from heterosexism equally, nor do all LGB people experience homophobia in the same way.

As with the various minorities we have already studied, discrimination against LGB people is global. In many places LGB relationships are criminalized, with penalties that include jail, death sentences, and torture. Antigay hate crimes occur even in societies whose laws seem relatively more open and tolerant, and it is common to find a variety of family-related privileges for heterosexuals, resulting in economic hardships for gay and lesbian families. Institutions including family, religion, politics, education, and the economy are all impacted by homophobia, even though popular culture and the media at times may project a more optimistic picture for LGBs than actually exists. By the end of this chapter, you will be familiar with issues of central concern in the history and development of sexual orientation inequality, and will be able to understand how stratification operates in this particular area of social life.

SEXUAL ORIENTATION, SEXUAL IDENTITY, AND SEXUAL BEHAVIOR

Sexual orientation refers to the gender or genders to which a person is predominantly attracted—physically, emotionally, and affectionately. We refer to people who are attracted to the opposite sex as heterosexual, while those who are mainly oriented toward same-sex partners are referred to as lesbian if female and gay if male. Someone who is attracted to both genders is bisexual.

These definitions might seem simple enough, but it is important to note that sexual orientation can be subtle and complicated: People don't always fall into one and only one category. For example, in Chapter 11, we noted that a person's biological sex does not always match his or her gender. How does a person, born male but gendered feminine

---

Sexual orientation refers to the gender or genders to which a person is sexually attracted.

(a male-to-female transgender person), identify his or her sexual orientation if attracted to other women? Lesbian? Heterosexual? Bisexual? What about the person who identifies as heterosexual but has had same-sex encounters? Or the celibate person who identifies as bisexual? These are probably not the images that come to mind when you think about sexual orientation, but they serve to illustrate the range of possibilities.

Furthermore, we need to distinguish between sexual orientation and **sexual identity**, or the way people think about themselves as sexual beings. A person who identifies as a heterosexual still may be physically attracted to members of the same gender, at least occasionally, and someone who identifies as gay or lesbian may sometimes be attracted to the opposite sex.

Sexual orientation and sexual identity are closely connected, but neither has a one-to-one correspondence with the other or with actual sexual behavior. Just as there are many virgins or celibate people (behavior) who identify as heterosexual (identity) but are attracted to members of the opposite sex (orientation), there are others who identify as bisexual, gay, or lesbian, yet have never actually had sexual relations or shared other physically affectionate acts with a person of the same sex. Some people may think of themselves as "bicurious" if they have had only or predominantly heterosexual relations but have considered or imagined—but not necessarily engaged in—sexual activity with members of their gender.

Still other people may have performed physical and sexual acts that do not correspond with their avowed sexual orientation. These include gay individuals who engage in relations with the opposite sex because it is a social norm, and heterosexually identified individuals who have engaged in same-sex sexual behaviors to satisfy a temporary physical need but do not feel an emotional attachment strong enough to justify a gay or lesbian identity. Remember that the definition of sexual orientation includes an emotional as well as physical or sexual orientation, and that these dimensions aren't always consistent with each other.

Figure 12.1 explores some of these relationships, based on the findings of a 2013 survey of a nationally representative sample of LGB individuals. The sample was asked, "Who are you attracted to?" (sexual orientation), and responses are presented by the stated sexual identity (gay, lesbian, or bisexual) of the individual. The results illustrate our point that sexual orientation and sexual identity are closely but not perfectly connected.

Virtually all gay men (91%) said that they are attracted "only or mostly" to other men, but lesbians were less unanimous: Only 80% said they were only or mostly attracted to other women, and 13% said they were "somewhat" more attracted to other women. Interestingly, about 3% of the self-identified lesbians said they were equally attracted to both men and women, and 2% said they were more attracted to men!

The self-identified bisexuals were, as their sexual identity suggests, quite variable in their sexual orientation. Roughly equal percentages of male bisexuals were more sexually attracted to men (32%), to women (32%), and to both sexes equally (28%).

FIGURE 12.1 Sexual Attraction by Sexual Identity (LGB Individuals Only)

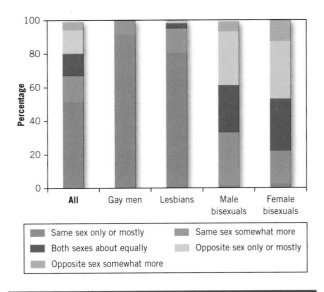

SOURCE: Pew Research Center (2013d, p. 81). Reprinted with permission of Pew Research Center.

In contrast, a substantial number of bisexual women (34%) were more attracted to men, while 20% were more attracted to women and 31% were attracted to both sexes equally.

If nothing else, these results suggest that the relationship between sexual orientation and sexual identity is neither simple nor straightforward. Suffice it to say that the terms *lesbian*, *gay*, and *bisexual* refer to socially constructed identities and social statuses that are by no means exhaustive or mutually exclusive in terms of representing the range of relationships that exist in human sexuality. Nonetheless, the social divisions between those who are deemed heterosexual and those who are not does affect the allocation of societal resources—particularly in the institutions of politics, economy, family, and religion, just to name a few. These are the inequalities we focus on in this chapter.

SEXUAL ORIENTATION INEQUALITIES, MINORITY-GROUP STATUS, AND IDENTITY

As with any minority group, classification as nonheterosexual brings stigma and marginalization, handicaps that people generally try to avoid if they are able. This threat of stigma can complicate the relationship between sexual identity and actual behavior because people may be reluctant to publically take on the sexual identity that fits their behavior or emotions, in an effort to avoid sanctions.

Sexual identity refers to the way people think about themselves sexually.

To illustrate, recall the cases of Mary Farrell and Hector Gonzalez, presented in Chapter 1. Mary identifies as a lesbian and is effectively married to another woman but is not fully "out" in her role as schoolteacher. Hector is (or perhaps was) bisexual, a sexual orientation he has shared with his wife but not his parents. Mary and Hector are comfortable with who they are sexually but choose to be discreet about sharing the details of their sexual identities with everyone in their lives, much as an African American who is passing for white (or a member of the Burakumin who is living in the larger society; see Chapter 9) would be circumspect about revealing all personal information.

Research on sexual behavior and desires, undertaken by Alfred Kinsey and his colleagues as early as the 1940s, revealed that nearly 40% of the population admitted to experiencing some kind of same-sex desire and/or behavior, and this estimate has been replicated fairly consistently in subsequent studies (Ellis, Burke, & Ames, 1987; Kinsey, 1948). This suggests that nonheterosexual behaviors and desires are quite common and that many people are avoiding the stigma that full sexual disclosure might bring.

In recognition of the complicated and uncertain relationships between sexual orientation, sexual identity, and actual behavior, many scholars of sexuality have argued that sexual orientation should be regarded as a continuum rather than a series of discrete categories. Such a schema would more accurately describe the variety of sexualities and behaviors that exist in the population. However, the gay/straight dichotomy has become an influential dimension of societal stratification of resources, both cultural and institutional, that greatly influences individual's association with particular identities. We will, as a matter of convenience, use it throughout this chapter.

In Chapter 11, we discussed how some women of color opted for the term *womanist* rather than *feminist*. They argued that the simple "male/female" dichotomy was inadequate because it did not account for the myriad, crucial differences— by race, age, class, region, and so forth—between the genders. In the same fashion, we cannot simply discuss gays, lesbians, and bisexuals but must recognize the intersections with other social categories. For example, research has found that people of color who practice same-sex behavior are more reluctant to identify with the terms *gay* and *lesbian* than are whites (Pathela et al., 2006; Wolitski, Jones, Wasserman, & Smith, 2006). People of color have invented labels such as "same-gender loving," "in the life," and "on the down low" to refer to their various sexual identities and practices, in part because taking on yet another socially stigmatized identity when they are already racial minorities seems too daunting (Boykin, 2006).

VISIBILITY AND IDENTITY: GENDER TRAITS AND SEXUAL ORIENTATION

We should note some of the similarities and differences between the social visibility of members of the LGB minority and those of other groups we have considered. It may appear that gays and lesbians have more options for remaining invisible and avoiding the sanctions and limitations associated with minority-group status, unlike people of color, who typically have no control over their social visibility.

As we have discussed, however, many multiracial persons are assumed to be one race but are another or a mix of others. Likewise, some people may attempt to conceal their nonheterosexuality but are unable to do so, perhaps due to certain mannerisms that are culturally assumed to be associated with being gay or lesbian.

It is important to note the connection here between gender and sexual orientation. In many cultures, men who enact what is considered to be feminine behavior are assumed to have a gay sexual orientation, and, likewise, "masculine" behavior in a woman might suggest that she is a lesbian. Indeed, some LGB persons may reveal their sexual orientation by exhibiting such culturally embedded behaviors, sometimes even unconsciously or without meaning to do so. However, there is no one-to-one correspondence between gender-opposite behavior and sexual orientation. This is one reason why we chose to discuss transgender persons in our chapter on gender (Chapter 11), since they can be of any sexual orientation.

Many LGB men and women exhibit gender traits that are similar to those conventionally associated with their biological sex. A popular sitcom from the late 1990s/early 2000s called *Will and Grace* provides a token example of this sexual orientation/gendered behavior distinction. A male character named Jack exhibits more feminine behavior than his more masculine friend Will, yet both of them share a gay sexual orientation (although they are not a couple). Jack may provide an example of a person who is unable to conceal his sexual orientation no matter how hard he tries. It is easier for Will to choose to live "in the closet" due to his gender-conforming behavior in other areas of his life besides dating and relationships. Gender roles are as diverse within the LGB population as within the "straight" population.

Assumptions are often made about a person's sexual orientation based on his or her conformity or lack thereof to gender-appropriate behavior for that culture. Indeed, some victims of "antigay" hate crimes have been targeted because of what the assailant(s) perceived as gender-nonconforming behavior, even when the victim(s) were actually heterosexual (Mooney, Knox, & Schacht, 2010). Thus, a minority sexual-orientation status may be conferred on a person by society whether or not it is accurate; however, this happens less frequently than the assumption that persons are heterosexual, due to heterosexuality being the dominant status in society.

HISTORY AND BACKGROUND OF SAME-SEX RELATIONSHIPS

Same-sex relations have existed throughout time, but a distinct social identity based on sexual orientation—and even the word

NARRATIVE PORTRAIT

Black or Gay?

Keith Boykin, author of *One More River to Cross: Black and Gay in America.*

Keith Boykin is a best-selling author, columnist, TV commentator, political activist, crusader for gay rights, and lawyer. Over the course of his very active life, he has served as a media consultant in the Clinton White House, a professor of political science, and the cofounder and president of the National Black Justice Coalition, an organization committed to fighting racism and homophobia. Boykin "came out" when he was in law school, and in this passage he describes his relationships with African Americans, the gay community, and his own family.

ONE MORE RIVER TO CROSS

Keith Boykin

I have often been asked by blacks and gays alike which group I most closely identify with. I have been black for far longer than I have known I am gay, so I think I understand African-American culture better than gay culture. In addition, the gay community...has long been dominated by white men, so as a black person I have felt ostracized by that world. But at the same time, I do not believe many in the black community fully understand or accept me either. As a result, I've spent a great deal of my time and energy as an

openly gay black man shuttling back and forth between my two identities.

It took time to learn about the dark realities of both communities. I had felt so liberated when I first came out that I began to immerse myself in the so-called gay lifestyle, slowly, unknowingly, and destructively absorbing characteristics of a culture that devalued me because of my color. I later learned how white gays had excluded African Americans, denying them entry into nightclubs, ignoring their contributions to the gay political movement, and reinforcing straight society's stereotypes and prejudices.

At the same time, the black community made my life difficult as well. When I lived in the closet, I suffered the oppression of living a lie, and once I came out, I faced a different prejudice, one based on fear and dislike. The more out I was, the more at risk I became. At first, some "straight" black men I knew observed me from afar with both curiosity and trepidation, as though they were examining a dangerous animal in the jungle. Others seemed afraid even to talk to me, apparently fearing that they, too, would be labeled gay by their association with me. When I hung out with certain black male classmates in law school, some would almost immediately begin talking about their girlfriends, as if to let me know they were straight. Being out, I learned, sometimes meant being marginalized by one's own communities....

Ultimately, it was the black lesbian and gay community that reaffirmed my existence...and taught me to love myself as a mirror image of these others. Within this group, I felt I could be a whole person rather than just a gay man or just a black man. I felt the comfort of unqualified love and acceptance that I had never really felt in other communities. Many of the black lesbians and gay men I met came from backgrounds different from my own. We had different jobs, interests, and desires. Yet I did not feel ostracized for not being "black enough" or for not being "gay enough."...

Years of hiding my sexual identity from myself and others had diminished my sense of self-worth. But in the black gay community I found a support group, if not a family, willing to love me and accept my love for them regardless of our differences....On the one hand, I wanted to return home to my family and to the black community; but on the other hand, I was unsure whether I would be welcomed by either once they learned who I really was. I followed the road in my heart, and I started on my way home.

I soon learned that the assumptions I had made were not always accurate. By assuming my family would react negatively to my homosexuality, I made this reality somewhat self-fulfilling. By dodging and tiptoeing around the issue, I thought I could protect both myself and them from...painful and bitter discussions....Instead, by not challenging anyone to confront the reality of my identity and my place in the family, I only made it harder for us all. But as I began to come out to family members, I learned to do something I had never been able to do before—to love. I learned to love myself enough so that I could open up and love other people, and I learned to love my family enough to be honest with them in spite of the consequences.

SOURCE: Boykin (1997, pp. 26–28).

Questions to Consider

1. Compare Boykin's experiences with Leslie Feinberg's from Chapter 11 and with Carla's and Tim Wise's from Chapter 1. What similarities and differences can you find in these memoirs? Who is the least uncertain about who they are? Who is the most? Why?

2. How do Boykin's experiences and thoughts illustrate the importance of the intersectionality perspective? How would his story change if he were uneducated? Female? Hispanic? Why?

---

homosexual—did not emerge until the latter part of the 19th century (Pincus, 2011). In reviewing the history of same-sex relations, it becomes clear that a crucial determining factor of how such relationships are conceptualized—and an interesting connection with the preceding chapter on gender—is

society's relative degree of openness toward women's economic independence. A society's views toward same-sex relations are deeply influenced by whether women are seen as fully intelligent and capable human beings and whether they are able to support themselves without male companionship.

ANCIENT GREECE

In ancient Greece, relations between persons of the same sex were typically just one of many ways of exploring sexual attraction. There were norms for the socially appropriate ways an older male could mentor a young person, and these norms varied by social class and the gender of the protégé. Particularly among the elite, it was acceptable for a young man to be "wooed" by an older man, and this could even be a sign of prestige if the man interested was of high social standing (Hubbard, 2003).

Women were perceived as intellectually inferior, and men were socialized to expect little more than idle conversation with them. Rather, they were encouraged to take up strong emotional–physical bonds with other men, with whom they could explore all the great questions of the world. When they courted women, it was primarily for securing a wife with whom they would procreate. As seems to be the case across many times and social spaces, a man was expected to choose a younger woman for these purposes.

Ancient Greece was a patriarchal society, where men made the rules and women's humanity was not fully acknowledged or respected. However, the writings of the poet Sappho indicate that some erotic yearnings also existed between women. Sappho grew up on the Greek island of Lesbos and

©iStockphoto.com/GeorgiosArt

A representation of Sappho, the Greek poet whose residence on the isle of Lesbos may be the origin of the term "lesbian."

ran a school for girls there. In fact, when the word *lesbian* was coined much later, it was said to emerge from Sappho's Lesbos heritage (Sappho & Lombardo, 2002).

As with most societies where women were marginal figures in political and public life, women in ancient Greece who desired an education pursued their studies in a sex-segregated environment, where they forged emotional connections with one another through learning and sharing their intellectual curiosity, not unlike the relationships among educated men described by Plato. However, the fact that Sappho's poetry describes erotic feelings for women as well as for men underscores the conclusion drawn by most scholars of male–male relations in ancient Greece: Same-sex relations did not stand out as deviant and existed alongside a range of other forms of sexual and romantic expression.

By today's standards, one might observe the intimate relations of ancient Greece and categorize them as "bisexual"; however, doing so would misinterpret history and apply a modern concept that does not really fit the social structure and norms of that period (Halperin, 1989). Because sexual behavior is governed by both biological drives and social constraints, it would be more accurate to say that certain forms of same-sex relations were approved and encouraged, particularly when they fostered political and intellectual connections, because they did not pose a threat to procreation. As one translator of Sappho's poetry noted, the poet seemed to have loved men, women, and music, in equal measure (Sappho & Carson, 2003).

The writings that have survived from ancient times frame various aspects of life with passionate language of longing and desire, heartache and heartbreak, and the genders of the various protagonists and antagonists in the stories are not always of central concern. However, once social ideologies—religious, political, and otherwise—began to confine people's relationships in particular ways, a quite different framing of what forms of sexuality were considered appropriate began to appear. People's behaviors adapted accordingly.

SEPARATE SPHERES: AGRARIAN TO INDUSTRIAL SOCIETY

As we have seen, an agrarian society demands high levels of fertility and larger families to supply the labor power required to meet the demands of a preindustrial technology. In agrarian societies, sexual behaviors were exclusively channeled to the marital unit. The agrarian Victorian, Puritan, and colonial societies all featured highly restrictive social norms regarding sexuality. Whether it was adultery with an opposite-sex partner or intimate relations with a same-sex partner, all were forbidden in equal measure as a sin and a crime (D'Emilio, 1998).

Within these rigid boundaries, same-sex intimacy continued. In Victorian England, where women were almost entirely isolated from men, women created intimate bonds and desires for other women, sometimes even consummated in what they referred to as "marriage" to each other (Marcus, 2007).

By the late 19th century, many of the women involved in the suffrage movement and those who had the economic means to pursue a profession were realizing they could not do the work they found most meaningful while fulfilling the duties of a "wife." Some of these women—negatively labeled as "spinsters" by society—found emotional and sometimes physical companionship with other women. The founding of several elite women's colleges (Vassar, Smith, Wellesley, and Bryn Mawr) in the late 1800s facilitated these connections among independent-minded women. Some of these affluent women even formed households that were sometimes referred to as "Boston marriages." Records left behind by the participants in these relationships demonstrate that emotional bonds definitely existed, though the exact nature of the sexual relations in these households cannot always be determined (Faderman, 1991).

Late-19th-century developments in same-sex relations can also be tied to the emergence of urbanization, industrialization, and capitalism. Rigid norms regarding sexuality and gender relations still ruled society, but the decline of the agrarian family and the movement of the population from rural villages to urban areas allowed people—mainly men but women as well—some latitude in developing their personal and sexual identities. With the shift from labor-intensive agrarian technology to capital-intensive industrial technology, a man did not need a house full of farmhand children to survive economically.

These forces combined in many cities to create a distinctly "gay" subculture among men—primarily in New York, San Francisco, and Washington, D.C. By the 1920s, there were certain urban areas where men could find each other for intimate relations (D'Emilio, 1998). Not all women were elite enough to fashion themselves an educated "Boston marriage," but there are records of working-class women who lived in "marriages" with each other—one disguised as a man to find work in the city (D'Emilio, 1998; Faderman, 1991). Key figures of the Harlem Renaissance have left behind writings to attest to the fact that this urban center included same-sex relations among people of color as well (Schwarz, 2012).

These men and women, increasingly labeled "homosexual" by their society, knew they were engaging in behavior that bucked conventional norms. The aforementioned Puritanical church law, as well as state law, labeled their behavior sinful, criminalized it, and relegated homosexuals to the fringes of "respectable" society—or well beyond those fringes. At the same time, science and medicine were coming to see homosexuality as a disease. Bolstered by the shared rejection of same-sex relations across institutions, the state and law enforcement authorities repressed, censored, and arrested persons who engaged in homosexual behavior or who advocated for understanding and tolerance. The result was that the "gay community" remained largely invisible, underground, and covert.

FROM WORLD WAR II AND THE McCARTHY ERA TO CIVIL RIGHTS

World War II was a watershed for nonheterosexual minority groups, as it was for so many others. The war increased opportunities for many types of same-sex relations. With men away at war and women encouraged by the political propaganda of the day to do their patriotic duty and enter the workplace en masse, same-sex associations—some intimate and sexual—practically became the rule rather than the exception. Even people who did not live in larger cities began to be exposed to opportunities for nonheterosexual relations. For nonheterosexuals who had previously lived quietly, privately tormented by their own desires, this period provided them the possibility of no longer feeling alone with their secret.

Yet repression loomed large, both during the war and into the following years. At best, psychoanalysts strove to "cure" those deemed "homosexual" of their "illness"; at worst, the political "witch hunts" of the 1940s and 1950s, led by U.S. Senator Joe McCarthy, pulled them from their jobs and threw them in jail. Although McCarthy is best remembered for targeting suspected communists, close to 5,000 Americans were dismissed from military and civilian positions between 1947 and 1950 due to their alleged sexual orientation (Faderman, 1991).

Bars that were undercover gay/lesbian gathering places continued to be subjected to police raids and harassment in the 1940s and 1950s. Because the people found at these bars were widely framed as "sexual perverts" and deviants, there was not much societal concern for the police abuses and injustices that took place during and after these raids. Both men and women were routinely sexually abused by officers, and their word was often disregarded in courts of law. There was little legal recourse for those targeted by these raids (D'Emilio, 1998; Faderman, 1991).

A political consciousness did begin to form in the gay community at this time, and some key protest organizations were founded as people started to speak out publically against these injustices. However, severe social stigmas were still attached to LGB persons, and no legal protections existed in any state to shield those living with same-sex partners from being fired from their jobs or even jailed for their private activities. Thus, those who dared to be "out" often faced severe repercussions. Even when people were beaten and killed for their sexual orientation, the justice system remained unsympathetic to those they considered "perverts" and "outcasts" (D'Emilio, 1998). In fact, not until after the turn of the present century would same-sex behavior even in private be federally decriminalized.

THE 1960S AND BEYOND: GROWING VISIBILITY, BACKLASH, AND HIV/AIDS

Intolerance of LGBs began to soften in the latter half of the 20th century, as did other forms of prejudice and racism (see Chapter 3). One major milestone occurred in 1973 when the American Psychiatric Association removed homosexuality from its list of mental illnesses, where it had been for nearly a century (Bayer, 1987). This decision helped reduce the stigma attached to gays and lesbians, and removed one of the primary rationales for their exclusion and marginalization in the larger society.

Several pioneering sociological works, including Howard Becker's *Outsiders* (1963) and Erving Goffman's *Stigma* (1963), also helped reduce prejudice against gays and lesbians by presenting compelling arguments about the crucial role of social construction in deciding what is deviant and what is not. These works encouraged open conversations about various forms of human behavior and relationships previously considered taboo in the larger society.

Furthermore, the fact that sexual activity between adults was not always aimed at procreation was made more public by Supreme Court decisions such as *Griswold v. Connecticut* (1965), which made it legal for married couples to obtain contraception, and *Eisenstadt v. Baird* (1972), which made contraception available to unmarried persons (Dudley, 2006).

Developments such as these challenged the traditional societal consensus regarding gays and lesbians just as the civil rights movements began to raise cultural awareness about injustice against minorities. Several states began to decriminalize same-sex behavior in the 1970s (D'Emilio, 1998), and LGB people became more socially visible across a range of cultural and institutional spaces.

This increasing tolerance was hardly unanimous, however. A movement of political and religious conservatism often called the Religious Right rose to prominence and influence in the 1980s. Led by men such as Jerry Falwell, a Baptist preacher and the founder of Liberty University, and Pat Robertson, chair of the Christian Broadcasting Network, this movement targeted gay and lesbian behavior as one of many social ills to which it was morally opposed. There were also legal setbacks. In 1986, for example, the U.S. Supreme Court, in the case of *Bowers v. Hardwick*, upheld a Georgia state law that criminalized private, consensual same-sex behavior, a victory for traditional morality and a setback for gays and lesbians (Carpenter, 2012). Thus, it seemed the gains of the 1960s and 1970s threatened to be reversed, and echoes of the pariah and "pervert" stigmatization of the McCarthy era returned to prominence.

The most important development in the antigay backlash of the 1980s, on many levels, was the HIV/AIDS epidemic. The disease became associated in the public consciousness with gay men, despite the fact that many types of people carried and spread the virus, and transmitted it in many other ways besides through intimate relations.

Quilts memorialize victims of the AIDS epidemic.

National Institutes of Health

The stark losses of the AIDS-related epidemic provoked concern in the hearts of not only LGB persons but others as well. This sympathetic concern was strengthened by the case of Ryan White, a young boy who had hemophilia and passed away after contracting HIV/AIDS through a blood transfusion, and by Elizabeth Taylor's publically expressed support for victims of the disease, one of whom was her good friend and fellow actor Rock Hudson. These were just two of many voices that worked in the 1980s to raise national and global awareness about AIDS.

In the view of many, the social stigma associated with HIV/AIDS hampered the medical community's ability to develop public health solutions. In response, playwright Larry Kramer founded the organization ACT UP (AIDS Coalition to Unleash Power) in New York City in 1987 (U.S. Department of Health and Human Services, 2011). As the organization's name suggests, there was an urgency among both LGB persons and their allies to take to the streets to raise public awareness about the disease. Thus, the health crisis renewed the social stigma attached to gays and lesbians but also brought together those concerned about injustice against LGB persons.

COMING OUT

Increasing AIDS awareness, growing visibility of the LGB minority, and increasing tolerance in the larger community led many people, both famous and ordinary, to publically reveal their sexual orientation during the last decades of the 20th century. Note that **"coming out"** refers only to nonheterosexuals: The term highlights both the privileged status of heterosexuality and the relative invisibility of sexual orientation as a social status and dimension of inequality. Just as whiteness is often assumed to be the unspoken norm, so, too, is heterosexuality in most cultures around the world. Essentially, the act of coming out transforms an invisible minority status into a visible one.

The first National March on Washington for Gay and Lesbian Rights was held on October 11, 1987. In commemoration of

---

Coming out refers to the act of a nonheterosexual person publically disclosing his or her sexual identity.

The first National march on Washington for gay and lesbian rights, 1987.

that date, October 11 was chosen to celebrate the first National Coming Out Day a year later. By 1990, Coming Out Day was recognized in all 50 states (Human Rights Campaign, 2013).

One of the most important causes addressed by the organizers of the national coming out campaign was civil rights protection for gays and lesbians. At this time, hardly any U.S. state or city included sexual orientation in its civil rights laws, making employment discrimination against LGB persons perfectly legal. The organizers thought that the courage required to "come out," and the risks incurred by those who did, would attract allies, make LGB people more visible, and build momentum for the expansion of civil rights law to include this "new" minority.

This strategy is supported by research—consistent with the contact hypothesis introduced in Chapter 3—that shows one of the strongest predictors of support for gay rights is a personal relationship with someone who is gay or lesbian (Hinrichs & Rosenberg, 2002). Although the LGB population is still a small minority, it is probable that many people are acquainted with someone who is LGB, even though they may not be aware of it (Leff, 2011; Pincus, 2011). The logic of National Coming Out Day is to increase visibility and cause more people to recognize their connections to LGB people. The more widespread this recognition, the greater the support for civil rights protection.

RECENT DEVELOPMENTS

LGB visibility is much greater today than ever before in U.S. history, and because of the social movement activity we will outline in the next section, this group has experienced many political, legal, and cultural advancements. Due to these gains, more LGB persons feel comfortable coming out. Indeed, contemporary media portrayals, along with the improved political climate, seem to be giving Americans the impression that there are many more gay and lesbian people than there actually are. Respondents to a Gallup poll estimated that the group is as large as 25% of the total U.S. population (Franke-Ruta, 2012).

(Other surveys show that Americans also overestimate the proportion of the population that consists of African Americans and other people of color).

Of course, the levels of acceptance and tolerance vary markedly from region to region and between more rural and more metropolitan areas. This variation was demonstrated by an innovative research project conducted by Harvard economist Seth Stephens-Davidowitz (2013), based on a combination of Facebook, Google, and other data. The researcher looked at both rural and urban areas to see if gay men were "public" (e.g., stated their sexual orientation on their Facebook profiles) or "private" (e.g., searched the Internet for gay porn) and found that the key variable was residence in a "tolerant" state, or a state that supported gay marriage initiatives. Rhode Island was rated as the most tolerant (joined by several other northeastern and western states), and Mississippi (along with all other southern states except Florida) was the least tolerant. The findings suggest that many rural and southern Americans (and others) continue to remain in the closet due to fear of social stigma and other potential repercussions (Stephens-Davidowitz, 2013).

Urban centers in the United States and other Western nations have been the most visible embodiments of LGB culture in recent times, but such research reminds us that LGB persons are everywhere and that their lives can be especially difficult in areas where "the closet" is the norm. As of late 2013, 16 nations (mainly European) had legalized gay marriage (Masci, Sciupac, & Lipka, 2013). At the same time, in some nations today, sex between two persons of the same sex is punishable by life in prison or even death (Kordunsky, 2013).

A recent study of LGB life in rural America shows that members of the nonheterosexual minority deal with their surrounding communities in a variety of ways (Johnson, 2013). While some LGB persons—such as Evelyn and Hope, whose vignette opened this chapter—are fighting to have their families recognized legally, others are still struggling simply to live without fear of attack by fellow citizens. Everywhere, LGB activists and their allies continue to seek equal rights, both for themselves and for those who are unable to come out of the closet.

QUESTIONS FOR REFLECTION

1. Since same-sex relations have existed throughout human history, why was the term *homosexuality* coined only relatively recently?

2. What ideologies create societal resistance to homosexuality, and how have science and religion played a role? In what ways were these ideologies similar to and different from those that stigmatized people of color?

3. What factors converged to lessen social stigma against LGB persons over time, and where is such lessening most and least evident?

GAY LIBERATION MOVEMENTS

In this section, we review the various movements for gay liberation in the United States over the past century. There have been three distinct phases in these movements, and we use the Stonewall Rebellion of 1969—a direct and violent reaction to the police harassment of gay and lesbian bar patrons—as the benchmark to separate the first two. The third phase, which we date from the turn of the present century, encompasses many political achievements for gay rights both in the United States and worldwide.

HOMOPHILE ORGANIZATIONS (PRE-STONEWALL)

We already mentioned the shift to an urban-industrial economy that, by the 1920s, created social spaces in which a distinct gay community could develop. In turn, these communities allowed for the growth of a **collective identity,** or a shared understanding of one's place in the social order, which is an important prerequisite for the formation of social movement organizations. With the rise of an urban gay culture, gays and lesbians became increasingly cognizant of the need to organize for social change. Knowing they were a small numerical minority, they understood that they would need to secure allies to reach their goals.

Spurred by the desire to challenge the McCarthy-era homosexual witch hunt, the Mattachine Society first organized in 1951 in Los Angeles. This organization took its name from the masked mythological creatures of medieval times that were rumored to be homosexual. The Mattachine Society was founded by men who wanted to educate the public about gay men and convince society that they were just as deserving of the right to live and work without fear of harassment as were other Americans.

The Mattachine Society engaged with allies in the medical community, particularly sexuality researchers associated with Kinsey who were beginning to uncover the range of sexual desires present in the "normal" human psyche. Eventually, they would become known as part of the "homophile" movement. They engaged in public service to their community with the hopes of counteracting the caricature of them in the wider society that branded them as deviant and disposable (D'Emilio, 1998).

Although the Mattachine Society aspired to advocate for all, regardless of gender, its membership was mainly men. Lesbians also began to organize for political and protest activity but responded to different social situations. For example, there was a social class divide between the elite educated women and the working-class lesbians who gathered in bars, often with one partner being a "butch"—dressing in men's clothing and passing as male—and the other a "femme." Middle- and upper-class lesbians of the day tended to look down on the lesbian working-class bar culture and instead sought to create an alternative gathering space for women similar to the social clubs where married women interacted and engaged in community service. Out of this desire, the Daughters of Bilitis formed in 1955 in San Francisco, just a few short years after the Mattachine Society (D'Emilio, 1998; Faderman, 1991).

The primary aim of both the Mattachine Society and the Daughters of Bilitis was assimilation into the wider society, and they strove to counteract the severe repression of the 1950s. Chapters of both organizations sprung up in several major cities across the country, connected by newsletters, but concerns for safety and retribution prevented the organizations from pursuing mass membership.

Then, the turbulent 1960s brought a change in tactics. Inspired by civil rights organizations such as the Student Nonviolent Coordinating Committee and Congress of Racial Equality, as well as feminist groups such as the National Organization for Women, new leadership challenged homophile organizations to be less "genteel" and more confrontational, more demanding of basic rights and respect.

This new direction eventually culminated in the Stonewall Rebellion, a spontaneous and violent reaction to a 1969 police raid on the Stonewall Inn, a bar in Greenwich Village, New York City. As we have noted, such raids were common in cities across the nation, but this time the gay community fought back. A crowd gathered and fought the police in the streets of Greenwich Village, and hostilities continued, sporadically, for several nights thereafter. The gay community had sent a message: It would no longer tolerate police harassment and mistreatment. The event has been compared to France's Bastille Day and the fall of the Berlin Wall, in terms of its significance for the gay rights movement (Carter, 2005; D'Emilio, 1998).

Perhaps most interesting about the Stonewall Rebellion is that those responsible represented a distinct shift from the socioeconomic profile of the homophile organizations that preceded it. The clientele at the Stonewall Inn, particularly those who fought back against the police, included mostly blacks, Latinos, and the working class.

The participants also did not fit the assimilationist profile that the homophile organizations strove to promote—educated, successful, and "just like heterosexuals" in every way but choice of partner. Rather, they were drag queens and other types that sought to accentuate their differences from the mainstream (Duberman, 1994). This is one of many reasons why the Stonewall Rebellion is considered a turning point for the movement.

Collective identity is the shared understanding of one's place in society.

The Stonewall Rebellion, 1969.

GAY LIBERATION MOVEMENT (POST-STONEWALL)

The final three decades of the 20th century saw some progress toward inclusion and equal rights, but the movement was hardly linear. After Stonewall, the homophile organizations faded into the background, giving way to gay rights groups or coalitions. By the time an anniversary march honoring the Stonewall Rebellion took place in 1970 (eventually becoming an annual gay pride parade), two groups—the Gay Liberation Front and the Gay Activist Alliance—had formed. These groups often used direct-action tactics to confront politicians or institutions that refused to serve gay people (D'Emilio, 1998).

The 1970s saw the development of an array of major gay organizations—some cultural, others more political. The cultural organizations included gay/feminist bookstores, gay choruses, and gay or gay-friendly churches—specifically, the Metropolitan Community Church, United Church of Christ, and Unitarian Universalists. The latter two churches existed well before the 1970s but passed gay-inclusive resolutions and began to hire openly gay ministers. Periodical publications such as *The Empty Closet, The Advocate, The Lesbian Connection,* and *Journal of Homosexuality* all began circulation in the 1970s and are still in print today. Bisexual-focused organizations also appeared for the first time starting in this decade. The more community building that occurred, the more political organizing was possible (Eaklor, 2008).

Several political milestones were reached in the 1970s: an openly lesbian Massachusetts House representative, another on the Ann Arbor City Council, and an openly gay city supervisor in San Francisco named Harvey Milk, famously portrayed by Sean Penn in the 2008 film. The same year Milk was elected (1977), the White House held its first meeting with lesbian and gay leaders, and the Gay Rights National Lobby was founded in 1978 (Eaklor, 2008).

This greater visibility resulted in stronger alliances beyond the LGB community. For example, a group called Parents and Friends of Lesbians and Gays was started in New York City by the mother of a gay man and continues to have many chapters across the country—both urban and rural (Bernstein, 2008). Several municipalities and states began rescinding their antisodomy laws and adding sexual orientation to their anti-discrimination ordinances (Eaklor, 2008). The 1970s were the first decade of notable political and legal advancements in LGB equality.

If the 1970s were a decade of action, the 1980s were a time of reaction, mostly to the efforts, led by politically and religiously conservative elements, to resist the gay liberation movement. For example, ACT UP and National Coming Out Day were formed in resistance to the Supreme Court decision mentioned previously that upheld state antisodomy laws.

By the early 1990s, the momentum of the movement was reinvigorated. Embracing an identity outside of the mainstream but also committed to equal rights, groups such as Queer Nation and Lesbian Avengers formed, with an emphasis on lack of conformity to the status quo. These groups began to thrive, while at the same time, more politically centered organizations, such as the Human Rights Campaign, picked up the fight to become more involved with the political process. In 1992, the Human Rights Campaign endorsed its first presidential candidate, Democrat Bill Clinton (Eaklor, 2008).

During the Clinton era of the 1990s, the gay rights movement attracted many allies among heterosexuals. Just as the civil rights movement enlisted support from white antiracists, the gay liberation movement also worked to gain heterosexual allies. From Clinton's campaign promise to end the ban on gays in the military (with Democratic Party support) to MTV's show *The Real World* featuring an openly gay cast member, the early 1990s clearly thrust LGB persons into the cultural and political mainstream. In the late 1990s, a variety of media events, including the coming out of Ellen DeGeneres in 1997, continued this pattern (Eaklor, 2008).

Allies are sometimes also activated in times of crisis, as with AIDS in the 1980s. In the 1990s, antigay hate crimes drew more media attention and outraged many people, regardless of their political and religious orientations. When gay (and HIV-positive) Wyoming college student Matthew Shepard was beaten to death in 1998, many allies—particularly among adolescents and college students—took note. Although the first gay–straight alliance had formed nearly a decade before, the number of youth gay–straight alliances (at both the university and high school levels) soared after Shepard's death (Miceli, 2005). Youth have been consistently more supportive of gay rights (Pew Research Center, 2013b), a pattern we also see with prejudice toward other types of minority groups (von Hippel, Silver, & Lynch, 2000). Yet youth are rarely in a position to shape public policy. Gay–straight alliances often faced resistance from parents, school administrators, and community members (Miceli, 2005).

While support for gay rights was gaining ground among the younger generation at the end of the 20th century, the baby-boom generation—which made up most of the political elite—was not as receptive. President Clinton's initial promises regarding civil rights for gays ended up in political compromises that were in some cases worse than before he took office. For example, Clinton had pledged to allow gays to serve openly in the military, but the compromise policy—"Don't Ask, Don't Tell"—that began in 1993 eventually resulted in more than 13,000 discharges. A disproportionate number of those discharged due to sexual orientation were also racial minorities and women (O'Keefe, 2010). Many in positions of power were not ready for significant policy changes that would remove discrimination from LGB persons' lives.

In the 1990s, it seemed that every step forward for LGB rights was countered by a step back. On one hand, the Hawaii Supreme Court ruled (in *Baehr v. Miike*, 1996) that it was unconstitutional to exclude same-sex couples from the right to marry, and a host of European countries (e.g., Denmark, Norway, Sweden, and the Netherlands) began to offer domestic partner benefits.

On the other hand, reactions to these advances resulted in President Clinton signing the Defense of Marriage Act (DOMA) in 1996 (Eaklor, 2008). This law disallowed any federal recognition of same-sex marriages whatsoever and also upheld states' rights to refuse to recognize same-sex marriages performed in other states, even though no state recognized same-sex marriage at the time (Hawaii voters had overturned the 1996 ruling by constitutional amendment by 1998). Also in 1996, the Employment Non-Discrimination Act failed to pass, by a narrow 49–50 vote in the U.S. Senate (Eaklor, 2008). This law would have banned discrimination based on sexual orientation or sexual identity.

Although the progress was spotty, by the close of the 20th century, the struggle for LGB equality was irrevocably on the national and global radar, particularly in the Western industrialized world. In the new millennium, the gay liberation movement would focus increasingly on mobilizing its allies, in both likely and unlikely places: from Log Cabin Republicans—a gay rights organization formed in a political party not typically supportive of the movement—to Coretta Scott King (Martin Luther King Jr.'s widow), who publicly encouraged civil rights activists to join the gay liberation movement. By the end of the century, the allies that had been collected would lay the groundwork for the successes to come in the next decades.

LGBT AND QUEER POLITICS (NEW MILLENNIUM)

The new millennium is when the LGBT (lesbian, gay, bisexual, and transgender) movement began to reap the fruit of its labors from the prior decades. The youth who came of age in the 1990s, when mainstream pop culture opened significantly toward nonheterosexuals, had grown old enough to begin to exert some political influence, and the movement began to center its efforts on the state rather than federal level. Vermont became the first state to offer civil unions to same-sex couples in 2000, and Massachusetts became the first state to allow gay marriage in 2004, with New Hampshire, Vermont, Connecticut, Iowa, and Washington, D.C., following by the end of the decade (PBS, 2011). In the meantime, several nations that had already been granting civil unions and partnerships moved to full marriage equality: The Netherlands was the first (2001), followed by Belgium (2003), Spain and Canada (2005), South Africa (2006), Norway and Sweden (2009), and Portugal, Iceland, and Argentina (2010) (BBC News, 2013).

Marriage equality was not the only priority of the movement, however. Not every person in the LGBT community aspired to mimic heterosexual lifestyles, and many, in a variety of U.S. states and other nations, remained focused on very basic issues: the right not to be fired from their jobs or attacked, jailed, or even murdered because of their sexual orientation. The work of building a safe society, where the rights of LGBTs are truly protected across all institutions, continues—often at the local level and often with very small steps.

Victories for gay rights at the national level did begin to accrue, however. In 2003, for example, the U.S. Supreme Court, in the case of *Lawrence v. Texas*, overturned the 1986 ruling that upheld state antisodomy laws (Eaklor, 2008). Also, the election of President Barack Obama in 2008 set the stage to move beyond the Clinton presidency's compromises on gay rights.

For example, in a partial reversal of DOMA, Obama signed an act in 2009 that allowed same-sex partners of federal employees to receive some of the benefits routinely available to marital partners. In the same year, Obama signed the Matthew Shepard Act, which updated the 1969 federal hate crimes law to include gender expression, sexual identity, and disability. By the close of the decade, with the support of the Senate, Obama also repealed the Don't Ask, Don't Tell law that effectively excluded gays from the U.S. military (PBS, 2011). Upon his election for a second term, Obama also made history by being the first president to make mention of gay rights in an inaugural address, using "Selma, Seneca Falls, and Stonewall" to invoke black, women's, and gay liberation struggles, respectively (Walshe, 2013).

The new millennium brought more political and legal victories than ever before for LGBTs, but social movement organizations continued to raise awareness about many other issues that, although perhaps less central in the mainstream media, were still considered necessary to create full equality. As illustrated in our opening vignette about Hope and Evelyn, in the absence of marriage equality in a majority of states, laws against gay adoption threaten the stability of children already being raised in same-sex homes. Further, courts are still revoking custody from gay parents without consulting the plethora of social science evidence demonstrating no adverse effects (and even more positive effects) on children of same-sex parents (Pappas, 2012). And without full marriage equality, U.S. citizens with same-sex partners who are immigrants face barriers to solidifying their families. The work of the new millennium social movement continues on these and a variety of other family-formation legal issues.

THE ROLE OF YOUTH AND QUEER LIBERATION

As with the black civil rights movement, the feminist movement, and others, college students have often been the force propelling action in the gay liberation movement. While middle and high schools formed gay–straight alliances, LGBT and **queer** student groups organized at colleges and universities in the late 20th and early 21st century. The term *queer* is used in this context to represent an umbrella collection of people whose gender expression and/or sexual identity and practice do not fall in line with societal norms. While the "gay" rights movement typically brings to mind men attracted to men and/or women attracted to women, a "queer" movement is meant to bring to mind a wider range of possibilities. Indeed, organizing around the word *queer* can transform allies from supporters or cheerleaders to an actual part of the aggrieved/minority group.

Bisexual, transgender, and even some practicing heterosexual people may be more inclined to favor the "queer" label because they feel it is more inclusive of various forms of gender and/or sexual expression that fall outside the bounds of the traditional heterosexual norm. For example, a man who carries a purse, gets his nails done, dyes his hair, and wears earrings may proudly consider himself "queer" even though he identifies as a heterosexual and has always had female partners. A bisexual woman may consider herself queer to distance herself from lesbians who appear to be trying to look and act just like heterosexuals in their everyday lives or to emphasize her commonality with other lesbians despite the fact that she currently has a male partner. A female-to-male transgender person may still feel "queer" despite the fact that to the outside world, his choice of a female partner appears to make him a conforming heterosexual. The term *queer* can be deployed in many ways.

The practice of reclaiming words that were once used as derogatory slurs against them is a common practice of many minority groups, and LGBT people's use of the word *queer* falls in line with this pattern. As with other "reclaimed" slurs, not everyone in the minority group feels comfortable with embracing the term, as for some it may too strongly represent a painful history of oppression. Age, class, and education levels, among other experiences, are often related to a person's willingness to use the term *queer*. But even by using the acronym LGBT, as opposed to the "gay liberation" groups of a previous era, the newer movement indicated a historical transition.

And while youth are more supportive of gay rights than other groups are, there is still much danger in being young and gay in a heteronormative society. The widely publicized case of 18-year-old Rutgers student Tyler Clementi's suicide, after his roommate cyberbullied him about his sexual orientation, brought to light in 2010 a long-standing problem of antigay harassment among youth (Allen, 2010). Coming out is easier in some places than others, and some youth are kicked out of their homes when they come out to their parents, resulting in a disproportionate number of homeless youth being LGBT (Ray, 2006). Youth are more likely to attempt suicide if they are LGBT and even more likely if they are also nonwhite (Harrison-Quintana & Quach, 2013). Groups such as the National Gay and Lesbian Task Force, the Gay Lesbian Straight Education Network, and the It Gets Better Project continue to work to end chronic problems such as bullying, suicide, and homelessness among youth as the new millennium continues.

QUESTIONS FOR REFLECTION

1. What distinct connotations do the terms *homosexual*, *gay*, and *queer* suggest? What would you predict the goals of a social movement organization to be depending on which of the terms it used to label itself?

2. Before reading this text, what was your impression of the gay rights movement and what it has accomplished? How would you revise your impression after reading this brief history?

3. In what ways have race, class, gender, and geographic location shaped the gay rights movement?

RECENT TRENDS AND ISSUES

Social change tends to come in spurts. While the biggest waves of political and legal victories for women and African Americans happened in earlier decades, most positive change for LGB persons, particularly in Western industrialized nations, has been more recent. Several public policy issues for gay men and lesbians hang in the balance today. Two particularly volatile areas are the legal recognition of same-sex families and the integration of LGB service members into the U.S. armed forces. Here we cover recent developments in both of these areas, as well as a third issue particularly relevant to the intersectionality lens we have carried throughout this text—how race and racism impact LGB communities and their struggle for civil rights.

Queer refers to gender expressions and identities that do not conform to societal expectations.

SAME-SEX MARRIAGE

As our opening vignette about Hope and Evelyn demonstrates, without full marriage equality, same-sex couples will continue to be denied a number of privileges, regardless of the evidence they might possess to prove they are a family. As of the 2000 Census, more than 250,000 children in the United States were being raised by same-sex couples, and that number is expected to increase—with many of those families residing in states where marriage is not an option for them (James, 2011). Hundreds of rights and privileges come to a couple upon marriage in the United States—including parental rights to any child born to or adopted by the other partner, federal tax benefits, immigration privileges, and spousal immunity (not having to testify against one's partner in court), just to name a few. These rights are unavailable to same-sex couples (although, in some cases they may be able to file legal motions that approximate certain of these rights, but only if their particular state allows it), and this stark imbalance has motivated LGB activists to make marriage equality one of the movement's central goals.

Interestingly, the pathway that gay marriage has traveled resembles the road toward legalizing interracial marriage in the United States. Certain states were in the forefront of recognizing and affirming interracial marriage long before the U.S. Supreme Court struck down all state bans of interracial marriage in 1967 (*Loving v. Virginia*). When the Supreme Court ruled that interracial marriage bans were unconstitutional, 17 states (mostly southern) still forbade it (Monifa, 2008). However, several states had already removed their interracial marriage bans—some immediately after the Civil War ended and others following the 1948 desegregation of the military and the end of World War II. As of this writing, 18 states plus Washington, D.C., allow gay marriage, and the vast majority (13) of those states changed their laws after 2010 (National Gay and Lesbian Task Force, 2014). Thus, changes are happening at a rapid-fire pace, and we should not expect that pace to lessen.

The states that have approved gay marriage as of 2014 are not just those in the Northeast or just the more urban states. For example, Iowa, Minnesota, and Utah are all on the list. While in the late 20th century, one might have had to venture to a major urban area to find gay acceptance, now in the second decade of the 21st century, the majority of the population seems supportive. Gallup has been polling Americans since 1996 on whether or not they support gay marriage, and starting in 2011, those who approve have accounted for at least 50% of respondents each year (Jones, 2013). Although the U.S. Supreme Court has avoided a ruling as sweeping as *Loving v. Virginia*, which would make any state law banning same-sex marriage unconstitutional, in June of 2013 it ruled that DOMA must be struck down, resulting in the extension of federal benefits to any same-sex couple married in a state that allows it (Hurley, 2013).

The U.S. Supreme Court has been reluctant to take a more definitive position on gay marriage for both political and

Jeri Andrews and Amy Andrews display their marriage license in Seattle, December 2012.

religious/moral reasons. Chief Justice Roberts, appointed by Republican President George W. Bush, took great care in the case striking down DOMA to make clear that individual U.S. states had the right to define marriage as they saw fit (Hurley, 2013). The Republican Party platform still opposes same-sex marriage, and most major figures in the party adhere to this platform. Moreover, virtually all the fundraising and lobbying organizations allied with the Republican Party, especially those that have a religious base, oppose same-sex marriage. With the exception of the American Israel Public Affairs Committee, all other top religious lobbying groups—the U.S. Conference of Catholic Bishops, the Family Research Council, and the National Organization for Marriage—oppose gay marriage (Kaleem, 2011). Also, a sizable segment of the U.S. population, particularly the older and more religious portion, still opposes marriage equality.

However, it is important to note that many, especially younger, Republicans and religious Americans are supportive of marriage equality. Several prominent public figures known to be either religious or Republican (or both)—such as Marie Osmond, Colin Powell, Laura Bush, and Dick Cheney—have spoken out in favor of gay marriage, often because they have a family member who is gay or lesbian (Stolberg, 2013). Some Americans may confuse a legal marriage—through which tax, health insurance, and other benefits are secured—and a religious marriage, which is up to individual churches to grant or deny for their own reasons and not subject to interference by the state.

Several American churches were performing holy unions between same-sex couples long before such marriages were legal anywhere in the States, and they continue to do so today. United Church of Christ, Unitarian Universalists, and Metropolitan Community Church all perform such marriages nationwide, and most Reform Jewish synagogues and several Lutheran churches (a denomination that allows autonomy of individual congregations) will do so as well. Episcopalian churches are variable on this issue, and the Methodist Church is split in vigorous debate over the matter (Zoll, 2014). Even if the United States granted civil marriage to same-sex couples at the federal level, no church could be forced to perform such ceremonies, due to the separation of church and state. Yet sometimes there is confusion on this matter, causing concern for those who oppose marriage equality on moral or religious grounds.

Similar to the NAACP (National Association for the Advancement of Colored People) Legal Defense Fund's work to obtain civil rights for African Americans in the 20th century, U.S. organization Lambda Legal supports cases across the country that seek equality for LGB people in employment, health insurance, and other areas, including marriage. As of 2014, there were 47 different gay-marriage–related cases spanning 24 different states, and the organization was hopeful that at least one would finally make it to the highest court of the nation (Wolf, 2014). This is an area where groundbreaking rulings have been constant in the past decade, and one should not expect this movement to subside in the near future.

SEXUAL ORIENTATION IN THE U.S. MILITARY

President Harry Truman desegregated the military via executive order in 1948 but only after many years of back-and-forth compromise and pressure from the political/civil rights movement (Moskos & Butler, 1997). Similar maneuvering preceded the eventual repeal in 2010 of the Don't Ask, Don't Tell (DADT) policy that barred nonheterosexuals from the military.

With two ongoing wars (in Afghanistan and Iraq) in the early 2000s, U.S. military forces were strained, and there was even talk of reinstituting a draft. It was becoming more difficult to justify the removal of able-bodied service members, despite the concern over whether having openly gay members would fracture the cohesion of units. Indeed, similar concerns were raised when racial integration of the military was proposed, and in the 1940s, Gallup polls showed that the American public was about two thirds against such a change (Herek, Jobe, & Carney, 1996).

As more states began to allow same-sex marriage, couples with one partner in the military began seeking the same benefits as heterosexual couples. Moreover, several of the nations allied with the United States—including Great Britain, Canada, Australia, Israel, and the Netherlands—had integrated their military forces by 2010. These countries even discovered unanticipated benefits—what sociologists refer to as positive latent consequences—of this policy change. For example, Great Britain reported that the amount of unfilled positions in its military was cut in half, and retention rates improved because the gay members were less likely to leave the service to start families or have children (Shaughnessy, 2010). Although President Obama could have simply signed an executive order as Truman did in 1948, the bill went through Congress, getting both Senate and House approval in late 2010, and was signed into law by Obama in 2011 (Bumiller, 2011; Foley, 2010).

One of the advantages of a relatively authoritarian organization such as the military, with a clear chain of command, is that policies such as desegregation can take hold relatively quickly and without extensive protest. While both pro and con voices from within the military spoke out when the policy was being debated, all military leaders made clear that whatever became the law of the land, it would be their duty to enforce it. Although the Pentagon could not extend federal benefits to partners and families of gay service members until the U.S. Supreme Court repealed DOMA in 2013 (with the *U.S. v. Windsor* ruling), the repeal of DADT brought immediate change to the culture of the U.S. military, and by the anniversary of the repeal, there was little contention to report (Tungol, 2012).

The major areas of continued legal battles will be the overturning of dishonorable discharges issued under the DADT years (1993–2011) and the acquisition of veterans' benefits for families/partners of those discharged. A group called OutServe–SLDN (Servicemembers Legal Defense Network) provides legal assistance for such persons, as various cases/bills attempting to remove barriers to these rights continue to move through both the courts and Congress (Reilly, 2013; Terkel, 2011). It remains to be seen whether a glass ceiling for LGBT service members will persist in the highest ranks of the military, as it has done for other minorities (Smith, 2010). As we have seen, there is a difference between legal desegregation and the cultural and structural shifts to full integration at all levels of any organization.

RACE, RACISM, AND SEXUAL ORIENTATION

When California voters repealed same-sex marriage via a ballot initiative in 2008, the allegation was made that the record turnout of African American voters (due to Obama's presidential candidacy) was in part responsible for this antigay legal setback. Immediately after the vote, LGB activists and their allies gathered to protest the new law (Proposition 8), and black lesbian and gay protesters reported being called racial epithets during the march (Bates, 2008). This incident illustrates a microcosm of a larger and ongoing tension between African American and gay rights groups, despite the fact that both movements share much in common. Not all African Americans see gay liberation as connected with their own struggles against racism, and, conversely, some elements of the gay liberation movement have not been inclusive of racial minorities.

Some conservative religious African Americans have been outspoken about their disagreement with the parallels often drawn between equal rights for people of color and equal rights for LGB people; they contend that being black is not analogous to being gay. When President Obama changed his position to support same-sex marriage, a group of black pastors organized in protest (Merica, 2012). Due in part to media coverage of such events, public perception often holds that

A protest against Proposition 8 in California.

African Americans are just as, or even more, homophobic than whites. Yet, along with the majority of Americans, blacks have been steadily evolving as a whole in their views on this issue. An ABC–*Washington Post* poll demonstrated that by 2012, 59% of African Americans supported gay marriage, compared with only 41% in 2008 (James, 2014).

Many contend that framing African Americans as largely antigay is an unfair characterization of a diverse racial community. As early as 1989, black feminist writer bell hooks pointed out that there are certain forms of exaggerated expression among black communities—such as The Dozens, a game in which the participants exchange playful zingers against "your momma," among many other potential targets—that are meant to be taken in fun and not intended with the vitriol that a literal reading of them might suggest. Just as she argued that the "gangsta rap" of that era was no more misogynistic than the "high-culture" films being produced by whites, hooks also maintained that black public talk about gays was doing less harm than the antigay public policies put forth by the predominantly white political institution. And she also pointed out that, in practice, black communities were hardly ignorant of the vital presence of LGB members in their own local neighborhoods, whether or not they were always fully understood (hooks, 1999).

Studies have confirmed the complexity of African American views about homosexuality. In his review of several surveys and polling results over the late 20th and early 21st century, Gregory Lewis (2003) found a consistent trend: Controlling for education and religion, African Americans were no more disapproving of homosexuality than were whites. Regardless of race, religiosity tends to decrease approval and education tends to increase approval of homosexuality. To the extent that African Americans are less educated and more religious than whites as a whole, their tendency to disapprove of homosexuality can trend slightly higher. Interestingly, though, African Americans were more likely than whites to agree that LGB persons deserved legal protection from employment discrimination, regardless of whether or not they considered homosexuality

a sin. In other words, in theory, blacks might disagree slightly more with homosexuality, but in legal and political practice, they are more likely than whites to support public-policy measures for LGB rights (Lewis, 2003).

Indeed, virtually all well-known African American civil rights activists have spoken out in support of the gay liberation movement. Coretta Scott King, late widow of Martin Luther King Jr., spoke out in favor of same-sex marriage as early as 1998 (PBS, 2011). The NAACP in 2012 also issued a public statement supporting Obama's position on same-sex marriage, with Rev. Al Sharpton and other clergy also expressing agreement. And U.S. Attorney General Eric Holder has labeled the current movement for LGB rights as the next phase of the civil rights movement (Apuzzo, 2014). This framing extends the legal struggles for civil rights beyond who marries whom to encompass the equality of all persons before the law, in terms of employment, fair housing, and access to medical care and survivor benefits for one's dependents.

Yet, just as women of color resented racism in the feminist movement, so, too, have black gay and lesbian activists found that the gay liberation movement has not always included them, or understood the unique experiences of their communities. Indeed, some African American LGB people have found that the gay rights movement has "used" them for political support when necessary, yet not reciprocated when it was time to work on the concerns of people of color (Bates, 2008; Warren, 2011). Some LGB people of color feel more comfortable in coethnic communities, despite the stigma they may face there due to their sexual orientation, because they have been so badly hurt by racism in the LGB movement (Boykin, 2006).

Since both groups face prejudice and discrimination, some may have elevated expectations of LGB people, thinking they should be more open-minded than others regarding racism. The fact that interracial couples are actually more common in the gay community than in society at large only adds to this expectation (Jayson, 2012). However, research shows that racism can also be present even within close interracial relationships (Childs, 2005; Korgen, 2002; O'Brien & Korgen, 2007). Partners of color may feel "exoticized" and objectified in ways that are dehumanizing. And white partners may see their partner of color as an "exception" (e.g., "You're not like the rest of them") and still hold onto racial prejudices about the rest of their partner's group.

On a macro level, LGB persons of color—not unlike women of color in the feminist movement—can find their unique concerns overshadowed by a white-centered public policy agenda. To counteract this marginalization within the gay liberation movement, several national-level groups—such as the National Black Justice Coalition, founded in 2003, and Gay Men of African Descent, founded in 1986—exist in the United States. Although same-sex marriage may be the public policy campaign getting the most media attention, communities of color have for centuries found creative ways of family formation when the state would not recognize their relationships—such as "jumping the broom" as an indigenous way of recognizing black family ties during slavery. As such, when one visits the websites of LGBT organizations of color, one tends to find less of a focus on same-sex marriage and more of a focus on issues of physical health and safety, such as HIV/AIDS outreach and antibullying and suicide-prevention programs. Far from seeing an either/or question of "racial equality" versus "gay equality," LGBT persons of color in such organizations stress the importance of recognizing the interconnectedness of both types of minority statuses. However, this remains an ongoing struggle for those who refuse to recognize the relationship between the two, whether in blatant or more subtle ways.

QUESTIONS FOR REFLECTION

1. Which of the above three issues most directly impacts you—through your family and/or your local community? If you became a policymaker, which would you feel was the most urgent to address and why?

2. Do you feel that marriage equality—so often in the news—is the most important issue facing LGB people today? Why or why not? If not, which issue (including those not covered above) would you say warrants the most pressing attention in terms of LGB inequality?

3. What role has religion played in the above issues, as well as in the inequalities discussed in other chapters of this text? How has religion fueled continued discrimination? How has it supported movements toward equality?

HOMOPHOBIA AND HETEROSEXISM

As we have seen in previous chapters, prejudice and discrimination exist in many different forms, and the prejudice and discrimination directed at LGB persons is likewise multifaceted.

The term **homophobia** refers to the more attitudinal dimension: It literally means hatred or fear of gays and lesbians. Homophobia can be blatant and overt, but, like other forms of prejudice we have discussed, it can also be subtle and indirect.

Sometimes homophobia manifests itself in the fear of being mistaken as gay or lesbian. Take the case of Charles Butler, in prison for the hate crime of killing Billy Jack Gaither, a gay man. Butler claims that he likes gay people and has even hung out with them. But when Gaither allegedly propositioned Butler and his friend Steven Eric Mullins, the two felt that Gaither had crossed a line, insulted their heterosexual identity, and deserved to be beaten for it. One might expect perpetrators of antigay hate crimes to be filled with feelings of hate and rejection for all gay people; yet this case illustrates a more expansive definition of homophobia, which sociologist Michael S. Kimmel describes as "the fear that people might get the wrong idea about you" (Malis, 2000).

Some forms of homophobia spring from the inability to deal with one's secret desires and feelings of attraction toward members of the same sex, similar to the inability of highly authoritarian people to deal with their hostility toward their parents (see Chapter 3). People who feel uncomfortable with the idea that others of their sex may be romantically attracted to them may be homophobic and in denial of their own feelings.

Heterosexuality is the dominant ideology in U.S. society, and it can affect even LGB people, who are, after all, socialized into the same culture as are people with a heterosexual orientation. This is called **internalized homophobia,** and it occurs when persons who are attracted to members of the same sex are repulsed in various ways by their own attraction, consciously or subconsciously. In the most extreme cases, internalized homophobia may cause people with an LGB sexual orientation to carry out antigay hate crimes, but these feelings can also manifest themselves in more subtle ways, such as not wanting to be seen around other gay people or referring to oneself as a "very straight-acting gay," so as not to be associated with other LGB persons.

These feelings of rejection and even loathing for one's own group can be found in other groups as well, including women who think that men are inherently smarter or better equipped to be leaders and people of color who feel that whiteness is more desirable or attractive (see "Gender and Physical Acculturation: The Anglo Ideal" in Chapter 9). Minorities commonly experience feelings of rejection for their own group because they, too, are exposed to the dominant ideology, which marginalizes and denigrates their own experiences.

Research demonstrates that men are more likely to be homophobic than women (Herek, 1988). Additionally, homophobia tends to increase with age and decrease with education (Lewis, 2003). This suggests that homophobia is learned, like many (possibly all) other forms of prejudice, and can be unlearned, perhaps through education or more frequent equal-status contact situations.

In Chapter 1, we distinguished between the individual (micro) and group or societal (macro) levels of analysis (see Table 1.1). We also said that we would use *prejudice* to refer to individual thoughts and feelings and *ideological racism* to refer to similar phenomena at the macro level of analysis.

In this chapter, we can make an analogous distinction. Homophobia is a form of prejudice and refers to an individual's

---

Homophobia is prejudice directed at LGB persons.

Internalized homophobia refers to the repulsion some people feel in response to their own feelings of attraction to other members of their sex.

---

thoughts and feelings. At the group and societal level of analysis, we will use the term **cultural heterosexism** to refer to the ideology that upholds heterosexuality as the norm and confers societal privilege on heterosexual relationships.

Cultural heterosexism is maintained, in part, by the ways we socialize youngsters to expect heterosexuality in themselves as well as those around them. Adrienne Rich (1980) has referred to this practice as *compulsory heterosexuality*. We socialize young girls to look forward to the day when they will marry their Prince Charming, not necessarily due to homophobia but through an unquestioned adherence to custom. However, this creates a climate in which girls and women who may not be attracted to Prince Charming are made to feel out of place—or may not even realize they are attracted to other females, because they are socialized not to recognize that desire in themselves.

Cultural heterosexism is also encouraged in adults. It is present in water-cooler conversations when coworkers ask each other if they had any dates (implicitly meaning dates with a member of the opposite sex) over the weekend. Such conversations are a way of connecting with others, but they have the latent (and probably unintended) consequence of marginalizing individuals who may want to share the news about their same-sex date but are reluctant to do so in an environment where their existence is inadvertently written off or discounted.

When we describe a female baby as "flirting" when she is affectionate with a boy or man, we are also practicing cultural heterosexism. Teachers who ask their students about their "mom and dad" are another good example (though this practice also excludes a host of other possible family forms, not just those headed by same-sex parents). Cultural heterosexism is present in myriad well-intentioned conversations that inadvertently exclude LGB persons and their experiences.

In Chapter 1, we also identified another dimension of analysis and differentiated "doing" from thinking and feeling. Discrimination refers to the unequal treatment of others by individuals, and at the group or societal level of analysis, institutional discrimination refers to patterns of unequal treatment built into the everyday operations of society. We have seen many examples of institutional discrimination, and, when applied to LGB people, we can also use the term **structural heterosexism**, which refers to ways heterosexual people, relationships, and families receive unequal material and institutional privileges.

To illustrate, the U.S. General Accounting Office concluded that DOMA denied more than 1,000 rights, privileges, and benefits to same-sex couples (Bedrick, 1997), including

---

Cultural heterosexism refers to the ideologies that uphold heterosexuality as normative.

Structural heterosexism refers to the ways heterosexual relationships are allocated more resources, opportunities, and privileges.

---

access to Social Security benefits, advantageous tax deductions, and less costly medical insurance plans. Also, as of 2013, a majority of U.S. states (29) did not provide any legal protection against being fired from one's job due to sexual orientation (Bloomberg Editors, 2013). Over the years, organizations and companies such as Cracker Barrel and the Boy Scouts of America have made national news for their exclusionary hiring policies, but they are not alone (Chatel, 2013). These patterns of institutional discrimination or structural heterosexism allow heterosexuals and opposite-sex married couples to enjoy a host of privileges not unlike the male and white privileges we have outlined in previous chapters.

QUESTIONS FOR REFLECTION

1. Can you identify examples of homophobia, cultural heterosexism, and structural heterosexism from your own experiences or from something you have seen in the news media, in movies, or on television?

2. Which is the most serious problem for LGB individuals: homophobia, cultural heterosexism, or structural heterosexism? Why? Could any one of these exist in the absence of the other two? How?

ASSIMILATION AND PLURALISM

In this section, we use many of the concepts from previous chapters to assess the situation of the LGB minority group. As usual, the discussion is organized around the concepts of acculturation and integration.

ACCULTURATION

In this chapter, as in Chapter 11, we change our usual approach to acculturation. Usually, we have discussed the ways minority groups learn the culture of the dominant group. Here, we reverse directions and examine the increasing inclusion of LGB people in the dominant culture.

The meaningful inclusion of LGB persons into mainstream culture has been quite recent. Historically, mass media either ignored the group or treated it as "comic relief." For example, sitcoms sometimes featured men cross-dressing or using a gay "cover" but only to get closer to women and only for laughs. It was not until the past several decades that mainstream TV shows began to portray gays and lesbians as family members or as people with love interests. At about the same time, talk shows such as *Oprah* and *Donahue* began to include lesbian and gay guests as panelists (Eaklor, 2008).

By the end of the 1990s, the term *culture wars*—popularized by presidential candidate Patrick Buchanan in a 1992

Several actual events are listed below. In the space provided, classify each as an example of homophobia, cultural heterosexism, or structural heterosexism, and briefly explain your reasoning. Some incidents may be ambiguous and include elements of more than one concept.

INCIDENT	CONCEPT	EXPLANATION
1. A middle school bully uses antigay slurs to taunt another boy on the school bus.		
2. Making conversation at the sandbox in the local playground, a neighborhood parent asks your child where her "mom and dad" live.		
3. You receive an offer for free tickets to a local amusement park. The only catch is that you must take a tour of a timeshare development with your opposite-sex spouse.		
4. The school textbook that lists the spouses of all American astronauts does not include Sally Ride's female partner of 27 years.		
5. A man's coworker tells him about a place where lots of beautiful women hang out after work: "You'll love it," the coworker says.		
6. A father does not feel comfortable that one of his 16-year-old son's best friends is gay, and he discourages his son from inviting this friend to his birthday party.		
7. The local youth baseball league does not allow gay or lesbian coaches.		

NOTE: Your instructor may ask you to complete this assignment as a group discussion.

TURN THE PAGE TO FIND OUR ANSWERS

Republican National Convention speech—became widely used to characterize the struggle between increasingly mainstream LGB visibility and those who opposed it. Many well-known public figures were daring to "come out" during the decade—from Candace Gingrich (U.S. House Speaker Newt Gingrich's daughter) to popular musicians such as k.d. lang and Melissa Etheridge and actors such as Nathan Lane and Ellen DeGeneres (Eaklor, 2008; Handy, 1997).

This increasing visibility, including the publication of children's books such as *Heather Has Two Mommies* and *Daddy's Roommate*, prompted a conservative backlash. Sponsors cancelled their support of certain TV shows, and protests were held at public libraries to express disapproval of gay-friendly material and content ("After Protest," 1998; Taffet, 2013). Yet the groundswell could not be quieted, and Americans of all ages and classes were increasingly exposed to LGB people in a variety of cultural settings.

Perhaps one of the most striking indicators of the vast cultural shift between the 1990s and the present is the difference in the pattern of protesting today. In the 1990s, companies such as Wendy's and JCPenney pulled their advertisements from the Ellen DeGeneres show when she came out. In 2014, in contrast, companies have publically disassociated themselves from organizations that could be seen as antigay. For example, the Disney Corporation pulled its funding from the Boy Scouts of America because of its discrimination against gay troop leaders (Frizell, 2014). Other major companies such as AT&T spoke out about Russia's antigay laws both before and during the Sochi Winter Olympics (Elliott, 2014). Today, it is clear that many corporations perceive it as to their benefit to position themselves as being for gay equality.

Indicators of progress toward LGB cultural assimilation can also be found in an institutional arena especially well-known for homophobia—sports. Previously, most news stories about gay athletes concerned their coming out after retirement. In recent years, in contrast, the focus has been on highly placed athletes coming out while they are still active.

NBA player Jason Collins announced his sexual orientation in *Sports Illustrated* in 2013, and Michael Sam, a college football player and NFL draft prospect, made his sexual orientation

INCIDENT	CONCEPT	EXPLANATION
1. A middle school bully use antigay slurs to taunt another boy on the school bus.	Homophobia	This is both an individual action and an expression of negative feelings.
2. Making conversation at the sandbox in the local playground, a neighborhood parent asks your child where her "mom and dad" live.	Cultural heterosexism	The comment is based on the assumption that opposite-sex couples are "normal."
3. You receive an offer for free tickets to a local amusement park. The only catch is that you must take a tour of a timeshare development with your opposite-sex spouse.	Structural heterosexism	A benefit (the free tickets) is being denied to same-sex couples.
4. The school textbook that lists the spouses of all American astronauts does not include Sally Ride's female partner of 27 years.	Cultural heterosexism	The omission illustrates the marginalization of same-sex relationships.
5. A man's coworker tells him about a place where lots of beautiful women hang out after work: "You'll love it," the coworker says.	Cultural heterosexism	The coworker is making assumptions about sexual orientation.
6. A father does not feel comfortable that one of his 16-year-old son's best friends is gay, and he discourages his son from inviting this friend to his birthday party.	Homophobia	Like #1, this is both an individual action and an expression of negative feelings.
7. The local youth baseball league does not allow gay or lesbian coaches.	Structural heterosexism	A benefit (the opportunity to coach) is being denied to lesbians and gays.

public in 2014, prompting an avalanche of mainstream media attention (Branch, 2014). In anticipation of more such announcements in the future, all four of the major professional sports leagues—NBA, NFL, MLB, and NHL—have included sexual orientation in their nondiscrimination policies and have instituted various policies to foster inclusive cultures in their organizations (Klein & Battista, 2013). This inclusion of and support for gay athletes may increase the acceptance of LGB people in the society as a whole, much as African American athletes such as Jesse Owens, Jackie Robinson, and Arthur Ashe assisted in the further integration of their group.

While the media and sports have a tremendous impact on culture, the lives of everyday people—not just superstars—should also be considered. As we have noted earlier, in the past decade alone, American's attitudes have shifted considerably toward support of gay marriage, with youth becoming a driving force in this change. Other surveys have shown increasingly favorable views of LGB Americans and decreases in the percentage of adults who say they would be "very upset" if their children came out to them as gay or lesbian (Drake, 2013; Pew Research Center, 2013b).

The pace of cultural change regarding acceptance of the LGBT minority in recent years is clearly unprecedented; however, we must be careful not to mistake a rapid increase with full acceptance. When a sample of LGBT Americans were asked if they felt there was "a lot" of acceptance in society for them, only 19% said yes, and many reported being made to feel unwelcome in various social settings, including places of employment and churches (Drake, 2013).

Also, even though they are encountering a more tolerant society than did prior generations, LGBT youth are still facing a hostile cultural climate in many areas of the United States, as evidenced by their alarmingly high rates of suicide attempts. In a 2012 survey of more than 10,000 youth ages 13 to 17 of all sexual orientations, the LGBT respondents were twice as likely to report some kind of physical bullying and more than 90% of all the youth surveyed said they hear some kind of negative message at school about being gay. Further, nearly half of all the youth surveyed felt that their particular community was not accepting of gay people (Human Rights Campaign, 2012).

LGB persons live in grave danger of physical attacks and harassment in many parts of the world, including the United States, and the level of cultural heterosexism remains high. Yet the increasing pace of change in the United States has at least given some hope to LGBT youth: Although only 49% of the youth surveyed felt that they could lead a happy life in their current hometown, 83% said they believe they will be happy "eventually" (Human Rights Campaign 2013).

Attitudes Toward LGBTs in Global Perspective

Attitudes about LGBT people vary widely across the globe. Some nations recognize same-sex marriages and have instituted strong civil rights protections for LGBT citizens. In other nations, homosexuality is criminalized and demonized, punishable by harsh prison terms or even death.

The map in Figure 12.2 outlines the diversity in levels of acceptance of nonheterosexuals. It is based on representative samples from 39 nations across the globe. Respondents were asked, "Should society accept homosexuality?"

In the blue nations, more than 55% of respondents replied "yes" to the question, with the highest levels of support in Spain (88%) and Germany (87%). Acceptance was generally highest in western Europe, North America, and Australia. Central and South American nations also frequently scored above the 55% mark.

The nations colored in red, on the other hand, scored lower than 45% on the question and were strongly opposed to homosexuality. The lowest levels of acceptance were in Asia, the Middle East, and, especially, Africa. The nations of Pakistan (2% "yes"), Senegal (3% "yes"), and Nigeria (1% "yes") were virtually unanimous in their rejection of homosexuality.

Acceptance of homosexuality has increased in recent years in many nations: Levels of acceptance in both the United States and Canada increased about 10% between 2007 and 2013. Other nations have remained consistently opposed. There is no worldwide trend toward greater acceptance.

Russia (16% "yes"), in particular, has repeatedly made world headlines in recent years with its campaign to ban "homosexual propaganda," especially in the run-up to the 2014 Olympics in Sochi. The strongest resistance to gays and lesbians, however, has been in the Muslim world and in Africa. In 2014, for example, Nigeria enacted a law that prescribed a 10-year prison term for public displays of same-sex relationships. In the more Muslim areas of northern Nigeria, the penalty for homosexuality is death by public stoning (Nossiter, 2014). Also in 2014, Uganda (4% "yes") passed a law that punishes homosexuality with a life sentence and provides jail terms for groups convicted of promoting homosexuality (McConnell, 2014).

What accounts for this mixed pattern of support and rejection? Not surprisingly, religiosity might explain much of the variance: The nations most accepting of homosexuality tend to be more secular, and those most opposed tend to be highly religious. There is a pervasive pattern of greater acceptance among the young, which might suggest a higher level of tolerance in the future. However, in predominantly Muslim nations and African nations, overwhelming majorities of *all* age groups agree that homosexuality should be rejected (Pew Research Center, 2013a, pp. 6–7).

Questions to Consider

1. What other variables besides religiosity might help account for the differences in acceptance of homosexuality? Which of the theories of intolerance and prejudice that we have reviewed might be useful?

2. What predictions can you make about future levels of tolerance for gays and lesbians around the globe? Does the future for greater acceptance appear bright or dim? Why?

FIGURE 12.2 Views on Homosexuality Worldwide

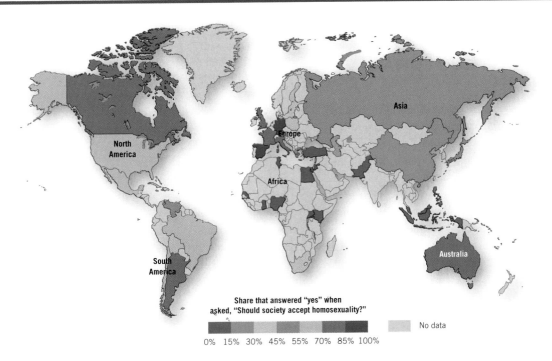

Share that answered "yes" when asked, "Should society accept homosexuality?"

0% 15% 30% 45% 55% 70% 85% 100%   No data

SOURCE: Fisher (2013a).

FIGURE 12.3 Geographic Distribution of the LGBT Population, 2012

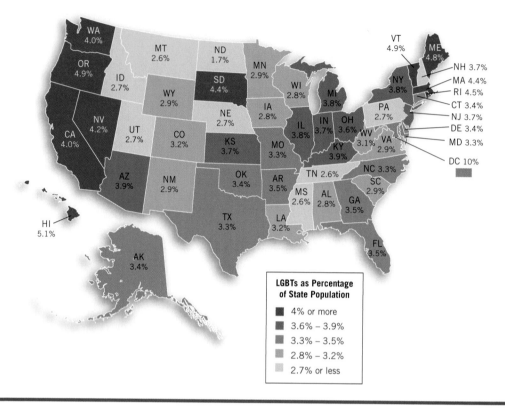

LGBTs as Percentage of State Population
- 4% or more
- 3.6% – 3.9%
- 3.3% – 3.5%
- 2.8% – 3.2%
- 2.7% or less

SOURCE: Gates and Newport (2013).

Taken together, these shifts indicate an increase in the incorporation of this particular minority group into the culture of the dominant society, if not full acceptance. Clearly, as we will explore in the next section, major issues of inequality remain.

SECONDARY STRUCTURAL ASSIMILATION

In this section, we will assess the status of the LGB minority following our usual format. However, a couple of problems limit the analysis. First, one of our primary sources of information is not available, because the U.S. Census Bureau does not, of course, collect information on sexual orientation or sexual identity, although it does collect information on same-sex households, as we will see below. Second, an unknown percentage of the members of the LGB group are still, to some extent, "in the closet." Thus, it is very difficult to ascertain even the most basic information (the size of the group, for example) with certainty.

However, a number of recent studies do provide some insight into the extent of secondary structural assimilation for the LGB minority. The studies are limited in some ways, and, in particular, they use a variety of measures and definitions in their assessment of the LGB community. For example, some are based on people living together as same-sex couples, not on the entire group. Nonetheless, it is possible to develop some

useful conclusions regarding some of the dimensions of structural integration.

Size of Population, Racial and Ethnic Composition, and Residential Patterns. A recent survey estimates the LGBT group at 3.4% of the adult U.S. population. These results are based on a very large, representative sample of more than 120,000 people who were asked, "Do you personally identify as gay, lesbian, bisexual, or transgender?" This seems to be a reasonable estimate of group size, but recognize that it is based on sexual identity, not sexual orientation or behavior. A different methodology or definition might yield somewhat different estimates of the size of the group.

A different study, based on an analysis of household data collected during the census, shows that the number of same-sex–couple households increased by 80% between 2000 and 2010, double the rate of growth of opposite-sex married-couple households (Gates, 2012, p. 1). It seems likely that a large part of this very rapid rate of apparent growth reflects greater openness about claiming an LGB identity, as opposed to an actual increase in group size.

Every racial and ethnic group is represented among LGB Americans, in roughly the same proportions as in the general population. We presented information about the racial/ethnic mix of the U.S. population in Figure 1.1, and a recent survey shows that the LGBT population has a similar composition: About two thirds are white, 15% Latino, and 12%

FIGURE 12.4 Educational Attainment for the General Population and LGBT Americans

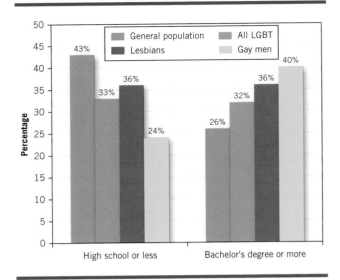

SOURCE: Pew Research Center (2013d, p. 4).

African American (Pew Research Center, 2013d, p. 4). As we mentioned previously, a much higher percentage of same-sex couples (20.6%) than heterosexual couples (9.5%) are interracial or interethnic (Gates, 2012, pp. 2–5).

LGBT persons live in every corner of the United States, from the smallest village to the largest metropolis. Figure 12.3 shows that the percentage of each state's population that identifies as LGBT ranges from a low of 1.7% in North Dakota to highs of 5.1% in Hawaii and 10% in Washington, D.C. The variation from state to state is not large, but there is a pattern in these figures. With the exception of South Dakota, every state in which the percentage of LGBT persons exceeds 4% has laws that prohibit discrimination based on sexual orientation, and many recognize same-sex marriage or domestic partnerships in their legal codes (Gates & Newport, 2013).

Education. LGBT Americans have higher levels of educational attainment than the general population, as displayed in Figure 12.4. They are less likely to be at the lower level of education and, particularly for gay men, more likely to have a college degree or more.

Figure 12.4 refers to all LGBTs. A different study used census data to compare the educational profiles of same-sex couples (defined as households in which the same-sex residents describe each other as husband or wife or domestic partner) with those of opposite-sex couples (Kastanis & Wilson, 2012). The researchers found that same-sex couples were more likely to have a college degree—consistent with Figure 12.4—but that this pattern varied markedly by race or ethnic group. Half the white same-sex couples had completed college compared with about a third of the white heterosexual couples, and as we saw in Chapter 9, Asian American couples—both same sex and heterosexual—were the most educated group (p. 3). However,

again consistent with earlier chapters, the levels of education for African Americans, Native Americans, and Hispanic Americans were markedly lower, although the same-sex couples in each group were more educated than the opposite-sex couples.

Political Power. As such a small minority, LGB Americans have relatively little influence on the political institution. As we have seen, however, political power is a function of group organization as well as sheer numbers, and LGB groups have been able to impact local and city elections, especially in the larger metropolitan areas.

In terms of ideology and party preference, LGBT Americans tend to be liberal and Democrat. However, these preferences are not unanimous, and the community is diverse and split on many issues. A 2012 national survey showed that 44% of LGBT Americans identified themselves as Democrats, but 43% were political independents and 13% identified with the Republican Party. Similarly, 45% of LGBT Americans say they are liberals, but 20% describe themselves as conservative. As in the general population, conservative LGBTs are more religious, older, and more likely to be white (Gates & Newport, 2012).

Income and Poverty. Earlier research tended to find that LGBT Americans were at a disadvantage in terms of income and other measures of affluence, consistent with other marginalized groups. Figure 12.5 confirms that LGBT persons are more likely to be low income and less likely to be high income. This is not consistent with the relatively high levels of educational attainment of the group (see Figure 12.4) and suggests that LGBT Americans are getting lower rewards for their investment in human capital. This pattern is similar to the situation for women (see Figure 11.4), and we discuss it in more detail below.

FIGURE 12.5 Annual Family Income for the General Population and LGBT Americans

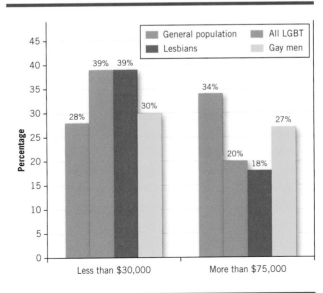

SOURCE: Pew Research Center (2013d, p. 4).

FIGURE 12.6 Median Incomes for Same-Sex and Opposite-Sex Couples by Racial and Ethnic Group, 2010

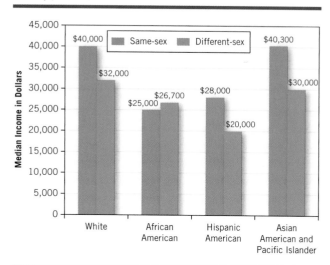

SOURCE: Kastanis and Wilson (2012, p. 8).

The pattern of income inequality changes when we look at couples as opposed to individuals. Figure 12.6 displays census data showing that, for all racial and ethnic groups except African Americans, same-sex couples average higher incomes than do heterosexual couples. (The difference for African Americans, although contrary to the other groups, was only about $1,700, the smallest difference of the four groups.) Note how the differences between groups echo patterns we have observed in previous chapters. For both same- and opposite-sex couples, white and Asian Americans have higher incomes than do African Americans and Hispanic Americans. Thus, the outlines of the patterns of inequality in the larger society are echoed in the LGB community.

Figure 12.7 displays levels of poverty for couples and repeats the patterns displayed in Figure 12.6: Inequality in economic distress varies by race and ethnicity among LGB Americans as it does in the larger society. White and Asian American couples have lower poverty levels than do African American and Hispanic American couples, and levels of poverty are especially high for gay, male, African American couples.

The picture painted by the information in this section is somewhat unclear, in part because the data are based on different units of analysis (couples vs. individuals). However, one idea that may knit the picture together is discrimination and disadvantage, especially in jobs and income.

Consider disposable income, rather than total income. The fact that gay and lesbian couples cannot be legally married in so many states means that they experience a variety of disadvantages in how they must spend their income. They have higher costs for medical insurance—a major expense for most Americans—since they can't take advantage of the discounts

offered by family plans. They also tend to pay higher income taxes. Imagine two families with identical incomes of $45,000 and two children. One family is heterosexual and legally married; the other is a same-sex couple. Using standard deductions for child care and other expenses, the heterosexual couple would claim a $50 refund on their federal income taxes. The gay couple would owe about $2,100 (Capehart, 2012). The two families might be equal in gross salary but not in their actual disposable income. This puts a new perspective on the income data and suggests some of the costs of being gay in America.

Another major issue for LGBT people is job discrimination. Members of this group sometimes face agonizing choices about revealing their sexual orientation during job searches for fear that it will limit their opportunities, as detailed in the second Narrative Portrait in this chapter. In fact, there is evidence from research, some using the powerful audit study methodology (see Chapter 5), of a tendency to pass over LGBT candidates for jobs (Movement Advancement Project, Human Rights Campaign, & Center for American Progress, 2013).

On the job, LGBT people often face hostile workplaces, harassment, bullying, and worse. Also, one of the patterns that limits upward mobility for women (see Chapter 11) also applies to gays and lesbians: They may not have the same chance to network with colleagues and bosses, and such contacts can provide crucial links to opportunities to increase skills and knowledge and to prepare for jobs at higher levels. Discrimination in the workplace, both subtle and open, may explain the apparent gap between preparation for work, as measured by education, and actual rewards, as shown in the income data in Figure 12.5.

FIGURE 12.7 Poverty Rates for Same-Sex and Opposite-Sex Couples by Racial and Ethnic Group, 2010

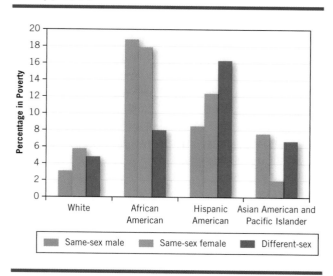

SOURCE: Badgett, Durso, and Schneebaum (2013, p. 11).

NARRATIVE PORTRAIT

Negotiating the Job Market

Jenny Strauss had just graduated college in 1989, but even though she lived in relatively tolerant San Francisco, she feared that her job prospects would be diminished by the fact that she was lesbian. When she got her first job, she remained "in the closet" to her boss and coworkers, but when she began a relationship, she felt that she could no longer live a lie and found the courage to reveal her sexual orientation.

She eventually moved on to jobs with companies that were more open to diversity, and she married and started a family. Today, she and her spouse are happy and secure, but as we saw in the vignette that opened this chapter, this state of affairs is not typical for same-sex families across the nation.

FAMILIES LIKE OURS

Jenny Strauss

My [first] boss, an evangelical woman, openly disapproved of "aberrant" lifestyles. She wasn't unkind, and although I learned a lot from her, I definitely felt that I couldn't be open. About a year into the job I met a woman, and shortly afterward decided that I couldn't hide anymore. Because I had kept this essential part of me a secret (for fear of being treated differently, or worse, mistrusted), no one had a clue, and so I had to formally come out to my boss and coworkers. Palms sweating and heart racing, I went to each of them and said, "I have something to tell you. I'm a lesbian." It was awful! I felt like I was giving them permission to judge me. I felt self-conscious...and nervous to the point of feeling sick to my stomach. In fact, my boss, who was shocked, told me she didn't agree with my "lifestyle choices." This is a woman with whom I had built a good relationship, and yet, now there was this strange rift between us. After that, I swore I would be open from the start, and only work where I would be accepted for who I am.

I left that job to work at Levi Strauss & Company...—one of the few companies at the time known to be gay-friendly.... Altogether, I spent seven years at Levi's. While there, I met my partner, Em, and we've been together 16 years and legally married since 2008.

In the mid-1990s I left Levi's to work for a boutique advertising agency, but was laid off during the dot-com bust when I was pregnant with our first child. Em was also laid off during this period. Thank goodness I was on her benefits...or we would have been in terrible shape. In the end, I took an entry-level job and a huge pay cut just to make ends meet and be close to home and my child.

Em and I now have two children. We have good jobs, and a good life. I work for an LGBT-friendly...company, SunPower, which has a nondiscrimination policy covering both sexual orientation and gender identity/expression. A few transgender employees have transitioned at work, and the company recently added sex reassignment surgery to our health benefits package. SunPower also offers domestic partner benefits....

I feel very grateful that times have changed enough that many companies, not just one, recognize families like ours and I look forward to the day when no matter where someone lives in the country, they feel safe coming out at work.

SOURCE: Movement Advancement Project et al. (2013, p. 23).

Questions to Consider

1. Are there companies in your area that offer the sorts of benefits that Jenny and Em enjoy? How could you identify these companies?
2. Does your state or city have laws prohibiting discrimination on the grounds of sexual orientation?

PRIMARY STRUCTURAL ASSIMILATION

Gordon's model of assimilation cites marital assimilation as the final stage of the assimilation process, and in previous chapters we have applied this idea to a variety of American minority groups. As with women in Chapter 11, this criterion does not apply to LGBTs. Thus, we will consider other areas of primary assimilation—such as family and friendships—where LGB people still face barriers to full acceptance.

Earlier, we noted the survey result showing that Americans were much less likely in 2013 to be "very upset" if their child came out to them as gay or lesbian. Nevertheless, LGB adults report that coming out to their parents is extremely difficult. About a third of them have not disclosed their sexual orientation to their mothers, and roughly half have not told their fathers (Drake, 2013).

Between fear of parental rejection and the social stigma and bullying of peers, it is no wonder that LGB youth have a higher risk of attempted suicide, substance abuse, and depression. Yet those who did not report family rejection were less likely to experience those negative outcomes (Ryan, Huebner, Diaz, & Sanchez, 2009). Indeed, when family, peer, and community are supportive, LGB youth grow up to be well adjusted (Savin-Williams, 2001). Thus, acceptance at the primary level is crucial to this particular minority group's mental and physical health, especially at young ages. At any age, however, being able to be "out" to one's family and friends relieves an enormous amount of stress and avoids a host of difficulties, both psychosocial and physical. Indeed, although reported as stressful initially, most LGB adults found that coming out to their parents did not significantly alter their relationships with them (Drake, 2013).

Having a personal relationship with someone who is gay or lesbian increases support for legal equality (Morales, 2009). One study also found that people who had recently become supportive of same-sex marriage cited knowing someone gay or lesbian as the number one reason for their change of mind (Pew Research Center, 2013b). Even when controlling for other variables known to affect people's views on LGB equality, such as religion and political affiliation, the effect of knowing someone gay or lesbian remains significant, a finding that lends support to the contact hypothesis (Lewis, 2011).

The number of people who say they know someone LGBT has increased in recent years, from 61% of adults in 1993 to 87% in 2013. Moreover, nearly a quarter of Americans surveyed in 2013 said they know "a lot" of gay or lesbian people (Drake, 2013). Even the social networking site Facebook reported that about 70% of its users have someone gay or lesbian on their friend list (Fowler, 2013). Figures such as these are striking for a minority group that accounts for such a small segment of the total U.S. population.

Although the 2010 U.S. Census found that less than 1% of all households were headed by a same-sex couple, such households are on the rise, and more than 100,000 of them have their own children (Lofquist, Lugailia, O'Connell, & Feliz, 2012). As the number of children who live in households with gay or lesbian parents continues to grow, we can expect the number of adults who know someone who is LGB to increase as well.

Despite the significant headway LGB persons have made in recent decades in terms of coming "out" in their families, building their own families, and developing cross–sexual-orientation friendships, many Americans remain steadfastly antigay. Outside the United States, as our Comparative Focus box demonstrated, there are many places where primary structural assimilation is an elusive goal.

QUESTIONS FOR REFLECTION

1. Would you say that LGB people are now fully included in American culture? Are they more included in popular culture and the media than in everyday life? If so, why does this difference exist?

2. Comparing the evidence presented in this chapter and Chapter 11, are LGB people closer to secondary structural integration than women are? What are the key challenges facing the LGB minority in the quest for equality?

CONCLUSIONS AND IMPLICATIONS FOR DOMINANT–MINORITY RELATIONS

As with many of the groups we have considered over the course of this text, the LGB minority has made a great deal of progress in recent years, but much remains to be done before full acceptance, assimilation, and equality are achieved. Like other minorities, LGB people face discrimination and inequalities in the distribution of material resources (jobs and income, for example) and in the protections offered by civil rights law. Unlike other minorities, however, part of the challenge facing LGB people is moral and cultural.

Fifty years ago, after decades of struggle and turmoil, American society formally rejected the Jim Crow system of segregation and its racist past. Through legislation, court decisions, and the changed thinking of millions of ordinary people, the United States recommitted itself to one of the most fundamental of its founding principles: equal treatment for all under the law, regardless of race, color, creed, national origin, or gender. As we have seen, in many ways our society continues to fall short of actually implementing this principle, but the importance of this moral consensus cannot be understated. The 1960s was a watershed decade in American history, and it is almost impossible to imagine a return to those days.

A similar moral and cultural debate now faces the nation: Should this same principle of equality be extended to gays and lesbians? Should same-sex couples be recognized as having legal marriages? Should antidiscrimination laws be extended to include sexual orientation? Is this a time when another fundamental shift in America's thinking—another watershed—will occur?

It seems that popular support for gay rights is building in this nation, and some observers even argue that marriage equality and full civil rights are just a matter of time. However, there is powerful, well-funded, and well-organized opposition to these changes, and it is clear that the traditional views of homosexuality as sinful and a form of deviance and mental illness retain considerable strength.

The nation is clearly committed to racial and gender equality (at least in principle). Will this moral and cultural consensus be extended to LGBs?

SUMMARY

This summary is organized around the Learning Objectives listed at the beginning of this chapter.

 12.1 Identify and analyze the difference between sexual orientation, sexual identity, and sexual behavior or practices.

Sexual orientation refers to the gender or genders to which a person is attracted, while sexual identity refers to how people think about themselves as sexual beings. The two concepts are closely but not perfectly related, and neither is perfectly related to sexual practices or behaviors.

 List and explain the key events that have impacted how lesbian, gay, and bisexual persons are viewed by society and have experienced society.

Same-sex relations are ancient but have been expressed and perceived differently in different eras and types of societies. In ancient Greece, same-sex relations between men were normative and accepted. In agrarian societies, the need for large families placed a huge premium on heterosexual relations, but same-sex relations existed even in the most straight-laced and prudish societies. As societies began to industrialize and urbanize, more social spaces were created where same-sex relations could exist, and gay subcultures emerged in larger cities. In postindustrial society, LGB people are more visible than ever before and have become increasingly accepted, although strong opposition to homosexuality persists among the more religious and conservative.

 Describe key moments in the struggle for gay liberation.

The modern U.S. gay liberation movement began with the formation of several "homophile" organizations in the 1950s. Perhaps the key event in the movement's history was the Stonewall Rebellion in 1969, which marked the beginning of a more activist, confrontational, inclusive approach. After Stonewall, a variety of organizations emerged to lead the struggle and attract allies. Successes were sporadic in the 1980s and 1990s, but the movement enjoyed a number of successes in the new century, including the spread of marriage equality at the state level and the Supreme Court decision that invalidated DOMA. Continuing issues for the movement include marriage equality and protections against discrimination in work and other institutions.

 Identify and explain the patterns of sexual orientation inequality in society today.

Information is less available for the LGB minority than for other groups, but patterns of inequality in income and poverty can be documented. As is the case with some other minorities, LGB people seem to enjoy lower returns (income) on their investments in human capital (education). Also, same-sex couples must often spend a higher percentage of their incomes on health care and taxes.

 Describe how race, class, gender, and religion impact sexual-orientation inequality.

The patterns of inequality in the LGB community reflect those in the larger society. For example, African Americans and Hispanic Americans are at a greater disadvantage than white Americans and Asian Americans. The gay and lesbian communities reflect the larger society in other ways as well and are divided by racism and other cultural values. Heterosexism and homophobia affect different subgroups of LGB people in different ways.

KEY TERMS

collective identity 358	homophobia 365	queer 361	structural
coming out 356	internalized	sexual identity 351	heterosexism 366
cultural heterosexism 366	homophobia 365	sexual orientation 350	

REVIEW QUESTIONS

1. Define and explain the terms *sexual orientation* and *sexual identity*. How do they relate to sexual practices and behaviors?

2. How has changing subsistence technology affected the LGB minority? What are the key differences between the agrarian, industrial, and postindustrial levels of development for this group?

3. Summarize the history of the gay liberation movement. Why do we distinguish between pre- and post-Stonewall eras? What are the most important victories and setbacks for gay liberation since 1990?

4. Summarize and explain each of the three issues for LGB people analyzed in this chapter (marriage equality; service in the military; and race, racism, and sexual orientation).

5. What are homophobia and heterosexism? How do these compare and contrast with prejudice, discrimination, institutional discrimination, and ideological racism?

6. Apply the concepts of acculturation, secondary structural assimilation, and primary structural assimilation to the LGB minority. How does the application of these concepts differ for this group compared with other groups we have considered?

Sharpen your skills with SAGE edge at edge.sagepub.com/healey7e

SAGE edge for students provides a personalized approach to help you accomplish your coursework goals in an easy-to-use learning environment.

The following resources are available at SAGE edge:

Current Debates: Whose Rights Should Prevail?

Many Americans, especially the more religious and politically conservative, find homosexuality offensive and believe that it is morally wrong. What should happen when these views clash with laws that require equal treatment? Which should prevail: religious values or civil rights?

On our website you will find an overview of the topic, the clashing points of view, and some questions to consider as you analyze the material.

Public Sociology Assignments

Public Sociology Assignments provide opportunities for students to address directly and personally some of the issues raised in this text.

There are four assignments for Part IV on our website. In the first assignment, students use the information available from the Pew Research Center to examine religion as a source of diversity in American life. In the second assignment, groups of students will analyze the lyrics of popular songs. Do the lyrics reflect stereotypes of racial or ethnic groups? What messages are being conveyed about gender or sexual orientation?

The third assignment focuses on a film and website that probe the reality of bullying in America's schools. The fourth assignment is an analysis of the thousands of languages around the world that are in danger of becoming extinct.

Contributed by Linda M. Waldron

Internet Research Project

This Internet Research Project has two parts, and you are urged to complete both. In the first, you will search the Internet for information on several controversial questions related to this chapter; in the second, you will add to the profiles of LGB people. It is particularly important to rely on trusted, scientifically based sources for these projects. Your instructor may ask you to discuss your findings in small groups.

For Further Reading

Please see our website for an annotated list of important works related to this chapter.

CHAPTER-OPENING TIMELINE PHOTO CREDITS

1948: Library of Congress Prints and Photographs Division

1969: NY Daily News/Getty Images

1979: Wikimedia Commons

1987 (AIDS quilt): National Institutes of Health

1987 (National March on Washington): Associated Press

2008: Wikipedia

2009: Official White House Photo/Pete Souza

2014: Reuters/Marcus Donner

13 DOMINANT–MINORITY RELATIONS IN CROSS-NATIONAL PERSPECTIVE

LOC

BATTLE OF BELMONT. NOV. 23? 1899. BOER-BRITISH WAR.

State of Israel's National Photo Collection

timeline

1899
British and Dutch factions fight each other in the Boer War for control of South Africa.

1918
Yugoslavia is created.

1948
The state of Israel is established by the UN as the Jewish homeland, resulting in full-scale wars between Israel and its neighbors in 1948, 1967, and 1973.

1890   1900   1910   1920   1930   1940   1950

1916
The Easter Rebellion leads to the creation of an independent Republic of Ireland. The new nation encompasses most of the island, but the largely Protestant northern counties remain part of Great Britain.

1939–1945
6 million Jews and at least 6 million others, including Roma, Slavs, and the handicapped, are murdered by the Nazi German state.

1948
The National Party, the primary political vehicle of the Afrikaans, or Dutch, segment of the white community, comes into control of South Africa. The system of apartheid is subsequently constructed to firmly establish white superiority.

1953
Josip Broz Tito, a leader of anti-Nazi guerrilla forces during World War II, becomes Prime Minister of Yugoslavia.

LOC

German Federal Archive

I pause in the central square of Uzhgorod, a city on the western edge of Ukraine. It is early evening, and the streets are crowded as people hurry through the cold, on their way home or to one of the numerous bars for an after-work drink. It is 2006, and I am here for a semester at the university, trying to acclimate to this ancient, recently Soviet, formerly Hungarian, formerly Czechoslovakian, strangely (to me) cosmopolitan city.

If I listen closely to the passing crowds, even my untutored ear can hear multiple languages besides Ukrainian: Russian, Czech, Romanian, Hungarian, Slovak, and probably others. I know that almost everyone in the city speaks at least two of these languages, and some, especially the more educated, speak English (thankfully!).

LEARNING OBJECTIVES

By the end of this chapter, you will be able to do the following:

13.1 State and explain the central themes of this text.

13.2 Summarize the overall pattern of ethnic variability around the globe and identify which regions are most and least diverse.

13.3 Summarize the dominant–minority situations outlined in this chapter, including the history and present situation, and apply the central concepts developed in this text to each case.

LOC

1979
Egypt, formerly committed to the destruction of the Jewish state, signs a peace accord with Israel.

Wikimedia Commons

1992–1995
More than 200,000 Bosnian Muslims are killed by Serbs and Croats in Yugoslavia.

Wikimedia Commons

1994
Nelson Mandela is elected President of South Africa.

1998
The "Good Friday Agreement" is signed, establishing a new power-sharing arrangement for the governance of Northern Ireland in which both Protestant and Catholic parties would participate.

1960 1970 1980 1990 2000 2010 2020

1960s
The Catholics of Northern Ireland begin a civil rights movement, seeking amelioration for their minority status. Protestants, fearing loss of privilege and control, resist attempts at reform, and the confrontation escalates into violence.

1960s
A militant pluralistic movement begins in Quebec.

1960s
Canada reforms its restrictive immigration policy that favored whites, leading to a steady influx of newcomers from Latin America, the Caribbean, and Asia.

1980
Referendums supporting a politically autonomous Quebec fail. A similar referendum fails in 1995, but only by a very thin margin.

1990
F. W. de Klerk, the leader of the National Party and the prime minister of the nation, begins a series of changes that eventually ends apartheid in South Africa.

1994
Paramilitary groups of the Republic of Ireland and Northern Ireland declare a cease fire and begin to negotiate with each other.

1994
Approximately 800,000 ethnic Tutsis are killed by Hutu rebels is Rwanda.

Copyright World Economic Forum

1998
A terrorist attack on a shopping area in Omagh, Northern Ireland, leaves nearly 30 people dead.

From where I stand, I can see the old synagogue, abandoned after World War II when only a few hundred Jews—survivors of the Holocaust and a tiny remnant of a once large, bustling community—returned to the area. In the 1950s, the Soviets, practicing their brand of anti-Semitism, stripped the building of all religious symbols and turned it into a concert hall.

I can hear a Roma boy of about 10 singing nearby. He belts out a melody and accompanies himself on a beat-up guitar. People mostly ignore him, but he manages to score an occasional coin or two from those not too afraid to get close to a Gypsy. He looks cold and unkempt, but I have learned that he is probably better off than the hundreds of Roma children in the orphanages scattered throughout the countryside.

The group makeup of the city reflects its complicated past and its geographic centrality. For centuries, it has been a crossroads for cultures and languages, armies and traders. The diversity constantly surprises me, but it is just one of the countless ways ethnicity, language, culture, and race are blended around the globe. •

—Joe Healey

Early in this text, we developed a set of concepts and hypotheses to help analyze and understand dominant–minority relations. Our analytical framework has been elaborated and applied to the creation and evolution of a variety of minority groups across U.S. history. Although our concepts have proven their usefulness, it is important to recognize that, up to this point, they have been tested against the experiences of just a single nation. Just as you would not accept an interview with a single person as an adequate test of a psychological theory, you should not accept the experiences of a single nation as proof for the sociological perspective developed in this text. However, if our ideas can be applied to dominant–minority situations in other societies, we will have some assurance that the dynamics of intergroup relations in the United States are not unique and that our conclusions have some general applicability.

In this chapter, we will first briefly review the ideas that have guided our analysis. Then, after looking at an overview of diversity around the globe, we will apply our ideas to a variety of societies. It is not possible to investigate every nation in the world, but we will focus on "trouble spots" or societies with dominant–minority group conflicts that have been widely publicized and are therefore familiar to most people. For purposes of comparison, we have also included several societies in which group relations are thought to be generally peaceful.

We want to be very clear as to the limits of this "test." The sample of societies is small and is not representative of all human societies across time and space; therefore, the test will not be definitive. Before final conclusions can be reached, we

need much more research on a broad array of societies, drawn from a variety of time periods, regions, levels of development, and cultural backgrounds. Just as important, information about many of our most crucial concepts (e.g., the degree and nature of prejudice or discrimination) is simply not available for many societies. Without precise, trustworthy information, our tests will necessarily be informal and impressionistic. At any rate, you can rest assured that the conclusions reached in this chapter—and in this text—will not be the final word on the subject.

A BRIEF REVIEW OF MAJOR ANALYTICAL THEMES

Before commencing our cross-national tour, it will be useful to review the major analytical points developed in this text. These ideas were summarized as seven themes in the introduction to Part III and have been used extensively throughout the text; thus, a brief review will be sufficient here.

One theme that has been constantly stressed is the importance of the initial contact situation between groups. The characteristics of the initial meeting (particularly the nature and intensity of the competition and the balance of power between the groups) can shape relations for centuries. We have also found that the fates of minority groups created by colonization and conquest are very different from those of minority groups created by immigration. As we have seen repeatedly in U.S. history, colonized or conquered minority groups are subjected to greater rejection, discrimination, and inequality, and become more completely mired in their minority status. Positive change is more difficult to accomplish for conquered or colonized groups, especially when the group is racially or physically different from the dominant group.

As we examine in this chapter the most difficult and explosive group conflicts from around the globe, you will notice that their origins are often in contact situations in which the colonizers were white Europeans and the eventual minority groups were peoples of color. This pattern of dominance and subordination reflects the conditions under which the present world system of societies was created. By the 1400s, the nations of Europe were the most technologically advanced in the world, and they used their superiority to explore, conquer, and sometimes destroy much of the rest of the world. The conflicts between whites and nonwhites around the globe today—and many of the conflicts between peoples of color—are one legacy of this enormous burst of European power and energy.

Of course, the present pattern of white dominance is also an accident of history. Nations have been conquering, enslaving, persecuting, and oppressing their neighbors since there were nations. When neighboring societies differed in some visible way, prejudice, racism, and systems of inequality based on group membership often followed the military conquests.

The early days of the Industrial Revolution.

The unique contribution of Europeans to this ancient pattern was that their era of conquest and colonization was made possible by breakthroughs in shipbuilding, navigation, and other technologies that enabled them to spread their influence far wider and more permanently than could any previous colonizers. The nations of Europe (and the British in particular) were able to rule much of the world until very recent decades, and many ethnic and racial conflicts today were born during the era of European colonialism (see Wallace, 1997).

A second important theme is that dominant–minority relationships tend to change most rapidly and dramatically when there are changes in the level of development or the basic subsistence technology of the larger society. For example, industrialization not only revolutionized technology and modes of production; it also transformed group relationships in Europe, in the United States, and, eventually, around the globe. In Europe, the growth of industrial technology stimulated massive waves of immigration, beginning in the 1820s, and the new technology helped European nations dominate the world system of societies in the 19th century and much of the 20th century.

In the United States, the industrial revolution led to a transition from paternalistic to rigid competitive group relations, starting in the 19th century. In the latter half of the 20th century, continuing modernization led to the present era of fluid competitive group relations. The blatant racism and overt discrimination of the past have become more moderate, taking on milder, more ambiguous forms that are more difficult to identify and measure. Very importantly, this evolution to less repressive forms of group relations has been energized, in large part, by the protest activities of minority-group members and their allies.

Contact situations, subsistence technology, assimilation and pluralism, prejudice, racism, and institutional discrimination are all central to understanding the past and present situations of U.S. minority groups. To what extent are these themes and concepts applicable to group relations around the world?

QUESTIONS FOR REFLECTION

1. What is a contact situation, and why is it important?

2. Why do group relationships change when a society undergoes a change in subsistence technology?

A SNAPSHOT OF GLOBAL DIVERSITY

Before we begin to consider individual nations, it will be helpful to look at diversity around the globe. Figure 13.1 presents one view, based on ethnicity. As you can see, the nations of Africa, with their multitude of tribes, languages, and cultures, tend to rank highest on diversity.

This pattern partly reflects the colonization of the continent by European powers: Virtually all of Africa has been, at one time or another, a colonial possession of a European nation. The African national boundaries of today were drawn for the convenience of—and sometimes at the whim of—the European masters.

Also, in many cases, part of the governing strategy of European conquerors was to incorporate different ethnic

FIGURE 13.1   Ethnic Diversity Around the Globe

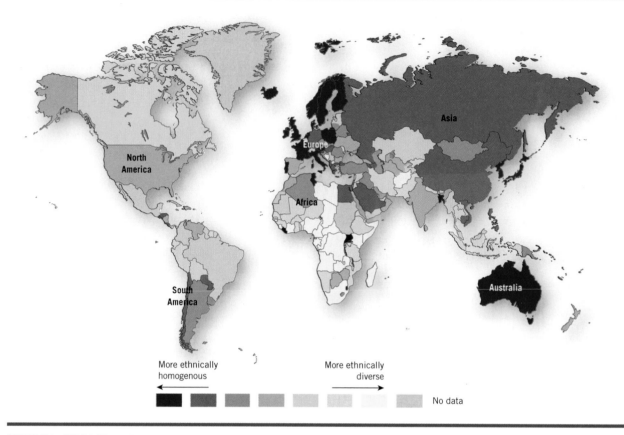

SOURCE: Fisher (2013b). This map is based on Alesina, Devleeschauwewr, Easterly, Kurlat, and Wacziarg (2002).

groups in the same colony and pit one against the other, using a "divide-and-conquer" strategy to solidify their own rule. This strategy, as we shall see in the case study of Rwanda, often resulted in prolonged tragedies.

Europe is the least diverse region of the globe, but the most homogeneous nations, according to this measure, are Japan and North and South Korea. The nations of North and South America are fairly diverse, with the United States scoring in the middle range and Canada scoring higher (largely, as we shall see, because of the large French-speaking population).

Maps such as Figure 13.1 are interesting and useful for identifying broad patterns, but they should not be taken too literally. For one thing, the data used to compute the scores are old, sometimes stretching back to the early 1990s. Also, as we have seen, ethnicity—like race—is a social construction, and any attempt to measure it (especially across political, cultural, and social lines) is bound to be somewhat arbitrary. Still, the map is a useful starting point and reminds us that the United States is not the only nation (far from it!) to confront issues of group relations.

QUESTIONS FOR REFLECTION

1. Why do African nations tend to be so diverse?

2. All other things being equal, would you prefer to live in a more diverse or less diverse society? Why?

A GLOBAL TOUR

We begin our world tour of group relations with Canada, our neighbor to the north, and then continue east, spanning the globe and returning to the Western Hemisphere for a discussion of Brazil.

CANADA

Citizens of the United States often see Canada as simply a colder version of their home society, a perception sustained by the enormous impact the United States has had on everyday social, economic, and political life in Canada. In fact, dominant–minority situations in the two societies do share some similarities, both historically and at present. But the two societies are quite different. For example, although black Africans were enslaved in colonial Canada, the institution never took on the economic, political, or social significance it assumed in the United States (see the Comparative Focus in Chapter 4).

Perhaps the most obvious difference between the two nations is that, for much of its history, the most significant minority-group issue in Canada has been cultural and linguistic, not racial. Virtually since its inception, Canadian society has been divided into two major language groups, French speaking and English speaking. French speakers (or Francophones) are the minority group and are concentrated in the province of Quebec. Nationally, French speakers make up about 21% of the population, but they are about 78% of the population of Quebec (Statistics Canada, 2013).

In our terms, issues of assimilation and pluralism separate the two linguistic and cultural groups. French Canadians have preserved their language and culture in the face of domination by English speakers for more than 200 years, and they continue to maintain their traditions today.

Although French Canadians tend toward pluralism, they are not unanimous about the type of relationship they want with the larger society. At one extreme, some Francophones want complete separation between Quebec and English-speaking Canada: Their goal is to make Quebec an independent nation. Others would be satisfied with guarantees of more autonomy for Quebec and some national recognition of the right of the French-speaking residents to maintain their language and culture.

What caused the conflict between French- and English-speaking Canadians? It will not surprise you that the answer begins with the contact situation between the English and French in Canada. Throughout the 1600s and 1700s, France and England (and other nations) fought for control of North America. The French were eliminated as a colonial power in 1759 when the British captured Quebec City and Montreal and ended the French and Indian War (as it is called in the United States).

The French who remained after the war were largely concentrated in what is now Quebec, and they became the ancestral community to today's Quebecois (French speakers of Quebec). The French community was organized around small farms; a rural, traditional, relatively low-income lifestyle; and the Catholic Church. The victorious British Protestants took control of the economic and political institutions of the region and became the ruling elite classes.

A militant pluralistic movement began in the 1960s in Quebec. The French-speaking residents were still clearly a minority group, and there were marked differences in wealth, education, occupational profile, and political power between French and English speakers in the province. Industrialization and urbanization had tended to raise the educational levels and aspiration of the Quebecois, and a nationalistic movement—with some similarities to the Black Power, Brown Power, and Red Power movements that developed in the United States in the same decade—emerged and began to grow in power.

The Parti Quebec became the major vehicle for the expression of Quebecois nationalism and the movement for a politically autonomous Quebec. Referendums in support of separation were held in 1980 and 1995. Both failed but the latter only by a very thin margin.

The status of Quebec's French-speaking residents has continued to rise in recent decades, and they have gained more economic and political power, but issues of control of resources and wealth continue to animate the struggle. Quebec is still attempting to work out its relationship with the rest of the nation, and the desire for separation is alive and well. Additional referenda on the issue of separation may take place in the near future.

In addition, Canada faces a number of other minority-group issues, most of which will be familiar to citizens of the United States. For example, after years of maintaining a restrictive immigration policy that favored whites, Canada reformed its laws in the 1960s. Since that time, there has been a steady and large influx of newcomers from the same areas that supply immigrants to the United States: Latin America, the Caribbean, and Asia.

Also, the native peoples of Canada share many problems and inequities with American Indians in the United States. Many live on remote reservations (called "reserves") that have high levels of poverty and unemployment and low levels of health care and educational opportunities.

Even though they are different from those of the United States, Canada's problems of group relations can be analyzed in familiar terms. Some Canadian minority groups (French speakers and Canadian Indians, or First Nations people) originated in conquest and colonization and have been victimized by discrimination and rejection for centuries. Especially since the 1960s, members of these groups have actively protested their situations, and some reforms and improvements have been made.

Other groups consist of recent immigrants who share much in common with similar groups in the United States. In fact, despite the clear and important differences between the nations, Canada faces many of the same issues that confront U.S. society: questions of unity and diversity, fairness and equality, assimilation and pluralism.

NORTHERN IRELAND

Other nations face issues similar to those faced by Canada, but with different levels of intensity, urgency, and lethality. In Northern Ireland, the bitter, violent conflict between

The Easter Rebellion, Dublin, Ireland, 1916.

Protestants and Catholics has some parallels to Canadian and U.S. group relations and has been closely watched and widely reported. Thousands of people have lost their lives during the struggles, many of them victims of terrorist attacks.

The roots of this conflict lie in armed hostilities between England and Ireland that began centuries ago. By the 1600s, England had colonized much of Ireland and had encouraged Protestants from Scotland and England to move to what is now Northern Ireland to help pacify and control the Catholic Irish. The newcomers, assisted by the English invaders, came to own much of the land and control the economy and governing structure of the northern regions of the island.

Over the centuries, the Protestants in the north of Ireland consolidated their position of power and separated themselves from the native Catholic population in the school system, in residential areas, and in most other aspects of society. Law and strong custom reinforced the subordinate position of Catholics, and the system, at its height, resembled Jim Crow segregation. That is, it was a system of rigid competitive relations (see Chapter 5) in which the Protestants sought to limit the ability of Catholics to compete for jobs, political power, housing, wealth, and other resources.

The British ruled Ireland as a colony for centuries but never succeeded in completely subordinating the Irish, who periodically attempted to gain independence through violent rebellions. These efforts came to partial fruition in the 1920s when an uprising that began with the Easter Rebellion of 1916 led to the creation of an independent Republic of Ireland. The new nation encompassed most of the island, but the largely Protestant northern counties, most of the province of Ulster, remained part of Great Britain.

The partition of the island into an overwhelmingly Catholic Republic of Ireland and a largely Protestant Northern Ireland set the stage for the troubles that reached a boiling point in the 1960s. The Catholics of Northern Ireland began a civil rights movement, seeking amelioration for their minority status. Protestants, fearing loss of privilege and control, resisted attempts at reform, and the confrontation escalated into violence.

Decades of riots, assassinations, bombings, occupation by the British Army, mass arrests, hunger strikes by prisoners, and terror attacks ensued. Both the Catholic and Protestant communities produced extremist, heavily armed terrorist groups (e.g., the Irish Republican Army for the Catholics and the Ulster Defence Association for the Protestants) that coordinated attacks on the other side. The level of violence rose and fell over the decades, but there seemed little reason to hope for peace. Until, in the 1990s, it began to happen.

In 1994, the paramilitary groups on each side declared a cease-fire, and the parties began to negotiate with each other. Four years later, in 1998, the Good Friday Agreement was signed, but only after an extremely difficult negotiation process. This accord, made possible in large part by the involvement and support of Great Britain, the Republic of Ireland, and the United States, established a new power-sharing arrangement for the governance of Northern Ireland in which both Protestant and Catholic parties would participate.

The new governing arrangement has survived several difficult crises, including a terrorist attack on a shopping area in Omagh, Northern Ireland, in August 1998 that left nearly 30 people dead. In that same year, a referendum in support of the arrangement passed with overwhelming agreement in both Northern Ireland and the Republic, and a stable and workable solution to the troubles seems to have been reached.

Note that in this case, as in the case of relations between Quebec and the rest of Canada, both the dominant and the minority groups are of the same race. The deep divisions are, on the surface, linguistic and cultural (English speaking vs. French speaking) and religious (Protestant vs. Catholic). In both nations, however, these divisions are highly correlated with social class position, access to education and jobs, and political power. That is, Catholics in Northern Ireland—like the French-speaking residents of Quebec—are a minority group that has been victimized by intense, systematic, and persistent discrimination and prejudice.

What was at stake in these struggles was not simply the survival of a culture or religion. These clashes were so bitter, so deadly, and so difficult because they also concerned the distribution of real resources and questions about who gets what and how much.

GERMANY

In the annals of intergroup relations, Germany is infamous as the site of the greatest atrocities against minority groups in history. In the 1930s and 1940s, the Nazi leadership of the nation attempted to eradicate the Jewish community (and several

Survivors of the Nazi concentration camps.

The Roma: Europe's "True Minority"

Professor Andria D. Timmer studies the Roma of Europe and, especially, of Hungary. She lived and worked in Roma communities in Hungary for several years while conducting research.

Dr. Andria D. Timmer

FIGURE 13.2 Roma Population in Europe, 2009

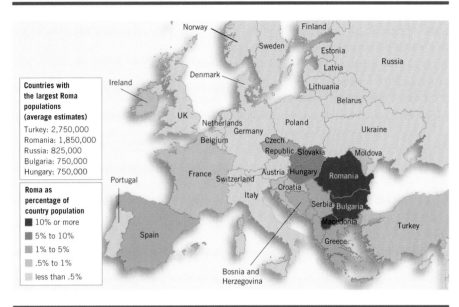

Countries with the largest Roma populations (average estimates)
Turkey: 2,750,000
Romania: 1,850,000
Russia: 825,000
Bulgaria: 750,000
Hungary: 750,000

Roma as percentage of country population
■ 10% or more
■ 5% to 10%
■ 1% to 5%
■ .5% to 1%
□ less than .5%

The Roma (often called "Gypsies") live throughout the world, but they are most populous in Europe. They can be found in every European nation, and their geographic distribution is depicted in Figure 13.2. According to many historical documents, the Roma have been part of central and eastern European society since at least the 14th century, when they arrived in several migratory waves from India. Despite the fact that they have lived in Europe for more than half a millennium, they are still treated as recent immigrants in many respects. Thus, the Roma illustrate the point made by Gordon (see Chapter 2) and many others that length of residence in a country is not necessarily related to a group's ability to assimilate and gain acceptance.

The Roma do not form one singular group but comprise several different ethnic enclaves. In most cases, members of these groups share little in common and are more similar to the majority members of the country in which they reside than to one another. However, from a pan-European perspective, they are often considered a single group. To understand how these different peoples get grouped together, it is necessary to return to the definition of *minority group* provided in Chapter 1 of this text. We will use the first two elements of the definition to help us examine the situation of the Roma in Europe.

The first, and most important, defining characteristic of a minority group is disadvantage or inequality, and this is something that all Roma groups have in common. Violence and intolerance toward Roma are an ever-present reality. Roma neighborhoods are often lacking in basic amenities, such as running water and regular trash collection. As an egregious form of discrimination, Roma youth are frequently educated separately from their majority-group peers and, as a result, receive lower-quality education that leaves them unable to compete in the job market. Unemployment rates for the Roma stand somewhere between 70% and 95%, depending on region.

The second defining characteristic of a minority group is a visible trait or characteristic. Linguistic, genetic, and ethnographic evidence shows that the Roma ancestors migrated out of northern India sometime between the 7th and 10th century. Therefore, contemporary populations share physical features with Indian populations, especially in regard to skin color. Otherwise, there is little that culturally ties the Roma to India, and, as mentioned previously, there are few cultural characteristics that tie all Roma groups together. Very few—apart from Traveler groups of England and Ireland, who are not Indian descendants—still practice the stereotypical nomadic lifestyle. Many have lost the use of their native tongue or use it only in the privacy of their homes.

The deep divide between Roma and non-Roma in Europe is largely the result of a long history of isolation and segregated living. Government and civil-sector programs have done little to address the segregated living but have, for the most part, endeavored to improve living conditions in Roma settlements. They have helped build new houses and sponsored environmental cleanup projects, but there are few programs to integrate Roma families into the larger national communities in which they reside. As long as residential segregation, prejudice, and discrimination persist, Europe will remain divided and the Roma will remain isolated and segregated.

Questions to Consider

1. Are the Roma a "typical" minority group? How do they compare to African Americans or Native Americans? What important differences and similarities can you identify?

2. What stereotypes do Americans hold about "Gypsies"? Where do these ideas come from? In Chapter 3, we noted that stereotypes tend to fall into two categories: one for groups that occupy a low status and the other for groups that are "too" successful. Into which category do American stereotypes of the Roma fall? Why?

other groups) and nearly succeeded. Six million Jews died in the concentration camps.

Since the end of World War II, modern Germany has broken from its racist past, democratized, industrialized, and modernized. It is a global leader politically and economically, and has one of the world's best-trained and most-educated workforces. Germany has worked hard to atone for the Nazi's attempted genocide of Jews. It has, for example, paid reparations to the state of Israel in partial compensation for the atrocities of World War II and is Israel's leading trading partner in Europe. Germany also funds a variety of cultural exchange programs between the two nations.

Today, Germany faces new dominant–minority group challenges. Like the United States, Canada, and other western European nations, Germany has become a highly desirable destination for immigrants, who come to satisfy the demand for both unskilled, cheap labor and "high-tech" professionals (see the Comparative Focus in Chapter 8).

Besides the demand in various parts of the job market, immigrants are also pulled to Germany (and many other European nations) by the low rate of population growth. Birthrates are low throughout western Europe, and Germany's birthrate is actually lower than its death rate (Population Reference Bureau, 2013). If this condition continues, Germany will begin to lose population.

Based on the patterns we have documented in the United States, we would predict that high rates of immigration would be accompanied by episodes of racist violence, and it is easy to find neo-Nazi hate groups, hate crimes, and violent attacks against immigrants and other minority-group members in Germany (and other European nations) in recent years. These attacks include bombings, killings, beatings, and myriad other forms of violence and brutality.

The most sensational of these attacks involved a gang of three neo-Nazis who allegedly murdered at least nine people from immigrant backgrounds and robbed at least a dozen banks to finance their activities. Two of the members of the so-called Zwickau Cell of the National Socialist Underground committed suicide as they were about to be captured, but the third, Beate Zschaepe, went on trial for these crimes in December 2013 (Schofield, 2013).

Also, anti-Semitism is still a fact of life in Germany and may be increasing there and across Europe. A recent survey of Jews in eight European nations found that 66% thought that anti-Semitism was a "very big" or "fairly big" problem in their country. Percentages ranged from a high of 85% in France to a low of 48% in the United Kingdom. Germany was intermediate, with a percentage of 61% (European Union Agency for Fundamental Rights, 2013, pp. 15–16).

Another survey found that anti-Semitic sentiments had increased just between 2009 and 2012 in four of the seven nations surveyed. Support for such sentiments ranged from a low of 17% in the United Kingdom to a high of 63% in Hungary. In this survey, Germany ranked toward the bottom,

with 21% supporting prejudiced statements (Anti-Defamation League, 2012, p. 18).

Hate crimes, neo-Nazis, and anti-Semitic sentiments are part of everyday life in Germany, other European nations, and the United States, as well as across the globe. They seem to have some common causes: high rates of immigration combined with economic uncertainty for working-class, less educated males, and strong traditions of racism and intolerance. Still, the memory of the Holocaust gives special resonance to attacks on minority groups in Germany.

SWITZERLAND

Although our focus is on the ethnic and racial trouble spots, it is also important to consider societies in which group relations are generally peaceful and conflict is comparatively minimal. One such society is Switzerland. Swiss society incorporates three major and distinct language and cultural groups: French speakers, German speakers, and Italian speakers. Each language group resides in a particular region of the country and enjoys considerable control of its local affairs. In our terms, Switzerland is a pluralistic society in which the groups are separate both culturally and structurally. That is, at the local level, the groups have neither acculturated nor integrated. Each group maintains its unique cultural and linguistic heritage, and its separate institutional and organizational structures.

At the national level, political power and economic resources are shared in proportion to the size of each group. The leaders of the different groups are careful to cooperate in national affairs and maintain the sense of proportional sharing and fundamental fairness. With the combination of cooperation at the national level and autonomy at the local level, Switzerland is able to function effectively as a multicultural, multilingual society.

Perhaps the key to Swiss success in combining diversity and unity is that none of the three major groups was forced to join the nation by military conquest or coercion. The groups joined together voluntarily and created this pluralistic nation for mutual advantage. Thus, for the three major groups that make up Swiss society, there is no history of conquest or subordination and no patterns of structured inequality, prejudice, or resentment.

FORMER YUGOSLAVIA

The case of Switzerland indicates that peaceful and prosperous pluralistic societies can be created, but this is not typical of multigroup societies. Conquest and coercion are more common than voluntary cooperation, and the potential for rancor, conflict, and violence tends to be high, as demonstrated by the former nation of Yugoslavia.

As we saw in the introduction to this chapter, eastern Europe is a region of immense ethnic, linguistic, and religious diversity. Travel, trade, and warfare have mixed and scattered groups, and over the centuries, nations and empires have come and gone. The former nation of Yugoslavia exemplifies both the diversity of the region and the complexities of intergroup conflict and cooperation.

The history of the modern nation of Yugoslavia is both short and complex. When it was created in 1918, at the end of World War I, the nation encompassed a variety of ethnic groups, each with its own language, religion, history, and memories of grievances against other groups. The larger groups include Croats (who are mainly Roman Catholic), Serbs (primarily Eastern Orthodox), and Bosnians (roughly half Muslim, half Christian). Each of these groups had a home territory (see Figure 13.3) in which it was the numerical majority. For example, in 1992, Croatia was 78% Croatian, and Serbia was 85% Serbian. Bosnia was the most diverse of the former Yugoslav states. In 1992, about 44% of the population of Bosnia was Muslim, 39% was Serb, and 17% was Croat (Remington, 1997, p. 275).

During World War II, Yugoslavia was one of the bloody battlegrounds, and each of these groups took sides. German forces invaded the region and created a puppet government in Croatia. The Croatian allies of the Nazis participated not only in the persecution of Jews but also in a campaign against the Serbs residing within their reach. Concentration camps were constructed and mass executions carried out. By the end of the war, the fascist Croatian government had murdered hundreds of thousands of Serbs. However, the Croats were not alone in their atrocities. Their campaign against Serbs provoked anti-Croatian violence in Serbia; hostility and resentment between the two groups had grown to new heights by the end of the war.

World War II also saw the emergence of Josip Broz Tito as a leader of anti-Nazi guerrilla forces. After the war, Tito became the chief architect of the modern nation of Yugoslavia. Tito's design incorporated many of the same elements that make Switzerland a successful pluralistic society. Postwar Yugoslavia comprised several different subnations, or republics, each of which was associated with a particular ethnic group. Power at the national level was allocated proportionately, and each region had considerable autonomy in the conduct of its affairs.

A major difference between Yugoslavia and Switzerland, however, lies in the contact situation. Whereas Switzerland was formed on a voluntary basis, Yugoslavia was first created by post–World War I diplomatic negotiations and then re-created at the end of World War II by the authoritarian regime of Tito. The nation was held together largely by the forcefulness of Tito's leadership. After his death in 1980, little remained to preserve the integrity of the Yugoslavian experiment in nation building. The memories of past hostilities and World War II atrocities were strong, and the separate republics began to secede from the Yugoslav federation in the 1990s.

Self-serving political and military leaders in Serbia and in the other former Yugoslavian states inflamed prejudices and antipathies. Vicious conflicts broke out throughout the region, with the worst violence occurring in Bosnia. Bosnia's attempt

FIGURE 13.3 States of Former Yugoslavia

to establish its independence was opposed by Serbia and by the Serbian and Croatian residents of Bosnia, both of whom formed armed militias. Bosnia became a killing field as these different contingents confronted each other. The Serbs began a campaign of "ethnic cleansing" in Bosnia in 1992 and committed the worst excesses. In the areas of Bosnia where they could establish control, Serbs mounted a campaign to eliminate non-Serbs by forced relocation or, if necessary, by wholesale massacre. Concentration camps appeared, houses were torched, former neighbors became blood enemies, women were raped, and children were killed along with their parents.

The Serbs were not alone in resorting to tactics of mass terror and murder. Croats used the same methods against Bosnian Muslims, and Bosnians retaliated in kind against Serbs. By the time relative peace was established in Bosnia in 1995, more than 200,000 people had died in the murderous ethnic conflict. Many of these patterns of vicious brutality reappeared in the conflict between Serbia and Kosovo that began in 1999 and was ended by the armed intervention of the United States and its North Atlantic Treaty Organization allies.

The disintegration of the former Yugoslavia into savage ethnic violence is one of the nightmarish episodes of recent history. Unfortunately, it is not unique.

RWANDA

In the spring of 1994, the tiny African nation of Rwanda sprang into international headlines. Rwanda's two ethnic groups, the Hutus and Tutsis, had a long history of mutual enmity and hatred, but the attacks that began in 1994 reached new heights of brutality. Perhaps 800,000 people—perhaps many more—were murdered, and millions fled to neighboring nations (Gourevitch, 1999, p. 83). Accounts by witnesses and survivors told of massacres with rifles, machetes, rocks, and fists. No one was spared in the killing frenzy. Elderly people, pregnant women, and small children were executed along with the men in what became one of the most horrific, unimaginable episodes of intergroup violence in world history.

What caused this outburst? As seems to be the case whenever intense ethnic violence occurs, colonization and conquest are part of the explanation for the brutal confrontation between the Hutus and Tutsis. European nations began colonizing Africa in the 1400s, and the area that became Rwanda did not escape domination. Germany established control over the region in the late 1800s. Following its defeat in World War I, Germany lost its overseas possessions, and Belgium became the dominant power in the region. Both European powers valued Rwanda for its mild climate and fertile soil. The native population was harnessed to the task of producing agricultural products, especially tea and coffee, for export.

The European colonizers attempted to ease the difficulty of administering and controlling Rwanda by capitalizing on the long-standing enmity between the Tutsis and Hutus. In a classic case of divide and conquer, Germany placed the Tutsis in a position to govern the Hutus, a move that perpetuated and intensified hostilities between the tribes. The Belgians continued the tradition and maintained the political and economic differentials between the tribes.

Throughout the colonial era, mutual tribal hostilities were punctuated by periodic armed clashes, some of which rose to the level of massacres. In the early 1960s, the era of direct European political colonialism ended, and two nations were created in the region: Rwanda was dominated by the Hutus, and neighboring Burundi by the Tutsis. Hostilities did not stop at this point, however, and the short histories of these two new nations are filled with shared conflicts. What portion of these conflicts is international and what portion domestic is difficult to determine, because a substantial number of Tutsis continued to reside in Rwanda and many residents of Burundi were Hutu. In other words, the borders between the two nations were drawn arbitrarily and do not reflect local traditions or tribal realities.

In the early 1990s, a rebel force led by exiled Tutsis invaded Rwanda with the intention of overthrowing the Hutu-dominated government. The conflict continued until the spring of 1994, when the plane carrying the Hutu president of Rwanda was shot down, killing all aboard. This was the incident that set off the massacres, with Hutus seeking revenge for the death of their president and attempting to eliminate their Tutsi rivals. In another of the great nightmarish episodes of the 20th century, perhaps as many as half the Tutsis in Rwanda died in the confrontation, and millions more fled for their lives. Although surely not a complete explanation for these horrors, the history of intertribal enmity and competition for power and control enhanced and magnified by European colonialism

Nelson Mandela casts his ballot in the first free and open South African election.

is part of the background for understanding them—if such an understanding is possible.

Since 1994, Rwanda has enjoyed relative calm. Violent ethnic clashes, however, have continued across the African continent, and the nightmare of genocide has struck Darfur, the Central African Republic, and Somalia, among other nations.

SOUTH AFRICA

Not all stories are nightmares, and the dreary litany of hatred, conflict, and violence occasionally takes a surprising twist. As recently as the late 1980s, the Republic of South Africa was one of the most racist and discriminatory societies in the world. A small minority of whites (no more than 10%) dominated the black African population and enjoyed a level of race-based privilege rarely equaled in the history of the world.

Today, although enormous problems of inequality and racism remain, South Africa has officially dismantled the machinery of racial oppression, enfranchised nonwhites, and elected three black presidents. Even in a world where change is rapid and unpredictable, the end of state-supported racism and race-based privilege in South Africa is one of the more stunning surprises of recent times.

Some background will illuminate the magnitude of the change. Europeans first came into contact with the area that became the nation of South Africa in the 1600s, at about the time when the British were establishing colonies in North America. First to arrive were the Dutch, who established ports on the coast to resupply merchant ships for the journey between Asia and Europe. Some of the Dutch began moving into the interior to establish farms and sheep and cattle ranches. The "trekkers," as they were called, regularly fought with indigenous black Africans and tribes moving into the area from the north. These interracial conflicts were extremely bloody and resulted in enslavement for some black Africans, genocide for others, and a gradual push of the remaining black Africans into the interior. In some ways, this contact period resembled that between European Americans and Native Americans, and in other ways, it resembled the early days of the establishment of black slavery in North America.

In the 1800s, South Africa became a British colony, and the new governing group attempted to grant more privileges to blacks. These efforts stopped far short of equality, however, and South Africa continued to evolve as a racially divided, white-dominated society into the 20th century. The white community continued to be split along ethnic lines, and hostilities erupted into violence on a number of occasions. In 1899, British and Dutch factions fought each other in the Boer War, a bitter and intense struggle that widened and solidified the divisions between the two white communities. Generally, the descendants of the Dutch have been more opposed to racial change than have the descendants of the British.

In 1948, the National Party, the primary political vehicle of the Afrikaans, or Dutch, segment of the white community, came into control of the state. As the society modernized and industrialized, there was growing concern about controlling the majority black population. Under the leadership of the National Party, the system of apartheid was constructed to firmly establish white superiority. In Afrikaans, *apartheid* means "separate" or "apart," and the basic logic of the system was to separate whites and blacks in every area of life: schools, neighborhoods, jobs, buses, churches, and so forth. As we pointed out in Chapter 5, apartheid resembled the Jim Crow system of segregation in the United States, except it was even more repressive, elaborate, and unequal.

Although the official government propaganda claimed that apartheid would permit blacks and whites to develop separately and equally, the system was clearly intended to solidify white privilege and black powerlessness. By keeping blacks poor and powerless, white South Africans created a pool of workers who were both cheap and docile. Whites of even modest means could afford the luxuries of personal servants, and employers could minimize their payrolls and their overhead. Of the dominant–minority situations considered in this text, perhaps only American slavery rivals apartheid for its naked, unabashed subjugation of one group for the benefit of another.

Note that the coming of apartheid reversed the relationship between modernization and control of minority groups that we observed in the United States. As the United States industrialized and modernized, group relations evolved from paternalistic to rigid competitive to fluid competitive forms (see Table 5.2), each stage representing a looser form of control over the minority group. In South Africa after 1948, group relations became more rigid and the structures of control became stronger and more oppressive. Why the difference?

Just as whites in the U.S. South attempted to defend their privileged status and resist the end of de jure segregation in the 1950s and 1960s, white South Africans were committed to retaining their status and the benefits it created. Although South Africans of British descent tended to be more liberal in matters of race than those of Dutch descent, both groups were firmly committed to white supremacy. Thus, unlike the situation in the United States at the end of Jim Crow segregation, in which white liberals and non-Southerners put considerable pressure on the racist South, there was little internal opposition to the creation of apartheid among South African whites.

Furthermore, South African blacks in the late 1940s were comparatively more powerless than blacks in the United States in the 1950s and 1960s. Although South African black protest organizations existed, they were illegal and had to operate underground or from exile and under conditions of extreme repression. In the United States, in contrast, blacks living outside the South were able to organize and pool their resources to assist in the campaign against Jim Crow, and these activities were protected (more or less) by the national commitment to civil liberties and political freedom.

A final difference between the two situations has to do with numbers, as we pointed out in Chapter 5. Whereas in the United States blacks are a numerical minority, they were the great majority of the population in South Africa. Part of the impetus for establishing the rigid system of apartheid was the fear among whites that they would be "swamped" by the numerical majority unless black powerlessness was perpetuated. The difference in group size helped contribute to the "fortress" mentality among some white South Africans: the feeling that they were defending a small (but luxurious) outpost surrounded and besieged by savage hordes who threatened their immediate and total destruction. This strong sense of threat among whites, and the need to be vigilant and constantly resist the least hint of racial change, is part of what made the events of the 1990s so remarkable and unexpected.

The system of racial privilege called apartheid lasted about 40 years. Through the 1970s and 1980s, changes within South Africa and the world in general built up pressure against the system. Internally, protests by blacks against apartheid began in the 1960s and continued to build in intensity. The South African government responded to these protests with violent repression, and thousands died in the confrontations with police and the army. Nonetheless, anti-apartheid activism continued to attack the system from below.

Apartheid also suffered from internal weaknesses and contradictions. For example, jobs were strictly segregated, along with all other aspects of South African society. In a modern, industrial economy, however, new types of jobs are constantly being created and old jobs are continually lost to mechanization and automation, making it difficult to maintain simple, caste-like rules about who can do what kinds of work. Also, many of the newer jobs required higher levels of education and special skills, and the number of white South Africans was too small to meet the demand. Thus, some black South Africans were slowly rising to positions of greater affluence and personal freedom even as the system attempted to coerce and repress the group as a whole.

Internationally, pressure on South Africa to end apartheid was significant. Other nations established trade embargoes and organized boycotts of South African goods. South Africa was banned from the Olympics and other international competitions. Although many of these efforts were more symbolic than real and had only minor impacts on everyday social life, they sustained an outcast status for South Africa and helped create an atmosphere of uncertainty among its economic and political elite.

In the late 1980s, these various pressures made it impossible to ignore the need for reform any longer. In 1990, F. W. de Klerk, the leader of the National Party and prime minister of the nation, began a series of changes that eventually ended apartheid. He lifted the ban on many outlawed black African protest organizations, and, perhaps most significant, he released Nelson Mandela from prison. Mandela was the leader of the African National Congress, one of the oldest and most important black organizations, and he had served a 27-year prison term for actively protesting apartheid.

Together, de Klerk and Mandela helped ease South Africa through a period of rapid racial change that saw the franchise being extended to blacks, the first open election in South African history, and Mandela's election in 1994 to a five-year term as president. After his presidency, Mandela continued to grow in stature on the world stage, hailed as the key individual who prevented a race war in South Africa and as a symbol of racial democracy and justice. His passing in December 2013 was met with virtually universal grief.

In 1999, Mandela was replaced by Thabo M. Mbeke, another black South African. Mbeke was reelected in 2004 but ousted in September 2008 after a bitter struggle with African National Congress rival Jacob Zuma, who became president in 2009. Zuma is a charismatic figure with strong support among the rank-and-file of the party, but his standing has been compromised by allegations of corruption, charges of rape, and other scandals.

The future of South Africa remains unclear. Although the majority black population now has political power, deep racial divisions remain. In many urban and white residential areas, South Africa maintains a First-World infrastructure, but the black population continues to live in Third-World poverty.

In 2010, South Africa hosted the soccer World Cup and expanded airports, improved roads, and built hotels and stadiums to provide first-class facilities for the hordes of fans who attended the matches. The event went off smoothly and was generally considered a triumph as South Africa presented its best multiracial, unified face to the world.

What the world didn't see was that much of the black population continues to live in apartheid-era townships—pockets of deep, grinding poverty with no running water, electricity, or sewage, poor or nonexistent medical care, and grossly overcrowded and understaffed schools. Things may be getting better for black South Africans: One report concludes that the black middle class has doubled in size since 1993 and the percentage of blacks in the middle class has increased from 8% to almost 14% in the same time period. Furthermore, the income gap between whites and blacks has declined. Still, the average annual income (in U.S. dollars) for black households was just under $7,000 in 2012, about one sixth of the annual income for white households (Cohen, 2012).

The problems of racial and class inequality facing South Africa are enormous, and this experiment in racial reform might still fail. However, should it succeed in meeting these challenges, the dramatic transition away from massive racism and institutionalized discrimination could still provide a model of change for other racially divided societies.

THE MIDDLE EAST

The tense, often violent relations between Israelis, Palestinians, and other Arabs are yet another example of the complex, long-lasting conflicts that seem to defy the most concerted, best-intentioned efforts at conciliation. Hatred, terrorism, and pledges to fight to the death are common in these conflicts and deeply complicated by the fact that they involve nation-states and global alliances as well as dominant and minority groups. Relations between groups in the Middle East are perhaps the most complex and ancient of any around the globe.

As with many of the situations considered in this chapter, present-day conflicts in the Middle East have their origins in military conquest. Following World War II and the horrors of the Holocaust, European Jews pushed for the establishment of a Jewish state in their traditional homeland. This cause was strongly supported by the United Nations and United States, and Israel was founded in 1948.

Unfortunately, the Jewish homeland was established on land occupied by Arabs (Palestinians), who also regarded it as their rightful homeland. Thus began the dominant–minority (Israeli–Palestinian) situation that continues today and is further complicated by relations between Israel and the other nations of the Middle East.

One difference between this and other intergroup struggles is the span of time involved. Although the modern state of Israel encompasses the traditional Jewish homeland, few Jews have lived in this area for the past 2,000 years. Jews were exiled

Palestinian activists confront Israeli soldiers during a demonstration.

There are some indications that a solution to the enmities in the Middle East is possible. In 1979, Egypt, formerly committed to the destruction of the Jewish state, signed a peace accord with Israel. More recently, Israel and representatives of the Palestinians have engaged in occasional peace talks and, most famously, signed an accord intended to lead to Palestinian self-rule in Oslo in 1993. The peace talks have been punctuated with violent uprisings by Palestinians ("Intifadas") and military responses by the Israeli Army. To say the least, negotiations have been extremely difficult and constantly threatened by violence, suicide bombings, attacks, and counterattacks.

Negotiations continue sporadically, but few can see an end to the ongoing conflicts. Of course, much the same point was made about South Africa until the dramatic events that led to the release of Mandela and the relatively peaceful transition to a racial democracy. The history of dominant–minority relations is filled with surprises, and, at least theoretically, a peaceful, permanent resolution remains a possibility.

HAWAII

Like Switzerland, Hawaii is often identified as a society that maintains peaceful group relations in the face of great diversity. This reputation justifies the inclusion of the islands in this global survey despite the fact that Hawaii is not a separate, autonomous nation.

The diversity of Hawaiian society is demonstrated, in part, by its racial makeup. The population of Hawaii is much more racially mixed than the general population of the United States. In the 2010 Census, for example, 24% of Hawaiians chose more than one category to describe their race, compared with less than 3% of the U.S. population as a whole.

Whites are a numerical minority on the island, accounting for about a quarter of the population. Asians are the single largest racial group, with Japanese Americans and Filipino Americans the largest Asian subcategories. Native Hawaiians are about 20% of the population. Other groups—Hispanic Americans, African Americans, and Samoans and other Pacific Islanders, among others—are also a part of the island social order.

The cultures and traditions of all these groups are evident in the mix of Hawaiian society and the rhythm of everyday life. The relatively low levels of prejudice, discrimination, and group conflict in the midst of this diversity are the bases for the sometimes glowing (and, many would argue, overstated) depictions of Hawaii as a racial paradise.

The comparatively high levels of tolerance seem unusual in a world that often features just the opposite. A brief review of the history of the islands provides some insight into the development of these peaceful relations, as well as the suggestion that the peaceful facade hides a grimmer reality.

Hawaii first came into contact with Europeans in 1788, but conquest and colonization did not follow the initial

from the region during the time of the Roman Empire and resettled in parts of Europe, Africa, and Asia. The Middle East has been Arab land for most of the past thousand years. Jews began to immigrate back to the area early in the 20th century, and especially after World War II and the founding of Israel, but they found a well-entrenched Palestinian Arab society on what they considered to be "their" land.

Warfare between the newly founded Israel and the surrounding Arab nations began almost immediately, and violent confrontations of one sort or another have been nearly continuous. Full-scale wars were fought in 1948, 1967 (the famous Six-Day War), and again in 1973. Israel was victorious in all three instances, and it claimed additional territory from its Arab neighbors (including the Golan Heights, the West Bank, and the Gaza Strip) to reduce the threat and provide a buffer zone. The wars also created a large group of refugees in the Arab countries neighboring Israel.

The Arabs who remained in Israel after the wars and in Israeli-occupied territories became a minority group. Israel has always pursued an official policy of assimilation, and some Arabs eventually became Israeli citizens, although most prefer to be classified as "permanent residents" rather than citizens, as a way of refusing to recognize Israel's sovereignty. Arabs make up about 20% of Israel's population of eight million (Israel Central Bureau of Statistics, 2014). The Palestinian population of Israel is supplemented with millions more living in the surrounding Arab nations.

Part of the complexity and intensity of this situation stems from the fact that the groups involved are separated along so many different lines: nationality, religion, language, ethnicity, history, and social class. In addition, because of the huge oil reserves in the region, the Israeli–Arab conflict has political and international dimensions that directly involve the rest of the world. The U.S. involvement in two separate invasions of Iraq; the war on terror following the September 11, 2001, attacks on the United States; the war in Afghanistan; and the difficult relationship between Iran and the West have added a level of complexity to the already tense relationships between Israel and its Arab neighbors.

contact. Early relations between the islanders and Europeans were organized around trade and commerce—not agriculture, as was the case in the United States, South Africa, Northern Ireland, and so many other places. Thus, the contact situation did not lead immediately to competition over the control of land or labor.

Also, the indigenous Hawaiian society was highly developed and had sufficient military strength to protect itself from the relatively few Europeans who came to the islands in these early days. Thus, two of the three conditions—competition and a differential in power—stated in the Noel hypothesis (see Chapter 4) for the emergence of a dominant–minority situation were not present in the early days of European–Hawaiian contact. Anglo dominance did not emerge until decades after first contact.

Contact with Europeans did bring other consequences, including smallpox and other diseases to which Native Hawaiians had no immunity. Death rates began to rise, and the population of Native Hawaiians fell from about 300,000 in 1788 to less than 60,000 a century later (Kitano & Daniels, 1995, p. 137).

As relations between the islands and Europeans developed, the land gradually began to be turned to commercial agriculture. By the mid-1800s, white planters had established sugar plantations, an enterprise that is extremely labor-intensive and has often been associated with systems of enforced labor and slavery (Curtin, 1990). By that time, however, there were not enough Native Hawaiians to fill the demand for labor, and the planters began to recruit abroad, mostly in China, Portugal, Japan, Korea, Puerto Rico, and the Philippines. Thus, the original immigrants of the Asian American groups we discussed in Chapter 9 often came first to the Hawaiian Islands, not to the mainland.

The white plantation owners came to dominate the island economy and political structure. Other groups, however, were not excluded from secondary structural assimilation. Laws banning entire groups from public institutions or practices, such as school segregation, are nonexistent in Hawaiian history. Americans of Japanese ancestry, for example, are very powerful in politics and have produced many of the leading Hawaiian politicians. (In contrast to events on the mainland, Japanese Americans in Hawaii were not interned during World War II.) Most other groups have taken advantage of the relative openness of Hawaiian society and have carved out niches for themselves in the institutional structure.

In the area of primary structural assimilation, rates of intermarriage among the various groups are much higher than on the mainland, reflecting the openness to intimacy across group lines that has characterized Hawaii since first contact. About 42% of all marriages in Hawaii from 2008 to 2010 crossed group lines, a much higher rate than for any other state (Wang, 2012, p. 10). In particular, Native Hawaiians have intermarried freely with other groups (Kitano & Daniels, 1995, pp. 138–139).

Although Hawaii has no history of the most blatant and oppressive forms of group discrimination, all is not perfect in the reputed racial paradise. There is evidence of ethnic and racial stratification, as well as prejudice and discrimination. Native Hawaiians, like Native Americans and other colonized groups, have developed organizations to pursue compensation for lands illegally taken and to resolve other grievances. There have been reports of attacks on whites by Native Hawaiians, incidents that some are calling hate crimes (Kasindorf, 2012). However, the traditions of tolerance and acceptance remain strong in the island state, even though it is not the paradise of mutual respect sometimes alleged.

BRAZIL

Brazilian and U.S. history run parallel in many ways. Both nations emerged from a contact situation that involved three racially distinct groups and a struggle for land and labor. In both cases, the group that became dominant was white, harsh treatment and disease devastated one of the defeated groups (the indigenous population), and the other group (blacks from Africa) was used for slave labor on plantations. In spite of these early parallels, the nations developed along different tracks, and race relations in modern Brazil are distinctly different from those in the United States.

Brazil is the largest nation in South America. Its territory stretches from the Atlantic Ocean deep into the interior and almost across the width of the continent, and its population of 190 million is racially and ethnically diverse. About 800,000 Indians survive, down from perhaps 5 million at first contact.

Brazil was a colony of Portugal until 1822, and Portuguese remains its primary language. The colonial history of Brazil began almost a century before Jamestown was established. In fact, the African slave trade on which the British colonies became so dependent in the 1600s and 1700s was originally created to provide slave labor for colonial Brazil in the 1500s (Curtin, 1990). Slavery was a central feature of the colonial Brazilian economy and was focused on sugar production in a plantation economy.

Unlike the United States, where slavery ended suddenly as a result of the Civil War, slavery in Brazil ended gradually. It was abolished in 1888, but preparations for the end had been under way for decades and the transition of slaves to free citizens was less wrenching than in the United States.

Today, race relations in Brazil are generally regarded as less problematic and confrontational than in the United States. A variety of theories have been advanced to explain the difference in group relations between the two nations (e.g., see Cottrol, 2013; Degler, 1971; Tannenbaum, 1947).

The issues cannot be fully explored in these few paragraphs, but we can make the point that the foundation for today's race relations may have been laid in the distant past, both before and during the contact situation. At the time Brazil was established, Portugal, unlike England, had had a long acquaintance

Listed below are some ethnic or racial "trouble spots" that were not covered in this chapter. For each, can you identify the region of the world, the groups involved in the conflict, and at least one key issue? For any given location, there may well be more than one issue, but we have tried to select the most prominent (at least in the headlines). How well do you think most Americans would do on this quiz?

AREA	REGION	GROUPS AND ISSUES
Chechnya		
Scotland		
Nigeria		
China		
Spain		
Mexico		

TURN THE PAGE TO FIND OUR ANSWERS.

with African cultures and peoples. In fact, Moors from North Africa ruled Portugal for a time. Thus, darker skin and other African "racial" features were familiar to the Portuguese and not, in and of themselves, regarded as a stigma or an indication of inferiority.

The relative absence of skin color prejudice also may be reflected in the high rates of intermarriage between Portuguese, Africans, and natives. The Brazilian colonists were mostly males, unlike their British counterparts, who were much more likely to immigrate in family groups, and they took brides from other groups. These intermarriages produced a large class of mulattos, or people of mixed race. Today, whites are slightly less than a majority of the population (47%), and blacks are about 8%. Most of the remainder of the population (about 43%) consists of *pardos*, or people of mixed-race ancestry (Instituto Brasileiro do Geografica e Estatistica, 2013).

Brazilian slavery tended to be more open than the North American variety. Brazilian slaves were freed at a much higher rate than British American slaves were, and there was a large class of free blacks and mulattos filling virtually every job and position available in the society.

In Brazil, slavery was not so thoroughly equated with race as it was in North America. Although slave status was certainly undesirable and unfortunate, it did not carry the presumption of racial inferiority. In North America, in contrast, antiblack prejudice and racism came into being as a way of rationalizing and supporting the system (see Chapter 4); slavery, blackness, and inferiority were tightly linked in the dominant ideology, an equation with powerful echoes in the present.

The results of the higher rates of racial intermarriage, large population of mulattos, and lower levels of racial

prejudice in Brazil are manifold. First, they helped sustain a way of thinking about race that is sharply different from North American practices. In Brazil and other parts of South and Central America, race is seen as a series of categories that have ambiguous, indeterminate boundaries. Black, white, and other colors shade into one another in an infinite variety of ways, and no hard or sharp borders mark the end of one group and the start of another.

In the United States, in contrast, race has traditionally been seen as a set of sharply delineated categories with clear, definite boundaries. One's race is determined by the social group one belongs to, regardless of appearance or actual ancestry, and everyone belongs to one and only one race. Thus, people who are raised in and identify with the black community—including people who "look white"—are black. In Brazil, on the other hand, people aren't forced into simple, dichotomous categories, and there can be a good deal of racial ambiguity and indeterminateness.

Second, after the end of slavery, Brazil did not go through a period of legalized racial segregation like the Jim Crow system or apartheid. Such a system would be difficult to construct or enforce when race is seen as a set of open-ended categories that gradually fade into one another. Racial segregation requires a simple racial classification system in which people are classified unambiguously into a single category. The more nuanced and subtle perception of race in Brazil is not conducive to a strict system of racial inequality.

It should be stressed that Brazil has not solved its dominant–minority problems. The legacy of slavery is still strong, and there is a very high correlation between skin color and social status. Studies consistently show that black Brazilians

AREA	REGION	GROUPS AND ISSUES
Chechnya	Eastern Europe	Separatism. Since the dissolution of the Soviet Union, Chechnya has fought two wars for independence. Besides cultural differences with Russia, Chechens are predominantly Muslim.
Scotland	Northern United Kingdom	Separatism. Scotland has been part of the United Kingdom for centuries, but there has always been strong sentiment to secede and become an independent sovereign nation. A variety of Scottish groups are pursuing this goal, and a referendum on the question is scheduled for the fall of 2014.
Nigeria	Western Africa	Discrimination against gays and lesbians (see Chapter 12). In January 2014, Nigeria passed a law that criminalized homosexuality and provided up to 14 years in prison for same-sex relationships.
China	East Asia	Separatism. Groups claiming to represent Uyghur, a predominantly Muslim area of western China, wish to gain their independence and make the province a separate, autonomous nation. There is also considerable support for separation and autonomy in Tibet, which has been a part of China since the 1950s.
Spain	Western Europe	Separatism. Many Basques, who live in the mountainous northern regions of Spain, desire their own independent nation. Basques are a distinct cultural and linguistic minority whose "home territory" stretches across the border to France.
Mexico	North America	Indigenous rights. The indigenous population of Mexico (about 15% of the total) is concentrated in the southern states of Oaxaca and Chiapas. They have numerous grievances, including land claims, discrimination, and racism.

Note the frequency of separatism as a goal in these trouble spots. Is this a testimony to the ability of groups to maintain their culture and distinct identity even when they have been part of a larger nation, sometimes for centuries? Will ethnicity ever fade away?

have higher poverty rates and lower educational attainment, levels of health, and incomes. Whites dominate the more prestigious and lucrative occupations and the leadership positions in the economy and politics, whereas blacks are concentrated at the bottom of the class system (Haan & Thorat, 2012; Marteleto, 2012).

Interestingly, Brazil has made a major commitment to increasing the opportunities available to the poor, a disproportionate number of whom are black or brown. For example, a program called Brazil Without Misery was launched in 2011 with the intent of eliminating extreme poverty by 2014, and the central government has instituted a variety of affirmative action programs intended to increase the enrollment of black students in the nation's universities.

Brazil is not a racial utopia, as is sometimes claimed. Racial discrimination, inequality, and racism are massive problems there, as they are in the United States. Still, the comparison between the two nations is instructive. Differences in the contact period and the development of race relations over time have resulted in a notably different form of group relations today.

QUESTIONS FOR REFLECTION

1. Which, if any, of these dominant–minority situations is new to you? Which was the most surprising to you? Why?

2. Do you think your peers are aware of the situations described in this section? How about most Americans? How would you explain the level of information (or interest) that people have in these matters?

ANALYZING GROUP RELATIONS

Our tour of group relations around the globe has been brief and highly selective in the stops we made. Nonetheless, some conclusions are possible.

Problems of dominant–minority relations are extremely common. It seems that the only nations that lack such problems are the relatively few (such as Sweden) that are homogeneous in their racial, cultural, religious, and linguistic makeup.

Still, many of these (including Sweden) have current issues with immigration.

Dominant–minority problems are highly variable in their form and intensity. They encompass genocide in the former Yugoslavia and Rwanda; hate crimes motivated by race, religion, or ethnicity in Germany (and many other nations); and complaints of racism, unfairness, and injustice virtually everywhere. Some long-standing minority grievances remain unresolved, and new problem areas appear on a regular basis. It seems unlikely that all these issues of group relations—and the many others not covered in this chapter—will be settled or otherwise fade away at any point in the near future.

As we have noted on a number of occasions, the most intense, violent, and seemingly intractable problems of group relations almost always have their origins in contact situations in which one group is conquered or colonized by another. Blauner's hypothesis seems well supported by this examination of dominant–minority relations around the globe.

The impact of modernization and industrialization on racial and ethnic relations is variable. Whereas these forces led to less rigid group relations in the United States, they had the opposite effect in South Africa until the 1990s. Furthermore, around the globe, ethnic and racial groups that were thought to have been submerged in the hustle and bustle of modern society have been reappearing with surprising regularity. The former Yugoslavia supplies some of the most dramatic examples of the seeming imperviousness of ethnicity to industrialization and modernization, but others can be found in Scotland, Belgium, Spain, the former Soviet Union, Mexico, China, Nigeria, Iraq, and scores of other nations. In each of these cases, pluralistic or separatist movements based on ethnic, racial, or religious groups are present and, in some cases, thriving.

It seems unlikely that even the most sophisticated and modern of nations will outgrow the power of ethnic loyalties at any point in the near future. In virtually all the cases discussed, whatever tendencies modernization fosters to reduce prejudice seem to be offset by memories of past injustices, unresolved grievances, a simple yearning for revenge, and continuing struggles over control of land, labor, and other resources. Ethnic and racial lines continue to reflect inequalities of wealth and power, and as long as minority-group status is correlated with inequality, ethnic and racial loyalties will remain powerful motivations for conflict.

As we have noted, ethnic and racial group conflicts are especially intense when they coincide with class divisions and patterns of inequality. For example, minority-group members in Canada, South Africa, and Northern Ireland command lower shares of wealth and political power, and have worse jobs, poorer housing, and lower levels of education. When a conflict arises in these societies, whether the problem is one of economics, politics, or a dominant–minority issue, the same groups face each other across the lines of division. The greater the extent to which issues and lines of fracture coincide and reinforce each other, the greater the threat to society as a whole and the more difficult it will be to manage the conflict and avoid escalation to its extremes.

With respect to the intensity and nature of dominant–minority problems, the United States is hardly in a unique or unusual position. Many nations are dealing with problems of assimilation and pluralism, diversity and unity, and some of these issues seem far more difficult and complex than those facing our society. Societies such as Switzerland and Hawaii help sustain the idea that relatively peaceful, comparatively just, and roughly equal group relations are possible even for very diverse nations. Our tour of the globe also shows that no racial paradises exist; even the multi-group societies with the most glowing reputations for tolerance are not immune to conflict, inequality, discrimination, and racism.

QUESTIONS FOR REFLECTION

1. Do the case studies in this chapter demonstrate the importance of the contact situation and subsistence technology? How?

2. Which is the most important of the major concepts applied in this text? Why?

SUMMARY

This summary is organized around the Learning Objectives listed at the beginning of this chapter.

 State and explain the central themes of this text.

Throughout the text, we have stressed the importance of the initial contact situation (especially competition, differential in power, and colonization vs. immigration); subsistence technology; assimilation; pluralism; and prejudice, discrimination, and racism.

 Summarize the overall pattern of ethnic variability around the globe, and identify which regions are most and least diverse.

The United States is one of many nations dealing with issues of diversity. African nations tend to be the most diverse, and western European nations tend to be the least.

13.3 Summarize the dominant–minority situations outlined in this chapter, including the history and present situation, and apply the central concepts developed in this text to each case.

Virtually all these dominant–minority situations began with a contact situation in which one group colonized another. In Canada, the groups were based on language and culture; in Northern Ireland, religion was the obvious dividing line; and in South Africa and Brazil, it was race. In all cases, however, the divisions go deeper and include differences in access to power, property, and prestige.

In all cases, perhaps especially in the Middle East, Northern Ireland, Rwanda, and former Yugoslavia, the group divisions are ancient and carry a heavy burden of history, memory, and old grievances. Unlike the United States, separatism,

self-determination, and group autonomy are major themes, especially in Canada, Northern Ireland, and the former Yugoslavia (and in the situations listed in the Applying Concepts exercise in this chapter). Immigration and assimilation are important factors in Germany, Canada, and many other nations.

The cases of Switzerland and Hawaii suggest the possibility that multigroup societies can have relatively peaceful group relations. The other cases seem to suggest the difficulty of achieving that goal.

REVIEW QUESTIONS

1. How do the cases reviewed in this chapter illustrate the importance of the contact situation and subsistence technology? How do modernization and industrialization affect group relations?

2. For each case study in this chapter, list the racial and cultural characteristics of the dominant and minority groups, the nature of the contact situation, and the type of competition that motivated the construction of minority status. What common patterns do you observe? How do the patterns relate to the concepts used throughout this text?

3. Switzerland, Hawaii, and Brazil are often cited as examples of multigroup societies that are relatively harmonious. How accurate are these characterizations?

Are there any common characteristics of their contact situations that might help account for the relative harmony?

4. Compare the development of dominant–minority relations in Brazil and the United States. What important differences and similarities can you identify? How do these differences and similarities affect contemporary relations?

5. What does this chapter say to you about the prevalence and persistence of minority inequality, prejudice, and racism? Will there ever be a time when the nations of the world are free of these problems? What would have to happen to achieve this peace?

STUDENT STUDY SITE

Sharpen your skills with SAGE edge at edge.sagepub.com/healey7e

SAGE edge for students provides a personalized approach to help you accomplish your coursework goals in an easy-to-use learning environment.

The following resources are available at SAGE edge:

Public Sociology Assignments

Public Sociology Assignments provide opportunities for students to address directly and personally some of the issues raised in this text.

On our website you will find four assignments in Part IV. In the first assignment, students use the information available from the Pew Research Center to examine religion as a source of diversity in American life. In the second assignment, groups of students will analyze the lyrics of popular songs. Do the lyrics reflect stereotypes of racial or ethnic groups? What messages are being conveyed about gender or sexual orientation?

The third assignment focuses on a film and website that probe the reality of bullying in America's schools. The fourth assignment is an analysis of the thousands of languages around the world that are in danger of becoming extinct.

Contributed by Linda M. Waldron

Internet Research Project

For this Internet Research Project, you will select any two of the dominant–minority situations covered in this chapter or listed in the Applying Concepts exercise and use the resources available on the Internet to update information and conclusions. Has the situation improved, or has it gotten worse? What course concepts seem to be of continuing relevance? Which are less relevant? The project will be guided by a series of questions, and your instructor may ask you to discuss your findings in small groups.

For Further Reading

Please see our website for an annotated list of important works related to this chapter.

CHAPTER-OPENING TIMELINE PHOTO CREDITS

1899: Library of Congress Prints and Photographs Division

1916: Library of Congress Prints and Photographs Division

1939–1945: German Federal Archive/Stanislaw Mucha

1948: State of Israel's National Photo Collection

1979: Library of Congress Prints and Photographs Division

1990: Copyright World Economic Forum

1992–1995: Wikimedia Commons/Paul Katzenberger

1994: Wikimedia Commons

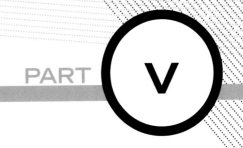

PART **V**

CHALLENGES FOR THE PRESENT AND THE FUTURE

Chapter 14 Minority Groups and U.S. Society:
Themes, Patterns, and the Future

Chapter 14 brings this text to a close. It looks back across the previous 13 chapters, summarizes our major themes and the information we have presented, and speculates about the future of group relations in America and the world.

We begin by revisiting the nine Americans we introduced in Chapter 1 and reexamining their diversity of race, ethnicity, gender, sexual orientation, and social class. Has your perspective on these individuals changed after reading this text? Are you more aware of how their differences reflect and mirror the American experience, in all its multiplicity?

We then review the major concepts we have employed throughout the text, including subsistence technology, the contact situation, group competition and power, intersectionality, and, of course, assimilation and pluralism. How has your understanding of these terms and ideas changed after reading this text? Do you feel comfortable applying these concepts and tracing their meanings?

We close with a consideration of what we regard as the major lessons of a sociological consideration of dominant–minority relations, in the context of American culture and contemporary forms of racism, prejudice, sexism, and homophobia. How do you respond to our points? How do they enrich your views on the subject? What are their limitations?

We are all too aware that we have raised many more questions in this text than we have answered. We hope that we have stimulated your interest in the vast and complex subject matter of dominant–minority relations and enhanced your ability to ask questions and seek answers on your own. If you finish this text with a stronger commitment to analytical thinking and careful evaluation—if you are less willing to settle for the everyday, superficial "explanations" that pass for understanding in so much of American life—we will have accomplished our most important goal.

14 MINORITY GROUPS AND U.S. SOCIETY

Themes, Patterns, and the Future

timeline

1960
The first U.S. public gathering of lesbians occurs at San Francisco's Daughters of Bilitis national convention.

1963
The March on Washington for Jobs and Freedom is attended by about 250,000 people. Martin Luther King, Jr. delivers his famous "I Have a Dream" speech.

1968
The American Indian Movement, an advocacy group, is founded.

1978
The American Indian Movement leads the Longest Walk, a spiritual walk across the country for tribal sovereignty and to protest anti-Indian legislation.

1955   1960   1965   1970   1975   1980

1955
The Daughters of Bilitis, a lesbian organization, is founded.

1955
Rosa Parks refuses to give up her seat on a bus to a white passenger, spurring the Montgomery bus boycott.

1960
Four black students in Greensboro, North Carolina, begin a sit-in at a segregated Woolworth's lunch counter. The event triggers many similar nonviolent protests throughout the South.

1965
César Chávez and Dolores Huerta found the United Farm Workers association.

1969
Patrons of the Stonewall Inn in Greenwich Village riot when police officers attempt to raid the popular gay bar.

1972
The American Indian Movement sponsors the Trail of Broken Treaties, a cross-country protest presenting a 20-point list of demands from the federal government.

Department of Labor

Throughout the previous 13 chapters, we have analyzed ideas and theories about dominant–minority relations, examined the historical and contemporary situations of minority groups in U.S. society, and surveyed a variety of dominant–minority situations around the globe. Now it is time to reexamine our major themes and concepts, and determine what conclusions can be derived from our analysis. •

LEARNING OBJECTIVES

By the end of this chapter, you will be able to do the following:

(14.1) Explain how the people profiled at the beginning of Chapter 1 exemplify the central themes and concepts of this text.

(14.2) Explain the relevance of our central concepts—especially subsistence technology, the contact situation, competition and power, and intersectionality—for American dominant-minority relations.

(14.3) Summarize the situation of each of the groups we have considered in terms of acculturation and integration.

(14.4) Explain the importance of a sociological perspective for understanding American dominant-minority relations.

Associated Press

Corbis

1987
The National March on Washington for Lesbian and Gay Rights draws over 500,000 people, making it the largest civil rights demonstration in U.S. history.

2004
Hispanic Americans become the largest minority group.

2008
The number of undocumented immigrants begins to decline in response to economic hard times in the U.S., falling to less than 11 million in 2012.

2012
Asians surpass Hispanics as the largest group of new immigrants in the U.S.

1965   1990   1995   2000   2005   2010

1979
An estimated 75,000 people participate in the National March on Washington for Lesbian and Gay Rights.

1995
The Million Man march is held in Washington, D.C. to place black issues back on the nation's political agenda.

2007
Massive demonstrations occur around the U.S. in support of immigrant rights.

Wikipedia

©iStockphoto.com/Coast-To-Coast

REVISITING
SOME AMERICANS

Let's begin with an exercise. Turn back to Chapter 1 and reread the biographies at the beginning of the chapter. After reading this text, you may see these nine people through different eyes: They represent a complex mix of privilege and disadvantage, and occupy a variety of positions in American society. Some are successful and affluent, but others are marginalized by their sexual orientation, religion, or race. Some are completely integrated into the primary job market, but others drift on the fringes in the informal, underground economy. Some, such as Juan Yancy, are bi- or multiracial and some, such as Hector Gonzalez, have a strong attachment to their cultural heritage. Others are uninterested in the stories of their ancestors' struggles.

Kim Park lives in an enclave economy, and Shirley Umphlett's life was profoundly affected by the "great migration" of African Americans from the rural South to the urban North. Mary Farrell's family history exemplifies the slow, generation-by-generation rise to middle-class status characteristic of so many European American immigrants, whereas George Snyder and Dennard Umphlett face the urban poverty and underclass marginality that confronts so many racial minority-group members today. William Buford III, in contrast, is wealthy and powerful, and argues that anyone could duplicate his success with sufficient diligence and hard work, conveniently forgetting that his wealth was inherited.

You might think that Buford's conclusions are not particularly insightful or informed, but his views are shared by millions of others in this society. Americans traditionally see success or failure as a matter of individual choice and personal effort. Blaming the victims of racism and discrimination for their situations can be comforting because it absolves the more fortunate of guilt or complicity in the perpetuation of minority-group poverty and powerlessness.

More accurate analyses and more compelling conclusions might be found in the thinking of people who are the victims of the system, because they are sensitized to the dynamics of racism and discrimination by their efforts to avoid victimization. We should recognize, however, that all nine of these Americans, like all of us, are victims in some ways and beneficiaries in others. Disadvantage and privilege are distributed in endlessly complex ways across the group matrices that structure our society.

We should also remember that our understandings are limited by who we are, where we come from, and what we have experienced. Our ability to imagine the realities faced by others is never perfect, and what we can see of the world depends very much on where we stand.

If we are to understand the forces that have created dominant–minority relationships in the United States and around the globe, we must find ways to surpass the limitations of our personal experiences and honestly confront the often ugly realities of the past and present. We believe that the information and ideas developed in this text can help liberate our sociological imaginations from the narrow confines of our own experiences and perspectives.

In this final chapter, we restate the general themes of this text, draw conclusions from the material we have covered, and speculate about the future. As we look backward to the past and forward to the future, it seems appropriate to paraphrase the words of the historian Oscar Handlin (1951): "Once I thought to write a history of the minority groups in America. Then, I discovered that the minority groups were American history" (p. 3).

THE IMPORTANCE
OF SUBSISTENCE
TECHNOLOGY

One of the most important sociological ideas we have developed is that dominant–minority relations are shaped by large social, political, and economic forces, and they change as these broad characteristics change. To understand the evolution of America's minority groups is to understand the history of the United States, from the earliest colonial settlement to the modern megalopolis. As we have seen throughout the text and in Chapter 13, these same broad forces have left their imprint on many societies around the globe.

Subsistence technology is the most basic force shaping a society and the relationships between dominant and minority groups in that society. In the colonial United States, minority relations were bent to the demands of a land-hungry, labor-intensive agrarian technology, and the early relationships between Africans, Europeans, and American Indians flowed from the colonists' desire to control both land and labor. By the mid-1800s, two centuries after Jamestown was founded, the same dynamics that had enslaved African Americans and nearly annihilated American Indians made a minority group out of Mexican Americans.

The agrarian era came to an end in the 19th century as the new technologies of the industrial revolution increased the productivity of the economy and eventually changed every aspect of life in the United States. The paternalistic, oppressive systems used to control the labor of minority groups in the agrarian era gave way to competitive systems of group relations. These newer systems evolved from more rigid forms to more fluid forms as industrialization and urbanization progressed.

As the United States grew and developed, new minority groups were created, and old minority groups, including women and lesbian, gay, bisexual, and transgender (LGBT) people, were transformed. Rapid industrialization, combined with the opportunities available on the frontier, made the

United States an attractive destination for immigrants from Europe, Asia, Latin America, and other parts of the world. Immigrants helped farm the Great Plains, mine the riches of the West, and, above all, supply the armies of labor required by industrialization.

The descendants of the immigrants from Europe benefited from the continuing industrialization of the economy, rising slowly in the social class structure as the economy grew and matured. Immigrants from Asia and Latin America were not so fortunate. Chinese and Japanese Americans survived in ethnic enclaves on the fringes of the mainstream society, and Mexican Americans and Puerto Ricans supplied low-paid manual labor for both the rural and the urban economy. For much of the 20th century, both Asian and Hispanic Americans were barred from access to dominant-group institutions and higher-paid jobs.

The racial minority groups, particularly African Americans, Mexican Americans, and Puerto Ricans, began to enter the urban working class after European American ethnic groups had started to move up in the occupational structure, at a time when the supply of manual, unskilled jobs was starting to dwindle. Thus, the processes that allowed upward mobility for European Americans failed to work for the racial minority groups, who confronted urban poverty and bankrupt cities in addition to the continuing barriers of racial prejudice and institutional discrimination.

Immigration to the United States has been quite high for the past several decades and has delivered highly educated professionals to help staff the postindustrial economy, along with large numbers of undocumented immigrants to supply workers for the secondary labor market and the irregular economy. This stream has evoked the usual American nativism and

Immigrants arriving at Ellis Island.

racism, along with intense debates—in the social sciences as well as in the general public—about the cost and benefits of the immigrants and their ultimate places in the social structure.

We can only speculate about what the future holds, but the emerging information-based, high-tech society is unlikely to offer many opportunities to people with lower levels of education and few occupational skills. It seems highly likely that, at least for the foreseeable future, a substantial percentage of racial and colonized minority groups and some recent immigrant groups will be participating in the mainstream economy at lower levels than will the dominant group, the descendants of the European immigrants, and the more advantaged recent immigrant groups. This outcome would be consistent with the segmented assimilation thesis, as discussed in Chapter 10. Upgraded urban educational systems, job training programs, and other community development programs might alter the grim scenario of continuing exclusion, but, as we discussed in Chapter 3, current public opinion on matters of race and discrimination makes creation of such programs unlikely.

The perpetuation of the status quo will bar a large percentage of the population from the emerging mainstream economy. Those segments of the African, Hispanic, and Asian American communities currently mired in the urban underclass will continue to compete with some of the newer immigrants for jobs in the low-wage, secondary labor market or in alternative opportunity structures, including crime.

Shifts in subsistence technology also helped transform gender roles and the situation of women. In the postindustrial era, women are heavily involved in the paid labor force and, because of the concerted, long-term efforts of the feminist movements, enjoy greater opportunities and more choices than ever before. However, as we have documented, women also face gender gaps in wages, glass ceilings, sexual harassment, and a variety of other issues and limitations. Women today are less constrained by institutional barriers, stereotypes, and presumptions of inferiority; yet what we have called the "invisible privileges" of maleness continue to operate across society, from intimate family relations to corporate boardrooms. Across the globe, the status of women continues to depend heavily on subsistence technology, and women in more agrarian societies face especially formidable barriers to gender equality.

As with other minority groups, nonheterosexuals have benefited from the greater tolerance and openness associated with more educated, more advanced industrial societies. The anonymity of urban spaces provided opportunities for gays and lesbians to find one another and begin to develop associations and form organizations, even when the labels of mental illness and stigmas of deviance and criminality were strongest. In recent decades, after considerable struggle and hard work, gay and lesbian Americans have reduced their marginalization and experienced a number of triumphs, including the growing acceptance of same-sex marriage. Much work remains to be done for LGBT people, however, especially in the areas of civil rights and legal protection against job discrimination.

THE IMPORTANCE OF THE CONTACT SITUATION, GROUP COMPETITION, AND POWER

We have stressed the importance of the contact situation—the conditions under which the minority group and dominant group first come into contact with each other—throughout this text. Blauner's distinction between immigrant and colonized minority groups is fundamental, a distinction so basic that it helps clarify minority-group situations centuries after the initial contact period. In Part III, we used Blauner's distinction as an organizing principle and covered American minority groups in approximate order from "most colonized" to "most immigrant." The groups covered first (African Americans and American Indians) are clearly at a greater disadvantage in contemporary society than are the groups covered last (especially immigrants from Asia with high levels of human capital) and the white ethnic groups covered in Chapter 2.

For example, prejudice, racism, and discrimination against African Americans remain formidable forces in contemporary America, even though they may have softened into more subtle forms. In contrast, prejudice and discrimination against European American groups such as Irish, Italian, and Polish Americans have nearly disappeared today, even though they were quite formidable just a few generations ago.

In the same way, contemporary immigrant groups that are nonwhite and bring few resources and low levels of human capital (e.g., Haitians) may experience segmented assimilation and find themselves in situations resembling those of colonized minority groups. Contemporary immigrant groups that are at the opposite end of the continuum (e.g., Asian Indians) are more likely to approximate the experiences of white ethnics and find themselves in some version of middle-class suburbia. The Internet research exercises presented at the ends of Chapters 6 through 10 should have given you information to assess some of these patterns.

Noel's hypothesis states that if three conditions—ethnocentrism, competition, and a differential in power—are present in the contact situation, ethnic or racial stratification will result. The relevance of ethnocentrism is largely limited to the actual contact situation, but the other two concepts help clarify the changes occurring after initial contact.

We have examined numerous instances in which group competition—or even the threat of competition—increased prejudice and led to greater discrimination and more repression. Recall, for example, the opposition of the labor movement

President Lyndon Johnson, the Reverand Martin Luther King, Jr. and Rosa Parks at the signing of the Voting Rights Bill, 1965.

(dominated by European American ethnic groups) to Chinese immigrants. The anti-Chinese campaign led to the Chinese Exclusion Act of 1882, the first significant restriction on immigration to the United States. There are parallels between campaigns for exclusion in the past and current ideas about ending or curtailing immigration. Clearly, some part of the current opposition to immigration is motivated by a sense of threat and the fear that immigrants are a danger not only to jobs and the economy but also to the cultural integrity of U.S. society.

Noel's third variable, differential in power, determines the outcome of the initial contact situation and which group becomes dominant and which becomes minority. Following the initial contact, the superior power of the dominant group helps it sustain the minority group's inferior position.

Minority groups, by definition, have fewer power resources, but they characteristically use what they have in an attempt to improve their situations. Improvements in the situations of American minority groups since the middle of the 20th century have been due in large part to the fact that they (especially African Americans, who typically led the way in protest and demands for change) finally acquired some power resources of their own. For example, one important source of power for the civil rights movement in the South during the 1950s and 1960s was the growth of African American voting strength in the North. After World War II, the African American electorate became too sizable to ignore, and its political power helped pressure the federal government to take action and pass the legislation that ended the Jim Crow era.

Minority status being what it is, however, each of the groups we have discussed (with the exception of the white ethnic groups) still controls relatively few power resources and is limited in its ability to pursue its own self-interests. Many of these limitations are economic and related to social class; many minority groups simply lack the resources to finance campaigns for reform or to exert significant pressure on political institutions. Other limitations include small group size (e.g., Asian American groups), language barriers (e.g., many Hispanic American groups), and divided loyalties within the group (e.g., Native Americans separated by tribal allegiances).

At any rate, the relative powerlessness of minority groups today is a legacy of the contact situations that created these groups in the first place. In general, colonized groups are at a greater power disadvantage than immigrant groups. Contact situations set agendas for group relations that continue to exert influence centuries after the initial meeting.

Given all we have examined in this text, it is obvious that competition and differences in power resources will continue to shape intergroup relations (including relations between minority groups themselves) well into the future. Because they are so basic and consequential, jobs will continue to be primary objects of competition, but plenty of other issues will divide the nation. Included on this divisive list will be debates about crime and the criminal justice system, welfare reform, national health care policy, school integration, bilingual education, immigration policy, and multicultural school curricula.

These and other public issues will continue to separate us along ethnic and racial lines because those lines have become so deeply embedded in the economy, in politics, in our schools and neighborhoods, and in virtually every nook and cranny of U.S. society. These deep divisions reflect fundamental realities about who gets what in the United States, and they will continue to reflect the distribution of power and stimulate competition along group lines for generations to come.

Of course, some of our most important concepts do not fit all dominant–minority group situations. For example, there is no "contact situation" for men and women, no time in history when one existed without the other. Similarly, it is impossible to identify a contact situation for heterosexuals and nonheterosexuals.

Still, both women and LGBTs fit Blauner's category of colonized minority group rather well. Patterns of inequality, marginalization, and denigration are easily documented, as we demonstrated in Chapters 11 and 12.

In the case of women, the system of oppression has been maintained and reinforced by highly visible physical markers of group membership, similar to the ways subordination is maintained for racial minority groups. For LGBT people, the dynamics of social visibility are more subtle and variable. However, as anyone who has "come out" can attest, visibility can bring fundamental changes in personal relations, occupational opportunities, and other areas of life.

Blauner's hypothesis may not be literally applicable to women and LGBTs, but Noel's concepts of power and competition are clearly central to the situations of both groups. They have both had to organize, acquire resources, and confront the bastions of privilege in the streets as well as the courtrooms to improve their situations and move closer to equality. Resistance to these movements has been constant and formidable, even though the long-term trend has been toward inclusion.

For women, the society made a formal (and, many would argue, partial and unfulfilled) commitment to equality many decades ago. The United States is currently embroiled in a deeply felt controversy over whether that commitment to equality should be extended to gays and lesbians, a struggle that reminds us that competition can be symbolic and cultural, and independent from the distribution of real resources such as jobs, income, and political representation. For LGBTs, the struggle for acceptance and an end to stigma and marginalization continues.

THE IMPORTANCE OF INTERSECTIONALITY

All too often, and this text is probably no exception, both dominant and minority groups are seen as unitary and undifferentiated. Although overgeneralizations are sometimes difficult to avoid, we want to stress again the diversity within each of the groups we have examined. Minority-group members vary from one another by age, sex, region of residence, level of education, urban versus rural residence, political ideology, and many other variables. The experience of one segment of the group (e.g., college-educated, fourth-generation, native-born Chinese American females) may bear little resemblance to the experience of another (e.g., illegal, male Chinese immigrants with less than a high school education), and the problems of some members may not be the problems of others.

One way we have tried to highlight the importance of this diversity is by stressing gender differentiation within each minority group. Studies of minority groups by U.S. social scientists have focused predominantly on males, and the experiences of minority women have been described in much less depth. All the cultures examined in this text have strong patriarchal traditions. Women of the dominant group, as well as minority women, have had much less access to leadership roles and higher-status positions and have generally occupied a subordinate status, even in their own groups. The experiences of minority-group women and the extent of their differences from minority-group males and dominant-group women are only now being fully explored.

As we have seen, generalizations about "all women" or "all men" seldom conform to reality, and we explored the gender dimension in depth in Chapter 11. We saw that struggles for gender equality have had to adapt to variations in experiences across race, class, and sexual orientation, and even to gender experiences that do not fit clearly into either the male or female categories. Only recently have feminist movements made attempts to frame issues in more inclusive terms, and some who might benefit from feminist organizing still may not feel that their concerns are represented by the movement. Since gender inequality remains a persistent problem worldwide, the extent to which feminist efforts are able to incorporate greater

Women have often taken the least desirable, lowest-status jobs, caring for the needs of others rather than their own families.

gender diversity will undoubtedly shape the relative success—both domestically and globally—of the movement.

Likewise, our consideration of gays, lesbians, and bisexual people made it clear that the experiences of members of these groups vary considerably by race, class, and gender. Two white men together in a household will tend to elevate that household's income, while the household income for two men of minority racial backgrounds or two women of any background will tend to mirror the patterns of inequality discussed in previous chapters. Moreover, gay liberation movements have faced challenges not unlike those of feminist groups, in that their efforts to alter public policy often privilege white, middle-class concerns over others.

Gender, class, race, ethnicity, and sexual orientation can combine and recombine to create especially heavy burdens for some. The women of every minority group have tended to take the least-desirable, lowest-status positions available in the economy, often while trying to raise children and attend to other family needs. They have been expected to provide support for other members of their families, kinship groups, and communities, often sacrificing their own self-interests for the welfare of others. At the other end of the continuum, white, Anglo, heterosexual, affluent, Protestant men have enjoyed—and continue to enjoy—a system of privilege and advantage so pervasive that it is invisible to its beneficiaries.

Fully understanding the complexities of inequality requires the recognition that Shirley Umphlett and Mary Farrell have different agendas in life, despite the fact that both are female. One woman must deal with modern racism, while the other must confront the realities of heterosexism; neither faces the world as a woman only. Likewise, Juan Yancy and William Buford III share a gender and little else. Similar comparisons and contrasts can be made for all nine of the Americans we introduced in Chapter 1 and revisited at the start of this chapter. Together, they suggest the outlines of difference and diversity in society, and the need to recognize the multiple realities that define each of us.

ASSIMILATION AND PLURALISM

It seems fair to conclude that the diversity and complexity of minority-group experiences in the United States are not well characterized by some of the traditional, or "melting pot," views of assimilation. For example, the idea that assimilation is a linear, inevitable process has little support. Immigrants from Europe probably fit that model better than other groups, but as the ethnic revival of the 1960s demonstrated, assimilation and ethnic identity can take surprising turns.

Also without support is the notion that there is always a simple, ordered relationship between the various stages of assimilation: acculturation, integration into public institutions, integration into the private sector, and so forth. We have seen that some groups integrated before they acculturated, others have become more committed to their ethnic or racial identity over the generations, and still others have been acculturated for generations but are no closer to full integration. New expressions of ethnicity come and go, and minority groups emerge, combine, and recombine in unexpected and seemingly unpredictable ways. The 1960s saw a reassertion of ethnicity and loyalty to old identities among some groups, even as other groups developed new coalitions and invented new ethnic identities (e.g., pantribalism among Native Americans). No simple or linear view of assimilation can begin to make sense of the array of minority-group experiences.

Indeed, the very desirability of assimilation has been subject to debate. Since the 1960s, many minority spokespersons have questioned the wisdom of becoming a part of a sociocultural structure that was constructed by the systematic exploitation of minority groups. Pluralistic themes increased in prominence as the commitment of the larger society to racial equality faltered. Virtually every minority group, including women and LGBTs, proclaimed the authenticity of its own experiences, its own culture, and its own version of history, separate from but as valid as those of the dominant groups. From what might have seemed like a nation on the verge of integration in the 1950s (at least for white ethnic groups), America evolved into what might have seemed like a Tower of Babel in the 1960s. The consensus that assimilation was the best solution and the most sensible goal for all America's groups was shattered (if it ever really existed at all).

Let's review the state of acculturation and integration in the United States on a group-by-group basis:

• African Americans are highly acculturated. Despite the many unique cultural traits forged in America and those that survive from Africa, black Americans share language, values and beliefs, and most other aspects of culture with white Americans of similar class and educational background. In terms of integration, in contrast, African Americans present a mixed picture. For middle-class, more-educated members of the group,

American society offers more opportunities for upward mobility and success than ever before. Without denying the prejudice, discrimination, and racism that remain, this segment of the group is in a favorable position to achieve higher levels of affluence and power for their children and grandchildren. At the same time, a large percentage of African Americans remain mired in urban poverty, and for them, affluence, security, and power are just as distant as they were a generation ago (perhaps even more so). Considering the group as a whole, African Americans are still highly segregated in their residential and school attendance patterns, and unemployment and poverty remain serious problems, perhaps even more serious than a generation ago.

- Native Americans are less acculturated than African Americans, and some tribes and organizations are trying to preserve American Indian cultures and languages. Overall, however, the strength and vitality of these traditions is probably decreasing. On measures of integration, there is some indication of improvement, but many American Indians are among the most isolated and impoverished minority-group members in the United States. One possible bright spot for some reservations lies in the further development of the gambling industry and the investment of profits in the tribal infrastructure to upgrade schools, health clinics, job training centers, and so forth.

- Members of the largest Hispanic American groups are also generally less acculturated than African Americans. Hispanic traditions and the Spanish language have been sustained by the exclusion and isolation of these groups within the United States and have been continually renewed and revitalized by immigration. Cubans have moved closer to equality than have Mexican Americans and Puerto Ricans, but they did so by resisting assimilation and building an ethnic enclave economy. Mexican Americans and Puerto Ricans share many of the problems of urban poverty that confront African Americans, and they are below national norms on measures of equality and integration.

The smaller Hispanic groups consist mostly of new immigrants who are just beginning the assimilation process. Many members of these groups, along with Mexican Americans and Puerto Ricans, are less educated and have few occupational skills, and they face the dangers of blending into a permanent urban underclass. Nonetheless, there is some evidence that these groups (or, more accurately, their descendants) may eventually find their way into the American mainstream (recall the debate over segmented assimilation in Chapter 10).

- As with Hispanic Americans, the extent of assimilation among Asian Americans is highly variable. Some groups (e.g., third- and fourth-generation Japanese and Chinese Americans) have virtually completed the assimilation process and compare favorably to national norms in terms of integration and equality, at least in terms of group averages. Some Asian American groups (the more elite immigrants from India and the Philippines) seem to be finding a place in the American mainstream. Other groups consist largely of newer immigrants with occupational and educational profiles that often resemble those of colonized minority groups, and these groups face the same dangers of permanent marginalization and exclusion. Still other Asian American groups (e.g., Korean Americans) have constructed ethnic enclaves and pursue economic equality by resisting acculturation.

- Only European American ethnic groups, covered in Chapter 2, seem to approximate the traditional model of assimilation. The development of even these groups, however, has taken unexpected twists and turns, and the pluralism of the 1960s and 1970s suggests that ethnic traditions and ethnic identity, in some form, may withstand the pressures of assimilation for generations to come. Culturally and racially, these groups are the closest to the dominant group. If they still retain a sense of ethnicity, even if merely symbolic, after generations of acculturation and integration, what is the likelihood that the sense of group membership will fade in the racially stigmatized minority groups?

- Different gender-role expectations continue to shape the socialization experiences of males and females throughout the life cycle and, in that sense, "acculturation" has not been accomplished. Women are equal to men on some measures of equality (e.g., education), but large gaps in other areas (e.g., income) persist. The gaps vary from group to group, but women in general continue to be disproportionately concentrated in less-well-paid occupations and continue to confront glass ceilings and other limits to their social mobility.

- As with women, the usual sociological meaning of acculturation does not fit the LGBT minority. However, it is clear that gays and lesbians are increasingly included in the popular culture of the dominant society. The patterns of inequality in the LGBT community generally follow those in the larger society, and, like women, LGBT people seem not to receive rewards proportionate to their degree of preparation for the job market. In most states, major inequalities persist between same-sex and heterosexual couples in terms of taxes and health care costs, and civil liberties and occupational discrimination continue to be issues of major importance.

For the racial and ethnic minority groups, assimilation is far from accomplished. The group divisions that remain are real and consequential; they cannot be willed away by pretending we are all "just American." Group membership continues to be important because it continues to be linked to fundamental patterns of exclusion and inequality. The realities of pluralism, inequality, and ethnic and racial identity persist to the extent that the American promise of a truly open opportunity structure continues to fail. The group divisions forged in the past and perpetuated over the decades by racism and discrimination will remain to the extent that racial and ethnic group membership continues to be correlated with inequality and position in the social class structure.

Along with economic and political pressures, other forces help sustain the pluralistic group divisions. Some argue that ethnicity is rooted in biology and can never be fully eradicated (e.g., see van den Berghe, 1981). Although this may be an extreme position, there is little doubt that many people find their own ancestries to be a matter of great interest. Some (perhaps most) of the impetus behind the preservation of ethnic and racial identity may be a result of the most vicious and destructive intergroup competition. In other ways, though, ethnicity can be a positive force that helps people locate themselves in time and space and understand their position in the contemporary world. Ethnicity remains an important aspect of self-identity and pride for many Americans from every group and tradition. It seems unlikely that this sense of a personal link to particular groups and heritages within U.S. society will soon fade.

Can we survive as a pluralistic, culturally and linguistically fragmented, racially and ethnically unequal society? What will save us from balkanization and fractionalization? Given our history of colonization and racism, can U.S. society move closer to the relatively harmonious models of race relations found in societies such as Hawaii?

As we deal with these questions, we need to remember that in and of itself, diversity is no more "bad" than unity is "good." Our society has grown to a position of global preeminence despite, or perhaps because of, our diversity. In fact, many have argued that our diversity is a fundamental and essential characteristic of U.S. society and a great strength to be cherished and encouraged. Sociologist Ronald Takaki (1993) ended his history of multicultural America, *A Different Mirror*, with an eloquent endorsement of our diversity and pluralism:

> As Americans, we originally came from many different shores and our diversity has been at the center of the making of America. While our stories contain the memories of different communities, together they inscribe a larger narrative. Filled with what Walt Whitman celebrated as the "varied carols" of America, our history generously gives all of us our "mystic chords of memory."
>
> Throughout our past of oppressions and struggles for equality, Americans of different races and ethnicities have been "singing with open mouths their strong melodious songs" in the textile mills of Lowell, the cotton fields of Mississippi, on the Indian reservations of South Dakota, the railroad tracks high in the Sierras of California, in the garment factories of the Lower East Side, the cane fields of Hawaii, and a thousand other places across the country. Our denied history "bursts with telling." As we hear America singing, we find ourselves invited to bring our cultural diversity [into the open], to accept ourselves. (p. 428)

To this heady mix of diversity in race, ethnicity, language, and culture, we must add the dimensions of gender and sexual orientation, and their infinite intersections and combinations

The diverse melodies of America's groups are sung by an infinitely variable chorus.

with group membership. The "varied carols" of American life are voiced by a complex, diversified chorus: The tune will not be the same for heterosexual, middle-class African Americans as for lesbian, Hispanic immigrants with low levels of human capital. How can we sort out this complexity? How can we answer the question we raised at the beginning of this text: What does it mean to be an American?

The question for our future might not be so much "Unity or diversity?" as "What blend of pluralism and assimilation will serve us best in the 21st century?" Are there ways society can prosper without repressing our diversity? How can we increase the degree of openness, fairness, and justice without threatening group loyalties? The one-way, Anglo-conformity mode of assimilation of the past is too narrow and destructive to be a blueprint for the future, but the more extreme forms of minority-group pluralism and separatism might be equally dangerous.

How much unity do we need? How much diversity can we tolerate? These are questions you must answer for yourself, and they are questions you will face in a thousand different ways over the course of your life. We do not pretend that the ideas presented in this text can fully resolve these issues or others that will arise in the future. As long as immigrants and minority groups are a part of the United States, as long as prejudice and discrimination and inequality persist, the debates will continue and new issues will arise as old ones are resolved.

As U.S. society attempts to deal with new immigrants, the varieties of gender expression, and unresolved minority grievances, we should recognize that it is not diversity per se that threatens stability but, rather, the realities of exclusion and marginalization, split labor markets, racial and ethnic stratification, urban poverty, and institutionalized discrimination. We need to focus on the issues that confront us with an honest recognition of the past and the economic, political, and social forces that have shaped us. As the United States continues to remake itself, an informed sense of where we have been will help us decide where we should go next.

MINORITY-GROUP PROGRESS AND THE IDEOLOGY OF AMERICAN INDIVIDUALISM

There is so much sadness, misery, and unfairness in the history of minority groups that evidence of progress sometimes goes unnoticed. Lest we be guilty of ignoring the good news in favor of the bad, let us note some ways the situations of American minority groups are better today than they were in the past. Evidence of progress is easy to find for some groups; we need look only to the relative economic, educational, and income equality of European American ethnic groups and some Asian American groups, or recall the election of President Barack Obama. The United States has become more tolerant and open, and minority-group members can be found at the highest levels of success, affluence, and prestige. Women are entering traditionally "male" occupations in large numbers, and American society has become increasingly inclusive of sexual-orientation minorities.

One of the most obvious changes is the decline of traditional racism and prejudice, sexism, and homophobia. As we discussed in Chapter 3, the strong racial and ethnic sentiments and stereotypes of the past are no longer the primary vocabulary for discussing race relations among dominant-group members, at least not in public. Similar shifts have occurred in attitudes toward women and LGBT people. Although prejudice in all its forms unquestionably still exists, Americans have become more circumspect and discreet in their public utterances.

The demise of blatant bigotry in polite company is, without doubt, a positive change; however, it seems that negative intergroup feelings and stereotypes have not so much disappeared as changed form. The old racist feelings are now being expressed in other guises, specifically in what has been called "modern" or "symbolic" racism and sexism: the view that holds that opportunity channels and routes of upward mobility in American society are open to all.

This individualistic view of social mobility is consistent with the human capital perspective and the traditional,

melting-pot view of assimilation. Taken together, these ideologies present a powerful and widely shared perspective on the nature of minority-group problems in modern American society. Proponents of these views tend to be unsympathetic to the plight of minorities and to programs, such as affirmative action, intended to ameliorate these problems. The overt bigotry of the past has been replaced by blandness and an indifference more difficult to define and harder to measure than "old-fashioned" racism, yet still unsympathetic to change.

This text has argued that the most serious problems facing contemporary minority groups, however, are structural and institutional, not individual or personal. For example, the paucity of jobs and high rates of unemployment in the inner cities are the result of economic and political forces beyond the control not only of the minority communities but also of local and state governments. The marginalization of the minority-group labor force is a reflection of the essence of modern American capitalism. The mainstream, higher-paying, blue-collar jobs available to people with modest educational credentials are controlled by national and multinational corporations, which maximize profits by automating their production processes and moving the jobs that remain to areas, often outside the United States, with abundant supplies of cheaper labor.

We have also seen that some of the more effective strategies for pursuing equality require strong in-group cohesion and networks of cooperation, not heroic individual effort. Immigration to this country is (and always has been) a group process that involves extensive, long-lasting networks of communication and chains of population movement, usually built around family ties and larger kinship groups. Group networks continue to operate in America and assist individual immigrants with early adjustments and later opportunities for jobs and upward mobility. A variation on this theme is the ethnic enclave found among so many different groups.

Survival and success in America for all minority groups has had more to do with group processes than with individual will or motivation. The concerted, coordinated actions of the minority community provided support during hard times and, when possible, provided the means to climb higher in the social structure during good times. Far from being a hymn to individualism, the story of U.S. minority groups—whether based on race, ethnicity, gender, or sexual orientation—is profoundly sociological.

A FINAL WORD

U.S. society and its minority groups are linked in fractious unity. They are part of the same structures but are separated by lines of color and culture and by long histories (and clear memories) of exploitation and unfairness. This society owes its prosperity and position of prominence in the world no less to the labor of minority groups than to that of the dominant group. By harnessing the labor and energy of these minority groups, the nation has grown prosperous and powerful, but the benefits have flowed disproportionately to the dominant group.

Since the middle of the 20th century, minority groups have demanded greater openness, fairness, equality, respect for their traditions, and justice. Increasingly, the demands have been made on the terms of the minority groups, not on those of the dominant group. Some of these demands have been met, at least verbally, and the society as a whole has rejected the oppressive racism of the past. Minority-group progress has stalled well short of equality, however, and the patterns of poverty, discrimination, marginality, hopelessness, and despair continue to limit the lives of millions.

As we face the 21st century, the dilemmas of America's minority groups remain perhaps the primary unresolved domestic issue facing the nation. The answers of the past—the simple faith in assimilation and the belief that success in America is open to all who simply try hard enough—have proved inadequate, even destructive and dangerous, because they help sustain the belief that the barriers to equality no longer exist and that any remaining inequalities are the problem of the minority groups, not the larger society.

These issues of equality and access will not solve themselves or simply fade away. They will continue to manifest themselves in myriad ways—through protest activities, rancorous debates, diffused rage, and pervasive violence. The solutions and policies that will carry us through these coming travails are not clear. Only by asking the proper questions, realistically and honestly, can we hope to find the answers that will help our society fulfill its promises to the millions who are currently excluded from achieving the American Dream.

The United States is one of many ethnically and racially diverse nations in the world today. As the globe continues to shrink and networks of communication, immigration, trade, and transportation increasingly link all peoples into a single global entity, the problems of diversity will become more international in their scope and implications. Ties will grow between African Americans and other peoples of color, agreements between the United States and the nations of Latin America will have direct impact on immigration patterns, Asian Americans will be affected by international developments on the Pacific Rim, organizations representing women

American groups celebrate a diversity of traditions and an endless array of realities. Here, an American flag is part of Chinese New Year.

and sexual-orientation minorities will develop more international ties, and so forth. Domestic and international group relations will blend into a single reality. In many ways, the patterns of dominant–minority relations discussed in this text already have been reproduced on the global stage. The mostly Anglo industrialized nations of the Northern Hemisphere have continuously exploited the labor and resources of the mostly nonwhite, undeveloped nations of the Southern Hemisphere. Thus, the tensions and resentments we have observed in U.S. society are mirrored in the global system of societies.

The United States is neither the most nor the least diverse country in the world. Likewise, our nation is neither the most nor the least successful in confronting the problems of prejudice, discrimination, and racism. However, the multigroup nature of our society, along with the present influx of immigrants from around the globe, does present an opportunity to improve on our record and make a lasting contribution. A society that finds a way to deal fairly and humanely with the problems of diversity and difference, prejudice and inequality, exclusion and marginalization, and racism and discrimination can provide a sorely needed model for other nations and, indeed, for the world.

SUMMARY

This summary is organized around the Learning Objectives listed at the beginning of this chapter.

14.1 Explain how the people profiled at the beginning of Chapter 1 exemplify the central themes and concepts of this text.

These brief biographies illustrate both the diversity and complexity of contemporary American society, including the divisions along the lines of class, race, ethnicity, gender, and sexual orientation. They display the varieties of acculturation and integration and the multiplicity of privilege and disadvantage. They also remind us of the often daunting difficulties of communicating across the diverse experiences and perspectives that animate contemporary society.

14.2 Explain the relevance of our central concepts—especially subsistence technology, the contact situation, competition and power, and intersectionality—for American dominant-minority relations.

Subsistence technology is the most basic force shaping society and group relationships. Agrarian technology created competition for land and labor, resulting in the subjugation of some groups and the near extermination of others. The evolution of subsistence technology through the industrial and post-industrial stages continued to shape the situation of minority groups—including women and LGBTs—and the nature of dominant-minority conflict.

The contact situation creates dynamics that can affect dominant-minority relations for centuries (or longer). We have analyzed these dynamics using Blauner's distinction between immigrant and colonized minority groups and Noel's concepts of ethnocentrism, competition, and power and we have seen the numerous ways in which minority groups today continue to be affected by their contact situation.

Intersectionality reminds us of the myriad ways in which we are each both privileged and disadvantaged and the multiple realities that shape our lives and opportunities. Although we have often generalized, we need to continually recognize the diversity within groups.

 14.3 Summarize the situation of each of the groups we have considered in terms of acculturation and integration.

The extent of acculturation and integration is highly variable from group to group. Of the racial and ethnic minority groups, only the descendants of the European immigrant groups have approached full assimilation. Each of the other groups we have considered ranks below white ethnics in terms of acculturation and integration and some of these groups (Hispanic and Asian groups in particular) have been affected by high rates of immigration in recent decades. Gender roles retain significant strength in American culture and women rank below men on many measures of integration and equality. The LGBT minorities seem to be gaining more acceptance but continue to face significant issues of inequality and marginalization.

14.4 Explain the importance of a sociological perspective for understanding American dominant-minority relations.

The sociological perspective locates the source of minority problems in the structure and everyday functioning of the larger society. It counters the individualistic view shared by many Americans and rejects the assumption that mobility and opportunity are equally open to all. It takes account of the history of dominant-minority relations, the evolving subsistence technology, globalization, and the changing political, cultural, and economic processes that structure modern societies. It provides a broad view of groups and social structures, grounded in evidence and research and guided by critical thinking and careful reflection.

STUDENT STUDY SITE

Sharpen your skills with SAGE edge at edge.sagepub.com/healey7e

SAGE edge for students provides a personalized approach to help you accomplish your coursework goals in an easy-to-use learning environment.

The following resources are available at SAGE edge:

Public Sociology Assignments

Public Sociology Assignments provide opportunities for students to address directly and personally some of the issues raised in this text.

The first assignment for this final chapter on our website leads students to identify and act on a problem in their neighborhood. The second assignment is a service-learning project in which students will research a local refugee group and then volunteer to help that community.

In the third assignment, students will explore privilege on their campus and engage with an organization that promotes a cause of interest to them. In the final assignment, students will explore the presentation of race, gender, ethnicity, class, and sexuality on the Internet.

Contributed by Linda M. Waldron

GLOSSARY

abolitionism: The movement to abolish slavery

acculturation: The process by which one group (generally a minority or immigrant group) learns the culture of another group (generally the dominant group); also called **cultural assimilation**

affective dimension of prejudice: The emotional or "feeling" dimension of individual prejudice. The prejudiced individual attaches negative emotions to members of other groups.

affirmative action: Programs designed to reduce the effects of past institutional discrimination or increase diversity in workplaces and schools

Alien Land Act: Bill passed by the California legislature in 1913 declaring that aliens who were ineligible for citizenship (effectively meaning only immigrants from Asia) were also ineligible to own land

Americanization: The model of assimilation in which groups are pressured to conform to Anglo-American culture (same as **Anglo-conformity**)

androgynous: Refers to a combination of "male" and "female" gender traits

Anglo-conformity: The model of assimilation in which groups are pressured to conform to Anglo-American culture (same as **Americanization**)

anti-Semitism: Prejudice or ideological racism directed specifically toward Jews

apartheid: The policy of extreme racial segregation formerly followed in South Africa

ascribed status: A position in society that is assigned to the individual, usually at birth.

Examples of ascribed status include positions based on ethnicity, race, and gender.

assimilation: The process by which formerly distinct and separate groups come to share a common culture and merge together socially

authoritarian personality: A theory that links prejudice to childhood experiences with stern, severe parents

Black Power movement: A coalition of African American groups that rose to prominence in the 1960s. Some central themes of the movement were Black Nationalism, autonomy for African American communities, and pride in race and African heritage.

bourgeoisie: The elite or ruling class in an industrial society that owns or controls the means of production

Bureau of Indian Affairs: The agency of the U.S. government that has primary responsibility for the administration of American Indian reservations

capital-intensive: Capital-intensive technology replaces hand labor with machine labor. Large amounts of capital are required to develop, purchase, and maintain the machines.

caste system: A closed system of stratification with no mobility between positions. A person's class at birth is permanent and unchangeable.

chattel: An item of personal property. In a system of chattel slavery, slaves were defined by law not as persons but as the personal property of their owners.

Chicanismo: A militant ideology of the Mexican American protest movement that appeared in the 1960s. The ideology took a critical view of U.S. society, made strong

demands for justice and an end to racism, expressed a positive image for the group, and incorporated other pluralistic themes.

Chicanos: A group name for Mexican Americans; associated with the ideology of Chicanismo, which emerged in the 1960s

Chinese Exclusion Act: Passed in 1882 by the U.S. Congress, banned virtually all immigration from China

civil rights movement: The effort of African Americans and their allies in the 1950s and 1960s to end de jure segregation in the South

cognitive dimension of prejudice: The "thinking" dimension of individual prejudice. The prejudiced individual thinks about members of other groups in terms of stereotypes.

collective identity: A shared understanding of one's place in society

colonized minority groups: Groups whose initial contact with the dominant group was through conquest or colonization

coming out: A public disclosure of sexual identity; usually reserved for nonheterosexuals

competition: A situation in which two or more parties struggle for control of some scarce resource

cultural assimilation: See **acculturation**

cultural feminism: The movement to change patriarchal values and norms

cultural heterosexism: Ideologies that uphold heterosexuality as normative

cultural pluralism: A situation in which groups have not

acculturated or integrated and each maintains a distinct identity

culture: All aspects of the way of life associated with a group of people. Culture includes language, beliefs, norms, values, customs, technology, and many other components.

culture of poverty theory: A theory asserting that poverty causes certain personality traits—such as the need for instant gratification—which, in turn, perpetuate poverty

de facto segregation: A system of racial separation and inequality that appears to result from voluntary choices about where to live, work, and so forth. Often, this form of segregation is really de jure segregation in thin disguise.

de jure segregation: Racial segregation that is institutionalized in local and state law

deindustrialization: The shift from a manufacturing economy to a service-oriented, information-processing economy

differential in power: Any difference between two or more groups in their ability to achieve their goals

discrimination: The unequal or unfair treatment of a person or persons based on their group membership

dissimilarity index: A measure of residential segregation. The higher the score, the greater the segregation, and scores above 60 are considered to indicate extreme segregation.

dominant group: The group that benefits from and, typically, tries to sustain minority-group subordination

double bind: A situation in which negative consequences ensue regardless of the choice that is made

enclave minority group: A group that establishes its own neighborhood and relies on a set of interconnected businesses for economic survival

equal status contact hypothesis: A theory of prejudice reduction asserting that equal status and cooperative contacts between groups will tend to reduce prejudice

ethclass: The group formed by the intersection of social class and racial or ethnic groups

ethnic minority groups: Minority groups identified primarily by cultural characteristics, such as language or religion

ethnic succession: The process by which white ethnic groups affected one another's positions in the social class structure

ethnocentrism: Judging other groups, societies, or cultures by the standards of one's own

extractive (or primary) occupations: Those that produce raw materials, such as food and agricultural products, minerals, and lumber; often involve unskilled manual labor, require little formal education, and are generally low paying

fatalism: The view that one's fate is beyond one's control

feminism: A variety of movements and organizations that have sought to reduce gender stratification

fluid competitive systems: Systems of group relations in which minority-group members are freer to compete for jobs and other scarce resources; associated with advanced industrialization

gender: The social characteristics associated with males or females

gender roles: Societal expectations regarding the behavior, attitudes, and personality traits for males and females

gender socialization: The processes by which boys and girls are taught expectations for appropriate gendered behaviors

genocide: The deliberate attempt to exterminate an entire group

glass ceiling: Discriminatory practices that limit opportunities for women and other minority groups to rise to higher levels in their careers, qualify for promotions, and earn higher salaries

glass escalator: An occupational setting in which the dominant group (e.g., men) enjoys a distinct advantage

hegemonic masculinity: The privileged, dominant expression of masculinity in a society

homophobia: Prejudice directed at lesbian, gay, and bisexual persons

homosocial reproduction: The tendency of male elites to select candidates for advancement who are most like themselves

huiguan: Associations in Chinese American society based on the region of China from which an individual or his or her family came. The *huiguan* performed a number of social and welfare functions.

human capital theory: Consistent with the traditional view of assimilation, this theory considers success to be a direct result of individual efforts, personal values and skills, and education.

ideological racism: A belief system asserting that a particular group is inferior. Although individuals may subscribe to racist beliefs, the ideology itself is incorporated into the culture of the society and passed on from generation to generation.

immigrant minority groups: Groups whose initial contact with the dominant group was through immigration

indentured servants: Contract laborers who are obligated to serve a particular master for a specified length of time

Indian Reorganization Act: Federal legislation passed in 1934 that was intended to give Native American tribes more autonomy

industrial revolution: The shift in subsistence technology from labor-intensive agriculture to capital-intensive manufacturing

institutional discrimination: A pattern of unequal treatment based on group membership that is built into the daily operations of society

integration: The process by which a minority group enters the social structure of the dominant society; also called **structural assimilation**

intermarriage: Marriage between members of different groups; same as **marital assimilation**

internalized homophobia: The repulsion some people feel in response to their own attractions to members of their same sex

intersectionality: A theoretical perspective in sociology that stresses the cross-cutting, linked nature of inequality and the multiplicity of statuses all people occupy

intersexed: People with the biological characteristics of more than one sex

Issei: First-generation immigrants from Japan

jigsaw method: A learning technique that requires cooperation among students

Jim Crow system: The system of rigid competitive race relations that followed Reconstruction in the South. The system lasted from the 1880s until the 1960s and was characterized by laws mandating racial separation and inequality.

labor-intensive: A form of production in which the bulk of the effort is provided by human beings working by hand. Machines and other labor-saving devices are rare or absent.

level of development: The stage of societal evolution. The stages discussed in this text are agrarian, industrial, and postindustrial.

machismo: A cultural value stressing male dominance, virility, and honor

manufacturing (or secondary) occupations: Occupations involving the transformation of raw materials into finished products ready for the marketplace. An example is an assembly line worker in an automobile plant.

marielitos: Refugees from Cuba who arrived in the United States in 1980

marital assimilation: Marriage between members of different groups; same as **intermarriage**

means of production: The materials, resources, and social relations by which the society produces and distributes goods and services

melting pot: A type of assimilation in which all groups contribute in roughly equal amounts to the creation of a new culture and society

middleman minority groups: Groups that rely on interconnected businesses, dispersed throughout a community, for economic survival

minority group: A group that experiences a pattern of disadvantage or inequality, has a visible identifying trait, and is a self-conscious social unit. Membership is usually determined at birth, and group members tend to form intimate relations within the group.

miscegenation: Marriage or sexual relations between

members of different racial groups

modern institutional discrimination: A more subtle and covert form of institutional discrimination that is often unintentional and unconscious

modern racism: A subtle and indirect form of prejudice that incorporates negative feelings about minority groups but not the traditional stereotypes

modern sexism: Like modern racism, an indirect, more subtle way of expressing prejudice against women

multiculturalism: A general term for some versions of pluralism in the United States. Generally, multiculturalism stresses mutual respect for all groups and celebrates the multiplicity of heritages that have contributed to the development of the United States.

New Immigration: Immigration from southern and eastern Europe to the United States between the 1880s and the 1920s

Nisei: Second-generation Japanese Americans

nonviolent direct action: The central tactic used during the civil rights movement in the South to defeat de jure segregation

Old Immigration: Immigration from northern and western Europe to the United States between the 1820s and the 1880s

Operation Wetback: A government program developed in the 1950s to deport illegal immigrants from Mexico

past-in-present institutional discrimination: Patterns of inequality or unequal treatment in the present that are caused by some pattern of discrimination in the past

paternalism: A form of dominant–minority relations often associated with plantation-based, labor-intensive, agrarian technology. In paternalistic relations, minority groups are extremely unequal and highly controlled. Rates of overt conflict are low.

patriarchy: Male dominance. In a patriarchal society, men tend to monopolize power and decision making.

pink collar: Those occupations that have been predominantly female

plantation system: A labor-intensive form of agriculture that requires large tracts of land and a large, cheap labor force. This was the dominant form of agricultural production in the American South before the Civil War.

pluralism: A situation in which groups maintain separate identities, cultures, and organizational structures

postindustrial society: A society dominated by service work, information processing, and high technology

power: The ability to affect the decision-making process of a social system

prejudice: The tendency of individuals to think and feel negatively toward others

prestige: The amount of honor or respect accorded a particular person or group

primary labor market: The segment of the labor market that encompasses better-paying, higher-status, more-secure jobs, usually in large bureaucracies

primary sector: Relationships and groups that are intimate and personal. Groups in the primary sector are small.

principle of third-generation interest: The notion that the grandchildren of immigrants will stress their ethnicity much more than the second generation will

proletariat: The workers in an industrial society

queer: A gender expression or identity that does not conform to societal expectations

race relations cycle: A concept associated with Robert Park, who believed that relations between different groups would go through predictable cycles, from conflict to eventual assimilation

racial minority groups: Minority groups identified primarily by physical characteristics such as skin color (e.g., Asian Americans)

rape culture: A patriarchal culture in which male violence and rape are tolerated

Reconstruction: The period of southern race relations following the Civil War. Reconstruction lasted from 1865 until the 1880s and witnessed many racial reforms, all of which were reversed during de jure segregation, or the Jim Crow era.

relocation camps: The camps in which Japanese Americans were held during World War II

repatriation: A government campaign begun during the Great Depression of the 1930s to deport illegal immigrants back to Mexico. The campaign also caused some legal immigrants and native-born Mexican Americans to leave the United States.

revolution: A minority-group goal. A revolutionary group wishes to change places with the dominant group or create a new social order, perhaps in alliance with other groups.

rigid competitive group system: A system of group relations in which the dominant group seeks to exclude minority groups or limit their ability to compete for scarce resources such as jobs

Sansei: Third-generation Japanese Americans

scapegoat hypothesis: A theory of prejudice that posits that under certain conditions, people will express their aggressions against substitute targets. When other groups are chosen as substitute targets, prejudice increases.

secondary labor market: The segment of the labor market that includes low-paying, low-skilled, insecure jobs

secondary sector: Relationships and organizations that are public, task oriented, and impersonal. Organizations in the secondary sector can be large.

segmented assimilation: The idea that assimilation can have a number of outcomes, in addition to eventual entry into mainstream society. Some groups may enter the middle class, but others may be permanently excluded, marginalized, and impoverished.

selective perception: The tendency to see only what one expects to see; associated with stereotyping in individual prejudice

separatism: A minority-group goal. A separatist group wishes to sever all ties with the dominant group.

service (or tertiary) occupations: Jobs that involve providing services. Examples include retail clerk, janitor, and schoolteacher.

sex: Refers to biological characteristics; see **gender**

sexism: Belief systems that label females as inferior and rationalize their lower status

sexual identity: The way people classify themselves sexually— for example, as lesbian, gay, or bisexual

sexual orientation: The gender to which a person is sexually attracted

sexual scripts: Gender-based verbal expectations

sharecropping: A system of farming often used in the South during de jure segregation. The sharecropper (often black), or tenant, worked the land, which was actually owned by someone else (usually white), in return for a share of the profits at harvest time. The landowner supplied a place to live and credit for food and clothing.

social classes: Groups of people who command similar amounts of valued goods and services, such as income, property, and education

social constructions: Perceptions shared by a group. These perceptions become real to the people who share them.

social distance: The degree of intimacy a person is willing to accept for members of other groups

social mobility: Movement up and down the stratification system

social structure: The networks of social relationships, groups, organizations, communities, and institutions that organize the work of a society and connect individuals to one another and to the larger society

socialization: The process of physical, psychological, and social development by which a person learns his or her culture

sojourners: Immigrants who intend to return to their countries of origin

split labor market theory: When the labor force is divided into a higher-paid segment composed of members of the dominant group and a lower-paid segment composed of minority-group members, higher-paid labor uses prejudice and racism to limit the ability of cheaper labor to compete for jobs.

stereotypes: Overgeneralizations that are thought to apply to all members of a group

stratification: The unequal distribution of valued goods and services (e.g., income, job opportunities, prestige and fame, education, health care) in society; the social class system

structural assimilation: See **integration**

structural heterosexism: Patterns of institutional discrimination whereby

heterosexual relations are allocated more resources, opportunities, and privileges

structural mobility: Rising occupational and social class standing that is the result of changes in the overall structure of the economy and labor market, as opposed to individual efforts

structural pluralism: A situation in which a group has acculturated but is not integrated

subsistence technology: The means by which a society satisfies basic needs. An agrarian society relies on labor-intensive agriculture, whereas an industrial society relies on machines and inanimate fuel supplies.

symbolic ethnicity: A sense of ethnicity that is superficial, voluntary, and changeable

termination: A policy by which all special relationships between the federal government and American Indians would be abolished

tongs: Secret societies in Chinatowns that sometimes fought with each other and with other organizations over control of resources

triple melting pot: The idea that structural assimilation for white ethnic immigrants took place within the context of the three major American religions

urban underclass: The urban lower classes, consisting largely of African Americans and other minority groups of color, which have been more or less permanently barred from the mainstream economy and the primary labor market

vicious cycle: A process in which a condition (e.g., minority-group inferiority) is assumed to be true and forces are then set in motion to create and perpetuate that condition

Yonsei: Fourth-generation Japanese Americans

REFERENCES

Aberson, Christopher, Shoemaker, Carl, and Tomolillo, Christina. 2004. Implicit Bias and Contact: The Role of Interethnic Friendships. *Journal of Social Psychology* 144:335–347.

Abrahamson, Harold. 1980. Assimilation and Pluralism. In Stephan Thernstrom, Ann Orlov, and Oscar Handlin (Eds.), *Harvard Encyclopedia of American Ethnic Groups* (pp. 150–160). Cambridge, MA: Harvard University Press.

Acuña, Rodolfo. 1988. *Occupied America* (3rd ed.). New York: Harper & Row.

———. 1999. *Occupied America* (4th ed.). New York: Harper & Row.

Adarand Constructors Inc. v. Pena, 515 U.S. 200 (1995).

Adorno, T. W., Frenkel-Brunswick, E., Levinson, D., and Sanford, N. 1950. *The Authoritarian Personality*. New York: Harper & Row.

After Protest by Pastor, Interest in Gay Books at Library Grows. 1998. *New York Times,* May 24. http://www.nytimes.com/1998/05/24/us/after-protest-by-pastor-interest-in-gay-books-at-library-grows.html.

Agbayani-Siewert, Pauline, and Revilla, Linda. 1995. Filipino Americans. In Pyong Gap Min (Ed.), *Asian Americans: Contemporary Issues and Trends* (pp. 134–168). Thousand Oaks, CA: Sage.

Alba, Richard. 1985. *Italian Americans: Into the Twilight of Ethnicity*. Englewood Cliffs, NJ: Prentice Hall.

———. 1990. *Ethnic Identity: The Transformation of White America*. New Haven, CT: Yale University Press.

———. 1995. Assimilation's Quiet Tide. *The Public Interest* 119:3–19.

Alba, Richard, and Nee, Victor. 1997. Rethinking Assimilation Theory for a New Era of Immigration. *International Migration Review* 31:826–875.

———. 2003. *Remaking the American Mainstream: Assimilation and Contemporary Immigration*. Cambridge, MA: Harvard University Press.

Aleiss, Angela. 2005. *Making the White Man's Indian: Native Americans and Hollywood Movies*. Westport, CT: Praeger.

Alesina, Alberto, Devleeschauwewr, Arnaud, Easterly, William, Kurlat, Sergio, and Wacziarg, Romain. 2002. *Fractionalization* (Harvard Institute Research Working Paper No. 1959). http://papers.ssrn.com/sol3/papers.cfm?abstract_id=319762.

Alexander, Michelle. 2012. *The New Jim Crow: Mass Incarceration in the Age of Colorblindness*. New York: New Press.

Allen, Jane E. 2010. Rutgers Suicide: Internet Humiliation Trauma for Teen. *ABC News,* September 30. http://abcnews.go.com/Health/MindMoodNews/rutgers-suicide-latest-linked-gay-humiliation/story?id=11766816.

Almquist, Elizabeth M. 1979. Black Women and the Pursuit of Equality. In Jo Freeman (Ed.), *Women: A Feminist Perspective* (pp. 430–450). Palo Alto, CA: Mayfield.

Alvarez, Rodolfo. 1973. The Psychohistorical and Socioeconomic Development of the Chicano Community in the United States. *Social Science Quarterly* 53:920–942.

American Civil Liberties Union. 2013. *The War on Marijuana in Black and White*. https://www.aclu.org/billions-dollars-wasted-racially-biased-arrests.

American Sociological Association. 2003. *The Importance of Collecting Data and Doing Scientific Research on Race*. Washington, DC: Author. http://www2.asanet.org/media/asa_race_statement.pdf.

Amott, Teresa, and Matthaei, Julie. 1991. *Race, Gender, and Work: A Multicultural History of Women in the United States*. Boston, MA: South End.

Andersen, Margaret L. 1993. *Thinking About Women: Sociological Perspectives on Sex and Gender* (3rd ed.). New York: Macmillan.

Andrews, Leslie. 2012. Why Augusta Matters. *Newsweek,* August 27. http://www.newsweek.com/why-augusta-matters-64527.

Anti-Defamation League. 2000. *Anti-Semitism in the United States*. http://www.adl.org/backgrounders/Anti_Semitism_us.html.

———. 2012. *Attitudes Towards Jews in Ten European Countries*. New York: Author. http://archive.adl.org/anti_semitism/adl_anti-semitism_presentation_february_2012.pdf.

Antin, Mary. 1912. *The Promised Land*. Boston, MA: Houghton Mifflin.

Anzaldúa, Gloria. 1999. *Borderlands/La Frontera: The New Mestiza*. San Francisco, CA: Aunt Lute Books. (Original work published in 1987)

Appelrouth, Scott, and Edles, Laura Desfor. 2012. *Classical and Contemporary Sociological Theory: Text and Readings*. Los Angeles, CA: Pine Forge Press.

Apuzzo, Matt. 2014. More Federal Privileges to Extend to Same-Sex Couples. *New York Times*, February 8. http://www.nytimes.com/2014/02/09/us/more-federal-privileges-to-extend-to-same-sex-couples.html?_r=0.

Arab American Anti-Discrimination Committee. 2002. *ADC Fact Sheet: The Condition of Arab Americans Post 9/11*. http://www.adc.org/terror_attack/9–11aftermath.pdf.

Aronson, Eliot, and Gonzalez, Alex. 1988. Desegregation, Jigsaw, and the Mexican-American Experience. In Phyllis Katz and Dalmas Taylor (Eds.), *Eliminating Racism: Profiles in Controversy* (pp. 301–314). New York: Plenum.

Aronson, E., and Patnoe, S. 1997. *The Jigsaw Classroom: Building Cooperation in the Classroom* (2nd ed.). New York: Addison-Wesley Longman.

Ashmore, Richard, and DelBoca, Frances. 1976. Psychological Approaches to Understanding Group Conflict. In Phyllis Katz (Ed.), *Towards the Elimination of Racism* (pp. 73–123). New York: Pergamon.

Associated Press. 2005. Asian Youth Persistently Harassed by U.S. Peers. *USA Today,* November 13. http://usatoday30.usatoday.com/news/nation/2005-11-13-asian-teens-bullied_x.htm.

Austin, Algernon. 2010. *Different Race, Different Recession: American Indian Unemployment in 2010* (Issue Brief 289). Washington, DC: Economic

Policy Institute. http://epi.3cdn.net/94a339472e6481485e_hgm6bxpz4.pdf.

Australian Bureau of Statistics. 2012. *The Health and Welfare of Australia's Aboriginal and Torres Islander People.* http://www.abs.gov.au/ausstats/abs@.nsf/mf/4704.0.

Baca Zinn, Maxine, and Eitzen, D. Stanley. 1990. *Diversity in Families.* New York: HarperCollins.

Baca Zinn, Maxine, and Thornton Dill, Bonnie (Eds.). 1994. *Women of Color in U.S. Society.* Philadelphia: Temple University Press.

Badgett, M., Durso, L., and Schneebaum, A. 2013. *New Patterns of Poverty in the Lesbian, Gay, and Bisexual Community.* Los Angeles: Williams Institute, UCLA School of Law. http://williamsinstitute.law.ucla.edu/wp-content/uploads/LGB-Poverty-Update-Jun-2013.pdf.

Baehr v. Miike, 910 P. 2d 112 (1996).

Bahadur, Nina. 2014. Dove "Real Beauty" Campaign Turns 10: How a Brand Tried to Change the Conversation About Female Beauty. *Huffington Post,* January 21. http://www.huffingtonpost.com/2014/01/21/dove-real-beauty-campaign-turns-10_n_4575940.html.

Ball, Richard. 2009. Social Distance in Japan: An Exploratory Study. *Michigan Sociological Review* 23:105–113.

Barreto, Manuela, and Ellemers, Naomi. 2005. The Perils of Political Correctness: Men's and Women's Responses to Old-Fashioned and Modern Sexist Views. *Social Psychology Quarterly* 68:75–88.

Barringer, Herbert, Takeuchi, David, and Levin, Michael. 1995. *Asians and Pacific Islanders in the United States.* New York: Russell Sage Foundation.

Bates, Karen Grigsby. 2008. Racial Divisions Challenge Gay Rights Movement. *NPR,* December 4. http://www.npr.org/templates/story/story.php?storyId=97826119.

Baumgardner, Jennifer, and Richards, Amy. 2000. *Manifesta: Young Women, Feminism, and the Future.* New York: Farrar, Straus & Giroux.

Bayer, Ronald. 1987. *Homosexuality and American Psychiatry: The Politics of Diagnosis.* Princeton, NJ: Princeton University Press.

Bayoumi, Moustafa. 2008. *How Does It Feel to Be a Problem?* New York: Penguin Books.

BBC News. 2013. Gay Marriage Around the World. http://www.bbc.co.uk/news/world-21321731.

Bean, Frank, and Stevens, Gillian. 2003. *America's Newcomers and the Dynamics of Diversity.* New York: Russell Sage Foundation.

Beaton, Anne, Tougas, Francine, and Joly, Stephane. 1996. Neosexism Among Male Managers: Is It a Matter of Numbers? *Journal of Applied Social Psychology* 26:2189–2204.

Becerra, Rosina. 1988. The Mexican American Family. In Charles H. Mindel, Robert W. Habenstein, and Roosevelt Wright Jr. (Eds.), *Ethnic Families in America: Patterns and Variations* (3rd ed., pp. 141–172). New York: Elsevier.

Beck, E. M., and Clark, Timothy. 2002. Strangers, Community Miscreants, or Locals: Who Were the Black Victims of Mob Violence? *Historical Methods* 35(2): 77–84.

Beck, E. M., and Tolnay, Stewart. 1990. The Killing Fields of the Deep South: The Market for Cotton and the Lynching of Blacks, 1882–1930. *American Sociological Review* 55:526–539.

Becker, Howard S. 1963. *Outsiders: Studies in the Sociology of Deviance.* New York: Free Press.

Bedrick, Barry R. 1997. Letter to Harry J. Hyde, Chairman, Committee on the Judiciary, House of Representatives, on the Defense of Marriage Act. Washington, DC: U.S. General Accounting Office, Office of the General Counsel. http://www.gao.gov/archive/1997/og97016.pdf.

Belkin, Lisa. 2012. Huggies Pulls Ad After Insulting Dads. *Huffington Post,* March 12. http://www.huffingtonpost.com/lisa-belkin/huggies-pulls-diaper-ads_b_1339074.html.

Bell, Daniel. 1973. *The Coming of Post-Industrial Society.* New York: Basic Books.

Bell, Derrick. 1992. *Race, Racism, and American Law* (3rd ed.). Boston: Little, Brown.

Benedict, Ruth. 1946. *The Chrysanthemum and the Sword: Patterns of Japanese Culture.* Boston: Houghton Mifflin.

Benjamin, Lois. 2005. *The Black Elite.* Lanham, MD: Rowman & Littlefield.

Berkowitz, Leonard. 1978. Whatever Happened to the Frustration-Aggression Hypothesis? *American Behavioral Scientist* 21:691–708.

Bernstein, Robert A. 2008. *Straight Parents, Gay Children: Keeping Families Together.* Cambridge, MA: Da Capo Press.

Bertrand, Marianne, and Mullainathan, Sendhil. 2004. Are Emily and Greg More Employable Than Lakisha and Jamal? A Field Experiment on Labor Market Discrimination. *American Economic Review* 94:991–1013.

Bird, Elizabeth. 1999. Gendered Construction of the American Indian in Popular Media. *Journal of Communication* 49:60–83.

Biskupic, Joan. 1989. House Approves Entitlement for Japanese-Americans. *Congressional Quarterly Weekly Report,* October 28, p. 2879.

Black-Gutman, D., and Hickson, F. 1996. The Relationship Between Racial Attitudes and Social-Cognitive Development in Children: An Australian Study. *Developmental Psychology* 32:448–457.

Blassingame, John W. 1972. *The Slave Community: Plantation Life in the Antebellum South.* New York: Oxford University Press.

Blau, Peter M., and Duncan, Otis Dudley. 1967. *The American Occupational Structure.* New York: Wiley.

Blauner, Robert. 1972. *Racial Oppression in America.* New York: Harper & Row.

Blessing, Patrick. 1980. Irish. In Stephan Thernstrom, Ann Orlov, and Oscar Handlin (Eds.), *Harvard Encyclopedia of American Ethnic Groups* (pp. 524–545). Cambridge, MA: Harvard University Press.

Bloomberg Editors. 2013. The End to Workplace Discrimination Against Gays. *Bloomberg,* April 24. http://www.bloombergview.com/articles/2013-04-24/the-end-to-workplace-discrimination-against-gays.

Blumer, Herbert. 1958. Race Prejudice as a Sense of Group Position. *Pacific Sociological Review* 1:3–7.

———. 1965. Industrialization and Race Relations. In Guy Hunter (Ed.), *Industrialization and Race Relations: A Symposium* (pp. 200–253). London: Oxford University Press.

Bobo, Lawrence. 1988. Group Conflict, Prejudice, and the Paradox of Contemporary Racial Attitudes. In Phyllis Katz and Dalmar Taylor (Eds.), *Eliminating Racism: Profiles in Controversy* (pp. 85–114). New York: Plenum.

———. 2001. Racial Attitudes and Relations at the Close of the Twentieth Century. In N. Smelser, W. Wilson, and F. Mitchell (Eds.), *America Becoming: Racial Trends and Their Consequences* (Vol. 1, pp. 264–301). Washington, DC: National Academy Press.

Bobo, Lawrence, Charles, Camille, Krysan, Maria, and Simmons, Alicia. 2012. The Real Record on Racial Attitudes. In P. Marsden (Ed.), *Social Trends in American Life: Findings From the General Social Survey Since 1973* (pp. 38–83). Princeton, NJ: Princeton University Press.

Bobo, Lawrence, and Kluegal, James. 1997. Status, Ideology, and Dimensions of Whites' Racial Beliefs and Attitudes: Progress and Stagnation. In Steven Tuck and Jack Martin (Eds.), *Racial Attitudes in the 1990s: Continuity and Change* (p. 101). Westport, CT: Praeger.

Bobo, Lawrence, and Tuan, Mia. 2006. *Prejudice in Politics: Group Position, Public Opinion, and the Wisconsin Treaty Rights Dispute.* Cambridge, MA: Harvard University Press.

Bodnar, John. 1985. *The Transplanted.* Bloomington: Indiana University Press.

Bogardus, Emory. 1933. A Social Distance Scale. *Sociology and Social Research* 17:265–271.

Bonacich, Edna. 1972. A Theory of Ethnic Antagonism: The Split Labor Market. *American Sociological Review* 37:547–559.

Bonacich, Edna, and Modell, John. 1980. *The Economic Basis of Ethnic Solidarity: Small Business in the Japanese American Community.* Berkeley: University of California Press.

Bonilla-Silva, Eduardo. 2001. *White Supremacy and Racism in the Post–Civil Rights Era.* Boulder, CO: Lynne Rienner.

———. 2003. "New Racism," Color-Blind Racism, and the Future of Whiteness in America. In Ashley Doane and Eduardo Bonilla-Silva (Eds.), *White Out: The Continuing Significance of Racism* (271–284). New York: Routledge.

———. 2006. *Racism Without Racists* (2nd ed.). Lanham, MD: Rowman & Littlefield.

Booth, Alan, Granger, Douglas, Mazur, Alan, and Kivligham, Katie. 2006. Testosterone and Social Behavior. *Social Forces* 86:167–191.

Bordewich, Fergus. 1996. *Killing the White Man's Indian.* New York: Doubleday.

Boswell, A. Ayres, and Spade, Joan Z. 1996. Fraternities and Collegiate Rape Culture: Why Are Some Fraternities More Dangerous Places for Women? *Gender and Society* 10:133–147.

Boswell, Terry. 1986. A Split Labor Market Analysis of Discrimination Against Chinese Immigrants, 1850–1882. *American Sociological Review* 51:352–371.

Bouvier, Leon F., and Gardner, Robert W. 1986. Immigration to the U.S.: The Unfinished Story. *Population Bulletin* 41(November): 1–50.

Bowen, Anna, and Patten, Eileen. 2013. *Hispanics of Cuban Origin in the United States: 2011.* Washington, DC: Pew Hispanic Center. http://www.pewhispanic.org/files/2013/06/CubanFactsheet.pdf.

Bowers v. Hardwick, 478 U.S. 186 (1986).

Boykin, Keith. 1997. *One More River to Cross: Black and Gay in America.* New York: Anchor Books.

———. 2006. *Beyond the Down Low: Sex, Lies and Denial in the Black Community.* Boston, MA: Da Capo Press.

Branch, John. 2014. NFL Prospect Michael Sam Proudly Says What Teammates Knew: He's Gay. *New York Times,* February 9. http://www.nytimes.com/2014/02/10/sports/michael-sam-college-football-star-says-he-is-gay-ahead-of-nfl-draft.html?_r=0.

Brennan Center for Justice. 2013. Voting Laws Roundup 2013. http://www.brennancenter.org/analysis/election-2013-voting-laws-roundup.

Briggs, Bill. 2013. Senator Seeks to Reform Military's "Unacceptable" Sex Abuse Policies. *NBC News,* May 16. http://usnews.nbcnews.com/_news/2013/05/16/18280367-senator-seeks-to-reform-militarys-unacceptable-sex-abuse-policies?lite.

Brittingham, Angela, and de la Cruz, G. Patricia. 2004. *Ancestry: 2000.* Washington, DC: U.S. Census Bureau. http://www.census.gov/prod/2004pubs/c2kbr-35.pdf.

Brody, David. 1980. Labor. In Stephan Thernstrom, Ann Orlov, and Oscar Handlin (Eds.), *Harvard Encyclopedia of American Ethnic Groups* (pp. 609–618). Cambridge, MA: Harvard University Press.

Bronson, Po, and Merryman, Ashley. 2009. Even Babies Discriminate: A NurtureShock Excerpt. *Newsweek,* September 14. http://www.newsweek.com/2009/09/04/see-baby-discriminate.html.

Brown, Anna, and Patten, Eileen. 2013a. *Hispanics of Colombian Origin in the United States, 2011.* Washington, DC: Pew Hispanic Center. http://www.pewhispanic.org/2013/06/19/hispanics-of-colombian-origin-in-the-united-states-2011/.

———. 2013b. *Hispanics of Dominican Origin in the United States, 2011.* Washington, DC: Pew Hispanic Center. http://www.pewhispanic.org/2013/06/19/hispanics-of-dominican-origin-in-the-united-states-2011/.

———. 2013c. *Hispanics of Salvadoran Origin in the United States, 2011.* Washington, DC: Pew Hispanic Center. http://www.pewhispanic.org/2013/06/19/hispanics-of-salvadoran-origin-in-the-united-states-2011/.

———. 2013d. *Statistical Profile: Hispanics of Puerto Rican Origin in the United States, 2011.* Washington, DC: Pew Hispanic Center. http://www.pewhispanic.org/2013/06/19/hispanics-of-puerto-rican-origin-in-the-united-states-2011/.

Brown, Dee. 1970. *Bury My Heart at Wounded Knee.* New York: Holt, Rinehart, & Winston.

Brown, Kendrick T., Brown, Tony N., Jackson, James S., Sellers, Robert M., and Manuel, Warde J. 2003. Teammates On and Off the Field? Contact With Black Teammates and the Racial Attitudes of White Student Athletes. *Journal of Applied Social Psychology* 33:1379–1404.

Brown, Rupert. 1995. *Prejudice: Its Social Psychology.* Cambridge, MA: Blackwell.

Brown v. Board of Education of Topeka, 247 U.S. 483 (1954).

Brunsma, David. 2005. Interracial Families and the Racial Identification of Mixed-Race Children: Evidence From the Early Childhood Longitudinal Study. *Social Forces* 84:1131–1157.

Bulwa, Demian. 2010. Mehserle Convicted of Involuntary Manslaughter. *San Francisco Chronicle*, July 9.http://www.sfgate.com/bayarea/article/Mehserle-convicted-of-involuntary-manslaughter-3181861.php.

Bumiller, Elisabeth. 2011. Obama Ends "Don't Ask Don't Tell" Policy. *New York*

Times, July 22. http://www
.nytimes.com/2011/07/23/
us/23military.html.

Bureau of Indian Affairs. 2005.
*2005 American Indian
Population and Labor
Report.* Washington, DC:
U.S. Department of the
Interior, Bureau of Indian
Affairs. http://www.bia.gov/
cs/groups/public/documents/
text/idc-001719.pdf.

Buriel, Raymond. 1993.
Acculturation, Respect
for Cultural Differences,
and Biculturalism Among
Three Generations of
Mexican American and
Euro-American School
Children. *Journal of Genetic
Psychology* 154:531–544.

Burns, Peter, and Gimpel,
James. 2000. Economic
Insecurity, Prejudicial
Stereotypes, and Public
Opinion on Immigration
Policy. *Political Science
Quarterly* 115:201–205.

Callimachi, Rukmini. 2005. Is
Nike Campaign Real About
Curves? *Salt Lake Tribune,*
August 19. http://www.sltrib
.com/business/ci_2954991.

Camarillo, Albert, and Bonilla,
Frank. 2001. Hispanics in
a Multicultural Society: A
New American Dilemma? In
N. Smelser, W. Wilson, and
F. Mitchell (Eds.), *America
Becoming: Racial Trends
and Their Consequences*
(Vol. 2, pp. 103–134).
Washington, DC: National
Academy Press.

Cameron, James. 2001. Social
Identity, Modern Sexism,
and Perceptions of Personal
and Group Discrimination by
Women and Men. *Sex Roles*
45:743–766.

Capehart, Jonathon. 2012. The
Income Inequality Faced by
LGBT Families. *Washington
Post,* February 2. http://
www.washingtonpost.com/
blogs/post-partisan/post/the
-income-inequality-faced-by
-lgbt-families/2011/03/04/
gIQAoInNkQ_blog.html.

Carpenter, Dale. 2012. *Flagrant
Conduct: The Story of
Lawrence vs. Texas.* New
York: W. W. Norton.

Carroll, Joseph. 2007.
Hispanics Support Requiring
English Proficiency for
Immigrants. Gallup. http://
www.gallup.com/poll/28048/
Hispanics-Support-Requiring
-English-Proficiency-
Immigrants.aspx.

Carter, David. 2005. *Stonewall:
The Riots That Sparked the
Gay Revolution.* New York:
St. Martin's Griffin.

Carter, Nancy M., and Silva,
Christine. 2010. *Pipeline's
Broken Promise.* New York:
Catalyst. http://www.catalyst
.org/publication/372/
pipelines-broken-promise.

Center for American Women
and Politics. 2011. *Gender
Differences in Voter Turnout.*
New Brunswick, NJ: Author.
http://www.cawp.rutgers
.edu/fast_facts/voters/
documents/genderdiff.pdf.

Central Intelligence Agency.
2013. *The World Factbook,
2013–14.* Washington, DC:
Author. https://www.cia
.gov/library/publications/the
-world-factbook/geos/xx.html.

Chan, Sucheng. 1990.
European and Asian
Immigrants Into the United
States in Comparative
Perspective, 1820s
to 1920s. In Virginia
Yans-McLaughlin (Ed.),
*Immigration Reconsidered:
History, Sociology, and
Politics* (pp. 37–75). New
York: Oxford University
Press.

Charles-Toussaint, G., and
Crowson, H. 2010.
Prejudice Against
International Students:
The Role of Threat
Perceptions and
Authoritarian Dispositions
in U.S. Students. *Journal of
Psychology* 144:413–428.

Chatel, Amanda. 2013. 7
Companies That Don't
Support Gay Rights.
Huffington Post, October 16.
http://www.huffingtonpost
.com/2013/10/16/anti-gay
-companies_n_4110344
.html.

Childs, Erica Chito. 2005.
*Navigating Interracial
Borders: Black–White*

*Couples and Their Social
Worlds.* Rutgers, NJ: Rutgers
University Press.

Chirot, Daniel. 1994. *How
Societies Change.* Thousand
Oaks, CA: Sage.

Cho, Sumi. 1993. Korean
Americans vs. African
Americans: Conflict and
Construction. In Robert
Gooding-Williams (Ed.),
*Reading Rodney King,
Reading Urban Uprising*
(pp. 196–211). New York:
Routledge & Kegan Paul.

Chou, Rosalind, and Feagin,
Joe. 2008. *The Myth of
the Model Minority: Asian
Americans Facing Racism.*
Boulder, CO: Paradigm.

Chowkwanyun, Merlin, and
Segall, Jordan. 2012. The
Rise of the Majority-Asian
Suburb. *CityLab,* August 24.
http://www.citylab.com/
politics/2012/08/rise
-majority-asian-suburb/
3044/.

Churchill, Ward. 1985. Resisting
Relocation: Dine and
Hopis Fight to Keep Their
Land. *Dollars and Sense,*
December, pp. 112–115.

Civil Rights Act of 1964, Pub.
L. 88-352, § 42 U.S.C.
2000 (1964).

Clark, M. L., and Person, Willie.
1982. Racial Stereotypes
Revisited. *International
Journal of Intercultural
Relations* 6:381–392.

Cofer, Judith Ortiz. 1995. The
Myth of the Latin Woman:
I Just Met a Girl Named
Maria. In *The Latin Deli:
Prose and Poetry* (pp. 148–
154). Athens: University of
Georgia Press.

Cohen, Adam, and Taylor,
Elizabeth. 2000. *American
Pharaoh, Mayor Richard J.
Daley: His Battle for Chicago
and the Nation.* New York:
Little, Brown.

Cohen, Mike. 2012. South
Africa's Racial Income
Inequality Persists, Census
Shows. *Bloomberg News,*
October 30. http://www
.bloomberg.com/news/2012
-10-30/south-africa-s-racial
-income-inequality-persists
-census-shows.html.

Cohen, Phillip. 2013. The
Problem With Mostly
Male (and Mostly Female)
Workplaces. *Atlantic
Monthly,* March 20. http://
www.theatlantic.com/sexes/
archive/2013/03/the
-problem-with-mostly
-male-and-mostly-female
-workplaces/274208/.

Cohen, Steven M. 1985. *The
1984 National Survey of
American Jews: Political
and Social Outlooks.* New
York: American Jewish
Committee.

College Enrollment in India
Expands Rapidly. 2012.
*Chronicle of Higher
Education,* August 22.
http://chronicle.com/blogs/
global/college-enrollment
-in-india-expands-rapidly/
34342.

Collins, Jason (with Franz Lidz).
2013. Why NBA Center
Jason Collins Is Coming Out
Now. *Sports Illustrated,* May
6. http://sportsillustrated
.cnn.com/magazine/
news/20130429/jason
-collins-gay-nba-player/.

Collins, P. H. 2000. *Black
Feminist Thought:
Knowledge, Consciousness,
and the Politics of
Empowerment* (2nd ed.).
New York: Routledge.

Conot, Robert. 1967. *Rivers of
Blood, Years of Darkness.*
New York: Bantam.

Conzen, Kathleen N. 1980.
Germans. In Stephan
Thernstrom, Ann Orlov,
and Oscar Handlin (Eds.),
*Harvard Encyclopedia of
American Ethnic Groups* (pp.
405–425). Cambridge, MA:
Harvard University Press.

Cook, Rebecca J. 2013. Human
Rights and Maternal Health:
Exploring the Effectiveness
of the Alyne Decision.
*Journal of Law, Medicine
and Ethics* 41:103–123.

Cornell, Stephen. 1987.
American Indians, American
Dreams, and the Meaning of
Success. *American Indian
Culture and Research
Journal* 11:59–71.

———. 1988. *The Return of
the Native: American Indian*

Political Resurgence. New York: Oxford University Press.

———. 1990. Land, Labor, and Group Formation: Blacks and Indians in the United States. *Ethnic and Racial Studies* 13:368–388.

———. 2006. *What Makes First Nations Enterprises Successful? Lessons From the Harvard Project.* Tucson, AZ: Native Nations Institute for Leadership, Management, and Policy.

Cornell, Stephen, and Kalt, Joseph. 1998. *Sovereignty and Nation-Building: The Development Challenge in Indian Country Today.* Cambridge, MA: Harvard Project on American Indian Economic Development. http://nni.arizona.edu/resources/inpp/2003_CORNELL.kalt_JOPNA_sovereignty.nation-building.pdf.

Cornell, Stephen, Kalt, Joseph, Krepps, Matthew, and Taylor, Johnathan. 1998. *American Indian Gaming Policy and Its Socioeconomic Effects: A Report to the National Impact Gambling Study Commission.* Cambridge, MA: Economics Resource Group.

Correll, Shelley J. 2004. Constraints Into Preferences: Gender, Status, and Emerging Career Aspirations. *American Sociological Review* 69:93–113.

Cortes, Carlos. 1980. Mexicans. In Stephan Thernstrom, Ann Orlov, and Oscar Handlin (Eds.), *Harvard Encyclopedia of American Ethnic Groups* (pp. 697–719). Cambridge, MA: Harvard University Press.

Cose, Ellis. 1993. *The Rage of a Privileged Class.* New York: HarperCollins.

Cottrol, Robert. 2013. *The Long Lingering Shadow: Slavery, Race, and Law in the American Hemisphere.* Athens: University of Georgia Press.

Cowan, Gloria. 2005. Interracial Interactions at Racially Diverse University Campuses. *Journal of Social Psychology* 145:49–63.

Cox, Oliver. 1948. *Caste, Class, and Race: A Study in Social Dynamics.* Garden City, NY: Doubleday.

Cribbs, S. E., and Austin, D. M. 2011. Enduring Pictures in Our Heads: The Continuance of Authoritarianism and Racial Stereotyping. *Journal of Black Studies* 42(3): 334–359.

Crow Dog, Mary. 1990. *Lakota Woman.* New York: HarperCollins.

Cuddy, A., Fiske, S., Kwan, V., Glick, P., Demoulin, S., Leyens, J.-C., et al. 2009. Stereotype Content Model Across Cultures: Towards Universal Similarities and Some Differences. *British Journal of Social Psychology* 48:1–33.

Curtin, Philip. 1990. *The Rise and Fall of the Plantation Complex.* New York: Cambridge University Press.

D'Alessio, Stewart, Stolzenberg, Lisa, and Eitle, David. 2002. The Effect of Racial Threat on Interracial and Intraracial Crimes. *Social Science Research* 31:392–408.

D'Angelo, Raymond. 2001. *The American Civil Rights Movement: Readings and Interpretations.* New York: McGraw-Hill.

Dao, James. 2013. In Debate Over Military Sexual Assault, Men Are the Overlooked Victims. *New York Times,* June 23. http://www.nytimes.com/2013/06/24/us/in-debate-over-military-sexual-assault-men-are-overlooked-victims.html?pagewanted=all.

Davis, Angela Y. 1983. *Women, Race and Class.* New York: Vintage Books.

Davis, Simon. 1990. Men as Success Objects and Women as Sex Objects: A Study of Personal Advertisements. *Sex Roles* 23:43–50.

de la Cruz, Patricia, and Brittingham, Angela. 2003. *The Arab Population: 2000.* http://www.census.gov/prod/2003pubs/c2kbr-23.pdf.

Debo, Angie. 1970. *A History of the Indians of the United States.* Norman: University of Oklahoma Press.

Degler, Carl. 1971. *Neither Black nor White: Slavery and Race Relations in Brazil and the United States.* New York: Macmillan.

Delk, John L., Madden, R. Burt, Livingston, Mary, and Ryan, Timothy T. 1986. Adult Perceptions of the Infant as a Function of Gender Labeling and Observer Gender. *Sex Roles* 15: 527–534.

Deloria, Vine. 1969. *Custer Died for Your Sins.* New York: Macmillan.

D'Emilio, John. 1998. *Sexual Politics, Sexual Communities: The Making of a Sexual Minority in the United States, 1940–1970* (2nd ed.). Chicago, IL: University of Chicago Press.

Deutsch, Barry. n.d. The Male Privilege Checklist. http://amptoons.com/blog/the-male-privilege-checklist/.

Deutsch, Morton, and Collins, Mary Ann. 1951. *Interracial Housing: A Psychological Evaluation of a Social Experiment.* Minneapolis: University of Minnesota Press.

Devine, Patricia, and Elliot, Andrew. 1995. Are Racial Stereotypes Really Fading? The Princeton Trilogy Revisited. *Personality and Social Psychology Bulletin* 21:1139–1150.

Dewan, Shaila. 2013. Immigration and Social Security. *New York Times,* July 2. http://economix.blogs.nytimes.com/2013/07/02/immigration-and-social-security/?_r=0.

Dinnerstein, Leonard. 1977. The East European Jewish Immigration. In Leonard Dinnerstein and Frederic C. Jaher (Eds.), *Uncertain Americans* (pp. 216–231). New York: Oxford University Press.

Dixon, Jeffrey. 2006. The Ties That Don't Bind: Towards Reconciling Group Threat and Contact Theories of Prejudice. *Social Forces* 84:2179–2204.

Dixon, Jeffrey, and Rosenbaum, Michael. 2004. Nice to Know You? Testing Contact, Cultural, and Group Threat Theories of Anti-Black and Anti-Hispanic Stereotypes. *Social Science Quarterly* 85:257–280.

Dollard, John, Miller, Neal E., Doob, Leonard W., Mowrer, O. H., and Sears, Robert R. (with Ford, Clellan S., Hovland, Carl Iver, and Sollenberger, Richard T.). 1939. *Frustration and Aggression.* New Haven, CT: Yale University Press.

D'Orso, Michael. 1996. *Like Judgment Day: The Ruin and Redemption of a Town Called Rosewood.* New York: Putnam.

Drake, Bruce. 2013. *How LGBT Adults See Society and How Society Sees Them.* Washington, DC: Pew Research Center. http://www.pewresearch.org/fact-tank/2013/06/25/how-lgbt-adults-see-society-and-how-the-public-sees-them.

Drogin, Richard. 2003. *Statistical Analysis of Gender Patterns in Wal-Mart Workforce.* Berkeley, CA: Drogin, Kakiki & Associates. http://www.walmartclass.com/staticdata/reports/r2.pdf.

Du Bois, W. E. B. 1961. *The Souls of Black Folk.* Greenwich, CT: Fawcett.

Duberman, Martin. 1994. *Stonewall.* New York: Plume.

Dudley, William. 2006. *Reproductive Rights.* Farmington Hills, MI: Greenhaven Press.

Duleep, Harriet O. 1988. *Economic Status of Americans of Asian Descent.* Washington, DC: U.S. Commission on Civil Rights.

Dwyer, R. 2010. Poverty, Prosperity, and Place: The Shape of Class Segregation in the Age of Extremes. *Social Problems* 57: 114–137.

Eaklor, Vicki. 2008. *Queer America: A GLBT History of the Twentieth Century.* Chicago, IL: Greenwood Press.

Eckholm, Erik. 2010. Congress Moves to Narrow Cocaine Sentencing Disparity. *New York Times*, July 28. http://www.nytimes.com/2010/07/29/us/politics/29crack.html?adxnnl=1&pagewanted=print&adxnnlx=1382103459-x0tOpZ4wq4IKuhvMAc5weg.

Egelko, Bob. 2009. BART Shooting Draws Rodney King Case Parallels. *San Francisco Chronicle*, January 15. http://www.sfgate.com/bayarea/article/BART-shooting-draws-Rodney-King-case-parallels-3176756.php.

Eisenstadt v. Baird, 405 U.S. 438 (1972).

Elias, Paul. 2010. "Greeter" Becomes Face of Fight vs Wal-Mart. *Huffington Post*, May 1. http://www.huffingtonpost.com/huff-wires/20100501/us-betty-v-goliath/.

Elkins, Stanley. 1959. *Slavery: A Problem in American Institutional and Intellectual Life.* New York: Universal Library.

Elliott, James R., and Smith, Ryan A. 2004. Race, Gender and Workplace Power. *American Sociological Review* 69:365–386.

Elliott, Stuart. 2014. AT&T Becomes First Major Advertiser to Protest Russia's Antigay Law. *New York Times*, February 4. http://www.nytimes.com/2014/02/05/business/media/att-becomes-first-major-advertiser-to-protest-russias-antigay-law.html.

Ellis, Lee, Burke, Donald, and Ames, M. Ashley. 1987. Sexual Orientation as a Continuous Variable: A Comparison Between the Sexes. *Archives of Sexual Behavior* 16:523–529.

Ellsworth, Scott. 1982. *Death in a Promised Land: The Tulsa Race Riot of 1921.* Baton Rouge: Louisiana State University Press.

Engels, Friedrich. 2010. *The Origin of Family, Private Property and the State.* New York: Penguin. (Original work published in 1884)

Ennis, Sharon, Rios-Vargas, Merarys, and Albert, Nora. 2011. *The Hispanic Population: 2010.* Washington, DC: U.S. Census Bureau. http://www.census.gov/prod/cen2010/briefs/c2010br-04.pdf.

Espinosa, Kristin, and Massey, Douglas. 1997. Determinants of English Proficiency Among Mexican Migrants to the United States. *International Migration Review* 31:28–51.

Espiritu, Yen. 1996. Colonial Oppression, Labour Importation, and Group Formation: Filipinos in the United States. *Ethnic and Racial Studies* 19:29–49.

———. 1997. *Asian American Women and Men.* Thousand Oaks, CA: Sage.

Essien-Udom, E. U. 1962. *Black Nationalism.* Chicago: University of Chicago Press.

European Union Agency for Fundamental Rights. 2013. *Discrimination and Hate Crimes Against Jews in EU Member States: Experiences and Perceptions of Anti-Semitism.* http://fra.europa.eu/sites/default/files/fra-2013-discrimination-hate-crime-against-jews-eu-member-states_en.pdf.

Evans, Sara M. 1979. *Personal Politics.* New York: Knopf.

———. 1980. *Personal Politics: The Roots of Women's Liberation in the Civil Rights Movement and the New Left.* New York: Vintage Books.

———. 1989. *Born for Liberty: A History of Women in America.* New York: Free Press.

Faderman, Lillian. 1991. *Odd Girls and Twilight Lovers: A History of Lesbian Life in Twentieth Century America.* New York: Columbia University Press.

Fadiman, Anne. 1998. *The Spirit Catches You and You Fall Down.* New York: Farrar, Straus, & Giroux.

Farley, John. 2000. *Majority–Minority Relations* (4th ed.). Englewood Cliffs, NJ: Prentice Hall.

Farley, Reynolds. 1996. *The New American Reality.* New York: Russell Sage Foundation.

Fausto-Sterling, Anne. 1993. The Five Sexes: Why Male and Female Are Not Enough. *The Sciences* (March–April): 20–24.

Faux, Jeff. 2004. NAFTA at 10: Where Do We Go From Here? *Nation* (February 2): 11–14.

Feagin, Joe. 2001. *Racist America: Roots, Current Realities, and Future Reparations.* New York: Routledge.

Feagin, Joe R., and Feagin, Clairece Booher. 1986. *Discrimination American Style: Institutional Racism and Sexism.* Malabar, FL: Robert E. Krieger.

Feagin, Joe, and O'Brien, Eileen. 2004. *White Men on Race: Power, Privilege, and the Shaping of Cultural Consciousness.* Boston: Beacon Press.

Fears, Darryl. 2007. Hate Crime Reporting Uneven. *Washington Post*, November 20, p. A3.

Federal Bureau of Investigation. 2013. Incidents and Offenses. In *Hate Crime Statistics, 2012.* Washington, DC: Author. http://www.fbi.gov/about-us/cjis/ucr/hate-crime/2012/topic-pages/incidents-and-offenses/incidentsandoffenses_final.

Federal Glass Ceiling Commission. 1995. *Good for Business: Making Full Use of the Nations Human Capital.* Washington, DC: Author. http://www.dol.gov/dol/aboutdol/history/reich/reports/ceiling.htm.

Feinberg, Leslie. 1996. *Transgender Warriors: Making History From Joan of Arc to Dennis Rodman.* Boston: Beacon Press.

Feliciano, Cynthia. 2006. *Another Way to Assess the Second Generation: Look at the Parents.* Washington, DC: Migration Policy Institute. http://www.migrationinformation.org/USfocus/display.cfm?ID=396.

File, Thom. 2013. *The Diversifying Electorate: Voting Rates by Race and Hispanic Origin in 2012 (and Other Recent Elections).* Washington, DC: U.S. Census Bureau. http://www.census.gov/prod/2013pubs/p20-568.pdf.

Firefighters Local Union No. 1784 v. Stotts, 467 U.S. 561 (1984).

Fisher, Mary. 2008. Does Campus Diversity Promote Friendship Diversity? A Look at Interracial Friendships in College. *Social Science Quarterly* 89:623–655.

Fisher, Max. 2013a. A Revealing Map of the Countries That Are Most and Least Tolerant of Homosexuality. *Washington Post*, June 5. http://www.washingtonpost.com/blogs/worldviews/wp/2013/06/05/a-revealing-map-of-the-countries-that-are-most-and-least-tolerant-of-homosexuality.

———. 2013b. A Revealing Map of the World's Most and Least Ethnically Diverse Countries. *Washington Post*, May 16. http://www.washingtonpost.com/blogs/worldviews/wp/2013/05/16/a-revealing-map-of-the-worlds-most-and-least-ethnically-diverse-countries.

Fisher v. University of Texas at Austin. 570 U.S. 11-345 (2013).

Fiske, S., Bergsieker, H., Russell, A., and Williams, L. 2009. Images of Black

Americans: Then, "Them," and Now, "Obama!" *Du Bois Review* 6:83–101.

Fitzpatrick, Joseph P. 1976. The Puerto Rican Family. In Charles H. Mindel and Robert W. Habenstein (Eds.), *Ethnic Families in America* (pp. 173–195). New York: Elsevier.

———. 1980. Puerto Ricans. In Stephan Thernstrom, Ann Orlov, and Oscar Handlin (Eds.), *Harvard Encyclopedia of American Ethnic Groups* (pp. 858–867). Cambridge, MA: Harvard University Press.

———. 1987. *Puerto Rican Americans: The Meaning of Migration to the Mainland* (2nd ed.). Englewood Cliffs, NJ: Prentice Hall.

Florida, Richard. 2011. The Geography of Hate. *The Atlantic*, May 11. http://www.theatlantic.com/national/archive/2011/05/the-geography-of-hate/238708/.

———. 2012. The Geography of Women's Economic Opportunities. *The Atlantic Cities*, January 11. http://www.theatlanticcities.com/jobs-and-economy/2012/01/how-economic-development-helps-worlds-women/907.

Foley, Elise. 2010. Don't Ask Don't Tell Repeal Passes Senate, 65-31. *Huffington Post*, December 18. http://www.huffingtonpost.com/2010/12/18/dont-ask-dont-tell-repeal_5_n_798636.html.

Fong, Eric, and Markham, William. 1991. Immigration, Ethnicity, and Conflict: The California Chinese, 1849–1882. *Sociological Inquiry* 61:471–490.

Fong, Timothy. 2002. *The Contemporary Asian American Experience* (2nd ed.). Upper Saddle River, NJ: Prentice Hall.

Fong-Torres, Ben. 1995. *The Rice Room: Growing Up Chinese; From Number Two Son to Rock 'n' Roll*. Plume: New York.

Forbes, H. D. 1997. *Ethnic Conflict: Commerce, Culture, and the Contact Hypothesis*. New Haven, CT: Yale University Press.

Forner, Philip S. 1980. *Women and the American Labor Movement: From World War I to the Present*. New York: Free Press.

Fowler, Geoffrey A. 2013. On Facebook, 70% of Americans Have a Gay Friend. *Wall Street Journal*, June 25. http://blogs.wsj.com/digits/2013/06/25/on-facebook-70-of-americans-have-a-gay-friend/.

Franke-Ruta, Garance. 2012. Americans Have No Idea How Few Gay People There Are. *The Atlantic,* May 31. http://www.theatlantic.com/politics/archive/2012/05/americans-have-no-idea-how-few-gay-people-there-are/257753/.

Franklin, John Hope. 1967. *From Slavery to Freedom* (3rd ed.). New York: Knopf.

Franklin, John Hope, and Moss, Alfred. 1994. *From Slavery to Freedom* (7th ed.). New York: McGraw-Hill.

Frazier, E. Franklin. 1957. *Black Bourgeoisie: The Rise of a New Middle Class*. New York: Free Press.

Frizell, Sam. 2014. Disney to End Funding for Boy Scouts Over Gay Leader Ban. *Time,* March 3.

Fry, Richard. 2007. *The Changing Racial and Ethnic Composition of U.S. Public Schools*. Washington, DC: Pew Hispanic Center. http://pewhispanic.org/files/reports/79.pdf.

Frye, Marilyn. 1983. *The Politics of Reality: Essays in Feminist Theory*. Freedom, CA: Crossing Press.

Gallagher, Charles. 2001. *Playing the Ethnic Card: How Ethnic Narratives Maintain Racial Privilege*. Paper presented at the Annual Meetings of the Southern Sociological Society, April 4–7, Atlanta, GA.

Gallup. 2013. *Race Relations*. http://www.gallup.com/poll/1687/Race-Relations.aspx.

Gans, Herbert. 1979. Symbolic Ethnicity: The Future of Ethnic Groups and Cultures in America. *Ethnic and Racial Studies* 2:1–20.

Garvey, Marcus. 1969. *Philosophy and Opinions of Marcus Garvey* (Vols. 1–2, Amy Jacques Garvey, Ed.). New York: Atheneum.

———. 1977. *Philosophy and Opinions of Marcus Garvey* (Vol. 3, Amy Jacques Garvey and E. U. Essien-Udom, Eds.). London: Frank Cass.

Gates, Gary. 2012. *Same-Sex Couples in Census 2010: Race and Ethnicity*. Los Angeles: Williams Institute, UCLA School of Law. http://williamsinstitute.law.ucla.edu/wp-content/uploads/Gates-CouplesRaceEthnicity-April-2012.pdf.

Gates, Gary, and Newport, Frank. 2012. LGBT Americans Skew Democratic, Largely Support Obama. *Gallup Politics*. http://www.gallup.com/poll/158102/lgbt-americans-skew-democratic-largely-support-obama.aspx.

———. 2013. LGBT Percentage Highest in D.C., Lowest in North Dakota. *Gallup Politics*. http://www.gallup.com/poll/160517/lgbt-percentage-highest-lowest-north-dakota.aspx.

Geiger, Kim. 2012. Rush Limbaugh's "Slut" Comment Draws Rebuke from All Sides. *Los Angeles Times,* March 2. http://articles.latimes.com/2012/mar/02/news/la-pn-rush-limbaugh-draws-rebukes-from-all-sides-20120302.

Genovese, Eugene D. 1974. *Roll, Jordan, Roll: The World the Slaves Made*. New York: Pantheon.

Gerson, Kathleen. 2009. *The Unfinished Revolution: Coming of Age in a New Era of Gender, Work and Family*. Oxford, UK: Oxford University Press.

Gerstenfeld, Phyllis. 2004. *Hate Crime: Causes, Controls, and Controversies*. Thousand Oaks, CA: Sage.

Gerth, Hans, and Mills, C. Wright (Eds.). 1946. *From Max Weber: Essays in Sociology*. New York: Oxford University Press.

Geschwender, James A. 1978. *Racial Stratification in America*. Dubuque, IA: William C. Brown.

Gilbert, D. L. 2011. *The American class structure in an age of growing inequality*. Thousand Oaks, CA: Pine Forge Press.

Glaeser, Edward, and Vigdor, Jacob. 2012. The End of the Segregated Century: Racial Separation in America's Neighborhoods, 1890–2010. New York: Manhattan Institute, Center for State and Local Leadership. http://www.manhattan-institute.org/html/cr_66.htm.

Glazer, Nathan, and Moynihan, Daniel. 1970. *Beyond the Melting Pot* (2nd ed.). Cambridge: MIT Press.

Gleason, Philip. 1980. American Identity and Americanization. In Stephan Thernstrom, Ann Orlov, and Oscar Handlin (Eds.), *Harvard Encyclopedia of American Ethnic Groups* (pp. 31–57). Cambridge, MA: Harvard University Press.

Goffman, Erving. 1963. *Stigma: Notes on the Management of Spoiled Identity*. New York: Simon & Schuster.

Goldstein, Amy, and Suro, Robert. 2000. A Journey on Stages: Assimilation's Pull Is Still Strong but Its Pace Varies. *Washington Post,* January 16, p. A1.

Gomez, Laura. 2008. *Manifest Destinies: The Making of the Mexican American Race*. New York: NYU Press

Gordon, M. M. 1964. *Assimilation in American Life: The Role of Race,*

Religion, and National Origins. New York: Oxford University Press.

Goren, Arthur. 1980. Jews. In Stephan Thernstrom, Ann Orlov, and Oscar Handlin (Eds.), *Harvard Encyclopedia of American Ethnic Groups* (pp. 571–598). Cambridge, MA: Harvard University Press.

Gourevitch, Philip. 1999. *We Wish to Inform You That Tomorrow We Will Be Killed With Our Families: Stories From Rwanda*. New York: Picador.

Gratz v. Bollinger, 539 U.S. 244 (2003).

Gray, David J. 1991. Shadow of the Past: The Rise and Fall of Prejudice in an American City. *American Journal of Economics and Sociology* 50:33–39.

Gray, Marion W. 2000. *Productive Men, Reproductive Women: The Agrarian Household and the Emergence of Separate Spheres During the German Enlightenment*. New York: Berghahn Books.

Grebler, Leo, Moore, Joan W., and Guzman, Ralph C. 1970. *The Mexican American People*. New York: Free Press.

Greeley, Andrew M. 1974. *Ethnicity in the United States: A Preliminary Reconnaissance*. New York: Wiley.

Green, Donald. 1999. Native Americans. In Antony Dworkin and Rosalind Dworkin (Eds.), *The Minority Report* (pp. 255–277). Orlando, FL: Harcourt-Brace.

Griswold v. Connecticut, 381 U.S. 479 (1965).

Grutter v. Bollinger, 539 U.S. 306 (2003).

Guilbault, Rose Del Castillo. 1993. Americanization Is Tough on "Macho." In Dolores La Guardia and Hans Guth (Eds.), *American Voices* (pp. 163–165). Mountain View, CA: Mayfield. (First published in "This World," *San Francisco Chronicle*, August 20, 1989)

Gutman, Herbert. 1976. *The Black Family in Slavery and Freedom, 1750–1925*. New York: Vintage.

Haan, Arjan, and Thorat, Sukhadeo. 2012. Addressing Group Inequalities: Social Policies in Emerging Economies' Great Transformation. *European Journal of Development Research* 24:105–124.

Hacker, Andrew. 1992. *Two Nations: Black and White, Separate, Hostile, Unequal*. New York: Scribner's.

Hainmueller, Jens, and Hiscox, Michael. 2010. Attitudes Toward Highly Skilled and Low-Skilled Immigration: Evidence From a Survey Experiment. *American Political Science Review* 104:61–84.

Hakimzadeh, Shirin, and Cohn, D'Vera. 2007. *English Language Usage Among Hispanics in the United States*. Washington, DC: Pew Hispanic Center. http://pewhispanic.org/files/reports/82.pdf.

Halberstam, David. 1998. *The Children*. New York: Fawcett Books.

Haley, Alex. 1976. *Roots: The Saga of an American Family*. New York: Doubleday.

Haller, William, Portes, Alejandro, and Lynch, Scott. 2011. Dreams Fulfilled, Dreams Shattered: Determinants of Segmented Assimilation in the Second Generation. *Social Forces* 89:733–762.

Halperin, David. 1989. *One Hundred Years of Homosexuality: And Other Essays on Greek Love*. New York: Routledge.

Hamer, Fannie Lou. 1967. *To Praise Our Bridges: An Autobiography of Fannie Lou Hamer*. Jackson, MS: KIPCO.

Handlin, Oscar. 1951. *The Uprooted*. New York: Grosset & Dunlap.

Handy, Bruce. 1997. Roll Over, Ward Cleaver and Tell Ozzie Nelson the News. Ellen

DeGeneres Is Poised to Become TV's First Openly Gay Star. Is TV Ready or Not? *Time*, April 14.

Hansen, Marcus Lee. 1952. The Third Generation in America. *Commentary* 14:493–500.

Harjo, Suzan. 1996. Now and Then: Native Peoples in the United States. *Dissent* 43:58–60.

Harrison-Quintana, Jack, and Quach, Chris (with Grant, Jaime). 2013. *Injustice at Every Turn: A Look at Multiracial Respondents in the National Transgender Discrimination Survey*. Washington, DC: National Gay and Lesbian Task Force.

Hartley, E. L. 1946. *Problems in Prejudice*. New York: Kings Crown.

Hawkins, Hugh. 1962. *Booker T. Washington and His Critics: The Problem of Negro Leadership*. Boston: D. C. Heath.

Heer, David M. 1996. *Immigration in America's Future*. Boulder, CO: Westview.

Hegewisch, Ariane, Liepmann, Hannah, Hayes, Jeffrey, and Hartmann, Heidi. 2010. *Separate and Not Equal? Gender Segregation in the Labor Market and the Gender Wage Gap*. Washington, DC: Institute for Women's Policy Research. http://www.iwpr.org/publications/pubs/separate-and-not-equal-gender-segregation-in-the-labor-market-and-the-gender-wage-gap.

Herberg, Will. 1960. *Protestant–Catholic–Jew: An Essay in American Religious Sociology*. New York: Anchor.

Herek, Gregory M. 1988. Heterosexuals' Attitudes Toward Lesbians and Gay Men: Correlates and Gender Differences. *Journal of Sex Research* 25(4): 451–477.

Herek, Gregory M., Jobe, Jared B., and Carney, Ralph M. 1996. *Out in Force: Sexual Orientation and the Military*. Chicago, IL: University of Chicago Press.

Higham, John. 1963. *Strangers in the Land: Patterns of American Nativism, 1860–1925*. New York: Atheneum.

Hill, Jane. 1995. Mock Spanish: A Site for the Indexical Reproduction of Racism in American English. *Language and Culture: Symposium 2*. http://language-culture.binghamton.edu/symposia/2/part1/.

Hines, Alice. 2012. Wal-Mart Sex Discrimination Claims Filed by 2,000 Women. *Huffington Post*, June 6. http://www.huffingtonpost.com/2012/06/06/walmart-sex-discrimination-women-_n_1575859.html.

Hinrichs, Donal W., and Rosenberg. Pamela J. 2002. Attitudes Towards Gay, Lesbian and Bisexual Persons Among Heterosexual Liberal Arts College Students. *Journal of Homosexuality* 43:61–84.

Hirschman, Charles. 1983. America's Melting Pot Reconsidered. *Annual Review of Sociology* 9:397–423.

Hirschman, Charles, and Wong, Morrison. 1984. Socioeconomic Gains of Asian Americans, Blacks, and Hispanics: 1960–1976. *American Journal of Sociology* 90:584–607.

———. 1986. The Extraordinary Educational Attainment of Asian-Americans: A Search for Historical Evidence and Explanations. *Social Forces* 65:1–27.

His Horse Is Thunder, Deborah, Anderson, Nate, and Miller, Darlene. 2013. *Building the Foundation for Success: Case Studies of Breaking Through Tribal Colleges and Universities*. Boston, MA: Jobs for the Future. http://www.jff.org/sites/default/files/publications/BuildingFoundationSuccess_ExSumm_040813.pdf.

Hoeffel, Elizabeth, Rastogi, Sonya, Kim, Myoung Ouk, and Shahid, Hasan. 2012.

The Asian Population: 2010. Washington, DC: U.S. Census Bureau. http://www.census.gov/prod/cen2010/briefs/c2010br-11.pdf.

hooks, bell. 1996. *Bone Black.* New York: Henry Holt.

———. 1999. *Talking Back: Thinking Feminist, Thinking Black.* Boston, MA: South End Press.

———. 2000. *Feminist Theory: From Margin to Center.* Cambridge, MA: South End Press. (Original work published in 1984)

———. 2013. Dig Deep: Beyond Lean In. *The Feminist Wire,* October 28. http://thefeministwire.com/2013/10/17973.

Hopcroft, Rosemary. 2009. Gender Inequality in Interaction: An Evolutionary Account. *Social Forces* 87:1845–1872.

Hostetler, John. 1980. *Amish Society.* Baltimore, MD: Johns Hopkins University Press.

Hovland, Carl I., and Sears, Robert R. 1940. Minor Studies of Aggression: Correlation of Lynchings and Economic Indices. *Journal of Psychology* 9:301–310.

How to Tell Your Friends From the Japs. 1941. *Time,* October–December, p. 33.

Hoxie, Frederick. 1984. *A Final Promise: The Campaign to Assimilate the Indian, 1880–1920.* Lincoln: University of Nebraska Press.

Hraba, Joseph. 1994. *American Ethnicity* (2nd ed.). Itasca, IL: F. E. Peacock.

Hubbard, Thomas K. 2003. *Homosexuality in Greece and Rome: A Sourcebook of Basic Documents.* Oakland: University of California Press.

Huber, Joan. 2007. *On the Origins of Gender Inequality.* Colorado Springs, CO: Paradigm.

Hughes, Michael, and Thomas, Melvin. 1998. The Continuing Significance of Race Revisited: A Study of Race, Class, and Quality of Life in America, 1972 to 1996. *American Sociological Review* 63:785–803.

Human Rights Campaign. 2012. *Growing Up LGBT in America: HRC Youth Survey Report Key Findings.* http://www.hrc.org/files/assets/resources/Growing-Up-LGBT-in-America_Report.pdf.

———. 2013. The History of Coming Out. http://www.hrc.org/resources/entry/the-history-of-coming-out.

Huntington, Samuel. 2004. *Who Are We? The Challenges to America's National Identity.* New York: Simon & Schuster.

Hurh, Won Moo. 1998. *The Korean Americans.* Westport, CT: Greenwood.

Hurley, Lawrence. 2013. Gay Marriage Gets Big Boost in Two Supreme Court Rulings. Reuters, June 26. http://www.reuters.com/article/2013/06/26/us-usa-court-gaymarriage-idUSBRE95P06W20130626.

Hyman, Herbert, and Sheatsley, Paul. 1964. Attitudes Toward Desegregation. *Scientific American* 211:16–23.

Ibish, Hussein (Ed.). 2003. *Report on Hate Crimes and Discrimination Against Arab Americans: The Post–September 11 Backlash.* Washington, DC: American-Arab Anti-Discrimination Committee. http://www.adc.org/hatecrimes/pdf/2003_report_web.pdf.

Iceland, John, Weinberg, Donald, and Steinmetz, Erika. 2002. *Racial and Ethnic Residential Segregation in the United States: 1980–2000* (U.S. Census Bureau, Series CENSR-3). Washington, DC: U.S. Government Printing Office. http://www.census.gov/prod/2002pubs/censr-3.pdf.

Instituto Brasileiro do Geografica e Estatistica. 2013. Table 1.3.1—Resident Population by Race, Age, and Sex. *Censo 2010.* http://www.ibge.gov.br/english/estatistica/populacao/censo2010/caracteristicas_da_populacao/tabelas_pdf/tab3.pdf.

Israel Central Bureau of Statistics. 2014. *65th Independence Day—More Than 8 Million Residents in the State of Israel* [Press release]. http://www1.cbs.gov.il/www/hodaot2013n/11_13_097e.pdf.

Jackman, Mary. 1978. General and Applied Tolerance: Does Education Increase Commitment to Racial Integration? *American Journal of Political Science* 22:302–324.

———. 1981. Education and Policy Commitment to Racial Integration. *American Journal of Political Science* 25:256–259.

Jackman, Mary, and Muha, M. 1984. Education and Intergroup Attitudes: Moral Enlightenment, Superficial Democratic Commitment, or Ideological Refinement? *American Sociological Review* 49:751–769.

Jackson, Beverly. 2000. *Splendid Slippers: A Thousand Years of an Erotic Tradition.* Berkeley, CA: Ten Speed.

Jacobs, David, and Wood, Katherine. 1999. Interracial Conflict and Interracial Homicide: Do Political and Economic Rivalries Explain White Killings of Blacks or Black Killings of Whites? *American Journal of Sociology* 105:157–180.

Jacobs, Harriet. 1987. *Incidents in the Life of a Slave Girl, Written by Herself* (Jean Fagan Yellin, Ed.). Cambridge, MA: Harvard University Press.

James, Susan Donaldson. 2011. Census 2010: One-Quarter of Gay Couples Raising Children. *ABC News,* June 23. http://abcnews.go.com/Health/sex-couples-census-data-trickles-quarter-raising-children/story?id=13850332.

———. 2014. Jason Collins and Michael Sam Redefine Black Manhood. *ABC News,* February 24. http://abcnews.go.com/Health/jason-collins-michael-sam-redefine-black-manhood/story?id=22650777.

Jamieson, David. 2012. Betty Dukes, Renowned Dukes v. Walmart Plaintiff, Takes Her Fight Back to Capitol Hill. *Huffington Post,* June 20. http://www.huffingtonpost.com/2012/06/20/betty-dukes-walmart-supreme-court_n_1613305.html.

Japanese American Citizens League. 2009. *Myths and Mirrors: Real Challenges Facing Asian American Students.* San Francisco, CA: Author. http://www.jacl.org/leadership/documents/MythsandMirrorsFinal.pdf.

Jayson, Sharon. 2012. Census Shows Big Jump in Interracial Couples. *USA Today,* April 26. http://usatoday30.usatoday.com/news/nation/story/2012-04-24/census-interracial-couples/54531706/1.

Jibou, Robert M. 1988. Ethnic Hegemony and the Japanese of California. *American Sociological Review* 53:353–367.

Joe, Jennie, and Miller, Dorothy. 1994. Cultural Survival and Contemporary American Indian Women in the City. In Maxine Zinn and Bonnie T. Dill (Eds.), *Women of Color in U.S. Society* (pp. 185–202). Philadelphia, PA: Temple University Press.

Johnson, Colin. 2013. *Just Queer Folks: Gender and Sexuality in Rural America.* Philadelphia, PA: Temple University Press.

Jones, James. 1997. *Prejudice and Racism* (2nd ed.). New York: McGraw-Hill.

Jones, Jeffrey M. 2013. Same Sex Marriage Support Solidifies Above 50% in U.S. *Gallup Politics.* http://www.gallup.com/poll/162398/

sex-marriage-support -solidifies-above.aspx.

Jones, N., and Bullock, J. 2012. *The Two or More Races Population: 2010.* U.S. Census Bureau. http://www.census.gov/ prod/cen2010/briefs/ c2010br-13.pdf.

Jordan, Winthrop. 1968. *White Over Black: American Attitudes Towards the Negro: 1550–1812.* Chapel Hill: University of North Carolina Press.

Josephy, Alvin M. 1968. *The Indian Heritage of America.* New York: Knopf.

Joyce, Amy. 2004. Still Outside the Good Ol' Boys Club: Women Continue to Be Discriminated Against in the Workplace, Study Finds. *Washington Post,* July 18. http://www.washingtonpost .com/wp-dyn/articles/ A56858-2004Jul17.html.

Kaleem, Jaweed. 2011. Religious Lobbying Groups Have Dramatically Increased in Washington: Study. *Huffington Post,* November 21. http://www .huffingtonpost.com/ 2011/11/21/religious -lobbying-groups_n_ 1105565.html.

Kallen, Horace M. 1915a. Democracy Versus the Melting Pot. *Nation* 100(February 18): 190–194.

———. 1915b. Democracy Versus the Melting Pot. *Nation* 100(February 25): 217–222.

Karlins, Marvin, Coffman, Thomas, and Walters, Gary. 1969. On the Fading of Social Stereotypes: Studies in Three Generations of College Students. *Journal of Personality and Social Psychology* 13:1–16.

Kasarda, John D. 1989. Urban Industrial Transition and the Underclass. *Annals of the American Academy of Political Science* 501:26–47.

Kasindorf, Martin. 2012. Racial Tensions Are Simmering in Hawaii's Melting Pot. *USA Today,* March 6. http:// usatoday30.usatoday.com/

news/nation/2007-03-06 -hawaii-cover_N.htm.

Kasinitz, Philip, Mollenkopf, John H., Waters, Mary C., and Holdaway, Jennifer. 2008. *Inheriting the City: The Children of Immigrants Come of Age.* New York: Russell Sage Foundation.

Kastanis, Angeliki, and Wilson, Blanca. 2012. *Race/ Ethnicity, Gender, and Socioeconomic Wellbeing of Individuals in Same-Sex Couples.* Los Angeles: Williams Institute, UCLA School of Law. http:// williamsinstitute.law.ucla .edu/wp-content/uploads/ Census-Compare-Feb-2014.pdf.

Katz, Michael B., and Stern, Mark J. 2008. *One Nation Divisible: What America Was and What It Is Becoming.* New York: Russell Sage Foundation.

Katz, Phyllis. 1976. The Acquisition of Racial Attitudes in Children. In Phyllis Katz (Ed.), *Towards the Elimination of Racism* (pp. 125–154). New York: Pergamon.

———. 2003. Racists or Tolerant Multiculturalists? How Do They Begin? *American Psychologist* 58:897–909.

Katz, Phyllis, and Taylor, Dalmas (Eds.). 1988. *Eliminating Racism: Profiles in Controversy.* New York: Plenum.

Katznelson, Ira. 2005. *When Affirmative Action Was White: An Untold History of Racial Inequality in Twentieth-Century America.* New York: Norton.

Kaw, Eugenia. 1997. Opening Faces: The Politics of Cosmetic Surgery and Asian American Women. In M. Crawford and R. Under (Eds.), *In Our Own Words: Readings on the Psychology of Women and Gender* (pp. 55–73). New York: McGraw-Hill.

Kaye, Jeffrey. 2010. *Moving Millions: How Coyote Capitalism Fuels Global*

Immigration. Hoboken, NJ: Wiley.

Kennedy, Randall. 2001. Racial Trends in the Administration of Criminal Justice. In N. Smelser, W. Wilson, and F. Mitchell (Eds.), *America Becoming: Racial Trends and Their Consequences* (Vol. 2, pp. 1–20). Washington, DC: National Academy Press.

Kennedy, Ruby Jo. 1944. Single or Triple Melting Pot? Intermarriage Trends in New Haven, 1870–1940. *American Journal of Sociology* 49:331–339.

———. 1952. Single or Triple Melting Pot? Intermarriage Trends in New Haven, 1870–1950. *American Journal of Sociology* 58:56–59.

Kephart, William, and Zellner, William. 1994. *Extraordinary Groups.* New York: St. Martin's Press.

Killian, Lewis. 1975. *The Impossible Revolution, Phase 2: Black Power and the American Dream.* New York: Random House.

Kinder, Donald R., and Sears, David O. 1981. Prejudice and Politics: Symbolic Racism Versus Racial Threats to the Good Life. *Journal of Personality and Social Psychology* 40:414–431.

King, Martin Luther, Jr. 1958. *Stride Toward Freedom: The Montgomery Story.* New York: Harper & Row.

———. 1963. *Why We Can't Wait.* New York: Mentor.

———. 1968. *Where Do We Go From Here: Chaos or Community?* New York: Harper & Row.

Kinsey, Alfred. 1948. *Sexual Behavior in the Human Male.* Philadelphia, PA: W. B. Saunders.

Kitano, Harry H. L. 1980. Japanese. In Stephan Thernstrom, Ann Orlov, and Oscar Handlin (Eds.), *Harvard Encyclopedia of American Ethnic Groups* (pp. 561–571). Cambridge, MA: Harvard University Press.

Kitano, Harry, and Daniels, Roger. 1988. *Asian Americans: Emerging Minorities.* Englewood Cliffs, NJ: Prentice Hall.

———. 1995. *Asian Americans: Emerging Minorities* (2nd ed.). Englewood Cliffs, NJ: Prentice Hall.

———. 2001. *Asian Americans: Emerging Minorities* (3rd ed.). Upper Saddle River, NJ: Prentice Hall.

Klein, Jeff Z., and Battista, Judy. 2013. Major Sports Leagues Prepare for the "I'm Gay" Disclosure. *New York Times,* April 11. http://www.nytimes .com/2013/04/12/sports/ hockey/nhl-announces -initiative-in-support-of-gay -athletes.html.

Kluegel, James R., and Smith, Eliot R. 1982. Whites' Beliefs About Blacks' Opportunities. *American Sociological Review* 47:518–532.

Kochhar, Rakesh. 2004. *The Wealth of Hispanic Households: 1996 to 2002.* Washington, DC: Pew Hispanic Center. http:// pewhispanic.org/files/ reports/34.pdf.

———. 2006. *Growth in the Foreign-Born Workforce and Employment of the Native Born.* Washington, DC: Pew Hispanic Center. http://pewhispanic.org/files/ reports/69.pdf.

Kochhar, Rakesh, Fry, Richard, and Taylor, Paul. 2011. *Wealth Gap Rises to Record Highs Between Whites, Blacks, and Hispanics.* Washington, DC: Pew Research Center. http://www .pewsocialtrends.org/files/ 2011/07/SDT-Wealth -Report_7-26-11_FINAL.pdf.

Kordunsky, Anna. 2013. Russia Not Only Country With Anti-Gay Laws. *National Geographic,* August 14. http://news.national geographic.com/news/ 2013/08/130814-russia -anti-gay-propaganda-law -world-olympics-africa-gay -rights/.

Korgen, Kathleen. 2002. *Crossing the Racial Divide: Close Friendships Between Black and White Americans.* Westport, CT: Praeger.

Kraditor, Aileen S. 1981. *The Ideas of the Women's Suffrage Movement: 1890–1920.* New York: W. W. Norton.

Krauss, Michael. 1996. Status of Native American Language Endangerment. In G. Cantoni (Ed.), *Stabilizing Indigenous Languages.* Flagstaff: Center for Excellence in Education, Northern Arizona University.

Kraybill, Donald B., and Bowman, Carl F. 2001. *On the Backroad to Heaven: Old Order Hutterites, Mennonites, Amish, and Brethren.* Baltimore, MD: Johns Hopkins University Press.

Kristofic, Jim. 2011. *Navajos Wear Nikes: A Reservation Life.* Albuquerque: University of New Mexico Press.

Kritz, Mary, and Girak, Douglas. 2004. *The American People: Immigration and a Changing America.* New York: Russell Sage Foundation.

Krysan, Maria, and Farley, Reynolds. 2002. The Residential Preferences of Blacks: Do They Explain Persistent Segregation? *Social Forces* 80:937–981.

Labaton, Stephen. 1994. Denny's Restaurants to Pay $54 Million in Race Bias Suits. *New York Times,* May 25. http://www.nytimes.com/1994/05/25/us/denny-s-restaurants-to-pay-54-million-in-race-bias-suits.html.

Lacy, Dan. 1972. *The White Use of Blacks in America.* New York: McGraw-Hill.

Lai, H. M. 1980. Chinese. In Stephan Thernstrom, Ann Orlov, and Oscar Handlin (Eds.), *Harvard Encyclopedia of American Ethnic Groups* (pp. 217–234). Cambridge, MA: Harvard University Press.

Lame Deer, John (Fire), and Erdoes, Richard. 1972. Listening to the Air. In *Lame Deer, Seeker of Visions* (pp. 119–121). New York: Simon & Schuster.

Lamont-Brown, Raymond. 1993. The Burakumin: Japan's Underclass. *Contemporary Review* 263:136–140.

Landale, Nancy, and Oropesa, R. S. 2002. White, Black, or Puerto Rican? Racial Self-Identification Among Mainland and Island Puerto Ricans. *Social Forces* 81:231–254.

LaPiere, Robert. 1934. Attitudes vs. Actions. *Social Forces* 13:230–237.

Lawrence v. Texas, 539 U.S. 558 (2003).

Le, C. N. 2005. Fleeing Dragon: The Refugee Experience of a Vietnamese Immigrant Family. In John Myers (Ed.), *Minority Voices: Linking Personal Ethnic History and the Sociological Imagination* (pp. 340–362). Boston: Pearson.

Lee, Sharon. 1998. Asian Americans: Diverse and Growing. *Population Bulletin* 53(2): 1–40. Washington, DC: Population Reference Bureau.

Leff, Lisa. 2011. Gay Population in U.S. Estimated at 4 Million, Gary Gates Says. *Huffington Post,* April 7. http://www.huffingtonpost.com/2011/04/07/gay-population-us-estimate_n_846348.html.

Lefkowitz, Bernard. 1998. *Our Guys: The Glen Ridge Rape and the Secret Life of the Perfect Suburb.* New York: Vintage.

Lenski, Gerhard E. 1984. *Power and Privilege: A Theory of Social Stratification.* Chapel Hill: University of North Carolina Press.

Lenski, Gerhard, Nolan, Patrick, and Lenski, Jean. 1995. *Human Societies: An Introduction to Macrosociology* (7th ed.). New York: McGraw-Hill.

Levin, Jack, and McDevitt, Jack. 1993. *Hate Crimes: The Rising Tide of Bigotry and Bloodshed.* New York: Plenum.

Levine, Lawrence. 1977. *Black Culture and Black Consciousness.* New York: Oxford University Press.

Levy, Jacques. 1975. *César Chávez: Autobiography of La Causa.* New York: Norton.

Lewis, Gregory. 2003. Black–White Differences in Attitudes Toward Homosexuality and Gay Rights. *Public Opinion Quarterly* 67:59–78.

———. 2011. The Friends and Family Plan: Contact With Gays and Support for Gay Rights. *Policy Studies Journal* 39:217–238.

Lewis, John (with D'Orso, Michael). 1999. *Walking With the Wind: A Memoir of the Movement.* New York: Harvest Books.

Lewis, Oscar. 1959. *Five Families: Mexican Case Studies in the Culture of Poverty.* New York: Basic Books.

———. 1965. *La Vida: A Puerto Rican Family in the Culture of Poverty.* New York: Random House.

———. 1966. The Culture of Poverty. *Scientific American* (October): 19–25.

Lewis, V. A. 2012. Social Energy and Racial Segregation in the University Context. *Social Science Quarterly* 93:270–290.

Lewis, Valerie, Emerson, Michael, and Klineberg, Stephen. 2011. Who We'll Live With: Neighborhood Composition Preferences of Whites, Blacks, and Latinos. *Social Forces* 89:1385–1408.

Lieberman, Robert. 1998. *Shifting the Color Line: Race and the American Welfare System.* Cambridge, MA: Harvard University Press.

Lieberson, Stanley. 1980. *A Piece of the Pie: Blacks and White Immigrants Since 1880.* Berkeley: University of California Press.

Lieberson, Stanley, and Waters, Mary C. 1988. *From Many Strands.* New York: Russell Sage Foundation.

Light, Ivan, and Bonacich, Edna. 1988. *Immigrant Entrepreneurs: Koreans in Los Angeles, 1965–1982.* Berkeley: University of California Press.

Lincoln, C. Eric. 1961. *The Black Muslims in America.* Boston: Beacon.

Ling, Huping. 2000. Family and Marriage of Late-Nineteenth and Early-Twentieth Century Chinese Immigrant Women. *Journal of American Ethnic History* 9:43–65.

Liptak, Adam. 2013. Supreme Court Invalidates Key Part of the Voting Rights Act. *New York Times,* June 25. http://www.nytimes.com/2013/06/26/us/supreme-court-ruling.html.

Locust, Carol. 1990. Wounding the Spirit: Discrimination and Traditional American Indian Belief Systems. In Gail Thomas (Ed.), *U.S. Race Relations in the 1980s and 1990s: Challenges and Alternatives* (pp. 219–232). New York: Hemisphere.

Loewen, James. 2005. *Sundown Towns: A Hidden Dimension of American Racism.* New York: Simon & Schuster.

Lofquist, Daphne, Lugailia, Terry, O'Connell, Martin, and Feliz, Sarah. 2012. *Households and Families: 2010.* Washington, DC: U.S. Census Bureau. http://www.census.gov/prod/cen2010/briefs/c2010br-14.pdf.

Logan, John, Alba, Richard, and McNulty, Thomas. 1994. Ethnic Economies in Metropolitan Regions: Miami and Beyond. *Social Forces* 72:691–724.

Logan, John, and Stults, Brian. 2011. *The Persistence of Segregation in the Metropolis: New Findings From the 2010 Census.* http://www.s4.brown.edu/us2010/Data/Report/report2.pdf.

Lopata, Helena Znaniecki. 1976. *Polish Americans.* Englewood Cliffs, NJ: Prentice Hall.

Lorber, Judith. 2001. *Gender Inequality: Feminist Theories and Politics* (2nd ed.). Los Angeles, CA: Roxbury.

Loving v. Virginia, 388 U.S. 1 (1967).

Lundquist, Jennifer Hickes. 2008. Ethnic and Gender Satisfaction in the Military: The Effect of a Meritocratic Institution. *American Sociological Review* 73:477–496.

Lurie, Nancy Oestrich. 1982. The American Indian: Historical Background. In Norman Yetman and C. Hoy Steele (Eds.), *Majority and Minority* (3rd ed., pp. 131–144). Boston: Allyn & Bacon.

Lyman, Stanford. 1974. *Chinese Americans.* New York: Random House.

Malcolm X. 1964. *The Autobiography of Malcolm X.* New York: Grove.

Malis, Claudia Pryor (Writer, Producer, and Director). 2000. *Frontline: Assault on Gay America* [Television broadcast]. Washington, DC: PBS. http://www.pbs.org/wgbh/pages/frontline/shows/assault/etc/script.html.

Mann, Charles. 2011. *1491: New Revelations of the Americas Before Columbus.* New York: Vintage Books.

Manning, Jennifer. 2013. *Membership of the 113th Congress: A Profile.* Congressional Research Service. http://www.senate.gov/CRSReports/crs-publish.cfm?pid=%260BL%2BR%5CC%3F%0A.

Mannix, Daniel P. 1962. *Black Cargoes: A History of the Atlantic Slave Trade.* New York: Viking.

Marable, Manning. 2011. *Malcolm X: A Life of Reinvention.* New York: Penguin.

Marcelli, Enrico, and Heer, David. 1998. The Unauthorized Mexican Immigrant Population and Welfare in Los Angeles County: A Comparative Statistical Analysis. *Sociological Perspectives* 41:279–303.

Marcus, Sharon. 2007. *Between Women: Friendship, Desire and Marriage in Victorian England.* Princeton, NJ: Princeton University Press.

Marosi, Richard. 2005. Death and Deliverance: The Desert Swallows Another Border Crosser, and Her Father Is Determined to Find Her Body. *Los Angeles Times*, August 7, p. A1.

Marteleto, Leticia. 2012. Educational Inequality by Race in Brazil, 1982–2007: Structural Changes and Shifts in Racial Classification. *Demography* 49:337–358.

Martin, Philip, and Midgley, Elizabeth. 1999. Immigration to the United States. *Population Bulletin* 54(2): 1–44. Washington, DC: Population Reference Bureau.

Marvasti, Amir, and McKinney, Karyn. 2004. *Middle Eastern Lives in America.* Lanham, MD: Rowman & Littlefield.

Marx, Karl, and Engels, Friedrich. 1967. *The Communist Manifesto.* Baltimore: Penguin. (Original work published 1848)

Masci, David, Sciupac, Elizabeth, and Lipka, Michael. 2013. *Gay Marriage Around the World.* Washington, DC: Pew Research Religion and Life Project. http://www.pewforum.org/2013/12/19/gay-marriage-around-the-world-2013.

Massarik, Fred, and Chenkin, Alvin. 1973. United States National Jewish Population Study: A First Report. In *American Jewish Committee, American Jewish Year Book, 1973* (pp. 264–306). New York: American Jewish Committee.

Massey, Douglas. 1995. The New Immigration and Ethnicity in the United States. *Population and Development Review* 21:631–652.

———. 2000. Housing Discrimination 101. *Population Today* 28:1, 4.

———. 2007. *Categorically Unequal: The American Stratification System.* New York: Russell Sage Foundation.

Massey, Douglas, and Denton, Nancy. 1993. *American Apartheid.* Cambridge, MA: Harvard University Press.

Mauer, Marc. 2011. Addressing Racial Disparities in Incarceration. *The Prison Journal* 91:875–1015.

McConahy, John B. 1986. Modern Racism, Ambivalence, and the Modern Racism Scale. In John F. Dovidio and Samuel Gartner (Eds.), *Prejudice, Discrimination, and Racism* (pp. 91–125). Orlando, FL: Academic Press.

McConnell, Tristan. 2014. Uganda's New Anti-Gay Law: Part of a Broader Trend in Africa. *National Geographic*, February 28. http://news.nationalgeographic.com/news/2014/02/140228-uganda-anti-gay-law-smug-homophobia-africa-world.

McDonald, Steve, Lin, Nan, and Ao, Dan. 2009. Networks of Opportunity: Race, Gender and Job Leads. *Social Problems* 56:385–402.

McDowell, Amber. 2004. Cracker Barrel Settles Lawsuit; Black Customers, Workers Reported Discrimination. *Washington Post,* September 10, p. E1.

McIntosh, Peggy. 1989. White Privilege: Unpacking the Invisible Knapsack. http://www.isr.umich.edu/home/diversity/resources/white-privilege.pdf.

McLaren, Lauren. 2003. Anti-Immigrant Prejudice in Europe: Contact, Threat Perception, and Preferences for the Exclusion of Migrants. *Social Forces* 81:909–936.

McLemore, S. Dale. 1973. The Origins of Mexican American Subordination in Texas. *Social Science Quarterly* 53:656–679.

McNickle, D'Arcy. 1973. *Native American Tribalism: Indian Survivals and Renewals.* New York: Oxford University Press.

McPherson, Miller, Smith-Lovin, Lynn, and Brashears, Matthew. 2006. Social Isolation in America: Changes in Core Discussion Networks Over Two Decades. *Social Forces* 71:353–375.

McTaggart, Ninochka, and O'Brien, Eileen. 2013. *Challenging the Face of Hip Hop: An Exploration of Gender and Representation in Hip Hop Culture.* Annual meeting of the Association for Asian American Studies, April 18, Seattle, WA.

McWilliams, Carey. 1961. *North From Mexico: The Spanish-Speaking People of the United States.* New York: Monthly Review.

Medoff, Marshall. 1999. Allocation of Time and Hateful Behavior: A Theoretical and Positive Analysis of Hate and Hate Crimes. *American Journal of Economics and Sociology* 58:959–973.

Meek, Barbara. 2006. And the Indian goes "How!": Representations of American Indian English in White Public Space. *Language in Society* 35:93–128.

Meissner, Doris. 2010. 5 Myths About Immigration. *Washington Post,* May 2, p. B2.

Merica, Dan. 2012. Black Pastors Group Launches Anti-Obama Campaign Around Gay Marriage. *CNN*, July 31. http://religion.blogs.cnn.com/2012/07/31/black-pastors-group-launches-anti-obama-campaign-around-gay-marriage/.

Merton, Robert. 1968. *Social Theory and Social Structure.* New York: Free Press.

Messner, Michael. 1990. When Bodies Are Weapons: Masculinity and Violence in Sports. *International Review of the Sociology of Sports* 25:203–218.

Miceli, Melissa. 2005. *Standing Out, Standing Together: The Social and Political Impact of Gay-Straight Alliances.* New York: Routledge.

Milkie, Melissa A. 1999. Social Comparisons, Reflected Appraisals, and Mass Media: The Impact of Pervasive Beauty Images on Black and White Girls' Self Concepts. *Social Psychology Quarterly* 62:190–210.

Miller, Neal, and Bugleski, R. 1948. Minor Studies of Aggression: The Influence of Frustrations Imposed by the Ingroup on Attitudes Expressed Towards Outgroups. *Journal of Psychology* 25:437–442.

Miller, Norman, and Brewer, Marilyn (Eds.). 1984. *Groups in Contact: The Psychology of Desegregation.* Orlando, FL: Academic Press.

Min, Pyong Gap (Ed.). 1995. *Asian Americans: Contemporary Trends and Issues.* Thousand Oaks, CA: Sage.

———. 2006. *Asian Americans: Contemporary Trends and Issues* (2nd ed.). Thousand Oaks, CA: Sage.

Mirandé, Alfredo. 1985. *The Chicano Experience: An Alternative Perspective.* Notre Dame, IN: University of Notre Dame Press.

Mirandé, Alfredo, and Enríquez, Evangelina. 1979. *La Chicana: The Mexican-American Woman.* Chicago: University of Chicago Press.

Mississippi Band of Choctaw Indians. 2011. *Tribal Profile.* Choctaw, MS: Office of the Tribal Miko. http://www.choctaw.org/aboutMBCI/tribalProfile.pdf.

Monger, Randall. 2012. *Nonimmigrant Admissions to the United States: 2012.* Washington, DC: U.S. Department of Homeland Security.

https://www.dhs.gov/sites/default/files/publications/ois_ni_fr_2012.pdf.

Monifa, Akilah. 2008. Interracial or Same Sex Marriage: Same Core Civil Rights Issues. *The Progressive,* June 12. http://www.progressive.org/mp_monifa061208.

Mooney, Linda, Knox, David, and Schacht, Caroline. 2010. *Understanding Social Problems.* Farmington Hills, MI: Cengage Learning.

Moore, Joan W. 1970. *Mexican Americans.* Englewood Cliffs, NJ: Prentice Hall.

Moore, Joan W., and Pachon, Harry. 1985. *Hispanics in the United States.* Englewood Cliffs, NJ: Prentice Hall.

Moore, Joan, and Pinderhughes, Raquel. 1993. *In the Barrios: Latinos and the Underclass Debate.* New York: Russell Sage Foundation.

Moquin, Wayne, and Van Doren, Charles (Eds.). 1971. *A Documentary History of Mexican Americans.* New York: Bantam.

Morales, Lymari. 2009. Knowing Someone Gay/Lesbian Affects Views of Gay Issues. *Gallup.* http://www.gallup.com/poll/118931/Knowing-Someone-Gay-Lesbian-Affects-Views-Gay-Issues.aspx.

———. 2010. Amid Immigration Debate, Americans' Views Ease Slightly. Gallup Politics. http://www.gallup.com/poll/141560/Amid-Immigration-Debate-Americans-Views-Ease-Slightly.aspx.

Morawska, Ewa. 1990. The Sociology and Historiography of Immigration. In Virginia Yans-McLaughlin (Ed.), *Immigration Reconsidered: History, Sociology, and Politics* (pp. 187–238). New York: Oxford University Press.

Morgan, Edmund. 1975. *American Slavery, American Freedom.* New York: Norton.

Morris, Aldon D. 1984. *The Origins of the Civil Rights Movement.* New York: Free Press.

Morris, Edward. 2005. "Tuck in That Shirt!" Race, Class, Gender, and Discipline in an Urban School. *Sociological Perspectives* 48:25–48.

Moskos, Charles, and Butler, John Sibley. 1997. *All That We Can Be: Black Leadership and Racial Integration the Army Way.* New York: Basic Books.

Motel, Seth, and Patten, Eileen. 2013. *Statistical Portrait of the Foreign-Born Population in the United States, 2011.* Washington, DC: Pew Hispanic Center. http://www.pewhispanic.org/2013/01/29/statistical-portrait-of-the-foreign-born-population-in-the-united-states-2011.

Movement Advancement Project, Human Rights Campaign, and Center for American Progress. 2013. *A Broken Bargain: Discrimination, Fewer Benefits and More Taxes for LGBT Workers (Full Report).* http://www.lgbtmap.org/file/a-broken-bargain-full-report.pdf.

Moynihan, Daniel. 1965. *The Negro Family: The Case for National Action.* Washington, DC: U.S. Department of Labor.

Mulligan, Thomas S., and Kraul, Chris. 1996. Texaco Settles Race Bias Suit for $176 Million. *Los Angeles Times,* November 16. http://articles.latimes.com/1996-11-16/news/mn-65290_1_texaco-settles-race-bias-suit.

Murguia, Edward, and Foreman, Tyrone. 2003. Shades of Whiteness: The Mexican American Experience in Relation to Anglos and Blacks. In Ashley Doane and Eduardo Bonilla-Silva (Eds.), *White Out: The Continuing Significance of Racism* (pp. 63–72). New York: Routledge.

Muslim West Facts Project. 2009. *Muslim Americans: A National Portrait.* Washington, DC: Gallup. http://www.gallup.com/strategicconsulting/153572/report-muslim-americans-national-portrait.aspx.

Myrdal, Gunnar. 1962. *An American Dilemma: The Negro Problem and Modern Democracy.* New York: Harper & Row. (Original work published 1944)

Nabakov, Peter (Ed.). 1999. *Native American Testimony* (Rev. ed.). New York: Penguin.

National Advisory Commission. 1968. *Report of the National Advisory Commission on Civil Disorders.* New York: Bantam Books.

National Center for Health Statistics. 2010. *Health, United States, 2010: With Special Feature on Death and Dying.* Hyattsville, MD: Author. http://www.cdc.gov/nchs/data/hus/hus10.pdf#061.

National Council on Crime and Delinquency. 2007. *And Justice for Some: Differential Treatment of Youth of Color in the Justice System.* http://www.nccdglobal.org/sites/default/files/publication_pdf/justice-for-some.pdf.

National Gay and Lesbian Task Force. 2014. Relationship Recognition Map for Same-Sex Couples in the United States. http://www.thetaskforce.org/reports_and_research/relationship_recognition.

National Indian Gaming Commission. 2011. NIGC Tribal Gaming Revenues. http://www.nigc.gov/LinkClick.aspx?fileticket=1k4B6r6dr-U%3d&tabid=67.

———. 2012. Gaming Revenue Reports. http://www.nigc.gov/Gaming_Revenue_Reports.aspx.

National Opinion Research Council. 1972–2012. *General Social Survey.* Chicago: Author.

National Origins Act, Pub. L. 139, Chapter 190, § 43 Stat. 153 (1924).

National Public Radio. 2004. *Immigration in America: Survey Overview.* http://www.npr.org/templates/story/story.php?storyId=4062605.

NationMaster. 2014. Education—Average Years of Schooling of Adults: Countries Compared. http://www.nationmaster.com/graph/edu_ave_yea_of_sch_of_adu-education-average-years-schooling-adults.

Neary, Ian. 2003. Burakumin at the End of History. *Social Research* 70:269–294.

Nelli, Humbert S. 1980. Italians. In Stephan Thernstrom, Ann Orlov, and Oscar Handlin (Eds.), *Harvard Encyclopedia of American Ethnic Groups* (pp. 545–560). Cambridge, MA: Harvard University Press.

Newport, Frank. 2013a. Gulf Grows in Black-White Views of the U.S. Justice System Bias. Gallup Politics. http://www.gallup.com/poll/163610/gulf-grows-black-white-views-justice-system-bias.aspx.

Newport, Frank. 2013b. In U.S., 24% of Young Black Men Say Police Dealings Unfair. *Gallup.* http://www.gallup.com/poll/163523/one-four-young-black-men-say-police-dealings-unfair.aspx?version=print.

Nishi, Setsuko. 1995. Japanese Americans. In Pyong Gap Min (Ed.), *Asian Americans: Contemporary Trends and Issues* (pp. 95–133). Thousand Oaks, CA: Sage.

Noel, Donald. 1968. A Theory of the Origin of Ethnic Stratification. *Social Problems* 16:157–172.

Nolan, Patrick, and Lenski, Gerhard. 2004. *Human Societies.* Boulder, CO: Paradigm.

Norris, Tina, Vines, Paula, and Hoeffel, Elizabeth. 2012. The American Indian and Alaska Native Population: 2010. *2010 Census Briefs.* Washington, DC: U.S. Census Bureau.

http://www.census.gov/prod/cen2010/briefs/c2010br-10.pdf.

Nossiter, Adam. 2014. Nigeria Tries to "Sanitize" Itself of Gays. *New York Times,* February 8. http://www.nytimes.com/2014/02/09/world/africa/nigeria-uses-law-and-whip-to-sanitize-gays.html.

Novak, Michael. 1973. *The Rise of the Unmeltable Ethnics: Politics and Culture in the 1970s.* New York: Collier.

O'Brien, Eileen, and Korgen, Kathleen. 2007. It's The Message, Not the Messenger: The Declining Significance of Black–White Contact. *Sociological Inquiry* 77:356–382.

Ogunwole, Stella. 2006. *We the People: American Indians and Alaska Natives in the United States.* Washington, DC: U.S. Census Bureau. http://www.census.gov/prod/2006pubs/censr-28.pdf.

O'Keefe, Ed. 2010. Minorities Disproportionately Discharged for Don't Ask Don't Tell Violations. *Washington Post,* August 17. http://www.washingtonpost.com/wp-dyn/content/article/2010/08/16/AR2010081605153.html.

Oldenburg, Ann. 2013. Miss America Nina Davulari Brushes Off Racist Remarks. *USA Today,* September 16. http://www.usatoday.com/story/life/people/2013/09/16/miss-america-nina-davuluri-brushes-off-racist-remarks/2819533.

Oliver, Melvin, and Shapiro, Thomas. 2006. *Black Wealth, White Wealth* (2nd ed.). New York: Taylor & Francis.

———. 2008. Sub-Prime as a Black Catastrophe. *American Prospect* (October): A9–A11.

Olivo, Antonio, and Eldeib, Duaa. 2013. Catholic Church Works to Keep Up With Growing Latino

Membership. *Chicago Tribune,* March 17. http://articles.chicagotribune.com/2013-03-17/news/ct-met-chicago-latino-catholics-20130317_1_latino-appointments-latino-candidates-priests.

Olson, James, and Wilson, R. 1984. *Native Americans in the Twentieth Century.* Provo, UT: Brigham Young University Press.

Omi, Michael, and Winant, Howard. 1986. *Racial Formation in the United States From the 1960s to the 1980s.* New York: Routledge & Kegan Paul.

Orfield, Gary, Kucsera, John, and Siegel-Hawley, Genevieve. 2012. *E Pluribus . . . Segregation: Deepening Double Segregation for More Students.* Los Angeles: Civil Rights Project. http://civilrightsproject.ucla.edu/research/k-12-education/integration-and-diversity/mlk-national/e-pluribus...separation-deepening-double-segregation-for-more-students.

Orfield, Gary, and Lee, Chungmei. 2007. *Historic Reversals, Accelerating Resegregation, and the Need for New Integration Strategies.* Los Angeles: Civil Rights Project, UCLA. http://www.eric.ed.gov/PDFS/ED500611.pdf.

Osofsky, Gilbert. 1969. *Puttin' On Ole Massa.* New York: Harper & Row.

Oswalt, Wendell, and Neely, Sharlotte. 1996. *This Land Was Theirs.* Mountain View, CA: Mayfield.

O'Toole, Molly. 2013. Military Sexual Assaults Spike Despite Efforts to Control Epidemic. *New York Times,* May 7. http://www.huffingtonpost.com/2013/05/07/military-sexual-assaults-2012_n_3230248.html.

Padavic, Irene, and Reskin, Barbara. 2002. *Women and Men at Work.* Thousand Oaks, CA: Pine Forge Press.

Pager, Devah, and Shepherd, Hana. 2008. The Sociology of Discrimination: Racial Discrimination in Employment, Housing, Credit, and Consumer Markets. *Annual Review of Sociology* 34:181–209.

Pappas, Stephanie. 2012. Gay Parents Better Than Straight Parents? What Research Says. *Huffington Post,* January 16. http://www.huffingtonpost.com/2012/01/16/gay-parents-better-than-straights_n_1208659.html.

Parish, Peter J. 1989. *Slavery: History and Historians.* New York: Harper & Row.

Park, Robert E., and Burgess, Ernest W. 1924. *Introduction to the Science of Society.* Chicago: University of Chicago Press.

Parke, Ross, and Buriel, Raymond. 2002. Socialization Concerns in African American, American Indian, Asian American, and Latino Families. In Nijole Benokraitis (Ed.), *Contemporary Ethnic Families in the United States* (pp. 211–218). Upper Saddle River, NJ: Prentice Hall.

Parrillo, Vincent, and Donoghue, Christopher. 2013. The National Social Distance Study: Ten Years Later. *Sociological Forum* 28:597–614.

Passel, Jeffrey, and Cohn, D'Vera. 2011. *Unauthorized Immigrant Population: National and State Trends, 2010.* Washington, DC: Pew Hispanic Center. http://pewhispanic.org/files/reports/133.pdf.

Passel, Jeffrey, Cohn, D'Vera, and Gonzalez-Barrera, Ana. 2012. *Net Migration From Mexico Falls to Zero—and Perhaps Less.* Washington, DC: Pew Hispanic Center. http://www.pewhispanic.org/files/2012/04/Mexican-migrants-report_final.pdf.

———. 2013. *Population Decline of Unauthorized Immigrants Stalls, May Have*

Reversed. Washington, DC: Pew Research Center. http://www.pewhispanic.org/2013/09/23/population-decline-of-unauthorized-immigrants-stalls-may-have-reversed.

Passel, Jeffrey, Wang, Wendy, and Taylor, Paul. 2010. *Marrying Out: One-in-Seven New U.S. Marriages Is Interracial or Interethnic*. Washington, DC: Pew Research Center. http://www.pewsocialtrends.org/2010/06/04/marrying-out/.

Pathela, P., Hajat, A., Schillinger, J., Blank, S., Sell, R., and Mostashari, F. 2006. Discordance Between Sexual Behavior and Self-Reported Sexual Identity: A Population-Based Survey of New York City Men. *Annals of Internal Medicine* 145:416–425.

PBS. 2011. Timeline: Milestones in the American Gay Rights Movement. http://www.pbs.org/wgbh/americanexperience/features/timeline/stonewall.

Pego, David. 1998. To Educate a Nation: Native American Tribe Hopes to Bring Higher Education to an Arizona Reservation. *Black Issues in Higher Education* 15:60–63.

Perez, Lisandro. 1980. Cubans. In Stephan Thernstrom, Ann Orlov, and Oscar Handlin (Eds.), *Harvard Encyclopedia of American Ethnic Groups* (pp. 256–261). Cambridge, MA: Harvard University Press.

Petersen, Williams. 1971. *Japanese Americans*. New York: Random House.

Peterson, Bill, and Pang, Joyce. 2006. Beyond Politics: Authoritarianism and the Pursuit of Leisure. *Journal of Social Psychology* 146:442–461.

Peterson, Bill, and Zurbriggen, Eileen. 2010. Gender, Sexuality, and the Authoritarian Personality. *Journal of Personality* 78:1801–1826.

Peterson, Mark. 1995. Leading Cuban-American Entrepreneurs: The Process of Developing Motives, Abilities, and Resources. *Human Relations* 48:1193–1216.

Pettigrew, Thomas. 1958. Personality and Sociocultural Factors in Intergroup Attitudes: A Cross-National Comparison. *Journal of Conflict Resolution* 2:29–42.

———. 1971. *Racially Separate or Together?* New York: McGraw-Hill.

———. 1980. Prejudice. In Stephan Thernstrom, Ann Orlov, and Oscar Handlin (Eds.), *Harvard Encyclopedia of American Ethnic Groups* (pp. 820–829). Cambridge, MA: Harvard University Press.

———. 1998. Intergroup Contact Theory. *Annual Review of Psychology* 49:65–85.

Pettigrew, Thomas, and Tropp, Linda. 2006. A Meta-Analytic Test of Intergroup Contact Theory. *Journal of Personality and Social Psychology* 90:751–783.

Pettigrew, T. F., Tropp, L. R., Wagner, U., and Christ, O. 2011. Recent Advances in Intergroup Contact Theory. *International Journal of Intercultural Relations* 35:271–280.

Pettigrew, Thomas, Wagner, Ulrich, and Christ, Oliver. 2007. Who Opposes Immigration? Comparing German and North American Findings. *Du Bois Review* 4:19–39.

Pettit, Becky, and Western, Bruce. 2004. Mass Imprisonment and the Life Course: Race and Class Inequality in U.S. Incarceration. *American Sociological Review* 69:151–169.

Pew Charitable Trust. 2008. *One in 100: Behind Bars in America 2008*. http://www.pewtrusts.org/uploadedFiles/wwwpewtrustsorg/Reports/sentencing_and_corrections/one_in_100.pdf.

Pew Hispanic Center. 2004. *Survey Brief: Assimilation and Language*. Washington, DC: Author. http://pewhispanic.org/files/factsheets/11.pdf.

———. 2005. *Hispanics: A People in Motion*. Washington, DC: Author. http://pewhispanic.org/files/reports/40.pdf.

———. 2013. *A Nation of Immigrants: A Portrait of the 40 Million, Including 11 Million Unauthorized*. Washington, DC: Author. http://www.pewhispanic.org/files/2013/01/statistical_portrait_final_jan_29.pdf.

Pew Research Center. 2007. *Muslim Americans: Middle Class and Mostly Mainstream*. Washington, DC: Author. http://pewresearch.org/assets/pdf/muslim-americans.pdf.

———. 2011. *Muslim Americans: No Signs of Growth in Alienation or Support for Extremism*. Washington, DC: Author. http://www.people-press.org/files/legacy-pdf/Muslim%20American%20Report%2010-02-12%20fix.pdf.

———. 2013a. *The Global Divide on Homosexuality*. Washington, DC: Author. http://www.pewglobal.org/files/2013/06/Pew-Global-Attitudes-Homosexuality-Report-FINAL-JUNE-4-2013.pdf.

———. 2013b. *Growing Support for Gay Marriage: Changed Minds and Changing Demographics*. Washington, DC: Author. http://www.people-press.org/2013/03/20/growing-support-for-gay-marriage-changed-minds-and-changing-demographics.

———. 2013c. *The Rise of Asian Americans*. Washington, DC: Author. http://www.pewsocialtrends.org/2012/06/19/the-rise-of-asian-americans.

———. 2013d. *A Survey of LGBT Americans: Attitudes, Experiences and Values in Changing Times*.

Washington, DC: Author. http://www.pewsocialtrends.org/files/2013/06/SDT_LGBT-Americans_06-2013.pdf.

Phillips, Ulrich B. 1918. *American Negro Slavery*. New York: Appleton.

Pincus, Fred. 2011. *Understanding Diversity: An Introduction to Class, Race, Gender, Sexual Orientation, and Disability* (2nd ed.). Boulder, CO: Lynne Rienner Press.

Pitt, Leonard. 1970. *The Decline of the Californios: A Social History of the Spanish-Speaking Californians, 1846–1890*. Berkeley: University of California Press.

Plessy v. Ferguson, 163 U.S. 537 (1896).

Pollard, Kelvin, and O'Hare, William. 1999. America's Racial and Ethnic Minorities. *Population Bulletin* 54(3): 29–39. Washington, DC: Population Reference Bureau.

Population Reference Bureau. 2013. *2013 World Population Data Sheet*. Washington, DC: Author. http://www.prb.org/pdf13/2013-population-data-sheet_eng.pdf.

Porter, Eduardo. 2005. Illegal Immigrants Are Bolstering Social Security With Billions. *New York Times*, April 5, p. A1.

Portes, Alejandro. 1990. From South of the Border: Hispanic Minorities in the United States. In Virginia Yans-McLaughlin (Ed.), *Immigration Reconsidered* (pp. 160–184). New York: Oxford University Press.

Portes, Alejandro, and Bach, Robert L. 1985. *Latin Journey: Cuban and Mexican Immigrants in the United States*. Berkeley: University of California Press.

Portes, Alejandro, and Manning, Robert. 1986. The Immigrant Enclave: Theory and Empirical Examples. In Susan Olzak and Joanne Nagel (Eds.), *Competitive*

Ethnic Relations (pp. 47–68). New York: Academic Press.

Portes, Alejandro, and Rumbaut, Rubén. 1996. *Immigrant America: A Portrait* (2nd ed.). Berkeley: University of California Press.

———. 2001. *Legacies: The Story of the Immigrant Second Generation*. New York: Russell Sage Foundation.

Portes, Alejandro, and Shafer, Steven. 2006. *Revisiting the Enclave Hypothesis: Miami Twenty-Five Years Later* (Working Paper No. 06-10). Princeton, NJ: Center for Migration and Development, Princeton University. https://www.princeton.edu/cmd/working-papers/papers/wp0610.pdf.

Posadas, Barbara. 1999. *The Filipino Americans*. Westport, CT: Greenwood.

Potok, Mark. 2013. The Year in Hate and Extremism, Southern Poverty Law Center. *Intelligence Report* (149). http://www.splcenter.org/home/2013/spring/the-year-in-hate-and-extremism.

Potter, George. 1973. *To the Golden Door: The Story of the Irish in Ireland and America*. Westport, CT: Greenwood.

Powers, Daniel, and Ellison, Christopher. 1995. Interracial Contact and Black Racial Attitudes: The Contact Hypothesis and Selectivity Bias. *Social Forces* 74:205–226.

Powlishta, K., Serbin, L., Doyle, A., and White, D. 1994. Gender, Ethnic, and Body-Type Biases: The Generality of Prejudice in Childhood. *Developmental Psychology* 30:526–537.

Prois, Jessica. 2013. Child Marriage on Rise as Global Crises Increase, New Study Says. *Huffington Post*, March 8. http://www.huffingtonpost.com/2013/03/08/child-marriage-international-womens-day_n_2838421.html.

Puzo, Mario. 1993. Choosing a Dream: Italians in Hell's Kitchen. In W. Brown and A. Ling (Eds.), *Visions of America* (pp. 56–57). New York: Persea.

Qian, Zhenchao, and Lichter, Daniel. 2011. Changing Patterns of Interracial Marriage in a Multiracial Society. *Journal of Marriage and Family*, 75:1065–1084.

Quaid, Libby. 2008. "Math class is tough" no more: Girls' skill now equal to boys. *USA Today*, July 25. http://usatoday30.usatoday.com/tech/science/mathscience/2008-07-24-girls-math-skills_N.htm.

Quast, Lisa. 2012. Thin is in for Executive Women: How Weight Discrimination Contributes to the Glass Ceiling. *Forbes*, August 6. http://www.forbes.com/sites/lisaquast/2012/08/06/thin-is-in-for-executive-women-as-weight-discrimination-contributes-to-glass-ceiling/.

Quigley, Mike. 2013. The Rights of our Daughters: Fighting for Global Reproductive Health. *Huffington Post*, November 1. http://www.huffingtonpost.com/mike-quigley/reproductive-rights_b_4181828.html.

Quillian, Lincoln. 2006. New Approaches to Understanding Racial Prejudice and Discrimination. *Annual Review of Sociology* 32:299–328.

Quillian, Lincoln, and Campbell, Mary. 2003. Beyond Black and White: The Present and Future of Multiracial Friendship Segregation. *American Sociological Review* 68:540–567.

Quinones, Sam. 2007. *Antonio's Gun and Delfino's Dream: True Tales of Mexican Migration*. Albuquerque: University of New Mexico Press.

Raabe, T., and Beelman, A. 2011. Development of

Ethnic, Racial, and National Prejudice in Childhood and Adolescence: A Multinational Meta-Analysis of Age Differences. *Child Development* 82(6): 1715–1737.

Rader, Benjamin G. 1983. *American Sports: From the Age of Folk Games to the Age of Spectators*. Englewood Cliffs, NJ: Prentice Hall.

Rastogi, Sonya, Johnson, Tallese, Hoeffel, Elizabeth, and Drewery, Malcolm. 2011. *The Black Population, 2010*. Washington, DC: U.S. Census Bureau. http://www.census.gov/prod/cen2010/briefs/c2010br-06.pdf.

Ray, N. 2006. *Lesbian, gay, bisexual and transgender youth: An epidemic of homelessness*. New York: National Gay and Lesbian Task Force Policy Institute and the National Coalition for the Homeless.

Raymer, Patricia. 1974. Wisconsin's Menominees: Indians on a Seesaw. *National Geographic*, August, pp. 228–251.

Read, Jen'nan Ghazal. 2004. Cultural Influences on Immigrant Women's Labor Force Participation: The Arab-American Case. *International Migration Review* 38:52–77.

Reaney, Patricia. 2010. Informal Work Networks New Form of Inequality: Study. Reuters, August 16. http://www.reuters.com/article/2010/08/16/us-women-work-networks-idUSTRE67F49820100816.

Reich, Michael. 1986. The Political-Economic Effects of Racism. In Richard Edwards, Michael Reich, and Thomas Weisskopf (Eds.), *The Capitalist System: A Radical Analysis of American Society* (3rd ed., pp. 381–388). Englewood Cliffs, NJ: Prentice Hall.

Reilly, Ryan J. 2013. Gay Veterans' Spouses Still Can't Get Benefits. *Huffington Post*, August 27. http://www.huffingtonpost.com/2013/08/27/gay-veterans_n_3825093.html.

Remington, Robin. 1997. Ethnonationalism and the Disintegration of Yugoslavia. In Winston Van Horne (Ed.), *Global Convulsions*. Albany: SUNY Press.

Reyna, Christine, Dobria, Ovidiu, and Wetherell, Geoffrey. 2013. The Complexity and Ambivalence of Immigration Attitudes: Ambivalent Stereotypes Predict Conflicting Attitudes Toward Immigration Policies. *Cultural Diversity and Ethnic Minority Psychology* 19:342–356.

Ricci v. DeStefano, 557 U.S. (2009).

Rich, Adrienne. 1980. Compulsory Heterosexuality and Lesbian Existence. *Signs: Journal of Women in Culture and Society* 5:631–660.

Ridgeway, Cecilia. 2011. *Framed by Gender: How Gender Inequality Persists in the Modern World*. New York: Oxford University Press.

Rifkin, Jeremy. 1996. *The End of Work: The Decline of the Global Labor Force and the Dawn of the Post-Market Era*. New York: Putnam.

Robertson, Claire. 1996. Africa and the Americas? Slavery and Women, the Family, and the Gender Division of Labor. In David Gaspar and Darlene Hine (Eds.), *More Than Chattel: Black Women and Slavery in the Americas* (pp. 4–40). Bloomington: Indiana University Press.

Rockquemore, Kerry Ann, and Brunsma, David. 2008. *Beyond Black: Biracial Identity in America* (2nd ed.). Lanham, MD: Rowman & Littlefield.

Rodriguez, Arturo. 2011. UFW Written Statement on House Judiciary Subcommittee on Immigration Policy and

Enforcement Hearing on "The H-2A Visa Program—Meeting the Growing Needs of American Agriculture?" http://ufwfoundation.org/_cms.php?mode=view&b_code=003002000000000&b_no=8777&page=14&field=..&key=&n=717.

Rodriguez, C. 2010. Parent-Child Aggression: Association with Child Abuse Potential and Parenting Styles. *Violence and Victims* 25:728–741.

Rodriguez, Clara. 1989. *Puerto Ricans: Born in the USA.* Boston: Unwin-Hyman.

Rodriguez, Clara, and Cordero-Guzman, Hector. 1992. Placing Race in Context. *Ethnic and Racial Studies* 15:523–542.

Rodriguez, Luis. 1993. *Always Running: La Vida Loca.* New York: Touchstone Books.

Roe v. Wade, 410 U.S. 113 (1973).

Roper Center. 2012. U.S. Elections: How Groups Voted in 2012. http://www.ropercenter.uconn.edu/elections/how_groups_voted/voted_12.html.

Rosenblum, Karen E., and Travis, Toni-Michelle C. 2002. *The Meaning of Difference: American Constructions of Race, Sex and Social Class, and Sexual Orientation* (3rd ed.). New York: McGraw-Hill.

Rosenfield, Michael. 2002. Measures of Assimilation in the Marriage Market: Mexican Americans 1970–1990. *Journal of Marriage and the Family* 64:152–163.

Rosich, Katherine. 2007. *Race, Ethnicity, and the Criminal Justice System.* Washington, DC: American Sociological Association. http://www.asanet.org/images/press/docs/pdf/ASARaceCrime.pdf.

Rouse, Linda, and Hanson, Jeffery. 1991. American Indian Stereotyping, Resource Competition, and Status-Based Prejudice.

American Indian Culture and Research Journal 15:1–17.

Royster, Deirdre. 2003. *Race and the Invisible Hand: How White Networks Exclude Black Men From Blue-Collar Jobs.* Berkeley: University of California Press.

Rumbaut, Rubén. 1991. Passage to America: Perspectives on the New Immigration. In Alan Wolfe (Ed.), *America at Century's End* (pp. 208–244). Berkeley: University of California Press.

Rupp, Leila J., and Taylor, Verta. 1987. *Survival in the Doldrums: The American Women's Rights Movement 1945–1960.* New York: Oxford University Press.

Russell, James W. 1994. *After the Fifth Sun: Class and Race in North America.* Englewood Cliffs, NJ: Prentice Hall.

Ryan, Caitlin, Huebner, David, Diaz, Rafael, and Sanchez, Jorge. 2009. Family Rejection as a Predictor of Negative Health Outcomes in White and Latino Lesbian, Gay, and Bisexual Young Adults. *Pediatrics* 123:346–352.

Saad, Lydia. 2010. Americans Value Both Aspects of Immigration Reform. Gallup Politics. http://www.gallup.com/poll/127649/Americans-Value-Aspects-Immigration-Reform.aspx.

———. 2013. Americans More Pro-Immigration Than in the Past. Gallup Politics. http://www.gallup.com/poll/163457/americans-pro-immigration-past.aspx.

Sadker, David, and Zittleman, Karen. 2009. *Still Failing at Fairness: How Gender Bias Cheats Girls and Boys in School and What We Can Do About It.* New York: Simon & Schuster.

Saenz, Rogelio. 2005. *The Social and Economic Isolation of Urban African Americans.* Washington, DC: Population Reference Bureau. http://www.prb.org/Articles/2005/

TheSocialandEconomicIsolationofUrbanAfricanAmericans.aspx.

Sanchirico, Andrew. 1991. The Importance of Small Business Ownership in Chinese American Educational Achievement. *Sociology of Education* 64:293–304.

Sandberg, Sheryl. 2013. *Lean In: Women, Work and the Will to Lead.* New York: Knopf.

Santiago, Esmeralda. 1993. *When I Was Puerto Rican.* Cambridge, MA: De Capo Press.

Sappho and Carson, Anne. 2003. *If Not, Winter: Fragments of Sappho.* New York: Vintage.

Sappho and Lombardo, Stanley. 2002. *Poems and Fragments.* Cambridge, MA: Hackett.

Satter, Beryl. 2009. *Family Properties: Race, Real Estate, and the Exploitation of Black Urban America.* New York: Henry Holt.

Savin-Williams, Ritch C. 2001. A Critique of Research on Sexual Minority Youths. *Journal of Adolescence* 24:5–13.

Schafer, John, and Navarro, Joe. 2004. The Seven-Stage Hate Model: The Psychopathology of Hate Groups. *The FBI Law Enforcement Bulletin* 72:1–9.

Schlesinger, Arthur M., Jr. 1992. *The Disuniting of America: Reflections on a Multicultural Society.* New York: Norton.

Schmid, Carol. 2001. *The Politics of Language: Conflict, Identity, and Cultural Pluralism in Comparative Perspective.* New York: Oxford University Press.

Schoener, Allon. 1967. *Portal to America: The Lower East Side, 1870–1925.* New York: Holt, Rinehart, & Winston.

Schofield, J. W., Hausmann, L. R. M., Ye, F., and Woods, R. L. 2010.

Intergroup Friendships on Campus: Predicting Close and Casual Friendships Between White and African American First-Year College Students. *Group Processes and Intergroup Relations* 13:585–602.

Schofield, Matthew. 2013. Far-Right Hate Crimes Creep Back into German Society. *Miami Herald,* December 24. http://www.miamiherald.com/2013/12/24/3834799/far-right-hate-crimes-creep-back.html.

Schuette v. BAMN, 572 U.S. 12-682 (2014).

Schulman, Michael. 2013. Generation LGBTQIA. *New York Times,* January 9. http://www.nytimes.com/2013/01/10/fashion/generation-lgbtqia.html?_r=0.

Schwartz, Mary Ann, and Scott, Barbara Marliene. 1997. *Marriages and Families: Diversity and Change* (2nd ed.). Upper Saddle River, NJ: Prentice Hall.

Schwarz, A. B. Christa. 2012. *Gay Voices of the Harlem Renaissance.* Bloomington: Indiana University Press.

Sears, David. 1988. Symbolic Racism. In Phyllis Katz and Dalmas Taylor (Eds.), *Eliminating Racism: Profiles in Controversy* (pp. 53–84). New York: Plenum.

See, Katherine O'Sullivan, and Wilson, William J. 1988. Race and Ethnicity. In Neil Smelser (Ed.), *Handbook of Sociology* (pp. 223–242). Newbury Park, CA: Sage.

Selzer, Michael. 1972. *"Kike": Anti-Semitism in America.* New York: Meridian.

Sen, Rinku, and Mamdouh, Fekkak. 2008. *The Accidental American: Immigration and Citizenship in the Age of Globalization.* San Francisco, CA: Berrt-Koehler.

Shannon, William V. 1964. *The American Irish.* New York: Macmillan.

Shapiro, Thomas, Meschede, Tatjana, and Osoro, Sam. 2013. *The Roots of the*

Widening Racial Wealth Gap: Explaining the Black-White Economic Divide. Waltham, MA: Institute on Assets and Social Policy, Brandeis University. http://iasp.brandeis.edu/pdfs/Author/shapiro-thomas-m/racialwealthgapbrief.pdf.

Shaughnessy, Larry. 2010. U.S. Allies Say Integrating Gays in the Military Was Non-Issue. CNN, May 20. http://edition.cnn.com/2010/US/05/19/us.allies.military.gays/.

Sheet Metal Workers v. EEOC, 478 U.S. 421 (1986).

Sherif, Muzafer, Harvey, O. J., White, B. Jack, Hood, William, and Sherif, Carolyn. 1961. Intergroup Conflict and Cooperation: The Robber's Cave Experiment. Norman, OK: University Book Exchange.

Sheth, Manju. 1995. Asian Indian Americans. In Pyong Gap Min (Ed.), Asian American: Contemporary Issues and Trends (pp. 168–198). Thousand Oaks, CA: Sage.

Sigelman, Lee, and Welch, Susan. 1993. The Contact Hypothesis Revisited: Black-White Interaction and Positive Racial Attitudes. Social Forces 71:781–795.

Simon, Julian. 1989. The Economic Consequences of Immigration. Cambridge, MA: Blackwell.

Simpson, George, and Yinger, Milton. 1985. Racial and Cultural Minorities: An Analysis of Prejudice and Discrimination. New York: Plenum.

Sklare, Marshall. 1971. America's Jews. New York: Random House.

Small, Mario Luis, Harding, David J., and Lamont, Michèle. 2010. Reconsidering Culture and Poverty. Annals of the American Academy of Political and Social Science 629:6. http://ann.sagepub.com/content/629/1/6.

Smedley, Audrey. 2007. Race in North America: Origin and Evolution of a Worldview (3rd ed.). Boulder, CO: Westview.

Smith, Barbara. 2000. Home Girls: A Black Feminist Anthology. New York: Kitchen Table Women of Color Press. (Original work published in 1983)

Smith, Christopher B. 1994. Back to the Future: The Intergroup Contact Hypothesis Revisited. Sociological Inquiry 64:438–455.

Smith, Irving, III. 2010. Why Black Officers Still Fail. Parameters 40(3): 32–47.

Smith, James, and Edmonston, Barry (Eds.). 1997. The New Americans: Economic, Demographic, and Fiscal Effects of Immigration. Washington, DC: National Academy Press.

Smith, Kevin, and Seelbach, Wayne. 1987. Education and Intergroup Attitudes: More on the Jackman and Muha Thesis. Sociological Spectrum 7:157–170.

Smith, Tom, and Dempsey, Glenn. 1983. The Polls: Ethnic Social Distance and Prejudice. Public Opinion Quarterly 47:584–600.

Snipp, C. Matthew. 1989. American Indians: The First of This Land. New York: Russell Sage Foundation.

———. 1992. Sociological Perspectives on American Indians. Annual Review of Sociology 18:351–371.

———. 1996. The First Americans: American Indians. In S. Pedraza and R. G. Rumbaut (Eds.), Origins and Destinies: Immigration, Race, and Ethnicity in America (pp. 390–403). Belmont, CA: Wadsworth.

Soares, Rachel, Combopiano, Jan, Regis, Allyson, Shur, Yelena, and Wong, Rosita. 2010. 2010 Catalyst Census: Fortune 500 Women Board Directors. New York: Catalyst. http://catalyst.org/publication/460/2010-catalyst-census-fortune-500-women-board-directors.

Social Science Data Analysis Network. n.d. Segregation: Dissimilarity Indices. CensusScope. http://www.censusscope.org/us/s40/p75000/chart_dissimilarity.html.

Southern Poverty Law Center. 2010. Ex-Skinhead Recalls Violent Past. Intelligence Report (140). http://www.splcenter.org/get-informed/intelligence-report/browse-all-issues/2010/winter/dark-angel.

Spicer, Edward H. 1980. American Indians. In Stephan Thernstrom, Ann Orlov, and Oscar Handlin (Eds.), Harvard Encyclopedia of American Ethnic Groups (pp. 58–122). Cambridge, MA: Harvard University Press.

Spickard, Paul. 1996. Japanese Americans: The Formation and Transformations of an Ethnic Group. New York: Twayne.

Spilde, Kate. 2001. The Economic Development Journey of Indian Nations. http://www.indiangaming.org/library/articles/the-economic-development-journey.shtml.

Stainback, Kevin, and Tomaskovic-Devey, Donald. 2012. Documenting Desegregation: Racial and Gender Segregation in Private-Sector Employment Since the Civil Rights Act. New York: Russell Sage.

Stampp, Kenneth. 1956. The Peculiar Institution: Slavery in the Antebellum South. New York: Random House.

Staples, Brent A. 1986. Black Men and Public Space. Harper's Magazine (December). http://harpers.org/archive/1986/12/black-men-and-public-space/.

Staples, Robert. 1988. The Black American Family. In Charles Mindel, Robert Habenstein, and Roosevelt Wright (Eds.), Ethnic Families in America (3rd ed., pp. 303–324). New York: Elsevier.

Statistics Canada. 2013. Population by Mother Tongue, by Province and Territory, Excluding Institutional Residents (2011 Census) (New Brunswick, Quebec, Ontario). http://www.statcan.gc.ca/tables-tableaux/sum-som/l01/cst01/demo11b-eng.htm.

Steinberg, Stephen. 1981. The Ethnic Myth: Race, Ethnicity, and Class in America. New York: Atheneum.

———. 2011. Poor Reason: Culture Still Doesn't Explain Poverty. Boston Review, January 13. http://www.bostonreview.net/steinberg.php.

Steinhauer, Jennifer. 2013. Sexual Assaults in Military Raise Alarm in Washington. New York Times, May 7. http://www.nytimes.com/2013/05/08/us/politics/pentagon-study-sees-sharp-rise-in-sexual-assaults.html?pagewanted=all&_r=0.

Stephens-Davidowitz, Seth. 2013. How Many American Men Are Gay? New York Times, December 7. http://www.nytimes.com/2013/12/08/opinion/sunday/how-many-american-men-are-gay.html?pagewanted=all&_r=0.

Stepick, Alex, Stepick, Carol Dutton, Eugene, Emmanuel, Teed, Deborah, and Labissiere, Yves. 2001. Shifting Identities and Intergenerational Conflict: Growing Up Haitian in Miami. In Rubén Rumbaut and Alejandro Portes (Eds.), Ethnicities: Children of Immigrants in America (pp. 229–266). Berkeley: University of California Press.

Stoddard, Ellwyn. 1973. Mexican Americans. New York: Random House.

Stolberg, Sheryl Gay. 2013. Prominent Republicans Sign Brief in Support of Gay Marriage. New York Times, February 25. http://www.nytimes.com/2013/02/26/

us/politics/prominent-republicans-sign-brief-in-support-of-gay-marriage.html?pagewanted=all.

Stoll, Michael. 2004. *African Americans and the Color Line.* New York: Russell Sage Foundation.

Stuckey, Sterling. 1987. *Slave Culture: Nationalist Theory and the Foundations of Black America.* New York: Harper & Row.

Swaine, Thomas, and Nishimoto, Richard S. 1946. *The Spoilage.* Berkeley: University of California Press.

Swim, Janet, and Cohen, Laurie. 1997. Overt, Covert, and Subtle Sexism: A Comparison Between the Attitudes Toward Women and Modern Sexism Scales. *Psychology of Women Quarterly* 21:103–119.

Swim, Janet, Mallett, Robyn, and Stangor, Charles. 2004. Understanding Subtle Sexism: Detection and Use of Sexist Language. *Sex Roles* 51:117–128.

Taffet, David. 2013. "Heather Has Two Mommies" Author Reflects on 25 Years. *Dallas Voice,* July 26.

Takaki, Ronald. 1993. *A Different Mirror: A History of Multicultural America.* Boston: Little, Brown.

Takao Ozawa v. United States, 260 U.S. 178 (1922).

Tanenbaum, Leora. 1999. *Slut! Growing Up Female With a Bad Reputation.* New York: Seven Stories Press.

Tannenbaum, Frank. 1947. *Slave and Citizen: The Negro in the Americas.* New York: Knopf.

Taylor, Jonathan, and Kalt, Joseph. 2005. *American Indians on Reservations: A Databook of Socioeconomic Change Between the 1990 and 2000 Censuses.* Cambridge, MA: The Harvard Project on American Indian Economic Development. http://www.hks.harvard.edu/hpaied/pubs/documents/AmericanIndianson

ReservationsADatabookofSocioeconomicChange.pdf.

Taylor, Paul, Cohn, D'Vera, Livingston, Gretchen, Funk, Cary, and Morin, Rick. 2013. *Second Generation Americans: A Portrait of Adult Children of Immigrants.* Washington, DC: Pew Research Center. http://www.pewsocialtrends.org/files/2013/02/FINAL_immigrant_generations_report_2-7-13.pdf.

Taylor, Paul, Lopez, Mark, Martinez, Jessica, and Velasco, Gabriel. 2012. *When Labels Don't Fit: Hispanics and Their Views of Identity.* Washington, DC: Pew Hispanic Center. http://www.pewhispanic.org/files/2012/04/PHC-Hispanic-Identity.pdf.

Telles, Edward. 2004. *Race in Another America: The Significance of Skin Color in Brazil.* Princeton, NJ: Princeton University Press.

Telles, Edward, and Ortiz, Vilma. 2008. *Generations of Exclusion: Mexican Americans, Assimilation, and Race.* New York: Russell Sage Foundation.

Terkel, Amanda. 2011. Lawmakers Press Pentagon to Give Veterans' Benefits to Service Members Discharged Under DADT. *Huffington Post,* February 4. http://www.huffingtonpost.com/2011/02/04/dadt-veterans-benefits-honorable-discharge_n_818555.html.

Theen, Andrew, and Staley, Oliver. 2012. Dartmouth to Create Task Force to Investigate Fraternity Hazing. *Bloomberg,* March 2. http://www.bloomberg.com/news/2012-03-02/dartmouth-to-create-task-force-to-investigate-fraternity-hazing.html.

Thompson, Becky. 1996. *A Hunger So Wide and So Deep: A Multiracial View of Women's Eating Problems.* Minneapolis: University of Minnesota Press.

Thornton, Russell. 2001. Trends Among American

Indians in the United States. In N. Smelser, W. Wilson, and F. Mitchell (Eds.), *America Becoming: Racial Trends and Their Consequences* (Vol. 1, pp. 135–169). Washington, DC: National Academy Press.

Tilly, Charles. 1990. Transplanted Networks. In Virginia Yans-McLaughlin (Ed.), *Immigration Reconsidered: History, Sociology, and Politics* (pp. 79–95). New York: Oxford University Press.

Treuer, Anton. 2012. *Everything You Wanted to Know About Indians But Were Afraid to Ask.* Borealis Books: St. Paul, MN.

Treuer, David. 2012. *Rez Life: An Indian's Journey Through Reservation Life.* New York: Atlantic Monthly Press.

Trevanian. 2005. *The Crazy Ladies of Pearl Street.* New York: Crown Books.

Tsai, Shih-Shan Henry. 1986. *The Chinese Experience in America.* Bloomington: Indiana University Press.

Tungol, J. R. 2012. "Don't Ask Don't Tell" One-Year Repeal Anniversary: 25 Amazing Moments. *Huffington Post,* September 20. http://www.huffingtonpost.com/2012/09/20/dont-ask-dont-tell-repeal-anniversary_n_1891519.html.

Udry, Richard. 2000. Biological Limits of Gender Construction. *American Sociological Review* 65:443–457.

United Nations. 2013. *The Millennium Development Goals Report, 2013.* New York: Author. http://www.undp.org/content/dam/undp/library/MDG/english/mdg-report-2013-english.pdf.

United Nations Department of Economic and Social Affairs, Population Division. 2013. *Population Facts* (No. 2013/2). http://esa.un.org/unmigration/documents/The_number_of_international_migrants.pdf.

United Nations Development Programme. 2013. *Mexico: Human Development Indicators.* New York: Author. http://hdr.undp.org/en/countries/profiles/MEX.

United Steelworkers of America, AFL-CIO-CLC v. Weber, 443 U.S. 193 (1979).

U.S. Bureau of Labor Statistics. 2013. Employment Status of the Civilian Non-Institutional Population by Race, Hispanic or Latino Ethnicity, Sex, and Age, Seasonally Adjusted. http://www.bls.gov/web/empsit/cpseea04.pdf.

U.S. Census Bureau. 1978. *Statistical Abstract of the United States, 1977.* Washington, DC: Government Printing Office.

———. 1990. Summary File 3. http://factfinder2.census.gov/faces/nav/jsf/pages/index.xhtml.

———. 1993. *Statistical Abstract of the United States, 1992.* Washington, DC: Government Printing Office.

———. 1997. *Statistical Abstract of the United States, 1996.* Washington, DC: Government Printing Office.

———. 2000a. Asian. *Mapping Census 2000: The Geography of U.S. Diversity* (pp. 62–71). http://www.census.gov/population/cen2000/atlas/censr01-108.pdf.

———. 2000b. Summary File 1. *Census 2000.* https://www.census.gov/census2000/sumfile1.html.

———. 2000c. Summary File 4. *Census 2000.* https://www.census.gov/census2000/SF4.html.

———. 2002. *Statistical Abstract of the United States, 2001.* Washington, DC: Government Printing Office.

———. 2004a. Ancestry. In *Census Atlas of the United States* (pp. 138–155). http://www.census.gov/population/www/cen2000/censusatlas/pdf/9_Ancestry.pdf.

———. 2004b. Population by Region, Sex, and Hispanic Origin Type, With Percent Distribution by Hispanic Origin Type, 2004. http://www.census.gov/population/socdemo/hispanic/ASEC2004/2004CPS_tab19.2.pdf.

———. 2005. *Statistical Abstract of the United States, 2005*. Washington, DC: Government Printing Office.

———. 2007. *Statistical Abstract of the United States, 2007*. Washington, DC: Government Printing Office. http://www.census.gov/compendia/statab/past_years.html.

———. 2008. 1990 Summary Tape File 3. http://factfinder.census.gov/servlet/DatasetMainPageServlet?_program=DEC&_tabId=DEC2&_submenuId=datasets_1&_lang=en&_ts=222966429406.

———. 2009. *American Community Survey 3-Year Estimates, 2007–2009*. http://factfinder2.census.gov/faces/nav/jsf/pages/index.xhtml.

———. 2010. *Statistical Abstract of the United States: 2010*. Washington, DC: Government Printing Office. http://www.census.gov/compendia/statab/2010/2010edition.html.

———. 2011a. *Statistical Abstract of the United States, 2011*. Washington, DC: Government Printing Office.

———. 2011b. *2010 Census [P.L. 94-171] Summary Files*. https://www.census.gov/rdo/data/2010_census.html.

———. 2012a. Most Children Younger Than Age 1 Are Minorities, Census Bureau Reports. News release. http://www.census.gov/newsroom/releases/archives/population/cb12-90.html.

———. 2012b. *National Population Projections: Summary Tables*. http://www.census.gov/population/projections/data/national/2012/summarytables.html.

———. 2012c. *Statistical Abstract of the United States, 2012*. Washington, DC: Government Printing Office. http://www.census.gov/compendia/statab/2012edition.html.

———. 2012d. *2010 Census American Indian and Native Alaska Summary File*. http://factfinder2.census.gov/faces/nav/jsf/pages/index.xhtml.

———. 2013a. *American Community Survey 3-Year Estimates, 2010–2012*. http://factfinder2.census.gov/faces/tableservices/jsf/pages/productview.xhtml?pid=ACS_sumfile_2010_2012&prodType=document.

———. 2013b. Educational Attainment—People 25 Years Old and Over, by Total Money Earnings in 2012, Work Experience in 2012, Age, Race, Hispanic Origin, and Sex (Table PINC-03). *Current Population Survey*. http://www.census.gov/hhes/www/cpstables/032013/perinc/pinc03_000.htm.

———. 2013c. Historical Income Tables: Household. *Current Population Survey*. http://www.census.gov/hhes/www/income/data/historical/household.

———. 2013d. Historical Income Tables: People. *Current Population Survey*. http://www.census.gov/hhes/www/income/data/historical/people.

———. 2013e. Historical Poverty Tables. *Current Population Survey*. http://www.census.gov/hhes/www/poverty/data/historical/index.html.

———. 2013f. Household Income Tables. *Current Population Survey*. http://www.census.gov/hhes/www/cpstables/032013/hhinc/hinc01_000.htm.

———. 2013g. Selected Characteristics of People 15 Years and Over, by Total Money Income in 2012, Work Experience in 2012, Race, Hispanic Origin, and Sex (Table PINC-01). *Current Population Survey*. http://www.census.gov/hhes/www/cpstables/032013/perinc/pinc01_000.htm.

———. 2013h. Selected Economic Characteristics (Table DP03). *American Community Survey, 2006–2012*. http://factfinder2.census.gov/faces/tableservices/jsf/pages/productview.xhtml?pid=ACS_10_SF4_DP03&prodType=table.

U.S. Commission on Civil Rights. 1976. *Puerto Ricans in the Continental United States: An Uncertain Future*. Washington, DC: Government Printing Office.

———. 1992. *Civil Rights Issues Facing Asian Americans in the 1990s*. Washington, DC: Government Printing Office.

U.S. Department of Health and Human Services. 2011. *Thirty Years of AIDS*. http://aids.gov/news-and-events/thirty-years-of-aids.

U.S. Department of Homeland Security. 2012. *Yearbook of Immigration Statistics, 2012*. http://www.dhs.gov/yearbook-immigration-statistics-2012-legal-permanent-residents.

U.S. Immigration and Naturalization Service. 1993. *Statistical Yearbook of the Immigration and Naturalization Service, 1992*. Washington, DC: Government Printing Office.

U.S. v. Windsor, 133 S. Ct. 2675 (2013).

Utah Supreme Court Rules That Non-Indian Members of Native American Church Can Use Peyote in Church Ceremonies. 2004. *New York Times*, June 23, p. A20.

Valentine, Sean, and Mosley, Gordon. 2000. Acculturation and Sex-Role Attitudes Among Mexican Americans: A Longitudinal Analysis. *Hispanic Journal of Behavioral Sciences* 22:104–204.

Van Ausdale, Debra, and Feagin, Joe. 2001. *The First R: How Children Learn Race and Racism*. Lanham, MD: Rowman & Littlefield.

van den Berghe, Pierre L. 1967. *Race and Racism: A Comparative Perspective*. New York: Wiley.

———. 1981. *The Ethnic Phenomenon*. New York: Elsevier.

Vargas-Ramos, Carlos. 2005. Black, Trigueño, White . . . ? Shifting Racial Identification Among Puerto Ricans. *Du Bois Review* 2:267–285.

———. 2012. Migrating Race: Migration and Racial Identification Among Puerto Ricans. *Ethnic and Racial Studies* 37:383–404. http://www.mixedracestudies.org/wordpress/?p=22819.

Vincent, Theodore G. 1976. *Black Power and the Garvey Movement*. San Francisco: Ramparts.

Vinje, David. 1996. Native American Economic Development on Selected Reservations: A Comparative Analysis. *American Journal of Economics and Sociology* 55:427–442.

Vock, Daniel. 2013. With Little Choice, Alabama Backs Down on Immigration Law. *Stateline*, October 30. Pew Charitable Trusts. http://www.pewstates.org/projects/stateline/headlines/with-little-choice-alabama-backs-down-on-immigration-law-85899516441.

von Hippel, William, Silver, Lisa A., and Lynch, Molly E. 2000. Stereotyping Against Your Will: The Role of Inhibitory Ability in Stereotyping and Prejudice Among the Elderly. *Personality and Social Psychology Bulletin* 26:523–532.

Voting Rights Act, 42 U.S.C. § 1971 (1965).

Wagley, Charles, and Harris, Marvin. 1958. *Minorities in the New World: Six Case Studies*. New York: Columbia University Press.

Walker, Alice. 1983. *In Search of Our Mother's Gardens: Womanist Prose*. New York: Harcourt.

Wallace, Michael, and Figueroa, Rodrigo. 2012. Determinants of Perceived Immigrant Job Threat in the American States. *Sociological Perspectives* 55:583–612.

Wallace, Walter. 1997. *The Future of Race, Ethnicity, and Nationality*. Westport, CT: Praeger.

Walshe, Shushannah. 2013. Obama Makes History by Citing Gay Rights in Inaugural Address. *ABC News*, January 21. http://abcnews.go.com/Politics/obama-makes-history-citing-gay-rights-inaugural-address/story?id=18275341.

Wang, Wendy. 2012. *The Rise of Intermarriage: Rates, Characteristics Vary by Race and Gender*. Washington, DC: Pew Research Center. http://www.pewsocialtrends.org/2012/02/16/the-rise-of-intermarriage.

Warren, Tamara. 2011. Gay Rights vs. Civil Rights. *Black Enterprise*, July 12. http://www.blackenterprise.com/lifestyle/gay-rights-is-a-civil-rights-issue/.

Warshaw, Robin. 1994. *I Never Called It Rape: The* Ms. *Report on Recognizing, Fighting and Surviving Date and Acquaintance Rape*. New York: Harper Perennial.

Washington, Booker T. 1965. *Up From Slavery*. New York: Dell.

Waters, Mary. 1990. *Ethnic Options*. Berkeley: University of California Press.

Wax, Murray. 1971. *Indian Americans: Unity and Diversity*. Englewood Cliffs, NJ: Prentice Hall.

Weeks, Philip. 1988. *The American Indian Experience*. Arlington Heights, IL: Forum.

Weil, Frederick. 1985. The Variable Effects of Education on Liberal Attitudes: A Comparative-Historical Analysis of Anti-Semitism Using Public Opinion Survey Data. *American Sociological Review* 50:458–474.

Weitz, Rose, and Gordon, Leonard. 1993. Images of Black Women Among Anglo College Students. *Sex Roles* 28:19–34.

Wellner, Alison. 2007. *U.S. Attitudes Toward Interracial Dating Are Liberalizing*. Washington, DC: Population Reference Bureau. http://www.prb.org/Publications/Articles/2005/USAttitudesTowardInterracialDatingAreLiberalizing.aspx.

West, Darrel. 2011. The Costs and Benefits of Immigration. *Political Science Quarterly* 126:427–443.

White, Deborah Gray. 1985. *Ar'n't I a Woman? Female Slaves in the Plantation South*. New York: Norton.

White, Michael, and Glick, Jennifer. 2009. *Achieving Anew: How New Immigrants Do in American Schools, Jobs, and Neighborhoods*. New York: Russell Sage Foundation.

White House. 2005. *Economic Report of the President*. Washington, DC: Government Printing Office. http://www.gpoaccess.gov/eop/2005/2005_erp.pdf.

Whiteman, Hilary. 2012. Akin "Legitimate Rape" Reaction, From the Congo to the Black Crickets. *CNN*, August 22. http://www.cnn.com/2012/08/22/world/akin-international-rape-reaction/.

Whiting, Robert. 1990. *You Gotta Have Wa*. New York: Macmillan.

Wilkens, Roger. 1992. L.A.: Images in the Flames; Looking Back in Anger: 27 Years After Watts, Our Nation Remains Divided by Racism. *Washington Post*, May 3, p. C1.

Williams, Christine L. 1992. The Glass Escalator: Hidden Advantages for Men in the "Female" Professions. *Social Problems* 39:253–267.

———. 2013. Glass Escalator, Revisited: Gender Inequality in Neoliberal Times. *Gender and Society* 27:609–629.

Williams, Gregory. 1995. *Life on the Color Line*. New York: Dutton.

Wilson, William J. 1973. *Power, Racism, and Privilege: Race Relations in Theoretical and Sociohistorical Perspectives*. New York: Free Press.

———. 1987. *The Truly Disadvantaged: The Inner City, the Underclass, and Public Policy*. Chicago: University of Chicago Press.

———. 1996. *When Work Disappears*. New York: Knopf.

———. 2009. *More Than Just Race*. New York: W. W. Norton.

Wirth, Louis. 1945. The Problem of Minority Groups. In Ralph Linton (Ed.), *The Science of Man in the World* (pp. 347–372). New York: Columbia University Press.

Wise, Tim. 2008. *White Like Me: Reflections on Race From a Privileged Son*. Brooklyn, NY: Soft Skull Press.

Wittig, M., and Grant-Thompson, S. 1998. The Utility of Allport's Conditions of Intergroup Contact for Predicting Perceptions of Improved Racial Attitudes and Beliefs. *Journal of Social Issues* 54:795–812.

Wogan, J. B. 2013. Alabama's Anti-Immigration Law Gutted. *Governing*, November 13. http://www.governing.com/news/headlines/gov-alabamas-anti-immigration-law-dies-amid-hunger-for-reform.html.

Wolf, Naomi. 2002. *The Beauty Myth: How Images of Beauty Are Used Against Women*. New York: Harper Perennial.

Wolf, Richard. 2013. Young People, Flip-Floppers, Fuel Surge Toward Gay Marriage. *USA Today*, March 21. http://www.usatoday.com/story/news/politics/2013/03/20/gay-marriage-pew-poll/2003545/.

———. 2014. Legal Fight for Gay Marriage Reaches Virginia Court. *USA Today*, February 5. http://www.usatoday.com/story/news/nation/2014/02/04/gay-lesbian-marriage-court-virginia/5193233/.

Wolfenstein, Eugene V. 1993. *The Victims of Democracy: Malcolm X*. New York: Guilford Press.

Wolitski, R. J., Jones, K. T., Wasserman, J. L., and Smith, J. C. 2006. Self-Identification as Down Low Among Men Who Have Sex with Men (MSM) From 12 US Cities. *AIDS and Behavior* 10:519–529.

Wong, Morrison. 1995. Chinese Americans. In Pyong Gap Min (Ed.), *Asian Americans: Contemporary Trends and Issues* (pp. 58–94). Thousand Oaks, CA: Sage.

Wood, Peter, and Chesser, Michele. 1994. Black Stereotyping in a University Population. *Sociological Focus* 27:17–34.

Woodward, C. Vann. 1974. *The Strange Career of Jim Crow* (3rd ed.). New York: Oxford University Press.

World Bank. 2013. Data: Mexico. http://data.worldbank.org/country/mexico.

Worsnop, Richard. 1992. Native Americans. *CQ Researcher*, May 8, pp. 387–407.

Wright, Richard. 1940. *Native Son*. New York: Harper & Brothers.

———. 1945. *Black Boy: A Record of Childhood and Youth*. New York: Harper & Brothers.

———. 1988. *12 Million Black Voices: A Folk History of the Negro in the United States*. New York: Viking Press. (Original work published 1941)

Wyman, Mark. 1993. *Round Trip to America*. Ithaca, NY: Cornell University Press.

Yamato, Alexander. 1994. Racial Antagonism and the Formation of Segmented Labor Markets: Japanese

Americans and Their Exclusion From the Workforce. *Humboldt Journal of Social Relations* 20:31–63.

Yancey, George. 1999. An Examination of the Effects of Residential and Church Integration on Racial Attitudes of Whites.

Sociological Perspectives 42:279–294.

———. 2003. *Who Is White? Latinos, Asians, and the New Black/Non-Black Divide.* Boulder, CO: Lynne Rienner.

———. 2007. *Interracial Contact and Social Change.* Boulder, CO: Lynne Rienner.

Yinger, J. Milton. 1985. Ethnicity. *Annual Review of Sociology* 11:151–180.

Zhou, Min. 1992. *Chinatown.* Philadelphia: Temple University Press.

Zhou, Min, and Logan, John R. 1989. Returns on Human Capital in Ethnic Enclaves: New York City's Chinatown.

American Sociological Review 54:809–820.

Zoll, Rachel. 2014. Methodists in Crisis Over Gay Marriage, Church Law. *MSN News,* February 9. http://news .msn.com/us/methodists -in-crisis-over-gay-marriage -church-law.

INDEX

⊛SAGE researchmethods

The essential online tool for researchers from the world's leading methods publisher

Find exactly what you are looking for, from basic explanations to advanced discussion

More content and new features added this year!

"I have never really seen anything like this product before, and I think it is really valuable."

John Creswell, University of Nebraska–Lincoln

Discover **Methods Lists**— methods readings suggested by other users

Watch video interviews with leading methodologists

Explore the **Methods Map** to discover links between methods

Search a custom-designed taxonomy with more than 1,400 qualitative, quantitative, and mixed methods terms

Uncover more than 120,000 pages of book, journal, and reference content to support your learning

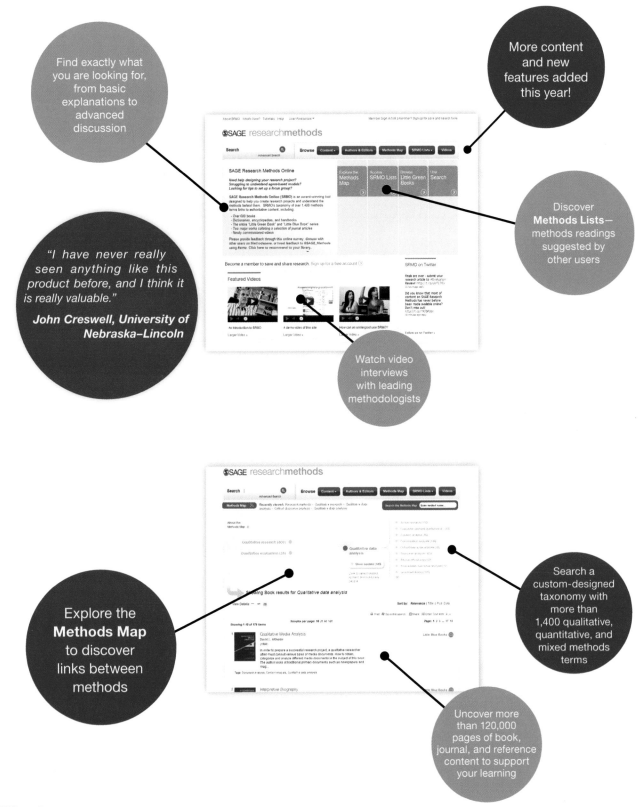

Find out more at
www.sageresearchmethods.com

ARCTIC OCEAN

Beaufort Sea

Baffin Bay

GREENLAND
(DENMARK)

RUSSIA

Bering Sea

CANADA

Hudson Bay

Labrador Sea

Gulf of Alaska

ST. PIERRE-MQ. (FR)

NORTH
PACIFIC
OCEAN

NORTH
ATLANTIC
OCEAN

UNITED STATES

BERMUDA
(UK)

MEXICO

Gulf of Mexico

THE BAHAMAS

CUBA

PUERTO RICO (US)
BRITISH VIRGIN ISLANDS
U.S. VIRGIN ISLANDS
ANGUILLA (UK)
ST. KITTS-NEVIS
ANTIGUA & BARBUDA
MONTSERRAT (UK)
GUADELOUPE (FR)
DOMINICA
MARTINIQUE (FR)
ST. LUCIA
BARBADOS
ST. VINCENT & THE GRENADINES
TRINIDAD & TOBAGO

DOM. REP.

JAMAICA

BELIZE
HONDURAS
HAITI

GUATEMALA
EL SALVADOR
NICARAGUA

N.E. ANTILLES (NE)
ARUBA
GRENADA

COSTA RICA
PANAMA

VENEZUELA

GUYANA
SURINAME
FRENCH GUIANA (FR)

COLOMBIA

NAURU

KIRIBATI

Equator

0°

ECUADOR

SOLOMON
ISLANDS

BRAZIL

TUVALU

TOKELAU (NZ)

AMERICAN
SAMOA
(US)

PERU

Coral Sea

WALLIS & FUTUNA
ISLANDS (FR)

SAMOA

BOLIVA

VANUATU

FIJI

FRENCH
POLYNESIA (FR)

PARAGUAY

NEW CALEDONIA (FR)

TONGA

COOK ISLANDS (NZ)

CHILE

NORFOLK ISLAND
(AUSTRALIA)

PITCAIRN ISLANDS (UK)

URUGUAY

RAPANUI / EASTER ISLAND
(CHILE)

Tasman Sea

SOUTH
PACIFIC
OCEAN

ARGENTINA

SOUTH
ATLANTIC
OCEAN

NEW ZEALAND

FALKLAND
ISLANDS
(UK)

SOUTH
GEORGIA
ISLAND
(UK)